T0236343

Communications
in Computer and Information Science   **742**

Commenced Publication in 2007
Founding and Former Series Editors:
Alfredo Cuzzocrea, Orhun Kara, Dominik Ślęzak, and Xiaokang Yang

More information about this series at http://www.springer.com/series/7899

Juan Carlos Figueroa-García
Eduyn Ramiro López-Santana
José Luis Villa-Ramírez
Roberto Ferro-Escobar (Eds.)

Applied Computer Sciences in Engineering

4th Workshop on Engineering Applications, WEA 2017
Cartagena, Colombia, September 27–29, 2017
Proceedings

 Springer

Editors
Juan Carlos Figueroa-García 🆔
Universidad Distrital Francisco José de
  Caldas
Bogota
Colombia

Eduyn Ramiro López-Santana 🆔
Universidad Distrital Francisco José de
  Caldas
Bogota
Colombia

José Luis Villa-Ramírez
Universidad Tecnológica de Bolívar
Cartagena
Colombia

Roberto Ferro-Escobar
Universidad Distrital Francisco José de
  Caldas
Bogota
Colombia

ISSN 1865-0929   ISSN 1865-0937 (electronic)
Communications in Computer and Information Science
ISBN 978-3-319-66962-5   ISBN 978-3-319-66963-2 (eBook)
DOI 10.1007/978-3-319-66963-2

Library of Congress Control Number: 2017952323

Printed on acid-free paper

This Springer imprint is published by Springer Nature
The registered company is Springer International Publishing AG
The registered company address is: Gewerbestrasse 11, 6330 Cham, Switzerland

Preface

The 4th Workshop on Engineering Applications (WEA 2017) focused on computer science, simulation, and its applications, while previous events aimed to be a forum for all practitioners of all kinds of scientific theories in engineering coming from academia and industry. WEA 2017 is now one of the flagship conferences of the Faculty of Engineering of the Universidad Distrital Francisco José de Caldas, in Bogotá, Colombia.

This year WEA 2017 was held at the Universidad Tecnológica de Bolívar in Cartagena, Colombia, and we received submissions on computer science topics such as software engineering, computer informatics, computational intelligence, intelligent computing, simulation systems, systems dynamics, systems modeling, IoT, and operations research. WEA 2017 concentrated on computer sciences and simulation systems, with miscellaneous applications in IoT and operations research. Therefore, the main topic of our conference was *Applied Computer Sciences in Engineering*.

WEA 2017 received 156 submissions from 14 countries. All submissions were rigorously peer-reviewed and 66 papers and 6 posters were accepted for presentation at WEA 2017. The Program Committee finally selected 59 high-quality papers to be included in this volume of Communications in Computer and Information Sciences (CCIS) proceedings published by SpringerNature.

The Faculty of Engineering of the Universidad Distrital Francisco José de Caldas, the Universidad Tecnológica de Bolívar, the Corporación Unificada Nacional (CUN), the Faculty of Engineering of the National University of Colombia, and the Universidad Libre in Colombia made a significant effort to guarantee the success of the conference. We would like to thank all members of the Program Committee and the referees for their commitment to help in the review process and for spreading our call for papers. We would like to thank Alfred Hofmann and Jorge Nakahara from SpringerNature for their helpful advice, guidance, and their continuous support in publishing the proceedings. Moreover, we would like to thank all the authors for supporting WEA 2017; without all their high-quality submissions the conference would not have been possible. Finally, we are especially grateful to the IEEE Universidad Distrital Francisco José de Caldas and Universidad Tecnológica de Bolívar student branches, the Institute of Industrial and Systems Engineers Chapter 985 (IISE) of the Universidad Distrital Francisco José de Caldas, the Laboratory for Automation and Computational Intelligence (LAMIC), the Expert Systems and Simulation (SES), the Laboratory for Development and Research in Networks and

Electronics (LIDER) research groups of the Universidad Distrital Francisco José de Caldas, and the Algorithms and Combinatory (ALGOS) research group of the National University of Colombia.

September 2017

Juan Carlos Figueroa-García
Eduyn Ramiro López-Santana
José Luis Villa-Ramírez
Roberto Ferro-Escobar

Organization

General Chair

Juan Carlos Figueroa-García — Universidad Distrital Francisco José de Caldas - Bogotá, Colombia

Finance Chair/Treasurer

Roberto Ferro-Escobar — Universidad Distrital Francisco José de Caldas - Bogotá, Colombia

Technical Chair

José Luis Villa-Ramírez — Universidad Tecnológica de Bolívar - Cartagena, Colombia

Publication Chair

Eduyn Ramiro López-Santana — Universidad Distrital Francisco José de Caldas - Bogotá, Colombia

Track Chairs

Edwin Rivas — Universidad Distrital Francisco José de Caldas - Bogotá, Colombia

Germán Andrés Méndez-Giraldo — Universidad Distrital Francisco José de Caldas - Bogotá, Colombia

José Luis Villa-Ramírez — Universidad Tecnológica de Bolívar - Cartagena, Colombia

Organizing Committee Chairs

Yesid Díaz-Gutierrez — Corporación Unificada Nacional (CUN)

José Luis Villa-Ramírez — Universidad Tecnológica de Bolívar - Cartagena, Colombia

Diego Suero — Universidad Libre - Colombia

Organizing Committee

Janna Gamboa — Universidad Distrital Francisco José de Caldas - Bogotá, Colombia

Rafael Ropero-Laytón	Universidad Distrital Francisco José de Caldas - Bogotá, Colombia
José Alejandro Parada-Calderón	Universidad Distrital Francisco José de Caldas - Bogotá, Colombia
Daniela Paola Torres-Ballestas	Universidad Tecnológica de Bolívar - Cartagena, Colombia

Program Committee

DeShuang Huang	Tongji University, Shanghai - Chinese Academy of Sciences, China
Jair Cervantes Canales	Universidad Autónoma de México, Mexico
Guadalupe González	Universidad Tecnológica de Panamá, Panama
Adil Usman	Indian Institute of Technology - Mandy, India
Rafael Bello-Pérez	Universidad de las Villas - Santa Clara, Cuba
Román Neruda	Czech Academy of Sciences of the Czech Republic - Prague, Czech Republic
Martin Pilat	Charles University - Prague, Czech Republic
Mabel Frías	Universidad de Camagüey - Camagüey, Cuba
Yurilev Chalco-Cano	Universidad de Tarapacá, Chile
Francisco Ramis	Universidad del Bío-Bío, Chile
Heriberto Román-Flores	Universidad de Tarapacá, Chile
I-Hsien Ting	National University of Kaohsiung, Taiwan
Ivan Santelices Manfalti	Universidad del Bío-Bío, Chile
Martha Centeno	University of Turabo, Puerto Rico
Aydee Lopez	Universidade Estadual de Campinas (UNICAMP), Brazil
José Luis Villa-Ramírez	Universidad Tecnológica de Bolívar, Colombia
Eugenio Yime	Universidad del Atlántico, Colombia
Oscar Acevedo	Universidad Tecnológica de Bolívar, Colombia
Germán Jairo Hernández-Pérez	Universidad Nacional de Colombia - Campus Bogotá, Colombia
Dusko Kalenatic	Universidad de La Sabana - Chía, Colombia
Yesid Díaz-Gutierrez	Corporación Unificada Nacional (CUN), Columbia
Diego Suero	Universidad Libre, Colombia
Jairo Soriano-Mendez	Universidad Distrital Francisco José de Caldas - Bogotá, Colombia
Juan Pablo Orejuela-Cabrera	Universidad Nacional de Colombia - Campus Bogotá, Colombia
Miguel Melgarejo	Universidad Distrital Francisco José de Caldas - Bogotá, Colombia
Alvaro David Orjuela-Cañon	Universidad Antonio Nario, Colombia
Javier Arturo Orjuela-Castro	Universidad Nacional de Colombia - Campus Bogotá, Colombia
Alonso Gaona	Universidad Distrital Francisco José de Caldas - Bogotá, Colombia

Carlos Osorio-Ramírez   Universidad Nacional de Colombia - Campus Bogotá,
                               Colombia
Elvis Eduardo Gaona   Universidad Distrital Francisco José de Caldas - Bogotá,
                               Colombia
Ignacio Rodríguez-Molano   Universidad Distrital Francisco José de Caldas - Bogotá,
                               Colombia
Elkin Muskus-Rincón   Universidad Central de Colombia - Bogotá, Colombia
Adolfo Jaramillo-Matta   Universidad Distrital Francisco José de Caldas - Bogotá,
                               Colombia
Carlos Franco-Franco   Universidad Católica de Colombia - Bogotá, Colombia
Diana Ovalle   Universidad Distrital Francisco José de Caldas - Bogotá,
                               Colombia
Henry Diosa   Universidad Distrital Francisco José de Caldas - Bogotá,
                               Colombia
Lindsay Álvarez-Pomar   Universidad Distrital Francisco José de Caldas - Bogotá,
                               Colombia
Gustavo   Universidad Distrital Francisco José de Caldas - Bogotá,
   Puerto-Leguizamón   Colombia
Frank Alexander   Universidad Nacional de Colombia - Campus Bogotá,
   Ballesteros-Riveros   Colombia
Sergio Rojas-Galeano   Universidad Distrital Francisco José de Caldas - Bogotá,
                               Colombia
Feizar Javier   Universidad Distrital Francisco José de Caldas - Bogotá,
   Rueda-Velazco   Colombia

Contents

Computational Intelligence

Simulation Systems

Internet of Things

Fuzzy Sets and Systems

Power Systems

Logistics and Operations Management

Miscellaneous

Computer Science

Unsupervised and Supervised Activity Analysis of Drone Sensor Data

Roman Neruda[1]([✉]), Martin Pilát[2], and Josef Moudřík[2]

[1] Institute of Computer Science, Czech Academy of Sciences,
Pod Vodárenskou věží 2, 182 07 Prague, Czech Republic
roman@cs.cas.cz
[2] Faculty of Mathematics and Physics, Charles University,
Malostranské náměstí 25, 110 00 Prague, Czech Republic
martin.pilat@gmail.com, j.moudrik@gmail.com

Abstract. This paper deals with methods for identification of drone activities based on its sensor data. Several unsupervised and supervised approaches are proposed and tested for the task of activity analysis. We demonstrate that sensor data, although quite correlated, are still prone to standard dimensionality reduction techniques that in fact make the problem hard for unsupervised methods. On the other hand, a supervised model based on deep neural network is capable of learning the task from human operator data reformulated as a classification problem.

1 Introduction

Activity analysis and recognition based on various sensor data has become an extensively studied area recently, especially with the advent of wearable devices. Typical examples of already well solved problems from this area include a recognition of walking and running based on accelerometer data from mobile phones or similar devices.

In robotics, the activity recognition is very important because it represent a first step in making robots more autonomous. The capability to analyze and understand robot sensor data allows to abstract from the continuous nature of sensor data towards abstract concepts of actions and states. This can close the gap between continuous control of the robot and planning robotic actions by formal methods. The separation is also in accord with modern hybrid control architectures for intelligent agents where distinct layers of control are defined operating on different domains [10].

A well trained activity recognition algorithm can also serve as a surrogate model of robotic behavior that operates on abstract layer of states and controls, and ultimately provides an autonomous robot capable of independent actions specified on high abstraction level.

In this paper we focus on applying machine learning methods to analyze logs of sensor data from a drone operated by a human operator. We apply methods of dimensionality reduction, k-means clustering, and a deep neural network in

© Springer International Publishing AG 2017
J.C. Figueroa-García et al. (Eds.): WEA 2017, CCIS 742, pp. 3–11, 2017.
DOI: 10.1007/978-3-319-66963-2_1

a standard machine learning workflow to mine the information about human operator actions from the sensor data.

The structure of the paper is as follows. In the next section we provide context of our work, related research, and also describe the data at hand. Section 3 briefly introduces the machine learning algorithms we are utilizing. Sections 4 and 5 represent the core of the paper where the results of unsupervised, and supervised approaches, respectively, are described. Finally, Sect. 6 provides discussion, conclusion and future work directions.

2 Background and Data

The activity analysis has been widely studied for decade mainly in the context of wearable devices and sensors monitoring human activity. Many machine learning approaches, both unsupervised and supervised have been used, for more details cf. survey [8], or more recent works [1,3]. However, the sensor data gathered from drone are usually more complex and diverse than the data obtained from human wearable sensors. Also the range of activities is more extensive for drones performing movements and maneuvers in 3D.

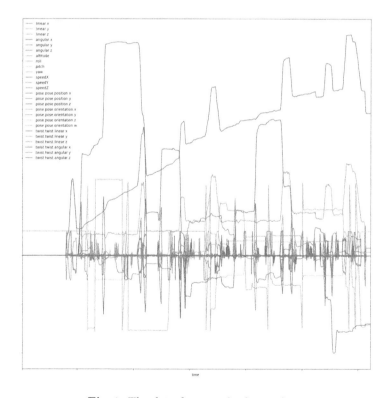

Fig. 1. The data from session2 overview.

For our experiments we have utilized data obtained from several recorded sessions of a drone operated by human in such a way that the whole spectrum of activities is covered in a data. The hardware platform used is the relatively inexpensive AR.Drone 2.0 by Parrot Inc. [7]. The operator controls the drone by sending pitch and roll angles and vertical and yaw speed. The drone tries to reach and maintain sent values until the next command arrives, which can happen with a frequency of 30 Hz. The collected data from the flight include the operators commands, as well as readouts from sensors. The sensors include gyroscope, accelerometer, magnetometer and ultrasound sensors, but the data is sent back as information about drone speed vector, azimuth, altitude and roll and pitch angles. The frequency of the sensor data varies between 15–200 Hz with transmission latency around 60 ms.

For more details about the hardware platform and data gathering procedure cf. [2], where the authors solve the same problem working with the same data. In the paper, they utilized several clustering methods as well the decision tree supervised learning applied on data preprocessed by clustering.

From several human operator sessions we have extracted two datasets that are used throughout this paper for our experiments (we refer to them as session1 and session2). The data have been cleaned, normalized, and the problem of different time scales and latencies have been also tackled by preprocessing. We have interpolated the data with lower frequency so that we have a complete set of features for every tick on a unified fine-grain time scale.

In general, after preprocessing, both data sets have between 12 000 and 15 000 data items and around 30 attributes sent from the drone. We drop several attributes describing internal states of the drone (battery, etc.) as well as wind information (experiments were performed indoors). Figure 1 illustrates the plotted data from session2 after complete preprocessing.

3 Methods Used

We use the Python programming language [9] for our experiments, the majority of machine learning methods is taken from the scikit-learn library, with the exception of deep neural network that uses the GPU-enabled Keras implementation.

For the dimensionality reduction we are using the standard principal component analysis (PCA) method, together with the t-distributed stochastic neighbor embedding (t-SNE) method that is quite time consuming, yet has shown impressive results in recent applications. For utilizing the t-SNE we downsized the data to 25% in order to keep realistic time performance.

Since the various clustering methods for this type of data have been studied in [2], we focus on the performance of clustering on low-dimensional projection of the data. A standard k-means clustering algorithm with varying cluster numbers have been used for this task [6].

For the supervised task we have performed experiments with the decision tree model, that usually serves as a baseline for its simplicity and speed. The results have been compared to random forests that represent a robust ensemble of partial decision trees [4]. Both models are classifiers, thus we train them to predict the operator command based on the context of other sensor data.

Finally, a deep neural network [5] have been trained to represent a surrogate model mapping operator inputs to sensor readouts in the future.

4   Unsupervised Learning Results

For the unsupervised learning methodology the goal was to investigate the possibility of using clustering not on the original many-dimensional data, but rather

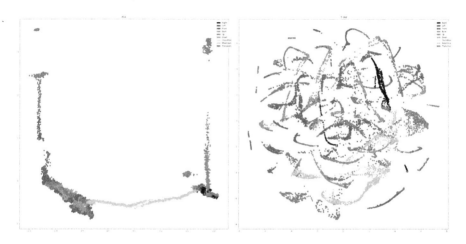

Fig. 2. PCA and t-SNE analysis of the sensor data session1. (Color figure online)

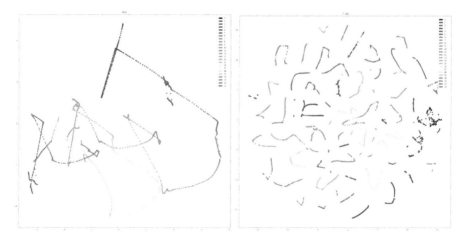

Fig. 3. PCA and t-SNE analysis of the sensor data session2. (Color figure online)

on the data reduced by dimensionality reduction. First, we applied the standard PCA procedure and the more sophisticated (and time exacting) t-SNE algorithm to perform projection of the data to 2 dimensions. Results can be seen on Figs. 2 and 3. Since the colors represent different operator commands, one would like to observe isolated regions of uniform-colored points that would be later suitable for clustering. In general we can observe that the t-SNE is not performing well on our data. The results of the PCA provide better geometrical projection overall.

The next step was to apply clustering on different 2D projections. We have decided for simple k-means clustering and we experimented with number of clusters ranging from 2 to 8. Also, the projections were selected as promising pairs

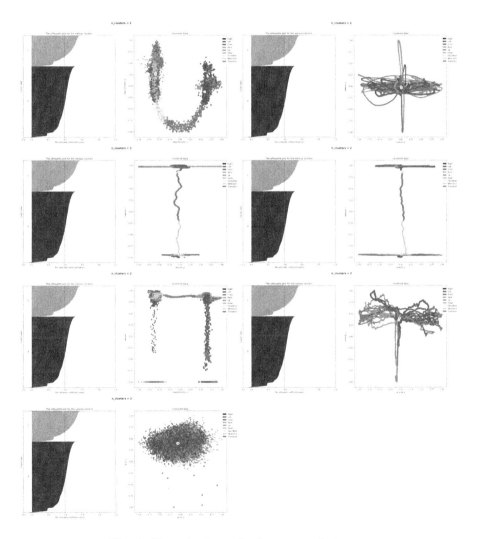

Fig. 4. Clustering in projection spaces, 2 clusters.

of different attributes based on the PCA and correlation results. The results are presented on Figs. 4 and 5 for number of clusters equal two or eight, respectively. We can conclude that while some of the projections seem to carry enough information about the actions relatively separated, the clustering was not able to make use of it in order to provide satisfying results. Varying number of clusters does not improve the situation too much, as in many cases, the clusters overlap.

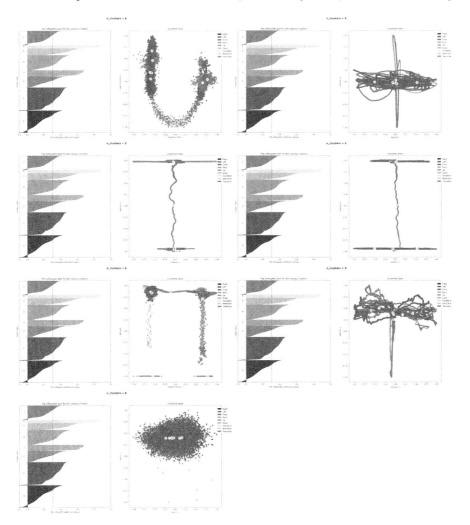

Fig. 5. Clustering in projection spaces, 8 clusters.

5   Supervised Learning Results

For the supervised learning approach we have performed two experiments. The first experiment compares the performance of decision tree with more robust model random forests. They both act as classifiers, thus the task for both models it to classify the operators command from the sensor readouts. Both training procedures were performed with 5-fold crossvalidation, the decision tree model has been set to maximum depth of 10, the random forest had up to 200 individual classifiers.

The results of the experiment are presented as confusion matrices showing the misclassification ratios for all category combinations in Fig. 6. It is not a surprise that the random forest performed better, the concrete values of the classification scores are 86.7418% (with 1.3197 error) for the decision tree, and 95.4083% (with 0.4652 error) for the random forest, respectively.

The experiment with the deep neural network has utilized the data in a different way than the previous one. Rather than classifying the current operator action, we want the network to act as controller, or a surrogate model of the drone. Thus, the task is to predict the next state (complete readout from sensors and controls) from the current and past ones. The history window has been chosen to 5, i.e. the network input consists of a sequence of 5 complete states, while the desired output is the future complete state of the sensors.

The network consist of four layers alternating perceptron units with RelU activation function, and dropout units. The training has been performed for 50 epochs using batches of size 16. We have split the data set into 5000 items of testing data (to measure the performance on previously unseen data) and the training data consisting of the rest, of approx 10 000 items. The results of this experiment are quite promising.

The network was able to train well, the mean square error on the test set went from the initial 3.0564 to the resulting 0.1129. We consider this result rather good, but for a complete evaluation of the quality of this result, more experiments are needed on different data.

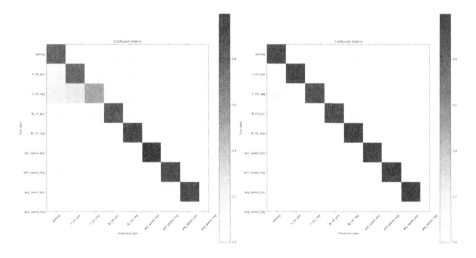

Fig. 6. Confusion matrices for decision tree and random forest classifiers on the session2 data.

6   Conclusion

In this paper we have applied machine learning procedures of dimensionality reduction, clustering and supervised learning by means of deep neural networks to raw drone sensor data. The motivation for our work is an action identification problem in the context of easily gathered data from drone controlled by a human operator. Based on our experiments we can conclude that unsupervised approach—represented by k-means clustering on data projected in two dimensions, in our case—does not provide sufficient results for action recognition. On the other hand, the two versions of supervised learning performed very well. The classification formulation of the task is handled well by the random forest which achieved 95% success rate in estimating the operator command. Also, the deep neural network model was successful in learning the input-output relationship for the surrogate formulation of our problem.

Still, several problems remain open for further research. The data we have utilized come from only a limited number of human operator sessions, thus there might be other flight situations not covered by the data sets. More variability in the data can result in a more general model. This should not be a problem, since the deep neural network model trained quite fast on the data at hand. Moreover, a larger data set can be better with respect to possible overtraining of the model. Which brings another consideration that maybe there can be an alternative—yet smaller—model that will perform similar or even better. Thus, more supervised learning techniques should be explored in the future with the focus on compact models.

Ultimately, for the application of formal methods for robot motion control and planning, it would be nice to come not only with action identification, but also to be able to parameterize it. That way, the robot can be in turn controlled by commands like 'fly forward 2 meters'. This approach will need to solve the possible clashes with existing drone firmware that already has some autonomous capabilities for balancing and hovering. The approach of supervisedly trained surrogate model, such as our deep neural network, in fact has the advantage that it already incorporates any hard-wired behavior of the drone. Thus, the model is implicitly tailored to hardware and software properties of the particular drone whose data have been used for training.

Acknowledgement. This research is supported by the Czech Science Foundation under the project P103-15-19877S.

References

1. Kwon, Y., Kang, K., Bae, C.: Unsupervised learning for human activity recognition using smartphone sensors. Exp. Syst. Appl. **41**(14), 6067–6074 (2014)
2. Barták, R., Vomlelová, M.: Using machine learning to identify activities of a flying drone from sensor readings. In: Rus, V., Markov, Z. (eds.) Proceedings of the Thirtieth International Florida Artificial Intelligence Research Society Conference, FLAIRS 2017, Marco Island, Florida, USA, 22–24 May 2017, pp. 436–441. AAAI Press (2017)

3. Bugdol, M.D., Mitas, A.W., Grzegorzek, M., Meyer, R., Wilhelm, C.: Human Activity Recognition Using Smartphone Sensors, pp. 41–47. Springer, Cham (2016)
4. Flach, P.: Machine Learning: The Art and Science of Algorithms That Make Sense of Data. Cambridge University Press, New York (2012)
5. Goodfellow, I.J., Bengio, Y., Courville, A.C.: Deep Learning. Adaptive Computation and Machine Learning, MIT Press, Cambridge (2016). http://www.deeplearningbook.org/
6. Hastie, T., Tibshirani, R., Friedman, J.H.: The Elements of Statistical Learning: Data Mining, Inference, and Prediction. Springer Series in Statistics, 2nd edn. Springer, New York (2009). http://www.worldcat.org/oclc/300478243
7. Krajník, T., Vonásek, V., Fišer, D., Faigl, J.: AR-drone as a platform for robotic research and education. In: Obdržálek, D., Gottscheber, A. (eds.) EUROBOT 2011. CCIS, vol. 161, pp. 172–186. Springer, Heidelberg (2011). doi:10.1007/978-3-642-21975-7_16
8. Lara, O.D., Labrador, M.A.: A survey on human activity recognition using wearable sensors. IEEE Commun. Surv. Tutorials 15(3), 1192–1209 (2013)
9. Müller, A.C., Guido, S.: Introduction to Machine Learning with Python: A Guide for Data Scientists. O'Reilly Media, Inc., Sebastopol (2016)
10. Wooldridge, M.J.: An Introduction to MultiAgent Systems, 2nd edn. Wiley, New York (2009)

Modeling, Control and Simulation
of a Quadrotor for Attitude Stabilization

Bárbara B. Carlos$^{(\boxtimes)}$, Antonio É.R.M. de Oliveira, Auzuir R. de Alexandria,
Rejane C. Sá, and Antonio W.O. Rodrigues

Instituto Federal do Ceará (IFCE), Fortaleza, Brazil
{barbara,ebano.rafael}@lit.ifce.edu.br

Abstract. Unmanned Aerial Vehicle (UAV) are increasingly playing an important role in various fields of application and their development, with the advancement and decreasing cost of technology, became simpler. In this paper we present a mathematical model for a quadrotor and different control strategies. The control task is based on the discretization of the system by Tustin's Method to achieve the angular stabilization of the quadrotor. The proposed approach shows the standard single loop and nested loop model, hierarchizing the mid-level attitude control, evaluating the performance of a P, PD and P-P controllers obtained by linearizing the plant's dynamics around an equilibrium point. Simulation results compared the proposed controllers providing a possible solution for future implementation.

Keywords: Quadrotor · Modeling · Discrete control · Simulation

1 Introduction

Although quadrotors do not have a complex structure, it is not simple to design their controllers. To address these difficulties, many researchers have attempted to approximate them to real dynamic models, or to linearize the system at certain points of operation, especially at hovering.

The quadrotor's dynamics is marked by underactuation (six degrees of freedom and only four actuators), large coupling between axes and unknown nonlinearities [1]. Works such as [2,3] are devoted to the determination of mathematical models that are more comprehensive and useful for both simulation and control problems. Other works, in addition to mathematical modeling, also present control techniques for these vehicles. Among these techniques, it is possible to cite the backstepping control of [4,5]; The comparison between PID control and LQR of [6]; And the robust fuzzy control technique of [7].

In [8], to the quadrotor's model is incorporated the dynamics of the engines as well as aerodynamics and gyroscopic effects. The control is made by separating the dynamics of the rigid body and the engine. Altug et al. [9–11] models the quadrotor using the Newton-Euler method and works with stabilization and trajectory control based on computational vision. Guenard [12] and Suter [13]

© Springer International Publishing AG 2017
J.C. Figueroa-García et al. (Eds.): WEA 2017, CCIS 742, pp. 12–23, 2017.
DOI: 10.1007/978-3-319-66963-2_2

also performed studies on the control of quadrotors based on the study of vision. Moktari [14] presents a nonlinear dynamic model for a quadrotor reasoned on Euler angles's control and observer of open-loop states. A controller based on feedback linearization techniques with a high order observer running in parallel applied to the quadrotor is presented by [15]. Dunfied [16] created a neural network controller for this type of aircraft.

The aim of this work is to obtain a controllable model of the attitude of a quadrotor for simulation. In the first part of the work, the quadrotor's attitude is mathematically modeled, presenting the conventions used, through the description of rigid-body dynamics. In the second part, the control strategy used, under two types of architecure, for the linearized model of both quadrotor and propulsion system is presented. Finally the simulation is performed on MAT-LAB/Simulink and the results are discussed.

2   Mathematical Modeling of the Quadrotor

2.1   Rigid-Body Dynamics

To describe the quadrotor's movements in space, two systems of reference are defined. Let $\{SR_A\}$ be a right-hand inertial frame, represented by unit vectors $\{\vec{x}, \vec{y}, \vec{z}\}$. Let $\{SR_B\}$ be a right-hand Body-fixed frame (BFF) denoted by the triad unit vectors $\{\vec{xb}, \vec{yb}, \vec{zb}\}$, as shown in Fig. 1.

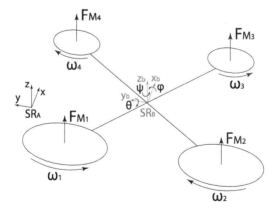

Fig. 1. Inertial and body-fixed frames representation (Source: Authors)

According the literature, the rotation of the BFF related to the inertial frame can be describe using three angles, commonly known as Euler Angles, represented for ϕ, θ and ψ.

$$\mathbf{\Psi} = [\phi, \theta, \psi]^T \tag{1}$$

The convention Z-X-Y is adopted to model the rotation of the quadrotor related to the inertial system. This convention produces the rotation matrix $^{\mathbf{B}}\mathbf{R_A}$.

$$^{\mathbf{B}}\mathbf{R_A} = \begin{bmatrix} cos\psi cos\theta - sin\phi sin\psi sin\theta & -cos\phi sin\psi & cos\psi sin\theta + cos\theta sin\phi sin\psi \\ cos\theta sin\psi + cos\psi sin\phi sin\theta & cos\theta cos\psi & sin\psi sin\theta - cos\psi cos\theta sin\phi \\ -cos\phi sin\theta & sin\phi & cos\phi cos\theta \end{bmatrix} \quad (2)$$

The angular velocity measured in the BFF frame is given by

$$^{\mathbf{B}}\mathbf{\Omega} = [p, q, r]^T \quad (3)$$

Where p is the angular velocity about x_b axis, q is the angular velocity about y_b axis and r is the angular velocity about z_b axis.

The rotational dynamics of a rigid body with m mass subjected to external forces applied to its center of mass can be defined by the Newtow-Euler formalism. Knowing that $^{\mathbf{B}}\tau$ e $\boldsymbol{I}$ are respectively the external torques and the moments of inertia of the rigid body, the governing equation is

$$\mathbf{I}\,^{\mathbf{B}}\dot{\mathbf{\Omega}} = -\,^{\mathbf{B}}\mathbf{\Omega} \times \mathbf{I}\,^{\mathbf{B}}\mathbf{\Omega} + \sum\,^{\mathbf{B}}\tau \quad (4)$$

where the inertia moments are given by the diagonal matrix

$$\mathbf{I} = \begin{bmatrix} I_{xx} & 0 & 0 \\ 0 & I_{yy} & 0 \\ 0 & 0 & I_{zz} \end{bmatrix} \quad (5)$$

Torques are the system control inputs, represented by τ_ϕ, τ_θ e τ_ψ. Each one is responsible for a certain motion on the frame: τ_ϕ the roll angle, τ_θ the pitch angle and τ_ψ the yaw angle.

When the vector in (3) and matrix in (5) are inserted into Eq. (4) the rates of the angular momentum components of the quadrotor, considering the gyroscopic effects (Ω) caused by the inertia of the rotors (I_r), can be found.

$$\dot{p} = qr\left(\frac{I_{yy} - I_{zz}}{I_{xx}}\right) + q\Omega\frac{I_r}{I_{xx}} + \frac{\tau_\phi}{I_{xx}} \quad (6)$$

$$\dot{q} = pr\left(\frac{I_{zz} - I_{xx}}{I_{yy}}\right) + p\Omega\frac{I_r}{I_{yy}} + \frac{\tau_\theta}{I_{yy}} \quad (7)$$

$$\dot{r} = pq\left(\frac{I_{xx} - I_{yy}}{I_{zz}}\right) + \frac{\tau_\psi}{I_{zz}} \quad (8)$$

These equations are nonlinear because they involve the multiplication of time-varying quantities. A linearization must be done in order to design the linear controllers. In this case, it is assumed conditions such as: (1) hovering state; (2) small angles ($\ddot{\phi} \sim \dot{p}; \ddot{\theta} \sim \dot{q}; \ddot{\psi} \sim \dot{r}$) and (3) absence of gyroscopic effect. Since

$(p \sim 0; q \sim 0; r \sim 0)$, it is possible to achieve a really simple group of equations to attitude control, described by

$$\ddot{\phi} = \frac{\tau_{\phi}}{I_{xx}} \tag{9}$$

$$\ddot{\theta} = \frac{\tau_{\theta}}{I_{yy}} \tag{10}$$

$$\ddot{\psi} = \frac{\tau_{\psi}}{I_{zz}} \tag{11}$$

2.2   Motors

The actuators are the components responsible for applying forces on the system to bring it to a desired state. In this case the actuators are the motors and propellers [17]. Brushless motors are used for all quadcopter platforms, where precise control of motor operation is required. A Brushless Direct Current Motor (BDCM) has a trapezoidal back EMF, and rectangular stator currents are needed to produce a constant electric torque [18]. Since this work combines the standard hierarchical control paradigm that separates the control into low-level motor control and mid-level attitude dynamics control, a BDCM model must be acquired.

Thrust. The instantaneous thrust of the quadrotor's motors as well as its instantaneous angular velocity are determined by the application of a pulse-width modulation (PWM) signal to a electronic speed controller (ESC) that is responsible for generating a three phase signal to the motor.

The thrust generated by each ith motor (F_{M_i}) can be modeled as

$$F_{M_i} = C_b \omega_i^2 \tag{12}$$

where ω_i is the angular velocity of the ith motor and C_b the thrust coefficient to be determined experimentally.

The measurement of the thrust/Duty Cycle and ω/Duty Cycle ratios can be done by varying the length of the PWM pulse in order to show a linear relationship between both ratios.

Torque. Each group of motor-controller-propeller contributes some torque about the body z axis. This torque is responsible for keeping the propeller spinning and also generating thrust. The instantaneous angular acceleration created by this action overcomes the frictional drag forces. This relation can be described as

$$\tau_{\psi} = \frac{1}{2} \rho A v^2 \tag{13}$$

where ρ is the fluid density of the environment, A is the cross sectional area of the propeller and v is the linear velocity. This implies that the torque for the ith motor (τ_{M_i}) opposed by an aerodynamic drag, according Newton's Second Law, is

$$I_M \dot{\omega}_i = \tau_{M_i} - \tau_{\psi} \tag{14}$$

For maneuvers where ω is constant, it is possible to assume that $\tau_{M_i} = \tau_\psi$, then

$$\tau_\psi = C_d \omega_i^2 + I_M \dot{\omega}_i \tag{15}$$

where I_M is the angular moment of the ith motor about the z axis, $\dot{\omega}_i$ is the angular acceleration of the propeller, and C_d is the drag coefficient that must be experimentally founded. For steady state, where $\dot{\omega}_i = 0$, the yaw torque is

$$\tau_\psi = C_d \omega_i^2 \tag{16}$$

Equation (16) can also be written in terms of thrust forces with using the relationship between thrust and drag coefficient. Thus,

$$\tau_\psi = \frac{C_d}{C_b} F_{M_i} \tag{17}$$

Doanç [19] provides a relation between both coefficients

$$\frac{C_b}{C_d} = \frac{1}{58} \tag{18}$$

Thus, the torque in the BFF can be generalized as

$$^{\mathbf{B}}_\mathcal{T} = \begin{bmatrix} C_b l(\omega_1^2 + \omega_2^2 - \omega_3^2 - \omega_4^2) \\ C_b l(-\omega_1^2 + \omega_2^2 + \omega_3^2 - \omega_4^2) \\ C_d(\omega_1^2 - \omega_2^2 + \omega_3^2 - \omega_4^2) \end{bmatrix} = \begin{bmatrix} \tau_\phi \\ \tau_\theta \\ \tau_\psi \end{bmatrix} \tag{19}$$

where l is the length from the center of the rotor to the geometric center of the quadrotor.

3   Control Strategy

The attitude controller is responsible for maintaining the 3D orientation of the quadrotor in a desired value. As done in the last section, the roll and pitch angles are zeroed to establish a hovering condition and yaw is set to an initial angle (ψ_0), which can be zero, maintained along any spatial displacement that one wishes to accomplish with the aircraft.

For a controller that is actually implementable it has to be a digital one, in this way it can be discretized and embedded into a microcontrolled platform. With this aim, it is required to have a digital model of all system to be controlled. In this case, the Motor-ESC-propellers's and quadrotor's plants.

The discretization of systems may be done using one of the three common approximations: Euler's method (EM), Backward difference (BD) or Tustin's Method (or trapezoidal method, TM). The difference between those three approximation methods, besides the crescent complexity of the algebra involved in using it, is the region of the complex plane that is mapped from s-plane to z-plane.

Considering the mapping of all the left-half plane of the s-plane, each approximation causes a different mapping region: EM maps a large region that includes non-stable region in z-plane, BD maps a region inside the unit circle and TM maps all left-half of s-plane onto the z-plane unit circle [20]. Thus, one has to choose which approximation method should be used analyzing the model's complexity as well as the pole location in the respective mapped region so the system be stable.

3.1   Plant Model

The quadrotor's attitude equations subsystem shows that ϕ, θ, ψ are forced directly by the input signals. Taking the Laplace Transform (LT) of Eqs. (9), (10) and (11), one obtains

$$\phi(s) = \frac{1}{I_{xx}} \frac{\tau_\phi(s)}{s^2} \tag{20}$$

$$\theta(s) = \frac{1}{I_{yy}} \frac{\tau_\theta(s)}{s^2} \tag{21}$$

$$\psi(s) = \frac{1}{I_{zz}} \frac{\tau_\psi(s)}{s^2} \tag{22}$$

These transfer functions are second order with two poles at the origin, which makes the system inherently unstable. As discussed in Sect. 3, it is necessary to discretize the quadrotor's plant and hence the controller using an approximation method. The discretization method chosen is TM because the algebra involved in the substitution of the s complex variable is not excessive, as the model is simple. This method is less risky than EM because the stable poles on s-plane cannot be mapped into unstable poles on z-plane. The designer must be aware that the sampling frequency also have influence in the position of the poles: the smaller, the nearer to the instability region the poles are.

3.2   Discrete Controller

The same approach applied to the discretization of the plant's model is applied to the controller. Many practical problems are solved with a PID controller [20] and, specifically for this system, a PD controller can also be used.

The continuous PD controller is given by

$$u(t) = K_P\, e(t) + K_D\, \frac{d}{dt} e(t) \tag{23}$$

where $u(t)$ is the control action, $e(t)$ is the difference between the reference signal and the process output, K_P and K_D are the proportional and derivative gains, respectively.

Applying the LT in Eq. (23) and then using TM approximation one obtains

$$\frac{U(z)}{E(z)} = K_P + K_D \frac{2}{T_s} \frac{z-1}{z+1} \tag{24}$$

4   Results and Discussion

4.1   Experimental System Identification

Inertial Properties. To calculate the moment of inertia tensor presented in Eq. (5), bifilar pendulum experiments are done according to [21] approach. The values obtained are $I_{xx} = 0.0062$, $I_{yy} = 0.0051$ and $I_{zz} = 0.0394$, in kgm^2.

Propulsion System. Motor-ESC-propeller unit models are identified experimentally. These models are algebraic, steady state ones, which implies that the transient state was considered the same for all four motors.

Experiments to acquire the ratios of ω/Duty Cycle and thrust/Duty Cycle are made to, based on Eq. (12), show a linear relationship between Force and angular velocity. Hence, estimate the thrust coefficient, C_b. In the first experiment, a tachometer is used to measure the angular velocity in RPM. In the second one, a balance is used to measure the force in grams. In both experiments, the duty cycle (d) is increased (from 8% to 9%; 0.10 resolution) and the respective measurements are taken. Using MATLAB's Curve Fitting Tool, angular velocity and force data of the motor are linearized. Both curves are presented in Fig. 2.

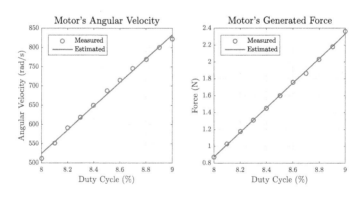

Fig. 2. Graphs of angular velocity versus duty cycle and force versus duty cycle (Source: Authors)

Considering that each ith motor can be represented by the same set of equations, the linear fit gives

$$\omega_i(d) = 308.8182 \cdot d - 19464.4 \quad \text{[rad/s]} \tag{25}$$

$$F_{M_i}(d) = 1.4598 \cdot d - 10.8051 \quad \text{[N]} \tag{26}$$

Using the collected data from the motor's angular velocity and force, plugging into Eq. (12) and taking the mean, it is possible to find the C_b coefficient. After that, using the result into Eq. (18), one obtains the C_d coefficient. The values obtained are $C_b = 3.4025 \times 10^{-6}$ and $C_d = 1.9735 \times 10^{-4}$.

4.2   Simulation of the System

Digitalizing Eq. (21) through TM, using a sampling frequency of 50 Hz, the quadrotor's digital transfer function become

$$\frac{\theta(z)}{\tau_\theta(z)} = 0.01961\frac{(z+1)^2}{(z-1)^2} \tag{27}$$

where torque $\tau_\theta(z)$ is the plant's input, which is proportional to the duty cycle increment sent for the controllers output $U(z)$, while the actual angle $\theta(z)$ is the system output.

The digital models for Eqs. (20) and (22) are omitted as they are basically represented the same way as Eq. (27), in respect to the poles and zeros positions.

Single Loop with Proportional Controller. In Fig. 3 is shown a block diagram of a single loop control of the system.

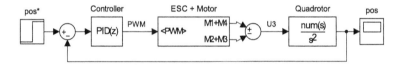

Fig. 3. Single loop control with P controller (Source: Authors)

A proportional controller was designed as first choice, basically to show that a single loop consisting of the angle position cannot be controlled with a proportional controller. In Fig. 4 is shown the root locus of the system continuous and discrete, whose system's closed loop poles are indicated in black, along with its step response with a digital controller.

Single Loop with Proportional-Derivative Controller. As a second solution, it is plausible to use a Proportional-Derivative controller, since the plant already has an integral action, which makes unnecessary the use of a controller like a PI or a PID.

In Fig. 5 can be seen that the controller forces the system poles to a stable region, producing a reasonable settling time, but also showing a slightly oscillatory behavior. The proximity of the poles with the unit circle, and the low gains values, makes the system behave like that. For this set up, the controller gains are $K_P = 7.5$ and $K_D = 0.025$, where the proportional gain is already large. Raising the gain of the controller will make the system less oscillatory, inducing a reduction on the overshoot, since the derivative gain will grow as well. However those gains are excessive, for real-world implementation this values may cause saturation of the controller's output, which means that the system will be working out of its operation region, for this reason, a PD controller is not an ideal option.

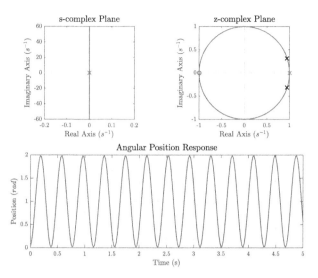

Fig. 4. Proportional controlled root locus and step response (Source: Authors)

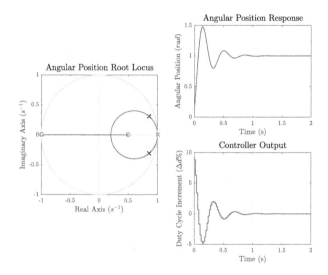

Fig. 5. Proportional-derivative controller root locus, system step response and controller signal (Source: Authors)

Nested Loop with P Controllers. As the controller gains are considered high for a single loop, and in order to maintain a good settling time for the angular position while having low oscillations, a nested loop architecture is proposed to control the angular position . On this approach, the inner loop controls the angular velocity whereas the outer loop controls the angular position. Such structure is shown in Fig. 6.

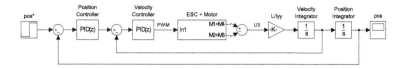

Fig. 6. Proportional controller root locus (Source: Authors)

For the nested loop control, both controllers are Proportional. Because of the quadrotor system structure, both loops already have an integrator which makes unnecessary a controller that presents an integral action. In Fig. 7, the root loci of both loops with Proportional controllers are shown as well as the responses for angular position and velocity to an unit step input.

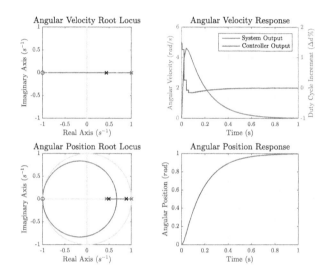

Fig. 7. Nested loop using proportional controllers (Source: Authors)

The gains for the proportional controllers designed are 0.3 and 5, for position and velocity respectively. This architecture achieved basically the same settling time while give a behavior less oscillatory. The fact that there is not a derivate action implies that the sensors noise does not affect the controller output as much as in single loop with PD controller. Besides the fact that the controllers are only proportional ones, which it is way more easier to implement in an embedded system.

5   Conclusion

This work proposes a mathematical modeling for a quadrotor with a single loop and nested loop control architecture to guarantee a prototype capable of stabilizing itself at hovering state. The linearized mathematical model was validated through simulation, using MATLAB/Simulink. The main goal of this research is evaluate the differences between control loops architectures for a quadrotor system using combinations of classical controllers, taking into consideration practical aspects of control systems design. Three architectures were presented and examined with respect to time response, controller's and system output. The system output response obtained for every architecture reflects on a distinct set of characteristic related to implementation. For the single loop with P controller, the system is inherent unstable, which means that the quadrotor is incapable of achieving the desired angle set point. On the other hand, for the single loop with PD controller, the location of the closed loop poles and zeros was able to bring the system to the stable region conducing to the set point convergence. Although the stability and a reasonable rise time have been achieved, for practical purposes, the derivative action can cause saturation of the controller's output given the noise in the sensors readings. Another aspect is that the computational cost in doing derivatives may decrease the code efficiency whether in execution time or space amount into memory program. For reduct the gains values, accommodation time and overshoot, the nested loop with P-P controllers is the most comprehensive choice. Although this approach requires additional sensors to provide feedback to the controllers, the cascaded architecture is a reasonable solution to the control system problem. Once the current technological developments related to the guidance systems provide cost-effectiveness, thanks to the miniaturization of the sensors, the cascade control architecture can be easily implemented in a quadrotor.

Future research will refine this approach using optimization, such as in Model Predictive Control (MPC), instead a classical one, but still maintaining a timescale separation of the different dynamic levels of the quadrotor.

Acknowledgement. The authors would like to express their gratitude to the Conselho Nacional de Desenvolvimento Científico e Tecnológico (CNPq) and Instituto Federal do Ceará (IFCE) for the research financial support.

References

1. Das, A., Subbarao, K., Lewis, F.: Dynamic inversion of quadrotor with zero-dynamics stabilization. In: IEEE International Conference on Control, pp. 1189–1194 (2008)
2. Sanca, A.S., Alsina, P.J., Cerqueira, J.: Dynamic modelling of a quadrotor aerial vehicle with nonlinear inputs. In: IEEE Latin American Robotic Symposium. LARS 2008, pp. 143–148 (2008)
3. Amir, M., Abbass, V.: Modeling of quadrotor helicopter dynamics. In: International Conference on Smart Manufacturing Application, pp. 100–105 (2008)
4. Bouabdallah, S., Siegwart, R.: Backstepping and sliding-mode techniques applied to an indoor micro quadrotor. In: International Conference on Smart Manufacturing Application, pp. 2247–2252 (2005)
5. Madani, T., Benallegue, A.: Sliding mode observer and backstepping control for a quadrotor unmanned aerial vehicles. In: American Control Conference, ACC 2007, pp. 5887–5892 (2007)

6. Bouabdallah, S., Noth, A., Siegwart, R.: PID vs LQ control techniques applied to an indoor micro quadrotor. In: Proceedings of 2004 IEEE/RSJ International Conference On Intelligent Robots and Systems, pp. 2451–2456 (2004)
7. Coza, C., Macnab, C.: A new robust adaptive-fuzzy control method applied to quadrotor helicopter stabilization. In: Annual meeting of the North American Fuzzy Information Processing Society, NAFIPS 2006, pp. 454–458 (2006)
8. Hamel, T., Mahony, R., Lozano, R., Ostrowski, J.: Dynamic modeling and configuration stabilization for an X4-flayer. In: 15th Triennial World Congress (2002)
9. Altuğ, E., Ostrowski, J.P., Mahony, R.: Control of a quadrotor helicopter using visual feedback. In: Proceedings of the 2002 IEEE conference on Robotics & Automation (2002)
10. Altuğ, E., Ostrowski, J.P., Taylor, C.J.: Quadrotor control using dual camera visual feedback. In: Proceedings of the 2003 IEEE conference on Robotics & Automation (2003)
11. Altuğ, E., Taylor, C.J.: Vision-based pose estimation and control of a model helicopter. In: International Conference on Mechatronics (2004)
12. Guenard, N., Hamel, T., Mahony, R.: A practical visual servo control for an unmanned aerial vehicle. IEEE Trans. Robot **24**, 331–340 (2008)
13. Suter, D., Hamel, T., Mahony, R.: Visual servo control using homography estimation for the stabilization of an X4-flayer. In: Proceedings of the 41st IEEE conference on Decision and Control (2002)
14. Moktari, A., Benallegue, A.: Dynamic feedback controller of Euler Angles and wind parameters estimation for a quadrotor unmanned aerial vehicle. In: Proceedings of the 2004 IEEE conference on Robotics & Automation (2004)
15. Benallegue, A., Mokhtari, A., Fridman, L.: Feedback linearization and high order sliding mode observer for a quadrotor UAV. In: Proceedings of the 2006 International Workshop on Variable Structure Systems (2006)
16. Dunfied, J., Tarbouchi, M., Labonte, G.: Neural network based control of a four rotor helicopter. In: IEEE International Conference on Industrial Technology (2004)
17. Henriques, B.S.M.: Estimation and control of a quadrotor attitude. Master's thesis, Universidade Técnica de Lisboa (2011)
18. Pillay, P., Khrishnan, R.: Modeling, Simulation and Analysis of Permanent-Magnet Motor Drives, Part II: The brushless DC motor drive, vol. 25, pp. 274–279 (1989)
19. Doanç, K.: Design of two wheeled twin rotored hybrid robotic platform. Master's thesis, Atilim University (2010)
20. Åström, K.J., Wittenmark, B.W.: Computer-Controlled Systems-Theory and Design, 3rd edn. Prentice Hall, Englewood Cliffs (1997)
21. Mattey, R.A.: Bifilar pendulum technique for determining mass properties of discos packages (1974)

Model and Design of the Embedded Hexapod Robot Aduka Used for Hazardous Environment Inspections

Edicarla P. Andrade[(✉)], Saulo M. Maia, Rejane C. Sá,
and José Luiz M. Uchôa Júnior

Laboratório de Inovação Tecnológica-IFCE, Fortaleza-Ce, Brazil
edicarla.andrade@gmail.com, saulommaia@gmail.com, rejanecsa@gmail.com,
jluizmujr@gmail.com

Abstract. A key to the advancement of robotics is to create more complex, flexible and sturdier robot structures and controllers. In order to accomplish this task it is crucial to first develop a 3D model that allows to make a robot well-designed and easily reconfigurable, where one can change its structure, add and remove degrees of freedom of legs, create and simulate new patterns of locomotion, and other adjustments. This research demonstrates the development of the embedded hexapod robot Aduka, a mobile robot powered by an embedded system. Using Beagle-Bone Black, other single boards and an operating system FreeBSD it can be remotely controlled by computers and mobile devices for hazardous environment inspections.

Keywords: Hexapod robot · 3D modeling · Single boards · FreeBSD · BeagleBone Black · Embedded robot

1 Introduction

Mobile robot systems will be an important asset in the future. A mobile robot not only has to execute predefined tasks programmed with, but also it must explore the unknown environment that might be pushed to work in [1].

The types of terrestrial mobile robots found in academic field are varied, among them are multi-legged and wheeled robots. A multi-legged robot has an advantage of being able to walk and explore rough terrain or obstacles that a wheeled robot would not have an easy access to or no access at all.

Multi-legged mobile robots have been studied since the 60's, including studies on modeling and development of a prototype with specific characteristics [2]. One can name different advantages for the use of multi-legged mobile robots, i.e. applications in military missions, inspection of complex or hazardous scenarios, forestry and agricultural tasks [3]. Particularly, hexapod robots offer a certain advantage of a more stable walking track compared to other multi-legged robots.

© Springer International Publishing AG 2017
J.C. Figueroa-García et al. (Eds.): WEA 2017, CCIS 742, pp. 24–35, 2017.
DOI: 10.1007/978-3-319-66963-2_3

In most robotics applications, the degree of mechanical complexity is one of the main reasons for failure and considerably increased cost and effort in developing something simple and robust. Research and laboratory environments do not impose certain limits on hardware and software components compared to real and unstructured locations, and this motivates the preference for a compact, energy-saving mechanical structure [4]. The use of 3D Computer Assisted Design (CAD) features assists a designer in the development of an appropriate geometric model and presents it to a user through a specific graphic interface, assisting in the process of building a more efficient prototype.

Decades ago mobile robots were controlled by heavy, large and expensive computer systems that could not be carried and had to be linked via cable or wireless devices. Today, however, one can build small mobile robots with numerous sensors and actuators that are controlled by inexpensive, small and light embedded computer systems that are carried on-board the robot [5].

This article seeks to show the development of the remotely operated embedded hexapod robot Aduka and its controlling system. 3D robot model, its physical structure, an embedded system, a hardware and software platform will be described in the following sections. Tests and their results are provided in the last section of this article.

2   3D Robot Model and Protoype

Although the ultimate goal is to build the actual robot, it is often useful to run simulations before its production. Simulations are easier to set up, cheaper, faster and more convenient to use. Construction and configuration of a new robot model in simulation environments takes only a few hours. The modeling of robotic systems in simulation software is much less expensive than the direct manufacture of the prototype, and allows a better exploration of the design, considering also that all the structure parameters are being displayed on the screen. The simulation allows you to use extremely complex algorithms, which would require a lot of time to run on microcontrollers in real robots [7].

2.1   3D Aduka Model

Aduka consists of a rigid body with six legs, each with two independent degrees of freedom (Fig. 1). The configuration described enables the tripod alternating movement in forward/backward and right/left directions allowing stability and synchronization during the movement process.

Solid Edge ST7 CAD technology software was used in the product development process including 3D drawing, simulation, manufacturing and project management of Aduka. This software guarantees an easy development of an integrated set of components such as robots. All investigations in a 3D environment such as collision detection, safety check, assembly weight and forces supported by the structure must be made before starting the production of the robot. By following these steps chances of failure are decreased significantly.

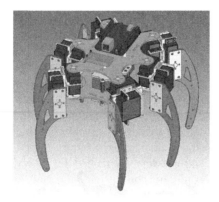

Fig. 1. 3D model of Aduka. Source: Authors (2017)

2.2 Aduka Prototype

The structure of the Aduka robot is made of silver aluminum. The robot is composed of an upper base (base 1) and a lower base (base 2). The leg of the robot is formed by a structure (base foot attachment) that connects the servo motor to the base of the foot. The robot has non-slip covers on its feet preventing it from sliding on the floor without actually moving.

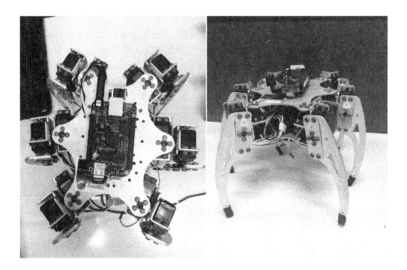

Fig. 2. Aduka Prototype - Upper and front views. Source: Authors (2017)

In terms of the robot leg configuration, Aduka was modified to have two degrees of freedom per leg instead of three degrees as it is usually a case in insects. Therefore, the robot has twelve servo motors. The piece used for the adaptation of three degrees of freedom to two degrees is shown also in Fig. 2.

3   Hardware Platform - Single Board Based System Behind Aduka

The hardware platform of Aduka is formed by the following single boards: PWM driver board, BeagleBone Black board and two voltage regulators. The use of single boards instead of one main controller is justified by the points below.

– Easy maintenance if one of the boards stop working;
– Dedicated hardware for different tasks;
– Easier to adapt new sensors and actuators;
– Easier to attach to the robot structure because they are smaller.

3.1   BeagleBone Black

Beaglebone Black is the central controller of Aduka, can be seen installed on top of the robot in the Fig. 2. This board performs two main tasks: communication with the peripheral PWM board and wireless communication with the client. A factor that drew attention to this particular board is its size (86.4 mm × 53.3 mm). It is ideal for use in a robot that is compact, lightweight and sturdy at the same time. Another factor considered for board choice was its ARM Cortex-A8 core processor with 512 MB of memory, and an open source community that allows the development of a more secure, stable, flexible (modular) code with more quality and especially accessible to all. In addition, this board has more than 40 pins for general use as I/O (GPIO), and even with this range of available peripherals it still runs on low voltage power of 210–460 mA at 5 V [8].

3.2   PWM Driver Board and Servo Motor

One of the limitations of BBB is the number of outputs of PWM, exactly four channels, though twelve outputs are required for the designed robot. One of the approaches to solve this issue is to demultiplex four PWM outputs and therefore generate signal for the 12 servo motors. However, this would create an additional effort for the main controller, because PWM signal must be kept in the servo motor to be matched in position. For this issue it was decided to use the PWM driver board which can control up to 32 servo motors simultaneously. In order to power the driver board and servos, two separate power supplies are necessary because more current required by servo motors than the processor can handle.

About the servo motors, these engines were chosen because are small and extremely powerful for thier size, and it also draws power proportional to the mechanical load, therefore, doesn't consume much energy.

3.3   Communication Protocol Between PWM and BBB Boards

To send values from BBB to driver board serial port communication was used where RX and TX channels are interconnected between the boards and a ground wire.

There are two different techniques to build the message with PWM values to be sent to the driver board. The first technique is to send PWM values one by one to output pins in the driver board, meaning if there are 12 servo motors to control one will have to send 12 messages. The protocol consists of: #, servo number to be controlled, P, servo position in PWM, # and T, time to servo perform the movement, formula $\#XPNTN\backslash R\backslash n$. The second approach is to send all values at the same time. One message will contain 12 PWM values. The protocol is very similar to sending PWM value one by one, where the difference is that instead of adding just one servo motor number and one PWM value, more motors can be added to the message. It can be seen in the following expression: $\#X1P1N1\# X2P2N2 \dots \# X32P32N32TN \backslash r\backslash n$. According to the manufacturer, servo numbers are decimal values between 1 and 32, PWM value ranges from 500 to 2500 corresponding to the value in μs of the pulse width and the time T varies between 100 and 999, the lower the number the faster the servo moves to the desired position. An example Table 1 below demonstrates different methods of sending data to the driver board.

Table 1. Methods of sending messages

Method	Message
First	$\#1P1500T350\backslash r\backslash n$
Second	$\#10P780\#12P940\#32P2500T480 \backslash r\backslash n$

3.4 Voltage Regulators and Batteries

According to the manufacturer, BBB should be powered by 12 V, the driver board by 6 up to 12 V and the servo motor by 4.8 up to 6 V. Since plates and servos have different voltages, it is necessary that the output voltage is regulated to feed the elements of the hardware platform. To accomplish this, following the idea of the project, a generic voltage regulator board called dsn2596 (CI LM2596) is used.

Another important observation is that the input voltage must be at least 1.5 V higher than the output voltage. The output voltage can vary between 1.25 V to 35 V, adjusted by a potentiometer present in the plate and the input voltage can vary between 3.2 V to 40 V.

4 Embedded System and Software Platform

One could ask why using a computer, i.e. Beagle Bone black board, to control the robot if the microcontrolled boards could easily have done the same task, the reason is the embedded system provides the robot with a more robust system that takes in account and overcomes inaccuracies and imperfections [5] of the environment and the communication between the robot (server) and the client.

4.1 Operating System FreeBSD and BeagleBone Black - Embedded System

FreeBSD is known and considered one of the most robust and secure multi-user and multi platform operating systems of modern computing. FreeBSD's native security features guarantee a DC/B3 EAL4 minimum level of certification assured by the Defense Advanced Research Projects Agency - DARPA [10]. This operating system supports the largest academic and government backbones in the world [11], one of the reasons to be chose as the operational system for Aduka. FreeBSD serves educational institutions, research, innovation and development foundations or companies around the globe. Unlike other free and open source projects available, FreeBSD is a complete operating system with its own kernel and userland.

FreeBSD is an operating system with unique safety features, performance, stability, and offers industry-leading technology standards. The current version of Aduka consists of a FreeBSD 11.0-CURRENT for ARM platform pre-compiled image to boot up, a BeagleBone Black board, revision C running Python scripts and routines powered by a battery bank. The first boot of FreeBSD in BBB is shown in the Fig. 3.

Fig. 3. First boot screen. Source: Authors (2017)

4.2 Client/Server Communication for Aduka

For a remote access to the robot, a client/server application was developed (Fig. 4) in C programming language. The server will be in the network created by a Wi-Fi dongle inserted to BBB. The server will execute a script that will interpret the messages sent by the client and provides a certain service that is available to every client that needs it.

The server in case the BBB, which acts as a provider of information to other sub-ordinate workstations, clients. The model enables us to run the modules across several different processors or machines connected through a computer network. The core of the architecture is a collection of server modules that

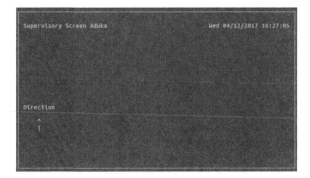

Fig. 4. Client screen. Source: Authors (2017)

provide resource sharing, access control, process synchronization and information sharing among the client modules [14].

In summary, aduka's communication system is shown in the Fig. 5. The client is represented by the PC and sends messages through wifi to the server indicating the directions the robot should move. The BBB (Server) interprets the message and sends the servo and position values to the driver board. The final step so the robot can move is the driver board decodes these values and generates PWM signals in the channels for the servo motors.

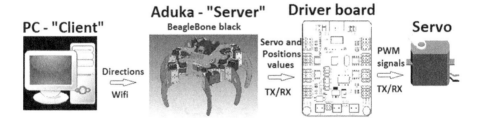

Fig. 5. Aduka's communication system. Source: Authors (2017)

5   Tests and Results

5.1   Tests with Simulated Robot

Using CAD, researchers managed modeling all the legs, bases, servomotors and their support. In addition, 3D simulation of Aduka movements allowed analyzes such as collision detection, safety check, assembly weight and forces supported by the structure. The force analyzes shown in Fig. 6 were performed to all legs to confirm that the servo motors could support and move the robot's structure.

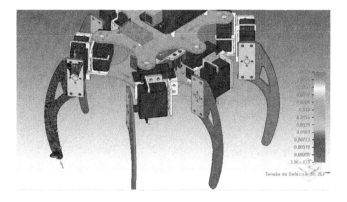

Fig. 6. Force analysis using CAD and 3D model. Source: Authors (2017)

The simulation environment provided a way of fine-tuning of movement synchronization of the servo motors through a timeline. Figure 7 shows the robot moving forward in the simulation environment. From time 0 to T1 the servos from the first set of legs move forward without the legs touching the floor while the legs of the second set give support to the robot. From time T1 to T2 the servos from the second set of legs move forward without the legs touching the floor while the legs of the first set give support to the robot. In the end of T2, all the legs are forward and touch the floor. From time T2 till T4, all the servos from the base move back, meaning that the mass center of the robot is moving forward. From time T4 to T5, the legs are moved to the initial positions. The length of the bar corresponds to how much the leg was moved in the simulation. For the other directions, i.e. backwards, left and right, more charts were created to analyze how to robot should move.

Fig. 7. Chart used to verify the synchronism of the movements. Source: Authors (2017)

To achieve a more stable movement, when testing the prototype, it was necessary to add more steps in the sequence, thus the legs would move slower and the robot could walk straight. The patterns of walking chose to simulate the system was 3×3 where 3 legs give the stability to the robot. There are other patterns,e.g. 4×2 where 4 legs down an 2 moving per step and move the robot leg by leg. Using these other walk patterns the robot walks more stable however slower than the 3×3 pattern chose for Aduka.

5.2   Tests with Prototype

Aduka can be classified as a computer-controlled robot according to Ferrari et al. [13] since it has no environmental feedback sensors and it is a robot without servo control, due to the go to goal movement.

Position matrices. In order for the robot to walk properly, the positions of the servo motors must be sent simultaneously. At first, the characteristics of the driver board were not explored in depth and the positions of the servos were sent one by one, proving to be a slow method and reducing the speed of the robot's movement. Therefore, direction matrices were created where the static torque was minimal and the robot was steady. Figure 8 brings the configuration of the direction matrices. The matrix rows represent the final legs configuration, in this case there are 4 different configurations. More rows there are in the matrix more slow the robot will walk but more stable and steady the walk will be. SP1, SP2, SP3 ...SP12 represent the PWM values and the matrix collumns represent each servo to be controlled and for Aduka there are 12 servos. The values of the position matrices were assembled sequentially and they were loaded into the message to be sent to the driver board by BBB, as a result the servos moved almost at the same time.

The final direction matrices (left, right, forward and backwards) were composed of position (PWM values) sequences that the legs of Aduka must be at so it can move steadily. According to [15], a statically balanced system avoids tipping and the ensuing horizontal accelerations by keeping its center of mass over the polygon of support formed by the feet. Due to a non-symmetrical and non-accurate structure, the position values were found after performing tests with the prototype, so it was possible to guarantee the position of the center of mass. It is worth noting that if the robot is disassembled the position matrices need to be updated. During initial tests the walking speed rate of the robot was of a less importance as long as the positions of the legs were correct. The stability could be seen when the robot had more legs touching the ground, however the robot would move slower and the current consumption was higher. In the following tests position values were modified for a better performance of the robot.

Stability versus velocity. In terms of structure validation the main items to be checked are servo motors, as they are responsible for the movement of the structure. For this purpose the relation velocity versus current consumption

Direction=[[S1P1, S2P1, S3P1, S4P1, S5P1, S6P1, S7P1, S8P1, S9P1, S10P1, S11P1, S12P1],
[S1P2, S2P2, S3P2, S4P2, S5P2, S6P2, S7P2, S8P2, S9P2, S10P2, S11P2, S12P2],
[S1P3, S2P3, S3P3, S4P3, S5P3, S6P3, S7P3, S8P3, S9P3, S10P3, S11P3, S12P3],
[S1P4, S2P4, S3P4, S4P4, S5P4, S6P4, S7P4, S8P4, S9P4, S10P4, S11P4, S12P4]]

Fig. 8. Aduka position matrices. Source: Authors (2017)

versus stability, was verified showing that the faster the motors rotate causing the robot to move faster, the greater the torque exerted by them, and according to Eq. 1, the greater the current flow through them supplied by the batteries.

$$\tau = k_t * I \tag{1}$$

where k_t is a constant and τ is torque.

Two factors were considered: the time it took to send new positions to servo motors and the time the servo motor took to reach the new position. The first factor was corrected by implementing a delay present in the robot code. The second factor was changed in the communication protocol message between BBB and the driver board. As a consequence, the robot walked more stable.

Power consumption versus velocity. To measure the performance of the batteries for the system, the first round of tests were performed in a stable and linear terrain, to simulate a first walk in a unknown terrain. At first, the robot had many "false steps" so non-slip covers (floor with low coefficient of friction) were attached to the robot legs. After this change, the robot had 45 min of power autonomy, the battery for the servos went down to 8 V and the battery for the boards went down to 10 V. The reason for the difference is that BBB and the driver board have a low power consumption, compared to servo motors. The performance of the servos after the battery went down to 8 V was inefficient, the robot lost stability because the motors did not have strength enough to move the structure.

The second round of tests with the prototype were focused in speed and power consumption. The conclusion was the faster the robot moved, the greater the battery consumption was and more unstable the robot appeared to be. To overcome this issue, the code was corrected so that the current did not exceed the peak of 2 Ah and that the robot remained stable but a little slower.

Finally, a test with imposed conditions (linear distance of 25 m, initial charge of the 12 V battery and non-stop walk) was performed. The robot took 8 min to walk the imposed distance, the average velocity was 3.1 m/min. For the power system, the number of motors running simultaneously influenced directly on the consumption of the battery due to the peaks of power requested by the servo motors. Another fact that justifies the high power consumption is the speed imposed the servo reaches to reach the next desired position (Fig. 9 - left).

The faster the motor rotates, the more current it will consume and more the batteries will be required. Then for a low energy path, a sequence of positions closer to each other is chosen to prevent the motor from turning quickly to reach the next position (Fig. 9 - right).

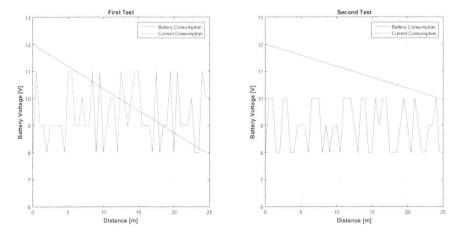

Fig. 9. Velocity and power consumption graphs. Source: Authors (2017)

To increase the power autonomy of the servos, the speed of the robot could be decreased and more powerful battery should be installed for the servo.

System communication. The control system and client/server communication did not show any fault being available to receive new direction information even when the robot could not complete a full step. The servo motors proved to be an adequate choice since they were able to support the weight of the robot and still generated the necessary force to be applied to move the robot. The main feature of this control system is that the robot can be controlled from any computer with the client program due to an ip configuration stablished for the robot.

6   Conclusion

The conception of Aduka was to offer Engeneering students a platform where they could study mechanics, electronics, dynamics, robotics, embedded systems, operational systems, programing language in one environment. In the end, the authors realized the potential of the work where you can use these simple but robust robots for the inspection of hazardous environments. As future works, the authors want to adapt a camera for visual inspection, create an mobile app with controllers and visual feedback, implement new controllers and improve the platform with sensors and actuators. Increasing the complexity of the system more knowledge is needed to accomplish the tasks given by the different environments.

References

1. Al-Jarrah, M.A.: Developing 3D model for mobile robot environment using mono-vision system. In: 2016 7th International Conference on Computer Science and Information Technology, CSIT 2016. IEEE (2016)
2. Demasi, D.: Modelagem dinâmica e de controle de um mecanismo de três de liberdade para aplicacao em um robô hexápode. Centro Federal de Educação Tecnológica Celso Suckow da Fonseca (2012)
3. Woering, R.: Simulating the first steps of a walking hexapod robot. University of Technology Eindhoven (2011)
4. Saranli, U.: Design, modeling and preliminary control of a compliant Hexapod Robot. In: Proceedings of the 2000 IEEE International Conference on Robotics & Automation, San Francisco, CA (2000)
5. Bräunl, T.: Embedded Robotics: Mobile Robot Design and Applications with Embedded Systems. Springer Science & Business Media, New York (2008)
6. Pedro N.J., Norberto, P.: CAD-based off-line Robot programming. In: Conference on Robotics, Automation and Mechatronics. IEEE (2010)
7. Olivier, M.: Cyberbotics Ltd., - Webots^{TM}: professional mobile robot simulation. Int. J. Adv. Robot. Syst. **1**(1), 40–43 (2004)
8. BeagleBone black foundation. http://beagleboard.org/black
9. ICCART.: LM2596 Step-down Voltage Regulator, DC-DC Step Down Adjustable Converter Power Supply Module (2016). http://www.iccart.com
10. Watson, R.N.M.: New approaches to operating system security extensibility. University of Cambridge, Computer Laboratory, Technical Report, UCAM-CL-TR-818 (2011)
11. Kerner, S.: FreeBSD, Stealth-Growth Open Source Project. InternetNews.com. http://internetnews.com/dev-news/article.php/3367381
12. Curti, J. C.: Análise de segurança em aplicações que utilizam plataformas UNIX e MS-Windows como Clientes e Servidores (2004)
13. Ferrari, D.G., Eto, R.M., Santos, N.M.: Classificação Geral dos Robôs. http://www.din.uem.br/ia/robotica/classif.htm
14. Dulimarta, H.S., Jain, A.K.: A client/server control architecture for robot navigation. Pattern Recogn. **29**(8), 1259–1284 . Elsevier, Amsterdam(1996)
15. Raibert, M.H.: Legged robots. Commun. ACM **29**(6), 499–514 (1986). ACM, New York

Subsampling and Pulse Reconstruction with High Frequencies Preservation

Andrés E. Jaramillo$^{(\boxtimes)}$ (iD) and Rafael M. Gutierrez (iD)

Universidad Antonio Nariño, Bogotá, Colombia
andres.jaramillo@uan.edu.co

Abstract. The conventional way to perform the sampling process of a signal requires the application of a filter to remove high frequency components in order to avoid the effect of frequency overlap. However, in many cases filtering the signal may mean important loss of information about signal details. This paper shows that under certain conditions on the sampling system and the sampled signal, it is possible to recover all the signal frequency components according to a sub-sampling and reconstruction process inspired in compress sensing. The study considered pulse signals with pulse duration much smaller than the total length of the signal.

Keywords: Compressed sensing · Subsampling · Pulse signals

1 Introduction

With the rapid development of information technology, supply and demand for information is increasing dramatically. This means important challenges to achieve high sampling and transmission rates, storing large amounts of data as well as new forms of analysis and use of information. The sampling criterion of Nyquist-Shannon represents a basic principle for the theory of sampling signals. This criterion implies that the sampling frequency should be at least twice the bandwidth of the input signal to accurately reconstruct the signal [1]. Usually, to meet this criterion the signals must be filtered, eliminating their high frequency components. However, in complex and nonlinear processes the information is, in principle, distributed throughout all the frequency range and filtering a signal of this kind can cause a loss of important information about signal details. In certain applications such as detection of micro-patterns in images [2, 3], this kind of information is just the most important, at least in certain regions of the image.

Recently, from the seminal works of Donoho [4], Candès, Romberg and Tao [5, 6], it has been developing a new theory which gives the possibility of achieving higher compression rates than those of the traditional compression standards, and also allowing a reconstruction of the original signal with higher precision. Under this new approach, called Compressed Sensing (CS) [7], the signal sampling is performed while the number of samples required to reconstruct the original is reduced without affecting any particular frequency component of the signal.

© Springer International Publishing AG 2017
J.C. Figueroa-García et al. (Eds.): WEA 2017, CCIS 742, pp. 36–46, 2017.
DOI: 10.1007/978-3-319-66963-2_4

This paper shows that it is possible to recover discrete pulse signals with all its frequency components from an efficient signal data sub-sampling, by using a sampling and reconstruction process similar to that of CS. For the type of signals considered, in general, high frequency components are not a small part of the information contained in the signal, corresponding to abrupt changes in the amplitude of the pulses themselves. The remaining content of this article is organized as follows. The next section reviews the basic concepts of the theory involved in this work. Section 3 presents the tests performed and the process are described. In Sect. 4 the results and analysis are presented. The final section is dedicated to the conclusions and future work.

2   General Framework

2.1   Subsampling and Reconstruction

In digital signal processing decimation or downsampling is the process by which the sampling frequency of a signal is reduced by an integer factor. In implementing this process on a digital signal, we obtain a signal with fewer samples than those of the original signal where intermediate samples are discarded and therefore the signal is smaller, it is compressed. The sampling theory of Nyquist-Shannon indicates that, in order to be able to make a good signal reconstruction from the subsampled signal, the original signal sampling should be limited in their frequency components. Therefore, first we must apply an anti-overlap filter to limit the frequency components of the original signal according to the maximum required by the sampling system. Once this process of filtering and sampling process is performed, for a conventional reconstruction process, it is no longer possible to recover the original signal with all its frequency components. Using interpolation filters, we can only recover the low frequency components, that is, the same original signal smoothed by the anti-overlap filter (Fig. 1).

Fig. 1. Subsampling and reconstruction using interpolation.

In this work we examine the processes of sampling and reconstruction applied to discrete signals of finite duration pulses. Such signals contain frequency components throughout the frequency range. From the results, it can be seen that under certain conditions it is possible to recover the high frequency components of pulse signals using optimization techniques similar to CS. Under the proposed approach, while sampling the original signal it is also accompanied by a smoothing operation however, here the reconstruction of the signal by the optimization process can recover all of the original signal components, including those of high frequency (Fig. 2).

pulse signal   reconstructed signal

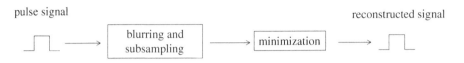

Fig. 2. Subsampling and reconstruction using minimization

2.2 Compressed Sensing

Compressed Sensing (CS), is a new concept in signal processing whereby it is possible to minimize the number of samples of a signal, while it is kept all the information necessary to precisely recover the original signal with a very high probability [8]. The main idea behind CS is to use the structure redundancies that occur in the signals. Because of these redundancies, the signals can be expressed in some domain, with a high number of coefficients close or equal to zero. This condition is known as sparsity and represents the only requirement on the nature of the signals to which we can apply this new concept. Moreover, to reconstruct a signal from their samples within CS, we need to apply iterative algorithms to solve an optimization problem.

In this paper, the sampling scheme and reconstruction is similar to the usual of SC. The sparsity condition of the input signal is assured, since they are considered discrete pulse signals for which most of its samples or data points are zero. Specifically, in the sampling stage we apply a sampling array based on Gaussian functions, and for the reconstruction we use an algorithm based on convex programming [9]. The algorithm minimize the norm $L_1 (\| x \|_1 = \sum_i x_i)$ on the signal to be reconstructed, g, subject to the condition $y = A \cdot g$, where A represents the sampling matrix, and y represents the sampled available signal. The L_1 minimization is a convex optimization problem and can be solved by interior point methods.

3 Numerical Experiments

3.1 Subsampling Process

The procedure followed in all tests is first a regular sampling by the application of the sampling function to the input signal using a Gaussian distribution, then the reconstruction from the sampled signal is performed using an optimization algorithm [10]. The samples of the sub-sampled signal are obtained by evaluating the dot product between the initial signal and the Gaussian sampling function. In Fig. 3 it is illustrated the sampling process applied to a rectangular pulse signal. The Gaussian sampling function is centered on the point at which the sample is generated. The other samples are obtained equivalently moving the Gaussian sampling function to each point and performing the dot product each time [11].

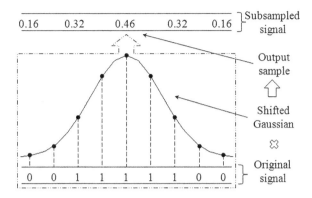

Fig. 3. Subsampling process of the signal: the dot product between the original signal and the shifted Gaussian sampling function generates each output sample.

In the reconstruction process we apply an optimization algorithm to minimize the L_1 on the signal to be reconstructed, g, we seek for $min \parallel g \parallel_1$, provided $y = A \cdot g$, where A is the sampling matrix, and y is the sub-sampled signal available. The rows of matrix A represent the sampling Gaussian function displaced by the sampling step. This sampling process generates a sub-sampled signal which is a mixture between shifted samples gathering information from different angles or positions of observation.

3.2 Sampling Function

The sampling function proposed in this work is a discrete normalized Gaussian function defined with the same length of the test signal. The sampling function f, on the discrete domain x, is defined as $f(x|p, \sigma) = \dfrac{1}{\sigma\sqrt{2\pi}} e^{\dfrac{-(x - p)^2}{2\sigma^2}}$, where p represents the sampling period and σ is the standard deviation. This function was chosen as an approaching simulation of the acquisition process of light intensity signals from an array of detectors in a row [12], where each detector capture radiation from a point with a spread Gaussian function representing the radiation intensity depending of the relative position of the source and the detector. For the numerical tests, both parameters take values in the domain of positive integers. According to the results obtained in this work, only for some particular combination of values of these two sampling parameters, the reconstruction or decompression is visually perfect. This is related to the spread and overlap of the shifting Gaussian sampling function which depends on both parameters.

3.3 Testing Signals

The first signals used for the numerical tests in this work were pulse signals, that is, signals with values different from zero only in a relatively short period compared to the total length of the signal. Pulse signals ensure the sparsity condition without the need of any previous transformation. The pulse signals considered in this work have a length of 1024 points with pulses lasting up to 24 points. Different pulse shapes were considered: constant, stepped, smooth and rapid variations, and signals with more than one pulse.

4 Results and Discussion

This section presents the results of a series of tests seeking for the ranges of values of the sampling process parameters p and σ, for which the high frequency components of the signal are recovered. As a global quantitative measure to determine the difference between the original signal and reconstructed signal we use the Root Mean Square Error (RMSE), which is the Euclidean distance between the reconstructed signal data points, x_i and the original signal data points, y_i, normalized by the total number of signal samples N, that is $RMSE = \sqrt{\dfrac{\sum_i (x_i - y_i)^2}{N}}.$

4.1 Tests

Test 1. Signal with a constant pulse of six samples duration. This test signal has a total length of 1024 points. The pulse has a constant height of 0.8 units and a duration of 6 points from the sample number 110 (Fig. 4). Since the value of the pulse amplitude does not affect the results, it was chosen arbitrarily. The length of the signal and the start and end points of the pulse are also chosen arbitrarily, though, sufficiently far from the extremes of the signal to fulfil the required sparsity condition of CS. It is also because the Gaussian sampling function is only defined on the same domain of the original signal

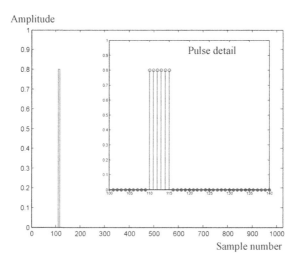

Fig. 4. Signal with a rectangular pulse: signal total length 1024 samples, pulse constant amplitude 0.8 in arbitrary units and duration of 6 samples from the signal simple number 110.

and it needs enough samples to the left and right of the focus simple in the original signal.

Applying the procedure described in the previous section with the Gaussian sampling function and using for the reconstruction process the minimization, we vary the sampling parameters σ and p, both in the signal sampling units, although in general, σ does not have to be an integer value. With the resulting signals we estimate the RMSE between the reconstructed signals and the corresponding original signal, and the overlap between neighbor Gaussian sampling functions separated by the sampling step p. The magnitude of the overlap is the sum of the amplitudes of the discrete common points of both neighbor Gaussian shifted one from the other by p points (Fig. 5).

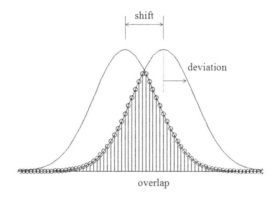

Fig. 5. Overlap of the Gaussian sampling function with itself shifted one step p.

As it is apparent, the relationship between p and σ determines the extent of the overlap indicating how strong it is for each pair of values of the two sampling parameters. If the overlap is too small, the necessary information to reconstruct data points of the signal between successive Gaussians may be insufficient, and if the overlap is too large the information from this data signal may become too redundant and reduces the likelihood to find the original signal. From a visual assessment of the similarity between the reconstructed signal and the original signal, a maximum acceptable value of RMSE was established to define overlap between limits for the values of the Gaussian sampling function parameters. The limit set by the previous criterion was RMSE $= 1E{-}06$ units. This value corresponds to a RMSE of 2.08E$-$05% relative to the total sum of amplitudes of the original signal. The overlap value obtained is indicated below.

Since linear increments in optimization has no any effect over optimal solutions, if a value of σ is kept fixed, the RMSE value does not exhibit a monotonous increase or decrease for increasing sampling step, p. As an example, Fig. 6a and b show RMSE in logarithmic scale as a function of the sampling step p for σ equal to 8 and 9, respectively. The range of values of p is limited by those when the RMSE is below the maximum value as indicated before. According to the limit value of RMSE, the minimum and maximum values for σ are 1 and 20, respectively. In this range, the minimum overlap is 0.4832 corresponding to $\sigma = 5$ and $p = 7$; and the maximum overlap is 0.7208 for

$\sigma = 7$ and $p = 5$. For a difference greater than 4 between σ and p, it is not possible to recover the original signal with an RMSE less than 1E−06.

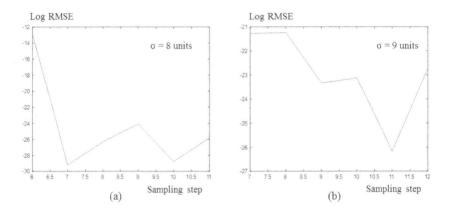

Fig. 6. Logarithm of RMSE as a function of sampling step, p, for σ equal to: (a) $\sigma = 8$ units, (b) $\sigma = 9$ units.

Test 2. Variable pulse signal. The test signal is pulse duration of six points with variable amplitude. In Fig. 7 it is shown the pulse shapes (left) with their corresponding frequency spectrum (right): (a) rectangular pulse; (b) smooth pulse but with abrupt start and end, thus containing high frequency components; (c) stepped pulse; and (d) pulse with arbitrary amplitude variations. The ranges obtained in the previous section to the rectangular pulse also apply to other forms of pulse considered in this test. In this test one set of values for the sampling parameters σ and p was found that enables a better reconstruction for all the pulse shapes considered. In Table 1 are presented the pulses shapes which has the best reconstruction (lower RMSE) with their corresponding pair

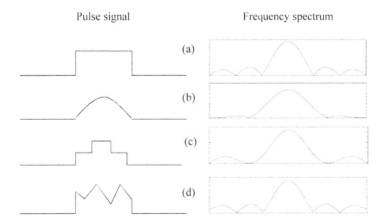

Fig. 7. Pulse shapes used for the numerical tests and their corresponding frequency spectrum. (a) Rectangular pulse, (b) Smooth pulse, (c) Stepped pulse, (d) Pulse with arbitrary amplitude variations.

of values of σ and p; other combination of values for the two sampling parameters do not meet the RMSE criteria.

Table 1. The letter indicates the only corresponding pulse shape of Fig. 7 meeting the RMSE criterion for the indicated values of the sampling parameters, σ and p; the other pair of values give larger RMSE.

σ	p					
	4	5	6	7	8	9
5	b	c	b	d	–	–
6	–	b	d	b	b	–
7	–	a	d	c	d	a
8	–	–	c	a	b	b

Test 3. Signal with a pulse of variable duration. In this test, in addition to the sampling parameters σ and p, the duration of the pulse d is considered as a variable parameter. The pulse amplitude is kept constant and the total length of the signal also 1024 data points. It was found that increasing the pulse duration decreases the possible values of σ and p, allowing a reconstruction with an RMSE less than the limit defined in Test 1. For $d \geq 17$ it is only possible to obtain a good reconstruction for $\sigma = p = 1$. Then for σ and p values larger tan 1, the pulse duration must be of maximum 16 points. In Fig. 8 are shown the maximum values of $\sigma = p$ for which the value of RMSE is below the limit defined in test 1, as a function of pulse duration, d.

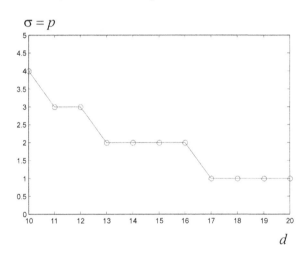

Fig. 8. Maximum values of $\sigma = p$, with RMSE below the limit defined in test 1, as a function of d.

Test 4. Signals with two pulses. In this test we consider two pulses of the same height and the same duration. The variable parameters are the pulse duration, d, and their separation, s (Fig. 9). The results show that for a reconstruction with RMSE less than the limit stated above, the pulse duration must be 12 points, regardless of the values of the sampling parameters σ and p. This implies a greater restriction than that obtained with a single pulse signal. Furthermore, in this case σ and p must be equal to 2.

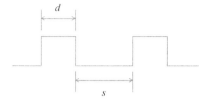

Fig. 9. Parameters of a signal with two pulses.

It was also found that when d is less than 12 points, the signal may have a smaller s and the overlap covers enough but not too much for a good reconstruction, equivalently to good conditions for the reconstruction of a larger pulse made of the sum of both smaller pulses. Specifically, for pulses up to $d = 8$ can be spaced a minimum of $d = 4$ points (with $\sigma = p = 2$), while for pulses of $d = 6$ can be spaced a minimum of $d = 1$ (with $\sigma = p = 2$).

4.2   Frequency Analysis

As it is known, the spectrum of a rectangular pulse signal has components of all the frequency range. This implies an overlapping effect of high frequency components in its spectrum is performed if subsampling of said signal. A common solution to avoid this effect is to apply a low-pass filter to remove the high frequencies of the signal to be sampled. This filtering process prevents the effect of overlap when sampling. However, in trying to recover the signal by a traditional demodulator filter what you get it is the smoothed signal, not the original signal with steep edges, that is, with its high frequency components.

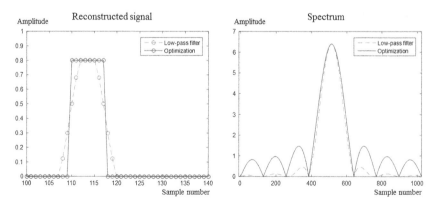

Fig. 10.   Reconstructed pulse signal (left) and its corresponding frequency spectrum (right) using a low-pass filter (dashed red line), and applying optimization (continuous blue line) (Color figure online).

According to the approach proposed in this paper, the anti-overlap filter is performed simultaneously with the sampling signal, and the process is represented by a sampling matrix formed by Gaussian functions. This same sampling matrix is then used to set a condition in the recovery of the original signal, which is effected by a minimization process. The results show that for some signals and values of the sampling parameters, it is possible to recover the original signal including the high frequency components with great accuracy. In Fig. 10 it is presented the spectrum of the recovered signal. As can be seen, a visual difference cannot be discerned from the original signal. In this case the RMSE value is 1.3350E-11.

4.3 General Discussion

Considering the RMSE limit equal to 1E−06, we found that it is possible to subsample and recover signals retaining high frequency components. Some results revels the relation between the parameters that characterize the pulses of the signals. For pulses of duration less than 12 points whose amplitude may vary in the range of the pulse duration, to obtain a RMSE below the defined limit, the parameter values of the Gaussian sampling function, width of the Gaussian and its shifting step, σ and p respectively, must be similar. For signals of a single pulse the difference of these two values has a maximum of 4 units, while for composite signals of several pulses the two parameters must be equal and their values must be maximum equal to 2 units. These results can be generalized to relative values of the different signal parameters: pulse duration, signal duration, number of pulses and pulses separation, and the sampling parameters, can be adjusted for a particular reconstruction precision of the signal in the high frequency content which represents the sharp contours traditionally loosed with other methods. On the other hand, it can also be seen that the reconstruction process is affected by the amplitude variations of the signal but not by its mean value.

5 Conclusion

In this work, we present a new technique for subsampling and reconstruction based on compressed sensing that can then rebuild discrete signals with high frequency components without having to undergo the Nyquist criterion. From the analysis of numerical experiments, it was found the conditions under which it is possible to reconstruct the discrete pulse signals with an error of less than a threshold approach chosen as RMSE = 1E−06. The conditions are expressed as different combinations of the most important parameters determining the process: step or sampling interval and the width of the sampling function which determines the overlap ratio in the sampling process; the pulse width and the size of the signal whose ratio determines the condition of sparsity.

As already mentioned, since all the tests signals meet the condition of sparsity in the initial domain, any transformation is not required to a different domain where the transformed signal is sparse. Future work will aim to generalize the results to non-scattered or disperse signals, requiring a transformation to a sparse representation as the compressed sensing techniques require.

As it is shown in Fig. 10, the proposed sub-sampling and reconstruction process recovers the original signal with very good fidelity respecting the information contained in high frequencies when the combination of parameters is appropriate. This can be useful in applications where the high frequency information is of great importance but in general lost by traditional methods, such as for details identification in low resolution images. This work is currently being developed.

Acknowledgments. This work was partially supported by Colciencias (Fondo Nacional de Financiamiento para la Ciencia, la Tecnología y la Innovación "Francisco José de Caldas") Project No. 1233-715-52363.

References

1. Proakis, J., Manolakis, D.: Digital Signal Processing: Principles, Algorithms and Applications, 4th edn. Prentice Hall, New York (2006)
2. Gutierrez, R., Cerquera, E., Mañana, G.: MPGD for breast cancer prevention: a high resolution and low dose radiation medical imaging. J. Instrum. 7(1), C07007 (2012)
3. Rodriguez, C., Gutierrez, R., Jaramillo, A.: Adaptive thresholding by region of interest applied to quality control of gas electron multiplier foils. In: XXI Symposium on Signal Processing, Images and Artificial Vision (STSIVA) (2016)
4. Donoho, D.: Compressed sensing. IEEE Trans. Inf. Theory 52(4), 1289–1306 (2006)
5. Candès, E., Romberg, J., Tao, T.: Robust uncertainty principles-exact signal reconstruction from highly incomplete frequency information. Trans. Inf. Theory 52(2), 489–509 (2006)
6. Candès, E., Romberg, J., Tao, T.: Stable signals recovery from incomplete and inaccurate measurements. Commun. Pure Appl. Math. 59(8), 1207–1223 (2006)
7. Davenport, M., Duarte M., Eldar Y., Kutynik, G.: Introduction to compressed sensing. In: Compressed Sensing: Theory and Applications, Cambridge University Press, Cambridge (2011)
8. Candès, E., Wakin, M.: An introduction to compressive sampling. IEEE Sig. Process. Mag. 25(2), 21–30 (2008)
9. Boyd, S., Vandenberghe, L.: Convex Optimization. Cambridge University Press, Cambridge (2004)
10. CVX Research Homepage. http://cvxr.com/cvx. Accessed 05 Mar 2017
11. Kröger, M., Rosenbaum, M., Sauer-Greff, W., Urbansky, R., Lorang, M., Siegrist, M.: Irregular sampling for X-ray imaging simulation. In: Signal Processing: Algorithms, Architectures, Arrangements, and Applications (SPA) (2015)
12. Grupen, C., Buvat, I.: Handbook of Particle Detection and Imaging. Springer, New York (2012)

Data Register for the Automobile Control Flow in Real-Time Using UAV

Gustavo Armando Guancha Taquez[1] (ID), Octavio José Salcedo Parra[1,2(✉)] (ID), and Brayan Steven Reyes Daza[2(✉)] (ID)

[1] Universidad Nacional de Colombia, Bogotá, D.C., Colombia
{gaguanchat,ojsalcedop}@unal.edu.co
[2] Internet Inteligente Research Group, Universidad Distrital Francisco José de Caldas, Bogotá, D.C., Colombia
bsreyesd@correo.udistrital.edu.co, osalcedo@udistrital.edu.co

Abstract. The world today combines a larger number of megacities, which are control nodes of the whole world. These megacities must provide to their inhabitants an efficient way to transport and that is the reason of this paper. It is intended to give a judgment of the acquisition, handling and processing of information that may be useful for an intelligent traffic system.

Keywords: UAV · Traffic · SAR · Windows media service

1 Introduction

Bogotá presented an annual increment of 12% in vehicles from 2002 to 2011, but the increment of infrastructure doesn't show up in a corresponding way [1, 2]. Among the many alternatives exposed in the literature is one that particularly will be study object in this work and it is the one that corresponds to the gathering of data flow and vehicular density by means of video transmission in real time to obtain a model that allows to display the state of the streets so an appropriate working of the traffic lights is given and decisions taking on the part of the conductive citizens of vehicles, whose data can be presented for example in mobile applications. The system that is sought could has extra advantages as the possibility of speeding up rescue works or of attention to victims in transit accidents.

DRONES or UAVs are an alternative to be considered, they allow a constant air monitoring with the advantage of possessing considerably bigger speeds to those of the vehicles for their ability of moving with freedom, so it is a tool of favorable data acquisition. This data acquisition system however requires of a data handling that allows interpreting the videos taken by the DRON, translating those in formative data, treatment that can be made by artificial vision followed by a statistical treatment that would allow a statistical model to predict vehicular flows [3].

© Springer International Publishing AG 2017
J.C. Figueroa-García et al. (Eds.): WEA 2017, CCIS 742, pp. 47–54, 2017.
DOI: 10.1007/978-3-319-66963-2_5

2   Architecture of the Design

The concept of the project is represented in the Fig. 1, which shows an UAV equipped with a video camera which transmission in real time to the earth station. While the images are recorded, they are also transmitted through wireless Internet to a fixed server that transmits to transit multiple authorities to make quick decisions on the identification of incidences.

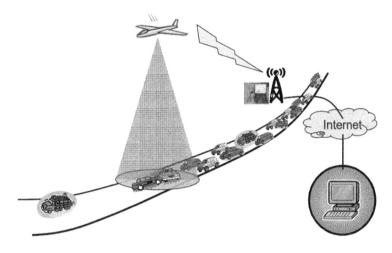

Fig. 1.   General view of the project [5].

After revising carefully several small models of UAV platforms including an option to develop a custom system, it is convenient to imitate the election that made of Western Michigan University in which existing small UAV is used that it is MTD III of MLB Company [5]. There is been keeping in mind the underlying factors as the budget and the time restrictions, registers and previous experiences, etc. It is a complete mini system UAV that operates in a stand-alone way and offers videotape of high quality data of images and of the sensors in real time. The 10 liberate airplane have a span of 6 ft, but it can be disassembled to occupy a box of "18 × 18 × 36". The airship can get ready for the flight in question of minutes but of course each mission is specified inserting a waypoints series in the earth station. It has autonomy in flight duration of until 6 h, field of the telemetry of 7 miles and a charge capacity of 4 lb.

3   Communication UAV-Earth

The connection module among the camera from UAV and the monitoring station to earth it is based on the design used by the office of the Department of Transport of Michigan who make use of the available communication networks to make the transmission toward the station to earth and being either exposed to end users in real time or saved for off-line later analysis [3]. Flagrantly one of the obstacles to surpass is the videotape data call in real time captured by the camera from UAV to the station to earth. The group of the University of Florida has implemented a system of surveillance of the air traffic that encodes the video data of an air view, and it transmits the sequences of videotape multimedia on an IP network microwaves, [6] it is given by expert that the station to earth has access to internet in an easy way by means of a communication tower or similar the viability of the broadband use is proven for the video transmission, the quality of wireless link and the security that one has in an environment of public network [3]. The system MLB MTD III include the radio frequency transmission device that connects the UAV with the control station in earth. The video images captured on board by the camera are transmitted to the team in the station to mobile earth, and it needs to be retransmitted the end users.

It can observe in the Fig. 2, how UAV captures images of video and transmits data to earth station. The station in earth receives the radio signal and transforms it into videotape of digital base band. A computer in earth has a system of wireless wired PC board to the network of some of the national operators, the program that encodes the flow of videotape of images in real time it is developed by Microsoft. The cellular national network is wired with a backbone of Internet. Lastly, the teams of the end users obtain the video images in Internet. The mobile operator provides mobility to the network.

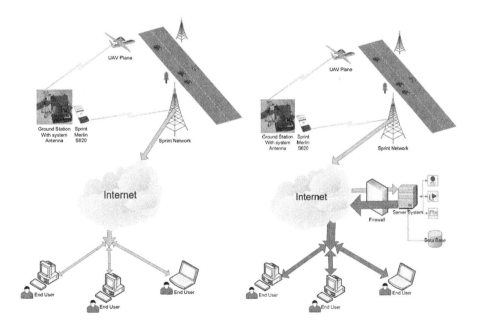

Fig. 2. Data transmission outline [5]

4   Data Transmission

The computer of the control station in mobile earth informs the end user of its IP address and the teams of the end users can open the reproducer of means to consent to the video-tape flow from this address IP. The mobile broadband service usually allocates a dynamics IP address for what differs from a connection application to another. There-fore, it should be informed at the final users of the IP address recently acquired in each connection. In the second scheme in Fig. 3, an additional server is used that serves as host of the data call connection. The server works with a fixed IP address that can be known a priori by the station to movable earth and for the end users. The computer in earth trans-mits the video to the server with a specific IP address, and the end user consents to the videotape from the server through this IP address. Besides the videotape streaming in

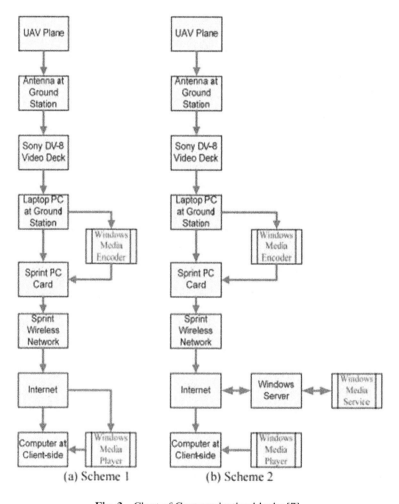

Fig. 3. Chart of Communication blocks [7].

address time server can store the videotape received in its hard disk for an off-line future analysis. The outline of the proposals in charts of blocks is exposed in the Fig. 3.

Protocols used in the video streaming for Windows Media 9 Series are User Datagram Protocol (UDP), Real-Time Protocol (RTP), Real Time Streaming Protocol (RTSP), Real Time Control Protocol (RTCP), Hypertext Transfer Protocol (HTTP) y Microsoft Media Server Protocol (MMS). The firewall is a hardware or software piece that controls the data flow of traffic based in the reception port, the IP address origin and the IP address destination. The information is related with its packages of data. Some secure servers can also control the additional data flow on the base of the protocols. For this project UAV, the ports allocation for Windows Streaming Mediates they are different and they depend in the ways of content distribution methods. Windows Media Service is one of the applications that have incorporated in Microsoft Windows Server 2003. The server system can provide a stable environment while Windows Media Service average is operand under conditions of real time. Windows Media Service has applied in the project UAV based on the following features:

- Setup of the bandwidth limits for the publication during the distribution content.
- To control the number of clients that consent to files of audio and videotape in a simultaneous way.
- To administer the global demands of bandwidth of the features of Services of Windows Media.
- To minimize the excessive demands on service of media distribution in the network for the appropriate setup and the features to optimization of media services.
- To decide in real time clients with authorized IP address.
- To provide features to average out several files to a single emission or in an only directory for a selective broadcasting.

Widows Media Service provides two types of methods: unicast and multicast to distribute the content of the media. Basically, the option of unicast establishes a videotape sequence from one to one among the server of Windows Media and each client system, considering that the option of multicasting delivery sends an only videotape sequence it can consent simultaneously from multiple users. This delivery method is easier of configuring and easier to work without a lot of network infrastructure (router, firewall, system settings). However, unicast is significantly an environment bandwidth. Because each client for the session of the server is separately a videotape sequence, the emission with 10 users would have 10 videotape sequences from the server to the clients, and the emission with 100 users it would have 100 sequence of videotape from the server to the clients [5].

5   Complementary and Alternative Solutions

Video Streaming could be a little annoying due to the limited bandwidth, and therefore it is convenient to think in that UAV can process on board the data captured by its camera and to transmit reports of lighter data for example simply the number and the coordinates of each one of the vehicles that observes in real time. It is then necessary to think in artificial vision techniques that allow to subtract features of the images and to infer on them.

5.1 Harris Corner Detection

The detection of corners is an approach used in the vision by computer systems to extract certain types of features and to infer the content of an image. The detection of corners frequently is used in the movement detection, image analysis, tracking in video, modeling 3D and recognition of objects among other. The detection of corners is overlapped with a more comprehensive topic: the detection of points of interest. It is an algorithm that searches to characterize the air images based on the identification of the edges. A corner can be defined as the intersection of two edges. It can also be defined as a point for which there are two addresses of dominant and different edges in a local vicinity of the point. A point of interest is a point in an image that has a defined position and it can be detected in a robust way. This means that a point of interest can be a corner but it can also be, for example, an isolated point of local maximum or minimum intensity, final of lines, or a point in a curve where the bend is locally maximum.

- Estimate of density features: In this stage, an algorithm characterizes and determines which are above a certain value.
- Refined detection based on the color: The idea is to reject objectives discriminating the color to avoid false alarms.
- Classification of objectives: The recognition of corners is useful but it is still weak and it needs of a refinement to classify objectives and to determine which of them are of interest, for the case it is the automobile.

The task could be completed in two steps: Extraction of Features and Classification techniques. It is necessary to have a census system on board UAV that monitor. It is a difficult task because the control in 3D and the complexity of the images. UAV requires fulfilling the necessity of bring images of wide covering so it should can to fly at considerable levels of height.

Synthetic Aperture Radar SAR is a processing unit that wants to merge the information obtained in sweepings of the antenna to generate a "virtual sweeping" being the result comparable to which would offer an antenna of more size. The use of SAR has been quite wide primarily in remote sense applications and cartography, then they are used to produce digital precise models of big areas and they are generally used for tracking of relatively immobile targets. On the other hand, the Moving Target Indication (MTI) is a model of radar operation to identify objectives in movement or amid clutter (English term that refers to the not wanted echoes in the electronic systems, mainly in reference to the radars) and they are appropriate for characterization of the traffic flow with the use of radars.

5.2 Generation of Static Profiles for Traffic Monitoring Using REAL-TIME with Videos from UAVs

The eye-in-the-sky project is proposed from the Florida South University which wants to make use of UAVs to gather data in real time with the objective of monitoring the vehicular traffic identifying quantities of vehicles in the streets measuring and valuing traffic patterns. Each UAV should have a system of vision and register on board to transmit them information to earth where would be the station to earth who is the one in charge of processing the data. For them it is convenient according to this study the use of cameras able to make dynamic automatic monitoring and for it there are cameras like PTZ of automatic capable tracking to discriminate the movement, or a combination of these factors- active the camera, the focus and changes in the field of view. Some features of this type of cameras are listed next:

- They can rotate around two axes, one horizontal and other vertical, as well as to come closer or far away (zoom) to focus an area or object in a manual or automatic way. Said in another way, this type of cameras can rotate in a vertical plan and in a horizontal plan, besides to come closer or to take in a manual or automatic way.
- It can be analog, of IP type or even hybrid merging both features. In the case of the cameras analog PTZ, the commands are generally transmitted through a pair of cables that are connected via RS232 or RS485 to a keypad or directly to the recording team and the video transmission is carried out through a coaxial cable or of an UTP cable with the use of a videotape balloon. In the case of the IP equipment, all the commands PTZ are sent through the same network cable that is used for the video transmission. Some of the features that can incorporate to a camera PTZ include:
- Electronic image stabilization (EIS) which helps to reduce the effect of the vibration in a videotape.
- Mask of privacy that allows to lock or to mask determined areas of the scene in front of visual display or recording.
- Auto-ensue: it is a feature of intelligent videotape that detects the movement of a person or object automatically and it follows it inside the field of covering of the camera.

The previous features facilitate the tracking of automobiles in an individual way in the hypothetical case that an individual tracking is required for example to an automobile to calculate the time that takes in crossing intersections, to cross bridges or to turn in some sense. The data gathered by means of video are used to conclude the parameters like capacity, density of vehicular flow, among other; that will be picked up historically to arrive to a simulation model that allows to model traffic conditions.

6 Results Comparing and Conclusions

Comparing the articles [4] and [5] of the bibliography, the first design supposes the use of a single transmission medium for which the end users make its connection and they share the speed of data of the connection of mobile broadband. The wireless connection is the bottle neck for the video signal transmission, the system can only support to a limited number of end users with acceptable speed of data. The sum of the maximum rates of data that the end users can have is smaller than the speed of data with the one that the earth control equipment UAV transmits to the server by means of a connection of mobile broadband. In the second scheme, the computer to mobile earth sends data to the server through the mobile broadband network. The server transmits the data to the teams of the end users through wire Internet. The maximum number of end users that can see the video depends simultaneously in the speed of data of the Internet connection for cable of the server that is much bigger than the wireless connection. Therefore, more equipment of the end users can receive the flow of videotape in a simultaneous way with acceptable speed of data.

SAR [7] has the advantage of adaptation to environmental changes, thanks to the system of vision on board UAV and the system on earth which has some algorithms that allow to do it; also, the uncertainty of the same one it bears to difficulties to take a faithful count of vehicles. The task of more effort in the project is the detection of vehicles by means of air images in automatic way that facilitates to characterize the streets. For it is primordial to have technical computational appropriate and organized that allow it. The use of radars on board UAVs allows capturing images of fields of big extensions without matter the climatic conditions and it doesn't require of any technology on board the vehicles, SAR offers a resolution of images from among one to two meters. However, the techniques for detection of vehicles don't have clarity and are under study [5, 7].

References

1. Movilidad en Cifras, Bogotá (2011). http://www.movilidadbogota.gov.co
2. Kanungo, A., Sharma, A., Singla, C.: Smart traffic lights switching and traffic density calculation using video processing. In: Recent Advances in Engineering and Computational Sciences (RAECS), pp. 1–6. IEEE, Chandigarh (2014). doi:10.1109/RAECS.2014.6799542
3. Puri, A., Valavanis, K., Kontitsis, M.: Statistical profile generation for traffic monitoring using real-time UAV based video data. In: Mediterranean Conference on Control & Automation, pp. 1–6. IEEE, Athens (2007). doi:10.1109/MED.2007.4433658
4. Chen, Y., Dong, L., Oh, J.: Real-time video relay for UAV traffic surveillance systems through available communication networks. In: Wireless Communications and Networking Conference, pp. 2608–2612. IEEE, Kowloon (2007). doi:10.1109/WCNC.2007.485
5. Ro, K., Oh, J., Dong, L.: Lessons learned: application of small UAV for Urban highway traffic monitoring. In: 45th AIAA Aerospace Sciences Meeting, pp. 7160–7178, Elsevier, Reno (2007)
6. Srinivasan, S., Latchman, H., Shea, J., Wong, T., McNair, J.: Airborne traffic surveillance systems—video surveillance of highway traffic. In: Second International Workshop on Video Surveillance & Sensor Networks (VSSN), pp. 131–135. ACM, New York (2004). doi: 10.1145/1026799.1026821
7. Bethke, K., Baumgartner, S., Gabele, M., Hounaman, D., Kemptner, E., Klement, D., Krieger, G., Erxleben, R.: Air- and spaceborne monitoring of road traffic using SAR moving target indicationproject TRAMRAD. In: International Society for Photogrammetry and Remote Sensing, pp. 243–259. Elsevier B.V., Wessling (2006). https://doi.org/10.1016/j.isprsjprs.2006.09.005

A Semi-supervised Speaker Identification Method for Audio Forensics Using Cochleagrams

Steven Camacho[(✉)], Diego Renza, and Dora M. Ballesteros L.

Universidad Militar Nueva Granada, Bogotá, Colombia
{u3900217,diego.renza,dora.ballesteros}@unimilitar.edu.co

Abstract. The general task in speaker identification for audio forensics is to identify the unknown speaker within an audio proof, who is suspected of a crime. Here, the voice of each person within a group of suspects is compared to the audio proof with the aim to determining which of them corresponds to the source. In this paper, a semi-supervised speaker identification method is proposed, which does not require a training stage. Also, the feature extraction is based on the use of cochleagrams for the previously selected words. The system can identify one or multiple suspects which have high similarity to the audio proof, or give a null response if none of the suspects satisfies a similarity threshold. The results of the proposed method are compared with the respective results of the same method but using spectrograms instead of cochleagrams. The performance of our system is measured through a confusion matrix (true and false positives, and true and false negatives) and global results are given in terms of overall accuracy and kappa index. According to several tests, our system has an overall accuracy higher than 0.97 and a kappa index around 0.78; this means a high confidence in the results of identification and rejection.

Keywords: Speaker identification · Audio forensics · Cochleagram · Correct identification · Correct rejection

1 Introduction

Speaker recognition is a useful tool in forensic sciences in areas such as law enforcement or national security, and it includes two main areas: speaker identification (SI) and speaker verification. The aim of SI is to identify an unknown speaker from a set of known speakers, whereas in speaker verification the task is to verify the identity of an unknown speaker [6,10]. SI for audio forensics consists in determining the person whose voice sounds the closest to the voice from an unknown person within an audio sample [12]. This has a special interest, since incorrect identification may incriminate an innocent person or discard a real participant in such conversation. The fundamental problem in the speaker identification process is about the voice signal: although it can be considered as a signature of its owner, it is not always the same because their characteristics can

© Springer International Publishing AG 2017
J.C. Figueroa-García et al. (Eds.): WEA 2017, CCIS 742, pp. 55–64, 2017.
DOI: 10.1007/978-3-319-66963-2_6

suffer unintentional variations (e.g. current health or aging) or intentional variations (e.g. distortion by an impersonation process), which can lead to incorrect conclusions about the identification of the suspect. Additionally, although the messages come from different people, some parameters such as entropy and statistical moments (e.g. average, variance, kurtosis and skewness) may be similar to each other [4,5].

Currently, there are numerous speaker recognition methods for verification purposes, which usually use a training phase and are usually based on techniques such as neural networks [3,7,16], fuzzy logic [9,11,18], genetic algorithms [8], ant colony optimization [14], Markov chains [2], and clustering [15]. These methods show excellent identification results (over 90%), but unfortunately their application in forensic audio is limited, since they require a data training stage with prior knowledge of the speaker, a situation that is not feasible in forensic practice. Quite the contrary, in the forensic field it is common for the suspect to pretend fake his voice in such a way that it can not be verified as participant in the audio given as evidence.

According to a study reported in 2016 by the International Criminal Police Organization (INTERPOL) [13], the speaker identification methods used by the intelligence agencies of countries worldwide can be classified into six categories: auditory, spectral, acoustic-phonetic, statistical, semi-supervised (human-assisted), and automatic. The first three categories are subjective and they are based on the opinion of an expert in phonetics, either by listening to the audio (auditory method), comparing the spectrograms of audio signals (spectrographic methods) or a combination of the two previous options (acoustic-phonetic approaches). In the fourth category, statistical approaches, the forensic performs measurements on the audio signals and calculate their statistical parameters. In semi-supervised cases, signal processing engineers and/or phonetic experts use algorithms for the identification of characteristics of audio signals, which allow to identify positively or negatively (rejection) the suspect. However, this requires a pre-processing step for extracting (manually) some utterances from the voice records. Finally, in automatic systems, the processing and analysis stages are performed objectively and without supervision. In six of the seven countries consulted by INTERPOL in Latin America, the identification of the speaker is done by using a subjective method, mainly the spectrographic method. Also, the study emphasizes that in the case of North America, work is mainly done with semi-supervised methods.

According to the above, the present work proposes a speaker identification model classified as semi-supervised method, which does not require a training stage, and therefore does not need prior knowledge of the people participating in the voice registers. Because the identification is done in a "blind" way, unlike the methods focused on verification, in the proposed method the system's response may be null (without identified suspect), with a single positive identification, or with multiple suspects identified from positively way. Based on the fact that the time-frequency analysis of the voice allows to find similarities or differences between individuals, and knowing that most of the energy of a speech signal is concentrated at low frequencies, the cochleagram of the voice records is used as the main feature. The cochleagram, unlike the spectrogram, is a graphical representation of the time-frequency intensities of the voice by using a non-linear frequency scale, so that at low frequencies a better resolution is obtained than it would be obtained with a spectrogram.

2   Cochleagram-Based Identification

The spectrogram is one of the most used options in speaker identification, since it allows the simultaneous visualization of time and frequency behaviour of a signal [1,12], in addition, it has been shown that even when an individual is capable of imitating the voice of another person (and sounds very similar), the spectrogram between them presents differences [17]. However, a spectrogram uses a linear scale for the frequency axis, showing with the same resolution level low and high frequencies. An alternative solution is to use gammatone filters, and to obtain a graphical representation with non-linear resolution of the time-frequency behaviour of the speech signal, known as the cochleagram [19].

An example illustrates the differences between these two methods. Figure 1 presents the spectrogram of the word "paz" pronounced by two women with perceptually similar voice. Visually, the similarity between the spectrograms is remarkable, showing some zones with high amplitudes (red) between 0 and 1.5 kHz.

On the other hand, Fig. 2 shows the cochleagrams of the same voice registers used in Fig. 1. In this case, there are visually appreciable differences related to the intensities and the level of curvature. In Fig. 2(a), there is only one red zone (around 602 Hz), while in In Fig. 2(b) there are two red zones, one of which is around 1190 Hz. In addition, the difference in curvature of the strokes is clear (the zone is flatter in Fig. 2(a) than in Fig. 2(b)).

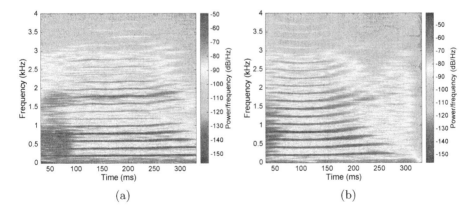

Fig. 1. Spectrograms for the word "paz" pronounced by two people with perceptually similar voice. (Color figure online)

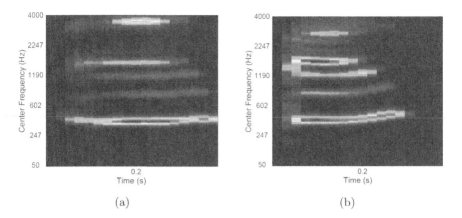

Fig. 2. Cochleagrams for the word "paz" pronounced by two people with perceptually similar voice. (Color figure online)

3   Proposed Method

The proposed model includes the following steps: word extraction, feature extraction, similarity estimation, global similarity, and thresholding (See Fig. 3). Each block is explained below.

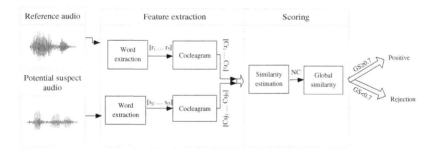

Fig. 3. Illustrative representation of the flow chart for speaker identification.

3.1   Word Extraction

This is a pre-processing stage and consists in the extraction of words from the audio provided as proof (reference). In order to make a comparison with different types of sounds (fricative, occlusive, nasal, among others), it is recommended to select at least five words, with different characteristics. These words must be pronounced by the potential suspects within a complete text, in order to avoid falsifying the voice by prior knowledge of the selected words. At the end of this stage we have the following sets of words (Eqs. 1 and 2).

$$ref = [r_1 \ r_2 \ r_3 \ r_4 \ r_5]$$ (1)

$$spk_j = [s_{j_1} \ s_{j_2} \ s_{j_3} \ s_{j_4} \ s_{j_5}]$$ (2)

where ref corresponds to the set of five words from the reference audio, and spk_j corresponds to the set of five words of the $j - th$ suspect.

3.2 Feature Extraction

The function of this block is to calculate the cochleagram of each input word, being this the main feature that will allow to define if the voice of a suspect matches or not with the reference audio. It should be noted here that it is proposed to use cochleagrams, not spectrograms, since the cochleagram allows a more specific visualization of the time-frequency characteristics at low frequencies of the signal, i.e. the spectrum where much of the voice signal energy is concentrated. However, the generalities of this method can also be used with spectrograms. The outputs of this block correspond to the set of cochleagrams from the reference audio ($C(ref)$, Eq. 3), and the set of cochleagrams from each suspect ($C(spk)$, Eq. 4).

$$C\left(ref\right) = [Cr_1 \ Cr_2 \ Cr_3 \ Cr_4 \ Cr_5]$$ (3)

$$C\left(spk_j\right) = [Cs_{j\_1} \ Cs_{j\_2} \ Cs_{j\_3} \ Cs_{j\_4} \ Cs_{j\_5}]$$ (4)

3.3 Similarity Estimation

From the cochleagrams originating from the reference audio and those from the potential suspects, the normalized correlation value (NC) between each pair of them is calculated; NC ranges from -1 and 1, being 0 when there is a null correlation, 1 when maximum correlation exists, and -1 when the data follow opposite trends (i.e. one signal is increasing and the other is decreasing). The outputs of this block are the NC values between each pair of cochleagrams, calculated by means of the Eq. 5.

$$NC\left(r, s_j\right)_i = \frac{\sum \left(Cr_i - \overline{Cr_l}\right)\left(Cs_{j\_i} - \overline{Cs_{J\_l}}\right)}{\sqrt{\sum \left(Cr_i - \overline{Cr_l}\right)^2}\sqrt{\sum \left(Cs_{j\_i} - \overline{Cs_{J\_l}}\right)^2}}$$ (5)

Here, i indicates the position of the word within the set of five selected words.

3.4 Global Similarity

Because a single word is not enough to completely characterize a speaker, the proposed method works with five words. These words are selected from the reference audio and must be pronounced by the suspects. Therefore, five NC values are obtained for each suspect. The objective of this block is to calculate a single value of similarity from the five results per suspect. This value will be called global similarity (GS) and calculated from Eq. 6.

$$GS_j = \frac{\left\langle \sum_{i=1}^{5} \left| NC\left(r, s_j\right)_i \right| \right\rangle - \min\left(\left| NC\left(r, s_j\right)_i \right| \right)}{4} \tag{6}$$

According to the above equation, to obtain the value of GS, we must first calculate the average of the absolute value of the four largest NC values per suspect; i.e., the minimum absolute value of NC is excluded. The reason for this exclusion is that poor audio quality (e.g. incomplete or poorly pronounced) can provide low NC values even if the suspect corresponds to the reference audio. Thus, by excluding the lowest value of NC, identification error is avoided due to this situation.

3.5 Thresholding

The input to this block corresponds to the GS value obtained in the previous block. Since the magnitude of each NC value is between 0 and 1, the value of GS also lies between 0 and 1. In this case, the closer the value of GS to 1, the greater the coincidence between the suspect and the audio reference. On the contrary, the lower its value (close to 0), the greater the certainty that the potential suspect and the reference audio do not match. According to preliminary tests, it was found that a GS value above 0.7 corresponds to the cases with a high probability that the potential suspect and the unknown person of the reference audio are the same person, for this reason this threshold value was selected for the positive identification of the subject. Mathematically, the classification is defined by means of Eq. 7.

$$ID = \begin{cases} positive & if \quad GS \geq 0.7 \\ rejection & if \quad GS < 0.7 \end{cases} \tag{7}$$

where ID corresponds to the potential suspect's identification status.

Based on the results from the classification block per suspect, the final step is to group the positive results. A positive result implies that the potential suspect is selected by the system given the match with the reference audio; a rejection result implies that the suspect's voice does not match the reference audio and therefore the suspect is discarded.

Using the proposed system the output can take one of the following options:

a. Null identification: no suspect is identified positively (the threshold is not exceeded).

b. Unique identification: the system selects a single suspect from the group provided by the forensic services.
c. Multiple identification: the system selects two or more suspects from the group.

4 Implementation and Evaluation of the Method

In the validation phase we used 10 databases, where each database has an audio proof and the corresponding audio recordings for the 25 suspects. Every database has ten audio recordings by word by suspect (trials), which means that there were 100 simulations (i.e. 10 databases * 10 trials). In each simulation, the aim was to compare the voice of each suspect with the audio proof and determine if each of them corresponds to the audio proof. After each simulation, the output is one of the following options:

- One suspect selected. It can be the right suspect (identified with the symbol ✓) or a wrong suspect (identified with the symbol ×).
- Several suspects selected: it follows the same notation of the above case. There is a symbol (✓ or ×) for every suspect selected.
- None of the suspects selected: in this case the output is null (identified with a question mark (?)).

The results of the proposed speaker identification method (i.e. using cochleagrams) after the 100 simulations are shown in Table 1. Each cell of this Table shows the number of identified suspects in each one of the trials for each database, and a ✓ if the suspect corresponds to the right suspect, and a × if the suspect does not. Additionally, a question mark (?) is showed in the cases where the system has not obtained any potential suspect.

Table 1. Identification results for the proposed speaker identification (cochleagram-based) after 100 simulations. 10 databases × 10 trials and 25 suspects by database.

	1	2	3	4	5	6	7	8	9	10
1	✓	✓	✓×	✓	✓	×	✓	✓	✓	✓
2	✓	✓	✓×	✓	✓	✓×	✓	✓	✓××	✓
3	✓	✓	✓×	✓	✓	✓×××	✓	✓	✓×	✓
4	✓	✓×××	✓	✓	✓	✓×××	✓	✓	✓×××××	✓××
5	✓	✓×	✓×	✓×××	✓	✓×	✓	✓	✓×××××	✓××
6	✓	✓×	✓×	✓×	✓×××	✓	✓×	✓	✓××	✓
7	✓	✓	✓	✓	✓×××	✓××××	✓	✓	✓××	✓
8	✓	✓××	✓×	✓	✓	✓××××××	?	✓	✓××	✓
9	✓	✓	✓	✓	✓×	✓×	✓	✓	✓××	✓
10	✓	✓×××	✓×	✓	✓××	✓××××	✓	✓	✓×	?

✓ right identification × wrong ? empty

Now, with the purpose of determining advantages and disadvantages of our proposal, we apply the proposed method using spectrograms. It means, the same blocks of the method are used (feature extraction, similarity estimation, global similarity, thresholding), but in the case of feature extraction the spectrograms of the audio signals are used instead of their cochleagrams.

With the same databases of the above results, we compute the performance using the spectrograms and the results are shown in Table 2.

Table 2. Identification results for the proposed speaker identification, but using spectrograms instead cochleagrams, after 100 simulations. 10 databases × 10 trials and 25 suspects by database.

	1	2	3	4	5	6	7	8	9	10
1	✓	?	?	?	?	?	?	?	?	?
2	✓	✓	?	?	?	✓	✓	?	?	?
3	✓	✓	?	?	?	✓	✓	?	?	?
4	✓	✓	?	?	?	✓	✓	?	?	?
5	✓	✓	?	?	?	✓	✓	?	?	?
6	✓	✓	?	?	✓	✓	✓	?	?	?
7	✓	✓	?	?	✓	✓	✓	?	?	?
8	✓	✓	?	?	?	✓	✓	?	?	?
9	✓	✓	?	?	?	?	✓	?	?	?
10	✓	✓	?	?	?	✓	✓	?	?	?

According to the results of Tables 1 and 2, we can deduce that:

- Using the spectrograms in the feature extraction, the probability of identifying a suspect that does not match with the audio proof is very low. However, the probability of identifying the right suspect is low, too.
- The total number of empty results significantly decreases if the system works with cochleagrams instead of spectrograms.
- The total number with correct identifications significantly increases if the system works with cochleagrams instead of spectrograms.

To assess the accuracy of our identification method, we use the error matrix evaluation method. Here, to determine the accuracy, error matrices are constructed by comparing the obtained results against the correct results (i.e. the correct suspect). Thereafter, Overall Accuracy (OA) and Kappa (κ) indices are calculated to evaluate the performance. OA is the sum of the suspects correctly classified divided by the total number of reference suspects, while κ index is a statistical measure of coincidence between two data, in this case, between the output identification results and the correct suspect.

According to the above, we summarize the results using the metrics OA (Overall Accuracy) and kappa (k) index. Using cochleagrams, the results are

0.97 and 0.78, respectively. In spectrogram case, the results are 0.975 and 0.38, respectively. It is worth noting that the kappa index severely punishes an incorrect result, for example an empty result or a unique response with a wrong suspect. For this reason, in terms of the kappa index, the system that uses cochleagrams has a significant improvement than the results with spectrograms.

5   Conclusion

In this paper we present a semi-supervised method of speaker identification. The inputs of the system are five words per suspect and five words of the audio proof; the output is one of the following options: unique from identification, several identifications, or empty identification. The steps of the method are feature extraction and scoring. In the extraction process, the cochleagrams of the inputs are calculated and then the normalized correlation of each pair is obtained. In the scoring step, a global similarity (GS) is calculated from the normalized correlations of the cochleagrams. Then, with a thresholding decision, the suspects that have high similarity to the audio proof are thereby selected.

According to the validation phase, it is found that the use of cochleagrams in the feature extraction step instead of spectrograms increases the probability to find the right suspect, and therefore, the number of empty results decreases significantly. As a disadvantage, wrong suspects can be identified together with the right suspect.

The most important advantage of our system is that it allows to identify the right suspect most of the times without a training phase. This is the great contribution of our work.

Acknowledgment. This work is supported by the "Universidad Militar Nueva Granada-Vicerrectoría de Investigaciones" under the grant IMP-ING-2136 of 2016.

References

1. Ajmera, P.K., Jadhav, D.V., Holambe, R.S.: Text-independent speaker identification using radon and discrete cosine transforms based features from speech spectrogram. Pattern Recogn. **44**(10), 2749–2759 (2011)
2. Alegre, F.L.: Application of ANN and HMM to automatic speaker verification. IEEE Lat. Am. Trans. **5**(5), 329–337 (2007)
3. Almaadeed, N., Aggoun, A., Amira, A.: Speaker identification using multimodal neural networks and wavelet analysis. IET Biometrics **4**(1), 18–28 (2015)
4. Ballesteros, L., Renza, D., Camacho, S.: An unconditionally secure speech scrambling scheme based on an imitation process to a Gaussian noise signal. J. Inf. Hiding Multimedia Sig. Process **7**(2), 233–242 (2016)
5. Ballesteros, L.D.M., Moreno, A.J.M.: A bit more on the ability of adaptation of speech signals. Revista Facultad de Ingeniería Universidad de Antioquia **66**, 82–90 (2013)
6. Campbell, J.P., Shen, W., Campbell, W.M., Schwartz, R., Bonastre, J.F., Matrouf, D.: Forensic speaker recognition. IEEE Signal Process. Mag. **26**(2), 95–103 (2009)

7. Daqrouq, K., Tutunji, T.A.: Speaker identification using vowels features through a combined method of formants, wavelets, and neural network classifiers. Appl. Soft Comput. **27**, 231–239 (2015)
8. Day, P., Nandi, A.K.: Robust text-independent speaker verification using genetic programming. IEEE Trans. Audio Speech Lang. Process. **15**(1), 285–295 (2007)
9. Devika, A., Sumithra, M., Deepika, A.: A fuzzy-GMM classifier for multilingual speaker identification. In: 2014 International Conference on Communications and Signal Processing (ICCSP 2014), pp. 1514–1518. IEEE (2014)
10. Hansen, J.H., Hasan, T.: Speaker recognition by machines and humans: a tutorial review. IEEE Signal Process. Mag. **32**(6), 74–99 (2015)
11. Hu, Y., Wu, D., Nucci, A.: Fuzzy-clustering-based decision tree approach for large population speaker identification. IEEE Trans. Audio Speech Lang. Process. **21**(4), 762–774 (2013)
12. Maher, R.C.: Audio forensic examination. IEEE Signal Process. Mag. **26**(2), 84–94 (2009)
13. Morrison, G.S., Sahito, F.H., Jardine, G., Djokic, D., Clavet, S., Berghs, S., Dorny, C.G.: Interpol survey of the use of speaker identification by law enforcement agencies. Forensic Sci. Int. **263**, 92–100 (2016)
14. Nemati, S., Basiri, M.E.: Text-independent speaker verification using ant colony optimization-based selected features. Expert Syst. Appl. **38**(1), 620–630 (2011)
15. Univaso, P., Ale, J.M., Gurlekian, J.A.: Data mining applied to forensic speaker identification. IEEE Lat. Am. Trans. **13**(4), 1098–1111 (2015)
16. Wu, J.D., Tsai, Y.J.: Speaker identification system using empirical mode decomposition and an artificial neural network. Expert Syst. Appl. **38**(5), 6112–6117 (2011)
17. Wu, Z., Evans, N., Kinnunen, T., Yamagishi, J., Alegre, F., Li, H.: Spoofing and countermeasures for speaker verification: a survey. Speech Commun. **66**, 130–153 (2015)
18. Xing, Y., Li, H., Tan, P.: Hierarchical fuzzy speaker identification based on FCM and FSVM. In: 2012 9th International Conference on Fuzzy Systems and Knowledge Discovery (FSKD), pp. 311–315. IEEE (2012)
19. Zhao, X., Shao, Y., Wang, D.: Casa-based robust speaker identification. IEEE Trans. Audio Speech Lang. Process. **20**(5), 1608–1616 (2012)

Automation of a Business Process Using Robotic Process Automation (RPA): A Case Study

Santiago Aguirre[1(✉)] and Alejandro Rodriguez[2]

[1] Pontificia Universidad Javeriana, Bogotá, Colombia
saguirre@javeriana.edu.co
[2] Outsourcing S.A., Bogotá, Colombia
alrodriguez@outsourcing.com.co

Abstract. Robotic Process Automation (RPA) emerges as software based solution to automate rules-based business processes that involve routine tasks, structured data and deterministic outcomes. Recent studies report the benefits of the application of RPA in terms of productivity, costs, speed and error reduction. Most of these applications were carried out on back office business process where the customer is not directly involved, therefor a case study was conducted on a BPO provider to verify the benefits and results of applying RPA to a service business process with front and back office activities. The results show that productivity improvement is the main benefit of RPA, nevertheless time reduction was not achieved on this case.

Keywords: Robotic process automation · RPA · Automation · Business process

1 Introduction

For the execution of business process, workers currently spend substantial time dealing with Enterprise Resourcing Planning (ERP), Customer Relationship Management (CRM), spreadsheets and legacy systems in manual repetitive tasks like tipping, coping, pasting, extracting, merging and moving massive amounts of data from one system to another.

Consider that some of these highly structured, routine and manual tasks could be handle by a robot, so that knowledge workers have more time for value added tasks. This is the promise or Robotic Process Automation (RPA) that emerges in the last five years as a set of software tools and platforms that can automate tasks on rules-based business process [1].

Recent case studies reports the benefits of the application of RPA in different business process [2, 3] and some authors [4, 5] propose the criteria for selecting the process for automation. One of these criteria is highly structured tasks, corresponding typically to back office business process like finance, procurement and human resources. On the research no studies have found that reveal benefits of the application of RPA on front office business process like selling, requirements handling or after sales support. Considering the above, the research question proposed on this paper is ¿What are the results on applying RPA to service business process with front and back office activities? For answering the

© Springer International Publishing AG 2017
J.C. Figueroa-García et al. (Eds.): WEA 2017, CCIS 742, pp. 65–71, 2017.
DOI: 10.1007/978-3-319-66963-2_7

question a case study was carry out on a business process of a Business Process Outsourcing (BPO) service provider.

This paper starts with a literature review of the RPA concept and evolution (Sect. 1), followed by the revision of different RPA applications (Sect. 2.2). On Sect. 3 a use case is analyzed in a business process that involves front and back office activities, to draw the results on Sect. 4 and finally conclusions and future work.

2 Literature Review and Related Work

2.1 Robotic Process Automation

According to Slaby [6], RPA is the technological imitation of a human worker with the goal of automating structured tasks in a fast and cost efficient manner. Even that the term "robot" brings to our minds visions of electromechanical machines, it is important to know that RPA is not a physical robot, it is a software based solution that is configured to carry out repetitive operational tasks and procedures that are used to be done by humans [7].

RPA can automate rules-based processes that involve routine tasks, structured data and deterministic outcomes, for example, transferring data from multiple input sources like email and spreadsheets to systems like ERP and CRM systems. Most applications of RPA have been done for automating tasks of service business process like validating the sale of insurance premiums, generating utility bills, paying health care insurance claims, keeping employee records up-to date, among others [7].

On the IT side, one "robot" equals to one software license. This robot is integrated across IT systems via front-end, as opposed to traditional software, which communicates with other IT systems via back-end so it is possible to integrate RPA with virtually any software used by a human worker, regardless of its openness to third party integration [3]. According to the Institute of Robotic Process Automation (IRPA) [8], RPA technology is not a part of a company's information technology infrastructure, but rather sits on top of it.

Some characteristics that distinguish RPA from other automation technologies like Business Process Management Systems (BPMS) are:

- RPA sits on the top of existing systems and access these platforms through the presentation layer, so no underlying systems programming logic is touched [5].
- In contrast to most BPMN modeling packages, RPA solutions do not require programming skills for software interface configuration. RPA is set to work by just dragging, dropping and linking icons.
- RPA doesn't create a new application and does not store any transactional data, so there is no need of a data model or a database like BPMS systems [5].

On the other hand, RPA is also different from cognitive automation. According to Willcocks and Lacity [7], Cognitive Automation is used to automate tasks and decisions that involve algorithms to interpret unstructured data resulting in a set of likely answers, as opposed to RPA that uses rules to process structured data and instructions. The outcome of cognitive automation is probabilistic, in RPA is deterministic, a single result.

A Capgemini [9] study suggest that an RPA software licence can cost between 1/3rd to 1/5th of the price of an full-time employee (FTE). Lacity and Willcocks [1] sustains that one robot can perform structured tasks equivalent to two to five humans. Although the benefits in cost savings that companies report with RPA [3], not every business process is suitable for its use. Fung [4] suggest some criteria of business process for RPA:

- *Low cognitive requirements.* Task that does not requires subjective judgment, creativity or interpretation skills.
- *High volume.* Tasks that are performed frequently.
- *Access to multiple systems.* Process that requires access to multiples applications and systems to perform the job.
- *Limited exception handling.* Tasks that are highly standardized with limited or no exceptions to handle.
- *Human error.* Tasks that are prone to human error due to manual labor.

According to these criteria, the strong candidates for RPA are back office areas that have processes that are more standardized than front office processes that require handling multiple exceptions. On the next section some case studies are analyzed.

2.2   Related Work

RPA applications have been reported over the last 5 years in business process like accounts payable, accounts receivable, travel expenses, fixed asset accounting, master data management, billing, keeping employee records, among others [2, 3, 5]. Most of these processes are back office or support processes for services where the costumer is not directly involved.

Telefonica O2 that launched on 2010 an RPA trial on two high-volume, highly standardized processes. One process was SIM swaps, a subprocess for replacing a customer's existing SIM with a new SIM but keeping his or her existing number. The other process was the application of a pre-calculated credit to a customer's account. On this process various software systems are needed. Telefonica compares using RPA versus BPMS for the automation finding that RPA for 10 automated processes would pay back in 10 months, in contrast, with the BPMS was going to take up to three years to payback [2].

Xchanging is a business process and technology services provider that applied RPA with one of its insurance customer. When brokers sell an insurance policy, they submit notices using a variety of inputs (email, spreadsheets, etc.) to Xchanging, which manages the multistep process of validating the sale. Previously, Xchanging's human operators managed the transactions manually. They organized the data, checked it for completeness and accuracy, worked with the insurance brokers to correct errors, extracted other necessary data from online sources, and then created and posted the official sales records. The structured parts of the process, including finding the errors, retrieving the online data, creating the official sales record, and notifying brokers when the process is complete, is managed by the robotic process automation software. Xchanging estimates cost savings averaging 30% per process [5].

Other case studies report the application of RPA in the finance industry [10], energy and BPO [7]. On the other hand, consulting firms like Deloitte [11] and Capgemini [9] conducted surveys that revealed that the main areas of RPA implementation will be: accounts payable, accounts receivable, travel and expenses, fixed assets and human resource administration. Capgemini survey [9] also revealed that the main measures for RPA success are: cost reduction, increasing process speed, error reduction and increasing compliance.

3   Case Study: RPA Application to a Business Process

The case study was conducted on a BPO provider firm located in Bogotá, Colombia. As part of its transformation strategy, this company created a Center of Excellence as a platform for process innovation, development of new services, better customer experience and organizational performance improvement, through process automation and deployment of new technologies.

RPA was pointed by some analyst as one of the new technologies that could thread traditional process outsourcing [6], but is also an opportunity for this industry therefor this BPO firm started by evaluating and prototyping this automation technology on some of its customer business process.

The use case was carried out on a process for generation of a payment receipt. The AS-IS process described on Fig. 1 starts when a customer calls and request the payment receipt, a front office agent creates the case on a CRM system. Then a back office agent open the case on the CRM, copy and paste the ID of the customer on the accounts receivable system and generates the payment receipt on a pdf file. The agent writes an email to the customer with the payment receipt attached and closed the case on the CRM.

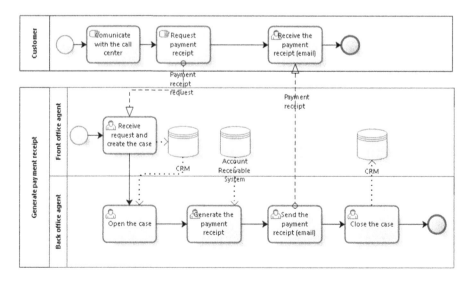

Fig. 1.   Generate payment receipt AS-IS process.

On Fig. 2 is the TO-BE automated process, where the back office activities were assumed by a software robot (RPA). After the case creation on the CRM is done by a front office agent, the robot access the CRM, copy the customer ID and paste it on the account receivable systems, generates de payment receipt, creates the email, send to the customer and finally close the case.

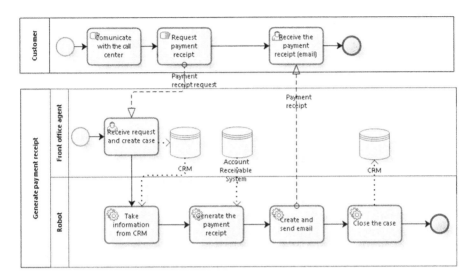

Fig. 2. Generate payment receipt TO-BE automated process

4 Results

For evaluating the results, the agents involved in the operation were divided in two groups, one group with RPA and the other group without RPA. On the group without RPA there was front and back office agents, on the group with RPA there were only front office agents because the robot perform the back office activities. The measures used for evaluating the results were case duration and productivity measured by the number of cases by agent on the evaluation period.

Table 1 shows the results on a one week evaluation period. The main benefit is productivity improvement measured by cases per agent, showing that the group with RPA could handle 21% more cases than the group without RPA. This productivity improvement is part of the benefits expected from RPA and for this BPO provider means that RPA could increase its capacity by 20% on this business process.

On the other hand, mean case duration was measured showing that the group with RPA has only 9 s less duration than the group without RPA. By surprise, reduction in terms of percentage is just 2%. One of the reasons for this is that some skill workers could perform the back office activities very fast, even faster that the software robot that imitates human behavior, with the difference that one license robot could perform several cases at the same time.

Table 1. RPA implementation results

Group with RPA	Number of Agents	22
	Mean case duration (seconds)	431
	Total number of cases	7163
	Cases per agent	326
Group without RPA	Number of Agents	13
	Mean case duration (seconds)	440
	Total number of cases	3505
	Cases per agent	270

5   Conclusions and Further Research

RPA is an automation technology based on software tools that could imitate human behavior for repetitive and non-value added tasks such as tipping, coping, pasting, extracting, merging and moving data from one system to another. The main benefits of RPA are cost reduction, increasing process speed, error reduction and productivity improvement.

When it comes to deciding on the use of RPA, companies should considerer that RPA is more suitable for high volume standardized tasks that are rules driven, where there is no need for subjective judgement, creativity or interpretation skills. Back office business process such as accounts payable, accounts receivable, billing, travel and expenses, fixed assets and human resource administration are good candidates for RPA. Also the back office part of customer service processes.

On the implementation side, it is important to consider that RPA doesn´t store any transactional data and does not require a database. RPA sits on the top of existing systems and access these platforms through the presentation layer. RPA solutions do not require programming skills for configuring the software as RPA interfaces work like BPMN modeling packages, by dragging, dropping and linking icons. Time and effort required to implement RPA are considerable less than automation technologies like BPMS.

The main benefit of RPA is cost reduction, based on productivity improvements as the case study reveals. Other benefits such as process agility are relative to the RPA configuration, hardware capacity and response time of the applications that the robot needs to access. Error reduction is also a measure, that although was not measured on the case study, could be improved by RPA.

RPA is one of the automation tools that need to integrate with other tools like BPMS and in the near future with cognitive automation tools. Technologies like IBM's Watson are being adopted for business process where unstructured information is analyzed for automating cognitive tasks. Future studies are required on how to combine these technologies.

References

1. Lacity, M., Willcoks, L.: What knowledge workers stand to gain from automation. Harvard Bus. Rev. (2015). https://hbr.org/2015/06/whatknowledge-workers-stand-to-gain-from-automation
2. Lacity, M., Willcocks, L.: Robotic process automation at telefónica O2. MIS Q. Executive **15**, 21–35 (2016)
3. Asatiani, A., Penttinen, E.: Turning robotic process automation into commercial success – case OpusCapita. J. Inf. Technol. Teach. Cases **6**, 67–74 (2016)
4. Fung, H.P.: Criteria, use cases and effects of information technology process automation (ITPA). Adv. Robot. Autom. **3**, 1–11 (2014)
5. Willcocks, L., Lacity, M.: Service Automation: Robots and the Future of Work. Steeve Brokes Publishing, Warwickshire (2016)
6. Slaby, J.: Robotic automation emerges as a threat to traditional low-cost outsourcing, HfS Res. 1–18 (2012). https://www.hfsresearch.com/report/robotic-automation-emerges-threat-traditional-low-costoutsourcing
7. Lacity, M., Willcocks, L.P.: A new approach for automating services. MITSloan Manag. Rev. **58**, 40–49 (2016)
8. Institute for Robotic Process Automation (IRPA): Introduction to Robotic Process Automation (2015). http://irpaai.com/introduction-to-robotic-process-automation-a-primer/
9. Capgemini Consulting: Robotic Process Automation-Robots conquer business processes in back offices (2016). https://www.de.capgemini-consulting.com/resource-file-access/resource/pdf/robotic-process-automation-study.pdf
10. Seasongood, S.: A case for robotics in accounting and finance. Technol. Account. Financ. Executive, 31–39 (2016)
11. Deloitte: The robots are coming (2015). https://www2.deloitte.com/uk/en/pages/finance/articles/robots-coming-global-business-services.html

Protocol Conversion Approach to Include Devices with Administration Restriction on a Framework of Reference of Management Network

Mauricio Tamayo García[✉], Henry Zarate, and Jorge Ortíz Triviño

Faculty of Engineering, Universidad Nacional de Colombia,
Av Carrera 30 No 45 03, Bogotá 111321, Colombia
{emtamayog,hzaratec,jeortizt}@unal.edu.co

Abstract. Considering the problem of handling devices with management limitations, the solution can be based on protocol conversion through finite-state converter in combination with the SNMP proxy agent functions and using the serial ports of legacy equipment and small devices with processing restrictions as sensors on a Ad Hoc network or Internet of Things. It reviews the framework of reference of management network, giving details of the challenges for the mentioned devices and the state of art of the existing solutions. This paper approximates to the proposed solution due to the research is in progress.

Keywords: Network management · SNMP · Proxy · Legacy systems · Protocol conversion · Finite-state converter · Ad Hoc · Serial communications

1 Introduction

Although, the major telecommunication devices are developed with management protocol support to their administration like SNMP (Simple Network Management Protocol), some of them have restricted access to their system variables through some management protocol or sometimes do not support it. This can happen for several reasons: (a) it does not consider it in the initial design, (b) the manufacturers develop own management applications as business model, (c) they are legacy systems which replacement can be expensive at the financial and operational level, or, (d) because their hardware is limited on processing and their resources are used in another kind of process.

This paper is an approach to the development of a solution that focus in the building of protocol converter SNMP to serial for integrating legacy devices or equipment with processing restrictions in a management network already constituted. It is necessary to resolve questions about its construction, implementation, diversity challenges, cost and scalability.

© Springer International Publishing AG 2017
J.C. Figueroa-García et al. (Eds.): WEA 2017, CCIS 742, pp. 72–83, 2017.
DOI: 10.1007/978-3-319-66963-2_8

In the Sect. 2, it explains briefly the framework of reference of the network management, the SNMP protocol as common element in the major of management networks and the serial communications advantages. In the Sect. 3, it is detailed the propounded problem for legacy systems and for elements with processing restrictions in an Ad Hoc network or Internet of Things (IoT). It explains some existing solutions like to use an independent software or to include additional hardware and the limitations that it implies. In the Sect. 4, it gives an approach to the solution based on a finite-state converter model that works together with the SNMP proxy features and its implementation in legacy systems and Ad Hoc networks. By last, in the Sect. 5, it describes the research scope and the possible use of its results.

2 The Framework of Management Network

The management systems in a telecommunications infrastructure refer to the activities, methods, procedures and tools that permit the operation, management, maintenance and provisioning [1] of the network. These systems permit to model management network environment such as organizational, information, functional and communications [2], each one performing a different role but complementary, where the operation variables and available services on the network are controlled and monitored, following and registering the components network performance to detect unexpected behavior to take actions to avoid failures or improve the services performance, control deviations and manage resources.

A network management system is based on the agent/manager model that consist in a manager, a managed system, a management information database and a network protocol [2] where the monitored parameters information of a devices are captured, controlled and registered, i.e., the percent of use of a processor, the temperature, the traffic level, among others.

2.1 Management Protocol

To administrate a telecommunications network, applications are used on which all the information coming from the devices or network services through management protocols like WMI (Windows Management Instrumentation), CMIP (Common Management Information Protocol), ANMP (Ad hoc network management protocol), NETCONF (Network Configuration) or SNMP. The last one is the most commonly used, both in IPv4 and IPv6, and it is part of the Internet protocols stack defined by the IETF (Internet Engineering Task Force) in recommendations RFC (Request for comments) that describe its definition, structure, architecture, syntax, applications, transport messages, coexistence between versions, and more; they have been updated according the protocol has evolved from version 1 to version 3.

The operational parameters of a devices or service are represented by resident objects on a management information base (MIB), defined in a structure management information (SMI) and using ASN.1(Abstract Syntax Notation One) format [3]. Each parameter or administration variable is a unique element detailed with an object id (OID), which follows the hierarchical tree format of SMI and it examines the device's MIB to get the wanted information. The data is registered in the management application to monitor, control and administration it. The challenge of this model is the way to handle devices without management network protocol support or equipment with restricted hardware to process this kind of functions.

2.2 Asynchronous Serial Communications

The serial ports are interfaces that transmit information one bit per time and they often use asynchronous protocols as RS232, RS485 or USB, although there are synchronous protocols too such as MIDI, SPI or microware. The serial ports are ideal for communications between embedded systems. They have some advantages as the exchange of any kind of information (they often are in sensors, switches, motor controllers, relays, displays, among others), the hardware is inexpensive, its format is not complex, cables can be very long (USB is an exception) and the wireless technology enables transmitting serial data [4]. Its main limitation is the transfer information rate.

The use of serial communications in telecommunications equipment has been extended like alternative method of control, diagnosis and debug. Some devices, like the legacy systems, can be only handled through this kind of interfaces, wherewith some management restrictions appear as mentioned in the next section.

3   The Challenge

What happens if a device in a telecommunications network is not managed, maybe because it is a legacy equipment that does not support any management protocol or because it is a sensor or a small device with limited resources? The reality is that it will be able to operate and provide its services, however, when problems occur in the network, it will not be possible to determine their origin or take contingent measures to solve or prevent the occurrence of incidents again.

Thus, when one wants to keep a historical record of the operating attributes of these equipment, it can only be done manually through remote control applications such as telnet, SSH or web access, whose results show values in real time, but with historical data limitations that entails: insufficient data, unreliable records, possible typing errors, inability to integrate the information captured with the management systems, nullity in correlation of events, forgetfulness in the capture of information by the operator, etcetera. With this, system performance information is not available, which is vital for making decisions about the proper management and operation of the telecommunications network.

In this way, there are also challenges in the integration of the different applications that are used both to manage and control, as well as to collect the operating information of the equipment in a communications infrastructure, and, in addition, a network has devices from different vendors, running management applications to each of them [1]. These considerations add risk factors that make the operation of systems more complex than it should be.

The previous challenges can be presented in different scenarios, so this research aims to address the conversion of management protocols in legacy systems, following a procedure whose result can be applied in agents of Ad Hoc networks with limited processing, such as mesh networks, IoT or embedded systems.

3.1 Legacy Systems

The Legacy systems are those devices, applications or services that are in a phase of "obsolescence" or are being replaced by new technologies, but the companies continue to use them because they have invested a lot of money in their purchase, their services are still active, they have returned the investment or because its replacement is very difficult to be critical in the operation [5].

An example of this challenge is in the satellite earth stations, whose topology is shown in Fig. 1. They are operating since several years, whose components as transmitters, amplifiers, converters, signals radio frequency controllers and others may lack of monitoring and they are not configured in the management network. These devices use serial communications for their control because the antennas are generally far from the baseband equipment, exceeding the distances allowed by other types of connections such as Ethernet.

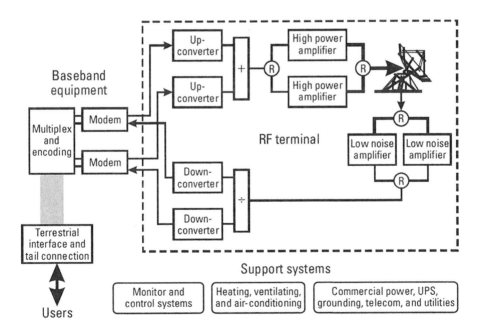

Fig. 1. Elements of an earth stations. The support systems use control and monitoring systems (Source: Elbert [6], p. 22)

An earth station can be operated locally or remotely, provided that it has an adequate monitoring and control design, which allows administrators to detect, diagnose and solve technical problems, as well as facilitates the execution of changes or configurations [6]. The facilities to do this are included within the devices, but they are not exploited when there are limitations of integration to the management infrastructure.

The most of the research that is done to include, maintain, or migrate legacy systems is focused on software rather than hardware, perhaps to replace a device may be easier than a specific application, although no less expensive. However, the results of such research can be associated to understand, for example, things that contribute to a successful migration process such as cost, duration, defects or capabilities [7]. In addition, the integration of legacy systems has other challenges besides technical ones that could be considered elements of user acceptance such as culture, information quality, utility, ease of use, compatibility, among others [8], and where organizational factors are very influential.

3.2   Sensors on Ad Hoc Networks

Another example of the administration challenges of devices with management limitations are the networks of wireless sensors or IoT, whose components have characteristics of heterogeneity, reduced energy consumption and particularities of wireless link [9] that must be considered for the development of any application. The sensors within an Ad Hoc, mesh or sensor network are designed to perform a specific function and due to their compact form factors have energy restriction that limits their lifetime or that of their batteries. Favorably there are working orientations [10] that seek to solve this limitation by designing the node and its wireless link as efficient as possible and using a strategy of collaboration between nodes.

Integrating these two concepts at the level of network management, it can be inferred that the approach of assigning optimal roles to the sensors to make them more efficient can leave out the management processes but there may be a collaborative method with an auxiliary node that supports and take charge of this service, so that the sensors are responsible for processing only the information relevant to your application.

3.3   Current Solutions

The market offers answers to the administration and monitoring challenges of telecommunications equipment without compatibility with the management protocols, developing drivers for each device and putting them to work on proprietary applications, such as Compass[1], Dataminer[2] or NetBoss XT[3], huge cost is high (depending on the number of equipment on the network, development

---

[1] http://www.kratosnetworks.com/products/network-management/compass.
[2] http://www.skyline.be/dataminer.
[3] http://netboss.com/page/netboss-xt.

requirements and administration functions, its cost is on range from \$100,000 to \$250,000 USD)[4] and generates the difficulty of using multiple applications in management systems.

There are also solutions based on the conversion of different protocols to SNMP using physical converters from serial to Ethernet such as ipConv[5], Red Lion[6] products or developments in embedded systems [11], but mostly used in industrial automation networks such as SCADA, in which protocols like Modbus, DNP3, PROFIBUS, among others are used. The use of these solutions allows migrating serial legacy systems to Ethernet networks, but they have scalability obstacles because of the use of a hardware element for each component to be included in the network and as its use has not been extended to telecommunications equipment, suppliers must develop to give full management of the devices and without the limitations offered by the mentioned protocols.

These are the reasons why the inclusion of legacy systems or equipment with hardware limitations, to a management network is expensive, restricted and often evaded.

4 Protocol Conversion

The challenges mentioned above, seen from the logical connectivity, can be summarized in a problem of incompatibility of communication processes, so the problem may treated with a software approach based on the conversion of protocols.

There are a variety of examples of protocol conversion, but there is no general theory that summarizes that procedure [12], however, there is an important development of formal models that can be used for the specification and accuracy of the conversion, seeing the incompatibility of protocols as a problem of syntax and semantics of messages that are exchanged for each protocol [13]. Since protocol conversion can take place in a huge diversity of environments, there are many methods that give different solution approaches such as protocol projection, Okumura approach, quotient approach [14] or multi-layer based OSI model through the normalization of the protocol and its requirements [15]. A specific option for the SNMP protocol is a proxy SNMP agent whose role is to translate requests, responses and notifications of management information and forward of those messages to the manager, using a suitable format [16].

4.1 Proposed Model

It is proposed the use of the finite-state converter model proposed by Lam [13], where it is sought to achieve interoperability between two protocols by

---

[4] Information based on actual quotes with each provider.

[5] http://ipcomm.de/product/ipConv/en/sheet.html.

[6] http://www.redlion.net/products/industrial-networking/communication-converters/.

constructing a common image protocol by adding functionalities using a finite-state machine. Considering the Fig. 2, where the SNMP protocol is called as P and the serial protocol as Q which handle different semantics and syntax, so that messages M and N can be understood by both parties, a protocol converter C must be used to translate messages so that interoperability can exist. Thus, the part of the network called PC can be seen as a process that interacts with P, whose state is defined by a tuple (s_1, s_2, m_1, m_2) where s_1 and s_2 are states of C and Q respectively, while m_1 and m_2 represent message sequence in the $P - C$ and $C - Q$ sections. The same logic is handled for QC.

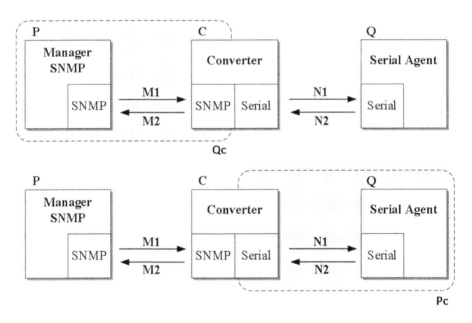

Fig. 2. Ways to see the conversion system. Exchange of messages between a P protocol and a PC process or between a Q protocol and a QC process (Source: own)

In the model, it is sought to break down each protocol at the flowchart level to understand how the messages enter and leave each node according to the internal events that appear in each one of them. Once you have these details, state machines are built to relate them.

4.2   Building the Relation

The challenge is considered as a problem of format and syntax incompatibility between both SNMP and serial protocols. So, a translation of the management information messages is done according to RFC3413 [16], making a preconfig-ured translation table (see Fig. 3), which will serve to make the mapping of management information through a direct translation approach as mentioned by Korner [17] in a conversion work similar to this research. In this case, the MIB for each device does not exist, so it must be created as per the parameters or attributes that can be measured in each equipment that is to be integrated into the management network, which, in turn, it will be related to a no rela-tional database (NoSQL), ideal to work on distributed systems with low capacity machines.

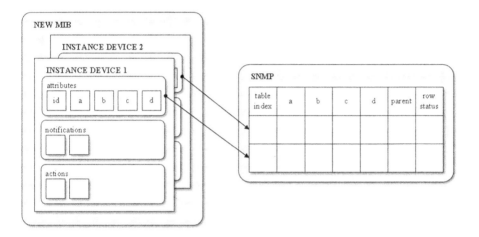

Fig. 3. Attributes translation approach of each device to SNMP (Source: Koerner [17], p. 351)

To construct the finite state machines of the SNMP and serial protocols (shown in the Fig. 4), are used: (a) a set of primitives that define the internal communications of the SNMP engine subsystems specified on the RFC3411 [18] for a SNMP agent, and (b) the exchange communication messages of the serial connections used in the flow control according to RS-232 specification [19], applying the most common configuration with TxD and RxD messages[7] and combined with the connectionless service primitives [20].

The converter protocol image is built through the flow of messages analysis and relating the states of each protocol where are executed the consult functions of the operational variables of the device ("*responding*" on SNMP and "*listening*" on serial) using the transition flows designed to establish transmission, reception and format states. The translation table (Fig. 3) is applied in the "*formating*" state.

---

[7] Another control signals, like RTS (resquest to send), CTS (clear to send), DTR (data terminal ready) or DSR (data set ready), are not considered because they are applied over modem communications, and that kind of connections are not part of the scope of this research.

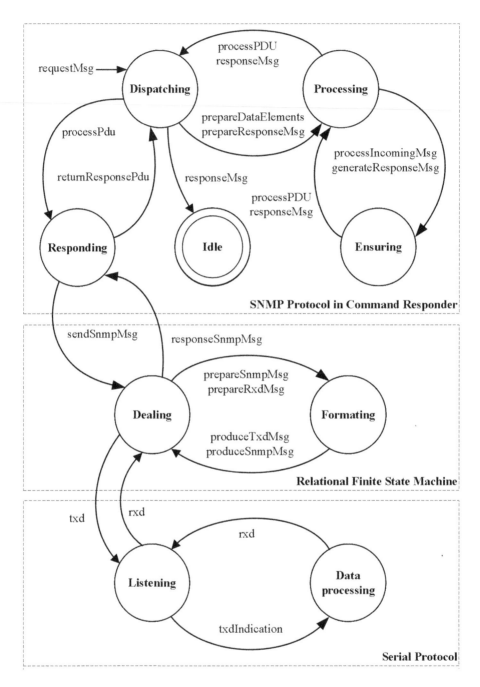

Fig. 4. The converter image protocol SNMP to serial design through finite state machines (Source: own)

4.3 Application on Ad Hoc Networks

To extend this model to Ad Hoc networks can be make if the proposed solution is seen as a protocol that can be executed in an agent that acts as a cluster header and in turn as an SNMP proxy that performs the translation functions between the main manager and the agents that are in that cluster, similar to the operation of the management systems in hierarchical networks where there are multiple intermediate managers who collect and process the information under their domain and then transmit it to a higher level. As shown in Fig. 5, there is a proxy agent for each cluster that exists on the network. This model of management in Ad Hoc networks is proposed by Chain, Jain and Singh [21] in whose work they use the ANMP as network management protocol.

Ad Hoc networks have different operating characteristics than infrastructure networks, so there are some additional challenges that are beyond the scope of this research but which may be useful for future work, such as mobility, integration with routing protocols, selection and change of clustered header agent, among others.

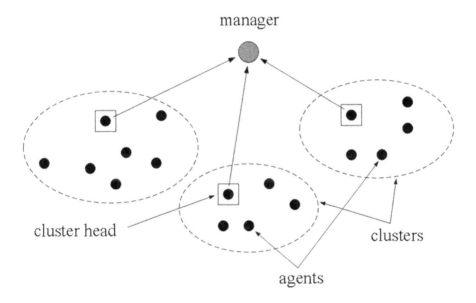

Fig. 5. Hierarchical architecture in an Ad Hoc network (Source: Chain, Jain y Singh [21], p. 1512)

5 Research Approach

The questions that are intended to solve with this research are: is it possible to develop a converser communications protocol serial to SNMP based on software to integrate legacy or process-constrained devices into the management network, what would be the appropriate implementation, how does it solve the diversity challenges, if it would be seen as an update to legacy systems with a low cost implementation and if it could be scalable to other types of heterogeneous interfaces or elements in a network.

To solve these questions and achieve the proposed objectives, the development has to be applied in devices of a satellite earth station (which are legacy systems) and wireless sensors to include them in applications of management that exist in the market; the converter protocol must have the sufficiency to relate the commands of administration and operation of the equipment, with a MIB where a unique OID is assigned for each variable, and of course; this solution should provide the ability to capture performance information, report events and modify operating parameters through the SNMP protocol.

5.1   Use of Results

The result of this research work may serve as an improvement tool in the administration and operation processes of the telecommunications infrastructure of companies that use legacy systems, making the monitoring of the operating variables more efficient because:

- It will facilitate the inclusion of the devices in the management systems that are already available using standardized protocols
- It will improve the quality of the service in availability issues since the online registration of the information will serve for early detection of incidents or to do reactive diagnosis, eliminating or reducing the downtime
- It will help in the control of changes because it will be possible to have remote access to the equipment avoiding the displacement of technical personnel to the places where the devices are
- Opportunities will be opened to eliminate, mitigate or transfer new risks that could appear and that otherwise would not be detected
- It will reduce the costs of operation and maintenance due to the automation of management processes and avoiding the purchase of new equipment or independent management systems

Acknowledgments. For the development of this paper, it took advantage of the members comments of the research group in dynamic telecommunications networks and distributed programming languages - TLÖN, and professor Oscar Agudelo from Universidad Nacional de Colombia.

References

1. Clemm, A.: Network Management Fundamentals, 1st edn. Cisco Press, Indianapolis (2006)
2. Miller, M.A.: Managing Internetworks with SNMP, 3rd edn. Wiley, Foster City (1999)
3. Case, J., McCloghrie, K., Rose, M., Waldbusser, S.: RFC 1441 Introduction to Version 2 of the Internet-standard Network Management Framework Status (1993)

4. Axelson, J.: Serial Port Complete: COM Ports, USB Virtual COM Ports, and Ports for Embedded Systems, 2nd edn. Lakeview Research LLC, Madison (2007)
5. Sommerville, I.: Software Engineering. Addison-Wesley, Boston (2011)
6. Elbert, B.R.: The Satellite Communication Ground Segment and Earth Station Handbook. Artech House Inc., Norwood (2001)
7. Huijgens, H., van Deursen, A., van Solingen, R.: Success factors in managing legacy system evolution: a case study. In: Proceedings of the International Workshop on Software and Systems Process, pp. 96–105 (2016)
8. Mathule, R.L., Kalema, B.M.: User Acceptance of Legacy Systems Integration, pp. 1–8 (2016)
9. Irastorza, J.A., Aguero, R., Gutierrez, V., Munoz, L.: Beyond management in Ad Hoc, heterogeneous WPAN environments: an experimental approach. In: 10th IEEE/IFIP Network Operations and Management Symposium, NOMS 2006, pp. 1–4 (2006)
10. Bhardwaj, M., Chandrakasan, A.P.: Bounding the lifetime of sensor networks via optimal role assignments. In: Proceedings, Twenty-First Annual Joint Conference of the IEEE Computer, Communications Societies, vol. 00(c), pp. 1587–1596 (2002)
11. Daogang, P., Hao, Z., Hui, L., Fei, X.: Development of the communication protocol conversion equipment based on embedded multi-MCU and Mu-C/OS-II. In: 2010 International Conference on Measuring Technology and Mechatronics Automation (ICMTMA), vol. 2, pp. 15–18 (2010)
12. Green, P.: Protocol conversion. IEEE Trans. Commun. **34**(3), 257–268 (1986)
13. Lam, S.S.: Protocol conversion. IEEE Trans. Softw. Eng. **14**(3), 353–362 (1988)
14. Calvert, K.L., Lam, S.S.: Formal methods for protocol conversion. IEEE J. Sel. Areas Commun. **8**(1), 127–142 (1990)
15. Sinha, R.: Conversing at many layers: multi-layer system-on-chip protocol conversion. In: 2015 20th International Conference on Engineering of Complex Computer Systems (ICECCS), pp. 170–173 (2015)
16. Levi, D., Meyer, P., Stewart, B.: RFC 3413 Simple Network Management Protocol (SNMP) Applications (2002)
17. Koerner, E.: Design of a proxy for managing CMIP agents via SNMP. Comput. Commun. **20**(5), 349–360 (1997)
18. Harrington, D., Presuhn, R., Wijnen, B.: RFC 3411 An Architecture for Describing Simple Network Management Protocol (SNMP) Management Frameworks (2002)
19. Jiménez, M., Palomera, R., Couvertier, I.: Principles of serial communication. In: Introduction to Embedded Systems, Chap. 9, 1st edn., pp. 475–536. Springer, New York (2014)
20. Hura, G., Singhal, M.: Data and Computer Communications. CRC Press, Boca Raton (2001)
21. Chen, W., Jain, N., Singh, S.: ANMP: Ad Hoc network management protocol. IEEE J. Sel. Areas Commun. **17**(8), 1506–1531 (1999)

Obstacle Evasion Algorithm for Clustering Tasks with Mobile Robot

César Giovany Pachón Suescún[1] ⓘ, Carlos Javier Enciso Aragón[1] ⓘ,
Marco Antonio Jinete Gómez[1] ⓘ, and Robinson Jiménez Moreno[2(✉)] ⓘ

[1] Universidad Piloto de Colombia, Bogotá, D.C, Colombia
{cesar-pachon1,carlos-enciso,marco-jinete}@upc.edu.co
[2] Universidad Militar Nueva Granada, Bogotá, D.C, Colombia
robinson.jimenez@unimilitar.edu.co

Abstract. This paper presents a proposal of obstacle evasion oriented to mobile robots in clustering tasks. For this case, polar coordinates are set for the movement of the mobile, the possible obstacles in the path are determined and imaginary boundaries are generated in each possible obstacle in order to delimit the path of the mobile between them. The algorithm developed under the Netlogo programming environment makes it possible to perform evasion and reach the clustering point efficiently.

Keywords: Clustering · Obstacle evasion · Mobile robot · Netlogo

1 Introduction

Clustering algorithms allow to perform different tasks of pattern recognition in data clustering, for instance, in [1], clustering validation techniques using cancer datasets are presented. However, clustering techniques are not biased only to datasets hence they are now being projected to navigation applications. For example, in [2], path-clustering techniques based on spatiotemporal restrictions are performed.

The analysis of trajectories and clustering of them has strong applications in systems of video surveillance [3], e.g., to determine trends in a particular path that can determine human-vehicle intersections and avoid accidents. Because of this, clustering applications can be found for vehicle [4] or aircraft trajectories [5].

Another application of clustering techniques in path planning is given in mobile robotics, where there are developments that seek to generate trajectories based on obstacle evasion to go from one point to another, as is the case of [6], also this is the objective proposed in [7], but in the latter case, a fuzzy clustering technique is used to delimit boundaries that will set the possible paths of the robotic mobile.

Algorithms such as those presented in [8, 9], which are based on a matrix system from the images captured in order to generate a path, generate a relatively high computational cost if they are implanted in programming languages not optimal for the use of matrices. In addition, they may be affected with the resolution in which the image is captured, since the larger the image, the longer the processing time. There are projects such as those implemented in [10] which use a global camera, or as seen in [11] that use

© Springer International Publishing AG 2017
J.C. Figueroa-García et al. (Eds.): WEA 2017, CCIS 742, pp. 84–95, 2017.
DOI: 10.1007/978-3-319-66963-2_9

a local camera, causing in this way that the strategy for the path planning has a dependence of the location of the camera. Investigations focused on the clustering of objects [12], in which the clustering zone depends more on the initial location of the objects to be grouped, can cause them to lose their usefulness in real applications where objects are needed in a particular zone.

Many of the simulations that exist in both the path planning and in clustering of objects usually obviate situations that can occur in an implementation in a real environment, as is the method of interaction with the medium [13], the intercommunication schemes between robotic agents [14] and collision with obstacles. In this project it was sought to take into account this type of situations, for which it was necessary to determine a procedure that was implemented in the general algorithm, which focused on the avoidance of obstacles for clustering tasks with easy adaptability to systems with global and local camera, scalability to a real environment and, because it has been developed in a generic way, it may allow its validation in multi-robot environments and collaborative applications.

This paper is developed in three sections, the first presents the materials and the methods used, the second presents the analysis of results and the final section gives the conclusions reached.

2 Materials and Methods

This paper discusses the development of an algorithm of evasion and clustering for a single mobile robotic agent, which must perform the path planning for its displacement from an object to the final location, avoiding obstacles in the path. The algorithm is developed in the NetLogo simulation environment, in order to verify its correct operation and to be able to have a future collaborative working environment, which is the strength of such simulation software, to work with multiple agents of the same or different class.

The projection of the algorithm starts from the initial idea of an agent that has a camera and, through image processing, locates objects with known dimensions in the work area, obtaining their polar coordinates with respect to the agent. This is the starting point of the algorithm, i.e. it starts from the base that the position of the objects with respect to the agent is known as well as the coordinates of the point of clustering. The agent must generate a strategy to move from each object to the point of clustering, then go to another object and return to the point of clustering and thus to finish the groupable objects. In Fig. 1, it can be seen the agent, the objects represented as a magenta square and the clustering area as a green square.

The initial problem that arises in the development of the algorithm is how to go from a point A (current location of the mobile) to a point B (location of the object), and then from the point B to a point C (clustering location) (Fig. 1). Because the polar coordinates are known at each of the points (B and C), where the agent must go, the agent would only need to rotate an angle α and move a distance h_1 to move to point B (see Fig. 2).

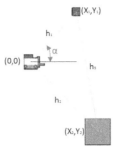

Fig. 1. Work area.

Fig. 2. Translation from point A to point B

Now it is desired to go from point B to point C, but the origin of the system and the orientation of the plane changed, therefore, it must be calculated the new position of C with respect to the new point of origin that is now located in B, taking into account the angle at which the agent is rotated.

For this calculation, the initial positions of A, B, C can be taken. Observing in Fig. 1, the coordinates of A are $(0, 0)$, but to calculate the coordinates of B and C, which are (X_1, Y_1) and (X_2, Y_2) respectively, it is necessary to perform the conversion of the known polar coordinates to rectangular ones, (see Fig. 3).

$$x_n = h \cos(\alpha)$$
$$y_n = h \sin(\alpha)$$

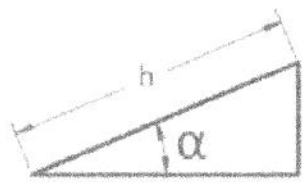

Fig. 3. Conversion from polar coordinates to Cartesian

Once these values are known, a subtraction is performed between the coordinates of C and those of B, with Eq. (1).

$$NC = (X_2, Y_2) - (X_1, Y_1) \tag{1}$$

In this way, the coordinates of B and those of C can be taken as $(0, 0)$ and as NC, respectively. Now to calculate h_3, which refers to the displacement from B to C, the magnitude of NC is calculated in (2).

$$h_3 = |NC| \tag{2}$$

Part of what is sought in this algorithm is to determine the different possible paths and which of them is the shortest, both translational and rotationally. When the agent rotates, it has two possibilities, the first is to rotate to the right and the second to the left, it will always be sought to rotate to the side where the angular displacement is the shortest, so if it is desired to calculate the angle of rotation from B to C, it must be assumed that the orientation of the agent is at 0°. With the function Atan2, the shortest angle can be calculated from 0°, but NetLogo lacks this function, so a simple Atan and a conditional are used, in order to achieve the same results as with the Atan2. If the angle is greater than 180°, 360° is subtracted from this angle, otherwise, if it is minor, no changes are made. The angle α_1 is subtracted from the result obtained in order to know the total angle that must be rotated to be in orientation to C. After calculating h_3 and α_2, it can be proceeded to rotate and move the agent to C (see Fig. 4). In this way if there were a point D, and we wanted to go from C to D, it would be proceeded to perform the same procedure that was done from B to C.

Fig. 4. Translation from point B to point C

The way in which it was decided to address the problem of collisions was proposing imaginary borders around each object, where their dimensions will be at least the radius of rotation of the mobile agent to implement, plus an extra safety factor given in centimeters, which can vary from 0 to the value that is deemed convenient, in order to ensure that, at any point on the frontier to which the agent is addressed, it will not collide with the object in question. To better understand a case of evasion, it will be made an analysis based on the possible scenario that can be observed in Fig. 5.

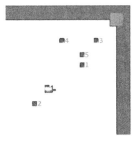

Fig. 5. Example of evasion

If it is wanted to go to object 3 and then take it to the clustering area, the agent would have to be able to evade the other objects, which would become obstacles for the agent. The first step to achieve this goal is to identify possible obstacles. The first parameter is if any of the objects is a distance greater than the target, then this is discarded as a possible obstacle. The next parameter refers to the maximum angle that the objects could be with respect to the objective, in order to discard those that exceed that angle in later calculations since these objects would not affect in the trajectory. In Fig. 6 it is possible to analyze a case in which an object is as close as possible to the agent, without hindering its rotation. If the agent wants to move to another point, the maximum angle that must be rotated to avoid colliding or that the object may obstruct the rotation of the agent after translation is 90°, therefore, this angular value is assigned as the maximum that objects can be relative to the target, so that they can be considered as possible obstacles.

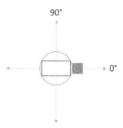

Fig. 6. Minimum angle to avoid an obstacle.

To calculate the angle between the target and each of the obstacles, this will be equal to the scalar product between the two vectors, divided by the product of their modules, and from this result, the arc cosine is calculated in (3).

$$\cos^{-1}\left(\frac{\overrightarrow{obj} \cdot \overrightarrow{obs}}{\left|\overrightarrow{obj}\right|\left|\overrightarrow{obs}\right|}\right) \tag{3}$$

Where $\overrightarrow{obj}$ refers to the target vector and $\overrightarrow{obs}$ to the obstacle vector.

Only objects that become possible obstacles in the path, the calculation of their borders is made. In Fig. 7, it can be seen that objects 1, 4 and 5 have points which represent the vertexes of their boundary.

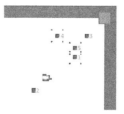

Fig. 7. Boundaries

In this case, the objects 5 and 1 share borders, therefore, when sharing borders are considered both as a single obstacle, and a new boundary is defined which will take into account for its dimensions the maximum and minimum points between boundaries of 5 and 1.

In Fig. 8a a special case is presented in which object A and B share boundaries but do not share with object C. In this case a new boundary is formed between the merging of A and B, this new resulting boundary shares boundaries with C (see Fig. 8b), therefore, in the algorithm designed, once two obstacles are merged it is proceeded to compare if this union shares a border with another obstacle, if so, they are combined again. Consequently, when C shares boundaries with the fusion between A and B, they generate a new one, and, what were initially 3 obstacles, are now treated as one (see Fig. 8c). This boundary treatment will avoid complex inter-object calculations of escape routes.

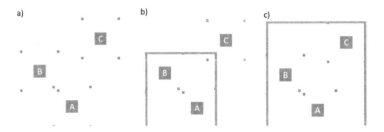

Fig. 8. Boundary union.

Once the final boundaries are set, which for reasons of simulation it is obviated to have to draw them, it is proceeded to calculate which are the possible obstacles that remained, in this case are 2 (object 4 and the union between 5 and 1), after this it is proceeded to calculate if the angle $\propto$ is contained between the maximum and minimum angles that form the boundaries of each obstacle with respect to the agent, (see Fig. 9).

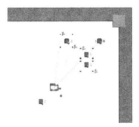

Fig. 9. Obstacles identification.

In this case only the union between 5 and 1 interfere with the trajectory of the agent, as 4 does not interfere, it is not considered as an obstacle. In case there are two or more obstacles that interfere in the path, only the one closest to the agent will be taken into account. Once the obstacle that interferes is identified, the evasion algorithm is performed. In this phase, 4 possible ways of evading the obstacle are established, these forms depend on the position of the object with respect to the agent (see Fig. 10).

- For case 1, it must be sought which is the lower corner of the obstacle boundary that is closest to the target.
- For case 2, it must be sought which is the upper corner of the obstacle boundary that is closest to the target.
- For case 3, it must be sought which is the left corner of the obstacle boundary that is closest to the target.
- For case 4, it must be sought which is the right corner of the obstacle boundary that is closest to the target.

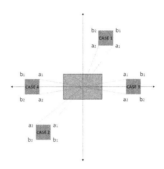

Fig. 10. Evasion cases.

Once the case is detected, it is proceed to move the agent to this point, in this example it can be seen that it is the case 1, and the lower corner closest to the target is the lower right, (see Fig. 11a).

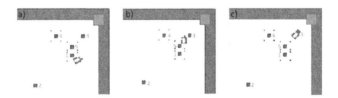

Fig. 11. Trajectory of evasion

Subsequently, the agent is moved to the corresponding point b, in this case b_1, as can be seen in Fig. 11b.

Once this point has been reached, it is necessary to calculate again whether there may be obstacles between the agent and the target, if this is the case, the same procedure for identifying and avoiding obstacles must be repeated. Since this is not the case, it is calculated the displacement to be made by the agent to the target, and move to this target point, (see Fig. 11c).

Finally, it is proceeded to calculate the path to the clustering zone, in which it must be also taken into account if there may be obstacles, if they exist, the evasion is done under the same algorithm, but since this is not the case, once the angle of rotation and the distance to be displaced have been calculated, the agent is taken along with the target to the clustering zone, (see Fig. 12).

Fig. 12. Displacement to the clustering zone.

Subsequent to this, in order to avoid having to evade a high number of obstacles, in the algorithm once the first object is taken to the clustering zone, the agent will bring the other objects from the closest to the farthest.

The case presented above refers if the agent was first for a specific object, but finally what is sought with this algorithm is to determine the shortest joint path, taking into account both linear and angular displacements. Therefore, an equation must be proposed in which the different possibilities of paths are calculated, and then compared and go through the shortest path, which is shown in (4).

$$Trajectory = Tra_{ag \to ob_i} + Tra_{ob_i \to za} + 2 * \left(\left(\sum_{n=1}^{numob} Trs_{za \to ob_n} \right) - Trs_{za \to ob_i} \right) \tag{4}$$

Where:

- $Tra_{ag \to ob_i}$ is a path from the agent to the object i.
- $Tra_{ob_i \to za}$ is path from object i to the clustering zone.
- *numob* refers to the number of objects in the environment.
- $Trs_{za \to ob_n}$ is the unobstructed path from the clustering zone to an object n.
- $Trs_{za \to ob_i}$ is the path without obstacles from the clustering zone to the object i.

In the equation it is initially assumed that the agent will be moved to get an object i, therefore, to take it to the clustering zone, it must be calculated the path to this object, and then from the object to the clustering zone. Whenever it is referred to trajectory, it is taken into account the displaced both linearly and angularly. As it is wanted to take all objects to this area, after carrying the first one, it should go from the closest to the farthest, therefore a summation of the paths from the zone of clustering up to each of the objects is proposed assuming that there are no obstacles, since it will go from the nearest to the farthest, to this sum it is subtracted the value of the trajectory without obstacles of the clustering zone until the object i, since it has already gone for that object, this result is multiplied by two because the path of the object n to the clustering zone must also be taken into account.

This calculation will be done by varying i from 1 to the number of objects. From all the results, it is calculated which is the smallest and therefore the value that had i in that result will be the object by which the agent must first be displaced in order to perform the shortest path.

3   Analysis and Results

For the validation of the algorithm, an interface was designed in which different variables related to the work area of the clustering task can be entered, (see Fig. 13).

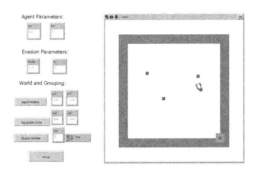

Fig. 13. NetLogo interface. (Color figure online)

In the parameters of the agent, it must be entered half the length and half the width of the mobile agent, since with these values the radius of rotation will be calculated and the boundaries will be established. In the evasion parameters, half the width of the objects is entered and a wanted extra safety factor to be added to the size of the boundaries. For the practical case, an ultrasound sensor that directionally detects the distance to the obstacle and this safety factor, delimits the maximum approach of the mobile to the object.

For the execution of the program, the initial position of the agent must be set, besides the zone of the surroundings where it is desired to group the objects, and finally the number of objects that are desired, they will come out with random coordinates inside the work area (area delimited by the red frame Fig. 13).

The operation of the algorithm can be seen in [15, 16], where, in a first situation, the agent groups up to 10 objects, and in the other, how the safety factor can cause the boundaries of the objects to merge and consequently the agent has a different path.

In all the tests except 3 specific situations, it was possible to group all the objects in the zone set, the situations that were presented are:

- The initial objective is contained within the boundaries of obstacles
- The agent is located at the boundary of the obstacles
- If a safety factor is entered high enough to cause the agent to be unable to move properly within the work area.

In order to check the speed of execution of the calculation of the trajectory according to the set evasion and clustering method, it is proceeded to propose four different scenarios in which the position of the clustering zone is changed in order to verify if this change can significantly affect the execution times, or these are due to some other factor, (see Fig. 14).

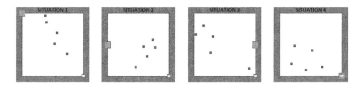

Fig. 14. Test scenarios

In order to accurately set the execution times, taking into account that in each test the positions of the objects change randomly, five different tests were performed for the same number of objects in each scenario. It should be noted that the tests were performed on a computer that does not operate the simulation in real-time, which can cause that the time increases if it is implemented in an embedded system due to its hardware limitations. In Table 1, the results obtained in each of the four situations can be observed, by varying the number of objects to be grouped.

Table 1. Processing time

Situation	Objects Number	Time 1(ms)	Time 2(ms)	Time 3(ms)	Time 4(ms)	Time 5(ms)	Average Time(ms)
1	5	10	9	12	8	9	9,6
1	10	21	19	24	18	25	21,4
1	15	36	37	36	35	37	36,2
1	20	57	51	53	62	57	56
2	5	8	9	11	7	8	8,6
2	10	18	18	22	16	16	18
2	15	38	33	39	42	35	37,4
2	20	56	49	53	53	55	53,2
3	5	7	10	8	7	9	8,2
3	10	19	20	17	15	14	17
3	15	42	30	32	41	42	37,4
3	20	60	56	68	51	59	58,8
4	5	10	10	7	7	8	8,4
4	10	19	17	21	17	20	18,8
4	15	33	42	41	33	41	38
4	20	53	59	57	63	53	57

As it can be seen in Table 1, the average times for different scenarios and the same number of objects do not vary significantly from one situation to another. The algorithm speed presents an approximate linear behavior between the average time and the number of objects, obtaining in the present situations of Table 1 a correlation higher than 0.97 between the data with respect to a trend line generated.

4   Conclusions

In the simulations performed, 3 specific cases were presented in which the algorithm was not as expected. In order to avoid the second situation corresponding to the fact that the agent was confined within the boundaries of the obstacles, it is advised to locate the initial position of the agent at the border or outside of the work area. For the third situation, a safety factor is entered that is high enough to cause the agent not to be able to move correctly in the work zone, so it is advisable that, according to the measures of the agent to be implemented, empirical tests are made to decide which the most appropriate safety factor is.

It is advised that, in case of an actual implementation, the clustering zone should be outside the work area, since it could present cases in which the accumulation of objects is such that interferes with the correct operation of the algorithm.

Observing in the simulations of the situations presented in Table 1, the execution times do not vary depending on the initial distance to which the agent is from the clustering zone, but of the obstacles that would be generated in the calculation of the most optimal path.

It should be noted that the algorithm is developed under conditions of reasonable use, including agent dimensions, number of objects and their size, safety factor, work area dimensions, among others. Therefore, setting appropriate ranges for the execution of the algorithm will depend on the user.

With the developed algorithm it is sought that this only needs the initial location of the objects with respect to the agent, causing in this way not to depend on the resolution of the image or on the image processing algorithm that previously would be implemented. In addition, it can be implemented with both global and local cameras, thus presenting greater adaptability to different types of clustering projects. It even allows the user to be the one to decide where they want the clustering zone, thus expanding their adaptation to real situations. If it is analyzed the processing times, it can be thought about the feasibility of adapting the algorithm to one with real-time image processing, thus allowing the development of human-machine interaction, multi-agent or collaborative algorithms.

References

1. Yu, Z., Kuang, Z., Liu, J., Chen, H., Zhang, J., You, J., Wong, H.S., Han, G.: Adaptive ensembling of semi-supervised clustering solutions. IEEE Trans. Knowl. Data Eng. **PP**(99), p. 1. doi:10.1109/TKDE.2017.2695615. 1 August 2017
2. Wu, H.R., Yeh, M.Y., Chen, M.S.: Profiling moving objects by dividing and clustering trajectories spatiotemporally. IEEE Trans. Knowl. Data Eng. **25**(11), 2615–2628 (2013). doi: 10.1109/TKDE.2012.249
3. Bak, Ç., Erdem, A., Erdem, E.: Clustering motion trajectories via dominant sets. In: 2016 24th Signal Processing and Communication Application Conference (SIU), Zonguldak, 2016, pp. 601–604. doi:10.1109/SIU.2016.7495812
4. Besse, P.C., Guillouet, B., Loubes, J.M., Royer, F.: Review and perspective for distance-based clustering of vehicle trajectories. IEEE Trans. Intell. Transport. Syst. **17**(11), 3306–3317 (2016). doi:10.1109/TITS.2016.2547641
5. Mcfadyen, A., O'Flynn, M., Martin, T., Campbell, D.: Aircraft trajectory clustering techniques using circular statistics. In: 2016 IEEE Aerospace Conference, Big Sky, MT, 2016, pp. 1–10. doi:10.1109/AERO.2016.7500601
6. Shantia, A., Bidoia, F., Schomaker, L., Wiering, M.: Dynamic parameter update for robot navigation systems through unsupervised environmental situational analysis. In: 2016 IEEE Symposium Series on Computational Intelligence (SSCI), Athens, 2016, pp. 1–7. doi:10.1109/SSCI.2016.7850238

7. Moreno, R.J., Lopez, D.J.: Trajectory planning for a robotic mobile using fuzzy c-means and machine vision. In: Symposium of Signals, Images and Artificial Vision - 2013: STSIVA - 2013, Bogota, 2013, pp. 1–4. doi:10.1109/STSIVA.2013.6644912
8. Mohammed, A.: Autonomous navigation of mobile robot based on flood fill algorithm. Iraq J. Electr. Electron. Eng. **12**(1), 79–84 (2016). E-ISSN 2078-6069
9. Burgos, D.A.T.: Planeamiento de trayectorias de un robot móvil. In: Enero 2006. [En línea]. http://tangara.uis.edu.co/biblioweb/tesis/2006/119245.pdf. [Último acceso: Junio 2017]
10. Murakami, K., Hibino, S., Kodama, Y., Iida, T., Kato, K., Naruse, T.: Cooperative soccer play by real small-size robot. In: Polani, D., Browning, B., Bonarini, A., Yoshida, K. (eds.) RoboCup 2003. LNCS, vol. 3020, pp. 410–421. Springer, Heidelberg (2004). doi: 10.1007/978-3-540-25940-4_36
11. Jiménez, F.J., Moreno, J.C., González, R., Rodríguez, F., Sánchez, J.: Sistema de visión de apoyo a la navegación de un robot móvil en invernaderos. In: XXIX Jornadas de Automática, 3–5 Septiembre. Tarragona, España (2008)
12. Gauci, M., Chen, J., Li, W., Dodd, T., Gross, R.: Clustering objects with robots that do not compute. In: Proceedings of the 2014 International Conference on Autonomous Agents and Multi-agent Systems, pp. 421–428, 5 May 2014. E-ISSN 978-1-4503-2738-1
13. Chatty, A., Kallel, I., Gaussier, P., Alimi, A.M.: Emergent complex behaviors for swarm robotic systems by local rules. In: 2011 IEEE Workshop on Robotic Intelligence Informationally Structured Space (RiiSS), pp. 69–76, 11–15 April 2011. doi:10.1109/RIISS. 2011.5945791
14. Kwon, J.W., Kim, J.H., Seo, J.: Consensus-based obstacle avoidance for robotic swarm system with behavior-based control scheme. In: 2014 14th International Conference on Control, Automation and Systems (ICCAS), pp. 751–755, 22–25 October 2014. doi:10.1109/ICCAS. 2014.6987879
15. Suescún, C.G.P., Aragón, C.J.E., Gómez, M.A.J., Moreno, R.J.: Youtube, Junio 2017. [En línea]. https://www.youtube.com/watch?v=LfxV1McBJRY&t=30s. [Último acceso: Junio 2017]
16. Suescún, C.G.P., Aragón, C.J.E., Gómez, M.A.J., Moreno, R.J.: Youtube, Junio 2017. [En línea]. https://www.youtube.com/watch?v=HBLqLI7yKWo. [Último acceso: Junio 2017]

A Web-Based Approach for Analyzing Microorganism Sequences

Hector Florez[1(✉)] and Karina Salvatierra[2]

[1] Universidad Distrital Francisco Jose de Caldas, Bogotá, Colombia
haflorezf@udistrital.edu.co
[2] Universidad Nacional de Misiones, Posadas, Argentina
karinasalvatierra@fceqyn.unam.edu.ar

Abstract. In biology, a mutation is a change in the nucleotide sequence of the genome of a microorganisms (e.g., virus, bacteria). Mutations play an important role in biological processes of microorganisms such as drug resistance. Analyzing these mutations becomes a challenge because microorganisms are described by a big amount of data that must be processed based on reference microorganisms data. Nowadays, scientists in health areas make these analyses manually or using standalone software that provide results in plain text formats, which limit their interpretations. In this paper, we present an approach for analyzing microorganism pathogens. The analysis is performed using the information contained in the nucleotide sequence and comparing it to reference sequences. This approach allows users to calculate changes of nucleotide and amino acid from selected sequences obtained using conventional Sanger and cloning sequencing techniques. The results of our approach are deployed using different visualization techniques that facilitate results interpretation.

Keywords: Bioinformatics · Pathogens · Mutations analysis

1 Introduction

The analysis of viruses, bacteria, fungi and parasites is important to research that lead to the knowledge of the behavior of each microorganism. Due to an increasing number of microorganism pathogen results are being generated from different studies, new medicine applications and bioinformatics tools are needed to promote the flow of these results into clinical practice, in order to improve patients' health. As more microorganism genomes are sequenced from conventional Sanger[1] and cloning sequencing techniques, computational analysis of these data has become increasingly important [1].

Microorganisms are characterized by their heterogeneity, which is based on the amount of processes such as nucleotide substitutions, deletions, insertions

---

[1] Sanger is a sequencing technique for obtaining the nucleotides (A, C, G, T) of microorganism genome.

© Springer International Publishing AG 2017
J.C. Figueroa-García et al. (Eds.): WEA 2017, CCIS 742, pp. 96–107, 2017.
DOI: 10.1007/978-3-319-66963-2_10

and rearrangements from genetic recombination events. When a microorganism infects a cell, it replicates its genetic information producing a new entity, which is able to infect other cells. In this replication process, some errors can occur in the copy of the genetic information (i.e., genome) of the microorganism. This change is known as mutation [2].

Mutations play an important role in both normal and abnormal biological processes such as: evolution, cancer, and the development of the immune system [3]. This is the reason of the great importance to develop computer-based systems that facilitate the analysis of sequences in order to identify nucleotide and amino acid changes.

The development of this type of tools is important not only to know the behavior of microorganisms in their changes of nucleotides and amino acids, but also as an instrument to support medical decisions supported by the prediction of drug resistance and phylogenetic inferences. Thus, the aim of the study presented in this paper was the development of an online bioinformatics approach that allows users to calculate changes in nucleotide and amino acid sequences, identifying their corresponding geographical genotype.

The rest of the paper is structured as follows. Section 2 presents the context of the study, which is related to microorganism sequencing and mutations. In Sect. 3, we present the related work of this research, which is compared to our approach. In Sect. 4, we present our approach for analyzing nucleotides and amino acid changes in microorganisms sequences. Section 5 presents the analysis results of our approach. Finally, Sect. 5 concludes the paper.

2 Microorganism Sequences and Mutations

A sequence of deoxyribonucleic acid (DNA) is a sequence of letters that represent the structure of a DNA molecule, with the ability to carry genetic information from generation to generation. The possible letters are A, C, G, and T, which symbolize the four nucleotide subunits of a DNA band (adenine (A), guanine (G), thymine (T) and cytosine (C)) [4].

A sequence is a set of any amount of nucleotides greater than four. Determining the DNA sequence of a microorganism is useful in the study of basic biological processes. In addition, DNA sequencing can be used to know the mutations generated in different microorganisms [5]. A mutation is defined as any change in the nucleotide sequence of the DNA, which may lead to the substitution of amino acids in the resulting proteins [2]. In some occasions, mutations are harmful and the microorganisms die before they can reproduce and pass the mutations to offspring. Nevertheless, in other occasions a mutation gives rise to a new trait that helps the microorganisms to survive [6].

Microorganisms reproduce very quickly and the genome of microbes is relatively small. Some microorganisms such as Escherichia coli has only about five million nucleotides and can divide every nine minutes. So for each new generation of microorganisms, there may be one or two mistakes in the genome [6].

A change in a single amino acid may be important when it occurs at an active site of a protein because said single amino acid change may imply a mutation that produce drug resistance. This change (mutation) is heritable and passed on to the progeny. The resistance capacity acquired by a microorganism as the result of a mutation, allows the microorganism to replicate and continue infecting new cells even in the presence of the drug. Because of this, a drug does not guarantee replication control of the resistant microorganism. Therefore, resistance analyzes help to make better decisions on the prescription of drugs of patients infected with a microorganism [7].

Sequences can be derived through the DNA sequencing process. DNA sequencing is a set of biochemical methods and techniques whose purpose is the determination of nucleotides (A, G, T and C) [8]. In order to obtain a set of sequences, several sequencing techniques can be used. These techniques provide a great amount of information about nucleotides. Thus, processing such information in a effective and efficient manner becomes an important need for biology researchers.

We have identified the following difficulties for processing data related to microorganisms sequences:

– Information available in some bioinformatics tools is often insufficient.
– Researchers need to get required input information (i.e., reference sequences) from external databases to perform analysis.
– Researchers have to use different bioinformatics tools to perform the complete analysis of desired data.
– There is a lack of integrated bioinformatics tools, for analyzing biological sequences.
– There is a lack of visualization techniques that allow an interactive way to manipulate the results of analyzed data.
– There is a lack of user-friendly interfaces in bioinformatics tools making them difficult to use and navigate.

3   Related Work

As mentioned in the previous section, recognizing mutations in the DNA sequences remains one of the most pressing problems in the analysis of microorganisms. Different approaches to analyze mutations have been developed, and there are several programs that are commonly used for this task. Some of these tools perform mutations prediction, relying only on the statistical parameters in the DNA sequence for mutation identification [9]. In contrast, homology-based methods rely primarily on identifying homologous sequences. Each of these methods has its own advantages and limitations.

For instance, Kalaghatgi et al. [10] present the project *Geno2pheno* (http://hcv.geno2pheno.org/index.php), which is a tool to identify mutations in hepatitis C virus (HCV) and to perform alignment of sequences to identify genotypes. Our approach allows researchers to identify mutations with detailed information regarding mutations positions, nucleotide and amino acid changes, as well as to identify a geographic genotype using phylogenetic trees.

Garriga et al. [11] present *DR SEQAN (Drug Resistance SEQuence ANalyzer)*, which is a tool to identify mutations in the human immunodeficiency virus (HIV). Nevertheless, it is coded in Visual Basic and thus it is not portable because it just runs on Windows-based platforms. Our approach is able to analyze different kinds of microorganisms and it is web-based, which implies that it is available from any platform. Similarly, Salvatierra et al. [12] presented *BMA*, which is another tool developed to identify nucleotide and amino acid changes.

In addition, other approaches have been developed to identify genotypes. For example, Rozanov et al. [13] present *The Genotyping tool at the National Center for Biotechnology Information* (http://www.ncbi.nih.gov/projects/genotyping/formpage.cgi), which has been designed to identify the genotypes of viral nucleotide sequences. Moreover, the *Dengue, Zika and Chikungunya Viruses Typing Tool* (http://www.bioafrica.net/software.php) also is able to identify genotypes in specific microorganisms (i.e., Dengue, Zika and Chikungunya). Our approach not only is able to identify genotypes of nucleotide sequences, but also variations of nucleotides and amino acids. McTavish et al. [14] have designed a sequence simulation software called *TreeToReads* (https://github.com/snacktavish/TreeToReads) to perform phylogenetic inference for emerging pathogens. The software was written in Python and requires a configuration file and two input files. However it needs the following dependencies to be executed: *Seq-Gen* [15], *Art* [16], and *Dendropy* [17]. Our approach may obtain phylogenetic genotypes and does not require any other bioinformatics tool.

4   Approach for Analyzing Microorganisms Sequences

We have designed and developed a web-based approach called *Pathogen Sequence Signature Analysis (PSSA)*. It allows researchers from health areas to analyze nucleotide and amino acid sequence variations, using sample sequences taken from infected patients. Said sequences are obtained through conventional Sanger sequencing. The analysis results may be used to identify the corresponding geographical genotype of each analyzed sequence.

The key element of the approach is the analysis algorithm that allows analyzing a large amount of sequences. To identify mutations, the algorithm compares the analyzed sequence to the reference sequence of genes of the desired microorganism. Reference sequences have been extracted from GenBank (https://www.ncbi.nlm.nih.gov/genbank/). For example, consider that a researcher needs to analyze 10 sequences taken from a patient, against the gene E1 of Chikungunya virus. Then, the algorithm splits each patient sequence into nucleotides and compare them to the nucleotides of the gene E1 of Chikungunya virus, where each gene can have several reference sequences. The *PSSA* algorithm is presented in Algorithm 1.

Based on the algorithm, *PSSA* obtains the mutation analysis results and presents them through the following alternatives:

– Online report. *PSSA* provides a report with all nucleotide changes including the amount of changes that matches specific nucleoties. In addition, it presents the changes of amino acids related to the nucleotides.

Algorithm 1. *PSSA* algorithm

for all ψ in Ψ **do**	▷ Ψ=Set of patient sequences to analyze
$\Phi_\psi \leftarrow split(\psi)$	▷ Φ_ψ=Set of nucleotides of the sequence ψ
for all λ in Λ **do**	▷ Λ=Set of sequences of the microorganism gene (e.g., E1 of Chikungunya)
$\Gamma_\lambda \leftarrow split(\lambda)$	▷ Γ_λ=Set of nucleotides of the sequence λ
for all ϕ in Φ_ψ, γ in Γ_λ **do**	
if ϕ != γ **then**	
$collect(\Omega, \phi, \gamma, pos)$	▷ Ω=Set of changes of nucleotides of the sequence ψ, pos=position of the change
end if	
end for	
end for	
end for	

- PDF report. *PSSA* provides a pdf report with the same information of the online report, but includes a summary that informs the amount of changes for each analyzed sequence.
- Force-Directed Graph. Based on this graph, *PSSA* displays the analysis results grouped by patients and clustered by the amount of changes of the analyzed sequences. This alternative is very useful because it enables researchers to find specific results among large amount of data.
- Phylogenetic analysis results. *PSSA* displays these results using two different visualization: Radial tree and Cartesian tree. They include the same information; however, both visualizations allow discovering different insights of the results.

PSSA has been supported by different artifacts (e.g., frameworks, libraries) that are presented by its component diagram (See Fig. 1). *PSSA* has been developed using PHP language. For the front end, *PSSA* uses Bootstrap (http://getbootstrap.com/) version 3.3.6, which is a popular HTML, JavaScript, and CSS framework for developing responsive web projects. In addition, JQuery (https://jquery.com/) version 1.12.3 has been used to support some specific JavaScript functionalities. Moreover, in order to present the results in a pdf file, *PSSA* uses ezpdf (https://github.com/rebuy-de/ezpdf/) version 0.0.9. Finally, the data is stored in a MySQL (https://www.mysql.com) database designed for this project.

As mentioned before, *PSSA* provides as output three different visualization techniques: force-directed graph, radial tree, and cardesian tree. These visualizations has been achieved supported by the project D3 (Data-Driven Documents) (https://d3js.org/) version 3.5.17, which serves to deploy data using fancy visualizations.

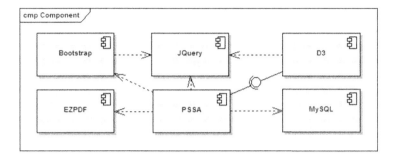

Fig. 1. Component diagram.

5 Results

PSSA is available in the web site http://pssa.itiud.org. Figure 2 presents a screen-shot of the project.

Once the researcher has accessed *PSSA*, he/she must access the menu *Sequence Analysis* to select the microorganism to be analyzed (e.g., Chikungunya). Then, *PSSA* presents the list of available genes. For example, for the microorganism Chikungunya, the genes *E1* and *E2* are displayed. *PSSA* offers two different types of analysis. On the one hand, by selecting the option *view reference sequences*, the user may perform mutation analysis, which analyzes nucleotide and amino acid changes in patient sequences regarding a specific microorganism gene. On the other hand, by selecting the option *view alternative sequences*, the user may perform phylogenetic analysis, which establishes the phylogenetic relationship between the submitted patient sequences and determines which genotype they belong to.

Once the desired analysis is selected, the user is asked to provide the patient sequences through FASTA format files. FASTA format is a text-based format to represent nucleotide sequences, in which amino acids are represented using single-letter codes. *PSSA* offers an example dataset that can be used to test the

Pathogen Sequence Signature Analysis

Pathogen Sequence Signature Analysis

The Pathogen Sequence Signature Analysis (PSSA) project is focused on performing computational analysis of nucleotides sequences of different microorganisms. This tool uses phylogenetic analysis to identify the Serotype/Clade and Genotype of selected microorganisms. Analyses may be performed on very large data sets. The report of the analysis per sequence contains a brief overview of the nucleotide changes that produce an amino acid change, followed by details of the phylogenetic analysis including a phylogenetic tree.

Fig. 2. Screenshot of *PSSA*.

system. The symbol '-' can be included in desired sequences in order to specify possible missing data; but tabs, blank spaces, and any other symbols than the ones used in these kind of sequences (i.e., A, C, T, G) are not accepted.

After patient sequences have been provided, the analysis algorithm is run. Later on, mutation analysis results and phylogenetic analysis results are presented.

5.1   Mutation Analysis Results

For mutation analysis, *PSSA* provides an online report that includes the nucleotide and corresponding amino acid changes for each patient's sequence. A fragment of this report is presented in Fig. 3. In this figure, the analysis informs in the left column, the amount of changes in nucleotides for the first sequence of the first patient. For instance, there are 2 changes from the nucleotie CTG to the nucleotide TTG. In the right column, the changes of amino acids[2] are presented highlighted in red. However, the list presents all changes of sets of three nucleotides that targets the same amino acid with te corresponding position.

Patient: E1_1.fas

1

Nucleotides	Amino Acid
CTG => TTG = 2	29: CTG (L) => TTG (L)
CTA => CTT = 1	33: CTA (L) => CTT (L)
TCA => TCT = 1	35: TCA (S) => TCT (S)
ACT => ACC = 2	37: ACT (T) => ACC (T)
GAG => GAA = 2	39: GAG (E) => GAA (E)
TAC => TAT = 1	51: TAC (Y) => TAT (Y)
GTC => GTT = 1	54: GTC (V) => GTT (V)
TGC => TGT = 3	68: TGC (C) => TGT (C)
AAA => AAG = 1	71: AAA (K) => AAG (K)
AAC => AGC = 1	72: AAC (N) => AGC (S)
GAC => GAT = 1	75: GAC (D) => GAT (D)
TTT => TTC = 3	87: TTT (F) => TTC (F)
GCT => ACC = 1	98: GCT (A) => ACC (T)
AAC => AAT = 1	100: AAC (N) => AAT (N)
GTA => GTG = 2	141: AAC (N) => AAT (N)
ACT => GCT = 1	144: GTA (V) => GTG (V)
GCC => GCT = 2	145: ACT (T) => GCT (A)
ATT => ATA = 1	146: GCC (A) => GCT (A)
GGT => GGC = 1	159: GCC (A) => GCT (A)
GTT => GTC = 1	162: ATT (I) => ATA (I)
GAT => GAC = 2	175: AAC (N) => AAT (N)
AAA => GAA = 1	182: GGT (G) => GGC (G)
GCT => TCC = 1	184: GTT (V) => GTC (V)
CCA => CCG = 1	192: TTT (F) => TTC (F)
TTA => CTA = 1	202: GAT (D) => GAC (D)
CTA => CTG = 1	211: AAA (K) => GAA (E)
CCC => CCT = 1	216: AAC (N) => AAT (N)
TTC => TTT = 4	225: GCT (A) => TCC (S)
CCC => CCA = 1	229: GTA (V) => GTG (V)
TCA => TCG = 1	232: CCA (P) => CCG (P)

Fig. 3. Online report of mutation analysis

---

[2] Amio acid are displayed in parenthesis. One amino acid can be obtained from different sets of three nuceotides.

Force-Direct Graph

Fig. 4. Force-direct graph

For example, in the position 29, the set of three nucleotides CTG which corresponds to the amino acid *Leucine* L has changed to the set of three nucleotides TTG which also corresponds to the amino acid *Leucine* L; nevertheless, in the position 72, independently the nucleotides, the amino acid *Asparagine* N has changed to *Serine* S and thus this position is highlighted.

The report can be sent to the user via e-mail in pdf format, and contains both a summary of the results and complete details of the analysis.

PSSA also provides the results through a force-directed graph, which presents each sequence as a node. The set of nodes deployed using the same color represents one patient (See Fig. 4). In addition, nodes that belong to each patient (i.e., nodes with the same color) are clustered based on the number of nucleotide and amino acid changes. This visualization helps researches in discovering insights regarding the analysis results because such results might be pretty large. For instance, when analyzing 10 patients each with 20 sequences, the pdf report might have up to 150 pages; consequently, finding specific results might become a challenge. However, based on the force-directed graph, desired results may be identified easily. For example, based on the graph presented in Fig. 4, the researcher can easily find that all sequences of the patient represented by dark green nodes have the same amount of changes, but the sequences of the patient represented by red nodes are clustered in four groups, which implies that these sequences are more interesting than the dark green ones. Thus, with this conclusion, the researcher may focus on the red patient reading the detailed results presented in the pdf report.

5.2 Phylogenetic Analysis Results

PSSA is also able to compare a query sequence to a set of reference sequences from known genotypes. Predefined reference genotypes exist for microorganisms pathogens. Then, researchers may used other available reference sequences. Phylogenetic analysis has been used to distinguish genotypes and/or subtypes of microorganisms, and to subtype new isolated strains by comparing them to existing reference and alternative sequences.

As a result, to perform phylogenetic analysis, *PSSA* might include various references sequences in which one of them play the role of the main reference sequence, and several alternative sequences. These reference and alternatives sequences are also obtained from the GenBank database. Thus, when performing this analysis, *PSSA* first analyzes all reference sequences and alternatives sequences against the main reference sequence. Later on, it analyzes patient sequences also against the main reference sequence. Finally, based on the analysis results, *PSSA* identifies the genotype of all patient sequences.

For example, Fig. 5 presents a fragment of an online report of the phylogenetic analysis results in which reference sequences and some alternatives sequences are displayed. As mentioned before, all sequences are analyzed against the main reference sequences, which in this case corresponds to *HM045811-Ross (ECSA)* and thus this sequence is fully displayed. For the other references sequences and all alternative sequences, the report presents the position and the nucleotide change. For instance, the alternative sequence *HM045800 (Asian)* has 60 changes: the first and second changes are presented in the positions 99 and 105 respectively. Both have *Thymine* T, but the main reference sequence has *Adenine* A.

Figure 6 presents another fragment of an online report of the phylogenetic analysis results in which some patient sequences are displayed. In this results, it is also possible to see which changes the analysis found for each patient sequence against the main reference sequence. For instance, the sequence *101* has 171 changes. The first six changes are:

- Position 54 has *Thymine* T, but the main sequence has *Adenine* A.
- Positions 69 and 85 have *Thymine* T, but the main reference sequence has *Cytosine* C.

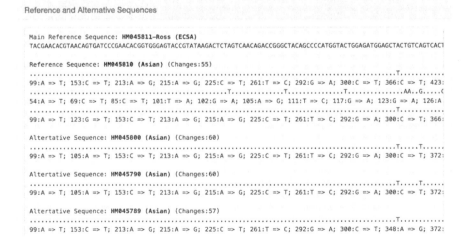

Fig. 5. Phylogenetic analysis. Reference and alternative sequences

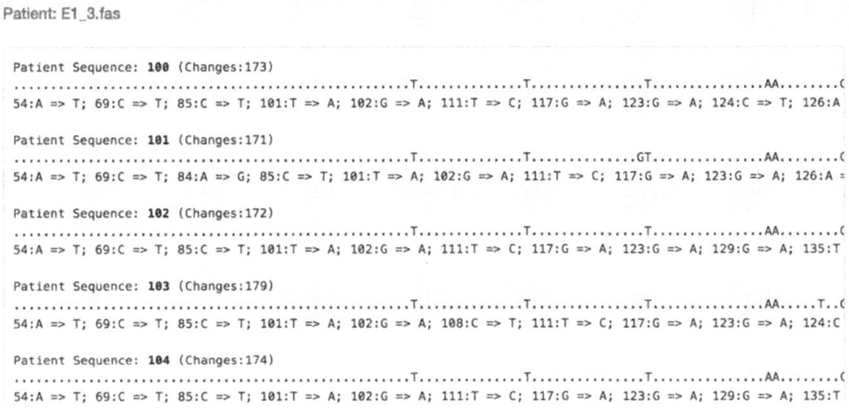

```
Patient: E1_3.fas

Patient Sequence: 100 (Changes:173)
...........................................T.............T...............T..............AA.......(
54:A => T; 69:C => T; 85:C => T; 101:T => A; 102:G => A; 111:T => C; 117:G => A; 123:G => A; 124:C => T; 126:A

Patient Sequence: 101 (Changes:171)
...........................................T.............T............GT..............AA.......(
54:A => T; 69:C => T; 84:A => G; 85:C => T; 101:T => A; 102:G => A; 111:T => C; 117:G => A; 123:G => A; 126:A =

Patient Sequence: 102 (Changes:172)
...........................................T.............T...............T..............AA.......(
54:A => T; 69:C => T; 85:C => T; 101:T => A; 102:G => A; 111:T => C; 117:G => A; 123:G => A; 129:G => A; 135:T

Patient Sequence: 103 (Changes:179)
...........................................T.............T...............T..............AA.....T..(
54:A => T; 69:C => T; 85:C => T; 101:T => A; 102:G => A; 108:C => T; 111:T => C; 117:G => A; 123:G => A; 124:C

Patient Sequence: 104 (Changes:174)
...........................................T.............T...............T..............AA.......(
54:A => T; 69:C => T; 85:C => T; 101:T => A; 102:G => A; 111:T => C; 117:G => A; 123:G => A; 129:G => A; 135:T
```

Fig. 6. Phylogenetic analysis. Patient sequences

– Position 84 has *Guanine* G, but the main sequence has *Adenine* A.
– Position 101 has *Adenine* A, but the main sequence has *Thymine* T.
– Position 102 has *Adenine* A, but the main sequence has *Guanine* G.

In addition, for phylogenetic analysis, *PSSA* presents the results by radial tree and cartesian tree to establish the phylogenetic relationship among sequences and to determine which genotype they belong to. This is achieved based on the alternative sequences of the analyzed gene. Figure 7 presents the cartesian tree when one patient were analyzed.

In this case, cartesian phylogenetic tree regarding Chikungunya viruses was generated by substitution model based on the nucleotide sequence of *E1* gene. Reference sequences of genotypes used are shown in distinct nodes in the cartesian tree: *West African (WAf)* with the code *HM045807*, *East/Central/South African (ECSA)* with the code *HM045811*, and *Asian* with the code *HM045810*. Thus, the cartesian phylogenetic tree shows the three genotypes separated clearly into different branches. Each node indicates each nucleotide sequence. Each sequence is abbreviated with patients ID and details of the amount of nucleotide changes. In addition, nodes that belong to each patient sequence are clustered based on the amount of nucleotide changes against the main reference sequences. In Fig. 7, we can observe one group of *E1_3* sequences. They are grouped together into the alternative sequence *HM045818*, which is a subclade[3] of the *WAf* genotype. However, other group of *E1_3* sequences were clustered into the subclade of the alternative sequence *AY726732*. Moreover, we can observe another group of *E1_3* sequences that belong to the subclade of the alternative sequence *HM045785*. Finally, another group of patient sequences are clustered together near the patient sequence *E1_3:102* directly related to the *WAf* genotype.

With this phylogenetic analysis, the researcher will be able to identify which genotype is circulating between patient sequences. Thus, the mutation combined

---

[3] In genetics, subclade is a term used to describe a subgroup.

Phylogenetic Tree

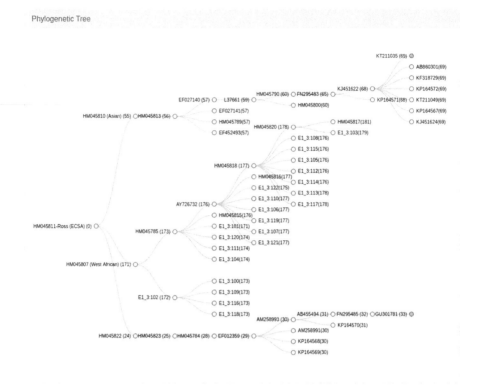

Fig. 7. Cartesian tree of phylogenetic analysis

with geographical information provides insights regarding the microorganisms infection, which is valuable information to public health.

6 Conclusion

Biomedical informatics is a relatively young discipline, which has evolved at an impressive rate by the continuous development of new software solutions and tools. Nevertheless, current tools remain having certain limitations that impede performing desired analysis by researchers. The development of bioinfomatics approaches contributes to public health needs because these approaches may offer analysis results that provide valuable insights useful to make decisions in epidemiology. Moreover, when such approaches are web-based deployed, additional features are offered to researchers such as availability, usability, scalability, among others. These features may improve analysis processes.

PSSA provides an automated computational algorithm that guarantees accurate and reliable detection of nucleotide and amino acid variations in microorganism sequences and provides various ways to visualize analyses results in order to ensure their proper understanding and interpretation. *PSSA* also allows the identification of the genotype of a microorganism by finding nucleotides and amino acid changes of patient sequences against to reference sequences of characterized microorganisms.

As future work, *PSSA* will be upgraded in order to allow analysis of new microorganisms such as *Denge*, and *Zika*.

References

1. Mount, D.: Bioinformatics: Sequence and Genome Analysis. Cold Spring Harbor Laboratory Press (2013)
2. Chen, J., Miller, B.F., Furano, A.V.: Repair of naturally occurring mismatches can induce mutations in flanking DNA. Elife **3**, e02001 (2014)
3. Rodgers, K., McVey, M.: Error-prone repair of dna double-strand breaks. J. Cell. Physiol. **231**(1), 15–24 (2016)
4. Alberts, B., Johnson, A., Lewis, J., Raff, M., Roberts, K., Walter, P.: Molecular Biology of the Cell. Garland Science, New York (2002). Chap. 4
5. Tang, Y.C., Amon, A.: Gene copy-number alterations: a cost-benefit analysis. Cell **152**(3), 394–405 (2013)
6. Murray, P.R., Rosenthal, K.S., Pfaller, M.A.: Medical Microbiology. Elsevier Health Sciences, London (2015)
7. Griffiths, A.: Modern Genetic Analysis: Integrating Genes and Genomes. Freeman, New York (2002)
8. Sanger, F., Nicklen, S., Coulson, A.R.: DNA sequencing with chain-terminating inhibitors. Proc. Natl. Acad. Sci. **74**(12), 5463–5467 (1977)
9. Hall, T.A.: Bioedit: a user-friendly biological sequence alignment editor and analysis program for windows. Nucleic Acids Symp. Ser. **41**(41), 95–98 (1999)
10. Kalaghatgi, P., Sikorski, A.M., Knops, E., Rupp, D., Sierra, S., Heger, E., Neumann-Fraune, M., Beggel, B., Walker, A., Timm, J., et al.: Geno2pheno [HCV]- a web-based interpretation system to support hepatitis c treatment decisions in the era of direct-acting antiviral agents. PLoS ONE **11**(5), e0155869 (2016)
11. Garriga, C., Menéndez-Arias, L.: DR_SEQAN: a PC/Windows-based software to evaluate drug resistance using human immunodeficiency virus type 1 genotypes. BMC Infect. Dis. **6**(1), 44 (2006)
12. Salvatierra, K., Florez, H.: Biomedical mutation analysis (BMA): Aasoftware tool for analyzing mutations associated with antiviral resistance. F1000Research **5**(1141), 1–9 (2016)
13. Rozanov, M., Plikat, U., Chappey, C., Kochergin, A., Tatusova, T.: A web-based genotyping resource for viral sequences. Nucleic Acids Res. **32**, 654–659 (2004)
14. McTavish, E.J., Pettengill, J., Davis, S., Rand, H., Strain, E., Allard, M., Timme, R.E.: Treetoreads-a pipeline for simulating raw reads from phylogenies. BMC Bioinf. **18**(1), 178 (2017)
15. Rambaut, A., Grass, N.C.: Seq-Gen: an application for the Monte Carlo simulation of dna sequence evolution along phylogenetic trees. Comput. Appl. Biosci. CABIOS **13**(3), 235–238 (1997)
16. Huang, W., Li, L., Myers, J.R., Marth, G.T.: Art: a next-generation sequencing read simulator. Bioinformatics **28**(4), 593–594 (2012)
17. Sukumaran, J., Holder, M.T.: Dendropy: a Python library for phylogenetic computing. Bioinformatics **26**(12), 1569–1571 (2010)

Design and Implementation of a Prototype of an Automatic Weather Station for the Measurement of Eolic and Solar Energy Resource

Brian Yesid Garzón Guzman[✉], María Fernanda Rincón Ceron,
Herbert Enrique Rojas Cubides, and Diego Julian Rodriguez Patarroyo

Universidad Distrital Francisco José de Caldas, Bogotá, Colombia
{brian.y.g,maria.m.f}@ieee.org

Abstract. This research document is focused on the design an implementation of a low cost Automatic Weather Station (AWS) in order to measure the environmental variables which are related to the wind an photovoltaic energy generation. This kind of structure, a weather station, entails more elements than sensors variables which are going to be measure, in such a way that it would be difficult because of data collection system, the information storage system process, the location of the AWS, the visualization system and the time of synchronization. This Process includes the proper selection of the sensors and each element, the analysis of the conditioning system, the construction of the entire prototype and the startup of this according to the environmental conditions of the position that will have the AWS.

Keywords: Sensor · AWS · Storage · Server · Information · Low-cost

1 Introduction

Measurement and study of meteorological variables has had an important relevance in different areas of our daily life such as agriculture, navigation, astronomy, power generation, among others. Also it is important to highlight that this type of research has allowed us to achieve a great efficiency advances in our labors since these variables are taken into account due to the fact they influence in the non-deterministic environmental phenomena that are presented all over the planet.

Taking into account the need to know the energy resource, we suggest the design, making of and implementation of an AWS not only to obtain wind and photovoltaic energy bases on the information received but also to produce friendly energy to the environment.

The main objective of the AWS is to provide information about environmental variables that would be used in the analysis of the appropriate energy resources with the goal of generate new energy. In addition, it is a paramount issue that the implementation of this tool, the use of international standards and guidelines for meteorological stations are applied according to World Meteorological Organization (WMO).

© Springer International Publishing AG 2017
J.C. Figueroa-García et al. (Eds.): WEA 2017, CCIS 742, pp. 108–118, 2017.
DOI: 10.1007/978-3-319-66963-2_11

In order to conclude, it is important to note that the implementation of an appropriated AWS, includes the selection of the sensors and some elements used to this project, the analysis of the monitoring systems, the design and building of the physical structure.

2 Concepts

According to WMO, meteorology is the study of the atmosphere and its phenomena. Through meteorology specialist study the meteorological variables which have great influence on the atmosphere behavior. In the course of this area they describe, analyze and predict some changes in the environment.

To carry out this study, meteorological stations are used as a location where observations and specific measurements of the different meteorological parameters are made using appropriate instruments in order to establish the atmospheric behavior in the different zones of the world. In Colombia, they are controller by the Institute of Hydrology, Meteorology and Environmental Studies (IDEAM, for its acronym in Spanish).

Measurements are made according to the station. Some variables are:

- Present time
- Past time
- Direction and wind speed
- Cloudiness
- Type of clouds
- Base height of clouds
- Visibility
- Temperature
- Relative humidity
- Atmospheric pressure
- Precipitation
- Snow cover
- Sun-light and/or solar radiation
- Soil temperature
- Evaporation

In relation to the location or measurement needs of these variables, an AWS should implement the union of different electrical sensors to obtain data of meteorological parameters, where the information is conditioned and then processed through a microcontroller or a microprocessor to be transmitted through a communication system automatically.

To meet the requirement, an AWS usually employs the following elements presented in the Fig. 1.

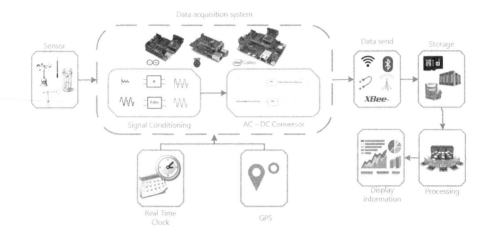

Fig. 1. Parts of an automatic weather station.

The main global standards for climatology and meteorology stations are given by the WMO. This document, guide No. 49, supports: "Technical Regulation: Volume I - General Meteorological Standards and Recommended Practices". This document is also related to the guidelines N°. 8: which says: "Guide to Meteorological Instruments and Methods of Observation" for meteorological stations, guiding with recommendations and advice for conducting meteorological observations and measurements; since it is a guide, the conditions of the procedures are not mandatory [1].

The WMO No. 8 presents all the conditions to emplacement, observers, metadata, instrument characteristics and other factors that must be taken into account when launching an AWS.

3   Methodological Design

We have proposed the implementation of the instruments corresponding to the variables bearing in mind the use that will have the information received from the station.

- Direction and wind speed (Anemometer and weather vane)
- Temperature (Thermometer)
- Relative humidity (Hygrometer)
- Atmospheric pressure (Barometer)
- Precipitation (Pluviometer)
- Solar radiation (Pyranometer)

In addition to the sensors that will be implemented as measuring instruments, other elements were used. They allowed us to know additional conditions of the measurement site and the acquisition and processing of the information. The connection scheme of the entire station is shown in Fig. 2.

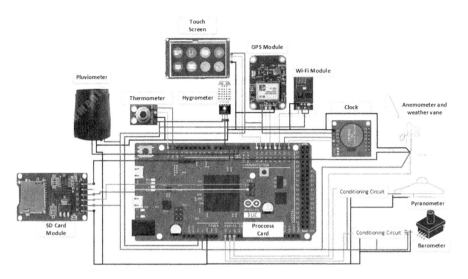

Fig. 2. AWS connection diagram

Each of the sensors was calibrated. This process was made in the 'Laboratorio de Radiometría Solar' of the 'Fundación Universitaria Los Libertadores', Bogotá. This laboratory has patron elements that had been used in different projects by several important companies.

In Latin America several similar research projects have been carried out. For instance, in the "Universidad de Los Andes" (Venezuela) – Transmitting data to a computer; the "Universidad de La Costa" (Colombia) – Embedded platform Arduino, the "Universidad de El Salvador" (El Salvador) – Global Positioning System - LCD display system; the "Universidad Autonoma de Zacatecas" (Mexico) – Internet monitoring; the "Instituto Politecnico Nacional" (Mexico) – Modular system, among others. These projects have been an important sourced for ours. We kept into account the better of each one in order to build a new prototype. In this opportunity peripheral elements and sensors were used.

3.1 Principal Architecture

For the main architecture, three boards were compared: Arduino (Due and Leonardo) and Tibbo. The Arduino Due board is used, mainly for its type of processing and the number of pins which allow to work, also several sensors and modules which will be useful in the processes; in addition an extensive bibliography about Arduino boards.

3.2 Sensors

Thermometer
The MLX90615SSG sensor was chosen because of its characteristics and compatibility with the conditions suggested by WMO. It is an infrared thermometer that allows

measurements of the environment temperature and objects without having contact with it, so at this point the option of performing panel temperature measurements is raised.

Hygrometer

The relative humidity sensor, DHT22, in addition to complying with the characteristics proposed by the WMO, it is easy to access and manipulate because of its implementation. It has an adaptation to be connected directly to the Arduino board, has only three pins, two for power and one for the digital output that connects to a digital pin of the Arduino board.

Barometer

The atmospheric pressure sensor, MPXM2102AS - SOIC 20, is a sensor that complies with the characteristics recommended by WMO and it is used in various projects as a barometer due to its accuracy. For its implementation a conditioning circuit is used for the output voltage of the same $(0 - 40)$ mV and to obtain an input on the Arduino DUE board within its working range $(0\ V - 3.3)\ V$.

Pyranometer

The sensor selected for the measurement of solar radiation was the Kipp & Zonen CMP3, because it had already been acquired for other projects, besides complying with the characteristics proposed by WMO, it is an equipment previously calibrated and ready for use. For its implementation it is used a circuit that allows to perform conditioning of the signal to work in the range of input signals of the data acquisition system.

Anemometer

For the wind speed sensor, anemometer, it was chosen to use the Novalynx 200-WS sensor as it complies with the conditions proposed by WMO and its acquisition is simple because it has been used in other educational institutions for other projects and has presented proper calibration results. This sensor also uses a conditioning circuit due to the equation in its datasheet.

Weather Vane

The vane is one of the simplest sensors, as it has magnetic elements to recognize the position of the shaft, emulating a potentiometer. The Novalynx 200-WS-04 sensor was chosen for its characteristics which satisfy the WMO criteria and because it is the easiest sensors to be acquired in the market. This sensor is also one of them implemented in complete meteorological stations that are part of the same company; so it is a company that allows us to trust that the use of the sensor will be suitable to implement it in a meteorological station.

Pluviometer

For the rain gauge, it is used the Rain Collector 260-7852; taking into account that it is a sensor of easy acquisition and which has been evidenced that it has been used in university projects with excellent results. This sensor has a circuit based on the balance of a rocker when completing its maximum weight and a counter to change sides on the balance.

3.3   Peripheral Elements

To complement the AWS process, the following peripheral devices are chosen, corresponding to the communication, data storage, data visualization, time synchronization and power systems.

Communication System

The communication is done via Wi-Fi between the AWS and the server. The ESP8266 Wi-Fi module, from Espressif Systems, it is a part of the Internet of Things (IoT) world, a world in which thousands of objects are now connected, not people. It is a module that can be directly connected to an Arduino board and can be programmed to work with or without an additional board. In this project, this element is used to connect the system to a web server, which storage all the information of the AWS (measured variables, date, time and geographical coordinates).

Storage System

Of all the technologies presented as information storage, the one with the best access for this project and with greater availability of storage is the memory card (SD), in this way it will be possible to perform analyzes later and that this information can be used for the principal objective that was created. This module allows using a micro SD memory in which the data received by the Arduino card is stored as backup and digitized in .csv files, which can be easily observed and processed in the Microsoft Excel application.

Display System

To display the AWS information, a touch screen is used to take advantage of its dual function and not use a keyboard as an additional element. The reference of the screen to use is Nextion of 2.4″, it has an HMI interface and with its own software to create the different applications, its handling is simple, where it does not use complicated programming code, its connection to the Arduino board is via the serial port.

Synchronization System

Having an AWS implies that the data recorded correspond to a certain date and time. The Arduino board does not have a real-time clock to know seconds, minutes, time, day, month and year. So, the AWS has a clock module, DS1307, that allows synchronizing the current time and knowing the information in real time, this module has a battery and its own circuit.

Location System

Since it is an AWS that can be located anywhere, its position may change, so it has a GPS module, Neo 6 m, which allows knowing the geographic location of the station, obtaining latitude and longitude data. With this information, can even calculate the time zone for the site where it is located to take into account the time difference from the time of the initial location that is Bogota. Additionally, it allows knowing the altitude in meters above sea level for the site where the station is located.

Power System

In situations in which the AWS can be connected to the network, there is a power adapter that will be directly connected to a socket and to the Arduino board. When the AWS is located in places with no electrical connection, it receives power from a set of panels and battery that are designed for the station.

3.4 Building

The used circuits have connections between the main system architecture, sensors, peripheral elements and the power system. For this, a PCB board, Fig. 3, was designed and built, which is located in the waterproof box, where the Arduino DUE development board and peripheral elements will be connected to 7 digital outputs, 7 analog outputs, 7 points of earth, 7 points of power at 3.3.V and 7 points of power at 5 V; this is due to the possibility that at some point changes are made to the sensors and all the sensors used are digital or all are analogous, it could equally happen with the level of voltage that feeds them.

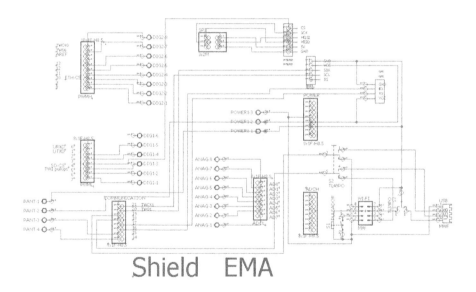

Fig. 3. Schematic diagram of connections

The making of the entire AWS was taken into account the views provided by WMO for the location of each of the sensors. For this reason, as it is usually used in meteorological stations, a tripod is designed to handle the heights recommended by WMO for temperature, radiation and wind speed and direction sensors (Fig. 4).

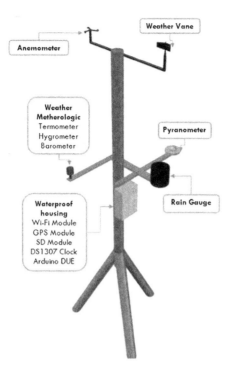

Fig. 4. Support tripod design

4   Implementation Analysis

This research project allowed us to use elements of easy implementation, application and acquisition in the market. They are some reason why during the process of its creation the technical viability was positive. Therefore, the economic investment in each of the elements is justified, in addition to the dedication of the time for its development and implementation.

Additionally, the elements used have extensive information on the web, since most of them are part of the current IoT world. It allows changes in its operation with the intention of improve or adapt the performance of each one. It means that in the future, modifications or improvements can be made to this project and this process will be possible due to all the easiness that can be found in the web and in the market. Suitable bibliographic resources for the realization of a new version of AWS will be willing as well.

5   Calibration Sensors

A Meteorological Station was used as a standard element to calibrate the sensors which is part of the 'Laboratorio de Radiometría Solar' of the 'Fundación Universitaria Los Libertadores', Bogotá. This station has an equipment from Novalynx Corporation, model 110-WS-16 with the following instruments

- Anemometer: 200-WS-01/02
- Rain gauge: 260-7852 Rain Collector
- Barometer: 100-WS-16BP
- Hygrometer: 110-WS-16TH
- Thermometer: 225-HMP50YA
- Weathervane: 200-WS-02/05
- Pyranometer: 100-6450

The synchronization of the information was checked taking as reference the time of each measurement and the graphs of each one of the variables measured. This took place after performing the manual process of the data of the station of the 'Fundación Universitaria Los Libertadores'.

5.1   Relative Humidity

See Fig. 5

- Standard deviation = 2.00   - Correlation coeff. = 0.85

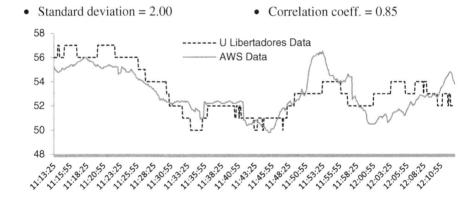

Fig. 5. Data compiled simultaneously in the AWS and the standard station to calibrate the relative humidity sensor

5.2   Temperature Standard

See Fig. 6

- Standard deviation = 1.43
- Correlation coeff. = 0.6

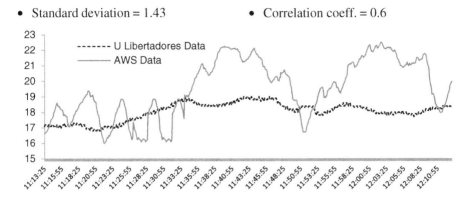

Fig. 6. Data compiled simultaneously in the AWS and the standard station to calibrate the temperature sensor

5.3   Atmospheric Pressure

See Fig. 7

- Standard deviation = 5.65
- Correlation coeff. = 0.98

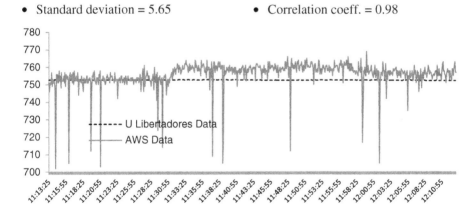

Fig. 7. Data compiled simultaneously in the AWS and the standard station to calibrate the pressure sensor. AWS data after sensor calibration

5.4   Solar Radiation

See Fig. 8

- Standard deviation = 117.72
- Correlation coeff. = 0.98

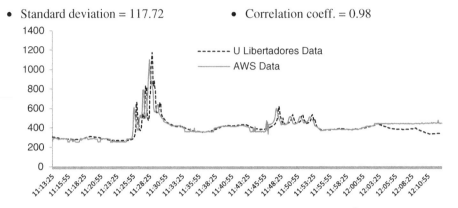

Fig. 8. Data compiled simultaneously in the AWS and the standard station to calibrate the solar radiation sensor. AWS data after sensor calibration

6   Conclusions

To conclude, throughout the evaluation process the WMO regulations were evaluated taking into account each suggestions given by the WMO, document No. 8 about sensors and other systems that are part of the AWS. The given characteristics in the datasheets were compared according to the standard rules.

Each of these sensors and peripheral elements were programmed and conditioned to function in a balance way as a whole system to get the goal, the measurement of the variables chosen from the beginning. The conditioning circuits were designed according to the datasheets of each of these sensors.

In addition to the implementation of AWS, the researchers designed an user's manual and an observer's manual to facilitate the access to manage of all elements in the station but the user had access to the screen only while observer was doing other activities.

As well as, it is very important to have a patron element for each sensors in order to verify the accuracy of the acquired information. Finally, cautions are suggested to preventive and maintain constant verification of each of the elements.

References

1. WMO: WMO No. 49: Technical Regulation: Volume I - General Meteorological Standards and Recommended Practices (2017)
2. Kodali, R.K., Sahu, A.: An IoT based weather information prototype using WeMos. In: Contemporary Computing and Informatics (IC3I) (2016)
3. Thakare, S., Shriyan, A., Thale, V.: Implementation of an energy monitoring and control device based on IoT. In: IEEE Annual India Conference (INDICON) (2016)
4. Saini, H., Thakur, A., Ahuja, S.: Arduino based automatic wireless weather station with remote graphical application and alerts. In: 3rd International Conference on Signal Processing and Integrated Networks (SPIN) (2016)

Assigning-Tasks Method for Developers in Software Projects Using up Similarity Coefficients

Sergio Ruiz[✉], Daniel Escudero, Jair Cervantes, and Adrián Trueba

Universidad Autónoma del Estado de México, Atlacomulco,
Estado de México, Mexico
jsergioruizc@gmail.com, piedraaO@hotmail.com,
chazarra17@gmail.com, atruebae@yahoo.com

Abstract. In the Software industry, big software projects are carried out with hundreds of developers. The fast change in technologies and development environments increase the complexity. Usually, there are project teams with a project leader. However, it is very difficult to know the profile of each developer. The development tasks also have their profile. Hence, it is necessary to assign each task to the most suitable developer. The erroneous assigning of tasks can cause delays and increase the project costs. Thus, a bad assigning of tasks can cause stress and low productivity. Therefore, we make a proposal to enhance tasks assignment to developers regarding the task and developer profiles. The task profile includes characteristics such as: knowledge, kind of task, complexity, experience, etc., in other aspects as codification: paradigm, programming language, version, etc. Using algorithms with similarity coefficients, we look for the best match to assign the tasks to developers. In this work, we used five techniques of similarity coefficient in order to find results and to recommend the best solution for this problem. We conclude that with the Sokal and Sneath technique we obtain better results to solve the problem.

Keywords: Matching · Software industry · Similarity coefficient · Profile of tasks · Profile of developer

1 Introduction

The reason that motivated the development of this work is the complexity that exists on assignment of tasks to the developers; mostly, in organizations that develop large and complex projects. The developers have different capabilities and abilities, called Profile of Developer (PD). Therefore, there are increasingly complex tasks with different characteristics that require new specialists, called Profile of Task (PT). Additionally, at least in Mexico, there is a high rotation of personal in the software project development companies.

The objective of this work is to create a method to support the assignment of tasks to the developers by the leaders or project managers. To fulfill the method, it is necessary for the project leader to generate a profile of each one of the developers. Then, when a new task is created, you must generate your profile. Our Model created

© Springer International Publishing AG 2017
J.C. Figueroa-García et al. (Eds.): WEA 2017, CCIS 742, pp. 119–128, 2017.
DOI: 10.1007/978-3-319-66963-2_12

for this purpose will do the matching by finding the most suitable developer for the task in question.

The proposed method for this work is the use of similarity coefficients to find the greatest similarity between PD and PT. Five similarity coefficients are used to constrain the results and determine the best alternative. An application has been created to help the project leader. This method is intended to achieve the assignment of tasks more optimally.

2   Similarity Coefficients

The similarity coefficients are more prolific than the similarity indexes. These coefficients are used to measure the association between samples. In contrast, with most distance coefficients, similarity measures are not metric, since two, A and B, samples may be found to be more similar to each other than the sum of their similarities to a distant C sample. Similarities cannot be used to locate samples relative to one another in a symmetric space. Also, they can be defined as those that measure the data of identical pairs between pairs of operative taxonomic units on a multi-state double character array.

The coefficient is a measure of similarity that satisfies the requirements of a scalar product between normalized vectors in a Euclidean space, which is called correlation coefficient.

The similarity coefficients are developed for binary data, of type presence-absence or 1-0. For binary data they are derived as a ratio that implies the number of attributes shared by a pair of entities related to the number of attributes involved in the comparison. In most of these coefficients, the values range from 0 (no similarity) and 1 (complete similarity) [1].

In binary coefficients, [2] affirm it is simple; the similarity between two samples is based on the presence or absence of certain characteristics in them. These descriptors may be environment variable or species. Therefore, the observations can be tabulated in a frequency table of 2×2. See Table 1.

Table 1. Frequency table of 2×2 [2].

Sample X2	Sample X1		
	1	0	
1	1, 1 (a)	1, 0 (b)	a + b
0	0, 1 (c)	0, 0 (d)	c + d
	a + c	b + d	(n) = a + b + c + d

From the Table 1, it gets the variables: *(a), (b), (c)* y *(d)*. The *(a)* when both values are 1's, *(b)* when the values are 1 and 0, *(C)* when the values are 0 and 1, *(d)* when both values are 0's. Finally, *(n)* is the total number of occurrences [2].

The Simple Comparison Coefficient (SMC) establishes the similarity between the two samples by counting the number of variables they both possess and dividing by the total number of variables. See Formula 1. This coefficient assumes that there is no difference between double zero and double one, so that the variable or attribute can get the value of zero or one indistinctly, this is giving the same value to absences or presences [2].

$$S_1(x_1, x_2) = \frac{a+d}{n} = \frac{a+d}{a+b+c+d} \tag{1}$$

The coefficient of Rogers and Tanimoto establishes that differences are more important than similarities. See Formula 2. This index produces values between zero and one [3].

$$D_2(x_1, x_2) = \frac{a+d}{a+2b+2c+d} \tag{2}$$

The Sokal and Sneath coefficient is proposed four measures which take into account the double zeros, See Formula 3. In this coefficient the joint occurrences have double value. This index provides values from 0 to 1 [4].

$$S_3(x_1, x_2) = \frac{2a+2d}{2a+b+c+2d} \tag{3}$$

The Hamman coefficient is the simple equality index except that the numerator is reduced by inequalities. You can also find it by the name of Index G. See Formula 4. This index produces values between -1 and $+1$ [5].

$$S_4(x_1, x_2) = \frac{(a+d) - (b+c)}{a+b+c+d} \tag{4}$$

Finally, the Jaccard coefficient gives the same value to all terms, and ranges from 0 to 1. See Formula 5 [6].

$$S_5(x_1, x_2) = \frac{a}{a+b+c} \tag{5}$$

The coefficient of similitude has been used in bio-informatics, pattern recognition, signal processing, file comparison and text correction. With the Distance of Levenshtein to know the distance between two words [7]. See the Table 2. The distance is 4, because among both words there are 4 different characters.

Table 2. Distance of Levenshtein [7].

U	N	I	V	E	R	S	A	L	L	Y
=	=	=	=	=	=	=	x	x	x	x
U	N	I	V	E	R	S	E	–	–	–

In this case, the distance is determined by the number of letters that need to be added, deleted or changed for getting two words are equal. When the two words or phrases are equal, then the distance is 0 [7].

We find the work of [8], where similarity metrics are applied for case-based project management, to find previous historical cases that provide knowledge.

The work of [9] seeks to detect the degree of similarity over short texts. For this, two different approaches are proposed to carry out this task. On one hand, they propose unsupervised methods based on algorithms that were originally created to solve the task of biological chain alignment. These algorithms are made to recognize a pair of sequences and find the main similarities between them. These algorithms are given semantic information to be used, not biological sequences, but in texts.

Another work [10] seeks to find similarity between leaves of plants from 150 characteristics. From a vector characteristic of a new leaf, it is compared with a set of 22767 vectors of the identified plants. The objective is to identify the new plant based on the characteristics of the leaf.

3   Proposed Method

3.1   Profile of Task

In this research, it is not intended to make a classification, but the application of a metric that allows finding the greatest similarity between the profile of a task and a developer.

Firstly, the PT was defined. The projects leader will create the profile of each task. Secondly, we have the profile of the task, we can search which developer has most similar profile and match them. The profile of some tasks can be seen in Table 3.

When the characterization exists the value is 1 and when the characterization does not exist the value is 0. Using a form, the project leader generates the task profiles, immediately it is captured on an application and the application makes the matching.

Thus, the first task has the next pattern: 01000100000001000010001010010100, and the second task: 00000100100100000000001000100101010. Then, each task has its own pattern.

3.2   Profile of Developer

The PD has 32 0's and 1's. The first developer has the next pattern: 00100110000000000010101010010101. Each developer will have their profile defined in the company and will be considered when assigning a task. See Table 4.

3.3   Choice of Similarity Metrics

When a new task is generated the Method for Matching Tasks and Developers (MMTD) compares the task with all the profiles of developers. Its aim is to find a developer who has greater similarity with the task. The task is assigned to the developer with the greatest similarity. See Table 5.

Table 3. Profiles of tasks.

	Profile of tasks	1	2	3	4	5
1	Requeriments management	0	0	0	0	0
2	Analysis of requeriments	0	0	1	1	1
3	Requeriments definition	0	1	0	0	0
4	Architecture of software design	0	1	0	0	0
5	User interface design	1	0	0	0	0
6	Model of data desing	0	0	1	0	0
7	Modelled with UML	0	0	0	1	1
8	Front-end programming	1	0	0	0	0
9	Back-end programming	0	0	0	1	0
10	Structured paradigm	0	0	0	0	0
11	Programming OO paradigm	1	0	0	1	0
12	Functional programming paradigm	0	0	0	0	0
13	Logical programming paradigm	0	0	0	0	0
14	Unit tests	0	0	1	0	0
15	Integration testing	0	0	0	0	0
16	Testing of acceptance	0	1	0	0	0
17	Software installation	0	0	0	0	0
18	Software configuration	0	0	0	0	0
19	Desktop software	0	1	1	0	1
20	Mobile software	1	0	0	0	0
21	Web system	0	0	0	1	0
22	Minimal experience	0	0	0	0	0
23	Regular experience	0	0	1	1	0
24	High experience	1	1	0	0	1
25	English language - low	0	0	1	0	0
26	English language - regular	0	0	0	1	0
27	English language - high	1	1	0	0	1
28	Individual task	0	0	1	1	1
29	Collective task	1	0	0	0	0
30	Task on office	0	1	1	0	0
31	Task on home office	1	0	0	1	0
32	Software documentation	0	1	0	0	1

3.4   Matching of Tasks and Developers

The Method for Matching Tasks and Developers has been created as a tool for this problem. The application compares the pattern of a task with all the patterns of the developers.

The MMTD takes the profile of the task and search a developer profile with the greatest similarity and it assigns the task to the developer, achieving the most suitable assignment.

Table 4. Profiles of developers.

	Profile of developers	1	2	3	4	5	6	7	8	9	10
1	Requirements management	0	0	1	0	0	0	1	0	0	0
2	Analysis of requirements	0	0	1	1	1	1	1	0	0	1
3	Requeriments definition	1	0	0	1	0	0	0	0	0	0
4	Architecture of software design	0	0	0	1	0	0	0	1	0	0
5	User interface design	0	1	0	0	0	0	1	0	0	1
6	Model of data design	1	1	0	0	0	1	1	0	0	0
7	Modelled with UML	1	0	1	1	0	1	1	0	0	0
8	Front-end programming	0	1	0	0	0	0	0	0	0	0
9	Back-end programming	0	0	0	0	0	0	0	1	0	0
10	Structured paradigm	0	0	0	0	0	0	0	0	0	1
11	Programming OO paradigm	0	1	1	0	0	0	0	0	0	0
12	Functional programming paradigm	0	0	0	0	0	0	0	0	0	0
13	Logical programming paradigm	0	0	0	0	0	0	0	0	0	0
14	Unit tests	0	0	0	0	1	0	0	0	0	0
15	Integration testing	0	0	0	0	1	0	0	0	0	0
16	Testing of acceptance	0	0	0	1	1	0	0	1	0	1
17	Software installation	0	0	0	0	0	0	0	0	0	0
18	Software configuration	0	0	0	1	1	0	0	0	0	0
19	Desktop software	1	1	1	1	1	1	1	0	1	0
20	Mobile software	0	1	0	0	0	0	0	0	0	0
21	Web system	1	1	1	1	0	1	1	1	0	0
22	Minimal experience	0	0	0	0	0	0	0	0	0	0
23	Regular experience	1	0	1	0	0	1	1	0	0	1
24	High experience	0	1	0	0	1	0	1	1	0	0
25	English language - low	1	0	0	0	0	0	0	0	0	0
26	English language - regular	0	0	1	0	0	1	0	1	0	0
27	English language - high	0	1	0	1	1	0	0	0	0	1
28	Individual task	1	0	1	0	1	0	1	0	0	0
29	Collective task	0	1	0	0	0	1	0	0	1	0
30	Task on office	1	0	1	1	0	0	1	0	0	0
31	Task on home office	0	1	0	0	0	0	0	1	0	0
32	Software documentation	1	0	0	1	0	0	1	0	0	0

3.5 Matching Technics

For this work, five techniques have been used: SMC, Roger and Tanimoto, Sokal and Sneath, Hamman and Jaccard. The objective is to find the best technique with the best results. For to use these techniques, we apply the algorithm as in Algorithm 1.

Table 5. Patterns of profiles.

New task	Profiles of developers
01000100000001000010001010010100	00100110000000000010101010010101
	00001001001000000011100100101010
	11000010001000000010101001010100
	01110010000000010110100000100101
	01000000000001110110000100110000
	01000110000000000010101001001000
	11000010000000000011100110010001
	00010000100000010000100101000010
	00000000000000000001000000000001000
	01001000010000010000001000100000

Algorithm 1. Similarity coefficient.

```
Repeat from Task=1 to n
  Read pattern of PT
  // Extraction the values of a, b, c. and d.
  Repeat from Developer=1 to n
   Read pattern of PD
   // It count the values of a, b, d, and d
   If  PT[t][d] = 1 and PD[t][d]=1
     a=1
   If  PT[t][d] =1 and PD[t][d]=0
     b=1
     If  PT[t][d] = 0 end PD[t][d]=1
     c=1
     If  PT[t][d]=0 and PD[t][d]=0
     d=1
     a++, b++, c++, d++
   End of Repeat Developer
  // with the values of a, b, c, and d. It get the
similarity
  SMC = a + d / (a + b + c + d)
  RT = a + d / (a + 2b + 2c + d)
  SS = 2a + 2c / (2a + b + c + 2d)
  Ham= (a + d) - (b + c) / (a + b + c + d)
  Jac = a / a + b + c + d
End of Repeat Task
```

The algorithm gets the PT and it compares it with each PD to find the best assignment using matching. The project leader can find the ideal developer for each task of the project.

4   Results

With a sample of ten PD and five PT, the first task was analyzed. The results are similar; however, the technique with the highest similarity is Hamman, with 0.951. The best Developer for the Task 1 is the PD2. See Table 6.

Table 6. Results of Similarity coefficients of Task 1.

	a	b	c	d	SMC	R&T	S&S	Ham	Jac
PD1	0	8	10	14	0,438	0,280	0,609	−0,125	0,000
PD2	8	0	3	21	0,906	0,829	0,951	0,813	0,727
PD3	1	7	9	15	0,500	0,333	0,667	0,000	0,059
PD4	1	7	10	14	0,469	0,306	0,638	−0,063	0,056
PD5	2	6	7	17	0,594	0,422	0,745	0,188	0,133
PD6	1	7	7	17	0,563	0,391	0,720	0,125	0,067
PD7	2	6	10	14	0,500	0,333	0,667	0,000	0,111
PD8	2	6	5	19	0,656	0,488	0,792	0,313	0,154
PD9	1	7	1	23	0,750	0,600	0,857	0,500	0,111
PD10	2	6	4	20	0,688	0,524	0,815	0,375	0,167

In Fig. 1 Developer 2 can be seen as the most ideal. On the other hand, developer 1 is the lowest.

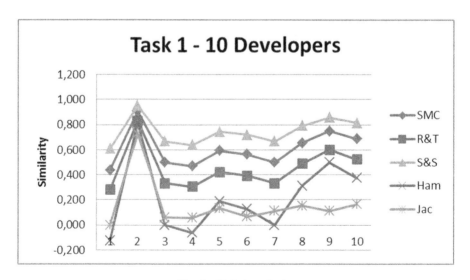

Fig. 1. Task 1 analysis.

For Task 2 analysis, Developer 4 is the most suitable. While, the Developer 1 and 6 are gets the lowest similarity. See Table 7. See also Fig. 2.

Table 7. Results of Similarity coefficients of Task 2.

	a	b	c	d	SMC	R&T	S&S	Ham	Jac
PD1	4	4	6	17	0,656	0,512	0,808	0,344	0,286
PD2	3	5	8	15	0,563	0,409	0,735	0,156	0,188
PD3	2	6	7	16	0,563	0,409	0,735	0,156	0,133
PD4	7	1	3	20	0,844	0,771	0,931	0,719	0,636
PD5	4	4	4	19	0,719	0,590	0,852	0,469	0,333
PD6	1	7	6	17	0,563	0,409	0,735	0,156	0,071
PD7	4	4	7	16	0,625	0,476	0,784	0,281	0,267
PD8	3	5	4	19	0,688	0,550	0,830	0,406	0,250
PD9	1	7	1	22	0,719	0,590	0,852	0,469	0,111
PD10	2	6	3	20	0,688	0,550	0,830	0,406	0,182

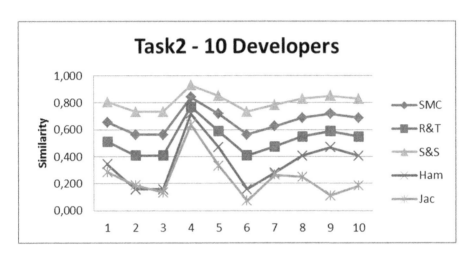

Fig. 2. Results of task 2.

Regarding the results of the five tasks and the ten developers the assigning it is as you see in Table 8. Specifying that, the corresponding tables and graphs the remaining tasks are not shown for reasons of space.

Table 8. Results of the five tasks

Matching tasks and
developers

Task	1	2	3	4	5
Developer	2	4	1	3	5

5 Conclusions

We conclude that MMTD can support project leaders on assignment of Tasks to Developers. Specially, in big development projects where hundreds or thousands of tasks take place. It can also support distributed projects. In this work, 32 characteristics have been included, but more characteristics could be added to the profiles to get a more precise matching. We recommended the technique Sokal & Sneath because sown similarity more high.

References

1. Rodríguez-Salazar, M.E., Álvarez-Hernández, S., Bravo-Núñez, E.: Coefficients of similarity. ed. Plaza y Valdés S. A. de C. V (2001). ISBN 968-856-901-1
2. Legendre, L., Legrende, P.: Numerical Ecology. Elsevier, Amsterdam (1983)
3. Rogers, J.S., Tanimoto, T.T.: A computer program for classifying plats. Science **132**, 1115–1118 (1960)
4. Sokal, R.R., Sneath, P.H.: Principles of Numerical Taxonomy. W.H. Freeman and Company, San Francisco (1963)
5. Hamann U. Merkmalsbestand und Verwandtschaftsbeziehungen der farinosae. Ein Beitrag zum System der Monokotyledonen Willdenowia, pp. 639–768 (1961)
6. Jaccard, P.: Nouvelles recherches sur la distribution florale. In: Bulletin de la Sociète Vaudense des Sciences Naturelles, vol. 44, pp. 223–270 (1908)
7. García, J.F.: Métricas de Similitud para Búsqueda Aproximada. Revista de Tecnologia, Facultad de Ingenieria de Sistemas, Universidad del Bosque, pp. 1–11 (2007)
8. Rodríguez, G., Berdún, L., Soria, A., Amandi, A., Macelo, C.: Análisis de Métricas de Similitud en Razonamiento Basado en Casos para Administrar Proyectos, ASAI 2015, 16° Simposio Argentino de Inteligencia Artificial (2015)
9. Álvarez, C.M.A.: Thesis: Detección de similitud semántica en textos cortos, Instituto Nacional de Astrofísica, Óptica y Electrónica Tonantzintla, Puebla (2014)
10. Ruiz, C.J.S., Cervantes, J.C., Juárez, R.R.H., Trueba, A.E.: Métricas de Similitud SMC, Jaccard y Roger & Tanimoto en la Identificación de Plantas, CIINDET, Morelos, México (2016)

Computational Intelligence

Segment and Fenwick Trees for Approximate Order Preserving Matching

Rafael Niquefa[1], Juan Mendivelso[2,3(✉)], Germán Hernández[4],
and Yoan Pinzón[5]

[1] Facultad de Ciencias e Ingeniería,
Politecnico Grancolombiano Institucion Universitaria,
Calle 57 # 3 - 00 Este, i Tower Bogotá, Bogotá, Colombia
rniquefa@poligran.edu.co
[2] Departamento de Matemáticas, Universidad Nacional de Colombia,
Bogotá, Colombia
jcmendivelsom@unal.edu.co
[3] Facultad de Matemáticas e Ingenierías,
Fundación Universitaria Konrad Lorenz, Bogotá, Colombia
[4] Departamento de Ingeniería de Sistemas e Industrial,
Universidad Nacional de Colombia, Bogotá, Colombia
[5] Departamento de Electrónica y Ciencias de la Computación,
Pontificia Universidad Javeriana, Cali, Colombia

Abstract. In this paper we combine two string searching related problems: the approximate string matching under parameters δ and γ, and the order preserving matching problem. Order-preserving matching regards the internal structure of the strings rather than their absolute values while matching under δ and γ distances permit a level of error. We formally define the $\delta\gamma$–order-preserving matching problem. We designed two algorithms for it based on the segment tree and the Fenwick tree, respectively. Also, we design and implement in C++ and an experimental setup to compare these algorithms with the naive solution and the $updateBA$ algorithm introduced in [22]. The data structure based algorithms show better experimental performance due to their better lower bound of $\Omega(n \lg n)$ complexity.

Keywords: String searching · Strings similarity metric · Fenwick tree · Binary indexed tree · Segment tree

1 Introduction

Stringology is the branch of computer science that is dedicated to the study of problems in which sequences are involved. One of the main problems of interest in stringology is *string matching*, which consists of finding the occurrences of a pattern within a text. Formally, the input of a string matching algorithm is a text T, of length n, and a pattern P, of length m. Both the text and the pattern are formed by the concatenation of symbols of a given alphabet Σ. This alphabet

© Springer International Publishing AG 2017
J.C. Figueroa-García et al. (Eds.): WEA 2017, CCIS 742, pp. 131–143, 2017.
DOI: 10.1007/978-3-319-66963-2_13

for the vast majority of practical applications can be considered as an ordered set of different symbols. The output of a pattern matching algorithm is the list of positions in the text T where the pattern P is found.

The strings will be considered throughout the paper as indexed from 0. A notation generally used to represent substrings in a string, and which we will adopt in this paper, is the following: Let $T_{0...n-1}$ represent a length-n string defined over Σ. The symbol at the position i of a string T is denoted as T_i. Also, $T_{i...j}$ represents the substring of the text T from the position i to the position j, i.e. $T_{i...j} = T_i T_{i+1} \cdots T_j$, where it is assumed that $0 \leq i \leq j < n$. In particular, we are interested in each length-m substring that starts at position i of the text, i.e. $T_{i...i+m-1}$, $0 \leq i \leq n - m$, which we call *text window* and denote as T^i in the rest of the paper. Then, the output of the exact string matching problem should list all the positions i, $0 \leq i \leq n - m$, such that $P_j = T_{i+j}$ for all $0 \leq j \leq m - 1$.

In this paper, two variants of the problem of exact search of patterns were combined: the $\delta\gamma$–matching problem and the order preserving matching problem. Both of them consider integer alphabets. The $\delta\gamma$–*matching* problem consists of finding all the text windows in T for which $\max_{0 \leq j \leq m-1} |P_j - T_{i+j}| \leq \delta$ and $\sum_{j=0}^{m-1} |P_j - T_{i+j}| \leq \gamma$. We can see that δ limits the individual error of each position while γ limits the total error. Then, $\delta\gamma$–matching has applications in bioinformatics, computer vision and music information retrieval, to name some. Cambouropoulos et al. [3] was perhaps the first to mention this problem motivated by Crawford's work et al. [6]. Recently, it has been used to make more flexible other string matching paradigms such as parameterized matching [17,18], function matching [19] and jumbled matching [20,21].

On the other hand, *order-preserving matching* considers the order relations within the numeric strings rather than the approximation of their values. Specifically, the output of this problem is the set of text windows whose natural representation match the natural representation of the pattern. The natural representation of a string is a string composed by the rankings of each symbol in such string. In particular, the ranking of symbol T_i of string $T_{0...n-1}$ is:

$$rank_T(i) = 1 + |\{T_j < T_i : 0 \leq j, i < n \wedge i \neq j\}| + |\{T_j = T_i : j < i\}|.$$

Then, the natural representation of T is $nr(T) = rank_T(0)rank_T(1)\cdots rank_T(n-1)$. Therefore, order preserving matching consists of finding all the text windows T^i such that $nr(P) = nr(T^i)$. Note that this problem is interested in matching the internal structure of the strings rather than their values. Then, it has important applications in music information retrieval and stock market analysis. Specifically, in music information retrieval, one may be interested in finding matches between relative pitches; similarly, in stock market analysis the variation pattern of the share prices may be more interesting than the actual values of the prices [15]. Since Kim et al. [15] and Kubica et al. [16] defined the problem, it has gained great attention from several other researchers [4,5,7–10,14].

Despite the extensive work on order-preserving matching, the only approximate variant in previous literature, to the best of our knowledge, was recently proposed by Uznański and Gawrychowski [12]. In particular, they allow k mismatches between the pattern and each text window. Then, they regard the number of mismatches but not their magnitude. In this paper, we propose a different approach to approximate order-preserving matching that bounds the magnitude of the mismatches through the $\delta\gamma$- distance. Specifically, δ is a bound between the ranking of each character in the pattern and its corresponding character in the text window; likewise, γ is a bound on the sum of all such differences in ranking. Thus, δ and γ respectively restrict the magnitude of the error individually and globally across the strings. We define $\delta\gamma$–*order-preserving matching* as the problem of finding all the text windows in T that match the pattern P under this new paradigm.

We first defined the notion of $\delta\gamma$–order preserving matching in [22]. Now, in this paper we provide a more formal definition in Sect. 2. In Sect. 3, we present two new algorithms for this problem: one based on segment trees and the other based on Fenwick trees. In Sect. 4, we describe the experiment performed to compare the algorithms with a naive solution and the algorithm *updateBA* introduced in [22]. The data structures based algorithms experimentally outperformed the other two. Finally, the concluding remarks are presented in Sect. 5.

2   Definition of $\delta\gamma$–Order Preserving Matching Problem ($\delta\gamma$–OPMP)

The motivation to define $\delta\gamma$–order-preserving matching stems from the observation that the application areas of order-preserving matching, mainly stock market analysis and music information retrieval, require to search for occurrences of the pattern that may not be exact but rather have slight modifications in the magnitude of the rankings. For example, let us assume that the text T presented in Fig. 1 is a sequence of stock prices and that we want to determine whether it contains similar occurrences of the pattern P (also shown in this figure). Under the exact order-preserving matching paradigm, there are no matches, but there are similar occurrences at positions and 1 and 11. In particular, $T_{1...8}$ and $T_{11...18}$ are similar, regarding order structure, to the pattern. This similarity can be seen even more clearly if we consider natural representations of these strings (also shown in Fig. 1).

Next we will formally define the $\delta\gamma$–*order-preserving match*, and with that definition we will define the $\delta\gamma$–*order-preserving matching ($\delta\gamma$–OPMP)*.

Definition 1 ($\delta\gamma$–order-preserving match). *Let $X = X_{0...m-1}$ and $Y = Y_{0...m-1}$ be two equal-length strings defined over Σ_σ. Also, let δ, γ be two given numbers ($\delta, \gamma \in \mathbb{N}$). Strings X and Y are said to $\delta\gamma$–order-preserving match, denoted as $X \overset{\delta\gamma}{\leadsto} Y$, **iff** $nr(X) \overset{\delta\gamma}{=} nr(Y)$.*

Example 1. Given $\delta = 2$, $\gamma = 6$, $X = \langle 10, 15,\ 19, 12,\ 11, 18,\ 23, 22\rangle$ and $Y = \langle 14, 17,\ 20, 18,\ 12, 15,\ 23, 22\rangle$, $X \overset{\delta\gamma}{\leadsto} Y$ as $nr(X) = \langle 1, 4,\ 6, 3,\ 2, 5,\ 8, 7\rangle$, $nr(Y) = \langle 2, 4,\ 6, 5,\ 1, 3,\ 8, 7\rangle$ and $nr(X) \overset{\delta\gamma}{=} nr(Y)$.

Problem 1 ($\delta\gamma$–order-preserving matching ($\delta\gamma$–OPMP)). Let $P = P_{0...m-1}$ be a pattern string and $T = T_{0...n-1}$ be a text string, both defined over Σ_σ. Also, let

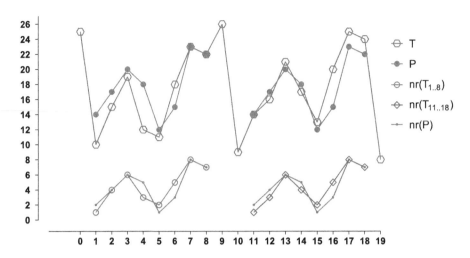

Fig. 1. Order preserving matching under $\delta\gamma$ approximation example.

δ, γ be two given numbers ($\delta, \gamma \in \mathbb{N}$). The $\delta\gamma$-*order-preserving matching problem* is to calculate the set of all indices i, $0 \leq i \leq n - m$, satisfying the condition $P \overset{\delta\gamma}{\approx} T^i$. From now on $\delta\gamma$-**OPMP**.

3   Algorithms for the $\delta\gamma$–OPMP

In this section, we present two algorithms that solve the $\delta\gamma$–Order preserving matching problem ($\delta\gamma$–OPMP): one that makes use of segment trees (Sect. 3.1) and the other utilizes Fenwick trees (Sect. 3.2).

3.1   Segment Tree Based Algorithm (*segtreeBA*)

The segment tree data structure is a powerful data structure with applications in many areas like in computational geometry [1,2] and graph theory. The segment tree data structure uses the divide and conquer approach to answer queries in ranges of an underlying array A. Every node in a Segment Tree is assigned a range and will contain the answer to the query for that specific range. We will use the segment tree data structure to solve the range minimum query (RMQ) problem, which consists in finding the index of the minimum value of the array in a given range, and we will be able to change elements of the array. Building a segment tree to solve the RMQ problem for an array A of length $|A|$ takes $O(|A|)$ space and time. The update and query operations both take $O(\lg |A|)$.

Based on this data structure, we propose the algorithm called *settreeBA* (see Fig. 2). It first calculates the natural representation of the pattern P (line 1 in Fig. 2). Then, it iterates over all possible position and tries to find $\delta\gamma$-order preserving matches in every one of them. The process of finding a match at position i in T is as follows: First the algorithm finds the smallest number

---

Algorithm 1: $\delta\gamma$–OPMP **segtreeBA**

Input: $P = P_{0...m-1}, T = T_{0...n-1}, \delta, \gamma$
Output: $\{i \in \{0, \ldots, n - m\} : T^i \overset{\delta\gamma}{\approx} P\}$
1. **Create as Array**: $P^{nr} \leftarrow nr(P)$
2. **Create as Array of size** m: $oldValue, changedIndex$
3. **Create as Segment Tree**: $minIndex \leftarrow buildSegTree(T, 0, n - 1)$
4. **Define**: $curDelta, curGamma, rank, idxT, idxP, nChanges$ **as integers**
5. $nChanges \leftarrow 0$
6. **for** $i = 0 \rightarrow n - m$ **do**
7.   **for** $rank = 1 \rightarrow m$ **do**
8. $idxT \leftarrow querySegTree(minIndex, i, i + m - 1)$
9. $idxP \leftarrow idxT - i$
10. $curDelta \leftarrow |rank - P^{nr}_{idxP}|$
11. $curGamma \leftarrow curGamma + curDelta$
12.   **if** $curDelta > delta \vee curGamma > gamma$ **then break loop**
13. $changedIndex_nChanges \leftarrow idxT$
14. $oldValue_nChanges \leftarrow T_{idxT}$
15. $nChanges \leftarrow nChanges + 1$
16. $updateSegTree(minIndex, idxT, \infty)$
17.   **for** $c = 0 \rightarrow nChanges - 1$ **do**
18. $updateSegTree(minIndex, changedIndex_c, oldValue_c)$
19.   **if** $rank > m$ **then report** i
20. $nChanges \leftarrow 0$

Fig. 2. Segment tree based algorithm: *segtreeBA*.

in the interval $[i, i + m - 1]$ (line 8); this value has the rank 1 in the sliding window T^i. It then uses the natural representation of P to check the δ and γ restrictions for the rank 1 in the window T^i. Then it prepares the segment tree for the next iteration; this is done by changing the smallest value in the interval $[i, i + m - 1]$ to infinity, so in the next iteration of the first inner loop the operation $querySegTree(minIndex, i, i + m - 1)$ finds the second smallest value in the same interval. This process is done for all the rankings from 1 to m.

In the second inner loop (lines 17 and 18 in Fig. 2), the values of T in the interval $[i, i+m-1]$ must be changed so that, in the next window, those contain the original values of T and no infinity. The arrays *oldValue* and *changedIndex* help in the process of restoring the segment tree. We are going to adapt the standard operations of the segment tree to this solution as follows:

- *buildSegTree*$(T, 0, n - 1)$: Builds a segment tree with $T_0, T_1, \ldots, T_{n-1}$ and returns the root node. The complexity is $O(n)$.
- *updateSegTree*$(minIndex, i, x)$: Sets T_i to x. The complexity is $O(\lg n)$.
- *querySegTree*$(minIndex, i, j)$: Returns the index of the minimum value among $T_i, T_{i+1}, \ldots, T_j$. If there are several minimum values, the leftmost (smallest index) is chosen. The complexity is $O(\lg n)$.

The complexity of *segtreeBA* can be computed as follows: In line 1 in Fig. 2, the algorithm creates the natural representation of the pattern with cost

$\Theta(m \lg m)$. In line 2 it creates two arrays of size m in $\Theta(m)$. In line 3 a segment tree is created in $\Theta(n)$. Then in the main loop it iterates over all $n - m + 1$ candidates. For each candidate it finds the elements with ranks from 1 to m using the segment tree. Finding the position of each rank in the window costs $O(\lg n)$. After each rank position is found, the algorithm checks if the $\delta\gamma$ restrictions holds for the current window (lines 10 to 12). If so, it continues with the next rank; if not, the algorithm breaks the inner loop and continues with the next search window (line 12).

Due to the fact that the segment tree is used to find the smallest element in an interval, the algorithm must $mark$ as ∞ the position of each rank. Then, in the next iteration, the next smallest element that is found, is the next rank. These changes are done in $O(\lg n)$ time (lines 13 to 16). Reversing those changes costs $O(m \lg n)$ (lines 17 to 18). In fact, the inner loops (lines 7 to 20) have a combined complexity of $O(m \lg n)$, but also have a lower bound of $\Omega(\lg n)$. The lower bound of this algorithm is then $\Omega(n \lg n)$, because in many cases it does not perform the m comparisons cost $O(\lg n)$. The total complexity of the algorithm is then $O(n + n \lg n + m \lg m + (n - m + 1)(m \lg n)) = O(nm \lg n)$, but with a lower bound of $\Omega(n \lg n)$.

3.2 Fenwick Tree Based Algorithm ($bitBA$)

The Binary Indexed Tree (BIT) or Fenwick tree, proposed by Peter M. Fenwick in 1994 [11], is a data structure that can be used to maintain and query cumulative frequencies. In particular, it is mainly used to efficiently calculate prefix sums in an array of numbers. Based on this data structure, we propose the algorithm called $bitBA$ (see Fig. 3). The BIT data structure could be considered then as an abstraction of an integer array of size n indexed from 1, i.e., a bit encapsulate $A = A_1 A_2 \cdots A_n$. The version we are going to use has two operations:

- $sumUpTo(tree, i)$: Returns $A_1 + A_2 + \ldots + A_i$. The complexity is $O(\lg n)$.
- $addAt(tree, i, x)$: Sums x to A_i. The complexity is $O(\lg n)$.

The algorithm has a preprocessing phase in which the data structures needed to solve the $\delta\gamma$–OPMP are created. This is done with a complexity of $\Theta(n + n \lg n + m \lg m)$. The term n is due to the creation of the BIT. The term $n \lg n$ is due to the creation of T^{nr} and the term $m \lg m$ is due to the creation of P^{nr}. In the searching phase, it iterates over all possible positions in the text T to find the existing matches. For each position i to be considered, the algorithm uses the BIT to get the rank of every symbol in the searching window $T_{i...i+m-1}$, and then each rank in the window is compared with each rank in P^{nr} to check if T^i is a $\delta\gamma$–order preserving match. This operation is evaluated using the function $isAMatch(P, T^i, \delta, \gamma)$; in particular, this function returns true *iff* $P \overset{\delta\gamma}{\leadsto} T^i$ and this takes $O(m \lg m + m)$.

Each rank calculation using the BIT costs $O(\lg n)$. Then the total complexity of the algorithm is $O(n \lg n + m \lg m + (n - m + 1)(m \lg n)) = O(nm \lg n)$. Similar to $segtreeBA$, $bitBA$ has a lower bound of $\Omega(n \lg n)$ because, in many cases, $bitBA$ does not perform the m comparisons of cost $O(\lg n)$. The total complexity of $bitBA$ is then $O(n + n \lg n + m \lg m + (n - m + 1)(m \lg n)) = O(nm \lg n)$, but with a lower bound of $\Omega(n \lg n)$.

In the preprocessing phase, the algorithm first creates the natural representations of the pattern P and the text T (P^{nr} and T^{nr}, respectively). Then, it creates a BIT which is an encapsulation of an array with n positions numbered from 1 to n. Then assigns 1 the positions $T_0^{nr}, T_1^{nr}, \ldots T_{m-2}^{nr}$ (Lines 1 to 5 in Fig. 3). In the searching phase, for each candidate position i, the algorithm computes the rank of each symbol $T_{i+j}, 0 \leq j \leq m - 1$ using $sumUpTo(i + j)$. After checking if there is a match at position i, the BIT must be updated in each iteration to consider symbol T_{i+m} (line 7 in Fig. 3). And the BIT must be updated so it does not consider the position i in the next search window (line 9 in Fig. 3).

Algorithm 2: $\delta\gamma$–OPMP bitBA

Input: $P = P_{0...m-1}, T = T_{0...n-1}, \delta, \gamma, \Sigma_\sigma$
Output: $\{i \in \{0, \ldots, n - m\} : T^i \overset{\delta\gamma}{\rightsquigarrow} P\}$
1. **Create as Array:** $T^{nr} \leftarrow nr(T)$
2. **Create as Array:** $P^{nr} \leftarrow nr(P)$
3. **Create as Array of size n:** bit
4. **for** $i = 0 \rightarrow m - 2$ **do**
5. $addAt(bit, T_i^{nr}, 1)$
6. **for** $i = 0 \rightarrow n - m$ **do**
7. $addAt(bit, T_{i+m-1}^{nr}, 1)$
8. $isAMatch(i, bit, T^{nr}, P^{nr}, \delta, \gamma)$ **then report** i
9. $addAt(bit, T_i^{nr}, -1)$

Fig. 3. BIT based algorithm: $bitBA$.

4   Experiments

In this section, we describe the experimental setup we designed to evaluate the performance of the proposed algorithms. We compare our algorithms with two baseline algorithms: The naive algorithm, which we call $naiveA$, and $updateBA$, presented in [22]. The former, whose time complexity is $\Theta(nm \lg m)$, considers all possible positions in the text and, for each one of them, verifies if there is a match in $\Theta(m \lg m + m)$ time. The latter algorithm, whose time complexity is $\Theta(nm)$, is based on linear update and verification.

We present the experimental framework (Sect. 4.1) and describe the data generation (Sect. 4.2). Then, we discuss the results obtained (Sect. 4.3). Finally we show the results of the experiments directed to detect how the algorithms $segtreeBA$ and $bitBA$ behave when in all the experiment instances the worst case came up (Sect. 4.4).

4.1   Experimental Setup

Here we describe the hardware and software used for the experiments. Then, we show how we vary the input parameters.

Hardware and Software. All the algorithms were implemented using C++. The computer used for the experiments was a Lenovo ThinkPad with a processor Intel(R) Core(TM) i7 4600u CPU @ 2.10 GHz 2.69 GHz and installed RAM memory of 8 GB. The computer was running 64-bit Linux Ubuntu 14.04.5 LTS. The C++ compiler version was g++ (Ubuntu 4.8.4-2ubuntu1 14.04.3) 4.8.4.

Parameters. It is clear that the defined problem has several parameters. They may change depending on the area of study in which the problem and string searching algorithms are applied. To show how our solution behaves with different configuration of the given parameters, we perform five types of experiments. In each experiment, we vary one of the given parameters n, m, δ, γ and σ, and let the other four parameters fixed at a given value. We chose the fixed values after several attempts via try and error to find values that produced results varying from no matches to matches near the value of n. For each experiment type, we performed five different experiments and took the median as the value to plot, making the median of five experiments the representative value for a experiment configuration of values n m, δ, γ and σ. The variation of the parameter values for each experiment type is presented in Table 1.

Table 1. Experimental values of n m, δ, γ and σ.

	Varying n	Varying m	Varying δ	Varying γ	Varying σ
n	$[3000, 60000] \Delta n = 3000$	10000	10000	10000	10000
m	40	$[30, 600]\ \Delta m = 30$	40	40	40
δ	10	10	$[0, 228]\ \Delta \delta = 12$	10	10
γ	60	60	60	$[0, 570]\ \Delta \gamma = 30$	60
σ	100	100	100	100	$[12, 240]\Delta \sigma = 12$

4.2   Random Data Generation

An experiment consists of two stages. The first stage is the pseudo-random generation of a text T of length n and the pattern P of length m. The second stage is the execution of the algorithms on the generated strings P and T. The random generation of each character of both the pattern P and the text T is done by calling a function that pseudo-randomly and selects a number between 1 and σ with the same probability for each number to be selected, i.e., all symbols have the same probability to appear in a position and for that reason, the count of each symbol on a generated string will be similar to the quantities of the others symbols in the alphabet.

4.3   Experimental Results and Analysis

The first result to highlight is the fact that, in every experiment, the naive algorithm always has the worst performance, as expected. The results shown in Figs. 4a, b and c show that the size of the alphabet and the parameters δ and γ have practically no impact on the execution time of any of the algorithms, they all show nearly constant time behavior. Figures 4d and f verify the theoretical complexity analysis that states that n and m are the parameters that really determine the growth in the execution time of all the algorithms. In Fig. 4d, m is a constant and n is a variable while in Fig. 4f, n is a constant and m is a variable. Also, for a clearer illustration, in Figs. 4e and g we only show the best two algorithms of Figs. 4d and f, respectively, on the same data. It is important to notice that, under these conditions, the graphs are expected to be linear and the experiments verify that.

In the figures where we show the result of varying the parameter n and the parameter m, (Figs. 4d–g), we can see that the best two algorithms are the based on data structures ($segtreBA$ and $bitBA$). This despite the fact that these two algorithms have a higher upper bound on their complexities in relation with the first two algorithms ($naiveA$ and $updateBA$). This result can be explained by the fact that the lower bound on the data structure based algorithms is considerably lower in comparison with the other two. The lower bound of the data structures based algorithms is $\Omega(n \lg n)$ and the lower bound of the $naiveA$ and $updateBA$ is the same as their upper bound which is $\Theta(nm \lg m)$ and $\Theta(nm)$ respectively. This can be understood by taking into account that the first two algorithms check for a match after a natural representation of every window is completely obtained; on the contrary, data structure based algorithms break the calculation of a given natural representation of a window if at some point the δ or γ restriction do not hold.

Given the result of the experiments, it is safe to say that the algorithms based on data structures are faster in most cases, especially if they are going to be used in applications where very few matches are expected to appear. This is due to their lower bound of complexity. We test two different implementations of the segment tree data structure: one based on classes and pointers, and the other based on an array. Finally we chose the array based as representative for the segment tree based solution and the experiments plots show their results. The array–based segment tree is almost twice time faster than the classes–based implementation.

4.4   Worst Case Experiments on $seegtreBA$ and $bitBA$

Taking into account that the first two algorithms, $naiveA$ and $updateBA$ both have complexities in θ–notation, i.e. their worst case is the same as their best case, the experiments described so far are enough for their experimental analysis. For the data structures based algorithms a more particular kind of experiment is needed, i.e. the worst case experimental analysis. For this algorithms the worst

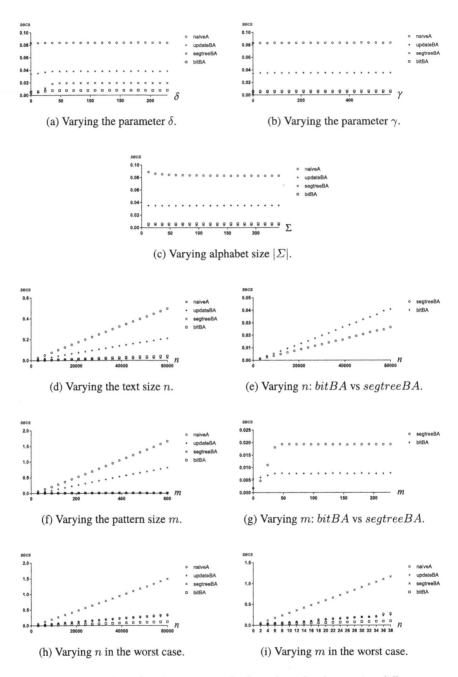

(a) Varying the parameter δ.

(b) Varying the parameter γ.

(c) Varying alphabet size $|\Sigma|$.

(d) Varying the text size n.

(e) Varying n: $bitBA$ vs $segtreeBA$.

(f) Varying the pattern size m.

(g) Varying m: $bitBA$ vs $segtreeBA$.

(h) Varying n in the worst case.

(i) Varying m in the worst case.

Fig. 4. Experimental results of comparing the four algorithm by varying different parameters.

case is when there is a match in every candidate position. An easy way to generate data for the worst case is when all the symbols in both the pattern P and the text T are the same. Other way to generate worst cases scenarios for this two algorithms is when either both P and T are strictly increasing or both are strictly decreasing. Results from this experiments show a fast degradation in experimental performance of the $segtreeBA$ algorithm, but a very slow degradation of the $bitBA$ algorithm. Results of this last experiments are shown in Figs. 4h and i.

5   Conclusions and Future Work

We define a new variant of the string matching problem, the $\delta\gamma$–order preserving matching problem ($\delta\gamma$–OPMP). This new variant provides the possibility of searching a pattern according to the relative order of the symbols as the order preserving matching problem. But we also gives more flexibility to the search allowing error in the individual ranking comparisons due to the parameter δ. And also the proposed problem gives a bound for the global error in the comparison of a pattern against a text window by γ. This new variant has at least the same applications as the order preserving matching problem.

We designed two algorithms: one based on the segment tree and another based on the Fenwick tree. They both have complexities of $O(nm \lg n)$ for their worst case and a $\Omega(n \lg n)$ lower bound. We implemented in C++ these algorithms and compared them with a naive solution and the $updateBA$ algorithm introduced in [22]. Their theoretical time complexity is $\Theta(nm \lg m)$. Our experimental results on randomly generated data show that in many cases, given the uniformly data generation, the proposed algorithms work faster than the $naiveA$ and the $updateBA$. One question that remains open is if an algorithm with better worst case time complexity than $O(nm)$ can be designed; other question that also remains open is that if an algorithm with better lower bound than $\Omega(n \lg n)$ can be obtained.

We show experimental results on the worst cases of the $bitBA$ and $segtreeBA$. We conclude that the degradation in performance in the $segtreeBA$ algorithm is much more notorious than the degradation of $bitBA$. A question remains, and is if we can device an experimental setup where the best worst–case algorithm, $updateBA$ experimentally beats the other three algorithms. Given the theory behind the big O notation, we can say that this experimental setup exist.

Our future work on this problem will be focused on the applications of $\delta\gamma$–order preserving matching. Specifically, we are interested in experiments with real data that verify some applications of this problem in music and finance. In music we can use it to search for a portion of a melody inside another music score; in finance, we can look for similar change patterns in the price of stock actions. It is important to notice that for specific applications more efficient algorithms could be designed based on the particularities of the chosen field (alphabet, language, etc.). Considering such particularities will also be part of our future work.

References

1. de Berg, M., Cheong, O., van Kreveld, M., Overmars, M.: More Geometric Data Structures, pp. 219–241. Springer, Heidelberg (2008)
2. Brass, P.: Advanced Data Structures. Cambridge University Press, Cambridge (2008). Cambridge books online
3. Cambouropoulos, E., Crochemore, M., Iliopoulos, C., Mouchard, L., Pinzon, Y.: Algorithms for computing approximate repetitions in musical sequences. Int. J. Comput. Math. **79**(11), 1135–1148 (2002)
4. Chhabra, T., Kulekci, M.O., Tarhio, J.: Alternative algorithms for order-preserving matching. In: Holub, J., Žďárek, J. (eds.) Proceedings of the Prague Stringology Conference 2015, pp. 36–46. Czech Technical University in Prague, Prague, Czech Republic (2015)
5. Chhabra, T., Tarhio, J.: Order-preserving matching with filtration. In: Gudmundsson, J., Katajainen, J. (eds.) SEA 2014. LNCS, vol. 8504, pp. 307–314. Springer, Cham (2014). doi:10.1007/978-3-319-07959-2_26
6. Crawford, T., Iliopoulos, C.S., Raman, R.: String-matching techniques for musical similarity and melodic recognition. Comput. Musicol. **11**, 71–100 (1998)
7. Crochemore, M., Iliopoulos, C.S., Kociumaka, T., Kubica, M., Langiu, A., Pissis, S.P., Radoszewski, J., Rytter, W., Waleń, T.: Order-Preserving Incomplete Suffix Trees and Order-Preserving Indexes, pp. 84–95. Springer, Cham (2013)
8. Crochemore, M., Iliopoulos, C.S., Kociumaka, T., Kubica, M., Langiu, A., Pissis, S.P., Radoszewski, J., Rytter, W., Walen, T.: Order-preserving suffix trees and their algorithmic applications. CoRR abs/1303.6872 (2013)
9. Crochemore, M., Iliopoulos, C.S., Kociumaka, T., Kubica, M., Langiu, A., Pissis, S.P., Radoszewski, J., Rytter, W., Waleń, T.: Order-preserving indexing. Theor. Comput. Sci. **638**(C), 122–135 (2016)
10. Faro, S., Külekci, M.O.: Efficient algorithms for the order preserving pattern matching problem. CoRR abs/1501.04001 (2015)
11. Fenwick, P.M.: A new data structure for cumulative frequency tables. Softw. Pract. Exp. **24**, 327–336 (1994)
12. Gawrychowski, P., Uznański, P.: Order-preserving pattern matching with k mismatches. Theor. Comput. Sci. **638**, 136–144 (2016)
13. Hasan, M.M., Islam, A., Rahman, M.S., Rahman, M.S.: Order Preserving Prefix Tables, pp. 111–116. Springer, Cham (2014)
14. Hasan, M.M., Islam, A., Rahman, M.S., Rahman, M.: Order preserving pattern matching revisited. Pattern Recogn. Lett. **55**(C), 15–21 (2015)
15. Kim, J., Eades, P., Fleischer, R., Hong, S.H., Iliopoulos, C.S., Park, K., Puglisi, S.J., Tokuyama, T.: Order-preserving matching. Theor. Comput. Sci. **525**, 68–79 (2014). Advances in Stringology
16. Kubica, M., Kulczyński, T., Radoszewski, J., Rytter, W.: WaleÅĎ, T.: A linear time algorithm for consecutive permutation pattern matching. Information Processing Letters **113**(12), 430–433 (2013)
17. Lee, I., Mendivelso, J., Pinzón, Y.J.: $\delta\gamma$-Parameterized Matching, pp. 236–248. Springer, Heidelberg (2009)
18. Mendivelso, J.: Definition and solution of a new string searching variant termed $\delta\gamma$-parameterized matching. Master's thesis, National University of Colombia, Bogota, Colombia (2010)
19. Mendivelso, J., Lee, I., Pinzón, Y.J.: Approximate Function Matching under δ- and γ- Distances, pp. 348–359. Springer, Heidelberg (2012)

20. Mendivelso, J., Pino, C., Niño, L.F., Pinzón, Y.: Approximate Abelian Periods to Find Motifs in Biological Sequences, pp. 121–130. Springer, Cham (2015)
21. Mendivelso, J., Pinzón, Y.: A novel approach to approximate parikh matching for comparing composition in biological sequences. In: Proceedings of the 6th International Conference on Bioinformatics and Computational Biology (BICoB 2014) (2014)
22. Niquefa, R., Mendivelso, J., Hernández, G., Pinzón, Y.: Order preserving matching under $\delta\gamma$-approximation. In: Congreso Internacional de Ciencias Básicas e Ingeniería (2017)

Algorithmic Trading Using Deep Neural Networks on High Frequency Data

Andrés Arévalo[1($\boxtimes$)], Jaime Niño[1], German Hernandez[1], Javier Sandoval[2], Diego León[2], and Arbey Aragón[1]

[1] Universidad Nacional de Colombia, Bogotá, Colombia
{ararevalom,jhninop,gjhernandezp,aaragonb}@unal.edu.co
[2] Universidad Externado, Bogotá, Colombia
{javier.sandoval,diego.leon}@uexternado.edu.co

Abstract. In this work, a high-frequency trading strategy using Deep Neural Networks (DNNs) is presented. The input information consists of: (i). Current time (hour and minute); (ii). The last n one-minute pseudo-returns, where n is the sliding window size parameter; (iii). The last n one-minute standard deviations of the price; (iv). The last n trend indicator, computed as the slope of the linear model fitted using the transaction prices inside a particular minute. The DNN predicts the next one-minute pseudo-return, this output is later transformed to obtain a the next predicted one-minute average price. This price is used to build a high-frequency trading strategy that buys (sells) when the next predicted average price is above (below) the last closing price.

Keywords: Short-term forecasting · High-frequency trading · Computational finance · Algorithmic trading · Deep Neural Networks

1 Introduction

Even tough financial markets have been focus of attention by investors worldwide, modeling and predicting prices of Financial Assets have been proved to be a very difficult task [4,10,12,13,16]. As time advances, two important families of techniques have been used for financial assets price modeling: The Analytical and the Machine Learning techniques. Analytical techniques are composed by statistical and stochastic models. Within statistical models like Linear Regression (LR), Multiple Linear Regression (MLR), Autoregressive Integrated Moving Average (ARIMA) and Generalized Autoregressive Conditional Heteroscedasticity (GARCH/N-GARCH). On the stochastic side models, Brownian Motion (BM), Diffusion, Poisson, Jumps, and Levy Processes are found. On the other hand, machine learning techniques include Decisions Trees, Artificial Neural Networks (ANN), Fuzzy Systems, Kernel Methods, Support Methods Machines (SVM) and recently, Deep Neural Networks (DNN), an extension of Artificial Neural Networks [4,10,14].

Since late 1980s, ANNs have been a popular theme in data analysis. Although ANNs have existed for long time and they have been used in many disciplines, only

© Springer International Publishing AG 2017
J.C. Figueroa-García et al. (Eds.): WEA 2017, CCIS 742, pp. 144–155, 2017.
DOI: 10.1007/978-3-319-66963-2_14

since early 1990s they started to be used for financial assets prices modeling [9]. The first known application of ANN in finance "Economic prediction using neural networks: the case of IBM daily stock returns" was published in 1988 [19].

ANNs are inspired by brain structure; they are composed of many neurons that have connections with each other. Each neuron is a processing unit that performs a weighted aggregation of multiple input signals. Depending on its inputs, a particular set of neurons are activated and propagate a transformed signal, through application of a non-linear function such as Unit Step, Hyperbolic Tangent, Gaussian, Rectified Linear, among others [6]. A Multilayer perceptron (MLP) is an ANN that consists of layers of neurons (an input, multiple hidden and an output layers). All neurons in a layer are fully connected to all neurons in the next layer. Therefore, the information always moves forward from inputs to outputs nodes [6].

The Universal Approximation Theorem says a MLP with a single hidden layer and enough neurons can approximate any function either linear or non-linear [6,7]. Nevertheless of their ability to approximate any function, ANNs have several limitations, because it gets stacked on local minimum avoiding the ANN to converge to optimal solution, causing that found weights and biases not necessary approximate the target data; furthermore, over-training causes over-fitting, which means the ANN tend to memorize training data, causing it to generalize poorly [17,22].

A Deep Neural Network (DNN) is a deep MLP (with many layers), which uses DL training techniques. In a DNN, data inputs are transformed from low-level to high-level features. As signals are propagated forward within the network, data is encoded in more complex features until it is capable of learning high level patterns, which are the ones of interest in this work. In recent years, Deep Learning (DL) has emerged as a very robust machine learning technique, improving the limitations of ANNs [2,17]. Furthermore, advances in hardware such as Graphics Processing Units (GPUs), make possible to accelerate training times for deep networks [2,3,11].

This paper is organized as follows: Sect. 2 presents some important definitions for this work. Section 3 describes data preprocessing done. Section 4 presents DNN modeling for forecasting the next one-minute average price. Section 5 describes trading strategy algorithm proposed. Section 6 presents strategy's performance. Section 7 presents strategy validation. Section 8 presents some conclusions and recommendations for future research.

2   Definitions

Below some important definitions are presented:

Log-return. Let p_t be the current closing price and p_{t-1} the previous closing price.

$$R = \ln \frac{p_t}{p_{t-1}} \cdot 100\% = (\ln p_t - \ln p_{t-1}) \cdot 100\% \tag{1}$$

Pseudo-log-return. It is defined as a logarithmic difference (log of quotient) between average prices on consecutive minutes. On the other hand, the typical log-return is a logarithmic difference between closing prices on consecutive minutes. Let $\overline{p_t}$ be the current one-minute average price and $\overline{p_{t-1}}$ the previous one-minute average price.

$$\hat{R} = \ln \frac{\overline{p_t}}{\overline{p_{t-1}}} \cdot 100\% = (\ln \overline{p_t} - \ln \overline{p_{t-1}}) \cdot 100\% \tag{2}$$

One-minute Trend Indicator. It is a statistical indicator computed as the linear model's slope ($price = at + b$) fitted on transaction prices for a particular minute, where t is time in milliseconds inside the particular minute; A small slope, close to 0, means that in the next minute, price is going to remain stable. A positive value means that price is going to rise. A negative value means that price is going to fall. Change is proportional to distance value compared to 0; if distance is too high, the price will rise or fall sharply.

3   Data Preprocessing

Data was taken from NYSE's TAQ database [8], all traded prices for Apple ordinary stock (ticker: AAPL) were downloaded from September 2nd to November 7th of 2008. Figure 1 show price behavior on this period.

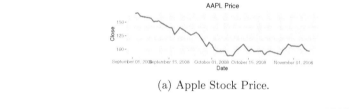

(a) Apple Stock Price.

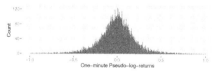

(b) Histogram of One-minute Pseudo-log-returns.

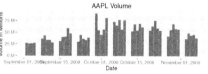

(c) Daily Trading Volume.

Fig. 1. Apple stock

The tick-by-tick dataset is composed by 14,839,395 observations. It has a maximum price on 173.5 dollars and a minimum one on 85 dollars. Figure 1b shows the one-minute pseudo-log-returns histogram. It is some symmetric with mean of -0.002961% and standard deviation of 0.282765. The maximum pseudo-log-return is 7.952000%, the minimum one is -7.659000%, the first quartile is -0.112200% and the third one is 0.108500. Given these properties, the pseudo-log-returns distribution can be approximated to a normal distribution.

Reviewed literature suggests that any stock log-returns follows approximately a normal distribution with mean zero [5,14,18]. As expected, the pseudo-log-returns distribution behaves like the normal distribution. For this reason, the best variables that describe the market behavior within a minute are the mean price and standard deviation of prices.

Figure 1c shows the daily trading volume. The 98.5% of transactions are carried out with less than $1,000$ shares with a mean equal to 165.58 ones. The minimum value is 100 and the maximum one is $5,155,222$ shares.

In order to check data consistency, all dates were working days (not holidays and not weekends). All times were during normal trading hours (between 9:30:00 am and 3:59:59 pm EST) and all prices and volumes were positive. Therefore, it was not necessary to delete or adjust records.

All data were summarized with a one-minute detailed level. Three time series were constructed from traded prices: **Average Price**, **Standard Deviation of Prices** and **Trend Indicator**. Each series has 19110 records (49 trading days $\times$ 390 minute per day).

4   Deep Neural Network Modeling

4.1   Features Selection

DNN's inputs were selected in four groups, explained as follows: Current Time, last n pseudo-log-returns, last n standard deviations of prices and last n trend indicators, where n is the window size. Current time group is composed of two inputs: **Current hour** and **Current minute**. The other three groups are composed of n inputs for each one. The number of DNN's inputs I are $3n + 2$. Following paragraphs describe each input group:

Current time: Literature reviewed did not include time as an input. However, hour and minute as integer values were chosen as two additional inputs, because financial markets are affected by regimes that occurs in certain minutes or hours during the trading day. This behavior may be explained by the fact that both human and automatized (machines) traders have strategies that are running in synchronized periods.

To illustrate this affirmation, Fig. 2a shows price changes that occurred at the first, third and sixth day. Approximately, in the minute 170, the stock was traded at the same opening price of corresponding day. Approximately, in the minute 250, the stock price fell 3 dollars relative to the opening price in these days. As these patterns, many more are repeated at certain time of day. In order to identify and to differentiate better these patterns, the current hour and current minute of day were added as additional inputs of DNN. These variables have 7 and 60 possible values ranging from 0 to 6 and from 0 to 59 respectively.

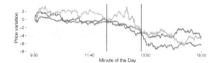
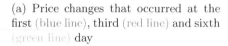
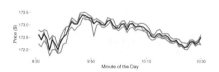

(a) Price changes that occurred at the first (blue line), third (red line) and sixth (green line) day

(b) First 60 Apple Stock Prices. Blue: High and Low. Red: Close. Black: Average.

Fig. 2. Temporal patterns of the time series (Color figure online)

Last n pseudo-log-returns: It is common to read works about forecasting financial time series with neural networks, which inputs are composed principally by untransformed observations. This is fine for several types of time series, but it is not advisable in financial time series forecasting, because when nominal prices are used, the neural network will train with special conditions (i.e. prices fluctuate between 120 and 170 dollars) and when it is tested against different market conditions (i.e. prices fluctuate between 90 and 120 dollars), overall performance should decline due to poor generalization.

In other words, the neural network learns to identify many static patterns that will be not appearing at all. For example, a pattern like when a price is over 150 dollars, raises to 150.25 dollars and falls to 149.75 dollars, then it will change to 150.50 dollars, could be found, but this pattern never will occur because in the closest future the prices fluctuates between 90 and 120 dollars. However, if prices are transformed into differences or logarithmic returns, not only data variance is stabilized, but also time series acquire temporal independence. For example, at the beginning of the selected period, a pattern, like when the price rises 25 cents and it falls 50 cents, then it will raise 75 cents, could be found and this pattern is more likely to occur in the future. Therefore, the last n one-minute pseudo-log-returns are inputs of DNN.

Last n standard deviations of prices: The last n one-minute standard deviations of prices are DNN inputs.

Last n trend indicators: The last n one-minute trend indicators are DNN inputs.

4.2   Output Selection of the Deep Neural Network

The DNN forecasts the next one-minute pseudo-log-return. As shown on Fig. 2b, the average price (black line) is the best descriptor of market behavior. The highest or lowest prices (blue lines) usually are found within a confidence range of average price, therefore the next highest and lowest prices can be estimated from a predicted average price. The closing price (red line) can be any value close to the average price; it coincides sometimes with the highest or lowest price. Unlike the average price, the highest, lowest and closing ones are exposed largely to noise or external market dynamics.

Since this work's objective is to learn market dynamic and to take advantage of it, forecasting average prices could be more profitable than forecasting closing prices. With a good average price forecast, it is known that traded prices will be equal to the average predicted at some point during the next minute.

4.3 Deep Neural Network Architecture

The architecture was selected arbitrarily. It has one input layer, L hidden layers and one output layer. Neuron number in each layer depends on input number I as well as hidden layers number L. In each hidden layer, the number of neurons decreases with a constant factor $\frac{1}{L}$. For example, with five hidden layers: Each layer will have I, $\lceil \frac{4}{5}I \rceil$, $\lceil \frac{3}{5}I \rceil$, $\lceil \frac{2}{5}I \rceil$, $\lceil \frac{1}{5}I \rceil$ neurons respectively. For example, with three hidden layers: Each layer will have I, $\lceil \frac{2}{3}I \rceil$, $\lceil \frac{1}{3}I \rceil$ respectively. The output layer always has one neuron. All neurons in hidden layers use a $Tanh$ activation function, whereas the output neuron uses a $Linear$ activation function.

4.4 Deep Neural Network Training

The final dataset is made up of $19109 - n$ records. Each record contains $3n + 3$ numerical values ($3n + 2$ inputs and 1 output). The final dataset was divided into two parts: training data (the first 85% samples) and testing data (the remaining 15% samples). It should be noted that to construct each record, only information from the past is required. Therefore, there is not look-ahead bias and this DNN could be used for a real trading strategy.

For this work, H_2O, an open-source software for big-data analysis [15] was used. It implements algorithms at scale, such as deep learning [1], as well as featuring automatic versions of advanced optimization for DNN training. Additionally, it implements an adaptive learning rate algorithm, called ADADELTA [1], which is described in [21].

4.5 Deep Neural Network Assessment

In order to assess DNN's performance, four statistics were chosen. Let be E real time series and F predicted series:

1. **Mean Squared Error:** $MSE = \frac{1}{n} \sum_{t=1}^{n} (E_t - F_t)^2$
2. **Mean Absolute Percentage Error:** $MAPE = \frac{100}{n} \sum_{t=1}^{n} \frac{|E_t - F_t|}{|E_t|}$
3. **Directional Accuracy:** Percent of predicted directions that matches the real-time series' direction. This measure is unaffected by outliers or variables scales. $DA = \frac{100}{n} \sum_{t=1}^{n} E_t \cdot F_t > 0$

5 Proposed Strategy

DNN predictions are used for building a high-frequency trading strategy: For each trading minute, it always buys (sells) a stock when the next predicted average price is above (below) the last closing price. When the price yields the predicted average price, it sells (buys) the stock in order to lock the profit. If the price never yields the expected price, it sells (buys) the stock with the last trading price of that minute (closing price), in order to close the position. Additionally, one cent is added/subtracted in order to consider or include the spread, which is the difference between the best quotes (best ask, best bid). Figure 3 shows the strategy flowchart.

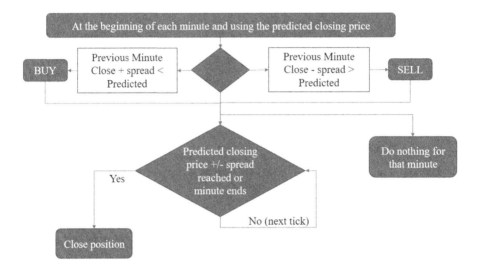

Fig. 3. Strategy flowchart

6   Experiment

6.1   Short-Term Forecasting

DNNs were trained only with the training data during 50 epochs each one. The chosen ADADELTA parameters were $\rho = 0.9999$ and $\epsilon = 10^{-10}$. On the other hand, DNNs were tested only with testing data.

Tables 1, 2 and 3 illustrate the average DNN performance using different sliding windows sizes (n lags) and number of hidden layers L. The number of neurons in each layer depends on the number of inputs $I = 3n+2$. In each hidden layer, the number of neurons decreases with a constant factor $\frac{1}{L}$. For example, five with hidden layers: Each layer will have I, $\lceil \frac{4}{5}I \rceil$, $\lceil \frac{3}{5}I \rceil$, $\lceil \frac{2}{5}I \rceil$, $\lceil \frac{1}{5}I \rceil$ neurons respectively. For example, with three hidden layers: Each layer will have I, $\lceil \frac{2}{3}I \rceil$, $\lceil \frac{1}{3}I \rceil$ respectively. All DNNs have a single output layer with only one neuron.

For each combination, ten different networks were trained. In each table, the best configuration was highlighted with a darker color. As shown on the Tables 1, 2 and 3, the best combinations are located leftward of x-axis and upward of y-axis, that is, the best yields are obtained by architectures that consider small sliding windows sizes and that are multi-layered.

Table 1. DNN performance: MSE

Mean Squared Error

Hidden Layers	2/8	3/11	4/14	5/17	6/20	7/23	8/26	9/29	10/32	16/50	32/98	64/194	128/386
10	0.0374	0.0367	0.0376	0.0377	0.0385	0.0389	0.0409	0.0395	0.0402	0.0425	0.0468	0.0411	0.0403
9	0.0376	0.0369	0.0374	0.0383	0.0379	0.0401	0.041	0.0443	0.0415	0.0435	0.0437	0.0431	0.04
8	0.0382	0.0383	0.0385	0.0382	0.0404	0.0405	0.0402	0.0391	0.0415	0.0451	0.0455	0.0437	0.0416
7	0.0375	0.0373	0.0398	0.0397	0.0425	0.0432	0.0454	0.0406	0.0434	0.0441	0.0452	0.0459	0.042
6	0.0378	0.037	0.0394	0.0389	0.0432	0.0386	0.044	0.0447	0.0384	0.0414	0.0467	0.0463	0.0445
5	0.0372	0.0372	0.037	0.0381	0.0402	0.0414	0.041	0.0406	0.0461	0.0465	0.0454	0.0484	0.0452
4	0.0371	0.0371	0.0384	0.0408	0.042	0.0429	0.0451	0.0429	0.0414	0.0463	0.0463	0.0518	0.0467
3	0.0379	0.037	0.0383	0.0401	0.0407	0.0402	0.0431	0.0419	0.0429	0.0476	0.0543	0.0537	0.0484
2	0.0375	0.0367	0.0375	0.0384	0.0395	0.0401	0.0416	0.0415	0.0439	0.0507	0.0657	0.0636	0.053
1	0.0375	0.037	0.037	0.0383	0.0383	0.0387	0.0395	0.0407	0.0417	0.0464	0.0697	0.0801	0.0631

Lags / Inputs

Colour
0.037 0.038 0.039 0.040

Table 2. DNN performance: MAPE

Mean Absolute Percentage Error

Hidden Layers	2/8	3/11	4/14	5/17	6/20	7/23	8/26	9/29	10/32	16/50	32/98	64/194	128/386
10	2.9889	2.9718	3.0467	2.9939	3.0086	3.0205	3.0369	3.0287	3.0669	3.0639	3.1986	3.2034	3.228
9	2.9813	3.006	3.0336	3.0174	2.9853	3.0178	3.0357	3.0505	3.0534	3.093	3.1778	3.2421	3.2154
8	3.0438	3.048	3.0332	3.017	3.0325	3.0219	3.0581	3.0535	3.076	3.1475	3.2404	3.2921	3.2851
7	2.9623	2.9598	3.0298	3.0108	3.0443	3.0589	3.0802	3.0569	3.067	3.1302	3.2843	3.3937	3.321
6	3.0209	3.0133	3.0385	3.0053	3.0849	3.015	3.077	3.0789	3.0566	3.1319	3.3208	3.559	3.4873
5	3.0022	2.9656	3.0029	2.9961	3.0268	3.0516	3.0524	3.0924	3.1295	3.2257	3.3462	3.7134	3.5793
4	2.9907	3.0079	3.0465	3.0377	3.1535	3.0723	3.1092	3.1051	3.136	3.2603	3.4148	3.8617	3.7227
3	2.9932	2.9871	3.0548	3.114	3.1212	3.1072	3.1518	3.1683	3.2015	3.4263	3.6435	3.8942	3.721
2	2.9834	2.9948	3.0463	3.0935	3.135	3.1925	3.2214	3.2565	3.3541	3.7606	4.469	4.3908	3.9831
1	3.0167	3.0441	3.0333	3.0752	3.0943	3.1248	3.1871	3.2803	3.3387	3.6736	4.8952	5.337	4.5948

Lags / Inputs

Colour
3.00   3.05   3.10

The best (lowest) MSE were achieved by almost all architectures using small sliding windows of four minutes or less, regardless of the number of hidden layers. The best (lowest) MAPE were achieved by architectures having four or more hidden layers. The best (highest) DA were achieved by architectures having four

Table 3. DNN performance: DA

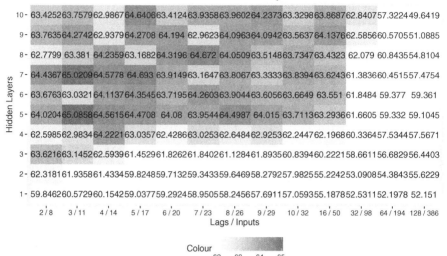

or more hidden layers. Also, when the number of layers increased, the DNNs achieved good MAPE and DA with larger sliding window sizes.

Comparing the figures, the best results were obtained by architectures having four to seven hidden layers, and sliding windows sizes of five or less minutes. Depending on training results, DNN performance may be better, but all networks converge with very similar and homogeneous results.

On average, the DNNs achieved approximately between 0.03 and 0.08 of MSE, between 2.95% and 5.33% of MAPE and between 49.64% and 65.08% of DA. The DNNs are able to predict these sudden rises or falls in price. This information may be useful for any trading strategy.

6.2   Strategy Simulation

For the effectiveness of the proposed strategy, it is required a DNN that has a good performance identifying the price direction. For this reason, the architecture with the best directional accuracy (DA) was selected: A DNN that uses a sliding window size of 3 min, and that have five hidden layers, 14 inputs and 1 output; Each hidden layer has 14, 12, 9, 6 and 3 neurons respectively.

Figure 4 shows the strategy performance during a trading simulation over testing data. The simulation did not consider transaction costs. Buying and selling the equivalent of a dollar in shares, the strategy accumulated approximately $0.28 in 8 trading days.

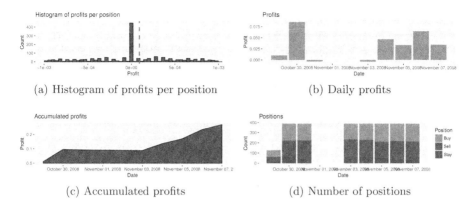

(a) Histogram of profits per position   (b) Daily profits

(c) Accumulated profits   (d) Number of positions

Fig. 4. Trading strategy performance

7 Strategy Validation

The dataset used in the experiment can be a little dramatic, since it belongs to a period in financial crisis. For this reason, it was decided to select a recent dataset and apply the same strategy using the same network architecture and same data split.

It is important to remember that this high-frequency trading strategy is only applicable to high liquidity stocks, because it requires to open and close

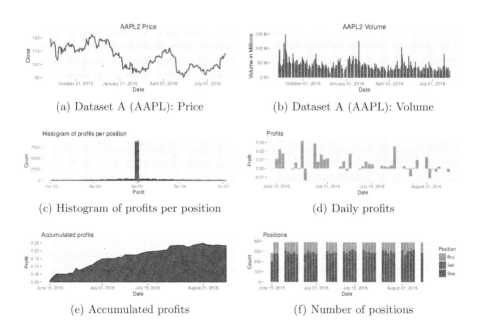

(a) Dataset A (AAPL): Price   (b) Dataset A (AAPL): Volume

(c) Histogram of profits per position   (d) Daily profits

(e) Accumulated profits   (f) Number of positions

Fig. 5. Dataset a (AAPL): trading strategy performance

positions in a time interval equal or less than one minute. Therefore, from the TAQ database of the NYSE [8], all trade prices for Apple ordinary stock (ticker: AAPL - 2016) were downloaded from the August 10th, 2015 to August 8th, 2016. Figure 5a shows the price and volume behavior of the second dataset.

A DNN with the selected architecture (5 hidden layers and a sliding window size of 3 min) was trained with the dataset A. The data set was split in the same way: The first 85% as training data and the remaining 15% as testing set. Figure 5 shows the strategy performance with the dataset A.

The simulation was performed with the same conditions of the previous experiment (only with the testing data, and the strategy buys or sells the equivalent of a dollar per trade). The strategy accumulated approximately \$0.25 in 38 trading days.

8   Conclusions

The strategy has a consistent performance, it turns out to be interesting and yields a good performance. The inclusion of time as an input, proved to be definitive for improving performance, further analysis of this effect is desirable.

Nevertheless, spreads were taken into account, it is desirable to extend the analysis including additional transaction cost. Furthermore, it must be refined in order to implement in a real environment, for example, it could analyze whether it closes its position in the next minute or it keeps it open in order to decrease transaction costs. The strategy can be extended by including other data sources, such as volume and news.

Traders collectively repeat the behavior of the traders that preceded them [20]. Those patterns can be learned by a DNN. The proposed strategy replicates the concept of predicting prices for short periods. Furthermore, adding time as a DNN input allows it to differentiate atypical events and repetitive patterns in market dynamics. Moreover, small data windows sizes are able to explain future prices in a simpler way.

Overall, the DNNs can learn the market dynamic with a reasonable precision and accuracy. Within the deep learning arena, the DNN is the simplest model, as a result, a possible research opportunity could be to evaluate the performance of the strategy using other DL model such as Deep Recurrent Neural Networks, Deep Belief Networks, Convolutional Deep Belief Networks, Deep Coding Networks, among others.

References

1. Arora, A., Candel, A., Lanford, J., LeDell, E., Parmar, V.: Deep Learning with H2O (2015)
2. Bengio, Y.: Learning deep architectures for AI. Found. Trends Mach. Learn. **2**(1), 1–127 (2009). http://dx.doi.org/10.1561/2200000006
3. Dalto, M.: Deep neural networks for time series prediction with applications in ultra-short-term wind forecasting. Rn (Θ1). http://centar.open.hr/_download/repository/KDI-Djalto.pdf

4. De Gooijer, J.G., Hyndman, R.J.: 25 years of time series forecasting. Int. J. Forecast. **22**(3), 443–473 (2006). https://doi.org/10.1016/j.ijforecast.2006.01.001
5. Härdle, W., Kleinow, T., Stahl, G.: Applied Quantitative Finance. Springer, Heidelberg (2002). https://doi.org/10.1007/978-3-662-05021-7
6. Haykin, S.: Neural Networks and Learning Machines. Pearson Education, Inc., Upper Saddle River (2009)
7. Hornik, K.: Approximation capabilities of multilayer feedforward networks. Neural Netw. **4**(2), 251–257 (1991). https://doi.org/10.1016/0893-6080(91)90009-T
8. Intercontinental Exchange Inc: TAQ NYSE Trades (2016). http://www.nyxdata. com/data-products/nyse-trades-eod
9. Kaastra, I., Boyd, M.: Designing a neural network for forecasting financial and economic time series. Neurocomputing **10**(3), 215–236 (1996). http://dx.doi.org/ 10.1016/0925-2312(95)00039-9
10. Krollner, B., Vanstone, B., Finnie, G.: Financial time series forecasting with machine learning techniques: a survey (2010). http://works.bepress.com/bruce_ vanstone/17/
11. Larochelle, H., Bengio, Y.: Exploring strategies for training deep neural networks. J. Mach. Learn. Res., 1–40 (2009). http://dl.acm.org/citation.cfm?id=1577070
12. Li, X., Huang, X., Deng, X., Zhu, S.: Enhancing quantitative intra-day stock return prediction by integrating both market news and stock prices information. Neurocomputing **142**, 228–238 (2014). http://dx.doi.org/10.1016/j.neucom.2014.04.043
13. Marszałek, A., Burczyński, T.: Modeling and forecasting financial time series with ordered fuzzy candlesticks. Inf. Sci. **273**, 144–155 (2014). https://doi.org/10.1016/ j.ins.2014.03.026
14. Mills, T.C., Markellos, R.N.: The Econometric Modelling of Financial Time Series. Cambridge University Press, Cambridge (2008). https://doi.org/10.1017/ CBO9780511817380
15. Nusca, A., Hackett, R., Gupta, S.: Arno Candel, physicist and hacker, 0xdata. Meet Fortune's 2014 Big Data All-Stars (2014). http://fortune.com/2014/08/03/ meet-fortunes-2014-big-data-all-stars/
16. Preethi, G., Santhi, B.: Stock market forecasting techniques: a survey. J. Theoret. Appl. Inf. Technol. **46**(1) (2012)
17. Schmidhuber, J.: Deep learning in neural networks: an overview. Neural Netw. **61**, 85–117 (2014). https://doi.org/10.1016/j.neunet.2014.09.003
18. Tsay, R.S.: Analysis of Financial Time Series, vol. 543. Wiley, New York (2005)
19. White, H.: economic prediction using neural networks: the case of IBM daily stock returns. In: IEEE International Conference on Neural Networks, pp. 451–458. IEEE (1988). https://doi.org/10.1109/ICNN.1988.23959
20. Wilder, J.W.: New Concepts in Technical Trading Systems. Trend Research, McLeansville (1978)
21. Zeiler, M.D.: ADADELTA: An Adaptive Learning Rate Method, p. 6 (2012). http://arxiv.org/abs/1212.5701
22. Zekic, M.: Neural network applications in stock market predictions-a methodology analysis. In: Proceedings of the 9th International Conference on Information and Intelligent Systems (1998). http://citeseerx.ist.psu.edu/viewdoc/download? doi=10.1.1.109.3374&rep=rep1&type=pdf

A Balancing Proposal for Population Variables in Multiobjective Problems: Towards Pareto's Frontier for Homogeneity

María Beatríz Bernábe Loranca[1]([✉]), Carlos Guillén Galván[1],
Gerardo Martínez Guzmán[1], and Jorge Ruiz Vanoye[2]

[1] Benemérita Universidad Autónoma de Puebla, Puebla, México
beatriz.bernabe@gmail.com, cguillen@fcfm.buap.mx, gmartinez54@hotmail.com
[2] Universidad de Guadalajara, Guadalajara, México
jorge@ruizvanoye.com

Abstract. Clustering is one of the most successful techniques for territorial design, location-allocation problems etc. In this type of problems, the parameters are usually optimized by means of a single objective. However, real applications are far from being solved without the application of multi-objective approaches. In this paper we present a bi-objective partitioning proposal to solve problems that involve census-based variables for territorial design (TD), known to be a high complexity computational problems. Two quality measures for partitioning are chosen, which are simultaneously optimized. The first quality measure obeys a geometrical concept of distances, whereas the second measure focuses in the calculation of balance for a descriptive variable. A formulation is included with a flexible notation for the second objective about variable population and this is our main contribution. Furthermore, our model allows for implementations in several languages and it is possible to reach quality solutions within a reasonable computation time.

Experimental tests show that it is possible to get results in the Pareto frontier, which is constructed with the approximate solutions generated by the chosen metaheuristic. In this case, one pilot test and its associated Pareto's front, is presented. These solutions are non-dominated and non-comparable with a similar mechanism on which the minima of a Hasse Diagram are reached.

Keywords: POS · Mutiobjetive partitioning · Pareto Frontier · Homogeneity

1 Introduction

Classification by partitioning is also known as automatic classification; however, a research line barely discussed in literature is the development of clustering methods for several data, which is the focus of this research.

K-medoids is a partitioning method that has overcome some limitations of the k-means clustering method; however both algorithms keep the high computational complexity in the presence of other restrictions. When the clustering

© Springer International Publishing AG 2017
J.C. Figueroa-García et al. (Eds.): WEA 2017, CCIS 742, pp. 156–166, 2017.
DOI: 10.1007/978-3-319-66963-2_15

process is performed around the medoids, the cost function may be treated as a geometrical compactness which is implicitly satisfied by the properties of this type of partitioning. However, the most important problems on territorial design (TD) call for restrictions other than geometrical compactness, such as homogeneity over certain variables, contiguity and connectedness, which must be optimized simultaneously. At this point, for a particular multi-objective problem we have focused our efforts in the simultaneous satisfaction of an additional restriction known as homogeneity for values or weights with descriptive variables, which is considered as another goal of interest together with compactness.

In this paper we introduce two quality measures expressed as cost functions that are optimized simultaneously: homogeneity and compactness.

The construction of the Pareto frontier is needed as in this case we must optimize two cost functions. In order to obtain the approximate non-dominated solutions, the order theory was studied along with some applications [1].

This paper is organized as follows: this introduction is Sect. 1. Section 2 presents concepts and definitions about multi-objective problems. In Sect. 3 we describe the problem from a mathematical standpoint, describing details of the cost functions for multi-objective partitioning. Section 4 describes Multi-objective Algorithm Homogeneity and finally, in Sect. 5 conclusions are presented.

2   Multiobjetive Problem (Basics Aspects)

The multi-objective formulation may be informally described as an optimization problem that presents two or more objective functions. The main disadvantage in this kind of problems when compared to a single objective model resides in the subjectivity of the solution found. A multi-objective problem doesn't have only one optimal solution, instead it generates a set of solutions that can't be considered different between the objectives it optimizes. The set of optimal solutions is the so-called Pareto Frontier (PF) where the frontier of solutions contains all the points that aren't exceeded in all of the objectives by another solution. This concept is called "dominance", thus the PF consists only of non-dominated solutions, then, a solution dominates another one if and only if, it is at least as good as the other in all of their objectives and is better in at least one of them.

These problems can be precised if the relationships between characteristics, restrictions and objectives are identified; it is then possible to express them as a mathematical functions. The improvement of all means that all the functions must be optimized simultaneously, leading to the following definition [2]:

Definition 1. *A multi-objective problem (MOP) can be defined in the case of minimization (and analogously for the case of maximization) as follows:*

Minimze $f(x)$ such that
$f : F \subseteq \mathbf{R}^n \to \mathbf{R}^q$, $q \geq 2$ with feasible region in
$A = \{a \in F : g_i(a) \leq 0, i = 1, \ldots, m\} \neq \emptyset$

The set A is known as feasible region and it is said that the problem is subject to the restrictions $g_i : \mathbf{R}^n \to \mathbf{R}$ that are any functions.

In multi-objective optimization a certain scheme has to be selected to define the improvement of one solution over another, frequently known as domination scheme and its definition is mainly based in the fact that the solution of a multi-objective problem it is not unique and therefore the decision maker must choose among a range of possible solutions that can't exceed each other, that is, that don't dominate each other. This concept may be clarified by thinking that in the real numbers field order is defined in a natural way. For $\mathbf{R}^n$, it's possible to extend the concept by means of the following definition:

Definition 2. *Given* $x = (x_k)$, $y = (y_k)$ *vectors in* $\mathbf{R}^n$, $x \preceq y$ *if and only* $x_k \leq y_k$ *for each* $k \in \{1, \ldots, n\}$, *where* $\leq$ *is the usual order in* $\mathbf{R}$.

2.1 Pareto Frontier

The domination relationship, known as Pareto domination is defined as follows:

Definition 3. *Given the multi-objective problem, minimize* $f(x)$ *where*

$$f : F \subseteq \mathbf{R}^n \to \mathbf{R}^q, \ q \geq 2$$

with $A \subseteq F$ *the feasible region. We say that a vector* $x^* \in A$ *is non-dominated or a Pareto optimum if there's no vector* $x \in A$ *such that* $x < x^*$.

Thus, the answer to the problem of finding the best solutions (the non-dominated solutions, where dominance is defined within the technique) in a multi-objective problem is what is called the solution set of the problem, and the set of values of the objective function with domain restricted to the vectors of the solution set (that is, the non-dominated vectors) is what we know as Pareto Frontier. In this way, the concept of set of non-dominated vectors, logically leads to the concept of partially ordered set.

Definition 4. *The set* E *of Pareto efficient solutions (also known as set of Pareto optimums) is defined as follows:*

$$E(A, f) := \{a \in F : \nexists b \in A, \ f(b) < f(a)\}$$

That is, the set of all the non-dominated vectors under the Pareto scheme. Summing up, the set of Pareto optimums is the solution space of the problem, and the Pareto Frontier is its image in relation to the function to optimize:

$$f : F \subseteq \mathbf{R}^n \to \mathbf{R}^q, \ q \geq 2.$$

A concept closely related with the Pareto Frontier is the Pareto optimum. The Pareto optimum as well as the Pareto Frontier are the framework over which the multi-criteria decision making is worked. The set of Pareto optimums for a given multi-objective problem is a partially ordered set (poset) when seen in a formal way [3]. In multi-objective problems the minimal elements are searched for in the solution space R n seen as a poset with the relation $\mathbf{R}^n$ given in Definition 3.

Definition 5. *Given A a set and $(\preceq)$ a partial order relationship over it, we call the couple $(A, \preceq)$ a **partially ordered set** also referred as **Poset**.*

Definition 6. *Given $(A, \preceq)$ a Poset, the subset $X \subseteq A$ it is said to be a **total order** or chain in relation to $(A, \preceq)$, if and only if $x \prec y$ or $y \prec x$ is met for each $x, y \in X$. In this case it is said that $(X, \preceq)$ is a totally ordered set.*

For partial order the domination relationship $(\prec)$ can be defined in the following way $x \prec y \Leftrightarrow x \preceq y \wedge x \neq y$.

When it happens that $x \npreceq y \wedge y \npreceq x$ it is said that they are not comparable, which is denoted by $x \| y$.

A **maximal element** of a partially ordered set P is an element P that isn't less than any other element. The term minimal element is defined in likewise.

Definition 7. *Let $(P, \leq)$ be a partially ordered set; $m \in P$ is a maximal element of P if the only $x \in P$ such that $m \leq x$ is $x = m$.*

The definition of a minimal element is obtained by replacing $\leq$ by $\geq$ [3,4].

Definition 8 *Maximal and minimal elements in a Hasse diagram.*
Let $(A, \leq)$ be a POS (partially ordered set). Let $m, n \in A$. Then

(1) n is a maximal element in A if and only if $(\forall x)(n \leq x \rightarrow n = x)$
(2) m is a minimal element in A if and only if $(\forall x)(x \leq n \rightarrow n = x)$

Intuitively, an element n of a POS $(A, \leq)$ is maximal of A if there isn't an element in A that is strictly greater than n. Analogously, an element m of A is a minimal of A if there isn't an element of A that is strictly less than m [4].

3   Multi-objetive Formulation Problem: Homogeneity Proposal

The compactness problem has been solved and good results were obtained, however homogeneity still has a few conflicts in time cost [5,6]. At this point, we present a new contribution for homogeneity that will help better develop implementations.

We have pointed out that we are interested in finding partitions of $\Omega = \{x_1, ..., x_n\}$ (geographical objects OG) that optimize both compactness and homogeneity, yet for this purpose some small adaptations to Definitions 1, 3 and 4 are required. Consider the collection of all the partitions of Ω: $\mathbf{P} = \{P : P \text{ is a partition of } \Omega\}$.

Let $f : \mathbf{P} \rightarrow \mathbf{R}^2$ be the function such that $f(P) = (C(P), H(P))$ where C and H are the compactness and homogeneity functions respectively, both with domain in $\mathbf{P}$ and values in $\mathbf{R}$.

The function of compactness C is given by

$$C(P) = \sum_{C \in \mathbf{P}} \sum_{i,j \in C} d(i,j) \tag{1}$$

Analytically the function of homogeneity H, the second objective is

$$V_j - \frac{1}{n} \sum_{i=1}^{n} v_{ij} = \frac{1}{n} \sum_{i=1}^{n} (V_j - v_{ij}) = H(P) \qquad (2)$$

In our case the Definition (2) about Sect. 2, is reduced to the following multi-objective problem:

Minimize $f(P)$ given that $f : \mathbf{P} \subseteq 2^{\Omega} \to \mathbf{R}^2$ with feasible region in

$$\mathbf{P} = \{P \subset 2^{\Omega} : P \text{ is partition of } \Omega\} \qquad (3)$$

where 2^{Ω} is the power set of Ω and $f(P) = (C(P), H(P))$.

Given the previous multi-objective problem we can include a partial order $\leq_P$ over the set of partitions $\mathbf{P}$ in the following way:

$$P \leq_P P' \text{ if and only if } f(P) \leq f(P'), \qquad (4)$$

where $\leq$ is the order given in Definition 2. Similarly to Definition 4, we say that a partition $P^* \in \mathbf{P}$ is non-dominated or a Pareto optimum if there isn't a partition $P \in \mathbf{P}$ such that $P <_{\mathbf{P}} P^*$, where $\leq_P$ is the strict order induced by the partial order $<_{\mathbf{P}}$.

Then the set of Pareto optimums $E(P, f)$ in our case is defined as:

$$(\mathbf{P}, f) = \{P \in \mathbf{P} : \nexists P' \in \mathbf{P} \text{ that meets } P' \leq_{\mathbf{P}} P\}. \qquad (5)$$

We can see that the set of the partitions $\mathbf{P}$ is generated from the finite set Ω then the image (Pareto Frontier) of the objective function f is finite and thus the Pareto Frontier is a discrete set.

Let $\Omega' = \{OG_1, OG_2, \ldots, OG_n\}$ be a set of n objects and $VC = \{X_1, X_2, \ldots, X_r\}$ a set of census variables that describe the geographical objects, where each X_i is a variable that depends on the objects set that takes real positive values $\mathbf{R}^+$. Given r intervals $I_j = [\alpha_j, \beta_j], j = 1, \ldots, r$ and the characteristic functions $\chi_{[\alpha_j, \beta_j]} : VC \to \{0, 1\}$,

$$\chi_{[\alpha_j, \beta_j]}(X) = \begin{cases} 1 \text{ if } X \in [\alpha_j, \beta_j] \\ 0 \text{ else} \end{cases} \qquad (6)$$

The participation matrix associated with the objects group Ω' with variables VC and conditions $I_j, (j = 1, \ldots r)$ is defined as the matrix $M = (v_{ij})$ sized $n \times r$ where

$$v_{ij} = \chi_{[\alpha_j, \beta_j]}(X_j) X_j(OG_i) \qquad (7)$$

Thus matrix M contains all values for the participating variables in the respective objects. If $v_{ij} = 0$ it is said that variable X_j does not participate in the OG_i (objects).

Once the participating variables are known, to homogenize groups the following calculations are performed:

Let us say that the variable of interest is X_j, an ideal average is obtained. Say that the ideal average is V_j, it should be that all groups have the same value.

As this, however, seldom happens in practice, then the actual average for each group $\frac{1}{n}\sum_{i=1}^{n} v_{ij}$ is calculated. This value is subtracted form the ideal average,

$$\frac{1}{n}V_j - \sum_{i=1}^{n} v_{ij} = \sum_{i=1}^{n}(V_j - v_{ij}) \tag{8}$$

By minimizing the absolute value for this difference, the cost for the target function may be obtained for homogeneity.

Let P_i : Localization, geographic location. If with P_i we associate the descriptive variable set, then:

$$P_i \rightarrow (V_1(P_i), V_2(P_i), V_3(P_i), \ldots, V_n(P_i)) = V(P_i) \tag{9}$$

where $i = 1, 2, 3, \ldots, n$ (number of geographics objects).

Let OG_i : Geographical Objects $= (P_i, V)$. To obtain a partition of compactness, minimizing object to centroid distance it is found that if k determines the number of groups, then the compactness function is defined as:

$$comp : ((\mathbf{R}^+)^{2k} \rightarrow \mathbf{R}^+, \ comp(P_1, P_2, \ldots, P_k) = \sum_{i=1}^{n} \sum_{P \in P_i} d(P, P_i); \ (centroid \ p)$$

where $d(P, P_i) = min\{d(P, P_j)\}$ y $j = 1, 2, \ldots, n$.

$$(\{P_1, P_2, \ldots, P_k\} \rightarrow \{G_{P_1}, \ldots, G_{P_k}\}) \rightarrow comp(\{G_{P_1}, \ldots, G_{P_k}\}) = \mathbf{f}_1 \tag{10}$$

To obtain a homogeneity grouping, minimizing the difference between the ideal average within the group and the actual average within the same group, the description would be:

$$P_i \rightarrow V_j(P_i) = v(P_i) \ y \ P_i = (long, lat) \ shows \ O_i = OG(P_i, \mathbf{V})$$

$$(\{P_1, \ldots, P_k\} \rightarrow_{j=1,\ldots,n} \{G_{P_1}, \ldots, G_{P_k}\}) \rightarrow hom(\{G_{P_1}, \ldots, G_{P_k}\}) = \mathbf{f}_2 \tag{11}$$

The homogeneity calculation is obtained as:

$$Ideal \ Value(\gamma_{P1,\ldots,Pk}) = (\frac{1}{k}\sum_{i=1}^{k} V_1(P_i), \ldots, \frac{1}{k}\sum_{i=1}^{k} V_n(P_i))$$
$$= \frac{1}{k}\sum_{j=1}^{k}(V_1(P_i), \ldots, V_n(P_i))$$
$$= \frac{1}{k}\sum_{i=1}^{k} \mathbf{V}(P_i) = \mathbf{V}_{average}(\gamma_{P1,\ldots,Pk}).$$

$$Actual \ average = (\gamma_{P1,\ldots,Pk})(\frac{1}{|G_{P1}|}\sum_{i=1}^{k} V_1(P_i), \ldots, \frac{1}{|G_{Pn}|}\sum_{i=1}^{k} V_n(P_i))$$
$$= \mathbf{V}_{actual \ value}$$

$$hom(P_1, \ldots, P_k) = ||\mathbf{V}_{actual \ average} - \mathbf{V}_{ideal \ average}|| \tag{12}$$

To associate this joint optimization problem of compactness and homogeneity of $y = \mathbf{f}(x) = (\mathbf{f}_1, \mathbf{f}_2)$, we have:

$$G(comp, hom)(P_1, P_2, \ldots, P_k) \rightarrow \{G_{P1}, \ldots, G_{Pk}\} = \gamma_{P1,\ldots,Pk} \rightarrow (comp, hom),$$

where X is a cartesian product between compactness and homogeneity, γ_{Pi} is a partition, and $i = 1, ..., k$ is the number of groupings.

From γ we wish to obtain a pair (comp, hom).

$$(P_1, ..., P_k) \quad \rightarrow \{G_{P1}, ..., G_{Pk}\}$$
$$= \gamma_{P1,...,Pk}$$
$$\rightarrow (comp(P_1, ..., P_k), hom(P_1, ..., P_k))$$

$$(P'_1, ..., P'_k) \quad \rightarrow \{G'_{P1}, ..., G'_{Pk}\}$$
$$= \gamma_{P'1,...,P'k}$$
$$\rightarrow (comp(P'_1, ..., P'_k), hom(P'_1, ..., P'_k))$$

$$(P^m_1, ..., P^m_k) \rightarrow \{G^m_{P1}, ..., G^m_{Pk}\}$$
$$= \gamma_{P^m_1,...,P^m_k}$$
$$\rightarrow (comp(P^m_1, ..., P^m_k), hom(P^m_1, ..., P^m_k))$$

The $m-th$ solution that minimizes $(comp, hom)$ is accepted. In this point, the Pareto Frontier has been obtained by experimental test under pilot implementations with another formulation for homogeneity, which was developed with Visual.net and the C programming language. Besides that, the Variable Neighborhood Search VNS metaheuristic has been included due do the combinatorial complexity related to our problem.

To "simultaneously" obtain the two values of the compactness-homogeneity function, the main idea is to first have a set of compact solutions available (the optimum and locals), and run the homogeneity process over said solutions as they are generated. This is achieved by the characteristics of VNS. Considering that in multi-objective problems the objective functions have the same dominion [6], to get the associated homogeneity value, and to simultaneously evaluate the two functions under the Pareto dominance (PD), it is necessary to review the complete set of solutions generated by VNS regardless if they are local optimums or the final "optimal" solution. In this point the homogeneity calculation is done over the complete set of compact solutions generated whilst the VNS process does not end. Finally, as the heuristic allows and for each iteration, this provides several pairs of solutions integrated by the compactness and homogeneity values (denoted as $(comp_i, hom_i)$). This means that at the same time that the solutions $(comp_i, hom_i)$ are generated by VNS and using the Pareto order, the solutions that fulfill this order are identified, thus finding a subset of solutions $(comp_k, hom_k)$, $k \leq i$, with a "special" non-dominated pair $(comp_{min}, hom_{min})$. This pair is said to be a distinguished element, named minimal in the Pareto frontier.

4   Multi-objetive Algorithm

We present the more relevant aspects of the VNS algorithm that minimizes compactness-homogeneity.

Algorithm 1. VNS - Compactness and homogeneity

> Require: n Number of objects to classify.
> Require: k Number of groups.
> Require: Val_i Value of the object i for the homogeneity variable.
> Require: MaxVNS Number of times that the neighborhood structures will be
> explored.
> Require: MaxLS Maximum number of iterations for local search
> kNeighborhood ← Generate a random number between 1 and n
> SolActual ← Generate a random solution found in the neighborhood structure
> kNeighborhood
> currentCost ← getCostComp(currentSol), getCostHom(currentSol)
> This pair of solutions must fulfill the "Pareto order"
> cont ← 1
> **while** cont < MaxV NS **do**
>   kNeighborhood ← 1
>   **while** kNeighbothood ← n **do**
>   SolCand ← Generates a random solution found in the the neighborhood struc-
> ture kNeighborhood
> SolCand ← LocalSearch(SolCand)
>   costCand ← getCostComp(SolCand), getCostHom(SolCand)
>   **if** costCand < currentCost **then**
>   currentSol ← SolCand
>   currentCost ← costCand
>   **else**
>   kNeighborhood ← kNeighborhood + 1
>   **end if**
>   **end while**
>   cont ← cont + 1
> **end while**
> return currentSol

Algorithm 2. getCostHom - Returns an integer that indicates how good the solution is in regard to homogeneity (the lower the value, the better)

> Require: Sol Solution to evaluate
>   total ← 0
>   cost ← 0
>   **for** i ← 1 to n **do**
>   ng ← Obtain the number of group which the object i belongs to
>   total ← total + V ali
>   totalGroupng ← V ali
>   **end for**
>   idealAverage ← total/k
>   **for** j ← 1 to k **do**
>   cost ← cost + $|totalGroupj - idealAverage|$
>   **end for**
>   return cost

Algorithm 3. getCostComp - Returns an integer that indicates how good the solution is in regard to compactness (the lower the value, the better)

       Require: Sol Solution to evaluate.
             $i \leftarrow 1$
             cost $\leftarrow 0$
    while $i \leq n$ **do**
        if GOi not a centroid **then**
            dmin $\leftarrow$ dist(Sol1,GOi)
            $j \leftarrow 2$
        while $j \leq k$ **do**
            if $dist(Sol_j, GO_i) < dmin$ **then**
            $dmin \leftarrow dist(Sol_j, GO_i)$
        end if
            $j \leftarrow j + 1$
    end while
            cost $\leftarrow$ cost + dmin
        end if
            $i \leftarrow i + 1$
  end while
  return cost

Algorithm 4. Local Search

    Require: Sol current solution.

            Solbest $\leftarrow$ Sol
            costSolbest $\leftarrow$ getCostComp(Solbest), getCostHom(Solbest)
    while iter $\leq$ MaxLS **do**
        SolCand $\leftarrow$ Generate a random neighbor solution of Solbest
        costSolCand $\leftarrow$ getCostComp(SolCand), getCostHom(SolCand)
        if costSolCand $<$ costSolbest **then**
        Solbest $\leftarrow$ SolCand
        iter $\leftarrow$ MaxLS + 1
      else
          iter $\leftarrow$ iter + 1
          end if
    end while
        return Solbest

Example: Assume that there is a government program to take care of education issues for the underage male population, in such a way that the distribution of this sector of the population must be known. Suppose that an expert on population problem asks for groupings of 2, 8, 32, 64 and 100 groups having 469 geographic objects (zones) to process. In accordance to the discussion in previous sections, the answer to a problem such as this one begins with the selection of the variables of interest. These variables have the nomenclature $\mathbf{X}+$ natural number or $\mathbf{Z}+$ natural number and they are retrieved from a database to form the partitioning matrix for homogeneity according to Eq. 4. The query to choose the variables that take part in the grouping is:

SELECT id AS Ageb, Z002 As Var
from cdata
WHERE (x001 BETWEEN (SELECT MAX(x001) FROM cdata) * 0 / 100 AND
(SELECT MAX(x001) FROM cdata) * 100 / 100) AND
(x003 BETWEEN (SELECT MAX(x003) FROM cdata) * 0 / 100 AND
(SELECT MAX(x003) FROM cdata) * 100 / 100) AND
(x007 BETWEEN (SELECT MAX(x007) FROM cdata) * 0 / 100 AND
(SELECT MAX(x007) FROM cdata) * 100 / 100)

In this problem, x001 is Male population under 6 years old, x003 is Male population between 6 and 11 years old, x007 is Male population from 15 to 17 years old and Z002 is Male population (Homogeneity Variable) The results can be seen in Figs. 1 and 2.

Test Number for two groups	Time (seconds)	Minimals	
1	180	4651927	5830
		4027761	7586
		3998703	35908
		8418672	1134
		3860558	203380
2	191	3896887	108510
		4062652	3962
		5221435	1090
		3896898	20122
3	199	4274664	5038
		3911128	101652
		3861364	210136
		4462969	2364
		4225945	7132
		3964625	39146
		4075477	18332
		3800188	313336
		4028417	33306
		3853377	298410
4	178	4060232	1012
		5098746	6
		3977408	1516
		3775415	84998
5	200	4099570	50674
		3939251	56028
		4132966	43278
		3830369	81072

Fig. 1. Solutions non dominated about description problem (masculine population).

In the next graphic, the Pareto Frontier is related to Fig. 2 where axis X is compactness and Y homogeneity.

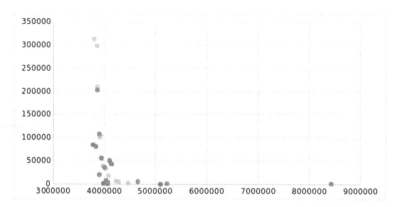

Fig. 2. Pareto Frontier related.

5   Conclusions

In this work a clear notation for partitioning with two objectives has been presented, in particular for homogeneity. The implementation of this model simplifies the incorporation of a VNS algorithm that adapts to the Pareto order relationship and allows for the obtaining of the Minima. Several tests have been made over OG where computing time is relatively short (4 min and 49 s for 469 objects, 10 groups and 8 census variables) and the Pareto frontier is acceptable given that it has been compared to Nodom [7]. In the future, the homogeneity procedure will be able to accept other kinds of data. Regarding the Pareto Frontier, the procedure has been refined to find more accurate Minima and in shorter computing time.

References

1. Acan, A., Lotfi, N.: A multiagent, dynamic rank driven multi-deme architecture for real-valued multiobjetive optimization. Artif. Intell. **48**(1), 1–29 (2017)
2. Ergohtt, M.: Multicriteria Optimization, 2nd edn., pp. 12–42. Springer, New York, Heidelberg (2005)
3. Lara, L.A.: Un estudio de las Estrategias Evolutivas para problemas Multi-objetivo: Tesis de Maestría en Ciencias en la especialidad de Ingeniería Eléctrica, pp. 12–29 (2003)
4. Grimaldi, R.: Discrete and Combinatorial Mathematics: An Applied Introduction, 880 pages. Addison-Wesley, Harlow (1994)
5. Bernabé, L., Coello, C.A., Osorio, M.: A multiobjective approach for the heuristic optimization of compactness and homogeneity in the optimal zoning. J. Appl. Res. Technol. **10**(3), 447–457 (2012)
6. Bernabé, L., Guillén, G.: Multi-objective variable neighborhood search to solve the problem of partitioning of spatial data with population characteristics. Computación y Sistemas **16**(3), 321–334 (2012)
7. CINVESTAV.   http://www.cs.cinvestav.mx/emoobook/nodom/nondomina-ted. htm. Accessed 26 June 2014

Ant Colony Algorithm for the Optimization of Semaphorization in One of the Most Congested Intersections in the Bogota City

Andres Cardenas[✉], Diana Toquica[✉], and Yesid Díaz-Gutierrez[✉]

Corporacion Unificada Nacional de Educacion Superior CUN, Bogotá, Colombia
{andres_cardenas,diana_toquica,yesid_diaz}@cun.edu.co

Abstract. One of the main problems in the big cities is traffic, both vehicles and motorcycles. Currently Bogotá D.C. (Capital of Colombia), has more than 8 million inhabitants, of whom the majority travels in private and public vehicles. In the interior of the city, it has been possible to identify sectors in which mobility generates a frequent chaos, given the number of vehicles that have to move there, including light vehicles and also cargo vehicles. The application of the Ant Colony algorithm is proposed to simulate the traffic at a specific time in an intersection in order to determine if it is possible to increase the flow of vehicles that circulate through said intersection, decreasing the time of exit of the vehicles. At the end of the article we present the results of the simulation which allow us to take a stand against the research and to confirm that the research process and, above all, the simulation process, allow us to make a decision about the way in which the times have been adjusted Of traffic lights at most of the intersections of the city of Bogotá.

Keywords: Ant colony algorithm · Traffic study · Semaphorization · Simulation models · Information flows

1 Introduction

The increase of motor vehicles in the city of Bogota D.C. (Automobiles, campers, trucks and motorcycles) to generate that in one way or another the system of the district collapses, mainly because its infrastructure presumably was not designed, from the beginning, to allow a fast and, above all, constant flow of Vehicles in the concrete sense of each of the tracks; Also the traffic light system is quite inefficient in terms of time allocation since it is very common to find that in an intersection can give "green light" to a crossing where there is no evidence of the presence of vehicles or motorcycles or simply change very fast The lights from red to green or vice versa, obstructing the flow in any of the senses. Taking into account the above, Bogota intersection 23 was selected, with the intention of carrying out a simulation that would allow us to draw conclusions about how efficient the current traffic light system could be at that point in the city. Two algorithms were then applied to achieve an adequate simulation: 1. The SIGCAP (A computer program for assessing the traffic capacity), which is currently widely used in scenarios requiring simulation by coprocessor and 2. The Ant colony algorithm, the

© Springer International Publishing AG 2017
J.C. Figueroa-García et al. (Eds.): WEA 2017, CCIS 742, pp. 167–178, 2017.
DOI: 10.1007/978-3-319-66963-2_16

Which is proposed for the control of the same. However, this research seeks to demonstrate the efficiency of the algorithms proposed, taking into account the flows of vehicles, as well as the travel times recorded at said intersection.

2 Problem Description

The problem of mobility in the city of Bogota is due to the system of Traffic at the intersections of In some cases handle response times or changes Of lights (Green, Yellow and Red) slow or too fast; In addition to the lack of prioritization when giving way to the tracks More congested, causing trances lost time. It is further desired to address the issue of The congestion in one of the main intersections of Bogota The AV. USME - AV. TO LL LLANO using an Ant colony algorithm, aiming to optimize Cycle and phase-to-phase times to Greater vehicular flow, and shorter time spent in the Vehicles at the intersection.

2.1 Intersection Characteristics

The intersection of CAREER 1 THIS BY STREET 81 A SOUTH is located in the south east of the city. CAREER 1 ESTE, is formed by a road for mixed traffic. It allows the circulation in north - south direction and vice versa. THE 81A SOUTH STREET, is formed by two roadways for mixed traffic, allows circulation in the west-east and vice versa. The total vehicular volume of the intersection for the gauging period is 29,410, the vehicle composition is: light 41.8%; Buses 20.9%; Trucks 16.7% and motorcycles 20.5%; The volume in equivalent vehicles is 40,075. Vehicle participation by access is: 25.8% north; South 21.2%; West 23.3%; And 29.7%. The hour of maximum demand at the intersection occurs in the morning between 06:00 to 07:00 with a volume of 3,400. Equivalent vehicles for a peak hour factor of 0.96 [1]. The control consists of four semaphore plans, these are adjusted between cycle time and phase intervals depending on the time of day. The way in which the different plans are established is with the analysis of flow, density, priority of ways among others that is done every four years by a group of engineers assigned to make the study; The last study that was done was in 2012 for which it was established that for the peak hours that are from 04: 30–09: 00, 11: 00–13: 00 and from 17: 00–21: 00, Plan 1, from 09: 00–11: 00 the plan 2, from 13: 00–16: 00 the plan 3 and for the rest of the hours the plan 4.

According to each of the plans indicated above, a TC variable is defined that defines the cycle time, on that same side the start data are tabulated, which are no more than the time for the cycle where the phase begins, too It establishes the end variable that is when the phase ends or the green light ends and finally the variable tv that is the time that the green signal lasts. Likewise, values are assigned to a column which shows the group of signals and also indicates the behavior for each signal with respect to the cycle time of the intersection, to see the position of each signal (see Fig. 1). The time for which each plan works is given in Table 1.

This way traffic is controlled is inefficient because the time has been established in relation to previous studies and not the current state in which the intersection is. In what way is it possible to implement an Ant colony algorithm to optimize the cycle and

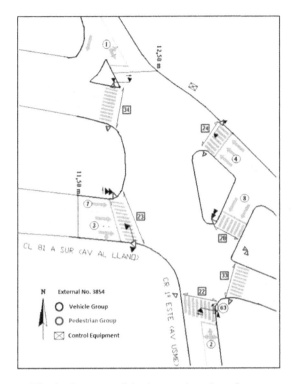

Fig. 1. Structure of the intersection. Own Source

Table 1. Operating time for each control

Daily plan	Hour	Minute	Plan - STR
WD1	4	30	1
	9	00	2
	11	00	1
	13	00	3
	16	00	4
	17	00	1
	21	00	4

phase times of the intersection CARRERA 1 THIS STREET 81 A SUR for its respective validation and comparison with the current method? The implementation of an Ant colony algorithm for the optimization of the response times of the simulated interception traffic lights located in the AV is proposed as specific objectives. USME - AV. TO THE PLAIN. Of the city of Bogota. Similarly, the use of the microscopic model to give a random behavior to each of the vehicles that will transit the simulated intercept, maintain a dynamic traffic flow in traffic simulation, as well as the comparison of the results obtained from the handling Of the traffic with the Ant colony algorithm and the SIGCAP algorithm (A computer program for assessing the traffic capacity). By studying a vehicular intersection and applying the electronic measurement devices used in large cities and a swarm algorithm in a simulated environment, it will allow analyzing different options from those currently used and in the end being able to generate more optimal plans that are forged through the study In real time of the different roads of the city. By optimizing travel times, the beneficiaries will be all the individuals of the population since on the one hand the drivers and passengers would arrive faster to their destination and the loss of time in traffic jams would be minimized. To achieve such a goal requires the development of simulations in which the variables and their relationship are analyzed, with the help of the available technologies which adapt to the necessity of the problem.

3   Traffic Dynamics

The flow of vehicles and the way to optimize it is one of the areas of concern for researchers and governmental entities, as the current delays cause great losses in the economy of the country and one way to improve it is to generate traffic control systems which can use The last advances made in artificial intelligence specifically in the behavior of swarms, electronics and mathematical models for the formal representation of the vehicular flow and its respective simulation that later allows to be implemented in real life.

In the following sections we will explain the dynamics of the traffic to be used in the simulation, clarifying the use of each equation that will serve to obtain the efficiency of the times selected with the algorithm, after all the relevant topics are detailed, The one that works the Ant colony algorithm, ending with a brief description of the technologies used.

3.1   Traffic Dynamics and Roling Horizont Method

The traffic flow is classified in two, interrupted and without interruptions, when talking about interrupted flow is when there are no traffic lights, signaling, reducers and others that affect the flow or if they are located at great distances as in the avenue Boyaca, The only factor affecting the flow is the behavior of the conductors. In the interrupted flow apart from the behavior of the drivers this is affected by several traffic lights and signs, in this case it is spoken of platoons and a platoons is the group of vehicles that leaves when the traffic light is in green.

There are two widely used ways in traffic simulation, these are macroscopic that gives a value for each group of vehicles at one time, the variables used are flow, density and speed which are averaged over the number of vehicles that passed in the road. And microscopic that gives a value for each pair of vehicles, the variables used are time headway and space headway. Next, the rules used for the arrival and departure of the vehicles are explained as well as the method used for the evaluation of the times.

3.2   Ants Colony Algorithm

The Ant colony algorithm has 4 versions of which vary in the way of updating the pheromone, has been applied to several combinatorial optimization problems such as traveling agent, vehicle routes, quadratic assignment among others, obtaining good results. The algorithm was inspired by the way ants look for food to take to the nest, at first they choose a random route and until they find no food they are not returned, in the path of food to the nest they deposit a chemical called pheromone that Evaluates the quality of the food with respect to the path so that the other ants are attracted or not to follow that path, the more pheromone is in the path, the choice of the path will become less random, as time passes the pheromone Is evaporating so if it is not very frequented the road is not going to choose, if you already have a source where the ants get the food they look for the shortest path, and this is the one that will accumulate more pheromone. This is represented by the experiment of the double bridge (see Fig. 2a) where in their first version they put two bridges of equal size, at the beginning the ants venture along a path, as time passes one of the roads accumulates more pheromone and this Is the one who continue to choose:

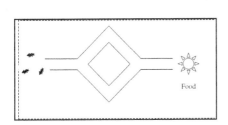

Fig. 2a. Double bridge of equal length. Marco Dorigo

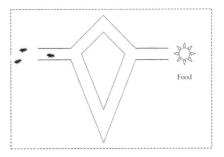

Fig. 2b. Double bridge with double length. Marco Dorigo

In Fig. 2b the second version of the experiment is shown, in this the lower bridge is twice as large as the upper one, and in doing the same process they observed that the ants after a time chose the shortest path due to the accumulation of pheromone.

When applying the behavior of the ants for the development of computational problems artificial ants are created that with the help of the pheromone they cross a graph, in mathematical terms its representation is the following one: (S, f, Ω) where "S" is the Set of possible solutions, "f" is the objective function and "Ω" are the rules for the problem, the objective is to find the optimal solution that minimizes "f". Although there are several versions for the algorithm all follow the same steps, the only difference is the way in which the pheromone is updated, the steps are as follows.

1. The routes are initialized. To traverse the graph, with the same amount of pheromone.

2. Solutions are built. Each ant builds a solution guided by pheromone levels, the solution is a set of nodes through which the ant passes, an ant goes from point i to j with probability (see Eq. 1)

$$p_{ij} = \begin{cases} \dfrac{T_{ij}^{\alpha}\eta_{ij}^{\beta}}{\sum_{l\in N_i}\tau_{il}^{\alpha}\eta_{il}^{\beta}}_{if\to J\in N_i} & {}^{if\to J\in N_i} \end{cases} \tag{1}$$

Where N_i are the places where we can go from i, η is the hejistic of iajy is the pheromone, α and β are positive values which describe the importance that will be given to the pheromone and the heuristic in this problem $\beta = 0$ since only the pheromone levels will be used to traverse the graph. 3. Update pheromone. First the pheromone evaporates (see Eq. 2).

$$\tau_{ij} \leftarrow (1 - \rho)\tau_{ij}, \forall(i,j) \in A \tag{2}$$

Where p is the evaporation coefficient and is in the range (0, 1), then the routes that were selected are added to pheromone (see Eq. 3).

$$\tau_{ij} \leftarrow \tau_{ij} + \Delta\tau_{ij} \tag{3}$$

τ_{ij} is the specific algorithm that determines the effectiveness of the solution and how much pheromone can be added, all versions follow the first step of evaporation what they change is how you add the pheromone. 4. Step 2 and 3 are repeated until the known condition is reached [2].

4 Simulator Modeling (Flowcharts)

The flow of vehicles and the way to optimize it is one of the areas of concern for researchers and governmental entities, as the current delays cause great losses in the economy of the country and one way to improve it is to generate traffic control systems which can use The latest advances made in artificial intelligence specifically in the behavior of swarms, electronics and model.

4.1 Main Flow

The main flow of the program starts with the initial data that will be given by the user, if these are not given they will be generated by default; The initial data are the time, the demand for each road, the number of ants to be used and the number of iterations per time choice in each phase. Having the demand for roadway continues to raise the vehicular flow which is stored in a file; This file will have the number of vehicles to simulate with the route to be performed in the simulation; The creation of the file is necessary since without this the sumo simulator does not work. Then the user chooses the type of algorithm with which to do the simulation in order to connect with SUMO and give him the type of control to execute, the simulation will be done until the time interval is finished or until there are no more vehicles To simulate, in the course of the simulation data are stored in a file that will be used later to fill the tables and make the comparison between algorithms. When the simulation is finished the data is represented in table by each access and intervals of every 15 s, and the totals are also generated in tables.

If the simulation was already done with both types of algorithms the program can be asked to make the comparisons which are number of vehicles per access and time that remained each vehicle that has been simulated in the two algorithms to leave the intersection. Comparisons are represented by graphs. If only one algorithm is simulated, only the number of vehicles per time interval of each access is plotted in graph.

4.2   SUMO Intersection Flow

To do the simulation in SUMO is necessary the creation of four files with different extensions which are nod that gives the coordinates of all the points that are going to be used, edge are the unions that exist between points, type the Type of road; In this go speed allowed number of roadways this can also be specified in edge, if not given is generated by default when using the command NETCONVERT; NETCONVERT creates the structure of the intersection, with which are allowed movements that in each road can be made if not given is also generated by default.

4.3   Control

The control of the traffic in SUMO can be done in two ways, one is adding the TLS (Traffic Light System) file for traffic control, which indicates the time of each phase,

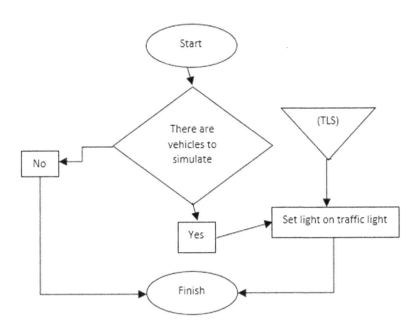

Fig. 3. SIGCAP flow diagram. Own Source

and once the cycle is finished, it is repeated until The simulation is finished in this file can be programmed several cycle plans, it is necessary to indicate the time at which each plan starts to work, if this file is not provided SUMO generates one by default but very unrealistic for traffic control. The second method is to use the TRACI interface which allows to communicate SUMO with a program that is executed in python for traffic control, in this case the program can request information as number of vehicles, and thus using an algorithm that has been written, Determine the time in each phase. Figure 3 shows the diagram for the semaphoric control using (TLS).

5 Simulator Modeling (Flowcharts)

At the start of a phase, the number of vehicles detected by each access in each lane is obtained. After this, the lane with the highest number of vehicles detected per road is chosen, in the case of the access 3 that has 3 lanes and the access 4 that Has three lanes it is chosen among those 6 lanes the lane that has more vehicles; Is done in this way because the accesses 3 and 4 share the same phase time. The same as just mentioned is done for the access 7 that has a lane and the 8 that has two lanes, for access one and two the lane is taken independently for each access; To see the structure of the intersection (see Fig. 1). This is done to get the time to empty the queues in each lane, which will be assigned as minimum time, and this value is multiplied by the flow that was in that interval and then divided by the headway obtaining the possible Number of vehicles arriving at that time; Then the time required to empty the lane with the new vehicles is assigned and the maximum and minimum time are subtracted to obtain the number of nodes that the graph will have at that level, and this is done for each access, If no vehicles were detected for the lanes that are part of the phase then they are not included in the graph, when the time is chosen for a phase the cycle time is analyzed after the time is obtained, this step is repeated.

"t_1" It is the time of the phase for the corresponding semaphore, the column represents in which phase that accesses are in green and which in red being the "t_n" the intervals of duration. As an illustration of how the graph is when the above data are obtained, the phase is assumed to be in access 1, and the times that are the subtraction between the maximum and minimum time are as follows: a1 = 3 A3, a4 = 2 a7, a8 = 2 a2 = 1. After the ants construct the solution is given a cost this is repeated until all the ants have their solution with its cost, after all have already done it is proceeded to update, and it is done to the already exposed until The number of iterations is reached.

6 Methodology

In the simulation no traffic accidents are contemplated, the maximum simulation time is one day and the minimum is 15 min, only one type of cars and motorcycles and two of buses and trucks are modeled, at the moment of running the simulation in Sigcap Can run at 0 ms but when running with the Ant colony algorithm the execution speed must be greater than 100 ms in order to appreciate the effectiveness of the algorithm proposed with the algorithm used. The only types of comparison to be developed are the number of vehicles per access per type of vehicle in a 15 s interval and the time it takes each vehicle to leave the intersection, in order to make this comparison it is necessary that the vehicle has Been simulated in the two algorithms.

7 Design

This phase of the project defines the components and classes that participate in the logical model of the system that will be implemented and support the functionality of the same.

7.1 Architecture Diagram

For the architecture of the software two components are used one that is the interface made in Python that in turn executes the algorithm colony of ants and another the simulator SUMO that is the one that shows the vehicles in the intersection, like the algorithm what gives are The traffic light times of the intersection it is necessary to connect the interface with SUMO, for this a TCP connection must be established on an appropriate port as shown in Fig. 4.

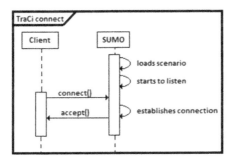

Fig. 4. Connect with SUMO. Marco Dorigo

The application sends commands through the interface TraCI to SUMO to control the traffic or to know the state of the intersection, after receiving the request SUMO responds with a Status -response and with additional information that depends on the request, after it is Has finished the simulation the client is responsible for closing it as shown in Fig. 5.

For the development of the application it is necessary to use four interfaces that are created for the application and one that is own of the simulator SUMO that is where the simulation is run.

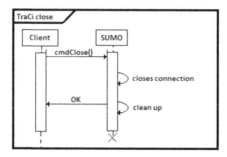

Fig. 5. Architecture diagram: close connection. Marco Dorigo

8 Tests

The simulation showed that the Ant colony algorithm is more efficient than the SIG-CAP, in order to arrive at this conclusion, the simulation was done with different data, obtaining in all cases a greater flow in each access and a shorter time of permanence in the intersection, in The present work only shows two of the tests to not make it very long but the reader can corroborate it when making their own simulations. Within the test conditions, the flow file is used by the two algorithms at the time of simulation, thus obtaining the same flow levels. For the execution of the algorithms will use a laptop with the following features: Operating System Windows 8.1, Python 2.7, Library PMW 1.6, Numpy 1.7 and Matplotlib 1.7. However, within the expected results is the fact of obtaining a greater flow and shorter stay time with the Ant colony algorithm compared to SIGCAP. Given the above, it is shown in Fig. 6a the times for the vehicles that were simulated in the two algorithms.

Particularly in Fig. 6b, the x-axis shows the number of the vehicle for which it is simulated in the two algorithms, in the label that in the center specifies that the red

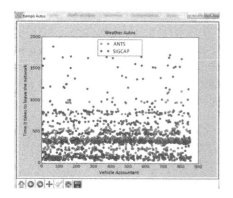

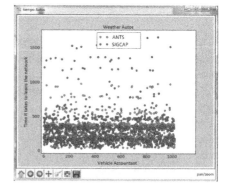

Fig. 6a. Car time graph. Case 1 (Color figure online)

Fig. 6b. Car time graph. Case 2 (Color figure online)

color is for the Ant colony algorithm and the blue one for SIGCAP, Here you can see that most of the red dots are below that of the blues which shows that with the implementation of the algorithm the times are reduced. Given the above and taking into account the Pseudocogic and its complexity, it is possible to pose the following pseudocode for the program, which basically is two cycles, where one of them is nested to the other and from there the operations of finding cycle, Evaluate cycle update pheromone, the pseudocode is shown in Fig. 7.

Input: Semaphore interval, activation; Cycle use sequence at traffic lights and queue which is the number of vehicles per access

Output: The optimum time for the phase

```
funcion simulacion(semaforos,activacionv,cola1):
   inicializargrafoh con intervalo semaforos
   inicializarnodost de grafoh
   tiempominimo=10000
   senalf=0
   para i=0 hasta numero de iteraciones
      listathotmigas igual vacia
      tiempomini=10000
      listaespera igual vacia
      para j=0 hasta numero de hormigas
         tsenal,tfase,rutan=Ciclo(grafoh,semaforos)
         cola=colas(tfase,activacionv,colai)
         costo=Costo(cola,activacionv,tfase)
         adicionarcosto,tsenal,rutan a la lista thormigas
         si costo<tiempomini
            senalf=tsenal
            tiempomini=costo
      sitiempomini<tiempominimo:
         senalf=tsenal
         tiempomonimo=tiempomini
      acFeromona(grafoh,thormigas,tespera,tiempomini)
   sa=senalf[0]+tiempo minimo de semaforos en posicion 0
   retornar sa
```

Fig. 7. Pseudocode of the program. Own Source

9 Conclusions

The SUMO Simulator is a powerful tool that allows to make microscopic simulations in a simple way and that also allows the interaction with the programming language python through the interface Traci which allows to generate code to control the semaphores using intelligent algorithms that optimize the process. The generation of the flows is generated taking into account the values that are assigned to each of the lanes that make up the intersection, these values are taken and the creation of the file is continued, which tells SUMO at what time a particular vehicle Is going to enter the intersection and at what speed. The Ant colony algorithm is inspired by the behavior of biological ants, in the way they communicate to optimize the process of finding food and bringing it to the nest, this communication process is based on depositing pheromones according to the quality of the ants. Food that was already in the distance of the path, thus changing the environment so that the other individuals realize and when making a choice of the way take into account the levels of pheromone in each of them.

Comparing the Ant colony algorithm with SIGCAP, it can be observed that the phase times for each semaphore are optimized, since in the same scenario where the same number of vehicles are generated, a greater flow is achieved and this in turn means that the time Total vehicle output will be lower.

References

1. Consorcio Monitoreo Tránsito y Transporte Urbano Bogotá: Toma de información de campo para el programa de monitoreo, seguimiento y planeación del tránsito y el transporte de Bogotá D.C (2012)
2. Dorigo, M., Stutzle, T.: Ant Colony Optimization. MIT Press, Cambridge (2004)

Intelligent Sampling for Colombian Soundscapes Using an Artificial Neural Network

Luis Quiroz[✉], Jairo Gómez, Oscar Agudelo, and Luis Tobón

Center of Excellence and Appropriation on the Internet of Things (CEA-IoT),
Pontificia Universidad Javeriana, Cali, Colombia
{laquiroz,jairoalejandro.gomez,oaagudelo,letobon}@javerianacali.edu.co
http://www.cea-iot.org/

Abstract. Information extracted from environmental sounds has been of great importance to the analysis of ecological complexity in natural ecosystems. However, the study of these sounds does not have a universal protocol for the sampling and reduction of large quantities of data that it produces. This paper proposes to use a neural network to optimize the sampling of soundscapes of three Colombian ecosystems. The neural network is trained to identify meaningful temporal windows for audio recording from previously gathered data. This method simplifies the acoustic complexity analysis.

Keywords: Soundscape ecology · Intelligent sampling · Artificial neural network · Environmental monitoring · Bioacoustics monitoring

1 Introduction

The automated acoustic monitoring is a promising tool in the soundscape research whose objective is to determine the condition, volume, variety, growth, interaction, and deterioration of species, measuring the health and effects of climate change in ecosystems [1]. Acoustic monitoring collects all sounds from the ecosystem, delivering detailed information about the distribution and variation of the dynamics of animal communities in time and space, helping researchers to better understand their behavior [2].

To collect acoustic data, audio from the ecosystem is recorded during long periods of time producing large amounts of data, which makes storage, processing, and analysis a difficult problem [3]. This problem can be mitigated using optimal sampling by minimizing the amount of data without compromising information quality. However, there is not a single universal protocol defining the best sampling windows for recording within each type of ecosystem.

Reducing the recording time is an important task to decrease hardware requirements in terms of computational power, memory, and power consumption. It is also important because it shortens the time required for digital signal processing and data analysis. However, the downside of reducing the recording

© Springer International Publishing AG 2017
J.C. Figueroa-García et al. (Eds.): WEA 2017, CCIS 742, pp. 179–188, 2017.
DOI: 10.1007/978-3-319-66963-2_17

time is that key information can be lost, producing distorted results about animal communities, and this is why, it is so important to identify the key time windows for making useful recordings in the ecosystem.

There are several studies of sonorous landscapes focusing on animal behavior [4], the relationship between sounds emitted by the ecosystem and its physical structure [5], the quantity and diversity of species [6], and the impact of human-produced noise [7]. However, acoustic sampling methods are empirical, there are a few studies about its optimization, and they can not be generalized because each ecosystem behaves in a different manner, and therefore, a customized protocol is needed to determine the sampling for each ecosystem.

The work of Pieretti [8] shows the problem of acoustic monitoring by performing a study on the information loss achieved with different recording windows in ecosystems located in Brazil. He identified an efficient period with a minimum sampling that yields a small information loss. The downside of the proposed method is that the sampling is fixed (recording during 1 min every 10 min, 1 min every 20 min or 1 min every 30 min during a day), which is not very efficient for ecosystems with non-periodical acoustic activity.

In this paper, authors propose an optimal sampling method using an artificial neural network that defines recording intervals or windows for three Colombian ecosystems. These intervals are adapted based on the inherent acoustic activity of the ecosystem, yielding little information loss.

2   Methodology

2.1   Area of Study

This paper analyzed three Colombian ecosystems:

Bahía Málaga is located on the Pacific Region of Colombia, between San Juan river and the Buenaventura's Bay, within the department of Valle del Cauca. It has an average temperature of 25 °C, an humidity of 88% and abundant rainfall. The National Natural Park Uramba Bahía Málaga is located within the Bay. It has a great diversity of animal species (frogs, lizards, snakes, corals, bony fish, among other).

Gorgona is located 35 km away from the Colombian Pacific Coast and it belongs to the municipality of Guapi which is part of the Cauca's department. It has a rainy weather with an average temperature of 28 °C and with a humidity of 90%. It has a National Natural Park, and a great variety of animal species (161 out of which 17 are endemic).

Chingaza is a National Natural Park located in the center of Colombia, in the eastern mountain range of the Andes between the departments of Cundinamarca and Meta. Its temperature oscillates between 4 and 22 °C and its climate is rainy. It has wetland ecosystems, forests and rain forests. It also has a variety of animal species (ducks, eagles, condors, spectacled bears, among others).

2.2   Acoustic Recordings

The recordings of the ecosystems were made in February and April because there is less rain during these months. Acoustic data were taken with an SM2 field recorder (SongMeter 2. Wildlife Acoustics, Inc., Massachusetts), which was programmed to record continuously from 00:00 to 23:59 h, with 5-minute intervals every 10 min. In total, 78 days (936 h) were recorded per ecosystem.

To reduce the amount of data, all days were analyzed to take an average day per week (a day with high acoustic activity and little noise), obtaining a total of 12 days (144 h).

(*Note: The Bahía Málaga ecosystem was recorded by researchers from Alexander Von Humboldt institute, an based on this ecosystem Gorgona and Chingaza ecosystem were recreated using two sets of atypical days where each one has its own behavior).

The recorder was placed in a central point of the ecosystem, on a tree at 1.5 m from the ground and away from vegetation to prevent interference. The SM2 recorder was configured with a sampling frequency of 44,100 Hz and with a resolution of 16 bits.

2.3   Processing of Acoustic Data

Each recording was normalized by its maximum amplitude value. For each minute of recording, a 512-point Fast-Fourier Transform (FFT) was applied on each time interval of 0.5 s, yielding a matrix with a total of 256 frequency bands in 120 time intervals.

The bioacoustic metric used was the Acoustic Complexity Index (ACI) because it correlates with the quantity and diversity of species within the ecosystems [4,5,9]. This index was applied to the S matrix that results from the FFT using (1), where d_f is the absolute value of the difference between two adjacent time instants in a single frequency band, namely $|S_{tf}|$ and $|S_{(t+1)f}|$.

$$d_f = \left| |S_{tf}| - |S_{(t+1)f}| \right| \tag{1}$$

Dimensions of S are $N \times M$, where N is the number of time intervals and M is the number of frequency bands. To get the index of each band, all d_f are summed and divided by the total sum $|S_f|$ according to (2).

$$ACI_f = \frac{\sum\limits_{t=1}^{N} d_f}{\sum\limits_{t=1}^{N} |S_{tf}|} \tag{2}$$

To get the value of the ACI_{total} index from the matrix, all indices from each frequency band are summed using (3).

$$ACI_{total} = \sum\limits_{f=1}^{M} ACI_f \tag{3}$$

For each recording, there are 5 values of ACI (1 per minute), which are then averaged to get a single value per recording. At the end of the day, this approach produces a signal with 144 values, representing the ACI index throughout the day. This signal is shown in Fig. 1.

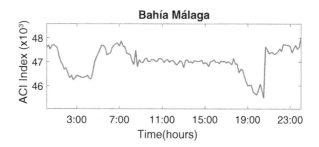

Fig. 1. ACI index of the Bahía Málaga ecosystem.

2.4   Artificial Neural Network

An Artificial Neural Network (ANN) was used to optimize the acoustic sampling in natural ecosystems, determining the time intervals or windows with strong changes in the acoustic richness on an average day. The architecture chosen for the ANN was a Multi-Layer Perceptron (MLP) based on its success in previous implementations.

2.5   Preprocessing

To reduce the ripples of the ACI signals before applying them to the ANN, a moving average window of length 5 was applied, and the results obtained are shown in Fig. 2.

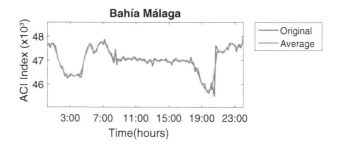

Fig. 2. Average of the ACI index in Bahía Málaga ecosystem.

The Matlab code used to implement the moving average was:

```
I=Indice ACI
for k=4:length(I)-4
    R(k)=mean(I(k-2:k+2))
end
```

Where R is the ACI signal without ripples.

2.6 Processing

An ANN was created with six neurons in the input layer, six neurons in the first hidden layer, six neurons in the second hidden layer, and six neurons in the output layer. Hidden layers were configured as fully connected, and the output had a sigmoid function. The network was created using the Matlab tool *"nnstart"*, and trained including Bayesian regularization.

Six continuous data points from the ACI signal are applied to the inputs for the neural network to analyze a one-hour window (each point represents 10 min). Each output neuron produces a 0 to avoid recording or a 1 to record.

2.7 Training

A total of 120 samples from Bahía Málaga were used to train the network. Data from Chingaza were used for validation and testing, and data from Gorgona were used to determine optimal sampling intervals to record in this ecosystem.

To train and validate the network, a manual labeling was required to indicate when the recorder should be OFF (0) or ON (1) both in Bahía Málaga and Chingaza. Intervals were labeled as 1 when data had differences with their neighbors (i.e.: when the index had a significant change in time), and 0 when data were similar to their neighbors (i.e.: when the index showed little variation in time) as shown in Fig. 3. There were 646 intervals marked with 0 and 794 intervals marked with 1.

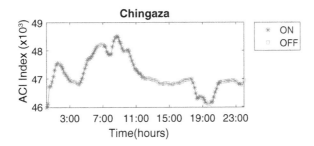

Fig. 3. Training data in Chingaza ecosystem.

2.8   Post-processing

The output of the ANN was a matrix of $6 \times n$ (where n is the number of recorded hours). Data within the matrix with values smaller than or equal to 0.5 were rounded to 0, while values above 0.5 were rounded to 1.

3   Results

The ANN was trained during 22 epochs or iterations. Its performance was evaluated using the Mean-Squared Error (MSE) shown in Table 1, where it can be observed that this value is relatively small when compared to the signal's values. The network can determine when the signal changes (i.e.: the ON state) and when it has the same value (i.e.: the OFF state) as shown in Fig. 4. The network reduced the number of samples from 144 to 79 (54.9%) in average.

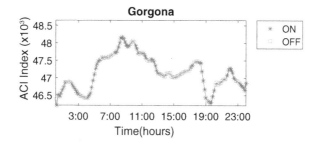

Fig. 4. Optimal sampling using the artificial neural network.

Table 1. Results of ANN training.

	Samples	MSE
Training	120	1.07×10^{-1}
Validation	60	1.28×10^{-1}
Test	60	1.17×10^{-1}

To create the sampling windows of the average days of Gorgona, recording intervals and their neighbors were concatenated, creating the length of each window. As minimum, each window could have 1 sample of length and in average about 6 or 10 samples, as shown in Table 2.

Averaging the recording instants of the five average days, the recording windows for the Gorgona ecosystem were determined. Resulting windows are shown in blue color in Fig. 5. These windows capture time intervals where the ACI index changes. Table 3 shows the initial and final time for each time window.

Table 2. Length of recording windows

	Number of windows	Window length		
		Maximum	Minimum	Average
Day 1	13	21	1	6
Day 2	8	24	1	10
Day 3	13	12	1	6
Day 4	14	12	1	6
Day 5	13	26	1	6

Table 3. Recording time for Gorgona

Windows		Windows	
Start	End	Start	End
01:00 am	01:20 am	12:10 am	13:00 am
02:10 am	03:00 am	01:10 pm	03:00 pm
04:10 am	05:20 am	05:10 pm	05:20 pm
06:10 am	06:20 am	06:10 pm	09:00 pm
07:30 am	08:40 am	09:40 pm	10:20 pm
11:00 am	11:30 am	11:10 pm	00:40 am

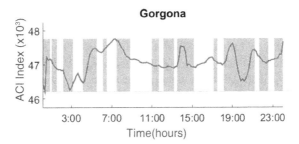

Fig. 5. Sampling windows for Gorgona ecosystem.

To analyze the information loss caused by the ANN, a signal without voids was reconstructed by using a zero-order-hold based on the data captured during the ON state, and it was compared to the original signal of an entire day. The result is shown in Fig. 6, producing a maximum absolute error of 0.12% while keeping a minimum correlation coefficient of 0.955 shown in Table 4.

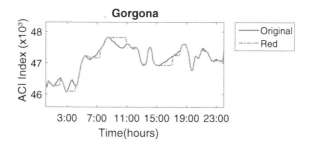

Fig. 6. Original signal vs. reconstructed signal from the artificial neural network.

Table 4. Absolute error and correlation coefficient of the neural network

Gorgona	Error (%)	Coefficient
Day 1	0.0993	0.9915
Day 2	0.1120	0.9551
Day 3	0.1051	0.9816
Day 4	0.0818	0.9917
Day 5	0.1221	0.9777

4   Conclusion

In this study, the acoustic sampling was optimized for three Colombian ecosystems: Gorgona, Chingaza, and Bahía Málaga. An artificial neural network was implemented to detect windows or intervals with strong changes in the acoustic activity. A Multi-Layer Perceptron was trained using Bayesian regularization. Obtained results indicate that the network provides windows with high detail, reducing recordings and causing little information loss. These windows do not have the same length and are not periodic, which allows them to adjust themselves to the acoustic characteristic of each ecosystem. The proposed method, can help researchers in sonorous landscapes to setup the automatic audio sampling of ecosystems. Future work will target other ways of reconstructing the acoustic signal to reduce even further the information loss.

5   Future Work

The intelligent sampling approach proposed from this study will be applied to a larger environmental monitoring project which aims to understand the ecosystem's bioacoustic behavior using the Internet of Things. The project will be hosted by the Center of Excellence and Appropriation on the Internet of Things (CEA-IoT) in Colombia, and it will be tested on the field using a sensor network based on mobile phones. A mobile application developed for this purpose

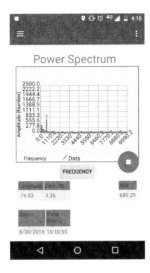

Fig. 7. Preliminary mobile application developed to collect and process audio from ecosystems.

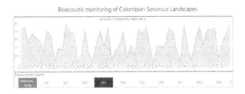

Fig. 8. Preliminary report to monitor the ecosystem's bioacoustic behavior using the Internet of Things.

will record audio of the ecosystem using the temporal intervals predicted by the neural network, compute the ACI index, extract the date and time (day, month, year, hour, minute, second), get the GPS position (latitude, longitude and altitude), and send resulting observations to the Cloud for storage and visualization. Authors have developed an early prototype of the mobile application that is shown in Fig. 7, which sends collected observations to Microsoft Azure for storage, and to a Power BI report that displays a time series of the ACI index from a Web browser. An image of the report developed so far is shown in Fig. 8.

Acknowledgment. Authors would like to acknowledge the cooperation of all partners within the Center of Excellence and Appropriation on the Internet of Things (*Centro de Excelencia y Apropiación en Internet de las Cosas, CEA-IoT*). Authors would also like to thank all institutions that supported this work: the Colombian Ministry for the Information and Communication Technologies (*Ministerio de Tecnologías de la Información y las Comunicaciones - MinTIC*), and the Colombian Administrative Department of Science, Technology and Innovation (*Departamento Administrativo de*

188 L. Quiroz et al.

Ciencia, Tecnología e Innovación - Colciencias) through the National Trust for Funding Science, Technology and Innovation Francisco José de Caldas (*Fondo Nacional de Financiamiento para la Ciencia, la Tecnología y la Innovación Francisco José de Caldas*), under project ID: FP44842-502-2015.

References

1. Farina, A.: Soundscape Ecology: Principles, Patterns, Methods and Applications. Springer Science & Business Media, New York (2013)
2. Van Parijs, S.M., Clark, C.W., Sousa-Lima, R.S., Parks, S.E., Rankin, S., Risch, D., van Opzeeland, I.: Management and research applications of real-time and archival passive acoustic sensors over varying temporal and spatial scales. Mar. Ecol. Prog. Ser. **395**, 21–36 (2009)
3. Aide, T.M., Corrada-Bravo, C., Campos-Cerqueira, M., Milan, C., Vega, G., Alvarez, R.: Real-time bioacoustics monitoring and automated species identification. PeerJ **1**, e103 (2013)
4. Farina, A., Pieretti, N., Morganti, N.: Acoustic patterns of an invasive species: the red-billed leiothrix (leiothrix lutea scopoli 1786) in a Mediterranean shrubland. Bioacoustics **22**(3), 175–194 (2013)
5. Farina, A., Pieretti, N.: Sonic environment and vegetation structure: a methodological approach for a soundscape analysis of a Mediterranean maqui. Ecol. Inform. **21**, 120–132 (2014)
6. Sueur, J., Pavoine, S., Hamerlynck, O., Duvail, S.: Rapid acoustic survey for biodiversity appraisal. PloS one **3**(12), e4065 (2008)
7. Joo, W., Gage, S.H., Kasten, E.P.: Analysis and interpretation of variability in soundscapes along an urban-rural gradient. Landscape Urban Plann. **103**(3), 259–276 (2011)
8. Pieretti, N., Duarte, M., Sous-Lima, R., Rodrigues, M., Young, R., Farina, A.: Determining temporal sampling schemes for passive acoustic studies in different tropical ecosystems. Trop. Conserv. Sci. **8**(1), 215–234 (2015)
9. Farina, A., Pieretti, N., Piccioli, L.: The soundscape methodology for long-term bird monitoring: a Mediterranean Europe case-study. Ecol. Inform. **6**(6), 354–363 (2011)

A Newton Raphson Based-Algorithm for Mitigation of Sags and Swells Using SVC and DSTATCOM on the IEEE 30-Bus System

Juan Camilo Caicedo Ulloa[✉], Jenny Elizabeth Roa Barragán, and Edwin Rivas Trujillo

Electrical Engineering Department, Faculty of Engineering, District University Francisco José de Caldas, Bogotá, Colombia {jccaicedou, jeroab}@correo.udistrital.edu.co, erivas@udistrital.edu.co

Abstract. This paper presents an analysis of the behavior of the IEEE 30-node distribution system in presence of short duration variations; specifically sags and swells are assessed before and after implementation of SVC (Static Var Compensator) and DSTATCOM (Distribution Static Compensator). The magnitude for sags and swells is selected according to what is specified in standard IEEE 1159: 2009 and NTC 5000: 2013. An algorithm is implemented in MATLAB to find the power flow solution based on the Newton-Raphson method, in which the SVC and DSTATCOM compensators are included. To validate the algorithm, a test for a 5-bus system, is conducted. In the IEEE 30-bus system, load values are changed in order to generate the sags and swells under analysis; the case study focuses on the behavior of node 10. The findings suggest that although the values of power delivered (or absorbed) by the SVC and DSTATCOM compensators for the same event are different, all nodes maintain voltage levels between 0.9 and 1.1 p.u.

Keywords: DSTATCOM · Newton-Raphson · Sag · Swell · SVC

1 Introduction

Electric power quality has driven significant attention within the field of electrical engineering due to the increase in energy demand as well as in the use of voltage waveform-degrading equipment (non-linear loads), which leads to phenomena such as sags (decrease or voltage dip), swells (voltage rises) and short duration voltage fluctuations.

According to standard IEEE 1159:2009 and NTC 5000:2013 [1, 2], the typical magnitude for sags, independent of their time span, is 0.1 to 0.9 p.u., where p.u. is the voltage value in a per-unit scale. However, the IEEE 30-bus system only allows dips down to 0.5, so the dynamic range for analysis is reduced to the interval 0.5–0.9. For Swells, this magnitude varies according to the time span, namely from 1.1 to 1.4 p.u. for time spans between 30 cycles to 3 s, and from 1.1 to 1.2 for time spans between larger than 3 s up to 1 min, the latter should be analyzed up to 1.3 p.u.

© Springer International Publishing AG 2017
J.C. Figueroa-García et al. (Eds.): WEA 2017, CCIS 742, pp. 189–200, 2017.
DOI: 10.1007/978-3-319-66963-2_18

For this analysis, the Newton-Raphson iterative method for solving the load flow is used and implemented in MATLAB. Therefore, only the magnitude values of sags and swells are considered.

In the last decade, authors like [3–6] have proposed the use of specific devices (e.g. FACTS - Flexible AC Transmission System) to reduce the impact of power quality problems. The main function of FACTS systems is to increase the capacity of control and power transfer in AC systems [7]. There is a variety of these controllers, classified according to the type of connection with the network and the type of compensation [8], namely compensators can be classified as: serial, parallel, series-series and series-parallel. However, some authors classify compensators according to their underlying power electronics technology [9]. A variant to the FACTS technology can be found in the application of these devices to distribution networks, also known as D-FACTS (Distributed Flexible AC-Transmission Systems). These systems are essentially improved versions of FACTS devices in terms of size and installation simplicity [10]. However, this article does not refer to construction or installation issues.

Table 1 provides a description and comparison of some compensators according to their type of connection with the network and their level of compensation, specifically: (✓) Low, (✓✓) Medium, (✓✓✓) High.

Table 1. Comparison of some compensators (Adapted [8])

Compensator	Connection	Load flow control	Voltage control	Transient stability	Dynamic stability
TCSC	Series	✓✓	✓	✓✓✓	✓✓
SSSC	Series	✓✓	✓	✓✓	✓✓
SVC	Parallel	✓	✓✓✓	✓	✓✓
DSTATCOM	Parallel	✓	✓✓✓	✓✓	✓✓
UPFC	Series-Parallel	✓✓✓	✓✓✓	✓✓	✓✓

As there is a variety of compensators, and also considering that for this study the objective is to evaluate system performance when compensators are included, the SVC, DSTATCOM and UPFC (Unified Power Flow Controller) compensators are the most suitable choice. However, in the literature, the application of UPFC has focused more on the transmission of power systems; for that reason the present study focuses only on the influence of SVC and DSTATCOM compensators (the latter being basically a STAT-COM but included in distribution systems, hence the addition of the letter "D") [11].

The SVC is a static reactive power compensator whose output is adjusted either to exchange capacitive/inductive current or to control specific parameters of the power system. In other words, the basic action of an SVC is to generate/absorb reactive power rapidly in response to a control signal. There are different models of the compensator for inclusion in power flows. Some existing models include variable shunt susceptance, angle firing and angle firing with integrated transformer [12]. For simplicity and ease of SVC inclusion in the study of load flow, the variable susceptance model has been selected. This model has also been selected by several authors [13, 14].

The DSTATCOM is a D-FACTS device, which performs network control by being parallel connected to one of the nodes. This compensator is similar to STATCOM; however, some differences can be observed in terms of construction and installation. In fact, the DSTATCOM is modeled like a STATCOM for its inclusion in power flows [11]. For inclusion of DSTATCOM in the load flow model, the power control mode and electrical model are considered [15, 16]. Among control modes, the following can be found: DSTATCOM-node voltage control, control of the absorbed power. In this study, the DSTATCOM-node voltage control has been selected.

Therefore, in this paper, a study of the behavior of a network is conducted by taking the IEEE system of 30 nodes as a case study when short duration voltage variations (sags and swells) occur. The behavior is analyzed before and after implementation of SVC and DSTATCOM.

2 Description IEEE 30-Bus System

The IEEE 30-bus system, is a representation of a small portion of the American electrical system (Midwestern United States). The data were provided in 1993 to become part of IEEE database [17].

This system has three generating units in the voltage levels of 132 kV; 2 synchronous capacitors in the voltage range of 11 kV; the remaining nodes are load nodes at 33 kV. The configuration parameters of the synchronous capacitors are equal to that of the generators; the main difference is that capacitors only inject reactive power to the system in order to control voltage levels. Figure 1 shows the system's diagram.

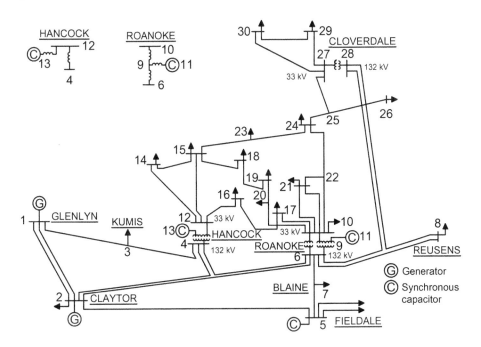

Fig. 1. IEEE 30-bus system [18]

3 MATLAB Algorithm

3.1 Power Flow: Newton-Raphson Method

The information for the analysis, mainly obtained from a study of power flows, corresponds to the magnitude and phase angle of the voltage on each bus (or node) and also to the active and reactive power flowing in each line. The power flow solution when applying the Newton-Raphson method was needed to use the implementation of an algorithm in MATLAB. This algorithm comprises the following steps:

(i) The initial data is recorded for voltage, angle, generated and demanded power, and the admittance matrix.

(ii) Known net-power values are calculated, corresponding to the difference between the generated power and the demanded power (Eqs. 1 and 2)

$$P_{Ni} = Pg - Pd \tag{1}$$

$$Q_{Ni} = Qg - Qd \tag{2}$$

(iii) Net powers are calculated by considering the Ybarra data (i.e. G: conductance and B: susceptance), the voltage and the angle of nodes (Eqs. 3 and 4).

$$P_{Ni(\text{Vk},\theta k)} = \sum_{k=1}^{n} V_i V_k (G_{ik} Cos(\theta_{ik}) + B_{ik} Sen(\theta_{ik})) \tag{3}$$

$$Q_{Ni(\text{Vk},\theta k)} = \sum_{k=1}^{n} V_i V_k (G_{ik} Sen(\theta_{ik}) + B_{ik} Cos(\theta_{ik})) \tag{4}$$

(iv) Power deltas are calculated; these deltas correspond to the difference between known net powers and calculated net powers.

(v) It is determined whether the error is less than specified. In this case, an error of $1e-5$ is specified. If the error is lower, the voltage and angle data obtained so far would correspond to the answer, otherwise the iterative process continues.

(vi) The functional matrix (i.e. J = Jacobian) is calculated. This matrix consists of sub-arrays H, N, J and L, which represent the power variations regarding voltages and angles.

(vii) Angle delta and voltage delta are calculated (i.e. $\Delta\theta$, ΔV). These delta values are obtained by multiplying the power-delta vector in (iv) by the inverse functional matrix (vi).

(viii) The new values of voltage and angle (for the next iteration) are calculated.

The algorithm, implemented in MATLAB, repeats this iterative process until the condition on the error is met.

3.2   Power Flow with DSTATCOM

The process for solving the power flow or load flow is similar to the process for solving the load flow without compensation. However, when including the DSTATCOM, a degree of complexity is added as two new conditions must be included; firstly, a condition relative to the active power, and secondly, another condition imposed by the control mode, which in this case corresponds to the voltage control. The inclusion of these two new conditions leads to having two new state variables, namely the DSTATCOM voltage and its angle (Vdstat and δ, respectively). These variables remain the same regardless of the control mode in which they work, as they are necessary to meet the reactive power injected by or absorbed from the DSTATCOM and so have an influence in the calculation of power flows.

In addition to this, also the dimensionality of the functional matrix increases. For every DSTATCOM, two columns (one for each state variable) are added as well as two rows (one for each condition). With the increase in the Jacobian matrix, not only do we have four subarrays (M, N, J, L), but also a total of 16 subarrays (H, N, J, L, A, B, C, D, E, F, G, I, K, M, O, P) are now obtained. The subarrays H, N, J, L, have small changes because not only the power lines are considered but also the conditions given by the compensator must be included.

Another difference derived from the inclusion of the compensator is that, apart from the initial data available for solving load flows, the data given by the compensator should also be considered (e.g. the reference voltage level (Vc), the angle (δ), and the conductance/susceptance values (Gdstat, Bdstat)). These values were assumed as they are simply unknown initial values. In this case the values assumed were: Vc = 1, δ = 0, Gdstat = 1, Bdstat = -10.

The process is similar to that described for the power flow without compensation; however, the following differences can be observed:

(i) After power calculation $(P_{Ni(Vk,\theta k)}, Q_{Ni(Vk,\theta k)})$ the values of ΔP and ΔQ are not calculated immediately; instead, a verification stage checks whether there is any compensator on that node, if so, a new value of power must be calculated with the DSTATCOM parameters, which are added to the calculated value (Eqs. 5 and 6).

$$
\begin{aligned}
P_{Ndst\,(Vdst,\delta dst)} = & V_k^2 G_{dstat} - V_k V_{dst}(G_{dst}Cos(\theta_k - \delta_{dst}) \\
& + B_{dst}Sen(\theta_k - \delta_{dst}))
\end{aligned}
\tag{5}
$$

$$
\begin{aligned}
Q_{Ndst(Vdst,\delta dst)} = & - V_k^2 B_{dst} - V_k V_{dst}(G_{dst}Sen(\theta_k - \delta_{dst}) \\
& - B_{dst}Cos(\theta_k - \delta_{dst}))
\end{aligned}
\tag{6}
$$

(ii) As there are two new conditions, the corresponding delta values (i.e. $\Delta P_{dstat}, \Delta V_c$) should be calculated.
(iii) The error not only considers ΔP, ΔQ values but also $\Delta P_{dstat}, \Delta V_c$ values.
(iv) Then the Jacobian matrix increases.
(v) Angle delta values as well as voltage delta values are calculated ($\Delta\theta$, ΔV) in addition to the values of $\Delta\delta$ and $\Delta Vdst$ to obtain new state variables.
(vi) New values of voltage and angle are calculated for the next iteration.

3.3   Power Flow with SVC

The process for finding the power flow solution including SVC is similar to the process for the power flow without compensation. However, when including the SVC as a shunt susceptance, the following differences must be considered:

(i) In addition to the initial values needed to solve the load flow without compensation, an initial value of Bsvc (susceptance shunt) should be assumed. In our case, a value of 0.001 was assumed (a value close to 0 assuming the network initially needed no compensation).

(ii) As in the DSTATCOM, after calculating the power values, the values of ΔP and ΔQ are not calculated immediately; instead, a verification stage should be implemented to verify whether there is a compensator at that node, if so, a new power value must be calculated with the parameters of the SVC, which is added to the previously calculated value (Eq. 7)

$$Q_{svc} = Q_k = -V_k^2 B_{svc} \tag{7}$$

(iii) If, when considering the value assumed for Bsvc, the error condition is not satisfied, a new value must be calculated. For such new calculation, the linearized version of the equation is used to calculate a value of ΔBsvc (Eq. 8)

$$\begin{bmatrix} \Delta P_{svc} \\ \Delta Q_{svc} \end{bmatrix}^{(k)} = \begin{bmatrix} 0 & 0 \\ 0 & Q_{svc} \end{bmatrix}^{(k)} \begin{bmatrix} \Delta \theta_k \\ \Delta B_{svc}/B_{svc} \end{bmatrix}^{(k)} \tag{8}$$

(iv) By using the value of ΔBsvc and the known value (which initially is 0.001), a new value can be calculated, which will be used in the next iteration (Eq. 9).

$$B_{svc}^{(k)} = B_{svc}^{(k-1)} + \left(\frac{\Delta B_{svc}}{B_{svc}} \right)^{(k)} B_{scr}^{(k-1)} \tag{9}$$

3.4   Validation Algorithm

To verify the functionality of the algorithm, a test for a network of 5 nodes was chosen [13]. Figure 2 depicts a situation in which the results for the load flows are known together with the value of the reactive power given by the SVC and DSTATCOM; also the resulting voltage levels on each node are shown after implementing these compensators in node 3 (i.e. "Lake").

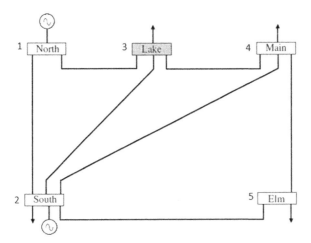

Fig. 2. Bus system [13]

The voltage and angle values given by the reference as well as the values obtained with the algorithm and the difference percentage (which was 0) are shown in Tables 2, 3 and 4.

Table 2. Validation algorithm. Power flow Newton-Raphson method

Node	Reference		Algorithm		Difference (%)	
	Voltage (p.u.)	Angle (Degrees)	Voltage (p.u.)	Angle (Degree)	Voltage (%)	Angle (%)
1	1,06	0,00	1,06	0,00	0,00	0,00
2	1,00	−2,06	1,00	−2,06	0,00	0,00
3	0,99	−4,64	0,99	−4,64	0,00	0,00
4	0,98	−4,96	0,98	−4,96	0,00	0,00
5	0,97	−5,77	0,97	−5,77	0,00	0,00

Table 3. Validation algorithm. Power flow with DSTATCOM

Node	Reference		Algorithm		Difference (%)	
	Voltage (p.u.)	Angle (Degrees)	Voltage (p.u.)	Angle (Degree)	Voltage (%)	Angle (%)
1	1,06	0,00	1,06	0,00	0,00	0,00
2	1,00	−2,05	1,00	−2,05	0,00	0,00
3	1,00	−4,83	1,00	−4,83	0,00	0,00
4	0,99	−5,11	0,99	−5,11	0,00	0,00
5	0,98	−5,80	0,98	−5,80	0,00	0,00

Table 4. Validation algorithm. Power flow with SVC

Node	Reference		Algorithm		Difference (%)	
	Voltage (p.u.)	Angle (Degrees)	Voltage (p.u.)	Angle (Degree)	Voltage (%)	Angle (%)
1	1,06	0,00	1,06	0,00	0,00	0,00
2	1,00	−2,05	1,00	−2,05	0,00	0,00
3	1,00	−4,83	1,00	−4,83	0,00	0,00
4	0,99	−5,11	0,99	−5,11	0,00	0,00
5	0,98	−5,80	0,98	−5,80	0,00	0,00

For power values, a difference of 2.98% was obtained. This difference is equivalent to 0.61 MVAR for the SVC, as shown in Table 5. This is due to the way the susceptance value is calculated from one algorithm to the other. In the reference algorithm, the Jacobian is affected, whereas the implemented algorithm requires no change in the Jacobian; instead, conditions (ranges) of the node voltages that should be compensated are established. The values of SVC are calculated according to such conditions.

Table 5. % Powers difference between reference and algorithm

	Reference	Algorithm	Difference (%)
Compensator	MVAR	MVAR	%
SVC	2,50	19,89	2,98
DSTATCOM	2,50	20,50	0,00

Based on these results, which were compared to reference data, and also understanding the causes of the observed difference in the values of SVC power, the implemented algorithm can be considered as valid.

4   Case Study Results

4.1   Load to Generate Sags or Swells

The values of Qd (to generate a sag) or Qg (to generate a swell) are modified on the node where the event is due to occur. Tables 6 and 7 indicate the required load values that were added to the existing load on node 10. The purpose of these modifications is to generate the sags and swells. That is, the values specified here do not include the load value that is already on the system.

Table 6. Load to generate sags in the algorithm on node 10

Magnitude Sag (p.u.)	Load (MVAR)	Sag (p.u.)
0,5	203	0,5454
0,6	195	0,6031
0,7	168	0,7037
0,8	123	0,8039
0,9	68	0,8924

Table 7. Load to generate swells in the algorithm on node 10

Magnitude Swell (p.u.)	Load (MVAR)	Swell (p.u.)
1,1	100	1,1015
1,2	200	1,2066
1,3	330	1,3078

4.2   Powers Delivered or Absorbed by the Compensators

The values of power delivered (to mitigate sags) or absorbed (to mitigate swell), as obtained with the algorithm for SVC and DSTATCOM are shown in Tables 8 and 9.

Table 8. Power delivered by SVC and DSTATCOM to mitigate sags on node 10

Magnitude Sag (p.u.)	Qdstatcom (MVAR)	Qsvc (MVAR)
0,5	211,32	201,46
0,6	203,40	190,36
0,7	175,99	162,77
0,8	130,66	121,80
0,9	75,39	60,25

Table 9. Power absorbed by SVC and DSTATCOM to mitigate swells on node 10

Magnitude Swell (p.u.)	Qdstatcom (MVAR)	Qsvc (MVAR)	Qdstatcom (MVAR)	Qsvc (MVAR)
1,1	92,54	101,90	92,76	122,28
1,2	191,86	202,79	220,77	253,32
1,3	320,25	333,40	391,06	425,35

4.3   Graphics

Figures 3 and 4 show the results of the sags and swells generated at node 10. Figures 5 and 6 show the results obtained with compensation when using DSTATCOM. Figures 7 and 8 show the results obtained with SVC.

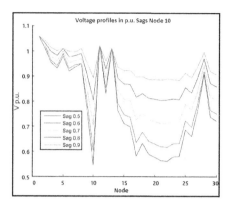

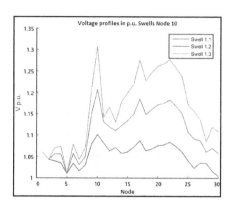

Fig. 3. Sags. Magnitude 0.5 to 0.9 p.u.

Fig. 4. Swells. Magnitude 1.1 to 1.3 p.u.

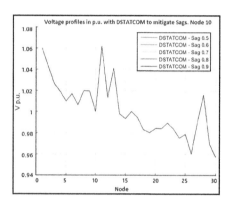

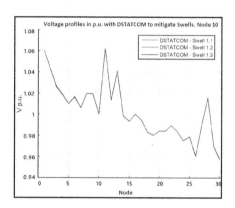

Fig. 5. DSTATCOM. Sags mitigation. Magnitude 0.5 to 0.9 p.u.

Fig. 6. DSTATCOM. Swell mitigation. Magnitude 1.1 to 1.3 p.u.

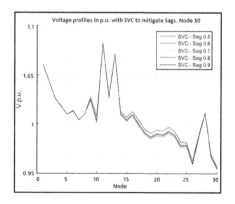

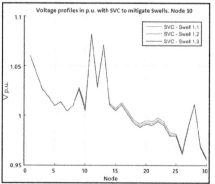

Fig. 7. SVC. Sags mitigation. Magnitude 0.5 to 0.9 p.u.

Fig. 8. SVC. Swell mitigation. Magnitude 1.1 to 1.3 p.u.

5 Analysis

When a sag or swell occurs in the bus system, for most nodes the voltage values are below 0.9 in the presence of a sag, or higher than 1.1 p.u. in the presence of a swell. These voltage variations tend to propagate more upstream than downstream with respect to the selected nodes.

With the graphs obtained, it can be seen that, for a sag of equal magnitude or a swell of equal magnitude (analyzed at the two nodes) the most significant impact to the system occurs when any of these variations is presented at node 10.

The values of power delivered or absorbed by compensating for the same event are different. However, when including these compensators, all the nodes within the network exhibit voltage levels between 0.9 and 1.1 p.u.

6 Conclusions

When a decrease or a rise in voltage on the network occurs, the event not only affects a single node (where the event actually occurs) but most nodes are affected. However, the SVC and DSTATCOM compensators help mitigate these problems. Additionally, although the powers that deliver or absorb the two compensators are different for the same event, both the SVC and the DSTATCOM meet the goal of leveling out or maintaining voltage levels between 0.9 and 1.1 p.u.

The use of D-FACTS devices could be an effective option provides an opportunity to improve an optimized the operation condition of power system by alleviating the distribution grids power quality problems. Thus, with the algorithm allows a sizing of the Value of the power delivered or absorbed by the SVC and DSTATCOM compensators, to mitigate short duration variations (Sags, Swells), keeping the voltage profiles within an acceptable range.

References

1. Institute of Electrical and Electronics Engineers: IEEE recommended practice for monitoring electric power quality. Institute of Electrical and Electronics Engineers (2009)
2. NORMA TÉCNICA NTC COLOMBIANA 5000 (2013)
3. Kazemtabrizi, B., Acha, E.: An advanced STATCOM model for optimal power flows using Newton's method. IEEE Trans. Power Syst. **29**, 514–525 (2014). doi:10.1109/TPWRS.2013.2287914
4. Goswami, A.K., Gupta, C.P., Singh, G.K.: Minimization of voltage sag induced financial losses in distribution systems using FACTS devices. Electr. Power Syst. Res. **81**, 767–774 (2011). doi:10.1016/j.epsr.2010.11.003
5. Jyotishi, P., Deeparamchandani, P.: Mitigate voltage sag/swell condition and power quality improvement in distribution line using D-STATCOM. J. Eng. Res. Appl. www.ijera.com
6. Ananth, D.V.N., Nagesh Kumar, G.V.: Mitigation of voltage dip and power system oscillations damping using dual STATCOM for grid connected DFIG. Ain Shams Eng. J. (2015). doi:10.1016/j.asej.2015.12.002
7. Rashid, M.H.: Power Electronics Circuits, Devices, and Applications, Mexico (2004)

8. Varma, S.: FACTS devices for stability enhancements. In: 2015 International Conference on Green Computing and Internet of Things (ICGCIoT), pp. 69–74. IEEE (2015)
9. Johnson, B.K.: Applications of FACTS (2011)
10. Santander-Hernandez, L.J., Angeles-Camacho, C.: Implementation of distributed compensation in the transmission lines design (D-FACTS). In: 2015 IEEE Thirty Fifth Central American and Panama Convention (CONCAPAN 2015), pp. 1–4. IEEE (2015)
11. Mehrdad, E.N., Hagh, T., Zare, K.: Determination of the performance of the distribution static compensator (D-STATCOM) in distribution network (2013)
12. Acha, E.: FACTS: Modelling and Simulation in Power Networks. Wiley, Chichester (2004)
13. Rao, B.V., Kumar, G.V.N.: Sensitivity analysis based optimal location and tuning of static VAR compensator using firefly algorithm. Indian J. Sci. Technol. 7, 1201–1210 (2014)
14. Debnath, A., Rualkima Rante, J.: Stability enhancement with SVC. Int. J. Comput. Appl. 72, (2013). 0975-8887
15. Adepoju, G.A., Komolafe, O.A.: Analysis and modelling of static synchronous compensator (STATCOM): a comparison of power injection and current injection models in power flow study. Int. J. Adv. Sci. Technol. 36 (2011)
16. Flexible AC Transmission Systems: Modelling and Control
17. Christie, R.: Power systems test case archive, 30 bus power flow test case. https://www2.ee.washington.edu/research/pstca/pf30/pg_tca30bus.htm
18. Power Systems Test Cases: IEEE 30 Bus Test Systems: Prof. F. Gonzalez-Longatt. http://www.fglongatt.org/Test_Systems/IEEE_30bus.html

A Wavelet-Based OFDM System Implemetation on GNURadio Platform vs. an FFT-Based

Sebastian Villalobos[1(✉)], Fabian Aldana[1], Ivan Ladino[2], and Ivan Diaz[3]

[1] Universidad Distrital Francisco Jos de Caldas, Bogota, D.C., Colombia
{svillalobosb,faaldanah}@correo.udistrital.edu.co
[2] Universidad Los Libertadores, Bogota, D.C., Colombia
idladinov@libertadores.edu.co
[3] Universidad El Bosque, Bogota, D.C., Colombia
iediaz@unbosque.edu.co

Abstract. This paper deals with the implementation of an OFDM system which uses wavelets as the carriers through the Discrete Wavelet Transform. It analyzes performance in terms of the Bit Error Rate (BER) for different values of signal-to-noise ratio in an Additive White Gaussian Noise (AWGN) wireless transmission environment. Additionally, it simulates the BER response for different bandwidths in the wavelet-based system, in order to reduce it, lessening it's BER performance until it equals the FFT-based, thus we achieved an improvement in spectral effieciency. To ensure the same testing conditions, both systems were implemented using the open source GnuRadio Software-Defined Radio (SDR) platform.

Keywords: Bandwidth · DWT · FFT · GNU Radio · Modulation · OFDM · SDR · Spectral · Efficiency · USRP

1 Introduction

An OFDM modulation system, simultaneously transmits parallel data through multiple carriers at different frequency ranges [1,2]. A conventional OFDM system uses Fourier complex exponentials as carriers. This is implemented through the FFT and IFFT [3]. In general, any set of functions that conform an orthonormal basis for a signal space can be used as the set of carriers [4]. Wavelet functions fulfill this property [5,6], hence they have been used for OFDM through the use of the Discrete wavelet Transform (DWT) [7]. A Wavelet OFDM system, transmits symbols in different wavelet spectra, which are stretched versions of a single spectrum determined by the used wavelet [8,9].

In this paper, we will first compare response for FFT and DWT modulation, using one refinement scale, 1024-FFT size and QAM-16, then, compare response for FFT and DWT modulation, using one refinement scale, 1024-FFT size and PSK-16. The comparison is again made with 2048-FFT for QAM-16 and PSK-16. In Sects. 2 through 4 we describe the foundations of these type of modulations. The implementation and results are shown in Sects. 5 and 6.

© Springer International Publishing AG 2017
J.C. Figueroa-García et al. (Eds.): WEA 2017, CCIS 742, pp. 201–211, 2017.
DOI: 10.1007/978-3-319-66963-2_19

2   Fourier-Based OFDM

In Fourier-based modulation, a set of N M-ary constellation data $X_m \mid 0 \leq m \leq N - 1$ is sent over N complex exponentials [4,10]. This is made by performing the IFFT on a vector of the data set X_m. The modulated output is the signal:

$$x_k = \sum_{n=0}^{N-1} X_n e^{j\frac{2\pi}{N}nk} \tag{1}$$

Where $\{x_k \mid 0 \leq k \leq N - 1\}$ is a signal in the discrete time domain, since X_m is assumed to be in the discrete frequency domain [11,12]. A cyclic prefix (CP) is added to minimize inter-symbol interference, and the discrete time signal is converted into an analog signal for transmission [13]. The reception side discretizes the signal, eliminates the CP and performs the FFT, to recover X_m as:

$$X_m = \sum_{k=0}^{N-1} x_k e^{-j\frac{2\pi}{N}km} \tag{2}$$

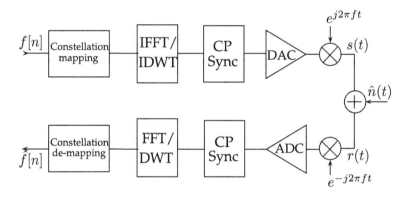

Fig. 1. OFDM transceiver

3   Wavelet-Based OFDM

Wavelet modulation [14,15] consists of multiplying the spectrum of constellation - modulated data by the spectrum of wavelet function $\psi_{j,0}.[n]$ [16,17]. Multi-scale wavelet modulation scheme is shown in Fig. 2. The incoming symbols are demultiplexed into N frames $c_{j,k}$ to be modulated by N scaled spectra $\{\tilde{\psi}(2^j\omega) \mid 0 \leq j \leq N - 1\}$, passing through successive processes of upsampling and circular convolution defined by the DWT [18,19]. The resulting spectrum for a scale j which multiplies the data spectrum $C_j(\omega)$ is given by:

$$\tilde{\psi}^j(\omega) = \tilde{G}(2^{N-j}\omega) \cdot \prod_{l=0}^{N-(j+1)} \tilde{H}(2^l\omega) \tag{3}$$

This function approximates the spectrum of the wavelet [20,21]. The data modulated in lower scales passes through more filtering stages which results in a better approximation for the function [22,23]. Data in the last modulating stage only goes through the high-pass filter H, which means at least one additional stage with a low-pass filter G is required in order to have $\tilde{\psi}^j$ at its worst

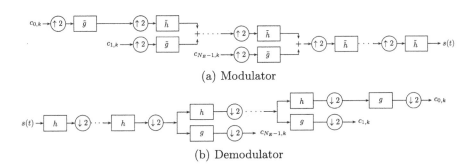

(a) Modulator

(b) Demodulator

Fig. 2. Wavelet-based OFDM

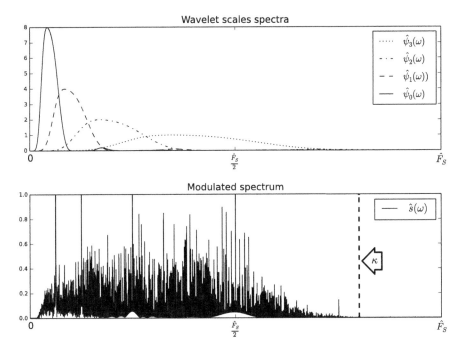

Fig. 3. Wavelet spectrum.

approximation. More stages like this can be added for refinement of the spectrum which means to introduce more samples per symbol [24,25]. The spectrum of the modulated signal is:

$$\hat{s}(\omega) = \sum_{j=0}^{N-1} \tilde{G}(2^{N-j}\omega) \prod_{l=0}^{N-j-1} \tilde{H}(2^l\omega)(\sum_{k=1}^{2^j} c_{j,k} \cdot e^{-i2^{N-j+1}\omega k}) \tag{4}$$

Figure 3 shows the wavelets spectrum and the modulated spectrum. The first filter H after the modulation stages limits the bandwidth to be $\frac{F_S}{2}$, where F_S is the sampling frequency. If this filter is not added, the bandwidth will be F_S, and there will be interference with the adjacent spectral period due to undersampling [26]. Any refinement stage, duplicates the samples of the signal and as a consequence, compresses the bandwidth to a half of the previous one. In general, after R refinement scales the bandwidth will be $\frac{F_S}{2^R}$. Demodulation is made through the inverse process IDWT, consisting of successive circular convolutions with complementary filters and downsamplings [27].

4   Spectral Efficiency

To estimate the spectral efficiency, the transmission symbol rate R_S and the used band width BW_{used} are required [28]. The wavelet-based modulation produces at least two samples per symbol for one refinement scale, whereas Fourier-based modulation can use one sample per symbol. To analyse them under the same conditions, it has been defined a normalized frequency $\hat{F}_S$ as $\hat{F}_S = \frac{F_S}{2^R}$. This represents the bandwidth for 2^R samples per symbol. In the Fourier case, it will be equivalent to modulating $\hat{N} = \frac{N}{2^R}$ symbols in an IFFT N-size [29].

4.1   Fourier-Based OFDM

In Fourier-based modulation, an N-size IFFT is applied to a vector of $\frac{N}{2^R}$ symbols which are transmitted in a time NT_S.

$$R_S = \frac{N}{2^R}\frac{1}{NT_S} = \frac{1}{\hat{T}_S} \tag{5}$$

The IFFT generates $\hat{N}$ complex exponential carrier with frequencies ranging from $-\frac{\hat{F}_S}{2}$ to $\frac{\hat{F}_S}{2}$ given by $\{\frac{n}{NT_S} \mid -\frac{\hat{N}}{2} \leq n \leq \frac{\hat{N}}{2}\}$ [30]. These are multiplied by a square window of size $\hat{N}T_S$. The spectrum corresponds to $\hat{N}$ sinc functions center at the different carrier frequencies so the useful bandwidth will be $\hat{F}_S + \frac{2}{\hat{N}T_S}$ including the two halves of the main lobes for the most lateral sync functions. The spectral efficiency η [12] is given by:

$$\eta = \frac{R_S}{BW_{util}} = \frac{1}{\hat{T}_S}\frac{1}{\hat{F}_S(1 + \frac{2}{\hat{N}})} \tag{6}$$

4.2   Wavelet-Based OFDM

For the wavelet-based system, every scale j carries 2^j symbols. Therefore for N_S scales, the number of symbols sent in a WOFDM frame is $2^{N_S} - 1$ [31]. The duration of the WOFDM symbol is the duration of the lowest scale symbol $T_S 2^{N_S + R} = \hat{T}_S 2^{N_S}$. Then, the bandwidth used may be expressed as a fraction κ of the total bandwidth [24], as shown in Eq. 7.

$$BW_{used} = \kappa \hat{F}_S \qquad (7)$$

The spectral efficiency in symbols per unit of frequency is given by:

$$\eta = \frac{R_S}{BW_{used}} = \frac{2^N - 1}{\hat{T}_S 2^{N_S}} \frac{1}{\kappa \hat{F}_S} = \frac{1}{\kappa} \frac{2^{N_S} - 1}{2^{N_S}} \qquad (8)$$

As N_S becomes large enough, the efficiency depends only on the fraction of the used bandwidth. Wavelet spectrum has a fast and flat decay, therefore it is not the necessary the disposal of $\hat{F}_S$ for sending most of the spectral information of a set of symbols. Figure 3 shows how κ can be set to narrow down the bandwidth to the useful bandwidth [32].

Figure 4 shows DWT and FFT spectra for the same sampling conditions, FFT consumes $\hat{F}_S$ in modulated frequency whereas the DWT consumes $2\hat{F}_S$ [31]. However, DWT spectrum is symmetrical since the filter coefficients are real, therefore

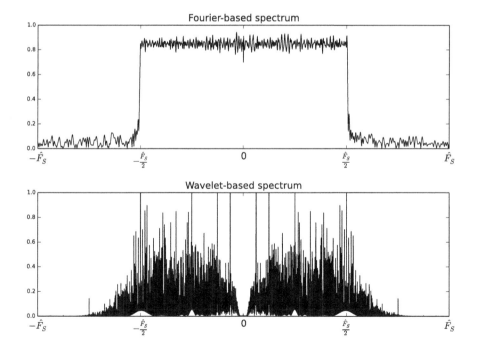

Fig. 4. Fourier-based and wavelet-based spectra.

it can be used in single-sideband having the same bandwidth as the FFT, which is not symmetrical. DWT spectrum has a fast decay, so the spectrum does not occupy the whole bandwidth $\hat{F}_S$, unlike FFT, and it can be narrowed down by κ.

5   Implementation

Implementation was made on GNU Radio Companion (GRC) [33,34]. The blocks for the Fourier system are by default in GNU Radio [35], whereas the modulator and demodulator for the wavelet-based system were developed [36].

5.1   Fourier-Based OFDM

The basis of the OFDM transceiver has been implemented using blocks of GNU Radio Companion according to the system in Fig. 1. We also implemented a synchronization block that uses Barker sequences for frame detection.

5.2   Wavelet-Based OFDM

The modulator and demodulator are implemented with GNU Radio blocks for GNU Radio Companion. The blocks are c++ classes implementing a method `general_work` [37] where all actual signal processing is done. Each block has five input parameters:

- `mod_scales`: Modulation scales (N)
- `ref_scales`: Refinement scales (R)
- `lor_taps/lod_taps`: Low-pass reconstruction/decomposition filter taps ($\hat{h}/h$)
- `hir_taps/hid_taps`: High-pass reconstruction/decomposition filter taps ($\hat{g}/g$)
- `gain`: Gain of the block (G)

The modulator block performs the reconstruction process shown in Fig. 2(a). Figure 5 shows the basic functionality of the block. To store the output of the filter at each stage an internal variable was created (`scale_output` (S)).

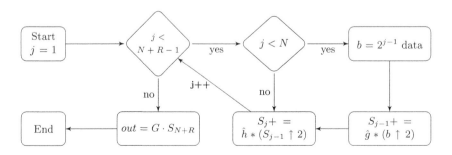

Fig. 5. IDWT.

The demodulator block performs the decomposition process of Fig. 2(b). Figure 6 shows the process. In this case `scale_output[L/H]` (S^L/S^H) has two subdivisions to store two outputs at each stage. After the convolution at each stage the output vector gets rotated $\frac{L_F}{2}$, where L_F is the number of taps; that rotation must be reversed before the next stage.

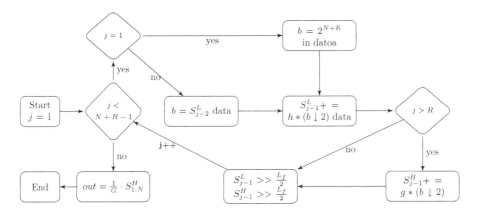

Fig. 6. DWT.

6   Bandwidth vs. BER

Random frames of 511-symbol were transmitted for the DWT and FFT systems mapped in 16-QAM and 16-PSK constellation. The Daubechies (Db8) wavelets [38] were used with 9 modulation scales, along with one and two refinement scales in order to have two and four samples per symbol. Equivalently used 1024 and 2048 FFT. The bandwidth was narrowed by a GNU Radio low-pass filter with cutoff frequency $\kappa \hat{F}_S$ and transition width $0.01\hat{F}_S$ and a hamming window.

Figures 7, 8, 9 and 10 show the Bit Error Rate to the Signal to Noise Ratio for different bandwidths. The Fourier-Based system presented, in fact, a better response in all cases than the wavelet-based. However, for a SNR sufficiently large it differs by less than 1% from the wavelet-based, making their responses practically equal.

Accordingly, the FFT presented a better response to noise than the DWT, however, in terms of bandwidth the DWT showed an improvement between 30% and 40% ($k = 0.7$, $k = 0.6$), representing a spectral efficiency gain of up to 43%. It is convenient to clarify than in FFT-based modulation it can not be reduced the bandwidth because the symbols are evenly distributed.

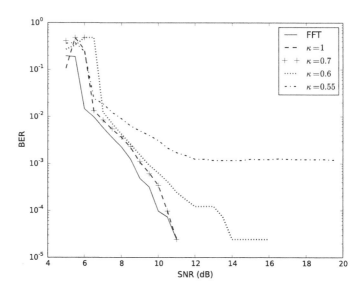

Fig. 7. BER-SNR-Bandwidth response for FFT and DWT modulation, using one refinement scale, 1024-FFT size and QAM-16.

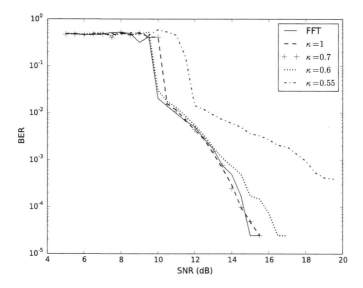

Fig. 8. BER-SNR-Bandwidth response for FFT and DWT modulation, using one refinement scale, 1024-FFT size and PSK-16.

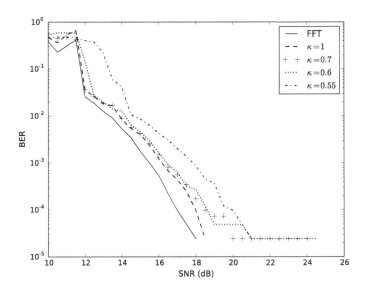

Fig. 9. BER-SNR-Bandwidth response for FFT and DWT modulation, using two refinement scales, 2048-FFT size and QAM-16.

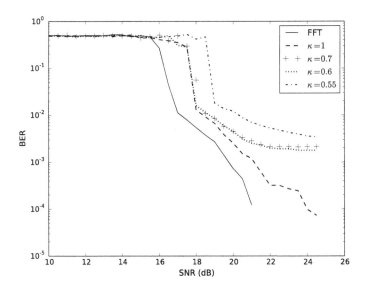

Fig. 10. BER-SNR-Bandwidth response for FFT and DWT modulation, using two refinement scales, 2048-FFT size and PSK-16.

7   Conclusion

We developed an OFDM System using the DWT as an alternative approach, managing to transmit bit frames successfully with a near zero Bit Error Rate. We observed that the FFT responds to noise practically equally than the DWT method under the same sample-per-symbol rate and bandwidth conditions, however, when used in single side band, the DWT allows a significant reduction in bandwidth without affecting the noise response. The information of symbols transmitted in one scale is distributed throughout the whole spectrum, producing a natural interleaving, and thus, more robustness against information loss; in contrast, for the FFT method, each symbol's spectral information is contained mainly in the piece of the spectrum assigned to each carrier. The most important feature in the wavelet spectrum is its fast decay, which causes nearly all of the information to be encompassed by the first lobe, whereas the FFT spectrum produces many lobes with a smaller decay rate; this is also important for implementation cost, since DWT spectrum will require lower order filtering. FFT implementation turns out to be more suitable for noisy environments, specially using a larger than one sample-per-symbol rate. DWT will force the use of more than one sample per symbol and is better for applications in channels with bandwidth limitations.

References

1. Intini, A.: Standard IEEE 802.1 (2000)
2. Sisul, G., Modlic, B., Kos, T.: 2005 Asia-Pacific Conference on Communications, pp. 720–724. IEEE, Western Australia (2005)
3. Corredor, O.F., Pedraza, L.F., Hernandez, C.A.: Visión Electrónica: algo más que un estado sólido 2(2), 86 (2011)
4. Proakis, J., Salehi, M.: Digital Communications, 5th edn. McGraw Hill, New York (2007)
5. Chun-Lin, L.: NTUEE. Taiwan 0(12) (2010)
6. Noelia, R.P.: Introducción a la teoría de wavelets. Master's thesis, Universitat de Barcelona (2005)
7. Gautier, M., Arndt, M., Lienard, J.: The Third Advanced International Conference on Telecommunications, AICT 2007, p. 19. IEEE (2007). doi:10.1109/AICT.2007. 21
8. Jiménez, M.D., Vidal, G.S.: La transformada wavelet: Una introducción. Master's thesis, Universidad Politécnica de Madrid E. T. S. de Ingenieros Industriales (2005)
9. Mallat, S.: A Wavelet Tour of Signal Processing, 3rd edn. Academic Press, London (2008)
10. Couch, L.W.: Sistemas de comunicación digitales y analógicos. Pearson Educación (2008)
11. Chide, N., Deshmukh, S., Borole, P.: Implementation of OFDM system using IFFT and FFT. Int. J. Eng. Res. Appl. 2009–2014 (2003)
12. Abdullah, K., Hussain, Z.M.: Australasian Telecommunication Networks and Applications Conference, ATNAC 2007, pp. 475–479. IEEE (2007)

13. Ghaith, A., Hatoum, R., Mrad, H., Alaeddine, A.: 2013 Third International Conference on Communications and Information Technology (ICCIT), pp. 225–229. IEEE (2013). doi:10.1109/ICCITechnology.2013.6579554
14. Guo, H., Burrus, C.S.: SPIE's 1996 International Symposium on Optical Science, Engineering, and Instrumentation, pp. 250–259. International Society for Optics and Photonics (1996)
15. Lankshmanan, M.K.: Reconfigurable and adaptive wireless communication systems based on wavelet packet modulators. Master's thesis, Technische Universiteit Delft (2011)
16. Mallat, S.: IEEE Trans. Pattern Anal. Mach. Intell. **11**(7), 674 (1989)
17. Sweldens, W., Schröder, P.: Building Your Own Wavelets at Home. Springer, Heidelberg (2000)
18. Jamin, A., Mähönen, P.: Wireless Commun. Mob. Comput. **5**(2), 123 (2005)
19. Daubechies, I., Heil, C.: Comput. Phys. **6**(6), 697 (1992)
20. Manglani, M.J.: Wavelet modulation in Gaussian and Rayleigh fading channels. Master's thesis, Virginia Polytechnic Institute and State University (2001)
21. Romero, H.A.R., Viáfara, J.M.R.: Avances en Sistemas e Informática **7**(1), 109 (2010)
22. Sweldens, W.: SIAM J. Math. Anal. **29**(2), 511 (1998)
23. Resnikoff, H.L., Raymond Jr., O., et al.: Wavelet Analysis: The Scalable Structure of Information. Springer Science & Business Media (2012)
24. Negash, B., Nikookar, H.: IEEE VTS 53rd Vehicular Technology Conference, VTC 2001, vol. 1, pp. 688–691. IEEE (2001)
25. Daubechies, I., Sweldens, W.: J. Fourier Anal. Appl. **4**(3), 247 (1998)
26. Manasra, G., Najajri, O., Arram, H.A., Rabah, S.: 2013 Palestinian International Conference on Information and Communication Technology (PICICT), pp. 77–82. IEEE (2013)
27. Van Bouwel, C., Potemans, J., Schepers, S., Nauwelaers, B., Van de Capelle, A.: Symposium on Communications and Vehicular Technology, SCVT 2000, pp. 131–138 (2000)
28. Ghaith, A., Hatoum, R., Mrad, H., Alaeddine, A.: 2013 Third International Conference on Communications and Information Technology (ICCIT), pp. 225–229 (2013). doi:10.1109/ICCITechnology.2013.6579554
29. He, Q., Schmitz, C., Schmeink, A.: Proceedings of the Tenth International Symposium on Wireless Communication Systems (ISWCS 2013), pp. 1–5. VDE (2013)
30. Nguyen, D.T.: Implementation of OFDM systems using GNU radio and USRP. Master's thesis, University of Wollongong (2013)
31. Asif, R., Abd-Alhameed, R.A., Oanoh, O., Dama, Y., Migdadi, H., Noars, J., Hussaini, A.S., Rodriguez, J.: 2012 International Conference on Telecommunications and Multimedia (TEMU), pp. 175–179. IEEE (2012)
32. Nerma, M.H., Kamel, N.S., Jeoti, V.: Sig. Process. Int. J. (2009)
33. GNU Radio: The free and open software radio ecosystem. http://gnuradio.org/redmine/projects/gnuradio/wiki
34. Reis, A.L.G., Barros, A.F., Lenzi, K.G., Meloni, L.G.P., Barbin, S.E.: IEEE Latin Am. Trans. **10**(1), 1156 (2012)
35. Bhat, N.S.: Int. J. Appl. Inf. Syst. **2**(7) (2012)
36. Gupta, D., Vats, V.B., Garg, K.K.: The Fourth International Conference on Wireless and Mobile Communications, ICWMC 2008, pp. 214–216. IEEE (2008)
37. Shane, D.: GNU radio tutorials: writing a signal processing block for GNU radio (2005)
38. Daubechies, I.: Commun. Pure Appl. Math. **41**(7), 909 (1988)

Particle Swarm Optimization Applied to the Economic Dispatch in a Power System with Distributed Generation, Study Case: IEEE 14 Nodes System

Juan David Gómez[(✉)], Luis Felipe Gaitan, and Edwin Rivas Trujillo

Universidad Distrital Francisco José de Caldas, Bogotá, Colombia
{juan.d.g,luis.f.g,erivas}@ieee.org

Abstract. This article presents an application of the Particle Swarm Optimization (PSO) on the optimization of the power flow in an IEEE system with 14 nodes, which has some nodes with distributed generation. In first place, the mathematical model used for the optimization of the electricity generation costs is defined. Afterwards, this model is applied in a study case with the IEEE system with 14 nodes and distributed generation.

Keywords: Optimal power flow · Particle Swarm Optimization · Distributed generation

1 Introduction

Optimal Power Flow (OPF) is one of the most dealt-with problems in the analysis of power systems. In 1962, Carpentier [1] introduces the power flow equations on the formulation of the Economic Dispatch (ED) [2]. There are different methods of optimization to solve the economic dispatch of the generation units of a power system. The methods based on artificial intelligence techniques have the advantage of considering various restrictions while finding multiple solutions for the optimization problem by performing a simulation and, hence finding the global optimum [3].

2 Particle Swarm Optimization

According to [4, 5], Particle Swarm Optimization (PSO) was developed by James Kennedy and Russell Eberhart in 1995 where the concept of non-linear function optimization is introduced with the purpose of understanding social behaviors. In 1998, Russel and Shi modify the optimization process by adding the inertia weight that balances the global and local search of the particles. If the inertia value is under 0.8, the local minimum can be found fast but it may not be the best solution because it has a reduced search area; if the value is over 1.2, it resembles a global search method that tries to explore new areas to find the global optimum, although it requires more iterations to finish the process. If the inertia value lies between 0.8 and 1.2, it has a higher probability to find a global optimum at an intermediate iteration cost [6].

© Springer International Publishing AG 2017
J.C. Figueroa-García et al. (Eds.): WEA 2017, CCIS 742, pp. 212–222, 2017.
DOI: 10.1007/978-3-319-66963-2_20

The main goal of this work is to perform the optimization of the cost of the combustible in a 14-node IEEE system with distributed generation subject to voltage and power restrictions in each one of the nodes using PSO.

According to [2], the equations and restrictions that must be satisfied to develop the problem are:

Total combustible cost function:

$$f(P_G) = \sum_{i=1}^{N_g} f_i(P_{Gi}) \tag{1}$$

Active power with the quadratic cost function:

$$f_i(P_{Gi}) = a_i P_{Gi}^2 + b_i P_{Gi} + c_i \tag{2}$$

Where $f(P_G)$ is the total production cost in \$/hour

$f_i(P_{Gi})$ is the i-th combustible unit cost function in \$/hour
$a_i b_i c_i$ are the cost coefficients of the i-th combustible unit
P_{Gi} is the real power delivered to the i-th unit in MW.

The quadratic cost function has three coefficients, a, b and c where a represents all the costs in terms of efficiency, b represents the costs that are proportional to the generated power and c represents the costs that are present even when there is no generation.

The restrictions that must be satisfied are the following: The power generated must be the same than the demanded power plus losses.

$$\sum_{i=1}^{N_g} P_{Gi} = P_D + P_L \tag{3}$$

$\sum_{i=1}^{N_g} P_{Gi}$ is the total system production
P_D is the demanded power
P_L are the system losses in MW
N_g is the number of generators in the system

The generation limits are restricted by:

$$P_{Gi}^{min} \leq P_{Gi} \leq P_{Gi}^{max} \tag{4}$$

P_{Gi}^{min} y P_{Gi}^{max} are the minimum and maximum power on the i-th generation unit.

3   Operation of PSO

PSO consists of a fixed number of particles that move in a determined searchpace, with a certain position and velocity, where each one of these particles is a possible solution. The optimization is performed in terms of the objective function when each particle knows its best position obtained during the process and is called thesonal Best (Pbest);

in the same way, the other particles know what is the bessition obtained by the group and is called the Global Best (Gbest) [7]. These values are used to calculate the new velocity values of the particles in the next iteration. The equations for the calculation of the velocity and position are [2]:

Velocity equation

$$v_i(k + 1) = v_i(k) + g_{1i}\big(p_i - x_i(k)\big) + g_{2i}\big(G - x_i(k)\big) \tag{5}$$

Position equation

$$x_i(k + 1) = x_i(k) + v_i(k + 1) \tag{6}$$

Where i is the particle number, k is the discrete time index, v is the velocity of the i-th particle, x is the position of the i-th particle, p is the best position found on the i-th particle and G the best position found by the swarm. Additionally, those equations have random numbers in the [0, 1] interval applied to the i-th particle [2].

Each particle changes position from the current one to the next one by modifying its velocity through the position equation until the number of desired iterations is reached.

To perform the PSO, the MATLAB software is used taking as a basis the Particle Swarm Optimization Toolbox. It was developed by Brian Birge in 2005 and received an update in 2006. Although it has not been updated in ten years, it remains a reference point in several works and investigation tools.

4   Use of PSO to Optimize the Economic Dispatch in the IEEE 30 Nodes

The IEEE 30-node system (Fig. 1) corresponds to an electrical network from middle East United States (New England) that has 6 generators, 41 transmission lines, 7 transformers and a system demand of 283.4 MW and 126.2 MVAR [8, 9]. The information of the total system conformation is found in [8]. The voltage limits are between 0.95 and 1.05 per unit.

The results obtained by the different authors using other optimization methods are summarized in Tables 1 and 2. The results achieved through PSO are listed in the last column to establish the comparison showing that the cost and the losses of PSO for the 30-node system are less than the values obtained through other methods. Some of the methods used by authors are the following:

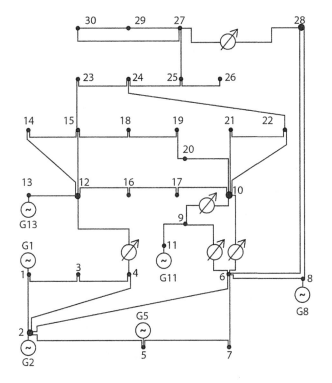

Fig. 1. IEEE 30 node system.

Table 1. Data obtained by different authors in a IEEE 30-node system (GA, MGA, GA-MGA, TABU, GAF OPF).

Node	GA	MGA	GA-MGA	Tabu	GAF OPF	PSO
PG1	175.27	180.19	183.75	176.00	174.96	173.28
PG2	54.00	48.13	46.77	48.76	50.35	48.03
PG5	19.45	21.56	21.23	21.56	21.45	21.31
PG8	12.77	12.30	15.75	22.05	21.17	24.47
PG11	16.12	15.35	10.71	12.44	12.66	12.35
PG13	15.11	15.13	14.40	12.00	12.11	12.00
Cost ($/h)	803.21	801.92	800.48	802.20	802.00	798.34
Losses	9.34	9.29	9.22	9.45	9.32	8.06

Tabu Search: It is an optimization method which uses local search to find the solution. In [10] it is used to get the optimal power flow due to its ability to avoid entrapment in local optimal solution.

Table 2. Data obtained by different authors in a IEEE 30-node system (GA OPF, RGA, EP, GA fuzzy, GA-MGA) vs. PSO.

Node	GA OPF	RGA	EP	GA Fuzzy	GA-MGA	PSO
PG1	175.64	174.0	173.84	178.17	183.75	173.28
PG2	48.94	46.80	49.99	45.16	46.77	48.03
PG5	21.17	22.00	21.38	20.65	21.23	21.31
PG8	22.64	23.90	22.63	21.29	15.72	24.47
PG11	12.43	11.00	12.92	15.16	10.71	12.35
PG13	12.00	14.50	12.00	12.00	14.40	12.00
Cost ($/h)	802.30	804.0	802.62	801.21	800.48	798.34
Losses	9.43	8.84	9.39	9.03	9.22	8.06

Genetic Algorithm (GA): According to [11], is a search algorithm based on the mechanics of natural selection and natural genetics and it belongs to the evolutionary algorithms. The main operators that can be used in the GA are crossover, mutation and selection. From here, some variation has been created.

Evolutionary programming (EP): It belong to the evolutionary algorithms being similar to the GA with a different structure and according to [12] the numerical parameters are allowed to evolve.

GA-Fuzzy: In [13] the authors explain that the crossover and mutation probabilities are governed by fuzzy rule base and therefore, that method has a faster convergence and lesser generation costs.

Refined Genetic Algorithm (RGA): It is another variation for the GA which uses the crossover and mutation probability and the dynamic hierarchy in order to make it more simple and effective [14].

Micro Genetic Algorithm (MGA): It's a variation who provides a closer and more exact solution than GA [11].

Hybrid GA-MGA: In [11], the authors propose a hybrid method using the GA to initialize the search and find a final solution with the MGA.

GAF: Genetic Algorithm Framework implements the genetic algorithm using C#.

Comparing the results obtained by the authors for the IEEE 30 node system, the highest value was 804 $/h and the lowest was 800,48 $/h, against the value obtained by PSO, which is 798.34 $/h. With this is verified that there is a reduction in the value obtained for the generation final cost implementing the PSO as a tool for the optimization process.

5   Use of PSO to Optimize the Economic Dispatch in the IEEE 14 Node System with Distributed Generation Sources

Taking the previous procedure as a reference, this methodology is replicated in the IEEE system of 14 nodes. The IEEE 14-node system (Fig. 2) corresponds to a portion of the American Electric Power System (in the Midwestern US) as of February 1962. It has 5 generators, 15 transmission lines and 4 transformers. This power system was simulated with the data supplied in [8].

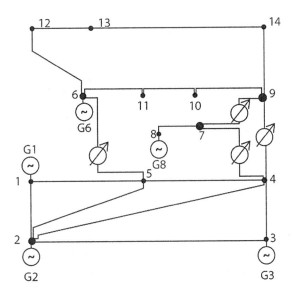

Fig. 2. IEEE 14 node system.

Five generators were added in the nodes indicated on Fig. 3 and their characteristics are detailed in Table 3. These new generators, present in the system, will always be delivering the total of their available generation since it is needed that their total capacity is considered when performing the optimization of the economic dispatch.

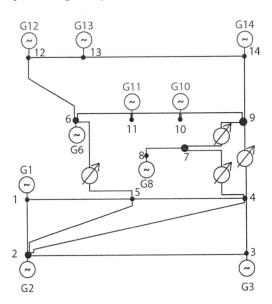

Fig. 3. Modified IEEE 14 node system.

Table 3. Data obtained by different authors in a IEEE 30-node system (GA OPF, RGA, EP, GA fuzzy, GA-MGA) vs. PSO.

Generator	Active power (MW)
Generator 10	9.00
Generator 11	3.50
Generator 12	6.10
Generator 13	13.5
Generator 14	10.6

With the purpose of maintaining the alternative generators on full load, the values of the coefficients a, b and c were adjusted in such manner that, when performing the optimization process, the algorithm guaranteed that these generators where dispatching at 100% of their capacity. This lead the dispatch of conventional generators to adjust to that condition and the values added to the initial IEEE 14-node system values. The coefficients used for the systems are shown in Table 4.

Table 4. Data obtained by different authors in a IEEE 30-node system (GA OPF, RGA, EP, GA fuzzy, GA-MGA) vs. PSO.

Generator	a	b	c	Pmin	Pmax
1	0.0050	2.45	105	10	160
2	0.0050	3.51	44.10	20	80
3	0.0050	3.89	44.60	20	50
10	0.0020	2.50	0	1	9.0
11	0.0020	2.50	0	1	3.5
12	0.0020	2.50	0	1	6.1
13	0.0020	2.50	0	1	13.5
14	0.0020	2.50	0	1	14.9

To perform the simulations, three scenarios have been established.

5.1 Conventional Scenario

In this scenario, only the load nodes are activated. They are associated to the spot-type loads present in the original power system.

5.2 Alternate Scenario

In this operation scenario, only the nodes that are associated to the new system generators are present.

5.3 Distributed Generation Scenario

In this operation scenario, the nodes that are activated are those with load as the new system generators.

Considering that there exists a subtle variation in the results of each PSO simulation due to the random nature of the particle generation when starting the simulation, 100 simulations were performed on each system.

The results were collected and the average of each value was calculated, they are summarized in Tables 5 and 6. Figures 4 and 5 gather the final results of the power and price variations for the conventional generators in the 14-node system.

Table 5. Results obtained for the alternate 14-node system.

Conventional			Alternative		
Gen	P (MW)	$/MWh	Gen	P (MW)	$/MWh
G1	143,684	560,251	G1	105,585	419,424
G2	70,026	314,410	G2	21,000	120,015
G3	50,0000	247,600	G3	40,225	205,166
			G10	9,000	22,662
			G11	3,500	8,775
			G12	6,100	15,324
			G13	13,500	34,115
			G14	14,900	37,694

Table 6. Results obtained for distributed 14-node system.

Conventional			Alternative		
Gen	P (MW)	$/MWh	Gen	P (MW)	$/MWh
G1	143,684	560,251	G1	130,963	511,616
G2	70,026	314,410	G2	44,455	210,018
G3	50,0000	247,600	G3	39,431	201,761
			G10	9,000	22,662
			G11	3,500	8,775
			G12	6,100	15,324
			G13	13,500	34,115
			G14	14,900	37,694

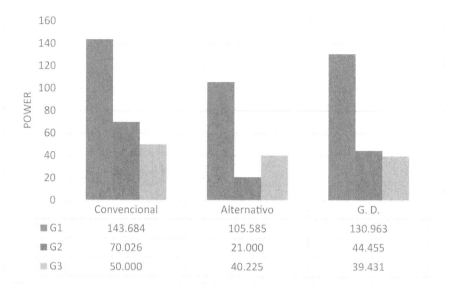

Fig. 4. Power variation for each generator.

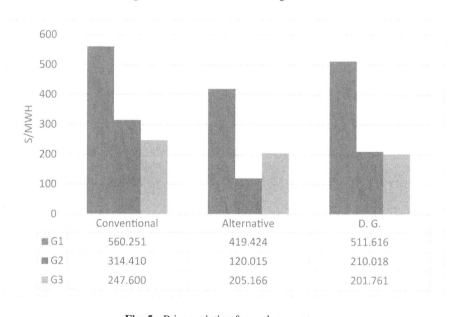

Fig. 5. Price variation for each generator.

Generator 1 is the biggest one of the system and presents a 26.52% power reduction and 25.14% cost reduction for the alternate system while the distributed generation system has an 8.85% power reduction and a 8.68% cost reduction. The previous results are explained by the distribution between the five generations units added in nodes 10, 11, 12, 13 and 14.

6 Conclusions

PSO has turned out to be effective in comparison to the results obtained for the genetic algorithms in terms of the total generation cost and the system losses.

The coefficients associated with the cost can be increased to resemble more to real operating conditions, with the purpose of having a more precise calculation in the prices.

The inclusion of distributed generation in the system brings a considerable reduction in the generation and, therefore, in the cost of conventional generators. However, distributed generation cannot always be at full load due to its random nature.

The results obtained for this study are related to distributed generation in general but the modelling could be performed for the different distributed generations that could enter the system for a more specific calculation.

References

1. Carpentier, J.: Contribution a l'étude du dispatching économique. Bulletin de la Société Française des Electriciens **3**, 431–447 (1962)
2. Frank, S., Rebennack, S.: A Primer on Optimal Power Flow: Theory, Formulation, and Practical Examples, Golden (2012)
3. Momoh, J.A., Adapa, R., El-Hawary, M.E.: A review of selected optimal power flow literature to 1993. I. Nonlinear and quadratic programming approaches. IEEE Trans. Power Syst. **14**(1), 96–104 (1999)
4. Schutte, J.F.: Particle Swarms in Sizing and Global Optimization. University of Pretoria (2001)
5. Kennedy, J., Eberhart, R.: Particle swarm optimization. In: Proceedings of IEEE International Conference on Neural Networks, vol. IV, 1942–1948 (1995)
6. Shi, Y., Eberhart, R.: A modified particle swarm optimizer. In: Proceedings of IEEE International Conference on Evolutionary Computation (1998)
7. Umapathy, P., Venkataseshaiah, C., Senthil Arumugam, M.: Particle Swarm Optimization with various inertia weight variants for optimal power flow solution. Discrete Dyn. Nat. Soc. **2010**, 15 (2010)
8. Electric Power Systems Analysis & Nature-Inspires Optimization Algorithms. http://www.al-roomi.org/power-flow. Accessed 10 Apr 2017
9. Montoya, D.: Formulación del Despacho Económico en el Mercado de Energía con Alta Penetración de Energía Eólica. Centro de Investigación y de Estudios Avanzados del Instituto Politécnico Nacional Unidad Guadalajara (2016)
10. Abido, M.: Optimal power flow using tabu search algorithm. Electric Power Compon. Syst. **30**, 469–483 (2002)
11. Kherfane, R., Younes, M., Kherfane, N., Khodja, F.: Solving economic dispatch problem using hybrid GA-MGA. Energy Procedia **50**, 937–944 (2014)
12. Yuryevich, J., Wong, K.: Evolutionary programming based optimal power flow algorithm. IEEE Trans. Power Syst. **14**, 1245–1250 (1999)

13. Ashish, S., Chaturvedi, D., Saxena, A.: Optimal power flow solution: a GAFuzzy system approach. Int. J. Emerg. Electr. Power Syst. **5**(2) (2006)
14. Paranjothi, S.R., Anburaja, K.: Optimal power flow using refined genetic algorithm. Electr. Power Compon. Syst. **30**(10) (2002)

Simulation Systems

Model for Logistics Capacity in the Perishable Food Supply Chain

Javier Arturo Orjuela-Castro[1,2,3(✉)], Gina Lizeth Diaz Gamez[1,3],
and Maria Paula Bernal Celemín[1,3]

[1] Universidad Distrital Francisco José de Caldas, Bogotá, Colombia
jorjuela@udistrital.edu.co, ginngamez@gmail.com,
pxdmaria92@hotmail.com
[2] Universidad Nacional de Colombia, Bogotá, Colombia
[3] GICALyT (Supply Chain Logistics and Treatability Group), Bogotá, Colombia

Abstract. Interest in fresh food has increased around the world. However, according to FAO losses of perishable food can reach 50%, depending on the logistics capabilities of the supply chain. A management model for transportation and warehouse capacities for the perishable food supply chain is proposed. The expansion of own capacity is evaluated in comparison to contracting 3PL in two scenarios: with and without cold chain. The model was developed within the system dynamics paradigm, modelled in iThink and evaluated through a case study of the supply chain of mango in Cundinamarca-Bogotá. The seasonality of the supply and its discrepancy with the demand is included in the model. The model allows the study of the logistic performance, quality, costs and responsiveness of the Mango Supply Chain.

Keywords: Logistics capabilities · 3PL · Cold system food · System dynamic model · Supply chain mango

1 Introduction

Logistics allows coordination between procurement, production and distribution [1]. Companies with world-class logistics capabilities achieve a competitive advantage by providing a superior service to their customers [2]. Competition requires the delivery of the appropriate product timely, in the right conditions and at the lowest cost, for which logistics capabilities are necessary [3]. The correct management of logistics capabilities generates operational efficiency, productivity and an increased value for the customer [4, 5]. [6] Identify three policies for planning logistics capabilities: An overcapacity to cover unforeseen demands; a capacity used in its totality even if demand is not met and, Ensuring that capacity and demand coincide. These logistical capabilities can be internal (organizational) or external (in SC) [4]. In the two large logistical processes, storage and transport, there is qualitative and quantitative logistical capacity. The quantitative capacity of storage or transport refers to the maximum number of cargo units that can be stored or transported [7]. Capacity planning and management minimizes the gap between the necessary capacity and the current one [8] in order to mitigate risks within the supply chain (SC). Companies have the choice of expanding logistics capacity through their

© Springer International Publishing AG 2017
J.C. Figueroa-García et al. (Eds.): WEA 2017, CCIS 742, pp. 225–237, 2017.
DOI: 10.1007/978-3-319-66963-2_21

own infrastructure or through the contracting of 3PL [9]. The interest in logistics out-sourcing is evidenced by the increase of companies that use logistic operators (3PL) to manage their logistics operations [10, 11] as it allows a reduction of costs, greater responsiveness, better customer service and decreased assets [12]. The importance of 3PL derives from *global markets, produced goods are transported over large distances, stored for varying periods of time at different locations along the supply chain (SC)* [13].

In perishable food supply chains (PFSCs), logistics management requires specific elements. The capacity must allow food preservation and speed in logistics processes in order to reduce losses. The organization must respond to unexpected situations related to logistical requirements, while still preserving quality [14]. In the PFSCs there are high requirements for qualitative logistics capabilities, given the use of vehicles and warehouses equipped with conservation technologies [15]. While in developed countries post-harvest food losses are low, in developing countries they are high due to a lack of adequate transportation, storage facilities, packaging, and handling techniques [16, 17]. The cold chain (CC) is a factor to consider in the management of qualitative logistic capacities in PFSCs, the shelf life of the food can be affected by temperature conditions [18]. A controlled temperature maintains the quality of the food [19]. Cold storage and transport is essential, it preserves quality and reduces the growth rate of microorganisms that cause damage [20, 21]. This method of conservation in PFSCs, for example for fruits or vegetables, allows the preservation of the organoleptic characteristics and keeps the products in a good state [22, 23].

In this article, we propose a model for the management of the logistics capacities for PFSCs in a dynamic environment, focused on storage and transport and the evaluation of the expansion of own capacity in comparison to contracting a 3PL, in two scenarios: with and without a cold chain. The model that evaluates the dynamics of the mango SC in Cundinamarca-Bogotá contemplates the discrepancy between supply and demand. In the model, the qualitative capacity is developed by means of a scenario where the warehousing and the vehicles, count or not with system of cold; On the other hand the quantitative capacity is posed as the available capacity expressed in square meters and vehicles by each one of the actors. The article is organized in two parts: first the model for capacity management of the PFSC that includes the dynamic problem and the Forrester model, and in a second part, the application of the model on the SC of mango presenting the chain and the results. In the end, there is a conclusion and a presentation of possible future works.

2   Model for the Management of Logistics Capabilities of the PFSC

Below, the dynamics of the chain and the model designed for the management of capacities of the PFSC is presented.

2.1   Dynamic Problem Description

The dynamics of the PFSC are represented by causal diagrams, which can be reinforcing (positive) or balancing (negative) [24]. The problem studied led to the proposition of the following hypothesis: *"The management of storage and transport capacities allows a greater approximation to the actual conditions of the PFSC by not considering capacity as an infinite variable, while the use of a cold chain system supports a decrease in levels of losses as well as the quantity missing and compliance in deliveries."* In Fig. 1, the causal diagram is presented. It is made up by the feedback cycles, logistics capacity, responsiveness, costs and quality.

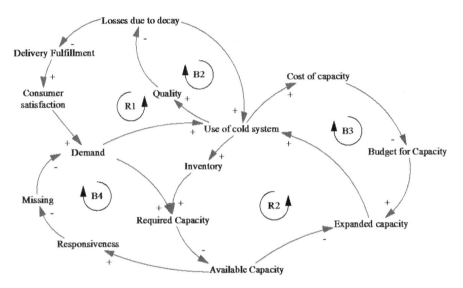

Fig. 1. Causal diagram of the logistic capacities of mango

The *quality cycle* conformed by R1 and B2, is about control measured in terms of losses. This is in turn linked to consumer satisfaction due to a higher quality in fresh or processed food. It is also affected positively when the cold system is implemented as it helps to preserve quality in transportation and storage. The *logistical capacity cycle* (R2) takes into account the required capacity and measures it against the available capacity in order to establish the capacity missing in terms of inventory and transport. In the case of the cold chain the level of inventory is expanded when the capacity. The *cost cycle* (B3): the higher the uses of cold system the higher are the capacity costs, lowering the budget. A higher budget allows for an expansion of capacity, which results in more cold system. The *cycle of responsiveness* (B4): based on a higher demand, more perishable and processed food is generated, which leads to a greater requirement of warehouses and transportation, reducing the available capacities, influencing the capacity of response and this in turn on the shortcomings that have a negative impact on demand.

2.2   Forrester Model for Supply Chain

A model was developed in System Dynamics using iThink 9.1.3 software. The PFSC consists of farmers, agroindustry, distributors, shopkeeper, hypermarkets and consumers [1]. Figure 2 shows the structure of the chain of food flows (blue arrows) and information flows (red arrows). This model is based on the models made by [1, 18, 25]. This model includes new agents in form of hypermarket, shopkeeper and a logistic operator that supplies transport capacity and warehousing, Fig. 2. In addition, several other modifications are included as presented below.

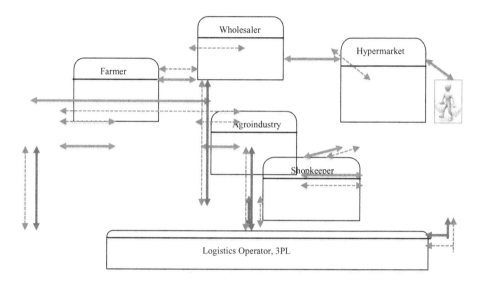

Fig. 2. Forrester diagram for the agro-industrial supply chain (Color figure online)

Variable discrepancy: In Eq. (1), when the supply of food is greater than the demand, the variable takes a positive value, in the opposite case it is negative, if they are equal, it will equal zero. This will affect the inventory level in warehousing.

$$Discrepancy = Food\_available\_of\_the\_agent\text{-}Demand \qquad (1)$$

Percentage of food for direct transport (% DT): Based on the food inventory level and the variable discrepancy, either the quantity to be stored or the quantity to be sent for direct transport in order to satisfy the demand is obtained (Eq. 2)

$$\%DT = IF(Discrepancia < = 0)\ THEN(1), ELSE(Demand/Quantity\_net\_available) \qquad (2)$$

When deciding what amount of food will be stored and what quantity will be transported directly, the model determines the amount of food to be stored in the own warehouse and the amount to be stored by the logistic operator.

Something similar occurs with transport when agents recur to 3PL vehicles after having exhausted its own capacity (Fig. 3). Figure 3 shows the farmer's use of own and subcontracted storage capacity. The formula (3) is used to determine the quantity of fruit that will be available in the own warehouse. The quantity that is stored in the own warehouse is restricted to the available capacity in square meters. The same procedure is carried out in the case of transport capacity. When there is no more own capacity the operator is used.

$$
\begin{aligned}
Food\ in\ &inventory\ in\ the\ farmer's\ own\ warehouse \\
= MIN\ &((Capacity\_of\_the\_warehouse\_of\_the\_farmer \qquad (3) \\
&* Converter\_in\_square\_meter),\ food\_in\_inventory\_of\_the\_farmer)
\end{aligned}
$$

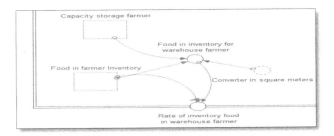

Fig. 3. Storage with own capacity

Discrepancy between food in transit and the demand (DTD) (4): the food leaves the warehouses because of perishability and to satisfy the demand, the latter is given by this variable. When the discrepancy is positive it gives the amount of food that will leave the stores to meet the demand.

$$
DTD = Demand\text{-}rate\_of\_food\_in\_transit \qquad (4)
$$

The model has the power to decide whether to expand the actor's own capacity or to continue subcontracting, for which the model follows a decision algorithm, Fig. 4. The algorithm is used for capacity expansion of warehouse or transport. In warehouse, extra square meters are acquired and in transport extra vehicles. The model will expand capacity according to the agent's available budget.

Scenarios: The model allows a simulation of the PFSC with and without the use of cold storage and cold transport system. The scenarios generate a different percentage of storage and transport losses in each of the PFSC agents, including 3PL. PFSC with CC will have half the losses compared to the other scenario, according to [26] the cold doubles the shelf life of perishable foods. In Fig. 5, Forrester is presented in order to calculate the losses of food in storage (LS), _the percentage of losses by decay_ (% LD) _and management_ (% LM), which will depend on the food.

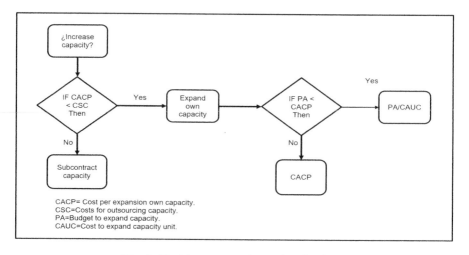

Fig. 4. Decision to expand capacity algorithm.

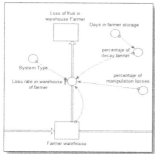

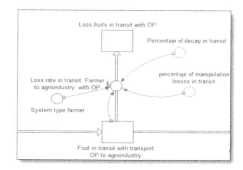

Fig. 5. Losses storage   **Fig. 6.** Losses transport

In addition, losses in transport (LT) are calculated. For the change of scenario, the *variable "type of system"* was included, Fig. 6. From the % LD and % LM the loss rate is calculated with Eq. (5), in which type of system 1 is the scenario not using cold and the scenario 2 is with the cold system. For this reason, when the system type is 2 the rate of losses is multiplied by 0.5. For transport, % LD corresponds to travel time.

$$Rate\ of\ losses\ in\ the\ agent's\ warehouse$$
$$= Warehouse\_of\_the\_agent * (\%LD\_agent + \%LM\_agent) \qquad (5)$$
$$* (IF\ (type\_of\_system = 1)\ THEN(1)\ ELSE(0.5))$$

3 Application of the Model on the Mango Supply Chain

The experimental design of this research follows the steps of the experimentation of [26], which raises 5 simulations for each proposed scenario, using a different seed value in each simulation. The used values are 1, 2, 3, 4 and 5, a DT = 0.5 was used. The simulation time was 20 years (7300 days) in order to see the long-term effect on logistics capabilities. For the input information of the model, surveys were used with the different actors of the Mango SC (SCM) during the years 2015–2016, using non-probabilistic snowball sampling. 30 surveys were carried out with producers, 10 with wholesalers, 2 with agroindustry, 10 with transporters, 2 with hypermarkets, retailers: 54 with shopkeepers and 40 with market place traders. The primary information was supplemented with reports from AGRONET, FAOSTAT and DANE as well as information from specific research of mango from fieldwork in the producing municipalities of Cundinamarca ASOHOFRUCOL and logistic work on the SC of fruit [27]. This information of the SCM in Cundinamarca-Bogotá allowed for the definition of the production area (ha) and yield (t/ha), seasonality of harvests (months), transit times between links (d), loading and unloading times, consuming population and consumption per capita for fresh fruit and pulp (g-inhabitant/d).

3.1 Fruit Chain: Mango

The mango is a fruit from the inter-tropical zone of juicy and sweet pulp. It is characterized by its good taste and its nutritional content [28]. The use of cold has a positive effect on climacteric fruits like mango, as it decreases the respiratory rate, the speed of biochemical reactions and enzymatic reactions. The CC preserves its quality [29]. With a temperature of 7–12 °C and relative humidity of 90%, a shelf life of 3 to 6 weeks in storage is achieved. The production of mango in Cundinamarca represents 34% of the total national production. It is one of the fruits with greatest demand [27]. In stock, the % LD of the mango will depend on its respiration rate, which varies according to the number of days that has passed. The number of storage days were modelled with a random variable, the LMs are a constant value for each agent, for farmers it is 2,9%, for wholesalers it is 5.6%, for hypermarket 5.76%, for shopkeeper 5.76% and for market places 5.6%, agroindustry 3,5%. For transport the % LD is the one that corresponds to one day as the duration of the trips is very short. The respiration rate is 0,41% in the case of not using a cold system and with a cold system it is 0.2%.

3.2 Results in the Supply Chain of Mango

The *quality* in the model is measured as a function of the amount of losses. The results are presented in Table 1. The reduction in total losses is 2.9% in the scenario with CC in comparison to without the cold chain. The main losses occur in the farmer's warehouse and in the 3PL. This is due to the excess supply in the harvesting season, generating an imbalance between supply and demand, increasing for the farmer with cold storage as storage times increase. Although the fruit lost in transport is a small share of the total, when the cold system is implemented, the loss of transport is reduced by 34.03%, as an effect of the all CC on the mango.

Table 1. Losses of transport and storage

Stage	Waste, millions of tons										
	Transport					Warehousing					Total
	From farmer	From agroindustry	From distributor	3PL	Sub-total	Farmer	Agroindustry	Shop	3PL	Sub-total	
No cold	30	5.0	4.0	1.9	**41**	5,837	166	279	5,983	**12,265**	**12,306**
Cold	19	4.3	2.2	1.4	**27**	5,978	13	28	5,902	**11,921**	**11,948**
Difference (%)	**35,67**	**13,60**	**44,0**	**25,3**	**34,03**	**−2.41**	**92,17**	**89,96**	1.35	2.80	2.90

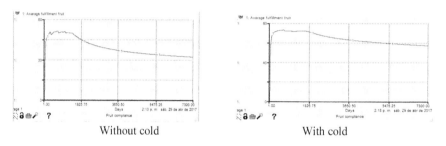

Without cold   With cold

Fig. 7. Demand average compliance percentage of supply chain mango.

The *response capacity* is measured in the model as the percentage of compliance and the percentage of non-compliance. Fruit compliance was 51% without cold system and 73%, with cold system, Fig. 7. Regarding non-compliance, both in fruit and in processed products, the indicator was better with a cold system, improving by 27.64% and 30.61% respectively.

Table 2. Losses of transport and storage by increase percentage demand

Increase percentage demand	Demand - Waste, millions of tons										
	Transport					Warehousing					Total
	From farmer	From agroindustry	From distributor	3PL	Sub-total	Farmer	Agroindustry	Shop	3PL	Sub-total	
0,25	9	1,5	1,1	0,56	**12**	6509	5,1	12	6522	**13048**	
0,5	14	2,7	1,7	0,98	**20**	6310	8,6	22	6313	**12654**	**12674**
0,75	17	3,6	2,0	1,23	**24**	6102	11,4	25	6107	**12246**	**12270**
1	19	4,3	2,3	1,47	**27**	5978	13,6	28	5903	**11922**	**11949**
2	26	6,7	3,2	2,28	**38**	5136	20,3	38	5144	**10339**	**10377**
3	27	6,6	3,5	2,31	**40**	4482	19,5	41	4490	**9033**	**9073**
4	45	10,9	6,3	3,61	**66**	3957	32,6	73	3969	**8031**	**8097**
5	49	12,0	6,8	3,93	**72**	3504	35,5	80	3517	**7137**	**7208**
6	67	12,9	10,0	4,22	**94**	3083	38,3	122	3098	**6342**	**6436**
7	70	13,7	10,5	4,47	**99**	2726	40,7	128	2741	**5635**	**5734**

Table 3. Losses of transport and storage by increase percentage supply

Increase percentage supply	Supply - Waste, millions of tons										Total
	Transport					Warehousing					
	From farmer	From agroindustry	From distributor	3PL	Sub-total	Farmer	Agroindustry	Shop	3PL	Sub-total	
0,25	854	7	-	0	**862**	854	7	11	857	**3.455**	**4.317**
0,5	2.430	12	-	0	**2.443**	2.430	12	23	2.435	**9.785**	**12.228**
0,75	4.140	11	-	0	**4.152**	4.140	11	19	4.145	**16.620**	**20.773**
1	5.898	14	0	0	**5.912**	5.898	14	28	5.903	**23.666**	**29.579**
2	12.988	15	0	0	**13.006**	12.988	15	35	12.994	**52.043**	**65.049**
3	20.091	15	0	0	**20.109**	20.091	15	35	20.096	**80.455**	**100.564**
4	27.193	15	0	0	**27.212**	27.193	15	35	27.199	**108.867**	**136.079**
5	34.295	15	0	0	**34.316**	34.295	15	35	34.301	**137.279**	**171.595**
6	41.398	15	0	0	**41.420**	41.398	15	35	41.404	**165.691**	**207.111**
7	48.501	15	0	0	**48.523**	48.501	15	35	48.506	**194.103**	**242.626**

Sensitivity analyses 1: It was done on losses, increasing the percentage demand and supply. For the case the demand, the losses in transport were increased due to a greater flows food, while in storage a decrease was observed given that there is a greater rotation in the warehouses. On the other hand, by increasing the supply, the losses increased in both transport and storage, since large quantities of fruit did not flow quickly, Tables 2 and 3.

Table 4. Expanded transportations and warehousing capacity of farmer

Increase percentage utility	Without cold		With cold	
	Expanded transportation capacity	Extended capacity of storage	Expanded transportation capacity	Extended capacity of storage
0,25	15	10.006	20.845	-
0,5	22	10.003	21.874	-
0,75	22	10.165	22.692	-
1	26	10.160	22.607	-
2	30	12.099	22.596	-
3	32	12.101	22.502	-
4	45	12.104	22.507	-
5	45	12.103	22.543	-
6	45	12.102	22.550	-
7	45	12.105	23.856	-

Sensitivity analyses 2: It was made for the farmer regarding his utility, for being the actor with less budget has for the expansion of his capacity, although the one that requires it the most. For the without cold scenario, there is an increase in the increased transport and storage capacity, while in the cold scenario, although transport capacity is increased, the storage capacity was not modified due to the high costs, Table 4.

The *costs of increasing capacity* per agent were measured for the two scenarios, agroindustry had greater investment in both scenarios, it was the only agent that decided to expand its storage capacity, it used more own capacity than subcontracted capacity. The farmer and the wholesaler were the other actors who incurred in the cost of expansion, but in transport. As well as in the agro-industry, the costs of the cold system are greater. The costs of expanding own capacity are lower than those of subcontracting, as there were actors who did not expand their capacities in any of the scenarios as a result of lower subcontracting costs, Table 5.

Table 5. Cost of capacity expansion (millions of pesos).

Stage	Farmer	Agroindustry	Distributor product	Total Agents	Warehouse 3PL	Transport 3PL	Total 3PL	Total SCM
No Cold	3,421	16,927	3,492	**23,840**	39,237	13,172,374	**13,211,611**	**13,235,451**
Cold	7,403	39,163	6,812	**53,379**	309,350	21,275,802	**21,585,152**	**21,638,531**
Difference %	116.4	131.4	95.1	123.9%	688.4	61.5	63.38%	63.49%

For all the actors, more is always stored with the CC. In transport the opposite occurs, more vehicles are used in the scenario without cold, but only slightly, the difference being between 10 and 15%. When cold is used, the losses are reduced. This results in fewer trips to comply with orders. The farmer and agroindustry are the only actors that use their own transportation capacity. All other actors use the 3PL operator;

Table 6. Expanding their capacity or subcontracting 3PL.

Performance measures	Stage	Total million (tons)	Farmer	Agroindustry	Wholesaler, Product Distributor	Hypermarket Shopkeeper
Extended Capacity of	Without Cold	10727	0	10727	0	0
Storage (m²)	With Cold	19238	0	19238	0	0
Difference %		-80%	0	-80%	0%	0%
Expanded Transportation	Without Cold	115	25,3	45,1	0	0
Capacity (vehicles)	With Cold	175	33	73,8	0	0
Difference %		-52,1%	-30,4%	-63,6%	0%	0%

the wholesaler does not transport fruit to its customers. The farmer and agroindustry expanded more with the CC scenario, by 30.4% and 63.6% respectively. Both are making more use of their own transport capacity than that of the operator. Table 6 shows the behaviour of capacity expansion in quantities, some actors did not expand their own capacity (farmer in storage, wholesalers in transport) because they were less expensive to subcontract to 3PL or perform very low storage, such as cross-docking. The fact that they do not increase their own capacity involved an expense in subcontracting.

4 Conclusions

A management model for logistics capabilities for the perishable food supply chain has been developed, which evaluates the expansion of own capacity in comparison to contracting a 3PL in two scenarios: with and without cold chain. It includes the seasonality of supply and its discrepancy with demand, allows the study of logistical capacity, quality, costs and the responsiveness. Losses in the PFSC can be reduced by the correct utilization of logistics capabilities and the implementation of a cold chain. The farmer is the actor that suffers the greatest amount of losses in transport and storage. Most of this effect happens due to oversupply caused by the harvest seasons, which causes farmers to store large quantities of fruit. The farmer and the agroindustry are the ones that expand their transport capacity the most. Agroindustry is the only actor that expands its storage capacity, gives priority to use its own capacity instead of using the capacity of the operator because it has the budget to do so. The farmer has no budget because his/her profit margin is low.

For future work the efficiency of the 3PL could be evaluated with regards to the agents of the SC comparing own logistic capacity against subcontracting with 3PL.

References

1. Orjuela-Castro, J.A., Caicedo-Otavo, A.L., Ruiz-Moreno, A.F., Adarme-Jaimes, W.: External integration mechanisms effect on the logistics performance of fruit supply chains. A dynamic system approach. Revista Colombiana de Ciencias Horticulas **10**(2), 311–322 (2016). (in Spanish)
2. Bowersox, D., Closs, D.J., Cooper, M.B.: Supply Chain Logistics Management, Igarss (2007)
3. Morash, E., Droge, C., Vickery, S.: Strategic logistics capabilities for competitive advantage and firm success. J. Bus. Logistics **17**, 1–22 (1996)
4. Sandberg, E., Abrahamsson, M.: Logistics capabilities for sustainable competitive advantage. Int. J. Logistics Res. Appl. **14**(1), 61–75 (2011)
5. Gligor, D.M., Holcomb, M.C.: The road to supply chain agility: an RBV perspective on the role of logistics capabilities. Int. J. Logistics Manag. **25**, 160–179 (2014)
6. Brockhoff, G., Marlies, G., Krome Dirk, M.: Logistics Capacity Management - A Theoretical Review and Applications to Outbound Logistics, FOM Hochshule, ild, p. 59 (2011)

7. Crainic, T.G., Gobbato, L., Perboli, G., Rei, W., Watson, J.-P., Woodruff, D.L.: Bin packing problems with uncertainty on item characteristics: an application to capacity planning in logistics. Procedia Soc. Behav. Sci. **111**, 654–662 (2014)
8. Becerra, M., Herrera, M., Orjuela-Castro, J.A.: Model for calculating operational capacities in service providers using system dynamics. In: System Dynamics Conference 31, Delft (2013)
9. Wang, L., Murata, T.: Study of optimal capacity planning for remanufacturing activities in closed-loop supply chain using system dynamics modeling, pp. 196–200 (2011)
10. Orjuela-Castro, J.A., Castro, O.F., Suspes, E.A.: Operators and logistics platform. Revista Tecnura **8**(16), 115–127 (2005). (in Spanish)
11. Liu, C.-L., Lyons, A.C.: An analysis of third-party logistics performance and service provision. Transp. Res. Part E Logistics Transp. Rev. **47**(4), 547–570 (2011)
12. Memon, M.A., Archimede, B.: Towards a distributed framework for transportation planning: a food supply chain case study. In: 10th IEEE International Conference on Networking, Sensing and Control (ICNSC), pp. 603–608 (2013)
13. Aguezzoul, A.: Third-party logistics selection problem: a literature review on criteria and methods. Omega **49**, 69–78 (2014)
14. Gou, J., Shen, G., Chai, R.: Model of service-oriented catering supply chain performance evaluation. J. Ind. Eng. Manag. **6**(1), 215–226 (2013)
15. Gebresenbet, G., Bosona, T.: Logistics and Supply Chains in Agriculture and Food (2004)
16. Vlachos, D., Georgiadis, P., Iakovou, E.: A system dynamics model for dynamic capacity planning of remanufacturing in closed-loop supply chains. Comput. Oper. Res. **34**, 367–394 (2007)
17. Orjuela-Castro, J.A., Herrera-Ramírez, M.M., Adarme-Jaimes, W.: Warehousing and transportation logistics of mango in Colombia: a system dynamics model. Revista Facultad de Ingeniería **26**(44), 71–84 (2016)
18. Orjuela-Castro, J.A., Casilimas, W., Herrera, M.: Impact analysis of transport capacity and food safety in Bogota. In: 2015 Workshop de Engineering Applications - International Congress on Engineering (WEA), Bogotá (2015). doi:10.1109/WEA.2015.7370138
19. Kuo, J.C., Chen, M.: Developing an advanced multi-temperature joint distribution system for the food cold chain. Food Control **21**(4), 559–566 (2010)
20. Vigneault, C., Thompson, J., Wu, S., Hui, K.P.C., Leblanc, D.I.: Transportation of fresh horticultural produce. Postharvest Technol. Hortic. **2**(1), 1–24 (2009)
21. Aung, M.M., Chang, Y.S.: Temperature management for the quality assurance of a perishable food supply chain. Food Control **40**, 198–207 (2014)
22. Orjuela-Castro, J.A., Pinilla-Ortiz, A.L., Rincón-Murcia, J.R.: Application of controlled atmosphere technology for the conservation of granadilla. Ingeniería **7**(2), 45–53 (2001). (in Spanish)
23. Orjuela Castro, J.A., Calderón, M.E., Buitrago Hernández, S.P.: The Agro-industrial Chain of Fruits, Uchuva and Tomato of tree, p. 191. Universidad Distrital Francisco José de Caldas, Bogota, D.C. (2006). (in Spanish)
24. Sterman, J.: Bussiness Dynamics: Systems Thinking. McGraw Hill, New York (2000)
25. Orjuela-Castro, J.A., Sepulveda-Garcia, D.A., Ospina-Contreras, I.D.: Effects of using multimodal transport over the logistics performance of the food chain of Uchuva. In: Workshop on Engineering Applications. Applied Computer Sciences in Engineering, pp. 165–177, September 2016
26. Sarimveis, H., Patrinos, P., Tarantilis, C.D., Kiranoudis, C.T.: Dynamic modeling and control of supply chain systems: a review. Comput. Oper. Res. **35**(11), 3530–3561 (2008)
27. Orjuela, J., Castañeda, I., Canal, J., Rivera, J.: Logistics in the fruit chain. Frutas y Hortalizas **39**, 10–15 (2015). (in Spanish)

28. Salamanca, G., Forero, F., Lozano, J.G., Díaz, C., Salazar, B.: Advances in the characterization, conservation and processing of the mango (Mangifera indica L.) in Colombia. Revista Tumbaga, 57–64 (2007). (in Spanish)
29. Wall, A., Olivas, F.J., Velderrain, G.R., González, A., De La Rosa, L.A., López, J.A., Álvarez, E.: Mango: agro-industrial aspects, nutritional/functional value and effects on health. Nutrición hospitalaria 31(1), 67–75 (2015). (in Spanish)

Dynamics of the Recycling Sector and the Generation of Waste in Bogotá

Nelson Riaño-Contreras[(✉)], William Velasquez-Melo[(✉)], and Germán Andres Mendez-Giraldo

Universidad Distrital Francisco José de Caldas, Bogotá, D.C., Colombia
{nerianoc,wvelasquezm}@correo.udistrital.edu.co,
gmendez@udistrital.edu.co

Abstract. The present simulation model represents and analyzes the dynamics of the recoverable solid waste stream in the Bogotá's recycling chain, characterizing the amount of waste collected per day, according to a number of recyclers that are in the daily activity.

This study is intended to provide guidance for decision-making district order, in politics and public operation of the recycling system as an input frequency in training and collection routes.

The model was developed through continuous simulation, using the computational tool Ithink, with which we represent the study system, which allows us to perform the analysis of the same, projections of the quantity of recyclable waste and capacity of collection by Part of the recyclers starting in 2017 until the year 2020.

The main achievement of the model is to be able to determine the most important variables to increase the efficiency in the collection of recyclable materials, which are given by the increase of the population of the recycling sector and its capacity of collection, transport, and storage. In addition to allowing to measure, the impact of the separation at the source on the efficiency of the collection system of recyclable solid waste generated per day, and whether or not this influences the amount of waste entering the landfill.

Keywords: Recycling · Solid waste · Dynamic systems · Continuous simulation

1 Introduction

Currently the Colombia's recycling sector is formalized, seeking to include the population whose activity is the solid waste recycling and that is in a condition of social and economic vulnerability, this based on the established in the Plans of Management Integral de Residuos – PGIRS (For its acronym in Spanish: Plan de Gestión Integral de Residuos Sólidos).

With [25] Decree 596 of 2016 issued by the Ministry of Housing, City and Territory of Colombia, the Recycling dynamics must change and become an orderly industrial process, allowing the start of a new industry contributing to the economy and environmental policies.

© Springer International Publishing AG 2017
J.C. Figueroa-García et al. (Eds.): WEA 2017, CCIS 742, pp. 238–249, 2017.
DOI: 10.1007/978-3-319-66963-2_22

The object of the simulation contemplates the middle part of the recycling chain, which is understood as a stage of collection and storage just before pre-transformation; We take data from the weighing records of the sub-management of the Special Administrative Unit for Public Services UAESP.

The estimation of waste types was considered according to the study Characterization of Residues generated in 2011 in Bogotá [24], carried out by the Special Unit of Public Administrative Services UAESP.

In spite of being grouped in organizations, the work done by each of the operators is individual and autonomous, since each individual decides the schedules, routes, and type of waste that wants to collect. Then Fig. 1 shows the recycling cycle.

| Waste generator | Recovery, collection and transportation | Storage | Pre-Transformation | Transformation |

Fig. 1. Shows the recycling cycle.

2 Literature Review

A model for the Chilean metropolitan area was constructed using systems dynamics and programmed in Powers [1]. The model integrates various components, such as population, socioeconomic status, waste collection, illegal waste landfills, transfer stations, and landfills. This model concludes that an informative and functional campaign, which increases recycled waste, has a significant impact on the amount of waste in landfills and over the costs associated with the production, collection, and disposal of household solid waste, in the metropolitan region of Chile. On the other hand, there was a model that simulates the impact of a strategy for the management of solid household waste in the urban area of the city of Huancayo (Junín Region in Peru). It was developed, based on the current management characteristics and proposing a model with the alternatives of recycling and composting in a treatment plant, prior to disposal in the landfill; this model integrates the various components involved, such as population, waste collection, illegal waste landfills, sanitary landfills, produced solid waste, population, segregation, financing, awareness and time [2]. Ibarra and Redondo [3] present a model developed with the methodology of the System Dynamics for the management of solid waste generated in educational institutions in which the variables are related to the amount of waste, the budget of the institutions and recycled waste. Fujii et al. [4], developed the concept of intelligent recycling, which is understood as the real implementation of urban symbiosis, i.e. the use of by-products (residues) of cities (urban areas) as raw materials; as alternatives or sources of energy for industrial operations [5] and propose a framework to facilitate the implementation of such a system. By making use of existing facilities and adopting closed-loop and semi-closed loop recycling processes, this system allows for flexible adaptations in changes in external factors. They develop an integrated model that combines both the collection model based on the geographic information system and a process model for an intelligent recycling center. The results of their simulation show that smart recycling can not only reduce carbon dioxide emissions but also reduce overall costs.

Recycling activities have shown a notable increase in the last decade due to the economic and environmental dimensions of sustainability. In particular, capacity planning at production facilities has become a key strategic issue affecting the profitability of the recycling industry [6]. Recycling is an important part of waste management (including different types of issues: environmental, technological, economic, legislative, social, etc.). Anghinolfi et al. [7] propose a dynamic decision model that is characterized by state variables, which correspond to the amount of waste in each container per day, and control variables that determine the amount of material collected in the area each day and the routes of a collection of vehicles. The objective function minimizes the sum of costs minus the benefits. Johansson [8] shows that the adoption of dynamic scheduling and routing policies can result in lower operating costs, shorter pick-up and transport distances, and reduced working hours than those resulting from static policies with fixed and predetermined routes, which are often employed by many residue collectors. Faccio et al. [9], who use an integrated vehicle routing model with real-time traceability data, introduce another approach. A heuristic model for routing optimization is presented to minimize different targets (i.e. the number of vehicles available, the And the total distance covered), taking into account the pattern of waste generation registered in a container, a supposed risk of oversizing and an optimum replenishment level parameter. Guariso et al. [10] propose a model of discrete events of a transfer station and its relations with the other terminals. Runfola and Gallardo [11], carry out a comprehensive review of concepts, characterization standards, methodologies of some official organisms, methodological proposals made by some researchers and methodologies applied in some studies of urban solid waste characterization. According to the review, it is noted there is no general or standard characterization methodology. It makes use of diverse criteria of sampling and precision, which means that a reference standard is not available at local, regional and international level. However, construction waste also deserves special treatment and a classification according to this activity, Mejía Urbaez [12], presents a simulation analysis for the comparison and quantification of residues.

At the industrial level, recycling has become particularly important, due to the possibility of some sectors recovering material and using it as part of their raw materials and inputs, in this way the concept of reverse logistics is born. Reverse logistics is the process of planning, executing and efficiently controlling the flow of raw materials, inventory in the process, finished products, and related information from the point of consumption to the point of origin, in order to recover value or perform a correct removal [13]. At present, companies have been interested in designing and implementing Reverse Logistics systems. The main reasons why companies carry out Reverse Logistics are economic benefits, legal pressures and the growing citizen culture regarding the issue of product returns [14–16]. Nativi and Lee [17] develop a work in which they consider the use of recycled material in the logistic process, and from the mathematical modeling, they evaluate the impact of the use of this material on environmental and economic indicators. Systems dynamics models are developed by different authors, applying reverse logistics, while some focus on system planning capacity and the effect of lead time [18], others evaluate a large number of scenarios focused on indicators such as Work in process (WIP), customer satisfaction and inventory levels [19]. Georgiadis and Vlachos [20] present a system dynamics model to represent a reverse logistics system that includes remanufactured products, in addition to analyzing the influence of aspects such as green image and environmental protection policies.

Recently, a relatively new paradigm has been developed for the simulation of systems with interactive agents, called Agent-Based Simulation (ABS). While the most accurate definition of ABS varies according to the field of study (even within the same field), the philosophy and uses of ABS are similar - to simulate interactions of autonomous objects (called agents) to identify, explain, generate, and Analyze emerging behaviors [21]. Meng et al. [22], in order to determine the most effective waste management policy for the classification and recycling of household solid waste, try to establish a simulation model that combines simulation techniques Multi-agent (MABS) with a social survey questionnaire. The results show that the policy of specific charges can improve the performance of residents' separation behavior, which is a more effective way to reduce household solid waste and increase the rate of collection of domestic recyclable resources. Shi et al. [23] propose a decision-making model based on agent-based simulation for effective planning of single-stream recycling programs (SSR) in this type of recycling system, all Recyclable materials are mixed in a wastebasket instead of being sorted by residents prior to collection. The simulation module performs two main tasks; In the first place, it identifies the various sources of uncertainties of the system and incorporates them into the SSR simulation model. Second, it compares and evaluates SSR alternatives (i.e., dual flow recycling) with respect to cost, bottleneck facilities and the types and capacities of the necessary processing facilities.

3 Proposed Model

The objective of the research is to understand the dynamics of recycling in Bogotá, based on historical data with information on a number of recyclers registered and the amount of material collected by them. In this way, to propose a tool that will improve policies that tend to reduce the levels of solid waste that reach the Sanitary Landfill, which for the city of Bogota DC is called Sanitary Landfill Doña Juana.

For the development of the simulation, the projection of the population and the generation per capita of waste from the year 2017 to the year 2020 are taken into account. The number of recyclers is identified as the random variable and the amount of material recovered as dependent on the collection capacity of the recycling sector.

3.1 Preliminary Data Analysis

The original database has data for the years 2014 and 2015; Distributed in 1'723,923 records, as follows; The year 2014: 897,279 records, and year 2015: 826,644 records.

To better understand the dynamics of recycling in Bogotá, it is decided, using conditional formulas of Microsoft Excel, to group recycle material recorded in different warehouses or weighing points and group the amount of material collected having as characteristic the day of the week.

3.2   The Treatment of the Data

It was demonstrated that the participation in the number of warehouses per locality remains constant from year to year, except for the localities of Ciudad Bolívar and Santa Fe, which allows us to assume the stability in the installed capacity for the reception of materials Recyclable.

Figure 2 shows that there is a difference in the collection dynamics in terms of the locality and the area of waste generation, from the point of view of the population of each locality. This leads us to conclude that the material that is collected is not possibly a random variable, but depends on a number of recyclers and that each day of the week has a different behavior.

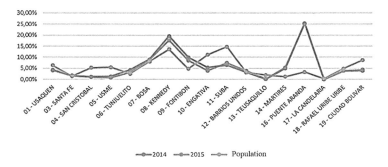

Fig. 2. Participation of recycled material by locality vs. population participation by locality

In Fig. 3, we see some data groups, which means that the recyclers per day do not follow a normal distribution. To do this, the ANOVA test will be applied to determine the grouping of the number of recyclers taking as reference on the day of the week in which a number of recyclers occur, taking into account that the dynamics of waste collection is influenced by the frequencies of Collection of material, not recycling, Synchronized with the frequencies of garbage collection in Bogotá.

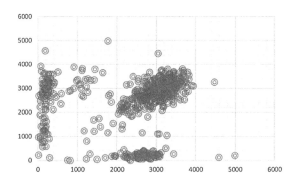

Fig. 3. Dispersion of variable recyclers.

3.3   Data Behavior

Sample Media: It is concluded that the mean of recyclers between the days of the week is not the same. To argue this conclusion, we performed ANOVA testing that rejects the main hypothesis asserting that the averages were the same for all days of the week. The box chart was also used, which supported the previous conclusion.

Normality: It is concluded that data on the quantity of recyclers do not follow a normal probability distribution. For this, a graphical representation Q-Q was performed, which showed values very far from the bisector of the coordinate axes and a Kolmogorov-Smirnov test, which yielded a test of significance 0.00.

Homogeneous Groups: By means of multiple comparisons, using the Scheffe test, the five groups of data were organized with which the simulation will be developed: Monday - Saturday, Tuesday - Wednesday, Thursday, Friday, Sunday; According to the level of significance given by the test for each of the groups.

Probability Distribution Functions: Following the tests mentioned above, the tests of goodness and fit were performed for each group of homogeneous data and in this way determine the probability distribution function that is most Adjusts to each of them.

Once found the probability functions for the number of recyclers in function of the day of the week, it is necessary to validate our initial assumption in which we understand that there is a dependence between the quantity of recyclers and the quantity of material recycled.

For this we apply the coefficient of Correlation of Pearson = 0.97. It is concluded that there is a correlation between the number of recyclers and the amount of material collected. The correlation between variables is positive, which means that they grow together, as we can see in Fig. 4.

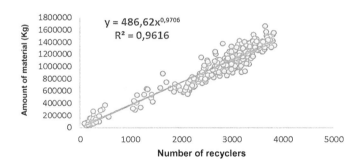

Fig. 4. Correlation between number of recyclers and amount of material

It was designed in Ithink, to simulate the recovery of potentially recyclable materials in the city of Bogota; With a projection of 4 years, counted from 2017. For this, the projections of population were used having as source the Secretariat of District Planning, to know the behavior of the population in the next years

Definition of the population: It is defined as a function that depends on time, taken to days as a unit of time and behaving under the equation:

$$Y = 276,6X + 7674089 \tag{1}$$

Where X is the day (projection period as of January 1, 2017).

Waste behavior: The solid waste of the city of Bogotá will behave in accordance with the PGIRS Solid Waste Management Plan, as follows:

years;   2017 and 2018: 0.92 kg per capita daily,
2018 and 2020, 0.93 kg per capita daily.

Number of recyclers: It is an independent random variable, which behaves according to the distribution probability functions.

Collected material to recycle: It is a function that depends on the number of daily recyclers and is defined by

$$Y = 486,62X^{0,9706} \tag{2}$$

Material to be landfilled: It is defined as the difference between the material produced and the material collected for recycling.

Daily efficiency of the system: It is defined as the level of collection of recyclable material collected in a period, on the potential of collecting recyclable material generated in the same period of study.

The model (see Fig. 5) consists of 5 modules defined by: Waste Generation, the waste separation module consisting of what in the different generation sources is achieved by separating waste, the waste recovery module through the Recyclers, the fourth module of generation of unrecovered material that goes to landfills and that constitutes the objective of the simulation. Finally the fifth module that deals with the indicators of the model.

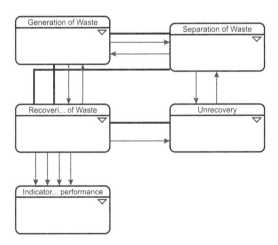

Fig. 5. General layout of logistic model in Ithink

Below is the construction of the model and its level of detail (see Fig. 6). We work with the random variables that associate the day with recyclers and waste recovery rate, additionally there are two variables that measure the daily efficiency of the system: It is defined as the level of collection of recyclable material collected in a period, on the potential of collecting recyclable material generated in the same period of study, these are the efficiency of recovery and the efficiency of recyclers.

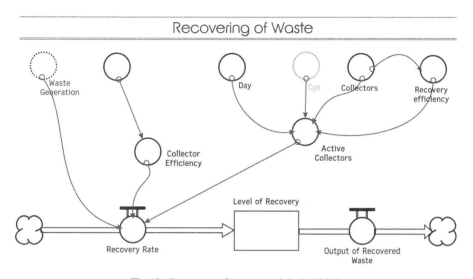

Fig. 6. Recovery of waste module in Ithink

Additionally there is a [26] collectors Mode parameter that indicates if these collectors are on foot and only manage to handle up to 50 kg/day of waste, or if they go in human traction vehicles that can collect up to 500 kg/day, The idisponen of mechanical vehicles of 1000 or 5000 kg/day.

Figure 7 shows the results of the model developed in IThink, in this case is much higher the rate of waste generated compared to what is recovered by the recyclers or what is obtained recovery at source (a). Therefore the percentages Fig. 7b, shows the high percentage of residues that go to the landfill.

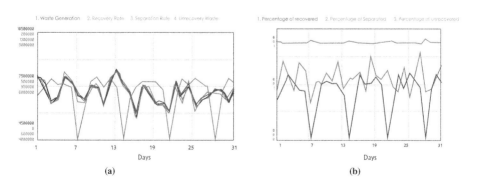

Fig. 7. Results of simulation model

4   Experimentation and Results

Three parameters are proposed for the design of scenarios: Number of recyclers, collector mode and waste separation factor that are generated in the source. All these values are related in Table 1, of these 60 experiments were constructed which were run In 5 replicates versus three measures of performance that are: Percentage of separation at the source, percentage of recovery obtained by the system of recyclers and percentage of material not recovered, that finally goes to landfills and that of course we want to minimize.

Table 1. Experimental setting.

Factor	No. Levels	Unit	Levels
Recyclers (collectors)	3	Unit	10000
			12500
			15000
Collector mode	4	N.A.	1: Manual
			2: Human traction vehicle
			3: Vehicle of 1 Tn
			4: Vehicle of 5 Tn
Recovery efficiency	5	%	14
			16
			18
			20
			22

The current rate of recycling or separation at the current source is 14% per cent, this percentage can be increased according to the public policies for presenting waste and awareness campaigns on separation at source, what which according to [25] Decree 596 of 2016 should be implemented by municipalities and municipal public service operators.

The maximum value estimated for the increase of said rate of separation at source is 22%, as established in [24] Characterization of Residential Solid Residues Generated in the City of Bogotá D.C 2011, made by the Special Administrative Unit of Public Services UAESP (Table 2).

Table 2. Sample scenarios developed.

Exp. No.	Collectors	Collector mode	Separation factor (%)	Separation (%)	Recovery (%)	Unrecovered (%)	Total cost
2	10000	1	16	14,4	1,2	84,4	$1.113.839.825
13	10000	3	18	16,2	23,8	60,0	$1.151.240.119
16	10000	4	14	12,6	84,7	12,8	$352.700.212
48	15000	2	18	16,2	14,8	69,0	$1.243.282.565
60	15000	4	22	19,8	85,4	11,4	$809.510.016

If it were to minimize the impact on the waste, it is obvious that the best performance experiment is the one with the largest number of recyclers, working with 5-ton trucks and also having the highest percentage of separation at source say 22%.

However, if the costs are considered, the result is no longer so attractive; Unfortunately, there are no studies that have determined all the cost factors for the different options. When no real cost estimator was available, data were collected from different sources such as the CGR operator, which is the operator of the Doña Juana Sanitary Landfill, and others were estimated, such as operating costs in the different modes and the different percentages of Separation. Of course these values are only approximate of what in reality can happen, being extremely difficult to estimate the value of separation in the source.

However it is difficult because of the high investment costs to equip all the collectors with trucks of 5 tons, for it modifies this scenario giving a mode of operation 3 and that does not in fact indicate that all the recyclers necessarily operating with vehicles with a cargo capacity of 1000 kg, if combinations of the average value are available, at the example level if 10% of recyclers do it manually (mode 1), 20% collect with vehicles of 65% with vehicles of 1000 kg of cargo and 5% with vehicles of 5000 kg of cargo, would be equivalent to having 100% with vehicles of 1000 kg of cargo.

The other proposal for improvement is to increase the base of recyclers since, although there are more than 10000 recyclers, there are no more than 3,500 working every day and no more than 400 on Sundays. This takes another factor called option (opt) for the development of scenarios, which contemplates 6 levels, the one of option 1 that is the normal one, option 2 that works with an average of the seventh part of the collectors in each day, the option 3 that works with an average of 20% of recyclers each day, option 4 that on average works with 25% of the recyclers; Option 5 that works with 35% and option 6 with the average 45% of recyclers each day.

The results of these new runs contemplate only working with mode 3 and in Table 3 again is shown a part of the scenario run including the best alternative.

Table 3. Sample scenarios developed.

Exp. No.	Option	Collectors	Separation factor (%)	Separation (%)	Recuperation (%)	Unrecovered (%)	Total cost
116	5	15000	0,14	12,6	58,1	29,4	$539.710.625
111	5	12500	0,14	12,6	55,4	32,0	$549.442.894
122	6	10000	0,16	14,4	60,5	25,1	$265.652.502
131	6	15000	0,14	12,6	75,1	12,8	$357.724.294

In this case the best option is where there is between 40% and 50% of the recyclers working every day in their work of collection with a means of work vehicle with cargo of 1000 kg, or in their absence the combination as the proposal and a source separation of 16%. This in addition to lowering the daily costs of operation means that only a quarter of the waste goes to the landfill.

5 Conclusions

By means of the present investigation we can conclude the following:
Even if the percentage of separation in the source (recycling) is increased and the goal set by the PGIRS is reached, to reach 22% per person; The collection capacity of recyclers is not enough to handle the volume of material generated.

The waste collection frequencies must be structured, as they depend on the routes of the recyclers and not being completely standardized, it is not possible to carry out an effective programming to collect all potentially recyclable material.

The material that is generated on Sundays is not always fully collected on Monday, in relation to potentially recyclable material.

It is clear that the factors subject to measurement such as the rate of separation at source as the recycling population and its efficiency are directly related to the recycling efficiency of the city, since if these do not grow simultaneously, no effect will be seen Positive.

It is necessary to arrive at an optimal mix between the parameters of separation at the source, number of recyclers and capacity of load of the recyclers to establish an efficient system at the lowest possible cost.

References

1. Vásquez, O.: Modelo de simulación de gestión de residuos sólidos domiciliarios en la Región Metropolitana de Chile. Revista de Dinámica de Sistemas **1**, 27–52 (2005)
2. Peña, A., Rojas, F.: Modelo Sistémico en la Gestión de Residuos Sólidos Domiciliarios en la Zona Metropolitana de Huancayo - Perú. Ingeniería y Tecnología (2013)
3. Ibarra, D., Redondo, J.: Modelo Sistémico para el Manejo de Residuos Sólidos en Instituciones Educativas en Colombia. 9° Encuentro Colombiano de Dinámica de Sistemas – 14 al 16 de septiembre de 2011, Bogotá – Colombia (2011)
4. Fujii, M., Fujita, T., Ohnishi, S., et al.: Regional and temporal simulation of a smart recycling system for municipal organic solid wastes. J. Clean. Prod. (2014). doi:10.1016/j.jclepro.2014.04.066
5. Geng, Y., Tsuyoshi, F., Chen, X.: Evaluation of innovative municipal solid waste management through urban symbiosis: a case study of Kawasaki. J. Clean. Prod. **18**, 993–1000 (2010). doi:10.1016/j.jclepro.2010.03.003
6. Georgiadis, P.: An integrated system dynamics model for strategic capacity planning in closed-loop recycling networks: a dynamic analysis for the paper industry. Simul. Model. Pract. Theory **32**, 116–137 (2013). doi:10.1016/j.simpat.2012.11.009
7. Anghinolfi, D., Paolucci, M., Robba, M., Taramasso, A.: A dynamic optimization model for solid waste recycling. Waste Manag. **33**, 287–296 (2013). doi:10.1016/j.wasman.2012.10.006
8. Johansson, O.: The effect of dynamic scheduling and routing in a solid waste management system. Waste Manag. **26**, 875–885 (2006). doi:10.1016/j.wasman.2005.09.004
9. Faccio, M., Persona, A., Zanin, G.: Waste collection multi objective model with real time traceability data. Waste Manag. **31**, 2391–2405 (2011). doi:10.1016/j.wasman.2011.07.005
10. Guariso, G., Michetti, F., Porta, F., Moore, S.: Modelling the upgrade of an urban waste disposal system. Environ. Model Softw. **24**, 1314–1322 (2009). doi:10.1016/j.envsoft.2009.04.008

11. Runfola, J., Gallardo, A.: Análisis comparativo de los diferentes métodos de caracterización de residuos urbanos para su recolección selectiva en comunidades urbanas. II Simposio I Iberoamericano de Ingeniería de Residuos (2009)
12. Mejia-Urbaez, Y.: Análisis mediante simulación para la comparación y cuantificación de residuos, pp. 45–65 (2017)
13. Diabat, A., Kannan, D., Kaliyan, M., Svetinovic, D.: An optimization model for product returns using genetic algorithms and artificial immune system. Resour. Conserv. Recycl. **74**, 156–169 (2013). doi:10.1016/j.resconrec.2012.12.010
14. Álvarez-Gil, M., Berrone, P., Husillos, F., Lado, N.: Reverse logistics, stakeholders' influence, organizational slack, and managers' posture. J. Bus. Res. **60**, 463–473 (2007). doi:10.1016/j.jbusres.2006.12.004
15. Rogers, D., Tibben-Lembke, R.: Going Backwards: Reverse Logistics Trends and Practices, pp. 147–164. Reverse Logistics Executive Council (1999)
16. Gallo, M., Murino, T., Romano, E.: The simulation of hybrid logic in reverse logistics network. Sel. Top. Syst. Sci. Simul. Eng. 378–384 (2010)
17. Nativi, J., Lee, S.: Impact of RFID information-sharing strategies on a decentralized supply chain with reverse logistics operations. Int. J. Prod. Econ. **136**, 366–377 (2012). doi:10.1016/j.ijpe.2011.12.024
18. Poles, R.: System dynamics modelling of a production and inventory system for remanufacturing to evaluate system improvement strategies. Int. J. Prod. Econ. **144**, 189–199 (2013). doi:10.1016/j.ijpe.2013.02.003
19. Özbayrak, M., Papadopoulou, T., Akgun, M.: Systems dynamics modelling of a manufacturing supply chain system. Simul. Model. Pract. Theory **15**, 1338–1355 (2007). doi:10.1016/j.simpat.2007.09.007
20. Georgiadis, P., Vlachos, D., Iakovou, E.: A system dynamics modeling framework for the strategic supply chain management of food chains. J. Food Eng. **70**, 351–364 (2005). doi:10.1016/j.jfoodeng.2004.06.030
21. Chan, W., Son, Y., Macal, C.: Agent-based simulation tutorial - simulation of emergent behavior and differences between agent-based simulation and discrete-event simulation. In: Proceedings of the 2010 Winter Simulation Conference (2010). doi:10.1109/wsc.2010.5679168
22. Meng, X., Wen, Z., Qian, Y.: Multi-agent based simulation for household solid waste recycling behavior. Resour. Conserv. Recycl. (2016). doi:10.1016/j.resconrec.2016.09.033
23. Shi, X., Thanos, A., Celik, N.: Multi-objective agent-based modeling of single-stream recycling programs. Resour. Conserv. Recycl. **92**, 190–205 (2014). doi:10.1016/j.resconrec.2014.07.002
24. Unidad Administrativa Especial De Servicios Públicos: Caracterización de los residuos sólidos residenciales generados en la ciudad de Bogotá D.C., pp. 24–58 (2012)
25. Decreto 596 de 2016. Bogotá D.C. (2016)
26. Corredor, M.: El Sector Reciclaje en Bogotá y su Región: Oportunidades para los Negocios Inclusivos, pp. 37–44 (2010)

A Hybrid System Dynamics and Fuzzy Logic Approach to Social Problem of Corruption in Colombia

Germán Andres Méndez-Giraldo[1],
Eduyn Ramiro López-Santana[1(✉)], and Carlos Franco[2]

[1] Universidad Distrital Francisco José de Caldas, Bogotá, Colombia
{gmendez, erlopezs}@udistrital.edu.co
[2] Universidad de la Sabana, Chía-Cundinamarca, Colombia
carlosfrfr@unisabana.edu.co

Abstract. This paper presents a system dynamics approach to the corruption problem in Colombia. The main causes were identified in service systems and their relation to drug trafficking. Each of these problems were modeled following the System Dynamics methodology, building causal diagrams and the simulation models that represent the dynamics of the factors that influence corruption such as: economic, political, social, psychological, and cultural factors. These factors are integrated in a general simulation model involving fuzzy logic in the inputs, which allows validating the behavior modeled and identify aspects to reducing the corruption in Colombia.

Keywords: Corruption · System dynamics · Drugs traffic · Public services · Fuzzy logic

1 Introduction

In recent years, there has been an increase in the recognition of the harmful effects of the problem of corruption on both economic growth and the welfare of society, with the latter evidencing indicators such as per capita income, literacy, infant mortality, among other aspects [1]. It has also increased the demand for practical strategies that effectively reduce this social problem, which in a few words is defined as the misuse of power.

Different studies of corruption have been carried out, characterizing in each of them different aspects of the problem such as: the factors that promote it [2–4]; the most frequent typologies [5–8]; the costs generated and others economic and social aspects derive; indicators of the measurement of corruption in specific periods of time [1, 9, 10]; and many others. Each of these elements has been analyzed from different perspectives, typifying political, economic, cultural variables, among others.

Table 1 summarizes the anti-corruption policies and measures in Colombia during the last five Governments. However, Colombia's efforts to reduce corruption have not been effective. Figure 1 shows the historical values of the Colombian Corruption

© Springer International Publishing AG 2017
J.C. Figueroa-García et al. (Eds.): WEA 2017, CCIS 742, pp. 250–262, 2017.
DOI: 10.1007/978-3-319-66963-2_23

Perception Index, where it can be seen that in the last two decades, it has not exceeded 40. Until 2011, the scale measured the Corruption Index from zero to 10 and from that year is measured from zero to 100, so the above data were taken to the new scale. It can be observed that it has not been possible to reduce this index in spite of the efforts of control by the Colombian government.

Table 1. Colombian government efforts to combat corruption (1990–2014).

Year	Government efforts to combat corruption
1990–1994	During the presidency of **Cesar Gaviria** (1990–1994), the approach was neoliberal, and a reform of civil service and public procurement was advanced to reduce opportunities for corruption. In addition, the constitutional change occurred and the new Constitution modified the control agencies, created the prosecution, the accusatory system and a regime of inabilities and incompatibilities for public workers. Other actions in the area of corruption prevention were internal control system, disciplinary regime and electoral reform
1994–1998	The Government of **Ernesto Samper** (1994–1998), made a Transparency Plan in which there was a greater role for the citizens. The evaluation of management and results was introduced with the creation of a National System for these purposes (Synergy), and the figure of codes of ethics was introduced. In addition, the first anti-corruption statute was issued (Law 190 of 1995). This changed the regime of public servants, penal and financial, to create more controls, allow a system of complaints and improve the quality of public information
1998–2002	In the Government of **Andrés Pastrana** (1998–2002), the Presidential Program of Fight against Corruption (PPFC) was created. Its director acquired in the media the title of anticorruption "Tsar". This program was placed under the Vice President of the Republic as a gesture to indicate the intention to give political priority to the issue and the possibility of acting on the entire executive branch. The program began with an approach combined prevention, control and sanction mechanisms and with the development of values such as efficiency and transparency
2002–2010	During the Government of **Álvaro Uribe** (2002–2010), a different course was taken on the subject of corruption. Among its first government actions was the creation of the Public Administration Renewal Program (PARP), which aimed to modernize the state, reduce costs and introduce principles of efficiency in the operation of public administration. The issue of the fight against corruption was relegated to second place, as shown by the nominations of directors for the Presidential Anti-Corruption Program, who were less important than their predecessors were and did not take forward significant actions
2011–2018	The Government of President **Juan Manuel Santos** (2010–present) created a High Presidential Office for Good Governance and gave new impetus to the issue, with the proposal of a new anti-corruption law and a work in progress to formulate an Anti-corruption policy since the Presidential Program. Norms have been issued to deal with this scourge (Anti-Corruption Statute, Anti-corruption Decree, Anti-Bribery Convention, Access to Information Law, etc.), cases are investigated and denounced in strategic sectors (Taxes, Health, Education); finally, the Secretary of Transparency was created to advise the President

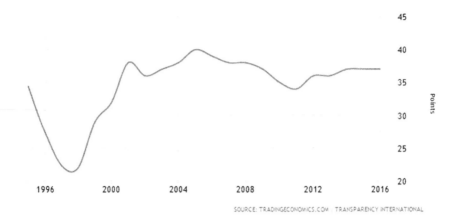

Fig. 1. Colombian corruption perception index (1990–2013).

The rest of this article is organized as follows: In Sect. 2, the followed methods to model are presented, after that, the general model of simulation. In Sect. 3, we present the results of experiments carried out with the simulation model in order to determine alternatives to reduce the corruption in Colombia. Finally, Sect. 4 presents the conclusions and lists some future research work.

2 Methods

In this section, we present the methodology used for the modeling process in which it will define the fuzzy sets for the causes of the corruption problem that are the inputs to the system dynamics model that is presented later.

2.1 Methodology

Figure 2 presents the main elements of the methodology used for the construction of the general model that describes the behavior of corruption in the Colombian case and which has been supported in the models developed in [11].

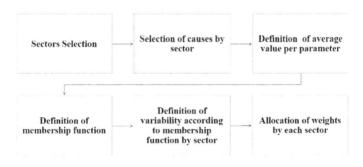

Fig. 2. Methodology of construction of the general model.

In the phase of sectors selection from the models presented by [11] it selects the most representative sectors that affect both the positive and negative increase in corruption, such as: Cultural (C), Economic (E), Drug Trafficking (DT), Political (P), Psychological (Ps), Services (Se) and Social (So) aspects. It is important to emphasize that both contracting and provision of services or drug trafficking models, have been included as high impact sectors in which the corruption is originated, as mentioned in [11]. These sectors constitute accumulators of information that favors or does not favor corruption and therefore, the model must have factors that allow its growth or decline.

In the phase of Selection of causes by sector, the main causes are chosen (they are not taken all of them because the objective is only to take the ones with the highest incidence in corruption) and then, it is defined if this cause becomes a factor of in-crease or decrease of the sector. That is why two types of relationship are defined according

Table 2. Causal sectors and causal relationships

Sector	Cause	Effect	Sector	Cause	Effect
C	Education	R	P	Centralization	C
C	Family	R	P	Institutional efficiency	R
C	Cultural heritage	C	P	Impunity	C
C	Individualism	C	P	Infiltration	C
C	Culture of trafficking of narcotics	C	P	Anti-corruption legislation	R
C	Cultural pressure	C	P	International pressure	R
C	Values	R	Ps	Social acceptance	C
DT	Absence of government	C	Ps	Anarchy	C
DT	Education	R	Ps	Greed	C
DT	Infiltration	C	Ps	Education	R
DT	Drug trafficking income	C	Ps	Intimidation	C
DT	Social investment	C	Ps	Power	C
DT	Culture of trafficking of narcotics	C	Ps	Bribery	C
DT	Poverty	C	Ps	Values	R
DT	International pressure	C	Se	Anarchy	C
DT	Values	R	Se	Absence of government	C
E	Smuggling	C	Se	Centralization	C
E	Economic growth	C	Se	Public funds for security	R
E	Drug demand	C	Se	Public investment	R
E	Unemployment	R	Se	Social investment	R
E	Social inequality	C	Se	Violence	C
E	Public funds for security	R	So	Social acceptance	C
E	Drug trafficking income	R	So	Anarchy	C
E	Public investment	C	So	Social benefits	C
E	Social investment	R	So	Distrust	C
E	Drug trafficking offer	R	So	Education	R
E	Poverty	C	So	Public information	R
E	Salary	C	So	Citizen participation	R
p	Absence of government	C	So	Violence	C

with what is proposed in the methodology of Systems Dynamics as expressed in publications such as [12–14], a reinforcing effect (R) or increase and a compensating effect (C) or of decreasing. Table 2 presents information related to this analysis.

In Table 2, it can be seen that some causes are part of several sectors and that may additionally have different increase or decrease effects, depending on the sector to which it impacts. This is of importance in the later stages of implementation of the methodology.

In the next phase of definition of values by each parameter, first, they were taken the statistics presented in [11]; after that, there were calculated the average values of the time series and transformed them into percentage terms. For these transformation was used a panel of experts and was considerate the causality analysis. Table 3 presents an example for three variables such as anti-corruption legislation, international pressure and centralization with respect to the source of information and its role of belonging. The other variables can be consulted in [11].

In the definition phase of the membership function it uses the concepts of fuzzy logic where mainly tries to classify the values of a variable in a linguistic attribute but based on the imprecision about its category since these are perceived differently by each person. The membership value used in this phase is as shown in Table 3.

Once the parameter value is identified, it is measured according to the membership function and calculated near functions when is required. In this case, the judgments of the experts or the use of the correlation index between variables, is used. Figure 3 shows how the qualitative membership function is and how the values are assigned (Low, Medium or High). These values are associated with the sector to which the parameter belongs.

Table 3. Estimation of values by parameter and category of membership functions

Parameter	Source of information	Membership function	
		Value	Interval
Anti-corruption legislation	Anticorruption Statute by which rules are adopted to strengthen mechanisms for prevention, investigation and punishment of acts of corruption and the effectiveness of the control of public administration Law 1474 of 2011	Null	0
		Low	0–30
		Medium	30–70
		High	70–100
		Value: 50	
International pressure	Primarily given by the USA and its certification in the fight against drug trafficking, on the other hand pressure from various Courts and NGOs. It is taken among many others to drug trafficking, political violence and foreign policy of the United States towards Colombia in the nineties [15]	High	70–100
		Medium	40–70
		Low	0–40
		Value: 70	
Centralization	According to what is seen of standards as well as the number of departments and municipalities, taken mainly from territorial decentralization in Colombia: situation and policy perspectives [16]	High	70–100
		Medium	30–70
		Low	0–30
		Value: 80	

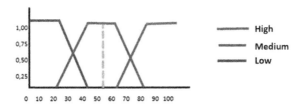

Fig. 3. Membership function of the variables to their sector.

In the definition phase of the variability according to the sector to which it belongs, it establishes the parameters, whose categories as already mentioned, can be Low, Medium or High and have the possibility of changing value. This variability value is necessary in order to adjust to the reality and to reduce the errors in the measures obtained in the previous stage. It also allows mitigating the influence of the interactions of the variables within the same sector, since a low influence relation could be more affected than a high influence relation within the same sector could. In this case, reinforcing and compensating influences are distinguished and therefore the variabilities are considered in the same sense. For the calculation of these variabilities is used a uniform random variable with an amplitude was taken in proportion to the averages of the membership functions. In addition, a confidence interval of 5% was considered compared to the mean estimated in the previous stage. In this way, a symmetric variability index is constructed, ranging from 5% to 15%.

Table 4 shows this variability by sector and influence relationship. It can be observed that these relations are valid because they are in the averages with a general value of variability of 8.5%, which in general is considered quite adjusted.

Table 4. Variability by sector

Sector	Loop	Variability%	Sector	Loop	Variability%
Cultural	R	10,00	Psychological	R	7,50
	C	7,50		C	8,33
Drug trafficking	R	8,33	Services	R	11,66
	C	8,75		C	6,25
Economic	R	10,00	Social	R	9,00
	C	9,5		C	6,75
Political	R	8,33			
	C	7,00			

Finally, in the sector weightings Assignment phase, it refers to the percentage incidence of the different parameters in a particular sector. It should be noted that for the same parameter different contributions could be made because their incidence changes between sectors or with the loop that it belongs. In any case, it is maintained that for each reinforcing or compensating effect the parameters contribute one hundred percent. These values are shown in Table 5.

Table 5. Assignment of weights by parameter and sector

Sector	Parameter	Loop	Weight %	Sector	Parameter	Loop	Weight %
C	Education	R	30	Ps	Social acceptance	C	10
	Family	R	35		Anarchy	C	10
	Cultural heritage	C	15		Greed	C	20
	Individualism	C	20		Education	R	70
	Culture of trafficking of narcotics	C	35		Intimidation	C	20
	Cultural pressure	C	30		Power	C	20
	Values	R	35		Bribery	C	20
E	Smuggling	C	10		Values	R	30
	Economic growth	R	40	Se	Anarchy	C	20
	Drug demand	C	15		Absence of Government	C	30
	Unemployment	C	10		Centralization	C	20
	Social inequality	C	10		Public funds for security	R	30
	Public funds for security	C	10		Public investment	R	30
	Drug trafficking income	C	10		Social investment	R	40
	Public investment	C	10		Violence	C	30
	Social investment	R	60	So	Social acceptance	C	20
	Drug trafficking offer	C	5		Anarchy	C	20
	Poverty	C	10		Social benefits	C	20
	Salary	C	10		Distrust	C	20
DT	Absence of government	R	10		Education	R	30
	Education	C	20		Public information	R	35
	Infiltration	R	10		Citizen participation	R	35
	Drug trafficking income	R	50		Violence	C	20
	Social investment	C	40	P	Absence of Government	C	25
	Culture of trafficking of narcotics	R	10		Centralization	C	15
	Poverty	R	20		Institutional efficiency	R	25
	International pressure	C	20		Impunity	C	30
	Values	C	20		Infiltration	C	30
					Anti-corruption legislation	R	25
					International pressure	R	50

2.2   General Simulation Model

The development of this model was carried out in the IThink continuous simulation software version 8.1, its comprehension becomes easier if one observes the general structure or high-level layer, as it is shown in Fig. 4.

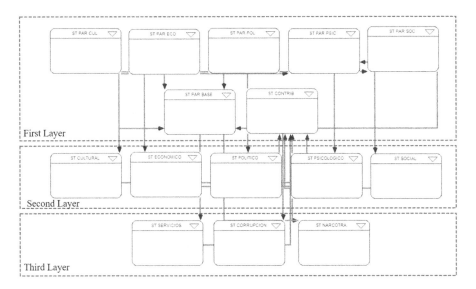

Fig. 4. General model of high level corruption.

The Diagram shows three levels or layers: The first, is about the parameters and corresponds to the five sectors defined above, also shows the parameters used in the drug trafficking model and the parameters used in the contracting and provision of services model; finally, the contribution of each sector is shown with the contribution weights. At the second level, the five sectors: Cultural, economic, political, psychological and social are affected by the corresponding parameters and their contributions or weights. At the third level, there are two other sectors modeled such as the contracting and provision of services and the drug trafficking; and finally, the sector of corruption model itself appears. The detail of each of these models can be found in [11].

3   Results

To carry out the validation, a qualitative measurement technique was used since there are no statistical measurements of the values of corruption. For this purpose, it wanted to show the trends of this measure in relation to changes in certain parameters of interest. Table 6 shows the implemented scenarios as well as the current values of the parameters involved.

Table 6. Values of the validation scenarios

Parameter	Current value %	Impact low%	Average impact%	High impact%	Very high impact%
Impunity	95	25	50	75	100
Social inequality	53	25	50	75	100
Values	70	25	50	75	100
Social investment	50	25	50	75	100
Narcotics demand	85	25	50	75	100
Drug trafficking revenues	95	25	50	75	100

As in the model, it considered random effects both for the contribution of sectors and for corruption, as well as for the proper conformation of each of the different factors: culture, politics, social, services, drug trafficking and psychological factors. Two runs are taken, one in which the net effects on corruption are lower (net negative change) and in the other where the net effects are higher (net positive change). First, the change in different contributions to increase or decrease corruption is analyzed.

Figure 5 shows the level of corruption in the typical conditions of the case in Colombia. Although it is a model that is varying with time, its levels do not move beyond certain controlled limits, both for the negative net change (Figure on the left), as well as for a positive net change (Figure on the right); and also remain in the time, which for this type of validation is 30 years.

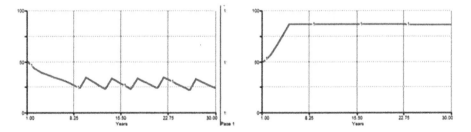

Fig. 5. Evolution of corruption under current (stable) conditions.

As is to be expected if the other parametric conditions are maintained unchanged (ceteris paribus) by increasing Impunity, corruption will increase or, if Impunity decreases, this value of corruption will decrease, see Fig. 6. In the particular case, the level of Impunity (in current model), has a value of 95%, this figure describes the four scenarios with levels of impunity corresponding to 25%, 50%, 75 and 100%. The figure on the left shows a net change from negative corruption and from the right a positive change. This factor of Impunity in the long term does not reflect significant changes in the decrease or increase of corruption, while it is inferred that in an environment of decreasing levels of corruption tends to control Impunity better and that on the contrary, in the case where corruption is favored, Impunity remains high.

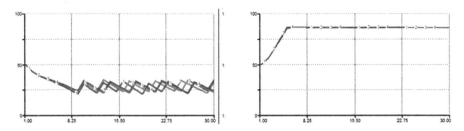

Fig. 6. Evolution of corruption in terms of impunity.

In the case of Social Inequality, the same type of analysis is done as in the case of the previous parameter, the results can be seen in Fig. 7. Currently it has a value of 53%.

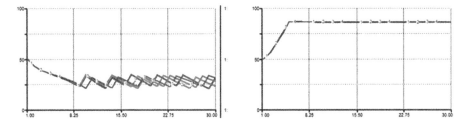

Fig. 7. Evolution of corruption in terms of social inequality.

The behavior of Social Inequality has a behavior similar to that of impunity, in which it is emphasized that when lowering inequality if the propensity to corruption is low, this impact is more noticeable than in the opposite case. The value of Social Inequality is moving with the same tendency that given by corruption. In the case of having a growth of corruption there is no difference in the line of changes in Social Inequality, that is to say that corruption is maintained in high values regardless of how much the inequality gap closes.

For the Values variable, the reference value is 70%. The scenarios are handled with the same values as in previous cases; the results are shown in Fig. 8. In this case, it is observed that if the propensity is to reduce corruption, when a high number of parameter named Value is obtained (Scenario 1). Then the corruption tends to increase when the values parameter is lowered indicating that these values have to be controlled so as not to trigger corruption. For other scenarios you have to adjust more the corruption to changes of this when the parameter of Values increase, that is to say it is kept more controlled when increasing the values. In the case of having a propensity to have high corruption, it is possible to perceive that it there is a possibility to reduce it, when having more Values. Therefore, it can be affirmed that the Values influence in any case in a way compensatory to the corruption, that is to say that they are due to stimulate the Values so that corruption tends to decrease.

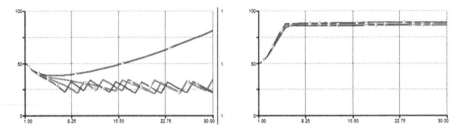

Fig. 8. Evolution of corruption in terms of values.

In social investment, the current value is 50%. The results for the four scenarios for both net negative effects and positive effects of corruption are given in Fig. 9. In this case, it is significant to show that if corruption is favored by the network (on the right) it obtains a relevant decrease effect, caused by the increase in social investment, unlike what happens when the network does not promote corruption and there is an indifference to this low level of corruption regarding this kind of investment.

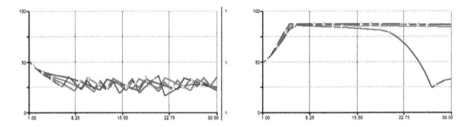

Fig. 9. Evolution of corruption in terms of social investment.

Drug Demand is currently at a level of 85% and changes in corruption against this parameter when keeping the rest constant, is observed in Fig. 10. In this case, when the net change in corruption is negative or positive, the effects of the Demand are not as noticeable as in previous analyzes. However, it is possible to differentiate the corruption curves maintain the trend according to the levels of Demand of Drugs, if Demand is low, the level of corruption falls slightly and if Demand rises this level of corruption rises slightly.

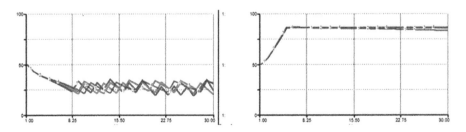

Fig. 10. Evolution of corruption according to the demand for drug trafficking.

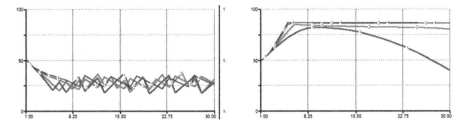

Fig. 11. Evolution of corruption in terms of income from drug trafficking.

For Drug Revenues, the value in the current situation analyzed is maintained at a value of 95% and the effects of changing this parameter can be seen in Fig. 11. In this case, if the contribution has a net change negative, the influence of changes in the Drug Revenues are not very noticeable, while if the net changes in corruption are positive, and is due to the reduction of income because it has a great incidence. Therefore, it is confirmed what many analysts proposed that it is to lower the Drug Revenues of this illegal activity, as this will reduce the reinforcing effects on corruption.

4   Conclusions

There is a wide and deep diffusion of studies of the social phenomenon of corruption; which are more of a qualitative rather than a quantitative character and when these investigations refer to values. They do it in an incomplete and isolated way, being their main contribution, the analysis of economic impact effect of the corruption over the public resource and private resources too, that in total go to the detriment of what could mean the availability of more resources to improve the welfare of society.

In order to show the effects of the first of the two main causes of corruption, that is to say, the contracting and provision of services, we conclude that the most influential is impunity added to the power conferred on political power in administrative structures and of management of quotas of personnel in the public entities. This compromises the actions of the officials supporting the people who get them the administrative positions favoring the clienteles. Likewise, there is a high level of impunity due to centralization and inadequate management of information, where most of the actions are unknown by the public and by the control bodies created by the state.

Public officials understand that they can execute corrupt acts that generate an extra income and that in the case of being discovered enjoy the favor of some politician who protects them. Because later on they will ask for reciprocity in other contracting process; then corruption increases because it is profitable for the official and because there are no effective mechanisms to avoid these acts.

As for the case of drug trafficking as an influential element for corruption, political and economic sectors are considered more influential, since this scourge influenced both. It is clear the influence that the drug trade had in the economic sector since on one hand, it stimulated positive economic growth, especially that of construction but unfortunately created an inflationary bubble in this sector; likewise, It deeply affects the economy of the country mainly with smuggling and laundering of assets.

As future work, a collection of information as input of the simulation models could be in order to validate the representation and determine factors that lead to the establishment of policies to reduce the damages derived from corruption. In addition, it is possible to explore the modeling and integration of agent-based simulation to explain the behavior of qualitative variables as an emergent effect of human interactions.

Acknowledgment. This work is partially supported by the Center for Research and Scientific Development of the Francisco José de Caldas District University (Colombia) under project No. 2-15-308-12.

References

1. World Bank: Anticorruption in Transition: A Contribution to the Policy Debate. World Bank Publications, Washington (2000)
2. Cobb, L., González, M.: Corruption as a system of vicious cycles intertwined: lessons from nation-lab (in Spanish). Secur. Def. Stud. Rev. **7**, 1–11 (2007)
3. Heidenheimer, A.J., Johnston, M., LeVine, V.T.: Political Corruption: A Handbook. Transaction Publishers, New Brunswick (2009)
4. Rose-Ackerman, S.: Corruption and governments: causes, consequences and reform (in Spanish). Siglo XXI de España Editores (2001)
5. Bautista, O.D.: Ethics for Corrupt: A Way to Prevent Corruption in Governments and Public Administrations (in Spanish). Desclée, Bilbao (2009)
6. Campos, J.E., Pradhan, S.: The Multiple Faces of Corruption: Vulnerable Aspects by Sector (in Spanish). The International Bank for Reconstruction and Development/The World Bank Publishers, Washington (2009)
7. Frattini, E.: ONU History of Corruption (in Spanish). Bubok Publishing S.L, Madrid (2009)
8. Estévez, A.: Theoretical reflections on corruption: its political, economic and social dimensions (in Spanish). Venezuelan Rev. Manag. **10**, 43–86 (2005)
9. Fan, C.S., Lin, C., Treisman, D.: Political decentralization and corruption: evidence from around the world. J. Public Econ. **93**, 14–34 (2009)
10. Smith, D.J.: A Culture of Corruption: Everyday Deception and Popular Discontent in Nigeria. Princeton University Press, Princeton (2007)
11. Méndez-Giraldo, G.A., López-Santana, E.R.: Social problem of corruption: perspective from the dynamics of systems (in Spanish). Universidad Distrital Francisco José de Caldas (2016)
12. Sterman, J.: Business Dynamics: Systems Thinking and Modeling for a Complex World. Irwin/McGraw-Hill, Boston (2000)
13. Forrester, J.W.: Industrial Dynamics. Pegasus Communications, Waltham (1961)
14. Méndez, G.: System Dynamics and Social Problems (in Spanish). Universidad Distrital Francisco José de Caldas, Bogotá (2012)
15. Bagley, B.: Drug trafficking, political violence and United States foreign policy toward Colombia in the 1990s (in Spanish). Colomb. Int. **49**, 5–38 (2000)
16. Maldonado, A.: Territorial decentralization in Colombia: situation and policy perspectives (in Spanish). In: FESCOL (2011)

Simulation of Fuzzy Inference System to Task Scheduling in Queueing Networks

Eduyn Ramiro López-Santana[1(✉)], Carlos Franco-Franco[2], and Juan Carlos Figueroa-García[1]

[1] Universidad Distrital Francisco José de Caldas, Bogotá, Colombia
{erlopezs,jcfigueroag}@udistrital.edu.co
[2] Universidad de la Sabana, Chía-Cundinamarca, Colombia
carlosfrfr@unisabana.edu.co

Abstract. This paper presents a simulation approach of the problem of scheduling customers in a queuing networks using a fuzzy inference system. Usually, in the queuing systems there are rules as round robin, equiprobable, shortest queue, among others, to schedule customers, however the condition of the system like the cycle time, utilization and the length of queue is difficult to measure. We propose a fuzzy inference system in order to determine the status in the system using input variables like the length queue and utilization. Our simulation shows an improvement in the performance measures compared with traditional scheduling policies.

Keywords: Fuzzy logic · Scheduling · Queuing theory · Utilization

1 Introduction

Generally, the manufacturing and service systems have items or customers waiting for been processing, for example the customers in a bank, patients in a health services, the data in computing and communication services, the raw material in a production system, among the others. In real-world systems, the process are complex and usually have several steps, configuring around each one of them, queues whose requirements are measured in terms of response times, throughput, availability and security [1, 2]. These are the queuing networks (QN), where the features as feedback loops, non-linearity, variability, product mixes, and routing add more complexity [3].

López-Santana, Franco & Figueroa-Garcia [2] study the problem to scheduling tasks in a queuing systems considering the condition based systems in terms the queue's length, utilization and the work in process involving the imprecision in their measurement process. Their proposed fuzzy inference (FIS) systems allocates a specific task according to the condition in the systems measured in terms of queue's length and server's utilization in a single queuing system with reprocess or feedback loop.

The purpose of this paper consists in apply the FIS proposed by [2] in a QN in order to determine the server to allocate a specific task for each station according to its queue's length and server's utilization.

© Springer International Publishing AG 2017
J.C. Figueroa-García et al. (Eds.): WEA 2017, CCIS 742, pp. 263–274, 2017.
DOI: 10.1007/978-3-319-66963-2_24

The remainder of this paper is organized as follows: Sect. 2 introduces the problem statement of scheduling task in a queuing system and presents a short background and related works. Section 3 describes the FIS based solution. Section 4 illustrates our application in an example. Finally, Sect. 5 concludes this work and provides possible research directions.

2 Problem Statement and Background

A queueing system (QS) is a setting which a customer (e.g., humans, finished goods, messages) arrives at a service facility, get served according to a given service discipline, and then depart [4]. A Queueing Network (QN) arises when the service is completed by several stages (or stations) where it is served in a sequential way. The complexity increases in QNs because we need to consider more variables like capacity, routing probabilities, variability, blocking, reprocessing, among others [3].

2.1 Overview of QS and QN

Figure 1 shows the process in a QS, where the customers enter to the QS and join a queue [5]. At certain times, a member of the queue is selected for service by some rule known as the queue discipline. The required service is then performed for the customer by the service mechanism, after which the customer leaves the QS. A QS could be characterized in terms of Kendall's notation [6], whose encoding under the following structure:

$$1/2/3/4 \tag{1}$$

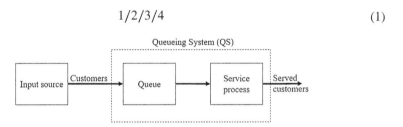

Fig. 1. The basic queuing system (source [5])

where 1 refers to the arrival process that can be Poisson (M), Deterministic (D) or general distribution different to Poisson (G); 2 is the service process that can be also M, D o G; 3 represents the number of servers by stage of process in the network, which can be single (represented by 1) or multiple (represented by s); and 4 states the system's capacity, infinite when it is empty or a K to indicate the queue's length.

According to [2], the standard terminology and notation in QS consider as the state of system the number of customers in the system. The Queue length (Ql) is the number of customers waiting for service to begin or state of system minus number of customers being served. $P_n(t)$ denotes the probability of exactly n customers in QS at time t, given number at time 0. s is the number of servers (parallel service channels) in the QS. λ_n is the mean arrival rate (expected number of arrivals per unit time) of new customers when n customers are in system and μ_n is the mean service rate for overall system (expected number of customers completing service per unit time) when n customers are in system. When λ_n is a constant for all n, this constant is denoted by λ. When the mean service rate per busy server is a constant for all $n \geq 1$, this constant is denoted by μ. (In this case, $\mu_n = s\mu$ when $n \geq s$, that is, when all s servers are busy.) Also, $\rho = \lambda/s\mu$ is the utilization factor for the service facility, i.e., the expected fraction of time the individual servers are busy, because $\lambda/s\mu$ represents the fraction of the system's service capacity $(s\mu)$ that is being utilized on the average by arriving customers (λ).

When a QS has recently begun operation, the state of the system (number of customers in the system) will be greatly affected by the initial state and by the time that has since elapsed. The system is said to be in a transient condition. However, after sufficient time has elapsed, the state of the system becomes essentially independent of the initial state and the elapsed time (except under unusual circumstances). The system has now essentially reached a steady-state condition, where the probability distribution of the state of the system remains the same (the steady-state or stationary distribution) over time. Queueing theory has tended to focus largely on the steady-state condition, partially because the transient case is more difficult analytically.

We assume that P_n is the probability of exactly n customers in queueing system. Then L is the expected number of customers in queueing system, it is computed by $\sum_{n=0}^{\infty} nP_n$, and L_q is the expected queue length (excludes customers being served), it is computed by $\sum_{n=s}^{\infty} (n - s)P_n$. In addition, W is the expected waiting time in system (includes service time) for each individual customer and W_q is the expected waiting time in queue (excludes service time) for each individual customer.

Assume that λ_n is a constant for all n. It has been proved that in a steady-state queueing process,

$$L = \lambda W. \tag{2}$$

It is known as Little [3]. Furthermore, the same proof also shows that

$$L_q = \lambda W_q. \tag{3}$$

The Eqs. (1) and (2) are extremely important because they enable all four of the fundamental quantities L, W, L_q, and W_q to be immediately determined as soon as one is found analytically.

2.2 Solution Techniques

A QN must be defined in terms of arrival and service rates, and routing probabilities or proportion in which classes of customers are transferred sequentially from one service stage to another. Particularly, the routing probabilities induces feedback cycles that increase complexity in the understanding of this type of systems.

A key feature of the QNs is whether these are open, closed, or mixed [2]. If the network permits the output of clients on the network then circular of default by the nodes required to complete the service, is considered an open network, otherwise it is considered a closed network. The network can receive different types of customers (multiclass) and can in turn be open for certain classes of customers and closed to other. Table 1 presents the scope of the analysis techniques described above, by specifying the types of customer and network that can be modeled with precision.

Table 1. Classification of analysis techniques scope of queueing networks

Analytical technique	Network topology	Customer type
Jackson networks	Open, closed	Single class
BCMP (Type I, II, III, IV)	Open, closed, mixed	Multiclass
Kingman's parametric decomposition	Open, closed, mixed	Multiclass, multi-class with retry
Mean value analysis	Open, closed	Single class
Equilibrium Point Analysis (EPA)	Open, closed, mixed	Multiclass, multi-class with retry

In the field of artificial intelligence, and specifically fuzzy inference systems and neuronal networks applied to QS and QNs, the research is scarce. Lopez-Santana et al. [2] presents some references who developed application in QS. Cruz [7] studies the problem of maximizing the throughput in QNs with general service time, finding the reduction in the total number of waiting areas and the service rate, through genetic algorithms multi-objective to find a feasible solution to the need of improve the service given the natural conflict between the cost and throughput. Other work is Yang and Liu [8], who develop a hybrid transfer function model that combines statistical analysis, simulation and analysis of queues, taking as input values the systems work rate, the performance variables throughput and work in process (WIP); the end result of the obtained model exposes the lack of fidelity of analytical models pre-set for this type of systems.

3   Solution Approach

López-Santana et al. [2] propose a Fuzzy inference system (FIS) which consists in a making decision process that consists of formulating the mapping from a given input to an output using fuzzy logic. Figure 2 shows a basic architecture of a FIS, which has as the output the cycle time (W) and the inputs the queue's length (Ql) and the utilization (u). This intuition is based in Kingman equation given by:

$$W = VUT \tag{4}$$

where, V refers to a variability in the system, U is the utilization and T is the time. Likewise, the Little Law in Eq. (1) refer that the W depends the L. Thus, we have two equations to determine the cycle time W and we propose to combine both in a FIS system involving the imprecision in the definition of the queue's length and the server's utilization.

For the Fuzzification and Defuzzification Interfaces we need to define the membership function (MF) for the inputs and output. For the queue's length we define three linguistic labels: small, medium, and large. Also, for the server utilization we use three

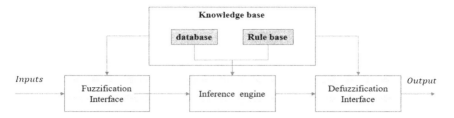

Fig. 2. Basic FIS architecture (source: [2])

linguistic labels: low, medium, and high. Figure 3 shows an example of the MFs for utilization (see Fig. 3(a)) and queue's length (see Fig. 3(b)). These MFs must be defined according to the system behavior. Figure 3(c) presents the MF for the cycle time W, where we state three linguistic labels: small, medium and large.

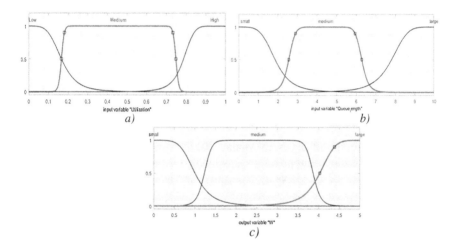

Fig. 3. Membership function of (a) utilization, (b) queue's length, and (c) cycle time W

Table 2 states the set of rules for the proposed FIS by [2].for each stage or station in a QN. For instance, if the utilization is low and the queue's length is large the cycle time is Large. The rest of rules works in a similar way. Figure 4 shows the rule based system and the response surface in graphs (a) and (b), respectively. For the response surface, we can observe as the utilization and queue's length increases the cycle time also increases. The proposed FIS is based on Mamdani inference system [9, 10] because this method is intuitive, has widespread acceptance and is well suited to human input.

Table 2. Rules based system for the proposed FIS

Utilization\Queue's length	Small	Medium	Large
Low	Small	Small	Large
Medium	Small	Medium	Large
High	Medium	Large	Large

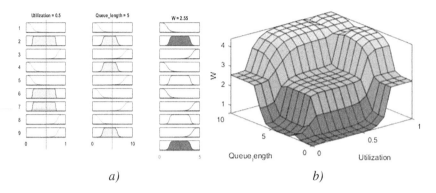

a)   *b)*

Fig. 4. Response of proposed FIS *(a)* rule base system, *(b)* response surface

This FIS system is evaluated in real time in a simulation process when a customer arrive to the queue, then a server l^* is determined as the server with the minimum value of W_l computed with the proposed FIS for all $l \in \{1, 2, .., s\}$ given as follows:

$$l^* = \mathrm{argmin}_{l \in \{1,2,...,s\}} \{W_l\}. \tag{5}$$

4 Experiments

We develop a prototype of a QN in Matlab 2017 using the toolbox of SimEvents. Figure 5*(a)* presents the prototype for a system with 4 servers each one with a queue, a single class of customer, the capacity is infinity, and rework is possible. Figure 5*(b)* shows the matlab function used to determine the selected queue in the scheduling process. The discipline in the queue is FIFO (First in First Out).

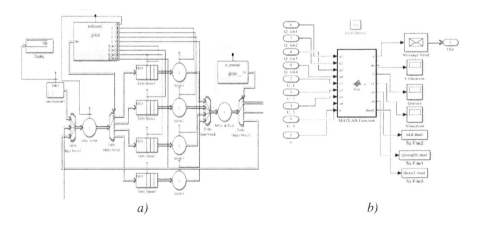

a)   *b)*

Fig. 5. Prototype for each station in QN. *(a)* single station, *(b)* matlab function to select the queue

Figure 6 presents the prototype of a QN with three stations. The first station has 4 servers, an input and rework probability of 0.2. Its outputs go to second and third stations with 0.3 and 0.5 probability, respectively. The second station has 3 servers, an additional input, rework probability of 0.15 and its outputs go to first station and third station with probability 0.4 and 0.45, respectively. The third station has 4 servers, rework and its outputs exit from the QN. Each station is a G/G/s system. For the first input in first station the inter arrival times follows a uniform probability density function U(0.4, 1.5). The second station, the probability density function is U(1.5, 3.5). For the services time the probability density functions are: U(1.5,2.5), U(1,7, 2.7) and U(2,2.8), for first, second and third stations.

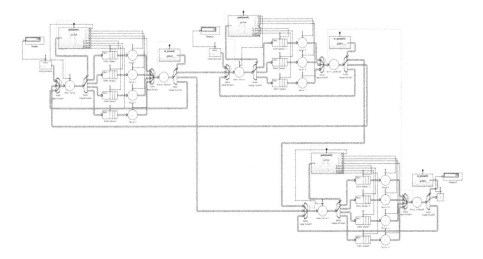

Fig. 6. Prototype of the QN example

In order to compare the performance of our approach we consider a round robin scheduling policy that consists in allocate a server in sequential way and equiprobable policy that consists in allocate any server with a same probability. We run a simulation of 500 unit times with a warm time of 100 min to transient condition.

Figures 7 and 8 show the results for the utilizations and queue's length, respectively, for equiprobable scheduling policy. Subfigures *(a)*, *(b)* and *(c)* present the results for stations 1, 2 and 3 respectively. The results show the evolution of the utilizations over the time where it can observed as the values trends to converge for a similar value, however some servers for each station have a high utilization because the scheduling policy does not observe the queue's length which it is high too. This scheduling policy does not observe the condition of the server and always assign the same work for all servers.

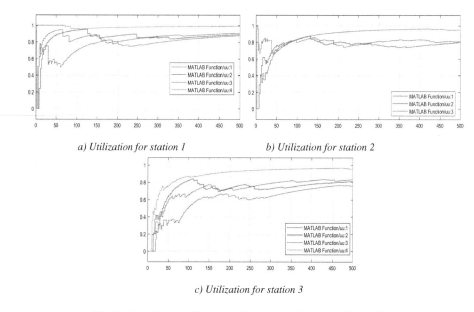

a) Utilization for station 1   b) Utilization for station 2

c) Utilization for station 3

Fig. 7.   Results of utilizations of equiprobable scheduling policy.

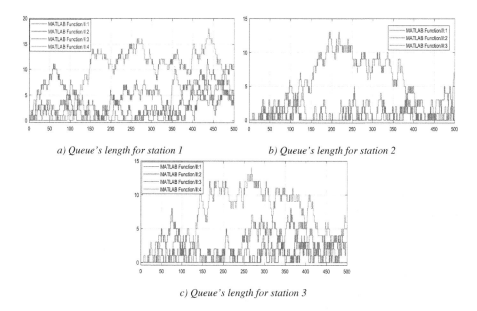

a) Queue's length for station 1   b) Queue's length for station 2

c) Queue's length for station 3

Fig. 8.   Results of queue's length of equiprobable scheduling policy.

The results of round robin scheduling policy are presented in Figs. 9 and 10, for utilizations and queue's length respectively. In similar way to equiprobable scheduling policy, the results are shown for each station and all servers. For this case, the results show as the utilization for all server for each station converges for a similar value and the queue's length is low compared with the equiprobable results. The queue's length is shorter for all time however this policy have not in to account the condition of the station and if a breakdown will occurs the allocation is the same for all jobs to processing.

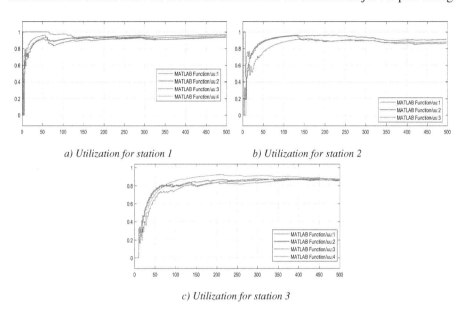

a) Utilization for station 1   *b) Utilization for station 2*

c) Utilization for station 3

Fig. 9. Results of utilizations for round robin scheduling policy

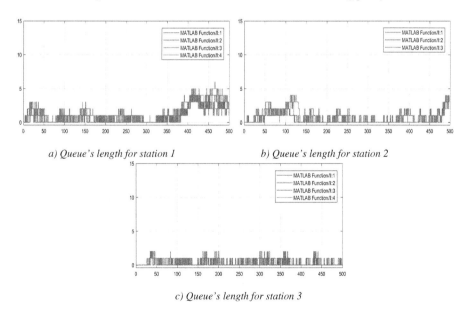

a) Queue's length for station 1   *b) Queue's length for station 2*

c) Queue's length for station 3

Fig. 10. Results of queue's length for round robin scheduling policy

Figures 11 and 12 show the results for the utilizations and queue's length, respectively, for FIS scheduling policy. Subfigures *(a)*, *(b)* and *(c)* present the results for stations 1, 2 and 3 respectively. The utilizations over the time converge for a similar value, and the queue's length is low for all time. This scheduling policy take into account

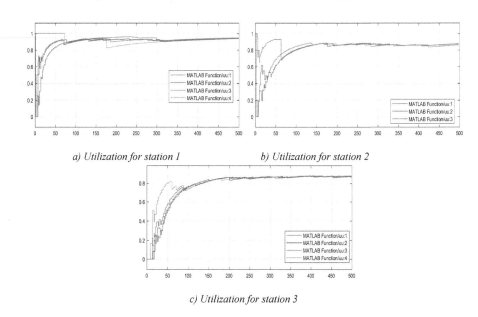

a) Utilization for station 1   *b) Utilization for station 2*

c) Utilization for station 3

Fig. 11. Results of utilizations for FIS proposed scheduling policy

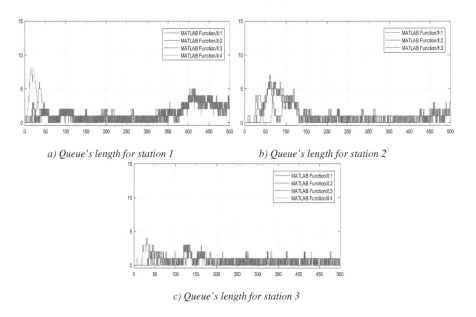

a) Queue's length for station 1   *b) Queue's length for station 2*

c) Queue's length for station 3

Fig. 12. Results of queue's length for FIS proposed scheduling policy

the condition of the server and always assign the work according to the minimum value of cycled time computed with the proposed FIS.

This results are consistent with the reported results by [2]. Moreover, the FIS approach converge faster than the traditional policies for all stations. In addition, for equiprobable policy the utilization and queue's length has a high variability for all stations while in round robin and FIS policies the results converge at the same value for all stations.

5 Conclusions

We focus on this paper in the problem of scheduling customers queuing networks using a FIS-based approach to select the customer in a single queuing system. Traditional scheduling policies works with different rules as round robin, equiprobable, shortest queue, among others, however the condition of the system does not consider. We propose an approach based in fuzzy inference system to scheduling customers or task in a queuing system depended of input variables like the queue length and the server utilization.

Our results evidence a better performance in utilization and queue length than round robin and equiprobable scheduling policies. In addition, our FIS approach could be consider more information like breakdowns, variability, blocking, among others, and to provide a condition based scheduling policies for queening networks.

As future works, we could be consider other variables as input for the FIS like breakdowns, variability and blocking. Also, it is possible to design a multi-agent system that allow the load balancing of tasks in queueing networks. Moreover, the validation in real-world case is possible, for example health services or call center services.

References

1. Lopez-Santana, E.R., Méndez-Giraldo, G.A., Florez Becerra, G.F.: On the conceptual design of multi-agent system for load balancing using multi-class queueing networks. In: 2015 Workshop on Engineering Applications - International Congress on Engineering (WEA), pp. 1–7 (2015)
2. López-Santana, E.R., Franco, C., Figueroa-García, J.C.: A fuzzy inference system to scheduling tasks queueing systems. In: Huang, D.-S., Hussain, A. (eds.) Intelligent Computing Theories and Application. pp. 286–297. Springer, Heidelberg (2017)
3. Hopp, W.J., Spearman, M.L.: Factory Physics - Foundations of Manufacturing Management. Irwin/McGraw-Hill, New York (2011)
4. Ross, S.: Introduction to Probability Models. Academic Press, London (2006)
5. Hillier, F.S., Lieberman, G.J.: Introduction to Operations Research. McGraw-Hill Higher Education, Boston (2010)
6. Kendall, D.G.: Stochastic processes occurring in the theory of queues and their analysis by the method of the imbedded Markov chain. Ann. Math. Stat. 24, 338–354 (1953)
7. Cruz, F.R.B.: Optimizing the throughput, service rate, and buffer allocation in finite queueing networks. Electron. Notes Discret. Math. 35, 163–168 (2009)

8. Yang, F., Liu, J.: Simulation-based transfer function modeling for transient analysis of general queueing systems. Eur. J. Oper. Res. **223**, 150–166 (2012)
9. Camastra, F., Ciaramella, A., Giovannelli, V., Lener, M., Rastelli, V., Staiano, A., Staiano, G., Starace, A.: A fuzzy decision system for genetically modified plant environmental risk assessment using Mamdani inference. Expert Syst. Appl. **42**, 1710–1716 (2015)
10. Alavi, N.: Quality determination of Mozafati dates using Mamdani fuzzy inference system. J. Saudi Soc. Agric. Sci. **12**, 137–142 (2013)

Estimation of Quantile Confidence Intervals for Queueing Systems Based on the Bootstrap Methodology

Rodrigo Romero-Silva$^{(\boxtimes)}$ⓘ and Margarita Hurtado

Faculty of Engineering, Universidad Panamericana, Mexico City, Mexico
rromeros@up.edu.mx

Abstract. This paper presents a simple methodology for estimating confidence intervals of quantiles in queueing systems. The paper investigates the actual probability density function of quantile estimators resulting of independent replications. Furthermore, we present a methodology, based on the concepts of bootstrapping, i.e., re-sampling and sub-sampling, to calculate the variability of an estimator without running different independent replications. Contrary to what overlapping and non-overlapping batching procedures suggest, we propose to randomly select data points to form a sub-sample, instead of selecting time-consecutive data points. The results of this study suggest that this proposal reduces the correlation between sub-samples (or batches) and overcomes the issue of normality.

Keywords: Bootstrapping · Non-overlapping batches · Confidence intervals · Discrete-Event Simulation · Quantiles

1 Introduction

Discrete-Event Simulation is a modeling paradigm that has proved useful in the analysis of any type of queueing system. By using Discrete-Event Simulation a variety of performance measures related to a queueing system can be estimated. Results stemming from this modelling paradigm are random by nature, creating the necessity of analyzing such results with statistical analysis techniques.

Estimating the value of a steady-state parameter and its confidence interval has proven to be difficult because it depends on an initial estimation of the simulation time needed to reach the steady-state and on the total simulation time needed to represent the steady-state.

Many statistical analysis techniques have been proposed to address the issue of estimating steady-state parameters. A great review of such proposals is presented in the book by Law [1] where two main approaches are described, namely, fixed-sample-size procedures and sequential procedures. Nevertheless, both approaches have been conceived with the objective of estimating mean values of the parameters. Mean values provide analysts with general information about the parameter but they lack the complete description of a random parameter. For example, the value of the mean cycle

© Springer International Publishing AG 2017
J.C. Figueroa-García et al. (Eds.): WEA 2017, CCIS 742, pp. 275–286, 2017.
DOI: 10.1007/978-3-319-66963-2_25

time of a manufacturing plant does not provide any information, on its own, about the risk of not fulfilling a specific delivery date.

Therefore, there exists a need to estimate more characteristics of a random variable, different from the mean. A series of parameters that can help understanding how a random variable behaves are the quantiles. Quantiles can help analysts to fit a probability distribution function to completely describe a random parameter [2].

In this regard, a number of studies have been concerned with proposing procedures to estimate quantiles of a random variable. The papers by Yang, Ankenman, and Nelson [2] and Chen and Zhou [3] use quantile estimation to model cycle time probability functions and approximate cycle time-throughput curves. On the other hand, Chen and Kelton [4] as well as Alexopoulos et al. [5], specifically propose sequential procedures to estimate a quantile of a random variate.

In order to consider the variability and the precision of the parameter estimator, confidence intervals need to be constructed. Typical confidence intervals estimations take into account the conclusions of the Central Limit Theorem [6], which states that sample means behave like a normal random variable. This conclusion has been extended to the estimation of confidence intervals for parameters different than the mean, such as, quantiles.

Alexopoulos et al. [5] provide an interesting argumentation for considering symmetric and typical confidence intervals calculations for quantiles. However, they also state that, to follow the procedure used to estimate confidence intervals for means in the estimation of quantile confidence intervals, three issues should be resolved, namely, bias on the sample estimators of the quantiles, skewness on the sample distribution of the estimators and correlation among estimators. Therefore, in this paper we present a study concerned with analyzing whether a procedure based on typical statistical simulation and on bootstrapping methods [7, 8] could help overcoming those previously mentioned issues.

The remaining of this paper is organized as follows. Section 2 presents a brief literature review while Sect. 3 describes the methodology used to build confidence intervals for quantiles based on the bootstrapping method. Section 4 presents the results of the study. Section 5 is concerned with a brief discussion about the implications of the study and suggestions for future research. Finally, Sect. 6 presents the conclusions.

2 Literature Review

The most typical procedure to calculate confidence intervals is the procedure used to calculate the confidence interval of the mean, based on the assumption that a sample's mean behaves like a normal distribution. This procedure, along with the procedures to estimate the confidence interval of a sample variance, the difference between two means and the proportion between two variances, are now standard procedures, which can be found in basic textbooks [6, 9].

On the other hand, the estimation of confidence intervals for quantiles has been mainly based on empirical and algorithmic approaches [10, 11] rather than on particular distributional assumptions [12, 13]. Thus, the bootstrap methodology has proven to be very efficient for calculating quantile confidence intervals in quantile regression procedures [14–16].

Despite the promise that bootstrap methods have provided to estimate confidence intervals of parameters with skewed distributions in simulations [17], few studies have used bootstrap methodologies for estimating confidence intervals of simulation outputs of queueing systems. One of those few studies is the one by Shiue et al. [18], where they study the mean waiting time for a M/M/1 queue. They found that the bootstrap percentile-t method [8] performs better than the normal confidence intervals.

In addition, Chu and Ke [19] investigate the confidence intervals of the mean time in system for a M/G/1 queue. They suggest that the percentile-bootstrap procedure [20] is the best performing procedure regarding largest coverage percentage or shortest average length, among various bootstrapping procedures. Finally, Zhang and Xu [21] extend the study by Chu and Ke by proposing a new procedure to calculate confidence intervals for different mean performance measures of an M/G/1 queue, which is based on fiducial empirical quantities. They suggest that their method performs better than the percentile-bootstrap methodology regarding coverage and length.

3   Bootstrapping the Results of a Steady-State System

As we have mentioned, there are two main approaches that have been used to estimate the parameters of a steady-state system for Discrete-Event Simulation: sequential and fixed-sample-size procedures. Sequential procedures give the best desired confidence interval "coverage", since the procedures stop whenever a desired objective, commonly related to the variance of the sample parameter estimation, is reached. Nevertheless, sequential procedures are more difficult to implement and could require larger sample sizes compared with fixed-sample-size procedures.

On the other hand, fixed-sample-size procedures are easier to implement but present the challenge of deciding the length of the simulation before any previous simulation results have been produced. For example, Alexopoulos et al. [5] use a Non-Overlapping Batch means (NBM) procedure to estimate quantiles. The biggest concern regarding this procedure is to set the length of each batch so as to minimize correlation among batch estimates. To overcome the issue of correlation among batch estimates, Law [1] suggests using the Replication/Deletion approach because each estimate will come from an independent set of random numbers. Nevertheless, the Replication/Deletion approach could produce biased estimates of the parameters as the length of the simulation is normally shorter than a NBM. Therefore, this study considers both approaches, namely, Replication/Deletion and NBM, while incorporating the notions of bootstrap to build confidence intervals.

3.1   Using a Replication/Deletion Approach

The advantage of the Replication/Deletion approach is that the correlation of estimators is minimized while its handicap is the bias of the estimator. Thus, a question that arises is: Which is the cause of the estimator bias? Either the simulation length is not long enough to capture the steady-state or the skewness of the parameter distribution is different than zero. To answer this question we developed a simulation experiment of an M/M/1 queue with a utilization factor of 0.8 ($\rho = 0.8$ and $\mu = 1$) measuring the customer time-in-system. A total of 100 different independent replications were carried out using the Simio simulation software [22]. A total of 50,000 entities were fixed as the simulation length (or sample size) following the suggestions by Chen and Zhou [3]. Furthermore, using Welch's [23] procedure for estimating the initial transient period we set the warm-up period to 10,000 total entities.

For each of the 100 replicates we calculated the 10, 30, 40, 50, 70, 85, 90, 95 and 99th percentiles for the time-in-system. With the aim of discovering whether there exists an estimator bias and skewness on the percentiles estimation, we calculated the mean, median and mode of the inter-replicate samples for each percentile, comparing them with the real values of the M/M/1 queue percentiles. Thus, the mean estimate was a simple calculation of the mean of all replicate percentiles:

$$\bar{X}_p = \frac{1}{100} \sum_{i=1}^{100} x_{pi} \tag{1}$$

where x_{pi} is the p percentile of the ith replicate.

If Y_p is the ordered set of all replication results for the p percentile where $y_{p1} < y_{p2} < y_{p3} < \ldots < y_{p99} < y_{p100}$, then the median of the p percentile was calculated as:

$$Median_p = \frac{y_{p50} + y_{p51}}{2} \tag{2}$$

The mode was calculated using the Half-Range Mode algorithmic method described in [24] using a bandwidth of 0.4. Interestingly, the median was found to be the most accurate estimate, when compared with the real percentile values.

Furthermore, we conducted a bootstrap procedure [7, 8] to find the confidence intervals of the median parameter. We created a re-sample of 1000 bootstrap balanced replicates [25] to build confidence intervals for the median estimator. Four different methods were used to calculate confidence intervals, namely, the normalized confidence interval method and percentile, pivotal (basic) and bias corrected bootstrap methods [26].

3.2 Simulating a Long Run

After conducting 100 independent replicates we carried out one long run for the M/M/1 queue with length 12,000,000 time units, which was the approximate length that Chen and Kelton [4] needed for estimating percentiles on their Zoom-In Algorithm. We considered a warm-up period of 10,000 entities. Following general bootstrap procedures, an initial estimate of each percentile (x_{p0}) was calculated using the complete dataset of the long run. The next steps of the procedure are only concerned on estimating the confidence intervals of x_{p0}.

Owing to the fact that the sample size was bigger than 9 million, a normal bootstrap procedure will be computationally burdensome. As an example, we tried to complete 100 bootstrap re-samples for the complete dataset of the long run using the R software [27].

This resulted in a memory allocation system error caused by the size of the re-samples, because the temporal file that was being built was bigger than 9 GB. Therefore, we considered the idea named Bag of Little Bootstraps (BLB) [28, 29] which suggests that it is not necessary to build bootstrap samples of the same size as the original sample size to preserve statistical correctness and validity of the results.

Using the concepts of BLB, we divided the complete simulation run results into various sub-samples of equal size with no replacement of data. However, contrary to what Overlapping Batch Means (OBM) or NBM procedures suggest, the data included on each sub-sample was not recorded in a consecutive order, that is, out of the n total data points that we have, we randomly select a subset of n, independently of the order in which they were recorded, into an R number of equally sized replicates. Thus, similarly to NBM, the size (B) of every bootstrap sub-sample will be equal to n/R. In order to build R samples of size B we randomly reordered n data points by defining as an ordering index a random uniform number between 0 and 1 for each data point. The idea behind the random reordering of data is that the correlation among the re-sampling parameter estimators will be smaller than the correlations between OBM and NBM estimators since batch estimators will not completely depend on the previous batch.

After the reordering has been carried out, then B adjacent data points will be considered as a sub-sample. Next, for each sub-sample i an estimation of x_{pi} will be calculated. The set of x_{pi} estimators will finally be used to build the bootstrap confidence intervals.

4 Results

4.1 Replication/Deletion Results

The first set of results came from the simulation of 100 independent replications where we calculated the mean, median and mode of the percentiles for each of the 100 replicates. Table 1 shows a comparison between the exact value of the percentile of the time-in-system with the sample estimators of the percentile calculated with the sample mean, median and mode. Table 2 shows that the best estimator for this particular experiment was the median as the sample probability distributions of the percentiles were not normally distributed. As an example of the distributional characteristics of sample percentiles, we build an histogram of the 70th percentile (not shown) for the 100 replications where we found that an Erlang distribution with parameter k = 6, exponential mean $\beta = 0.0884$ and minimum value equal to 5.52 was a good fit for the distribution of the sample of 70th percentile because the chi-squared goodness-of-fit test resulted in a p-value of 0.407.

Considering the 100 replications of the 70th percentile, we calculated a "normal" confidence interval, despite the fact that it was clear that the sample of the estimates was not normal. The estimations of bootstrap confidence intervals using 1000 re-samples of the median as well as the normal confidence interval are presented in Table 3, where "L" stands for the lower limit of the confidence interval and "U" represents the upper limit of the confidence interval. Additionally, Table 4 shows the confidence interval widths as a percentage of the estimate of the percentile. We can see

Table 1. Exact percentiles of a M/M/1 system compared with sample estimates of 100 replicates

Percentile	Exact	Mean	Median	Mode
10	0.5268	0.5285	0.5285	0.5302
30	1.7834	1.7896	1.7882	1.7645
40	2.5541	2.5632	2.5560	2.5173
50	3.4657	3.4794	3.4730	3.3924
70	6.0199	6.0506	6.0237	5.9392
85	9.4856	9.5407	9.5029	9.2289
90	11.5129	11.5782	11.5455	11.5804
95	14.9787	15.0562	14.9504	14.6646
99	23.0259	23.2433	22.8797	21.4533

Table 2. Percentage errors of sample estimators

Percentile	Mean	Median	Mode
10	0.3298%	0.3207%	0.6428%
30	0.3506%	0.2689%	−1.0607%
40	0.3570%	0.0731%	−1.4400%
50	0.3951%	0.2087%	−2.1156%
70	0.5109%	0.0642%	−1.3402%
85	0.5807%	0.1822%	−2.7062%
90	0.5669%	0.2831%	0.5865%
95	0.5174%	−0.1888%	−2.0965%
99	0.9446%	−0.6348%	−6.8295%
MPE[a]	0.5059%	0.0641%	−1.8177%
MAPE[b]	0.5059%	0.2472%	2.0909%

[a]MPE: Mean Percentage Error
[b]MAPE: Mean Absolute Percentage Error

Table 3. Confidence intervals' upper and lower limits built with the data from 100 independent samples

Method	10	30	40	50	70	85	90	95	99
Normal L	0.525	1.778	2.541	3.452	5.983	9.430	11.44	14.79	22.47
Normal U	0.532	1.798	2.571	3.494	6.065	9.576	11.64	15.11	23.28
Percentile L	0.525	1.769	2.531	3.445	5.974	9.409	11.43	14.75	22.43
Percentile U	0.531	1.801	2.580	3.510	6.093	9.613	11.63	15.12	23.50
Pivotal L	0.526	1.775	2.532	3.436	5.954	9.393	11.45	14.77	22.25
Pivotal U	0.532	1.808	2.581	3.501	6.073	9.597	11.65	15.14	23.32
Bias corrected L	0.525	1.772	2.532	3.449	5.983	9.429	11.44	14.80	22.48
Bias corrected U	0.530	1.801	2.577	3.504	6.082	9.610	11.61	15.12	23.43

Table 4. Confidence interval width as a percentage (%) of the percentile estimate

Method	10	30	40	50	70	85	90	95	99	Average
Normal	1.20	1.15	1.19	1.23	1.36	1.54	1.67	2.13	3.57	1.67
Percentile/Pivotal	1.18	1.83	1.88	1.86	1.98	2.15	1.73	2.47	4.69	2.20
Bias corrected	0.95	1.58	1.76	1.59	1.66	1.90	1.46	2.13	4.13	1.91

Table 5. Number of independent estimates covered by each confidence interval

Method	10	30	40	50	70	85	90	95	99	Average
Normal	22	13	10	13	13	14	17	15	12	14.33
Percentile	20	20	20	19	20	20	18	18	20	19.44
Pivotal	18	17	18	19	19	19	18	21	19	18.67
Bias corrected	17	17	17	17	16	17	15	17	16	16.56

that the "tightest" confidence interval is the normal interval while the "widest" intervals are both the percentile and pivotal intervals. Interestingly, the bootstrap sample of the medians did not behave as a binomial distribution with p = 0.5 as it was also skewed. All intervals included the real percentile value, although few of the 100 independent estimates were covered by the intervals (Table 5).

4.2   Long Run Results

The next results came from randomly sub-sampling the complete dataset from a long run. The most important issue regarding long run results is the issue of correlation among estimates, so we calculated the correlation coefficient of the 1000 sub-sample estimates of the studied percentiles for the time-in-system. Two correlation coefficients were calculated, namely, the correlation between the consecutive number of sub-sample and the sub-sample estimate value (Correl Obs) and the correlation between a sub-sample estimate value and the next consecutive estimate value, or Lag-1 correlation (Correl Lag1). The correlation coefficients are presented in Table 6.

Table 6. Correlation coefficients of 1000 sub-sample estimators

Percentile	Correl Obs	Correl Lag1
10	0.012	0.005
30	–0.025	0.024
40	–0.012	–0.033
50	0.013	0.000
70	0.000	0.017
85	0.001	0.014
90	–0.002	0.005
95	0.013	0.018
99	–0.031	0.000
Average	–0.003	0.006

Percentile estimators were calculated with the complete dataset of the long run resulting in only one estimator based on the overall percentile, as we followed some ideas of BLB. We additionally calculated the average value of the 1000 bootstrap percentile values only to compare both estimators. The values of both estimators are shown in Table 7 while the estimator errors are presented in Table 8. It can be seen that both estimates behave similarly since their percentage errors are very similar for all percentiles.

Table 7. Exact percentiles of a M/M/1 system compared with sample estimates of 1000 sub-samples

Percentile	Exact	Long run estimate	Sub-samples average
10	0.5268	0.5273	0.5278
30	1.7834	1.7841	1.7845
40	2.5541	2.5539	2.5540
50	3.4657	3.4659	3.4658
70	6.0199	6.0143	6.0139
85	9.4856	9.4575	9.4567
90	11.5129	11.4867	11.4851
95	14.9787	14.9686	14.9627
99	23.0259	23.1923	23.1570

Table 8. Percentage errors of sample estimators for 1000 sub-samples

Percentile	Long run estimate	Sub-samples average
10	0.101%	0.199%
30	0.040%	0.064%
40	−0.008%	−0.005%
50	0.004%	0.002%
70	−0.092%	−0.100%
85	−0.296%	−0.304%
90	−0.228%	−0.241%
95	−0.067%	−0.107%
99	0.723%	0.570%
MPE	0.020%	0.009%
MAPE	0.173%	0.177%

Different from the behavior of the estimators using 100 independent replicates, the estimators of the 1000 sub-samples behaved like a normal distribution. We conducted a goodness-of-fit chi-squared test for the 70th percentile data resulting on a p-value of 0.442, indicating a good fit.

Moreover, Tables 9 and 10 present the confidence interval calculations while Table 11 shows the coverage of the intervals. Similarly to the results from the 100 independent samples, the tightest interval comes from the normal confidence interval. Nevertheless, for the 1000 bootstrap sub-samples, the normal intervals did not include the exact value of the 70, 85, 90, 95 and 99th percentiles.

Table 9. Confidence intervals upper and lower limits built with the data of 1000 bootstrap re-samples

Method	10	30	40	50	70	85	90	95	99
Percentile L	0.494	1.718	2.477	3.367	5.869	9.239	11.204	14.562	22.146
Percentile U	0.562	1.849	2.632	3.564	6.174	9.716	11.800	15.415	24.217
Pivotal L	0.493	1.719	2.476	3.367	5.855	9.199	11.173	14.522	22.167
Pivotal U	0.561	1.850	2.631	3.565	6.160	9.676	11.770	15.376	24.238
Bias corrected L	0.498	1.730	2.485	3.385	5.901	9.269	11.242	14.634	22.386
Bias corrected U	0.556	1.840	2.620	3.549	6.155	9.670	11.763	15.370	24.100
Normal L	0.526	1.782	2.551	3.463	6.010	9.450	11.477	14.955	23.159
Normal U	0.528	1.786	2.556	3.469	6.019	9.465	11.496	14.982	23.225

Table 10. Confidence interval width as a percentage (%) of the percentile estimate

Method	10	30	40	50	70	85	90	95	99	Average
Percentile/Pivotal	12.84	7.36	6.08	5.69	5.07	5.04	5.19	5.70	8.93	6.88
Bias corrected	11.06	6.19	5.27	4.72	4.23	4.23	4.54	4.92	7.39	5.84
Normal	0.41	0.23	0.20	0.18	0.16	0.16	0.17	0.18	0.28	0.22

Table 11. Number of bootstrap sub-sample estimates covered by each confidence interval

Method	10	30	40	50	70	85	90	95	99	Average
Percentile	950	950	950	950	950	950	950	950	950	950.00
Pivotal	948	947	949	949	950	951	945	942	949	947.78
Bias corrected	900	900	900	900	898	899	899	899	896	899.00
Normal	46	53	50	57	34	44	53	46	46	47.67

5 Discussion

The most common assumption is that the Central Limit Theorem is applicable to different parameter estimators, other than the mean. After conducting experiments to estimate various percentiles of the time-in-system of an M/M/1 queue with independent replications, we found that the "normality" assumption does not hold true. Nevertheless, using the results of a long-run simulation by sub-sampling the complete dataset we found that a "normal" behavior in parameter estimators could very well depend on the methodology used for calculating the estimates.

Both the exponential distribution and the utilization factor of 0.8 could make the results of short-run simulations very dependent on the independent strings of random numbers utilized for each replicate, resulting in highly variable and somewhat skewed results. Thus, the Replication/Deletion approach seems to be helpful to capture the variability of short-runs of a queueing system, but does not seem to be the best method to approximate a steady-state value of a system's parameter. Clearly, the simulation length can always be increased while performing several replications; however, the time needed to complete various long-run simulations could be burdensome and; consequently, the number of replications of long-run simulations could be small because of time constraints, limiting the ability to draw conclusions about the variability of the estimator.

We think that the method proposed in this paper shows some promise in overcoming both the non-normality of the estimators and the correlation among the estimators. The non-normality of the estimator behavior is addressed by the bootstrap confidence-interval. Despite the fact that sub-sample estimators of the percentiles behaved like a normal distribution, the bootstrap confidence-intervals had better coverage of the estimators, compared with the normal confidence-interval.

Furthermore, the normal confidence interval did not include the exact value of the percentile as the sample size of 1000 and the small variance created a very "tight" confidence interval. This result is not surprising as the coverage of a normal confidence interval is only as good as the estimator and the resulting percentile estimator of one single long-run did not perform as well as the estimators from Chen and Kelton [4] and Alexopoulos et al. [5].

Nevertheless, the method proposed in this document performed well on building confidence intervals without assuming normality because the exact value of the percentiles was always included on the bootstrap confidence intervals built and with significantly less computation requirements than other methods. Thus, this method for building confidence intervals could be used in conjunction with sequential methods of quantile estimation.

On the other hand, the correlation among estimators is addressed by randomly selecting data points to build the sub-samples, instead of selecting time-consecutive data points. Thus, correlation created by state-dependency over time in queueing systems can be reduced by this procedure.

However, the random procedure to create sub-samples generates a limitation in the applicability of this procedure, as rate-dependent steady-state parameters cannot be estimated and analyzed. For example, direct measure and probabilistic behavior of throughput or revenue per hour cannot be estimated by this procedure because they are measures that depend on time-consecutive data points. Therefore, this methodology can only be used to calculate single-event steady-state parameters, such as, entity time-in-system and system's entity number-in-system.

Finally, more results are needed regarding different utilization factors and different queueing systems since this study only investigated an M/M/1 queue with a 0.8 utilization factor.

6 Conclusions

The main concern of this study was to propose a procedure to calculate confidence intervals for steady-state quantile estimators since the assumption of normality on a sample of quantile estimators could not be accurate. In order to investigate that assumption, we conducted an experiment of 100 independent replications of an M/M/1 queue to calculate various percentiles for the time-in-system. Results showed that the probability distribution function of such percentiles did not behave like a normal distribution.

We proposed a simple procedure to calculate confidence-intervals for quantile estimators based on notions from bootstrapping. The procedure consisted on carrying out one long-run simulation and creating randomized sub-samples of the complete dataset. The percentile estimates of the sub-samples were then used to build bootstrap confidence intervals. Results showed that bootstrap confidence intervals were not as dependent on a good estimator as the normal confidence interval, allowing for the exact value of the quantile being included on the estimated interval, making the confidence interval more useful for predicting the real value of the parameter. Worth noting is the fact that this procedure can only be used for calculating single-event steady-state parameters and not rate-dependent ones.

References

1. Law, A.: Simulation Modeling and Analysis, 5th edn. McGraw-Hill, New York (2014)
2. Yang, F., Ankenman, B.E., Nelson, B.L.: Estimating cycle time percentile curves for manufacturing systems via simulation. INFORMS J. Comput. **20**(4), 628–643 (2008). doi:10.1287/ijoc.1080.0272
3. Chen, N., Zhou, S.: Simulation-based estimation of cycle time using quantile regression. IIE Trans. **43**(3), 176–191 (2010). doi:10.1080/0740817X.2010.521806
4. Chen, E.J., Kelton, W.D.: Quantile and tolerance-interval estimation in simulation. Eur. J. Oper. Res. **168**(2), 520–540 (2006). doi:10.1016/j.ejor.2004.04.040
5. Alexopoulos, C., Goldsman, D., Wilson, J.R.: A new perspective on batched quantile estimation. In: Proceedings of the 2012 Winter Simulation Conference (WSC) (2012)
6. Walpole, R.E., Myers, R.H., Myers, S.L., et al.: Probability and Statistics for Engineers and Scientists, 9th edn. Pearson, New York (2011)
7. Hinkley, D.V.: Bootstrap methods. J. Roy. Stat. Soc. Ser. B (Methodol.) **50**(3), 321–337 (1988)
8. DiCiccio, T.J., Efron, B.: Bootstrap confidence intervals. Stat. Sci. **11**(3), 189–212 (1996)
9. Box, G.E.P., Hunter, J.S., Hunter, W.G.: Statistics for Experimenters: Design, Innovation, and Discovery, 2nd edn. Wiley, Hoboken (2005)
10. Chen, S.X., Hall, P.: Smoothed empirical likelihood confidence intervals for quantiles. Ann. Stat. **21**(3), 1166–1181 (1993)
11. Hutson, A.D.: Calculating nonparametric confidence intervals for quantiles using fractional order statistics. J. Appl. Stat. **26**(3), 343–353 (1999). doi:10.1080/02664769922458
12. Heo, J.-H., Salas, J.D.: Estimation of quantiles and confidence intervals for the log-Gumbel distribution. Stoch. Hydrol. Hydraul. **10**(3), 187–207 (1996). doi:10.1007/BF01581463

13. Heo, J.-H., Salas, J.D., Kim, K.-D.: Estimation of confidence intervals of quantiles for the Weibull distribution. Stoch. Environ. Res. Risk Assess. **15**(4), 284–309 (2001). doi:10.1007/s004770100071
14. Kocherginsky, M., He, X., Mu, Y.: Practical confidence intervals for regression quantiles. J. Comput. Graph. Stat. **14**(1), 41–55 (2005). doi:10.1198/106186005X27563
15. Karlsson, A.: Bootstrap methods for bias correction and confidence interval estimation for nonlinear quantile regression of longitudinal data. J. Stat. Comput. Simul. **79**(10), 1205–1218 (2009). doi:10.1080/00949650802221180
16. Wei, L., Wang, D., Hutson, A.D.: An investigation of quantile function estimators relative to quantile confidence interval coverage. Commun. Stat. Theor. Methods **44**(10), 2107–2135 (2015). doi:10.1080/03610926.2013.775304
17. Cheng, R.C.H.: Bootstrap methods in computer simulation experiments. In: Proceedings of the 27th Conference on Winter Simulation, WSC 1995, Arlington, Virginia, USA. IEEE Computer Society, Washington, DC (1995)
18. Shiue, W., Xu, C., Rea, B.C.: Bootstrap confidence intervals for simulation outputs. J. Stat. Comput. Simul. **45**(3–4), 249–255 (1993). doi:10.1080/00949659308811485
19. Chu, Y., Ke, J.: Confidence intervals of mean response time for an M/G/1 queueing system: bootstrap simulation. Appl. Math. Comput. **180**(1), 255–263 (2006). doi:10.1016/j.amc.2005.11.145
20. Efron, B., Tibshirani, R.: Bootstrap methods for standard errors, confidence intervals, and other measures of statistical accuracy. Stat. Sci. **1**(1), 54–75 (1986)
21. Zhang, Q., Xu, X.: Confidence intervals of performance measures for an M/G/1 queueing system. Commun. Stat. Simul. Comput. **39**(3), 501–516 (2010). doi:10.1080/03610910903484232
22. Kelton, W.D., Smith, J.S., Sturrock, D.T.: Simio and Simulation: Modeling, Analysis, Applications, 1st edn. Simio LLC, Sewickley, PA (2014)
23. Welch, P.D.: The Statistical Analysis of Simulation Results. In: Lavenberg, S.S. (ed.) The Computer Performance Modeling Handbook. Academic Press, New York (1983)
24. Bickel, D.R.: Robust estimators of the mode and skewness of continuous data. Comput. Stat. Data Anal. **39**(2), 153–163 (2002). doi:10.1016/S0167-9473(01)00057-3
25. Gleason, J.R.: Algorithms for balanced bootstrap simulations. Am. Stat. **42**(4), 263–266 (1988). doi:10.2307/2685134
26. Diciccio, T.J., Romano, J.P.: A review of bootstrap confidence intervals. J. Roy. Stat. Soc. Ser. B (Methodol.) **50**(3), 338–354 (1988)
27. The R Foundation: The R Project for Statistical Computing (2016). Accessed 30 Mar 2016
28. Kleiner, A., Talwalkar, A., Sarkar, P., et al.: The big data bootstrap. In: Proceedings of the 29th International Conference on Machine Learning, Edinburgh, Scotland, UK, 26 June–1 July 2012
29. Alin, A., Martin, M.A., Beyaztas, U., et al.: Sufficient m-out-of-n (m/n) bootstrap. J. Stat. Comput. Simul. **87**(9), 1742–1753 (2017). doi:10.1080/00949655.2017.1284847

Internet of Things

Design of a Robotic Hand Controlled by Electromyography Signals Using an Arduino Type Microcontroller for People with Disabilities

Karen Lemmel-Vélez[✉] and Carlos Alberto Valencia-Hernandez

Pascual Bravo University Institution, Medellín, Colombia
{karen.lemmel,carlos.valencia}@pascualbravo.edu.co

Abstract. This paper presents the development of a controlled robotic hand. The movement of the robot hand can be controlled by electromyography signals carrying out the steps of sensing, filtering, acquisition, digitization and processing of electromyographic signals together with the steps of power and control and drive equipment, thus achieving the development of a robotic hand. The robot controlled by Arduino nano, aiming to develop a control system with electromyography signals capable to control external devices such as prostheses and robots.

Keywords: Robotic hand · Electromyography signals · Arduino

1 Introduction

Nowadays, the design of robotic is an attractive area of research. [1] according to [2] "Robots have found an increasingly wide utilization in all fields, and they move objects with blurring speed, repeat performances with unerring precision and manipulate tasks with high dexterity". A robotic design can be influenced by a number of variables such as geometry of the manipulator, dynamics involved, the structural characteristics of the linkage system [1].

On the other hand in the world there are over 1 billion people with disabilities, which is about 15% of the world's population [3]. Persons with disabilities include those with long-term physical, mental, intellectual or sensory impairments which, by interacting with various barriers, may impede their full and effective participation in society, on an equal basis with others [4]; The World Health Organization (WHO) considers that disability is a global public health problem, a human rights issue and a priority for development [3]. In Colombia there are more than 850 thousand people with disabilities [5], that is, 2.3% of the population projected for 2013 [6] and in Medellín about 5.3% of the population in 2011 have some disability [7].

WHO as a plan of action to achieve a world in which all persons with disabilities, including children and their families, live in dignity and with equal rights and opportunities and are in a position to maximize their potential [3]; Sets out three objectives: (1) to eliminate obstacles and improve access to health services and programs; (2) strengthening and extending rehabilitation, habilitation, assistive technology, assistance and support services, as well as rehabilitation at the community level; (3) improving the

© Springer International Publishing AG 2017
J.C. Figueroa-García et al. (Eds.): WEA 2017, CCIS 742, pp. 289–299, 2017.
DOI: 10.1007/978-3-319-66963-2_26

collection of relevant and internationally comparable data on disability and enhancing research on disability and related services.

Worldwide the services of home automation and robotics provide from comfort the user with a considerable improvement in the quality of life because they reduce domestic work, increase well-being and provide a series of amenities [8], based on that and aiming at objective 2 of the WHO action plan on auxiliary technology, and to objective 3 where it is proposed to promote research, the design and construction of a robotic arm for persons with disabilities based on electromyography Signals is proposed as a solution to the comfort problems presented by people with physical disability.

This paper presents a simple based controlled robotic hand using Arduino nano embedded system as the core of this robot and also v3 sensor to interface the robot with the electromyography (EMG) signals. The robot does not require training because the robotic arm is fully controlled by the user

2   Literature Review

Disability is a general term that covers deficiencies, limitations of activity and restrictions of participation, a definition that includes both those who were born with difficulties and others who in the course of their lives due to accidents suffered mishaps [9], Disability is universal. It is quite likely that every person suffers it, either directly or in the person of a family member suffering from some type of functional limitation at one time or another, especially as they get older [3].

EMG signals are those that occur when tensing or distensing a muscle, and result from the chemical activity produced by the fibrous myosin protein. When contracting the muscles, an electric signal is generated (Fig. 1) of a few microvolts [10], that is, the functions performed by the human body are carried out by electric impulses [11].

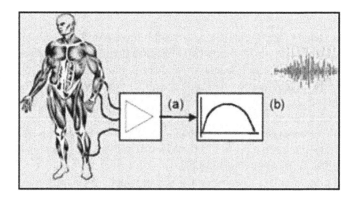

Fig. 1. Myoelectric signals generated by contracting or distracting muscles [10]

The past decade has seen a fast growing interest to develop various effective machine interfaces that can be invasive or noninvasive [12], robots have long been imaged as mechanical workers, cooperating with or even replacing people [2]. The robotic hand designed is influenced by a number of variables such as geometry of the manipulator, dynamics involved and the structural characteristics of the linkage system.

Typical teach-pendant in robots is a handheld control unit equipped with buttons or joysticks to manually send to desired positions, a screen to display the robot states, and a large red emergency stop button [2], in this case the control can be done using EMG signals an Arduino based microcontroller, Arduino is an open-source electronics proto-typing platform based on flexible, easy-to-use hardware and software [13]. The robot body was prepared mechanically and electrical components were chosen to be suitable to be used as a robotic hand. The robot is controlled using Arduino nano as the brain of the robot, connected to a v3 sensor for data adquisition.

3 Methodology

For the development of the robotic hand for People with disabilities based on electro-myography signals, the methodology described in Fig. 2 was followed.

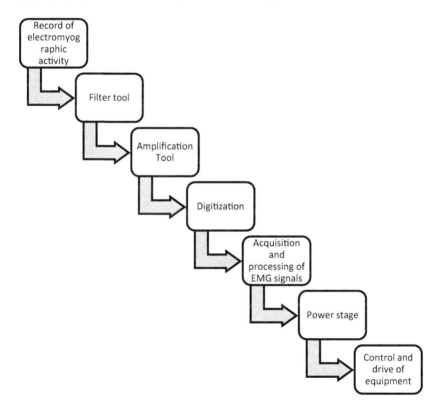

Fig. 2. Methodology for the analysis and development of the robotic hand for people with disabilities based on electromyography signals, adapted from [10].

4 Design of the Robotic Hand

The robot has been design to mimic the movement of a human hand. This section present a description of the hardware of the robot design.

4.1 Mechanical Design

Through the software CAD the mechanical design was simulated and the structure of the robotic hand defines, this software allowed us to modify and simulate the movement that defines the functionality of the hand and identified the elements that was used in the robotic hand.

The robotic hand composed by the structures of the proximal phalanges, intermediate phalanges and distal phalanges. In the construction was used the natural aluminum by its characteristic of low mechanical density, it is light and its easy manipulation.

For the structure that simulates the palm of the hand was chosen the nylon, artificial polymer belonging to the group of polyamides, highly resistant and lightweight that allows to reduce the weight to the servomotor of the wrist.

Figures 3, 4, 5, 6, 7, 8, 9, 10, 11 and 12 are the drawings of each element that compose the robotic hand, the Fig. 3 is the motor connecting rod this piece goes in the middle of the structure of the finger and allows to transmit the movement between the proximal phalanx and the intermediate phalanx.

Fig. 3. Motor connecting rod

The Conducted connecting rod is shown in the Fig. 4 this is in the middle of the structure of the finger and allows to transmit the movement of the intermediate phalanx to the distal phalanx.

Fig. 4. Conducted connecting rod

The piece that allows to perform the same rotational function performed by the human hand and is the coupling between the palm of the hand and the male coupling is in the Fig. 5.

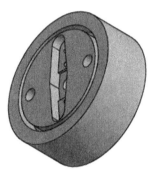

Fig. 5. Wrist

The male coupling (Fig. 6) supports the weight of the hand in a rotational sense, and joins the wrist with the cubit of the robotic hand.

Fig. 6. Male coupling

The piece shown in the Fig. 7 emulate the radius and ulna function allowing to accommodate the servomotor that gives the operation to the wrist and is the union between the complete structure of the hand with the structure of polypropylene where the stump is attached.

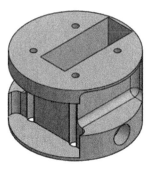

Fig. 7. Radius and ulna

Fig. 8. Distal phalanx

Fig. 9. Intermediate phalanx

The fingers from hand are composed by the elements shown in the Figs. 8, 9 and 10, distal phalanx, intermediate phalanx and the proximal phalanx respectively, the last one is placed in the structure of the hand and is in charge of transmitting the movement that comes from the servomotors and turn moves the connecting rods providing the total closing of the fingers.

Fig. 10. Proximal phalanx

The thumb (Fig. 11) is the piece allows the opponent's movement in relation to the other fingers, which allows a prehensile effect.

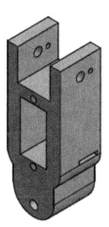

Fig. 11. Thumb

And finally the hand (Fig. 12) support the fingers and servomotors, its operation is also based on the prehensile grip.

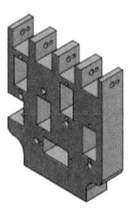

Fig. 12. Hand

4.2 Data Acquisition and Robot Control System

For the development of the robotic hand was used as sensor element a module of EMG of three derivations and adjustable gain, together with an Arduino nano to realize the data acquisition.

Two rechargeable 9 V batteries were used as power supply for the muscle sensor, the positive terminal of the first battery was connected to the pin +VS of the muscular sensor, then we connected the negative terminal of the first battery to the positive terminal of the second battery, Of these two terminals leaves the cable GND that was connected to the GND of the power supply of the muscular sensor; The negative terminal of the second battery was connected to the −VS of the muscle sensor as shown in Fig. 13.

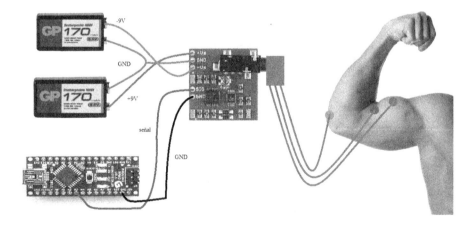

Fig. 13. Electrodes connection, sensor, Arduino.

The electrodes were connected one in the middle of the muscular body, another connected at one end of the same muscular body, and the last electrode was connect in a bony or non-muscular part but close to the body to be treated, taking as reference the front of the elbow.

In our case the electrodes of the first sensor is connected to the bicep muscle that is in charge of making the prehensile movement of the robotic hand, and the second muscle that is used is the triceps which is in charge of making the rotational movement of the hand.

For the filtering and amplification of the signal the 4 stages shown in Fig. 14. are used; Step 1 (Fig. 14a.) allows the signal to make full use of the feed rails, it also includes the possibility that small signals near the ground can be amplified without requiring dual supplies, step 2 (Fig. 14b.) made Full-wave precision rectifier, step 3 (Fig. 14c.) is composed of an active low-pass filter, the circuit amplifies and lets out low-frequency signals and blocks high-frequency signals. Finally step 4 is a feedback inverter amplifier (Fig. 14d.) where one of the amplifiers of the TL084 is used, an inverter amplifier is an amplifier that inverts the input voltage giving in turn an output gain that depends on its two Resistors in this case a variable resistance or tremor is used to give a variable value to the output gain.

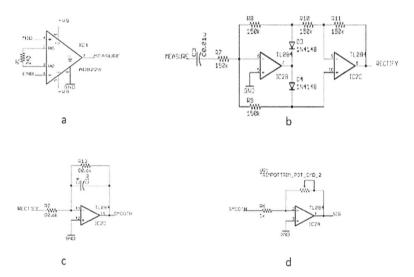

Fig. 14. Amplification and filtration step (a) Step 1, (b) Step 2, (c) Step 3, (d) Step 4. [14].

The signal amplificated and filtered goes to the Arduino nano where the control program runs. The final effectors are servomotors that received a PWM signal; with this, the hand can move as fallows, the servomotors of the fingers when detecting the value of the muscular sensor number one. The Arduino gives the instruction to close the robotic hand, as long as this is the presence of the value, if the value varies between the established ranges, the robotic hand has the ability to position itself at the angles established in the program. The servomotor of the wrist has the same function of the fingers; the difference is that the signal that allows to position this servomotor comes from the muscular sensor number two.

4.3   Project Overview

In this project, the hardware and software function are combined to make the system reliable. Arduino nano is the brain of this project and the V3 sensor is EMG signal captor. The project overview is as shown in Fig. 15.

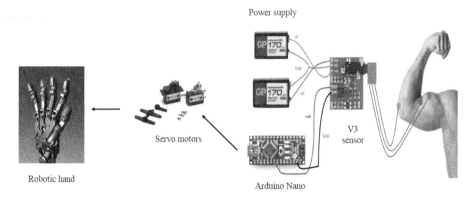

Fig. 15. Project overview

5   Conclusion

The use of low-cost electronic devices such as the Arduino allows improving the affordability of low-income people to robotic devices also the acquisition of electromyography signals using dry surface electrodes allows the recording of potentials of the muscular action at the same time and it is possible to capture electromyography signals for later use in power systems. The amplification and digitization of the electromyography signals are essential stages in the processing of signals of this type.

This experiment is scalable to any muscle in the body, making a suitable mechanical design of the part that you want to emulate. The utility of this system can be extended to other uses of exoskeletons, 3D simulations, and interaction with teleoperation among others.

In this study, we not only use electromyography signals as communication tool but also use them as control signals of external artificial devices, aiming to develop a control system with electromyography signals capable to control external devices such as prostheses and robots.

References

1. Hussain, S.B.: Design of a 3 DoF robotic arm. In: Sixth International Conference on Innovative Computing and Technology, pp. 145–149 (2016)
2. Deng, H., Xia, Z., Weng, S., et al.: A motion sensing-based framework for robotic manipulation. Robot Biomim. **3**, 23 (2016). doi:10.1186/s40638-016-0056-9

3. Organización Mundial de la Salud, Banco Mundial: Proyecto de acción mundial de la OMS sobre discapacidad 2014–2021: Mejor salud para todas las personas con discapacidad, pp. 1–27 (2014)
4. Ministerio de Salud y Protección Social: ABECÉ de la discapacidad, pp. 2–3 (2015)
5. Manuel, J., Calderón, S.: Mujer y Discapacidad en Colombia. Obs. Asuntos Género (2012)
6. Ministerio de Salud y Protección Social: Discapacidad, pp. 6–9 (2016)
7. de Medellín, A.: Indicadores de Discapacidad 2011, vol. 5 (2011)
8. Capel, A.R.: Diseño y desarrollo parcial de un sistema domótico para facilitar la movilidad de minusválidos (2005)
9. Salud, R.: La situación de personas discapacitadas en Colombia. El Espectador (2014)
10. Mario, R.R., Ángel, V.B., Gustavo, V.G., Luis, H.: GEYJR Detección y Acondicionamiento de Señales Mioeléctricas. In: 10° Congr Nac Mecatrónica, pp. 174–178 (2011)
11. González, I.A.C.: Diseño y Construcción de un Sistema Para la Detección de Señales Electromiográficas. Universidad Autonoma de Yucatan (2010)
12. Yoshioka, M., Zhu, C., Imamura, K., et al.: Experimental design and signal selection for construction of a robot control system based on EEG signals. J. Robot Biomim. **1**, 1–11 (2014). doi:10.1186/s40638-014-0022-3
13. Kadir, W.M.H.W., Samin, R.E., Ibrahim, B.S.K.: Internet controlled robotic arm. Procedia Eng. **41**, 1065–1071 (2012). doi:10.1016/j.proeng.2012.07.284
14. Advancer Technologies: Three-lead differential muscle/electromyography sensor for microcontroller applications. In: Three-lead Differ Muscle/Electromyography, pp. 2–5 (2013)

Irrigation System for Oil Palm in Colombia - An Internet of Things Approach

Ivan Baños Delgado$^{(\boxtimes)}$, Luz A. Magre Colorado, Erick Javier Argüello Prada, and Juan C. Martínez-Santos

Centro de Excelencia y Apropiación en Internet de Las Cosas (CEA-IoT), Universidad Tecnológica de Bolívar, Cartagena, Colombia
ivanalejandrobanos@gmail.com, luz0928@gmail.com, earguello@usb.ve, jcmartinezs@unitecnologica.edu.co

Abstract. In this article, we show a prototype of an irrigation system for oil palm plantations in Colombia. We make use of a predictive control model to improve the irrigation schedule. This model takes weather predictions from the Internet and uses them in the control model as a new variable to take into account when it comes to deciding whether the crops should be irrigated or not. A soil moisture sensor is used to both validate if the decision was correct and maintain the crop within the desired range of soil moisture. With this work, we want to give farmers the opportunity to embrace the Internet of Things (IoT) as a technology that can make their job easier and with better productivity in their plantations.

Keywords: Soil moisture · Internet of Things · Irrigation · Oil palm · Predictive control

1 Introduction

Consumption of fossil fuel resources leads to global warming and climate change, so avoiding emissions from fossil fuels has become a necessity over the last decades. Even when the contribution of biofuel production to development, social well-being and ecosystem preservation has been under an intense debate [1–3], biofuels have emerged as an environmentally-friendly energy alternative to prevent fossil fuel emissions. Throughout the world, the typical lipid feedstocks for biodiesel production are refined vegetable oils, and the choice of oil for biodiesel production depends on local availability and corresponding affordability [4].

Oil palm (*Elaeis guineensis*) is one of the most important crops used for biodiesel production in tropical countries. In Colombia, for instance, palm oil is the second agro-industrial export after sugar and molases as stated by Procolombia in its annual exportation report in 2016. A set of normative tools, such as statutory mandates and economic incentives that include price supports, subsidies, tax exemptions or preferential taxes, have been designed and implemented in order to promote the expansion of oil palm plantations in Colombia [5].

© Springer International Publishing AG 2017
J.C. Figueroa-García et al. (Eds.): WEA 2017, CCIS 742, pp. 300–311, 2017.
DOI: 10.1007/978-3-319-66963-2_27

This initiative points towards the replacement of 20% of diesel with biofuel by 2020, for which the Colombian oil-palm farmers association (FEDEPALMA) plans to increase annual CPO production sixfold to 3.5 Mt [6]. The production for the year 2015, was about 3.37 Ton/ha, which is slightly below the average (between 3.5–5 Ton/ha, according to Fedepalma's stadistics [7]).

With the system, We attempt to improve the productivity of crops by designing a system for controlling water irrigation. Accuracy errors can be avoided by automatizing the irrigation. Also, we can generate a dynamic control over crop's soil moisture level, which, along with other resources like the weather forecast and soil moisture sensors, may help not only achieving a better water use, but also saving money in resources and workforce.

This system is in a development stage as problems such as corrosion and temperature resistance in sensors, the presence of different soil textures to monitor, the poor Internet connection and infrastructure that are typically encountered in the agricultural sector of the country need to be addressed in order to come up with a more robust solution for this kind of plantations. After the prototyping stage, we are aiming at developing a full-custom device that allows farmers to get the most of their crops.

We divided this article in the following sections: in Sect. 2, we describe the reasons why this project should be executed; in Sect. 3, we summarize other authors' approach on this topic; in Sect. 4, we explain the process of designing the system (hardware and software) and how we implement and calibrate the soil moisture sensor used in this prototype; in Sect. 5, we show the results obtained in both the calibration process and the web application developed; finally, in Sect. 6, we discuss our results and future work.

2   Motivation

Despite recent research efforts, little is known about the actual water use of oil palm at the field level, as well as the minimum amount of water needed to obtain good yields [8]. What we know is that the oil palm is very sensitive to changes in the water levels in the soil where is planted, and that the amount of fertilizer depends on those water levels as well [9,10]. With respect to irrigation, Henson [11] underlines the importance of a comprehensive monitoring of soil and atmospheric conditions to maintain the crop yield despite the variability of weather conditions. Furthermore, the identification of functional relations between yield and crop water-use is crucial to develop an efficient water-management solution, which, in turn, must achieve a balance between what is desirable and what is practical. In this regard, we designed and developed an IoT-based solution for smart irrigation of oil palm crops by both taking advantage of the Cloud computing capabilities and defining a predictive control model for the irrigation scheduling. In addition, it may be deployed for not only agricultural purposes, but also gardening and landscaping purposes.

In Colombia, for the last 5 years, the harvesting of oil palm fruit has reached a maximum of 3.46 Ton/ha as shown in Fig. 1, which is below the world's average

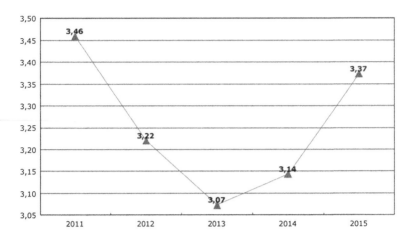

Fig. 1. Average performance of recollection for the last 5 years in Ton/Ha in Colombia.

(close to 4.0 Ton/ha). Another purpose of this work will be to improve the fruit production by defining and implementing a predictive control model able to create an irrigation schedule based on both the soil moisture of the crops and the weather predictions from *The Weather Channel*.

3   Related Work

The efficient use of available water resources requires the monitoring of environmental conditions that need to be fulfilled in order to obtain better productivity, such as the moisture, temperature (ideally between 28 °C and 30 °C) and pH (ideally between 4–6) of the soil [10,12]. Thus, it is possible to maintain the crop yield despite the variability of weather conditions by delivering the proper amount of water, where and when it is really needed. Real-time monitoring could be a demanding task because the amount of generated data tends to be enormous and if this data is not organized and properly processed, it will become meaningless. Hence, there is a need for high storage and processing capabilities, two of the hallmarks of Cloud computing. This term refers to a model for on-demand access to a shared pool of configurable computing resources (e.g., networks, servers, storage, applications, services, and software) that can be easily provisioned as and when needed [13]. Cloud computing has been used recently in the development of smart irrigation systems, like the one proposed by Sales et al. [14]. This system was intended to address a wide range of scenarios, such as agriculture, greenhouses, golf courses and landscapes. More recently, Vani and Rao [15] designed and developed a solution for automatically monitoring the soil moisture by exploiting Cloud computing and Android system capabilities. On the other hand, Lozoya et al. [16] present a predictive control irrigation model using the irrigation as the control input and evapotranspiration and deep percolation as given data, but they assume no rainfall. In this work, we take rainfall as a water source that can avoid irrigation in some cases. Also, for the irrigation scheduling, Saleem et al. [17] propose a Model Predictive Control framework for real-time irrigation scheduling, taking into account the limitations on water resources and climate data. In our proposed model, we assume that the availability of water does not represent an issue. The two previous work presented to control the scheduling, have not yet implemented their system, they have just simulated the results. In our system, we already propose an architecture and hardware/software design to implement it.

4 Our Approach

For our system, we needed to design both hardware and software implementations to achieve a good irrigation schedule. This will allow the soil of the crops to stay between the desired levels of moisture. When this is achieved, we produce an optimal growth of the oil palm in the long term, improving the production of the country. In the following, we will describe the design used for the system.

4.1 Model

To start making a suitable model for the crop studied, we must take into account the hydrological balance of the soil where the palm is cultivated. The hydrological balance is a model that describes the total amount of water stored in a certain location by adding the inflows on the crop and subtracting the outflows in the same area. As seen in Fig. 2, the inflows considered are the irrigation, precipitation and the capillary rise, and the outflows are the evapotranspiration, deep percolation and water runoff [18,19].

In our model, we assume that there is no shortage of water to irrigate the crops and that we will not exceed the field capacity. Given these assumptions, deep percolation and runoff are not taken into account for the hydrological balance model. With this information, our hydrological balance dynamics will be defined as Eq. 1:

$$\dot{\Theta}_{(t)} = ET_{c(t)} - I_{(t)} - R_{(t)} \tag{1}$$

Where $\dot{\Theta}_{(t)}$ is the variation of water in the root zone of the plant, $I_{(t)}$ is the water that comes in as irrigation, $R_{(t)}$ is rainfall and $ET_{c(t)}$ represents the evapotranspiration.

For the purpose of the irrigation scheduling, we need to maintain the soil moisture levels between the field capacity (FC) and the refill point (RP), this range is known as the Readily Available Water (RAW). In this range (Shown in Fig. 3) of soil moisture we find the optimal plant growth [20].

As we can see from Eq. 1, an important element of the hydrological balance is the evapotranspiration. This is a combination of the evaporation of water from the soil and the transpiration of the plants. The two processes represent loss of water and is often referred and studied as evapotranspiration [21]. The factors that mainly affect evapotranspiration are weather parameters, the crop characteristics,

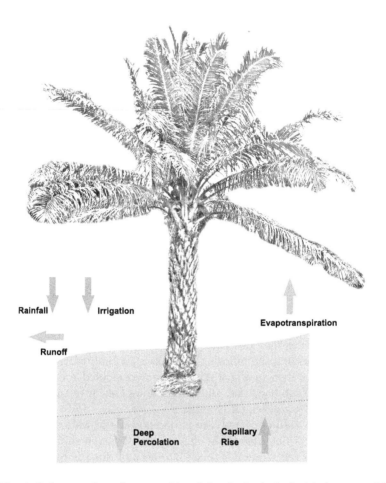

Fig. 2. Inflows and outflows considered for the hydrological balance model.

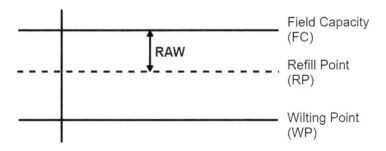

Fig. 3. Soil moisture levels. The crop moisture needs to be maintained between the RAW level.

management and environmental aspects. The evapotranspiration is described by Eq. 2. Where K_c is the crop coefficient and $ET_{o(t)}$ is the reference evapotranspiration (measured in mm/day). The latest depends on climatic parameters only and can be affected by dry, regular and rain season [21]. The crop coefficient (K_c) of mature oil palm is estimated to be between 0–8 and 1.0 [8,22].

$$ET_{c(t)} = K_c * ET_{o(t)} \tag{2}$$

With this information in mind, the hydrological balance dynamics can be written as shown in Eq. 3:

$$\dot{\Theta}_{(t)} = I_{(t)} + R_{(t)} - K_c ET_{o(t)} \tag{3}$$

We can write this continuous-time system as a state-space model like the one we show on Eq. 4:

$$\dot{\Theta} = A\Theta_{(t)} + BI_{(t)} + C \begin{bmatrix} ET_{c(t)} \\ R_{(t)} \end{bmatrix}$$

$$y_{(t)} = \Theta_{(t)} \tag{4}$$

The coefficients A, B, C and D are obtained from direct measurements on the field.

4.2 Design

The basic design of the implementation is depicted in Fig. 4. In this stage we used prototyping platforms such as Arduino UNO and Raspberry Pi 2. With all the issues fixed in the design, we can proceed to the construction of a full custom device that allows the system to be effective and low cost.

Hardware. The hardware in the solution, other than the cloud infrastructure that could be delegated to another entity, is the one that would be used in the field where the plantation is placed.

To interact with the environment, there should be a module capable of connecting the actuator and the sensor, and the capability to communicate with other devices. The actuators used in the system are relays to control an electrovalve to a water irrigation and fertilizer irrigation sub-system. The sensors are soil moisture, PH and environment humidity and temperature sensors.

A consideration that we must note, is if it's better to have a wired topology of the sensors in the field, or if it would be better to implement a wireless communication through the sensors. If we use 1-wire based sensors, we must consider the topology of the sensors and the gateway, because that affects the maximum length of cable that is allowed for a good communication. It is said that at a 750 m of cable length the communication will fail due to the delay of the response according to Maxim Integrated's guidelines for Reliable Long Line 1-Wire Networks.

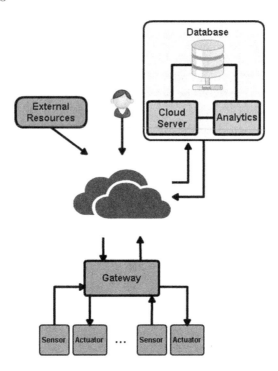

Fig. 4. Design of the application

Because of the limitations of the hardware in the nodes, there should be a gateway between the nodes and the application hosted in the cloud. This gateway should be resourceful enough to control a group of nodes and do other activities. The communication protocol is decided depending on the topography for the field, this could be done by Ethernet connection or 1-wire.

Software. The software should be capable of taking decisions based on the result of the transfer function which calculates the amount of water to reach the RAW level and the local precipitation prediction. In the following section, we will describe how these issues are addressed with the software.

The software in the end-mile node, where the sensor and actuators are connected, besides to accurately sense the data and communicate with the gateway and the actuators, should be capable of sending information if it senses a malfunction of things. However, it shouldn't take decisions, it should only receive orders from the gateway. The communication between the nodes and the gateway should be via Ethernet, because of the distance that makes non-viable to connect via GPIO or serial. There should be a two-way authentication method between the nodes and the gateway, and a protocol to maintain integrity, and confidentiality.

The main function of the gateway is to receive the information from the cloud about the precipitation prediction for each zone in the field, obtain the current information of the water level, and with these data and using the model, calculate the amount of water necessary to maintain the soil moisture in optimal levels. The gateway sends to the nodes the order to start and stop the electrovalve, and make sure that the water level reaches the RAW level. At the end of the irrigation, the gateway collects the information and send it to the cloud server to be persisted. If the gateway detects a wrong behavior given by a malfunction of one of the nodes or because the soil moisture reached the upper or lower limit of the accepted range defined previously, it should notify the cloud-server to generate the corresponding alarm to the stakeholders. The cloud server has two main functions, store the information, data and parameters needed in the system, and obtain the weather prediction for every zone and send it to the corresponding gateway when needed. The parametrization of the system should be done with an application hosted in the server that allows the administrator to set the information of the different elements of the systems, users and how are they identified and connected, and also which relationship exists between them. The application should allow to set the general parameters of the system such as information about the topography of the field, the connection string for the external resources, etc. The web application, should also allow to set manual events like a calendar for irrigation of water, and change the limits for the alarms, and the profile that should receive them, and add or remove elements from the system.

4.3 Implementation

For the implementation of the system, we used several frameworks due to the heterogeneity of the devices and infrastructure. In this first prototype, we present a system which is capable of sensing the soil moisture and control a Relay for the electro-valve.

For the hardware design of the system, we used Arduino UNO as the nodes that will collect the information from the soil moisture sensors. For the gateway, we used a Raspberry Pi 2. The latest sends the nodes' collected information to the web application.

We used an Arduino soil moisture sensor module, and a relay that will activate the electrovalve when it's needed. In this first stage of the project we used that sensor because it is low cost and easy to use in the small scenario we were making the prototype in. The issue that these sensors have, is that they damage rapidly, due to corrosion for being in a high humidity environment. Also, these sensors tend to fail at high temperatures, and this is a problem given that the oil palm must be between 28 °C and 30 °C. For the intended scenario of this project, we would need to use more specialized sensors that are suited to resist corrosion and high temperatures for a longer time such as the Decagon 10HS soil moisture sensor [23,24], the IMKO TRIME-PICO 64/32 [25] and the ML3 ThetaProbe [26]. Considering that most of the roots of an oil palm are found in the top 15–50 cm from the soil surface [27, 28], we can say that these sensors would work for this specific application.

The software for the nodes, the C based arduino framework was used to obtain the data and control the electrovalve. The *MD5.h* library was used to generate the MD5 hash, which is used to maintain integrity. The gateway software was built using *Mono* for Linux, with *c#* language. The client for the web services was built using the .Net web service reference libraries. The cloud server application was built with the .Net framework and internet information service to host the application. The presentation page was built using Razor, jquery and html5.

To calibrate the sensors for the specific soil type used for the oil palm, a multiple point calibration is used, where we need at least 10 samples of soil previously dried with different amounts of water in each of them. After calculating the volumetric water content of each sample, we can make a calibration curve to then perform a linear regression on it to obtain the slope and the intercept of the curve. This values help us calibrate the sensor for a specific soil type [29, 30].

The following step was to make the code for the nodes and the gateway to simulate the possible scenarios to verify the functionality of the system. The final step was to build the server infrastructure and the web application and later conduct a test for the full system.

5   Results

The data of the system are stored in the IoT irrigation system and can be visualized in http://ledswitch.botsolucionador.com/.

On the web page we show the last data sensed and a historic data posted as lines chart. In the application an upper and a lower level of humidity and the application will create an alarm to inform the interested and the administrator of the cultivation via email. The application let the administrator create irrigation events and show the results in a table.

The prototype has only been tested with one type of sensor, and simulated the water-valve with a relay. Also, the connection between the node and the gateway was proven with the serial port. Take notice that this is a work in progress, where we still need to include on our application many variables that affect the irrigation schedule.

6   Conclusions and Future Work

A prototype for an irrigation system to monitor the soil moisture of an oil palm plantation was designed, and a prototype was developed using a low cost soil moisture sensor, an Arduino UNO and a Raspberry Pi 2. This prototype allows the monitoring of the soil where the sensor is located. The application for the end user allows them to create events to irrigate the field at certain hours, given that if the soil is in an acceptable range of moisture, it will not water the palms. This prototype proves that the use of the Internet of Things in agriculture can save money in watering costs to the people working in the growth of the oil palm in Colombia. We also need to note that we are changing a technical activity (oil palm agriculture) to a research activity. When implementing this system into a real-life scenario, we would move from the Arduino Uno nodes to ATTiny 85 microcontrollers so the cost and the size of the nodes can be decreased [31]. Other variables that we could monitor and keep a registry of, are the temperature of the environment and the soil PH. This can be done with specialized sensor that can resist an outdoor environment with little to no maintenance.

The next step is to build a full custom device for the control of the irrigation. The device should have total awareness of the variables needed from the environment. Also, the system needs to be capable of generating events and alerts when the sensed values are not within the desired range.

Acknowledgment. The authors would like to acknowledge the cooperation of all partners within the Centro de Excelencia y Apropiación en Internet de las Cosas (CEA-IoT) project. The authors would also like to thank all the institutions that supported this work: the Colombian Ministry for the Information and Communications Technology (Ministerio de Tecnologías de la Información y las Comunicaciones - MinTIC) and the Colombian Administrative Department of Science, Technology and Innovation (Departamento Administrativo de Ciencia, Tecnología e Innovación - Colciencias) through the Fondo Nacional de Financiamiento para la Ciencia, la Tecnología y la Innovación Francisco José de Caldas (Project ID: FP44842- 502-2015).

References

1. Gasparatos, A., Stromberg, P., Takeuchi, K.: Biofuels, ecosystem services and human wellbeing: Putting biofuels in the ecosystem services narrative. Agric. Ecosyst. Environ. **142**(3), 111–128 (2011)
2. Escobar, J.C., Lora, E.S., Venturini, O.J., Yáñez, E.E., Castillo, E.F., Almazan, O.: Biofuels: environment, technology and food security. Renew. Sustain. Energy Rev. **13**(6), 1275–1287 (2009)
3. Chin, H.C., Choong, W.W., Alwi, S.R.W., Mohammed, A.H.: Issues of social acceptance on biofuel development. J. Clean. Prod. **71**, 30–39 (2014)
4. Knothe, G., Krahl, J., Van Gerpen, J.: The Biodiesel Handbook. Elsevier, Amsterdam (2015)
5. Acuña, A., Balcazar, V., Restrepo, S., Fernández, A., Infante Villarreal, A., Murgas, G., Mesa, D., et al.: Lineamientos de política para promover la producción sostenible de biocombustibles en colombiael biodiesel de palma en colombia. Technical report, Federación Nacional de Cultivadores de Palma de Aceite, Fedepalma, Colombia (2008)
6. Mesa, J.: La palmicultura colombiana de cara al 2020. Revista Palmas **21**(especial), 9–17 (2000)
7. González, A.C., Amaya, E.G.G.: Minianuario estadístico 2015. Technical report, Fedepalma, May 2015
8. Carr, M.: The water relations and irrigation requirements of oil palm (elaeis guineensis): a review. Exp. Agric. **47**(04), 629–652 (2011)

9. Roldán, J.R.B., Herrera, C.J.: Cuenta satélite piloto de la agroindustria de la palma de aceite: Palma en desarrollo, en producción y su primer nivel de transformación. Technical report, Departamento Administrativo Nacional de Estadística, October 2012

10. Mejía, J.: Consumo de agua por la palma de aceite y efectos del riego sobre la producción de racimos: una revisión de literatura. Revista Palmas **21**(1), 51–58 (2000)

11. Henson, I.E.: Modelling the impact of some oil palm crop management options. MPOB Technol. **29**, 52–59 (2006)

12. Gonzalez, J.: Panorama de la agroindustria de la palma de aceite en colombia y en la zona norte del país: Situación actual. Technical report, Fedepalma, June 2013

13. Buyya, R., Yeo, C.S., Venugopal, S., Broberg, J., Brandic, I.: Cloud computing and emerging it platforms: vision, hype, and reality for delivering computing as the 5th utility. Future Gener. Comput. Syst. **25**(6), 599–616 (2009)

14. Sales, N., Remédios, O., Arsenio, A.: Wireless sensor and actuator system for smart irrigation on the cloud. In: 2015 IEEE 2nd World Forum on Internet of Things (WF-IoT), pp. 693–698. IEEE (2015)

15. Vani, P.D., Rao, K.R.: Measurement and monitoring of soil moisture using cloud IoT and android system. Indian J. Sci. Technol. **9**(31) (2016)

16. Lozoya, C., Mendoza, C., Mejía, L., Quintana, J., Mendoza, G., Bustillos, M., Arras, O., Solís, L.: Model predictive control for closed-loop irrigation. IFAC Proc. Vol. **47**(3), 4429–4434 (2014)

17. Saleem, S.K., Delgoda, D., Ooi, S.K., Dassanayake, K.B., Liu, L., Halgamuge, M., Malano, H.: Model predictive control for real-time irrigation scheduling. IFAC Proc. Vol. **46**(18), 299–304 (2013)

18. Arnold, J.G., Allen, P.M., Bernhardt, G.: A comprehensive surface-groundwater flow model. J. Hydrol. **142**(1–4), 47–69 (1993)

19. Steduto, P., Hsiao, T.C., Raes, D., Fereres, E.: Aquacropthe FAO crop model to simulate yield response to water: I. concepts and underlying principles. Agron. J. **101**(3), 426–437 (2009)

20. McMullen, B.: SOILpak for Vegetable Growers, 1st edn. NSW Agriculture, Orange (2000)

21. Allen, R.G., Pereira, L.S., Raes, D., Smith, M., et al.: Crop evapotranspiration guidelines for computing crop water requirements-FAO irrigation and drainage paper 56. FAO, Rome **300**(9) D05109 (1998)

22. Arshad, A.M., et al.: Crop evapotranspiration and crop water requirement for oil palm in peninsular Malaysia. J. Biol. Agric. Healthc. **4**(16), 23–28 (2014)

23. Decagon Devices Inc.: 10HS soil moisture sensor, Rev. 1, July 2016

24. Spelman, D., Kinzli, K.D., Kunberger, T.: Calibration of the 10hs soil moisture sensor for southwest Orida agricultural soils. J. Irrig. Drain. Eng. **139**(12), 965–971 (2013)

25. IMKO Micromodultechnik GmbH: TRIME-PICO 64/32, Rev. 1, February 2010

26. Delta-T Devices Ltd.: ML3 ThetaProbe User Manual. Rev. 2., September 2016

27. Yahya, Z., Husin, A., Talib, J., Othman, J., Ahmed, O.H., Jalloh, M.B., et al.: Oil palm (elaeis guineensis) roots response to mechanization in Bernam series soil. Am. J. Appl. Sci. **7**(3), 343–348 (2010)

28. Verheye, W.: Growth and production of oil palm. In: Land Use, Land Cover and Soil Sciences. Encyclopedia of Life Support Systems (EOLSS). UNESCO-EOLSS Publishers, Oxford (2010)

29. Roth, C., Malicki, M., Plagge, R.: Empirical evaluation of the relationship between soil dielectric constant and volumetric water content as the basis for calibrating soil moisture measurements by TDR. J. Soil Sci. **43**(1), 1–13 (1992)
30. Baucke, F.G., Naumann, R., Alexander-Weber, C.: Multiple-point calibration with linear regression as a proposed standardization procedure for high-precision pH measurements. Anal. Chem. **65**(22), 3244–3251 (1993)
31. ATMEL Corporation: Atmel 8-bit AVR Microcontroller with 2/4/8K Bytes In-System Programmable Flash. Rev. 2586QAVR, August 2013

Industry 4.0 and Its Development in Colombian Industry

Kelly Viviana Bareño Sinisterra, Stefhania Mora Mejía[✉],
and José Ignacio Rodríguez Molano

Universidad Distrital Francisco José de Caldas, Bogotá, Colombia
kbareno@gmail.com, stefhaniamora@gmail.com,
jirodriguez@udistrital.edu.co

Abstract. This article describes the prospective in the Colombian industry related to the "Internet of things" and the concept of industry 4.0, using an analysis of different platforms implementation throughout several fields of the Colombian industries.

Keywords: Industry 4.0 · Industrial internet of things · Internet of things platforms · Big data

1 Introduction

In the Global context, taken decisions are the ones that define differential aspects stablishing the path followed by a company or an enterprise [1], those decisions rely upon tools of acquisition, collection, organization and analysis of information of the scenery of study. Which is why, this article claims to show up the current state of the IoT existing platforms in the studied area with their definition, characteristics and differential factors of the applications in several countries and regions around the globe such as success cases, and how these platforms which are developed to enhance the growth of 4.0 industry concept [2], aims to help to make decisions that determinate the future of companies in the current society of information and knowledge [3].

For reading and research convenience, this article, is organized as follows: Sect. 1, is a general introduction of the research; Sect. 2 contains the definitions and current state of key concepts, Sect. 3 discusses the characteristics of each consulted IoT platforms, Sect. 4 describes the development of platforms worldwide, Sect. 5 portrays Colombian case according to the authors investigation. Finally, Sect. 6 presents conclusions disaggregate from the paper content.

2 Conceptualization

2.1 Industry 4.0

Industry 4.0 is the designation for the fourth industrial revolution, consistent with the current trend of data exchange and automation in the technology industry. It includes cyber-physical systems, internet of things (IoT) and cloud computing [4].

© Springer International Publishing AG 2017
J.C. Figueroa-García et al. (Eds.): WEA 2017, CCIS 742, pp. 312–323, 2017.
DOI: 10.1007/978-3-319-66963-2_28

Industry 4.0 describes industry future as the establishment of internet and technological information based on interactive platforms [5], integrating each time more factors of scientific production, resulting in a more automated and connected industry. In addition to custom manufacturing industry 4.0 also incorporates information and manufacturing technology, meaning that the revolution will be dominated by intelligent manufacturing, through intelligent factories [6].

Talking about the fourth industrial revolution, the following Table 1 shows the evolution of industrial revolutions throughout history:

Table 1. Development of industry revolutions.

First industrial revolution	Began in the middle of the eighteenth century thanks to the steam engine that achieved the mechanization of the factory
Second industrial revolution	Started in the mid-nineteenth century, with the power to implement mass production on a large scale
Third industrial revolution	Ocurred in the mid-twentieth century through electrical and information technology to get automated manufacturing
Fourth industrial revolution	Based on the later evolution of the industry, according with physical system of cybernetics to develop new manufacturing methods

As mentioned, industry 4.0 is based on cyber-physical systems [5], that connect virtual spaces with physical realities, integrating computing, communication and storage capacity, reaching goods results of stability, security and acceptable efficiency in real time (Fig. 1).

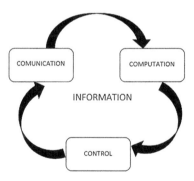

Fig. 1. Industry 4.0 structure. Adapted from [5]

Industry 4.0 structure works around three important concepts, computation, communication and control, to achieve interaction between the world and information in real time through feedback loops of engagement between computational and physical processes, with the purpose of increasing or expanding new functions, providing real time sensing, dynamic control and information feedback, among other characteristics.

A good comparison of the mechanism of the industry 4.0, could be a typical control system of an industrial process, in this case a variety of sensors and actuators are used to trace the comportment of a property of the system in actual time and transmit it to data center through the wireless networks technologies to establish electronic files of manipulation. Some of the sensors and actuators are shown in the following Table 2:

Table 2. Sensors and actuators used in the industry.

Sensors	Actuators
Temperature - Temperature	Light bulb or LED - Creates light
Light - Light/Dark	Heater - Increases temperature
Pressure - Pressure	Cooling unit - Decreases temperature
Moisture - Dampness/Dryness	Motor - spins things around
Water-Level - How full/empty a container is	Pump - Pushes water/air through pipes
Movement - Movement nearby	Buzzer/Bell/Siren - Creates noise
Proximity - How close/far is something	
Switch or button - If something is touching/ pressing it	

2.2 Internet of Things

Taking an overall vision, IoT is the acronym that refers to each object that has its own virtual identity and the potential capacity to integrate and interact independently in a network with any other individual or either between machines [7]. According with Cisco concept, internet of things is simply the point in time, when more things or objects than people get connected to internet.

It is a priority for asset-intensive companies to use their equipment to the maximum and optimally to become more profitable. Increasing the performance depends on several factors as the operation, design, plans of maintenance and the operational context, the modeling of these factors will allow better control over the asset. However, this is only possible with the existence of accurate information that allows to characterize the equipment. The applications of IoT technology on industries created the concept of IIoT (Industrial Internet of Things), which has three phenomena that characterize it, as shown in Table 3:

Table 3. IIoT phenomena.

Miniaturization	It makes that components of serves become smaller, providing connection of anything, anywhere
Infrastructure	Mobile telephony infrastructure that has a great coverage
Proliferation	Of applications and services that use the data generated of IoT

2.3 Big Data

In short words, big data can be defined as the management of the variety, volume and speed of data transferred, often used by the industry as a tool to automatically track the performance of IT systems and their behavior, and to innovate in business strategies and improve overall operational efficiency [8]. Also, big data are massive amounts of data that accumulate over time, difficult to analyze and manage using common database management tools [9]. In the same way Zdnet, interprets big data as tools, processes and procedures that allow an organization to create, manipulate and manage huge datasets and storage facilities, adding the concept of physical space to the Big Data dimension. The characteristics of the representative structure of Big Data will be shown below (Table 4):

Table 4. Four Vs for Big Data, representative characteristics.

Volume	Every day, companies record a significant increase in their data (terabytes, petabytes and exabytes), created by people and machines. Some companies generate terabytes of data every hour, every day of the year, which means, companies are flooded of data
Variety	It goes hand in hand with volume, because according to it and with technology development, there are many ways of representing data, it is the case of structured and unstructured data
Velocity	Of data creation, which measures the increase of software products developed (web pages, search files, social networks, forums, emails, among others)
Veracity	Level of confidence in data. One of the key challenges of Big Data is to ensure reliable data

3 Industry 4.0 Platforms

Nowadays, the success of a company that aims to implement industry 4.0 in its processes will depend of innovation capacity of companies [10], that goes hand in hand with interaction with other companies, through the development of platforms that make it easier for other companies to develop this philosophy. This paper will show the definitions, characteristics and advantages that each platform gives to the organization from its own development, taking into account that the platforms described here are in the first places in the ranking of worldwide demand.

3.1 Splunk

Definition: The Splunk platforms transforms machine generated data into valuable information, enabling companies to be more productive, profitable and secure [11].

Description: Splunk solutions can be describe through next cycle -Application distribution – Improved time of activity – Maintain SLA (Service Level Agreement) – Provides new information – Improve operations -Create performance information.

Relation with Big Data: Within the benefits offered by Splunk, big data plays an important role, because it allows to obtain and process the data generated by machines with one of the most complex and fastest areas of big data around the world, containing a record of all transactions, client behaviors, sensor readings, machine behaviors, security threats, fraudulent activities and so on, it is where Splunk helps discover the hidden value of all data generated by the machines, providing a unified method of organizing and extracting real time information from huge amounts of machine data from practically any source: Websites, enterprise applications, social networking platforms, application servers, hypervisors, sensors, traditional databases, and warehouses open source data.

IoT and IIoT Relation: it provides real time information on sensors, devices and industrial systems such as SCADA by providing a flexible and versatile platform for machine data generated by all sources connected in current networks.

3.2   Anella Industrial 4.0

Definition: This platform was born in Cataluña and developed by technology centers and local industries with the aim of providing a secure, stable and accessible framework for the exchange of cloud-IT services as a global solution to the expansion of the IIoT. This is a digital transformation tool that through a marketplace facilitates digitization of processes and industrial companies will be able to access to a catalog of digital services for the industry. It gives efficient, secure and scalable access to standard software solutions.

Description: Anella solution is represented by a cycle that aims to -Drive innovation -Facilitate infrastructure (in order to modify code) -Promote success stories and provide forums -Facilitate the adoption of new technologies -Participate of international forums and organizations.

3.3   Xompass Faas

Definition: This is an end-to-end solution that adds Edge Intelligence to thousands of assets in mining, water, power, oil, gas and power using cloud power.

Description: Platform oriented in three senses that facilitate to the company management of its operation from the advantages of the internet, big data, cloud computing and IIoT, allowing:

Rapid deployment, all assets can be connected in seconds, integrating them with existing control systems beyond the control layer, and is instantly available for implementation at every time.

Productivity improvement, the power of cloud and the new data management intelligence make it possible, to take better decisions in real time, which allow to operate assets efficiently, reducing product losses.

Downtime reduction, it is easier to avoid downtime with cloud-enabled predictive asset behavior models, by consolidating field data source, maintenance workforce is reduced, resulting in lower cost of preventive and corrective maintenance.

3.4   Microsoft Azure

Definition: Microsoft Azure is an open and flexible cloud platform to quickly build, deploy, and manage applications across a global network of Microsoft-managed datacenters. It provides the foundation for business and consumer applications that deliver a consistent way for people to store and share information easily and securely in the cloud, and access it on any device from any location [12].

Description: Microsoft Azure works through three tools and developers which include the platforms functions:

IaaS: Services oriented to the user, in order to have full control of virtual infrastructure. It includes everything related to servers (virtual machines), where to choose operating system (Windows Server, Linux, Oracle, Open Logic, etc.), number of processing cores, RAM capacity or virtual disks.

PaaS: Platform which is already created by Azure and it is also managed by itself. PaaS escalates, develops and manages the customer needs through the apps.

SaaS: Services where infrastructure and platform remain hide under a cape of abstraction.

3.5 Watson IoT Platform

Definition: It allows making sense to data to optimize operations, manage assets, rethink products and services, and transform customer experience [13].

Description: See (Table 5).

Table 5. Watson IoT platform solutions.

Analyze	Natural Language Processing: Automatically binds spoken words with meaning and intention of user
	Automatic learning: Automates data processing and classifies data according to priorities
	Image and video analysis: Monitor unstructured video channel data and image snapshots to identify scenes and patterns in video data
	Text Analysis: Survey unstructured textual data
Connect	Easily connection of chip devices to smart devices to their applications and industry solutions
Manage	Management of information and integration of external data
	Manage risk and collect information from IoT environment using sophisticated dashboards and alerts
Insert	Enter data from other data sources and platforms, to increase data of devices and perform additional analysis
Develop	Develop a variety of cloud services as data track record

4 Industry 4.0 Pioneer Countries

4.1 Germany

Germany works around "Internet + Manufacturing" [14]. This country is a leader in the deployment initiatives on Industry 4.0 through new technologies, which make possible digital transformation Germany, combines the participation of public administrations with the active role of companies, universities and research centers, to generate industry 4.0 ecosystems. An Example of this collaborative ecosystem is the project German National Academy of Science and Engineering (ACATECH) [5].

The Fraunhofer Institute of Industrial Engineering and automation in Germany predicts that in the country, industry 4.0 can improve productivity in a range of 20 to 30% points by 2025 [15]. In summary, the application for industry 4.0 represent an investment of 40 billion euros per year with a forecast of digital transformation of more than 80% of industries by 2021, with an efficiency increase of 18%, a cost reduction of 13% and a potential business growth of 425 billion euros in 2025 [16].

4.2   China

For the Asian country, the transitional program "Created in China" that evolves from the program "Made in China" as the complete transformation [5], establishes that manufacture future based on interactive platforms, internet and information technologies is going to be increasingly integrated to scientific and automated production factors, to networks creation and intellectuality added to standard of personalized manufacturing. In 2015, Chinese government promulgated "Made in China 2025" program, the Chinese version of Industry 4.0, which will be on the stage of history, in future development, directly related to the development of the industrial economy of China [5].

In this way, digitalization is an appropriate trampoline for China. According with official Chinese estimations, Industry 4.0 can increase productivity of China by 25 to 30% and reduce production losses in approximately 60% [17]. Moreover, according with a study of the Chinese Academy of Engineering (CAE), the Chinese income per capita could keep catch up with countries such as United States, Germany and Japan, by the year 2045 thanks to the accurate and total implementation of the fourth industrial revolution.

5   Industry 4.0 in Colombia

5.1   Contextualization

Colombia, at Latin American level, has the fourth position in Open Data Index. Bogota ranks within the top three smartest cities in Latin America, along with Sao Paulo and Mexico City. However, this regional positioning doesn't guarantee an "industrial revolution" considering the magnitudes of industry. Colombia has just opened the Center for Excellence and Internet Acquisition of Things, its first public-private research and innovation center of IoT; in which five public universities, eight national companies, three multinational technology companies (Intel, Hewlett-Packard Enterprise and Microsoft), Colciencias and the TIC Ministry joined forces to create developments in this technological field.

The business sector agrees that successful organizations are those that manage their digital universe to analyze behaviors, based on real data and using the concepts of "cloud computing" in which they can quickly access to information to make decisions, which follows the concept behind of Industry 4.0. While the state holds that technology is at hand, and that the way to use it has to be changed, it must pass from e-government to digital government. One major difficulty that Colombia has is that private companies do not use the technology properly, as they limit themselves in just having a web page, but without transforming their business model. Colombian companies use technology as a tool instead of a goal, wasting the technology is potential for innovation. This concludes that much remains to be done, recognizing the progress already made.

The challenge then is to understand that the development of the Colombian industry towards a higher level of intelligence and automatization is a task of everyone and that the way to achieve that is integrating government, companies and civil population in a perfectly related network. The government must also create suitable and optimum conditions to ensure sustainability of industry and support the entrepreneurship, characterized for its innovation and technology leverage to create value; all of which helps the government improves the life overall life quality of it is society by (allowing access to education for the entire population). Finally, the challenge for citizens and companies is to be ethical regarding the good acting and committing to generate shared value to society, realizing that ICT are not a luxury but a necessity to remain the market.

5.2 IoT Platforms Used in Colombia

In order to accomplish the objectives of the study, a survey was made for thirteen (13) companies, both private and public, with activity in the country with the purpose of having an overview of the real position of industries Colombia as was previously described. Most of the companies reviewed Industry 4.0 platforms, companies consulted covered areas of food production, manufacturing, mining, health, entertainment, services, sales, marketing, and collection and control of customs and taxes. Of the total of companies surveyed, it was found that only 23% of them do not use any platform to analyze company data, although those recognize the Industry 4.0 concept, while 47% of the companies affirmed to use two or more platforms simultaneously in different business areas (Fig. 2).

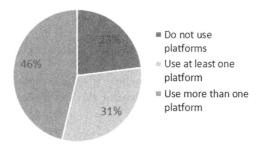

Fig. 2.   Usage of IoT platforms in companies consulted.

The next step consisted in identifying the top platforms currently used platforms by the companies and to verify, their versatility and the field of application (large or small scale within the internal structure of business) (Fig. 3).

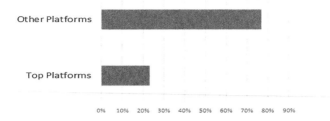

Fig. 3. Usage of IoT platforms reviewed and others.

At this point and taking into account the percentage of companies that use any data analysis platform, 77% of the sample claimed to use collection and analysis of data platforms with solid implementations, but from these implementations only 30.7% correspond to any of the platforms named in this review. The remaining 69.3% of these companies, were asked which platform they used, aiming to cover a greater depth regarding the type of platform, its characterization and why these platforms were preferred in comparison to top platforms of this paper (Table 6).

Table 6. Platform used by companies.

Platform	Usage %	Platform	Usage %
Sharepoint	12,50%	NOW	6,25%
Watson IoT platform		Oracle	
Orange		Cognos	
Eclipse	6,25%	Logtrust	
Bizagi		JDA	
Azure		Survella	
Tableau		Weka	
SQL server		Datamelt	

Nevertheless, 86% of these platforms are non-license, buffering financial expenses of paying a license periodically, according with data processing type preferred by each company. From the survey results, there is a tendency of companies that understand Industry 4.0 platforms as a simple support for processes, rather than a tool of decision making at management levels (Fig. 4).

As mentioned, 30.7% of the 13 companies surveyed that reported the use of the top named platforms return the next results: from five (5) of those companies just three (3) of them use two of the platforms (Fig. 5).

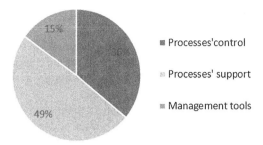

Fig. 4. Platforms usability.

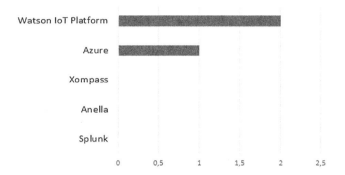

Fig. 5. Top platforms usage.

5.3 Implementation Barriers

Although it was previously said, Latin American levels stands out for the gradual reception of the most innovative business theories, not only in the case of platforms of Industry 4.0, but also of Big Data and business intelligence, among others [18]. Country evolution towards these tools of innovation and competitiveness is constrained by the high economic licenses costs of the best products (according with the ranking on global statistics by Capterra), and change resistance of which organizations are victims in adaptation processes [19].

6 Concluding Remarks

It is important to mention that companies that are leveraging their business model with this kind of tool are mainly B2B (Business to business) companies, those are too recent creation and are focused in generating value with services that improve the management indicators of large business companies. These companies are characterized because their founders are young people, who have mostly worked in large companies and have seen their specific needs, making the decision to solve those needs by building service.

Industrial revolutions throughout history have been characterized by the support, although late, of the government for its total implementation. The Colombian case of

Industry 4.0 requires a join effort of public sector headed by the government, businesses and the academy.

The commitment of the companies in investments related to Industry 4.0 platforms in the country should be understood as a requirement for the company is evolution and the increase of the value added to all the products and not only as a fashion industry or a mere global trend.

Open source tools are especially beneficial in Latin America because they are compatible with open data sources and have an attractive cost/benefit relation. On the other hand, licensed tools outstrip security platform correlation themes, technologies and algorithm capabilities to perform data analysis associated with security of technology platforms.

Finally, the dissemination, exhibition, consultation and research of technological tools that help to archive the fourth industrial revolution, development in general, are necessary to achieve the same development, this article is a sample and an attempt of it.

References

1. Devia, M., Gutiérrez, T.M.: Inteligencia de Negocios y su relación con la cultura Colombiana. Revista Redes de Ingeniería **7**(2), 1–8 (2016). Bogotá
2. Botia, D., Patiño, R., Ospina, E., et al.: Implementación Implementación de un Sistema Domótico Basado en una Plataforma de Internet de las Cosas. Décima Quinta Conferencia Iberoamericana en Sistemas. Cibernética e Informática, Ecuador (2016)
3. Rivoir, A.: La Sociedad de la Información y el Conocimiento hacia: un paradigma complejo. Las tecnologías de la información y la comunicación en el aula, Plan CEIBAL - MEC - Dirección de Educación, pp. 1–4. Uruguay (2015)
4. Huba, M., Kozak, S.: From e-learning to Industry 4.0. In: 2016 International Conference on Emerging eLearning Technologies and Applications (ICETA), pp. 103–108. Slovakia (2016). doi:10.1109/ICETA.2016.7802083
5. Cheng, G., Liu, L., Qianq, X., Liu, Y.: Industry 4.0 development and application of intelligent manufacturing. In: International Conference on Information System and Artificial Intelligence, Hong Kong (2016)
6. Baygin, M., Yetis, H., Karakose, M., et al.: An effect analysis of Industry 4.0 to higher. In: 2016 15th International Conference on Information Technology Based Higher Education and Training (ITHET), pp. 1–4. Turkey (2016). doi:10.1109/ITHET.2016.7760744
7. Suyama, T., Kishino, Y., Naya, F.: Abstracting IoT devices using virtual machine for wireless. In: 2014 IEEE World Forum on Internet of Things (WF-IoT), Seoul (2014). doi:10.1109/WF-IoT.2014.6803190
8. Xinhua, H., Jing, W., Yasong, L.: Big Data-as-a-Service: definition and architecture. In: 2013 15th IEEE International Conference on Communication Technology, pp. 738–742. China (2013). doi:10.1109/ICCT.2013.6820472
9. Camargo, J., Camargo, J., Aguilar, L.: Conociendo big data. Revista Facultad de Ingeniería **24**(38), 63–77 (2015). Bogotá
10. Shamim, S., Cang, S., Yu, H., et al.: Management approaches for Industry 4.0. A human resource management perspective. In: 2016 IEEE Congress on Evolutionary Computation (CEC), pp. 5309–5316. Canada (2016). doi:10.1109/CEC.2016.7748365
11. Griffin, D.: Splunk. Inf. Today **30**(11), 29 (2013)

12. Roth, J.: Microsoft Azure Subscription and Service Limits, Quotas, and Constraints, Microsoft Corporation (2105)
13. Davis, J.: IBM Buys the Weather Company in Watson IoT Push, Information Week (2015)
14. Lasi, H., Fettke, P., Kemper, H., et al.: Industry 4.0. Bus. Inf. Syst. Eng. **6**, 64 (2014)
15. Astarloa, A., Bidarte, U., Jimenez, J., et al.: Intelligent gateway for Industry 4.0-compliant production. In: IECON 2016- 42nd Annual Conference of the IEEE Industrial Electronics Society, pp. 4902–4907. Italy (2016). doi:10.1109/IECON.2016.7793890
16. Kovar, J., Mouralova, K., Ksica, F., Kroupa, J., et al.: Virtual reality in context of Industry 4.0. Proposed projects at Brno University of Technology. In: 2016 17th International Conference on Mechatronika (ME), pp. 1–7. Czech Republic (2016)
17. Wübbeke, J., Conrad, B.: Industrie 4.0: Will German Technology Help China Catch Up with the West? Mercator Institute for China Studies, China Monitor, China, issue 23 (2015)
18. Martínez, J.: La inteligencia de negocios como herramienta para la toma de decisiones estratégicas en las empresas. Análisis de su aplicabilidad en el contexto. Maestría thesis, Universidad Nacional de Colombia (2010)
19. Lueth, L., Patsioura, C., Williams, D., et al.: The current state of data analytics usage in industrial companies. Industrial Analytics, Digital Analytics Association Germany, pp. 38–49 (2016)

Power Monitoring Based on Industrial Internet of Things

Oscar Porto Solano, Leonardo Castellanos Acuña,
and Jose Luis Villa Ramírez[(⊠)]

Centro de Excelencia y Apropiación de Internet de las Cosas CEA-IoT,
Universidad Tecnológica de Bolívar, Cartagena D. T. y C., Colombia
oscports@gmail.com, castellanosleonardo7@gmail.com,
jvilla@unitecnologica.edu.co

Abstract. Monitoring has always been of crucial importance for industries, and it has been useful when getting notifications about critical parameters reaching threshold and alerts pertaining to failure of a specific device becomes a necessity. Traditional approaches are used to solve this problem, nevertheless generally deploy and maintenance the solutions based on that approaches are high-cost.

The Internet of Things (IoT) is a novel paradigm that covers a wide range of topics in the information-based era. One of the sectors which is particularly optimistic about the IoT future growth is the industry. This work aims to develop an IoT-based power-monitoring prototype as an alternative to the existing solutions. According with the last, a three-tier architecture for Industrial IoT applications is described and is used to implement the prototype. The presented solution is low-cost, enables real-time power-monitoring and allows to show the benefits of Internet of Things over Industrial tasks.

Keywords: Internet of Things · Modbus TCP · Industry · Power-monitoring

1 Introduction

Undoubtedly, the Internet of Things (IoT) has become one of the most frequently discussed topics between academics and practitioners. Essentially, this term conceptualizes an environment in which all kinds of objects are able not only to communicate with each other via Internet, but also to understand their context, interact with people, and take decisions. It is, then, a new model of information-sharing, ubiquitous computing and context-awareness that, if it is fully realized, will have a high impact on several aspects of users' everyday life, either from a personal/social or business perspective [1,2].

One of the sectors which is particularly optimistic about the IoT future growth is the industry. It is so much so that an important number of IoT projects have been conducted in a wide range of industrial systems and processes, thereby giving rise to a phenomenon dubbed the Industrial Internet of Things (IIoT)

© Springer International Publishing AG 2017
J.C. Figueroa-García et al. (Eds.): WEA 2017, CCIS 742, pp. 324–330, 2017.
DOI: 10.1007/978-3-319-66963-2_29

[3]. Lee and Lee [4] have identified three main categories for IIoT applications: (1) monitoring and control, (2) big data and business analytics, and (3) information sharing and collaboration. Monitoring has always been of crucial importance for industries, and it has been particularly useful when getting notifications about critical parameters reaching threshold and alerts pertaining to failure of a specific device becomes a necessity.

In this project a power monitoring prototype was built with IoT technologies which aims ubiquitously manage and monitoring the electrical behavior of several industrial equipment. Besides, preventive action could be taken with the collected information. Essentially, the goal of this study is to present an IoT-based system for real-time monitoring of current, voltage and/or any other electrical variable, such that an alert signal is generated when an undesirable electrical condition is presented.

The rest of the document is organized as follows. In Sect. 2, we briefly review previous work related to remote power monitoring. The architecture of the system is presented in Sect. 3. Section 4 describes the development devices selected for its construction and the results. The conclusions of this paper are summarized in Sect. 5.

2 Related Work

Power failures are particularly critical at sites where the environment and public safety are at risk, such as hospitals, sewage treatment plants and mines. They are also critical to a wide range of commercial and industrial processes. In seaports, for instance, it is necessary to provide an appropriate level of cargo safety when the goods to be shipped and/or consumed are perishable. This involves ensuring a permanent connection of reefer container to power supply source and detecting power failures in a fast and reliable way [5]. If quality features of refrigerated cargo are lost through ports fault, the port should pay compensation to the cargos owner. Occurrence of such situations may result in economic losses and damages to reputation of the port.

Over the last few years, a plethora of IoT solutions have been developed to solve a wide range of issues related to power monitoring [6–8]. In [9] a prototype which allows remote monitoring of energy consumption and provides alarms in case of power quality (PQ) event was developed, but its application is limited to residential environments. More recently, a remote monitoring solution through which industrial load status is automatically updated at a regular time frame was proposed in [10]. Some of its advantages are reduced power wastages, efficient monitoring and control, increased safety and less human-error related accidents. However, most of those solutions have been focused on monitoring power consumption rather than providing alerts when power failures occur. When alerts regarding power outages within an industrial environment are provided in fast and reliable way, the plant personnel are able to take immediate action to control damage and limit the consequences.

3 Industrial IoT Architecture

According to the reference architecture for Industrial Internet of Things described by the Industrial Internet Consortium [11] IIoT system contains 5 functional domains: Control, operation, information, application and business domain. Control domain represents the collection of functions that are performed by industrial control systems such as sensing and actuating. Operation domain aims execute monitoring and optimization task in the system. Information domain relates with the manage and storage of the data collected by the different domains. Application domain enable the system's interaction with people or applications. Finally the business domain supports business processes and procedural activities such as Customer Relationship Management (CRM) and Manufacturing Execution Systems (MES).

The IoT-based power monitoring system was developed according to the reference architecture mentioned previously. In our project the architecture was simplified (See Fig. 1). The architecture contains three tiers: Edge, platform and enterprise [11]. The tiers make use of three domains: Control, information and application. The functions of the tiers depend of the domain that these implement. The edge tier implements the control domain, it aims to collect the data from the sensors; the platform tier implements the information domain, it aims to receive the data from the edge tier and the data persisting; finally, the enterprise tier implements the application domain, it aims to show the information to the final user and to implement the logic and rules of the application.

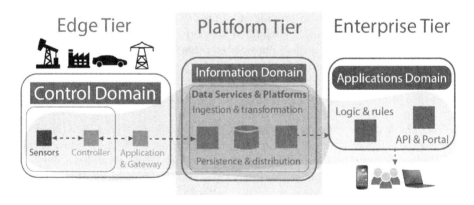

Fig. 1. IIoT Architecture based on [11].

Industrial sensors and IoT gateway makes part of the control domain. Industrial sensors are deployed over a local network and support MODBUS TCP protocol which enable to collect data from several industrial devices. To transfer the data of the measuring devices to a remote platform (Management application) an IoT gateway is used, which makes the transformation of the data from the MODBUS TCP protocol to the protocol that is necessary to establish the communication with the remote platform.

Information domain is based on a persistence entity, regularly a database but this depends of the design of the management application. Finally, the application domain contains the management application and the user interface. The management application is used to manage the data, to guarantee real-time monitoring and to customize alerts. Besides, data can be showed to the final user trough an user interface such as website or a mobile application.

One of the feature of the proposed architecture is to be customizable in each component of the domains, which enable to implement the architecture over different stages. Portability is another feature of the architecture since the control domain can be deployed over different locations and network topologies.

4 Implementation and Results

The proposed prototype aims to be flexible, portable, low-cost and reliable. To that end, a set of development boards were selected: A low cost single board computer (Raspberry Pi 2) was used as IoT gateway which manages the data acquired by an industrial sensing device (SENTRON PACK 3200) and then it sends the information to a cloud platform (UBIDOTS), which is responsible for the alert generation and allows access to historical data files. A Python script was developed and deployed in the IoT gateway to perform reading functions, unit conversions over the MODBUS TCP protocol and send the data to the management platform trough the REST protocol. (See Fig. 2).

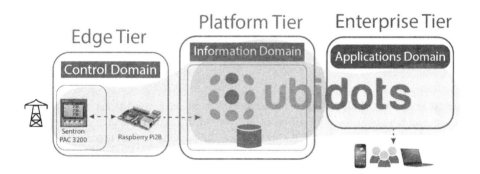

Fig. 2. Prototype implementation over proposed architecture

The power-monitoring prototype was tested with a star three-phase distribution electric power network. The three-phase RMS values of the measured phase voltage and line current are posted in UBIDOTS and can be visualized in real-time charts, as illustrated in Fig. 3d. With the data in UBIDOTS, two alarm situations were created. The first one is when the RMS value of the phase voltage is less than 100 V. The second one is when the RMS value of the line

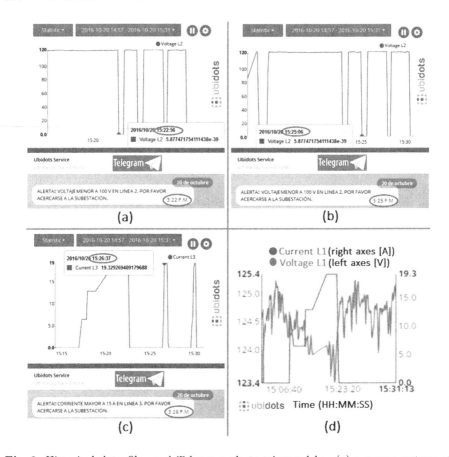

Fig. 3. Historical data files and Telegram alerts triggered by: (a) a power outage at 15:22, (b) a second power outage at 15:25, (c) a current peak at 15:26, and (d) real-time chart current vs voltage.

current is greater than 15 A. It is noteworthy that such conditions were defined for illustrative purposes, and different and/or additional alarm situations can be created from the account UBIDOTS to meet the specific requirements of the end user. The alerts can be sent to Telegram on a cell phone connected to Internet. Besides an Android App was developed to visualize the RMS value of the phase voltage and line current stored in UBIDOTS.

To test the alert generation process, a first power outage at 15:22, a second power outage at 15:25, and a current peak at 15:26 were simulated. The corresponding historical files and the Telegram alerts triggered by each of these events are shown in Figs. 3a, b and c, respectively. As can be seen, a Telegram alert appeared immediately after one of the previously defined alert situations was fulfilled.

Power monitoring problem can be solved with a traditional approach such as SCADA. Solutions based on SCADA are reliable and widely used in industry.

But the main inconvenient with this kind of solutions is the high cost of the implementation and maintenance. The proposed solution in this work exploits the benefits of IoT and can be implemented in big or small companies, because this makes use of low-cost elements and can be adapted to specific problems. The prototype described previously allows to show the mentioned benefits.

5   Conclusion

In this study, an IoT-based system for power monitoring, that is capable of sending alert messages when power failures occur, was presented. The system was developed over an architecture which exploits the benefits of the Internet of Things over industrial environments.

We should point out that the data capture process is performed through MODBUS/TCP protocol, so the proposed solution can be easily adapted to any other industrial application. Given that the Raspberry Pi can read values from holding registers of several power metering devices, the SENTRON PAC3200 can be replaced by any other device supporting MODBUS/TCP protocol. Alert conditions can be easily configured in the UBIDOTS platform, which allows end users to customize the rules for alert generation.

Future work includes the implementation of way to detect failures in the systems like lost of internet conexion, power cut, abnormal humidity or undesirable temperature conditions, etc. An little and low-cost batery is recommended to ensure continuous monitoring, even if a general power failure takes place. The IoT gateway can be improved adding support to another industrial protocols such as SNMP. The Android App can also be improved to integrate monitoring and alert generation.

Acknowledgment. The authors would like to acknowledge the cooperation of all partners within the Centro de Excelencia y Apropiación en Internet de las Cosas (CEA-IoT) project. The authors would also like to thank all the institutions that supported this work: the Colombian Ministry for the Information and Communications Technology (Ministerio de Tecnologías de la Información y las Comunicaciones - MinTIC) and the Colombian Administrative Department of Science, Technology and Innovation (Departamento Administrativo de Ciencia, Tecnología e Innovación - Colciencias) through the Fondo Nacional de Financiamiento para la Ciencia, la Tecnología y la Innovación Francisco José de Caldas (Project ID: FP44842-502-2015).

References

1. Atzori, L., Iera, A., Morabito, G.: The Internet of Things: a survey. Comput. Netw. **54**(15), 2787–2805 (2010)
2. Miorandi, D., Sicari, S., De Pellegrini, F., Chlamtac, I.: Internet of Things: vision, applications and research challenges. Ad Hoc Netw. **10**(7), 1497–1516 (2012)
3. Hartmann, M., Halecker, B.: Management of innovation in the industrial Internet of Things. In: ISPIM Conference Proceedings, p. 1 (2015). The International Society for Professional Innovation Management (ISPIM)

4. Lee, I., Lee, K.: The Internet of Things (IoT): applications, investments, and challenges for enterprises. Bus. Horiz. **58**(4), 431–440 (2015)
5. Filina, L., Filin, S.: An analysis of influence of lack of the electricity supply to reefer containers serviced at sea ports on storing conditions of cargoes contained in them. Pol. Marit. Res. **15**(4), 96–102 (2008)
6. Song, G., Ding, F., Zhang, W., Song, A.: A wireless power outlet system for smart homes. IEEE Trans. Consum. Electron. **54**(4), 1688–1691 (2008)
7. Lien, C.H., Bai, Y.W., Lin, M.B.: Remote-controllable power outlet system for home power management. IEEE Trans. Consum. Electron. **53**(4), 1634–1641 (2007)
8. Ashraf, Q.M., Yusoff, M.I.M., Azman, A.A., Nor, N.M., Fuzi, N.A.A., Saharedan, M.S., Omar, N.A.: Energy monitoring prototype for Internet of Things: preliminary results. In: Internet of Things (WF-IoT), 2015 IEEE 2nd World Forum, pp. 1–5. IEEE (2015)
9. Afonso, J.A., Rodrigues, F., Pereira, P., Gonalves, H., Afonso, J.L.: Wireless monitoring and management of energy consumption and power quality events. In: World Congress on Engineering 2015, pp. 338–343 (2015)
10. Ignatius, A.A., Samjay, D.C., Prathish, R., Rexy, A.I.: Automated monitoring of industrial loads using IoT and control using wireless technology. Middle East J. Sci. Res. **24**(S1), 55–58 (2016)
11. Industrial Internet Consortium: The Industrial Internet of Things Volume G1: Reference Architecture, Technical report (2017)

Design and Characterization of an Indoor Geolocator Using Beacons Captured by Bluetooth to Guide and Position People in a State of Visual Disability

Luis Eduardo Pallares[✉], Yesid Díaz-Gutierrez[✉], Edgar Krejci[✉], and Helmer Muñoz[✉]

Corporación Unificada Nacional de Educación Superior CUN, Bogotá, Colombia
{luis_pallares,yesid_diaz,edgar_krejci,helmer_munoz}@cun.edu.co

Abstract. Overcoming the barriers to access technology has been one of the main objectives that many institutes have planned for the inclusion of people with some type of disability. The technological developments have innumerable possibilities to create research projects that are inclusive, that is to say that it does not have difficulties to be used by people in a condition of visual disability, to achieve this, it is presented a solution to the problems of localization in Indoor space by using technology that is already available in any mobile phone through the use of Bluetooth Low Energy 4.0 and an application made in Android.

Keywords: Bluetooth · Android · Disability · Localization indoor

1 Introduction

The last census conducted by DANE in Colombia during 2005 shows 1,143,992 visually impaired people, who represent 43.5% of the total number of people with at least one disability, becoming one of the more frequent disabilities (see Fig. 1) according to Alejandra, A.M. (2013) from her work Characterization of persons with disabilities enrolled in institutions of care and rehabilitation. For visual impaired, one of the main problems is the spatial location of objects or things that surround them and are part of its environment so to have a better control of its location. The design developed in the Axon group, seeks to make an important contribution to solve the problem of Geolocation in confined spaces or Indoor, to achieve the above we will use Bluetooth 4.0 technology to manufacture access points [12] called Beacons and by developing a software application that can recognize these points and process the text of this information so to be translated by the TTS speech that guides the blind person; The application can basically talk and tell you where you are and thus guide you to avoid tripping and damaging your body by hitting any object you cannot see.

The technical development takes as reference the power signal of the reception signal that is commonly known as RSSI to measure distances and then can be triangulated, processed and transmitted to the blind person.

In this document it can be found in Sect. 3 the parameters and implementation of an HM-10 BLE 4.0 module as location beacons in interior spaces, measuring the power

© Springer International Publishing AG 2017
J.C. Figueroa-García et al. (Eds.): WEA 2017, CCIS 742, pp. 331–338, 2017.
DOI: 10.1007/978-3-319-66963-2_30

value of the RSSI received signal as well as the preparation of an app that implements text To speech, this API will help a person with visual impairment to process the information given by a Beacon of your location. In Sects. 4 and 5 we find the implementation and results obtained.

2   Description of the Problem

People with visual disabilities often have the need to improve their orientation using different aids, such as sense, touch, hearing and the use of the commonly known white stick, that allows him or her to extract information from the environment, this helps decision making as the case requires, such as when traveling independently, leading to the development of psychomotor, perceptive, cognitive and communication skills, which requires specialized staff that helps develop fine and gross motricity that aims to improve his reality.

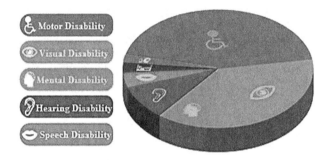

Fig. 1. Disability statistics in colombia (DANE source).

As shown in Fig. 1 it is necessary to investigate what up-to-date smartphone features are unused since there are often little exploited features that can help to develop applications that allow to solve and improve the skills of this type of population, therefore it is desired to address this problem using Bluetooth technology BLE 4.0 in the form of information points which can optimize the displacement and interaction with the space where this solution is implemented. To design the indoor geolocator device must have the following three aspects:

- An embedded device electronics system.
- A Bluetooth receiver system and it's App.
- A Beacon communication protocol, thus creating a powerful scenario where this technology of our mobile devices is applied.

3   Design and Modeling

3.1   Making the Beacon Access Point with an HM-10 BLE Module

A Beacon uses the following three customizable fields for identification [1, 2]:

- Universal Unique Identifier (UUID), 128 bits
- 16-bit Major
- Minor 16 bits

With these three fields, it can identify a Beacon point to use as a guide and for this; it can use three combinations for this purpose:

- Only UUID
- UUID and Major
- UUID, Major and Minor

The Minor (hexadecimal) number is the field that allows me to differentiate between one Beacon and the other (Fig. 2).

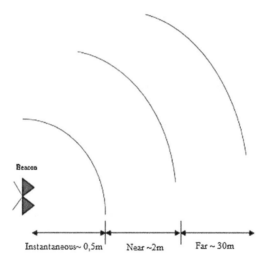

Fig. 2. Bluetooth ranges and areas.

These zones are defined to notify changes to applications when they are working in the background. In the foreground it is possible to obtain the exact distances to the Beacon by measuring the strength signal of the reception signal (RSSI) from the signal received from a Beacon, and comparing it with the signal value to a meter, which by default found in the Beacon and can be customized.

3.2   Configuration of the HM-10 Module as Beacon

To configure the HM-10 module as a Beacon, it is must enter the AT command mode via a USB to TTL converter. One of the features of the HM-10 module is that it can enter the serial mode automatically and a simple connection is enough as shown in Fig. 3.

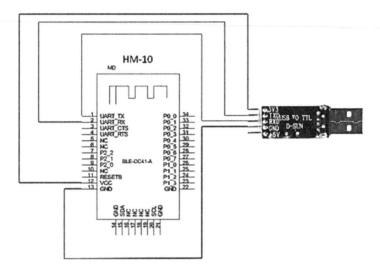

Fig. 3. Electrical connection of a HM-10 module with a TTL to USB converter

The sending of AT commands is done via a serial monitor, so you can configure the HM-10 module.

3.3   Equation for the Estimation of RSSI

The BLE HM-10 module comes configured to estimate the distance as a function of the power of the signal received, established and characterized at 1 m, this value corresponds to -59 dBm, the previous value is a direct consequence of propagation models statistic [3, 4], where the RSSI value is obtained by means of empirical parameters that intend to calibrate this value using measures in the environment and that allow to adjust them to the real conditions, of the previous one raises the following equation:

$$RSSI = -10n \log(x[m]) + A[dBm] \tag{1}$$

where n is the loss constant, which in neighboring regions (~ 2 m) is usually set to 2, in free space, A is the power in dBm referred to a meter (-59 dBm) and x is the distance between the transmitter and the measured transmitter in meters [5, 8]. Equation 1 can be written as follows, replacing the previous values:

$$RSSI[dBm] = -20 \log(x[m]) - 59dBm \tag{2}$$

With Eq. 2, the RSSI signal strength indicator versus the distance x in meters is plotted to observe its behavior, as shown below (Fig. 4).

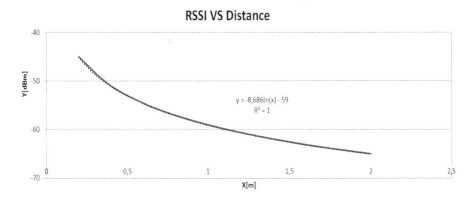

RSSI VS Distance

$y = -8,686\ln(x) - 59$
$R^2 = 1$

Fig. 4. Behavior of the intensity of the signal received RSSI with regard to the distance of the issuing point and receiver in a theoretical way.

3.4 App Components

The design of the App will be made using the suite IED Android Studio programmed in Java language (from her work I. Bluetooth SIG, Hans-on lab, Building an Android application for Beacons, 2015), the logic of the program is that it will identify a Beacon

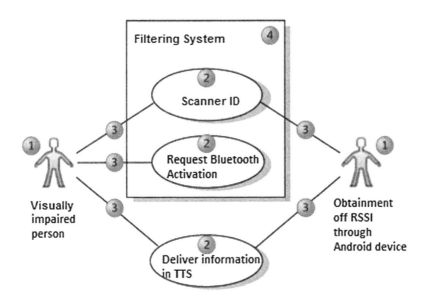

Fig. 5. Cases of use for the implementation

point, to estimate the distance to which it is, using the measured RSSI value. The components of the use case to take into account are:

1. Enable Bluetooth when the application starts.
2. Scanning and identification of the three Beacon fields (UUID, Major and Minor).
3. Obtaining the RSSI as the main parameter.
4. Use of a filter to improve accuracy (elimination of noise).
5. Use text to speech (TTS) to play audible messages for the recognition of access points, this can be carried out simply in Android through the API (Fig. 5).

4   Implementation

The model developed above is a theoretical parameter that will serve as a basis for estimating the position of a visually impaired person with respect to a Beacon information point, based on Eq. 3.

$$x[m] = 10^{-\left(\dfrac{RSSI[dBm] + 59dBm}{20}\right)} \tag{3}$$

Equation 3 is used to calculate the exact distance to the Beacon, by this method we can characterize and condition a specific place for a visually impaired person to develop with greater autonomy in that space [7].

5   Result

The tests were run with an HM-10 module, which was configured with a Beacon to send small packets, which will be interpreted by the test application.

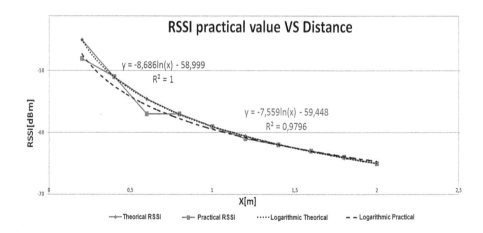

Fig. 6. Logarithmic trends and trend equation for the results obtained.

With this data, we calculate the absolute error of the distances obtained from the measurements made, it could improve the accuracy by calibrating the RSSI value, in this case the application can calibrate the value of RSSI measured at a distance of 1 m to obtain greater accuracy in the data obtained. The distance values that it is taken from the creation of a Beacon with an HM-10 module can be said to present errors of 20 cm as an approximate value due to the ambient conditions and other parameters that must be taken into account in a wireless measurement.

As it can see in the Fig. 6 the red color graph corresponds to the values measured from the data supplied by the application, the corresponding equation is on the left side, the blue graph corresponds to the theoretical values that is it obtained from Eq. 2 and whose equation resulting from the trend line is on the right side (Table 1).

Table 1. Experimental results and absolute distance error

X[m] Theorical	X[m] practical value	RSSI[dBm] theorical	RSSI[dBm] practical value	Absolute Error X[m]
0,2	0,28	−45,02	-48	0,08
0,4	0,36	−51,04	-51	0,04
0,6	0,71	-54,56	-57	0,11
0,8	0,77	-57,06	-57	0,03
1	0,95	-59	-59	0,05
1,2	1,27	-60,58	-61	0,07
1,4	1,44	-61,92	-62	0,04
1,6	1,68	-63,08	-63	0,08
1,8	1,87	-64,11	-64	0,07
2	2,09	-65,02	-65	0,09

To achieve the localization target the error can be controlled and improved considerably if we implement a noise filtering method to improve the precision of the instrument (a smartphone in this case) [9], which monitors the zone that surrounds the person with visual disability and manages the range of distances.

6   Conclusions and Future Work

The development of this project is very important since it allows people in a state of disability to be guided and positioned in an indoor environment without the need to use traditional walking sticks.

We can approach the location even more in a characterized space, it may be that the monitoring periods are done in real time, since usually the applications running in the background, deliver the information with some delay, that depends on the processor that is integrated in the mobile phone so this also affects the behavior of the results, but they are quite acceptable as the RSSI value tends towards a value and this leads us to estimate the distance, with the above it can develop a stable system so that a person with visual impairment can make use of the space according to the technological trends such as IoT, Wi-Fi, GPS, Bluetooth, etc. that aim toward an improved mobility in interior spaces avoiding or decreasing the amount of hits and blows that a visually impaired user can take in an unknown environment.

A future work would be to add an improvement to the traditional cane using this technology that integrates an appropriate hardware that allows the combination of different elements that are used and perceived by a visually impaired person.

As for the mobile application, continue to device accessibility strategies that allow all people, without exception, to use this type of content in an agile way, so that they are perceptible at any time, space and time without any difficulties.

Positioning systems using BLE can help position Drones in the detection of disasters or to supervise and monitor patients in the near space so that they arrive with exact precision to the sites within interior spaces. In addition to this technological application, in the commercial field, the detection of articles, the pattern of purchase patterns make this technology quite promising.

References

1. Madhavapeddy, A., Tse, A.: A study of bluetooth propagation using accurate indoor location mapping. In: Beigl, M., Intille, S., Rekimoto, J., Tokuda, H. (eds.) UbiComp 2005. LNCS, vol. 3660, pp. 105–122. Springer, Heidelberg (2005). doi:10.1007/11551201_7
2. Nirupama Bulusu, J.H.: Adaptive beacon placement. In: 21st International Conference on Distributed Computing Systems 2001, pp. 16–19. IEEE, April 2001. ISBN 0-7695-1077-9
3. Lau, L., Lee, B.G, Lee, S.-C., Chung, W.Y.: Enhanced RSSI-Based high accuracy real-time user location tracking system for indoor and outdoor eviroments. Int. J. Smart Sens. Int. Syst. 1(2), 1–12 (2008)
4. Oguejiofor, O.S: Outdoor localization system using RSSI measurement of wireless sensor network. Int. J. Innovative Technol. Exploring Eng. (IJITEE) 2, 1–6 (2013). ISSN: 2278-3075
5. Patwari, N.: Using proximity and quantized RSS for sensor. In: WSNA 2003 Proceedings of the 2nd ACM International Conference on Wireless Sensor Networks and Applications, pp. 20–29. ACM, New York (2003). ISBN: 1-58113-764-8
6. Pahlavan, K.: Wireless communications for office information networks. Commun. Mag. 23(6), 19–27 (1985). IEEE
7. Hassellöf, D.: Position determination using multiple wireless interfaces. KTH information and Communication Technology, Master of Science thesis, Sweden (2008)
8. Priyantha, N.B.: The cricket indoor location system, Ph.D. thesis, MIT Computer Science and Artificial Intelligence Laboratory, Cambridge, MA (2005)
9. Hashemi, H.: The indoor radio propagation channel. Proc. IEEE 81(7), 943–968 (1993)
10. Lin, T.N., Lin, P.C.: Performance comparison of indoor positioning techniques based on location fingerprinting in wireless networks. In: 2005 International Conference on Wireless Networks, Communications and Mobile Computing, 13–16 June 2005, vol. 2, pp. 1569–1574 (2005)
11. Kaemarungsi, K., Krishnamurthy, P.: Modeling of indoor positioning systems based on location fingerprinting, INFOCOM 2004. In: Twenty-third Annual Joint Conference of the IEEE Computer and Communications Societies, 7–11 March 2004, vol. 2, pp. 1012–1022 (2004)
12. Anastasi, G., Bandelloni, R., Conti, M., Delmastro, F., Gregori, E., Mainetto, G.: Experimenting an indoor bluetooth-based positioning service. In: 23rd International Conference on Distributed Computing Systems Workshops, ICDSW 2003, pp. 480–483 (2003)

Design and Implementation of an Energy Monitoring System for Buildings Based on Internet of Things Architecture

Edgar Villa[1], Julio Hurtado[2], and José Luis Villa[3]($\boxtimes$)

[1] Universidad Tecnolómica de Bolívar, Km 1, Via Turbaco, Cartagena, Colombia
edgar.villa.perez@gmail.com
[2] Department of Mathematics, Universidad Tecnolómica de Bolívar,
Km 1, Via Turbaco, Cartagena, Colombia
jhurtado@unitecnologica.edu.co
[3] Faculty of Electrical Engineering, Universidad Tecnológica de Bolívar,
Km 1, Via Turbaco, Cartagena, Colombia
jvilla@unitecnologica.edu.co

Abstract. Monitoring environmental variables in buildings is a first step to implement and provide services related to energy savings, comfort and safety among others issues. In this work we design and implement an Energy Monitoring System in order to achieve monitoring of environmental variables in buildings that use decentralized air conditioning systems. In particular, we focus on variables related with human comfort, such as room temperature, humidity, CO_2 and energy consumption of the air conditioning system. The system was implemented using low cost components and an Internet of Things Architecture. The field tests show the reliability of the proposed system.

1 Introduction

It is estimated that Heating Ventilation and Air Conditioning (HVAC) systems are responsible for approximately 40% of total building consumption [1]. In particular in Colombia, depending on the elevation of the cities, near to 40% of the households have air conditioning systems installed [2]. In consequence, several technologies have been proposed in order to reduce the impact of the high electric consumption that this kind of systems requires [3]. Among them, Building Automation Systems and Building Energy Management Systems arise as potential tools for reducing the energy consumption in buildings.

Broadly the air conditioning system can be classified in two broad categories: (1) Centralized air conditioning systems and (2) Decentralized systems. In general central systems provide better quality of indoor parameters and energy efficiency. However, central systems are costly to build but the operating costs tend to be low on large systems [4].

Our work is focused in design a monitoring and control platform that can be installed in public buildings that use decentralized air conditioning systems.

© Springer International Publishing AG 2017
J.C. Figueroa-García et al. (Eds.): WEA 2017, CCIS 742, pp. 339–348, 2017.
DOI: 10.1007/978-3-319-66963-2_31

In the literature, several approaches have been proposed. In [5] Zheng et al. use a hardware architecture for a Zigbee wireless network consisting of: sensor node, control node, gateway and server.

In [6], Nangtin et al., propose an alternative hardware architecture. Authors focus their work on the loss of energy in split air conditioners. They control the temperature considering the number of people and the position of the same ones. The control method uses a fuzzy Takagi Sugeno (T-S) model, where they regulate the speed of the evaporator and the on-off of the compressor. The hardware architecture contains: image processor, PLC, condenser and evaporator. It can be considered that the authors focus their attention directly on the compressor and the evaporator altering the original air circuit.

[7] presents an architecture based on the ADAM family of components from Advantech. With these components they acquire the data of the sensors and also in their architecture they use a PLC, to communicate it to the PC where the application is hosted.

2   Solution Architecture

Nissi Energy is the name of the platform of Hadware and Software, designed to reach the objective of the present study. The platform is intend for monitoring and controlling the energy consumed by mini Split or window air conditioners. In this section we present the Hardware Architecture and the Software Architecture.

2.1   Hardware Architecture

The hardware architecture forms a network of devices interconnected over an Ethernet network to provide monitoring and control services. The hardware devices are:

- Central server or server in the cloud
- Local mini server
- Cable/DSL modem
- Router
- Nissi Energy - Box
- Mobile devices or access computers.

In Fig. 1, it is observed that there is a "central server", which is the one that provides the services in the "cloud", to have access from Internet. The miniserver provides local services or functions (Intranet), the modem is the main communication element that gives access to the Internet. The router is used to expand the wireless network to those areas of difficult connection, the device "Nissi Energy-Box" is who performs the functions of data capture and control so it is worth noting that their communication can be wired or wireless, and Finally the mobile devices or access computers are those that are on the side of the client, they connect to the software and enjoy the benefits of the platform.

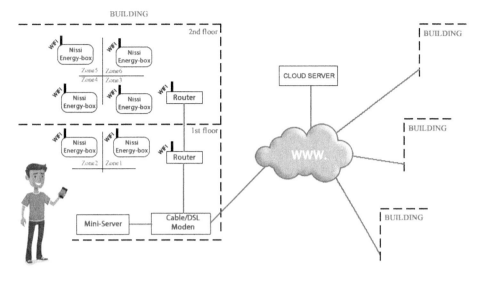

Fig. 1. Nissi Energy network architecture diagram.

Nissi Energy-Box is the primary data capture and control device. Which is conformed as shown in Fig. 2, by the following components:

– DC Source.
– Arduino Yun.
– Interface card (for the coupling of the sensors and the circuits of adaptation of the signals that make the interpretations by the Arduino Yun).
– Sensors and actuators for control.

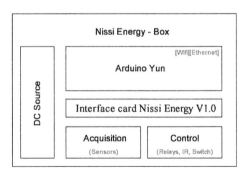

Fig. 2. Arquitectura hardware Nissi Energy Box.

2.2   Software Architecture

The software architecture consists of three applications mainly, see Fig. 3.

1. Software in the cloud
2. Intranet web software
3. "Nissi Energy-Box" acquisition and control software indispensable for data processing and control.

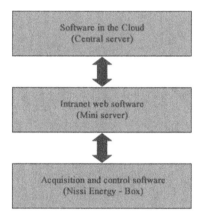

Fig. 3. Nissi energy software.

Starting with the domain or conceptual model (see Fig. 4), it is observed that for each company registered to Nissi Energy software, there are several buildings associated with it and each building has associated several users, where the program is assigned roles. A Mini Server device is associated with each building. Routers are assigned to each floor and depend on the scope of connectivity that is needed. Each zone is associated with a Nissi Energy-Box device. And the Nissi Energy - Box device monitors the electrical devices associated with each zone.

In general, three programs are developed to make the monitoring and control functions effective:

– Cloud Software - Nissi Energy.
– Local software or intranet - Nissi Energy.
– Nissi Energy Box software (Arduino).

Primary Server and Mini Server devices are running under the Ubuntu Operating System 16.04, and its execution environment is an Apache + PHP + MySQL + SSH server.

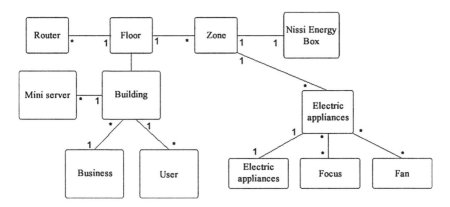

Fig. 4. Domain model diagram.

3 Implementation

3.1 Hardware Implementation

In the implementation of the hardware the main device "Nissi Energy-box" is described which must meet the requirements for this solution. The system requirements for monitoring and control are:

- Measure temperature.
- Measure humidity.
- Measure CO2.
- Measure CO.
- Measure voltage.
- Measure current.
- Measure power.
- Control three relays from 5 Vdc to 120 Vac.
- Infrared control for air control.
- Measure the state of the magnetic sensors.
- Store the history of the measurements taking into account the time.
- Allow communication to access history remotely.
- Allow communication to execute control functions via commands.

To meet the measurement and control requirements, the following circuits were designed:

- Voltage measuring circuit is a wave rectifier, with a voltage divider to adjust the signal to the input of the Arduino Yun.
- Current measuring circuit uses a differential amplifier with AD620AR followed by a full-wave rectifier with MC45588A operational amplifiers.
- Circuit connection of temperature and humidity sensors, CO2 and CO.

- Circuit to control the relays HJR-4102-L-05V that supports 3 A to 120 Vac, in it is a transistor for the activation, which works in switching and a protection or anti-return diode to protect the transistor.
- Infrared circuit consists of emitter LED and a resistance to reduce the voltage or power to the led.
- Circuit to measure the magnetic sensors.
- Linear regulated DC source circuit, consists of 4 regulators, two of them for integrated ones that handle input voltages of 5 Vdc and -5 Vdc; One for the sensors and the other for the Arduino Yun.

3.2   Software Implementation

In the implementation of the software were taken as functional requirements of the system:

1. Web interface and access control (Home, Company, Contact, Login)
2. System configuration (Manage user, Building registration, Zone settings, Network configuration.)
3. Monitoring (Power consumed, Voltage, Current, Humidity, Temperature, CO_2, CO)
4. Control (Air conditioners, Lights, Fans, Other)

In the characteristics of the system(see Fig. 5), the use of the framework "Administrator - Nissi Web, author Edgar Villa" is highlighted.

Features of the system:

- MySQL Database
- Framework "MVC- Administrator Nissi Web Author Edgar Villa"
- PHP programing language
- Apache http server
- SSH2 Server
- ubuntu OS

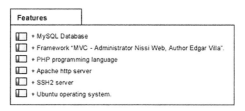

Fig. 5. Features of the system.

The "Administrator - Nissi Web" framework in your class diagram usually uses the MVC model (see Fig. 6).

The controller class is called "application", the model class is called "bdnissi", and the view class "Templater". There is only a small difference and it is necessary to implement a class for the communication that will be in charge of data acquisition and control of the system that we call "rednissi" (see Figs. 7 and 8).

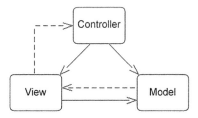

Fig. 6. Model View Controller MVC.

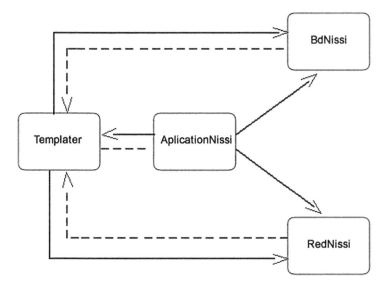

Fig. 7. Class model diagram.

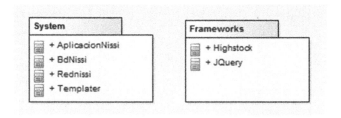

Fig. 8. Main classes of the external system and framework used.

Implemented Interfaces. The Login user interface in it controls user access. Depending on the type of user, the actions or links to which the user has permission are displayed in the menu.

The monitoring interface allows to choose the variable to be monitored according to the zone. The control interface allows the appliance to be switched on and off according to the zone (see Fig. 9).

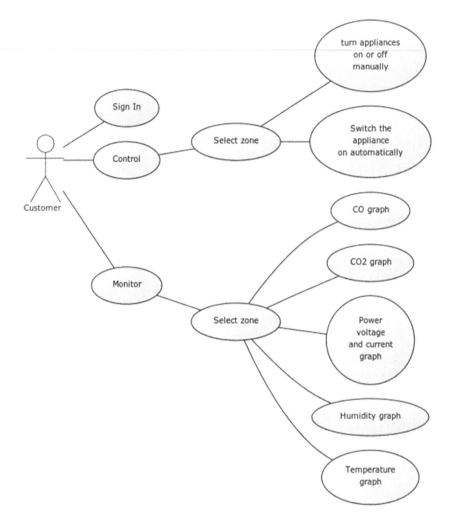

Fig. 9. Diagram of use monitoring and control.

Software Nissi Energy Box. It contains the software interface that interacts with the sensors and also the control interface.

- Measurement algorithms
- Communication algorithms
- Processing and storage algorithms
- Control algorithms (Local and remote)

The execution of the data capture is performed every 20 s through a function "timer" function included in the Arduino Yun (see Fig. 10).

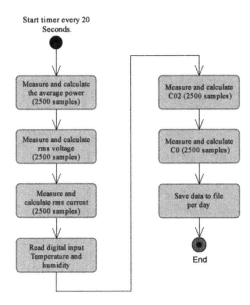

Fig. 10. Flow diagram, process performed in the "Timer of Arduino Yun" every 20 s.

4 Conclusions

In the present work, a monitoring system was designed, implemented and validated for the control applied to air conditioners. The architecture of hardware and software worked, but after it is emphasized that it is necessary to improve the stability of the network, this is achieved with algorithms and equipment thought specifically for tasks (central server and mini-server).

The implementation of the Nissi Energy platform in the Educational Establishment of the lumbreras del Maana Foundation leaves real results. Both the variables that were measured, as the power to verify the strengths and weaknesses of the system to make it more robust.

The system on the hardware side could improve performance to be able to perform more complex monitoring and control functions. At this time the libraries and functions load the Arduino Yun occupy much of the RAM memory, no space giving for the functions of infrared control. It should be noted that these control functions were tested with the single infrared and did work.

There are also other views to improve as the smaller material the "Nissi Energy-Box" component, and to design in detail that the maintenance of the parts can be done in a simple way.

Acknowledgement. The authors would like acknowledge the cooperation of all partners within the *Centro de Excelencia y Apropiación en Internet de las Cosas (CEA-IoT)* project. The authors would also like to thank all the institutions that supported this work: the Colombian Ministry for the Information and Communications Technology (*Ministerio de Tecnologías de la Información y las Comunicaciones - MinTIC*) and the Colombian Administrative Department of Science, Technology and Innovation (*Departamento Administrativo de Ciencia, Tecnología e Innovación - Colciencias*) through the *Fondo Nacional de Financiamiento para la Ciencia, la Tecnología y laInnovación Francisco Jewsé de Caldas* (Project ID: FP44842-502-2015), and Universidad Tecnologica de Bolivar under contract FI1602T2001.

References

1. Council of Australian Governments - COAG: Guide to Best Practice Maintenance & Operation of HVAC Systems for Energy Efficiency, Commonwealth of Australia (2012)
2. UPME: Caracterización Energética de los Sectores Residencial, Comercial y Terciario. Ministerio de Minas y Energa (2007)
3. Roth, K.W., Westphalen, D., Dieckmann, J., Hamilton, S.D., Goetzler, W.: Energy Consumption Characteristics of Commercial Building HVAC Systems Volume III: Energy Savings Potential. U.S. Department of Energy (2002)
4. Bhatia, A.: Centralized Vs Decentralized Air Conditioning Systems. Continuing Education and Development, Inc
5. Zheng, T., Qin, Y., Gao, D., Duan, J., Zhang, H.: A practical deployment of intelligent building wireless sensor network for environmental monitoring and airconditioning control. In: 2010 2nd IEEE International Conference on Network Infrastructure and Digital Content, p. 5 (2010)
6. Nangtin, P., Kumhom, P., Chamnongthai, K.: Adaptive actual load for energy in split type air conditioning. In: 2016 16th International Symposium on Communications and Information Technologies (ISCIT), p. 4 (2016)
7. Li, F., Lu, H.-Q., Zhou, H.: Design of intelligent monitoring system of air conditioning and ventilation system in distribution station with 10 kV power. In: 2012 China International Conference on Electricity Distribution, p. 4 (2012)

Fuzzy Sets and Systems

Generalization of Fuzzy Inference System Based on Boolean and Kleenean Relations FIS-BKR for Modelling and Control

Erika Zutta[⊠], Jhonattan Gantiva, and Jairo Soriano

Universidad Distrital Francisco José de Caldas, Bogotá, Colombia
erikzuttag@gmail.com, jlgantivar@correo.udistrital.edu.co,
josoriano@udistrital.edu.co

Abstract. Fuzzy logic emerges as an important tool in modelling control systems. For this reason, it is necessary to find methodologies involving fuzzy inference and allow to obtain levels of accuracy and interpretability accordance with design requirements. This paper proposes the generalization of a Fuzzy Inference System based on Boolean and Kleenean relations (FIS-BKR) from the conceptual expansion of the virtual actuator.

Keywords: Fuzzy logic · FIS-BKR · Modelling · Non-linear dynamic systems

1 Introduction

Several control applications look for the minimization of nondifferentiable nonlinearities due to their negative impact in the system performance leading to instability [11]. Subsequently, this kind of design can not assure the right operation in all situations, specially those involving hystereisis-backlash.

Backlash is a common nondifferentiable nonlinearity, showed in mechanical gear systems, electro-magnetic fields, mechanical actuators, electronic relay circuits, electrical drives and more physical systems [7]. By that, there is the need of study and description of backlash, in order to face its consequences and understand its possible applications, more than eliminate it [1]. This objective can be achieved from a modelling approach, using fuzzy inference systems that can provide precision and interpretability through the statement of implication rules.

One novel proposal of fuzzy inference system, originally known as fuzzy controller design using concretion based on Boolean relations (CBR) [9], proposed an implementation mechanism for fuzzy logic systems with design based on boolean tables as reference (from a logical reasoning approach), due to its high use in process control and ease of implementation. It was renamed Fuzzy Inference System based on Boolean and Kleenean Relations FIS-BKR, underlining the concretion module as the union (not integration) of Inference Engine and defuzzifier, including logical formulas within algebra of three elements (Kleenean algebra) [8].

© Springer International Publishing AG 2017
J.C. Figueroa-García et al. (Eds.): WEA 2017, CCIS 742, pp. 351–364, 2017.
DOI: 10.1007/978-3-319-66963-2_32

This paper is structured as follows: Sects. 2 and 3 introduce fuzzy inference systems Takagi-Sugeno (FIS-TS) and FIS-BKR. Section 3 also presents the expansion of the FIS-BKR proposing the process of concretion based on the concept of simple functions of fuzzy events beginning with the extension of Boolean tables to three elements tables (Kleenean tables) which satisfies the conditions of regularity. This expansion is used in the construction of a model of the nonlinearity of backlash that is found in Sect. 4, emphasizing in the modelling by logical reasoning and its advantages. Finally, the conclusions are presented and a future work point of view in Sect. 5.

2   Review of Fuzzy Inference System Takagi - Sugeno

The typical configuration of a Takagi-Sugeno fuzzy system (TS) [14] uses k input variables $x_1, x_2, \ldots, x_k$, where $x_i \in [a_i, b_i]$ and $i = 1, 2, \ldots, k$. Interval $[a_i, b_i]$ is split into N_i subintervals:

$$a_i = C_0^i < C_1^i < C_2^i < \cdots < C_{N_i-1}^i < C_{N_i}^i = b_i \tag{1}$$

There are N_i+1 input fuzzy sets on $[a_i, b_i]$ defined to fuzzify x_i, each denoted as $A_{j_i}^i$ $(0 \le j_i \le N_i)$ with their respective membership functions $\mu_{j_i}^i(x_i)$.

TS fuzzy sets use arbitrary fuzzy rules with linear consequent, as it is shown to h-th rule in (2):

$$\text{If } x_1 \text{ is } A_{h_1}^1, \cdots, \text{ and } x_k \text{ is } A_{h_j}^k \text{ then } y = p_0^h + p_1^h x_1 + \cdots + p_k^h x_k \tag{2}$$

where $p_0^h, p_1^h, \cdots, p_k^k$ are arbitrary constants chosen to each rule by designer, and y denotes the fuzzy system output. Using centroid defuzzifier considering a m rules base, it is found:

$$y = \sum_{h=1}^{m} \beta_h \cdot \left(p_0^h + p_1^h x_1 + \cdots + p_k^h x_k \right); \; \beta_h = \frac{\mu_{h_1}^1(x_1) \wedge \cdots \wedge \mu_{h_j}^k(x_k)}{\sum_{h=1}^{m} \left(\mu_{h_1}^1(x_1) \wedge \cdots \wedge \mu_{h_j}^k(x_k) \right)} \tag{3}$$

3   Expansion of Fuzzy Inference System Based on Boolean and Kleenean Relations FIS-BKR

A fuzzy inference system defined [8] as a function $\overrightarrow{y} = f(\overrightarrow{x})$ between a vector of input variables $\overrightarrow{x}$ and a vector of output variables $\overrightarrow{y}$ using a fuzzy inference mechanism, in which the concepts (sensors) are grouped by combinations given by logical reasoning process. Fuzzy Inference System based on Boolean and Kleene's relations, FIS-BKR, under the proposal of Salazar [8], the block diagram below sets out in Fig. 1.

Depending on the concepts (sensors) used it is possible to have overlap of control actions in the regions of operation, for which a given output may be greater than partial actions. The proposed model consists of r:

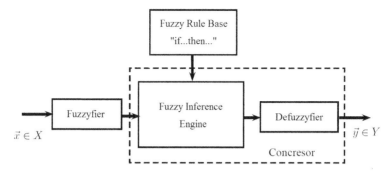

Fig. 1. FIS-BKR block diagram model [8].

3.1 Singleton Fuzzifier

The processing block input data, is defined by the membership function:

$$\mu_A\left(\overrightarrow{x}\right) = \begin{cases} 1, & \overrightarrow{x} = \overrightarrow{x^*} \\ 0, & \overrightarrow{x} \neq \overrightarrow{x^*} \end{cases} \tag{4}$$

where $\overrightarrow{x} = \langle x_1, \ldots, x_n \rangle \in X$ is the vector of input variables, $\overrightarrow{x^*} = \langle x_1^*, \ldots, x_n^* \rangle \in X$ is a particular value measured at fuzzifier entrance, and $X = X_1 \times \cdots \times X_n \subseteq \mathbb{R}_n$ is the input universe.

3.2 Rules Base

It is a implications set as *"if (antecedent) then (consequent)"*. In j-th output y_j $(j = 1, 2, ..., m)$ of output vector $\overrightarrow{y} \in Y$, where $\overrightarrow{y} = \langle y_1, \ldots, y_m \rangle$ and $Y = Y_1 \times \cdots \times Y_m \subseteq \mathbb{R}_m$, a h-th rule of the q rules base is:

$$If\ x_1\ is\ \overset{w_1}{\underset{s_1}{\bigwedge}} \tilde{A}_{s_i,h} \wedge \cdots \wedge x_i\ is\ \overset{w_i}{\underset{s_i}{\bigwedge}} \tilde{A}_{s_i,h} \wedge \cdots \wedge x_n\ is\ \overset{w_n}{\underset{s_n}{\bigwedge}} \tilde{A}_{s_n,h}\ then\ y_j\ is\ B_{j_h} \tag{5}$$

where $\tilde{A}_{s_i,h}$ $(i = 1, 2, \ldots, n)$ is noted as $A_{s_i,h}$ if the concept (sensor) is into the combination of possible fuzzy sets formulated on the i-th input universe X_i, or $\bar{A}_{s_i,h}$ if the concept (sensor) is out of the combination, and B_{j_h} is one of possible fuzzy sets formulated on j-th output universe Y_j, for h-th rule. Logical operations "and", "or" and "not" are given by standard fuzzy logic and/or classic logic, bearing in mind that logical operation "not" ($'$) depends on the application and it will satisfy the properties of monotonicity ($a \leq b$ implies $a' \geq b'$ for all $a, b \in [0, 1]$) and involution ($(a')' = a$ for all $a \in [0, 1]$). Fuzzy sets formulated on each input universe will obey some criterion and each fuzzy set B_h formulated on j-th output universe $Y_j \subseteq \mathbb{R}$ must have only one characteristic value $v \in Y_j$ denominated virtual actuator.

3.3 Inference Engine

This is responsible for adding the fuzzy implications of the rule base, transforms the degrees of membership in fuzzy sets of input universes into output truth values through process of inference. In the model proposed by Salazar [8], the inference procedure is performed by Approximation using classical logic, and by Extension to standard fuzzy logic using three-valued logic proposed by Kleene:

Thus, a logical formula $f_{h,j}$ is reduced using the disjunctive normal form (DNF, at left side), and using the conjunctive normal form (CNF, at right side):

$$f_{h,j} = \bigwedge_{i=1}^{n} \bigwedge_{s_i=1}^{w_i} \hat{A}_{s_i,h}; \qquad f_{h,j} = \bigvee_{i=1}^{n} \bigvee_{s_i=1}^{w_i} \check{A}_{s_i,h} \tag{6}$$

Then, the formula for h-th row of truth table, where j-th output has the value of 1 or u (in l rows in total), the formula for DNF (right) is:

$$f_{h,j} = \bigvee_{h=1}^{l_j} \bigwedge_{i=1}^{n} \bigwedge_{s_i=1}^{w_i} \hat{A}_{s_i,h} \tag{7}$$

Using CNF, the formula of h-th row of truth table, where j-th output has the value of 0 or u (in l rows in total), is obtained in a similar way.

3.4 Defuzzifier

This converts the truth values from inference engine in the output of fuzzy inference system. Here, outputs vector $\overrightarrow{y} \in Y$, where $\overrightarrow{y} = \langle y_1, \ldots, y_m \rangle$ and $Y = Y_1 \times \cdots \times Y_m \subseteq \mathbb{R}_m$, is found using a defuzzifier based on logical (Boolean and/or Kleenean) formulas. These formulas weigh the value of the respective virtual actuator. The j-th output y_j ($j = 1, 2, ..., m$), corresponding to j-th output universe Y_j where there are k virtual actuators $v_{p,j}$ ($p = 1, 2, ..., k$) being weighed by k logical formulas $f_{p,j}$ given by the inference engine:

$$y_j = f_{1,j} v_{1,j} + f_{2,j} v_{2,j} + \cdots + f_{k,j} v_{k,j} = \sum_{p=1}^{k} f_{p,j} v_{p,j} \tag{8}$$

where $v_{p,j}$ is the characteristic value of the output fuzzy set B_{p_j}, $f_{p,j}$ is the activation output, and the product $f_{p,j} v_{p,j}$ is the virtual output. The actuator element can take positive and negative values, depending on the specific case, and it can be considered as the discourse universe of consequent.

According to this model, the *concretor* term refers to the connection between the Inference Engine and Defuzzifier, making the concretion of the fuzzy information.

Virtual Actuator. Taking into account the analogy with the fuzzy inference system of Takagi-Sugeno (FIS-TS), as shown for h-th rule in (2), the numerator of β_h denotes a logical formula between the sets of universes of discourse that are activated in the h-th rule. The FIS-TS normalized, corresponds in its form to the output virtual FIS-BKR, although not in concept. Thus, for $p_1^h, \cdots, p_k^h = 0$ in q rules, the Fuzzy Inference System Takagi-Sugeno of zero order is obtained, in which the input universes discourses don't appear in the consequent but rather the values $p_0^1, \cdots, p_0^h, \cdots, p_0^q$. This may be associated with the current Fuzzy Inference System based on Boolean relations and Kleenean relations, in which virtual actuators are constant values, and therefore real values.

Moreover, there exists the analogy between FIS-BKR and the concept of simple function [6,10] within measure theory. A collection $\mathscr{F}$ of subsets of Ω (Ω is defined as an elementary events set) is a σ-algebra if the following conditions are satisfied: $\Omega \in \mathscr{F}$; if $A \subset \mathscr{F}$ then $A^c \in \mathscr{F}$; and, if $A_1, A_2 \ldots \in \mathscr{F}$ then $\bigcup_{k=1}^{\infty} A_k \in \mathscr{F}$.

Let M be an arbitrary non-empty set, and $\mathscr{M}$ is a σ-algebra of subsets of M. A set $A \subset M$ is measurable if $A \in \mathscr{M}$. A function $f : M \to \mathbb{R}$ is measurable if, for any $c \in \mathbb{R}$ the set $\{x \in M : f(x) \leq c\}$ is measurable, it is, belongs to $\mathscr{M}$. A function $f : M \to \mathbb{R}$ is named simple if it is measurable and the set of its values is at most countable. Let $\{a_k\}$ be the sequence of different values of a simple function f. Considering measurable sets $E_k = \{x \in M : f(x) = a_k\}$, and taking into account that $M = \bigsqcup_k E_k$ (disjoint union of E_k sets):

$$f = \sum_{k=1}^{N} a_k \chi_{E_k}, \; where \; \chi_{E_k}(x) = \begin{cases} 1 & \text{if } x \in E_k \\ 0 & \text{if } x \notin E_k \end{cases}. \tag{9}$$

χ_{E_k} is the characteristic function of each E_k set.

From the concept of simple function and its applicability (based on the knowledge obtained from the physical system given by Input/Output relationship and deriving its Characteristic Function), the concept of virtual actuator $v_{p,j}$ of (10) is extended, not only as a constant value to describe a linear relationship (identifying itself with a_k of (9)), but a real bounded function in terms of each input universe of discourse.

In this sense, the FIS-BKR concept can be generalized, so that defuzzifier block can be defined as follows:

"Fuzzifier converts truth values from inference engine at fuzzy inference system output. The outputs vector $\overrightarrow{y} \in Y$, where $\overrightarrow{y} = \langle y_1, \ldots, y_m \rangle$ and $Y = Y_1 \times \cdots \times Y_m \subseteq \mathbb{R}_m$, is found using a based in (Boolean and/or Kleenean) logical formulas fuzzifier. These formulas weigh the respective actuator value. The j-th output y_j ($j = 1, 2, ..., m$), corresponding to j-th output universe Y_j where there are k virtual actuators $v_{p,j}$ ($p = 1, 2, ..., k$) being weighed by k logical formulas $f_{p,j}$ given by inference engine:

$$y_j = \sum_{p=1}^{k} f_{p,j} v_{p,j} = \sum_{p=1}^{k} \left(\bigvee_{h=1}^{l_j} \bigwedge_{i=1}^{n} \bigwedge_{s_i=1}^{w_i} \hat{A}_{s_i,h} \right) v_{p,j} \tag{10}$$

Where $v_{p,j}$ is called virtual actuator, $f_{p,j}$ activation output, and $f_{p,j}v_{p,j}$ virtual output. Virtual actuator $v_{p,j}$ is a bounded real function of inputs vector $\overrightarrow{x} \in X$, where $\overrightarrow{x} = \langle x_1, \ldots, x_n \rangle$ and $X = X_1 \times \cdots \times X_n \subseteq \mathbb{R}_n$.
    A function that $v_{p,j}$ can take is the linear function in terms of input variables:

$$v_{p,j} = b_{p,j} + a_{1_{p,j}} x_1 + \cdots + a_{i_{p,j}} x_i + \cdots + a_{n_{p,j}} x_n \qquad (11)$$

with arbitrary constants "$b_{p,j}, a_{1_{p,j}}, a_{2_{p,j}}, \cdots a_{n_{p,j}}$".

4   Implementing the Proposal

An example design using extension FIS-BKR, a model of the nonlinearity of Hysteresis-Backlash is proposed, mechanically defined [2] as excess thickness of the tooth space of a gear on the other tooth in a mechanical coupling, presenting in two ways: if the tooth thickness is less than the value for null backlash, or if the distance between centres of operation is greater than for null backlash [4,13]. Backlash model is presented in Fig. 2a.

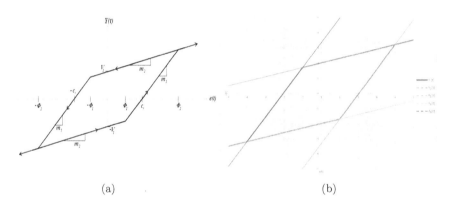

(a)   (b)

Fig. 2. (a) Characteristic typical function Backlash [3,12]. (b) Transfer characteristic showing the construction piecewise $Y(t)$ in terms of $e(t)$ in the Backlash model.

4.1   Principles of Modelling Using FIS-BKR

The model is carried out taking into account the principles of design using fuzzy inference systems CBR [5], then called FIS-BKR [8]: Partition of discourse universe using Boolean sets defining operation regions, and Monotonic and continuous switching between Boolean regions.
    From the above, the following issues arise to consider:

- For concepts ("sensors"), methodology to convert their boolean characteristics to fuzzy characteristics.
- Mechanism concretion (determination of virtual actuator).
- Restrictions and considerations present at the time of implementation.

4.2   Backlash Description

For an arbitrary sinusoidal input signal $e(t)$ $(e(t) = A\sin(\omega t))$, the output signal $Y(t)$ is obtained (Fig. 3), in which each constituent element in the response corresponds to each of the straight lines shown in Fig. 2b. Analysing this backlash response, for the case of a symmetrical characteristic and using its memory property in the calculation the output in a previous time t_d as described above, piecewise model is reached (12) and is presented in Fig. 2.

Fig. 3. Output $Y(t)$ of Backlash before a sinusoidal input a $e(t)$ sinusoidal.

Thus, generalizing to a symmetric model, $\Phi_{-1} = -\Phi_1$, $\Phi_{-2} = -\Phi_2$ y $V_{-1} = -V_1$, $e(t) \nearrow$ is defined as increasing when $\forall t | e(t+h) > e(t); h > 0 : e(t) \nearrow$ and decreasing $e(t) \searrow$ when $\forall t | e(t+h) < e(t); h > 0 : e(t) \searrow$:

$$Y(t) = \begin{cases} Y_1 = m_1(e(t) - c_r), & (e \nearrow) \wedge (\Phi_1 \le e < \Phi_2) \\ Y_2 = m_2 e(t) + V_1, & (e \searrow) \wedge (-\Phi_1 \le e) \\ Y_3 = m_1(e(t) + c_r), & (e \searrow) \wedge (-\Phi_2 \le e < -\Phi_1) \\ Y_4 = m_2 e(t) - V_1, & (e \nearrow) \wedge (e < \Phi_1) \end{cases} \qquad (12)$$

Rules Base to Obtain Backlash. After performing several tests with different number of sets, two boolean sets E_P y E_N are defined in the universe of discourse Error (referring to two sensors: positive error and negative error) with membership functions μ_P and μ_N, respectively, as shown in Fig. 4a and their mathematical description in (13), if the stipulated model is simplest would, it gains greater interpretability without losing accuracy:

$$\mu_P(e) = \begin{cases} 0, & e \le \Phi_2 \\ \frac{e - \Phi_1}{\Phi_2 - \Phi_1}, & \Phi_1 < e < \Phi_2 \ ; \\ 1, & e \ge \Phi_2 \end{cases} \quad \mu_N(e) = \begin{cases} 1, & e \le \Phi_{-2} \\ \frac{e - \Phi_{-1}}{\Phi_{-2} - \Phi_{-1}}, & \Phi_{-2} < e < \Phi_{-1} \\ 0, & e \ge \Phi_{-1} \end{cases} \qquad (13)$$

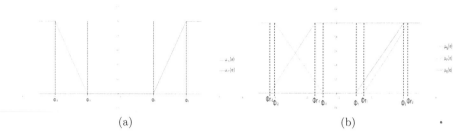

(a)   (b)   .

Fig. 4. (a) Membership functions of Kleenean sets in discourse universe Error $e\,(t)$ for the Backlash model. (b) Membership functions of Kleenean sets in discourse universe Error $e\,(t)$ and membership relation $\mu_R\,(e)$ corresponding to the auxiliary variable Delay R for Backlash model.

Delay Variable - Membership Relation. The concept of membership relation is set out in order to incorporate of prior state in the output. Therefore, an auxiliary variable R, is used, which reflects the output value given in a previous time t_d according to the memory property of the Backlash. Φ_{r_1}, $\Phi_{r_{-1}}$, Φ_{r_2} and $\Phi_{r_{-2}}$ parameters come from taking input $e\,(t)$ a sinusoidal signal of the form $e\,(t) = A\sin(\omega t)$ and from taking into account the t_d parameter:

$$\Phi_{r_1} = A\sin\left(\arcsin\left(\frac{\Phi_1}{A}\right) + \omega t_d\right); \qquad \Phi_{r_2} = A\sin\left(\arcsin\left(\frac{\Phi_2}{A}\right) + \omega t_d\right) \quad (14)$$

$$\Phi_{r_{-1}} = A\sin\left(\arcsin\left(\frac{\Phi_{-1}}{A}\right) + \omega t_d\right); \qquad \Phi_{r_{-2}} = A\sin\left(\arcsin\left(\frac{\Phi_{-2}}{A}\right) + \omega t_d\right) \quad (15)$$

The membership relation $\mu_R = \mu_R\,(e\,(t)\,, Y\,(t - t_d))$ that represents the auxiliary variable R for the Backlash model is illustrated in Fig. 4b:

$$\mu_R = \begin{cases} \dfrac{e(t) - \Phi_{r_1}}{\Phi_{r_2} - \Phi_{r_1}}, & \Phi_{r_1} \le e\,(t) < \Phi_{r_2}\ \wedge \\ & \{Y\,(t - t_d) = Y_4 \vee Y\,(t - t_d) = Y_1\} \\[4pt] 1, & \Phi_{r_{-1}} \le e\,(t)\ \wedge \\ & \{Y\,(t - t_d) = Y_1 \vee Y\,(t - t_d) = Y_2\} \\[4pt] \dfrac{e(t) - \Phi_{r_{-2}}}{\Phi_{r_{-1}} - \Phi_{r_{-2}}}, & \Phi_{r_{-2}} \le e\,(t) < \Phi_{r_{-1}}\ \wedge \\ & \{Y\,(t - t_d) = Y_2 \vee Y\,(t - t_d) = Y_3\} \\[4pt] 0, & e\,(t) \le \Phi_{r_1}\ \wedge \\ & \{Y\,(t - t_d) = Y_3 \vee Y\,(t - t_d) = Y_4\} \end{cases} \quad (16)$$

Using Boolean partitions within discourse universe of Error $e\,(t)$ and the auxiliary variable R, and defining control actions to continue modelling process using the FIS-BKR, rules base is proposed:

1. If error is negative (E_N) and R is activated, then r is deactivated.
2. (Auxiliary) If r is deactivated, then R is deactivated after a t_d timespan.
3. If error is not negative $(\bar{E}_N)$ nor positive $(\bar{E}_P)$ and R is deactivated, then r continues deactivated.
4. If error is positive (E_P) and R is not activated, then r is activated.
5. (Auxiliary) If r is activated, then R is activated after a t_d timespan.
6. If error is not negative $(\bar{E}_N)$ nor positive $(\bar{E}_P)$ and R is activated, then r continues activated.

Making the ternary coding of fuzzy sets and model Kleenean algebra, the truth table is obtained for the Backlash model in Table 1.

Table 1. Truth Kleenean table from the rule base for Backlash model

μ_N	μ_P	μ_R	r	Transitions
1	0	$\breve{0}$	0	$R \Downarrow$
$\breve{u}$	0	0	0	$N \downarrow$
$\breve{0}$	0	0	0	$N \Downarrow$
0	$\hat{u}$	0	$\hat{u}$	$P \uparrow; r \uparrow$
0	u	$\hat{u}$	u	$R \uparrow$
0	$\hat{1}$	u	$\hat{1}$	$P \Uparrow; r \Uparrow$
0	1	$\hat{1}$	1	$R \Uparrow$
0	$\breve{u}$	1	1	$P \downarrow$
0	$\breve{0}$	1	1	$P \Downarrow$
$\hat{u}$	0	1	$\breve{u}$	$N \uparrow; r \downarrow$
u	0	$\breve{u}$	u	$R \downarrow$
$\hat{1}$	0	u	$\breve{0}$	$N \Uparrow; r \Downarrow$

Symbols ˆ and ˘ indicate activation and deactivation, respectively.
Arrows $\Uparrow$ y $\Downarrow$ show Boolean (crisp) activation and deactivation.
Arrows $\uparrow$ y $\downarrow$ show Kleenean activation and deactivation

Transitions in Kleenean Table. The transition is defined as the sequential change having a variable one row to another. For example, in Table 1, from 1 to 2 row, E_N variable changes from 1 to u, where this change (transition) is defined as fuzzy deactivation or partial of E_N and is denoted $\breve{u}$ as an indication of sequentiality (of great importance in systems with memory). In this case, the transition does not have consequence in post-sequent, i.e. variable r in row 2 is the same in row 1. Another case occurs when a transition changes the output variable value, as is observed from 4 to 5 row wherein the transition from E_P

variable from 0 to u is denoted $\hat{u}$, which indicates this variable was activated and changes the value of r from 0 to u. In short, there are two possibilities:

– When the fuzzy activation of E_P occurs **after** that E_N has reached the boolean deactivation. For example, in Table 1 shows in rows 1, 3, 7 and 9 the Boolean conditions expressed in the rules, i.e. in the columns of the precondition no u values.
– When E_P fuzzy activation occurs **before** that E_N has reached the boolean deactivation.

Carrying out the process of extension of the table and simplification formulas [8], the output expressions are obtained using the graphical methodology presented in Fig. 5:

$$\mu_r(e) = \mu_{\bar{N}}(e) \wedge [\mu_R(e') \vee \mu_P(e)] = \mu_P(e) \vee [\mu_R(e') \wedge \mu_{\bar{N}}(e)], \qquad (17)$$

$$\mu_{\bar{r}}(e) = Y_{\bar{r}}(e) = \mu_N(e) \vee [\mu_{\bar{R}}(e') \wedge \mu_{\bar{P}}(e)] = \mu_{\bar{P}}(e) \wedge [\mu_{\bar{R}}(e') \vee \mu_N(e)]. \quad (18)$$

Under the proposal the FIS-BKR of first order, virtual actuators obey:

$$v_1 = m_2 e(t) + V_1; \qquad v_2 = m_2 e(t) + V_{-1} \qquad (19)$$

Thus, the model output $Y(t)$ is:

$$Y(t) = v_1 r + v_2 \bar{r} = m_2 e(t) + V_1(2r - 1) \qquad (20)$$

because $\bar{r} = 1 - r$.

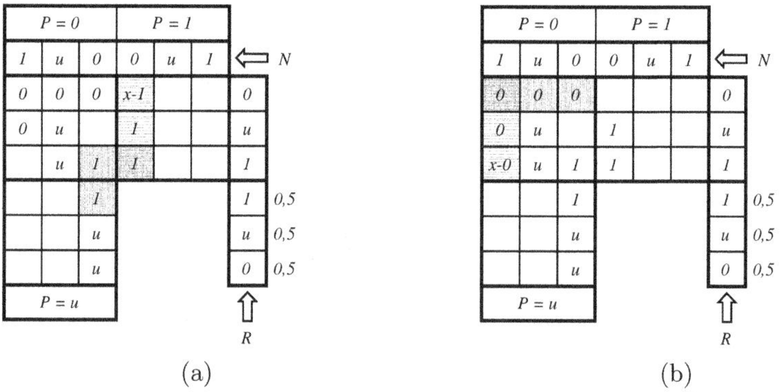

Fig. 5. Map to obtain reduced rows: associations of 1s (a) or 0s (b) through DNF or CNF.

Backlash Design Using Kleenean Algebra and Fuzzy Sets. Given backlash parameters c_r, m_1, m_2, V_1 and $-V_1$ (Fig. 2), and with the aim of perform some simplifications to achieve the backlash symmetry, points $(-\Phi_2, -\Phi_1)$ and (Φ_1, Φ_2) are defined as fuzzy sets parameters to negative error E_N and positive error E_P respectively, and the relationship among the straight lines Y_1, Y_2, Y_3 y Y_4. Therefore, it is just necessary to find the parameters Φ_1 y Φ_2. Through algebraic processing:

$$\Phi_1 = \frac{V_1 - m_1}{m_1 - m_2}; \qquad \Phi_2 = \frac{V_1 + m_1}{m_1 - m_2}. \tag{21}$$

Similarly, doing $Y_1 = 0$ in $e = c_r$:

$$c_r = \frac{\Phi_2 + \Phi_1}{2V_1 m_1 (\Phi_2 - \Phi_1)} \tag{22}$$

So, finding m_1 as Y_1 and Y_3 slope:

$$m_1 = m_2 + \frac{2V_1}{\Phi_2 - \Phi_1} \tag{23}$$

4.3   Simulation and Design

In order to simplify, $(-\Phi_1, u_1)$ and (Φ_2, u_2) points can be defined as cut-offs in the upper half plane of the characteristic function observed in Fig. 2 between Y_1 and Y_2 lines, and Y_3 and Y_4 lines, respectively, so that:

$$u_1 = m_2 \Phi_{-1} + V_1; \qquad u_2 = m_2 \Phi_2 + V_1 \tag{24}$$

Thus, finding m_1 as Y_1 and Y_3 slope:

$$m_1 = \frac{u_1 + u_2}{\Phi_2 - \Phi_1} = m_2 + \frac{2V_1}{\Phi_2 - \Phi_1} \tag{25}$$

Therefore, doing $Y_1 = 0$ in $e = c_r$:

$$c_r = \frac{u_1}{m_1} + \Phi_1 = \frac{\Phi_1 (m_1 - m_2) + V_1}{m_1} \tag{26}$$

Expressing the constant V_1 in terms of a percentage χ of input signal maximum amplitude A, and for a sinusoidal input as $e(t) = A \sin(\omega t)$, t_r is defined as the delay time between the zero crossing of $e(t)$ and zero crossing of output $Y(t)$ (27):

$$t_r = \frac{1}{\omega} \arcsin\left(\frac{c_r}{A}\right) \tag{27}$$

It is possible to use the Backlash model to make the design and simulation of a real system, if parameters of it are known, such as the time lag between a sinusoidal input and its corresponding output t_r, the m_1 and m_2 gains, and positive value of the output when the input zero, V_1, expressed as a proportion χ of the amplitude of the sinusoidal test input A.

Thereby:

$$c_r = A\sin(\omega t_r)\,; \qquad \Phi_1 = -\frac{\chi A - c_r m_1}{m_1 - m_2}\,; \qquad \Phi_2 = \frac{\chi A + c_r m_1}{m_1 - m_2}. \qquad (28)$$

Then the simulation results for the Backlash model with membership sets of Fig. 4, the output $Y(t)$ before sinusoidal arbitrary $e(t)$ in Fig. 6 for the simulation parameters that are shown in Table 2, and corresponding transfer characteristic in Fig. 6.

Table 2. Simulation parameters of Backlash Model

Parameter	Value	Parameter	Value
Φ_1	1	t_d	0,01
Φ_{-1}	−1	m_1	1,6333
Φ_2	4	Φ_{r_1}	1,0489
Φ_{-2}	−4	$\Phi_{r_{-1}}$	−1,0489
χ	0,4	Φ_{r_2}	4,0298
m_2	0,3	$\Phi_{r_{-2}}$	−4,0298
A	5	c_r	2,0408
ω	1	t_r	0,4204

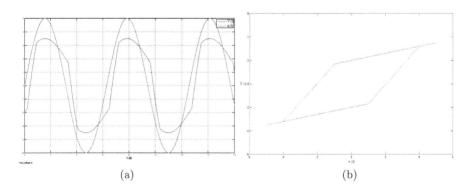

(a)   (b)

Fig. 6. (a) Simulation of Backlash model taking input magnitude $e(t)$ as an arbitrary sinusoidal signal. (b) Transfer characteristic of Backlash with previous considerations.

5 Conclusions

Proposed FIS-BKR generalization has its major advantage in allowing the system modelling (no matter if system has nondifferentiable nonlinearities) through logical analysis after experts knowledge and logical reasoning, enhanced by its design based on boolean and kleenean tables, in comparison with other fuzzy inference systems, and seeking for better precision and interpretability.

In this paper, by using the expansion to the FIS-BKR in the above example for the nonlinearity of Backlash, a consistent model was obtained, which could be used knowing the output characteristic of a physical system that presents this nonlinearity.

FIS-TS and FIS-BKR fuzzy models have proven to be a successful approach to dealing with nonlinear systems. Because their multi-modal essence in that simple submodels (typically linear submodels in the case of FIS-TS) are combined to describe the overall behaviour of the nonlinear system. Each fuzzy rule for FIS-TS has a linear dynamic model as part of the consequent that express the local dynamics of each, allowing linear analysis techniques. In the case of FIS-BKR, it is not limited to linear or polynomial analysis, because it can use real and bounded functions, according to constraints system and design requirements. Also worth noting that while FIS-TS for two neighbouring membership functions (the s_i-th and the $s_i + 1$-th) $\mu_{s_i} + \mu_{s_i+1} = 1$, for the FIS-BKR may have intervals the universe of discourse where this amount is different from one.

The generalization of the FIS-BKR allows to continue the investigation concerning the theoretical foundation of FIS-BKR, as modelling (such as application example in this article) and design tool in control systems, especially those ones with nondifferentiable nonlinearities like Backlash.

References

1. Cavallo, A., Natale, C., Pirozzi, S., Visone, C.: Limit cycles in control systems employing smart actuators with hysteresis. IEEE/ASME Trans. Mechatron. **10**, 172–180 (2005)
2. Quality Transmission Components: Section 14 (2010). http://www.qtcgears.com/Q410/PDF/techsec14.pdf
3. Corradini, M., Orlando, G., Parlangeli, G.: Robust control of nonlinear uncertain systems with sandwiched backlash. In: 44th IEEE Conference on Decision and Control and European Control Conference, CDC-ECC 2005, pp. 8112–8117 (2005). doi:10.1109/CDC.2005.1583475. http://ieeexplore.ieee.org/stamp/stamp.jsp?arnumber=1583475
4. Esbrook, A., Tan, X., Khalil, H.: Self-excited limit cycles in an integral-controlled system with backlash. In: American Control Conference (ACC), pp. 4736–4741 (2013). http://ieeexplore.ieee.org/stamp/stamp.jsp?arnumber=6580570
5. Espitia, H.E.: Aplicación del Concresor Basado en Relaciones Booleanas para Sistemas de Lógica Difusa Tipo Dos. Universidad Distrital Franciso José de Caldas, Bogotá, Colombia. Master's degree Thesis (2009)
6. Liu, W., Song, X., Zhang, Q.: (T) Fuzzy Integral of Multi-dimensional Function. In: 2010 Seventh International Conference on Fuzzy Systems and Knowledge Discovery (FSKD) (2010)

7. Nordin, M., Gutman, P.O.: Controlling mechanical systems with backlash - a survey. Automatica **38**(10), 1633–1649 (2002). http://www.sciencedirect.com/science/article/pii/S000510980200047X
8. Salazar, O.: Método de Diseñ y Optimizaciòn de Controladores Difusos FIS-BBR Cuasi-Estándar por medio de Lógicas Clásica y Trivalente de Kleene. Universidad Distrital Franciso José de Caldas. Master's degree Thesis (2014)
9. Soriano, J.J., González, O.L., Munar, F.V., Ramos, A.A.: Propuesta de concresor basado en relaciones booleanas. Ingeniería **10** (2001)
10. Stein, E.M., Shakarchi, R.: Real Analysis: Measure Theory, Integration, and Hilbert Spaces. Princeton University Press, Princeton (2009)
11. Tarbouriech, S., Queinnec, I., Prieur, C.: Stability analysis and stabilization of systems with input backlash. IEEE Trans. Autom. Control **59**(2), 488–494 (2014). doi:10.1109/TAC.2013.2273279. http://ieeexplore.ieee.org/stamp/stamp.jsp?arnumber=6558840
12. Vukic, Z.: Nonlinear Control Systems. CRC Press, New York (2003)
13. Yang, M., Tang, S., Tan, J., Xu, D.: Study of on-line backlash identification for PMSM servo system. In: IECON 2012–38th Annual Conference on IEEE Industrial Electronics Society, pp. 2036–2042 (2012). doi:10.1109/IECON.2012.6388745. http://ieeexplore.ieee.org/stamp/stamp.jsp?arnumber=6388745
14. Ying, H., Ding, Y., Li, S., Shao, S.: Comparison of necessary conditions for typical Takagi-Sugeno and Mamdani fuzzy systems as universal approximators. IEEE Trans. Syst. Man Cybernet. Part A Syst. Hum. **29**(5), 508–514 (1999). http://ieeexplore.ieee.org/xpls/abs_all.jsp?arnumber=784177

Fuzzy Logic System Based on Canvas Model to Evaluate the Initial Viability of a Business Proposal

Carlos Enrique Montenegro Marín$^{(\boxtimes)}$ ⓘ, Laura Daniela Acosta Contreras ⓘ, Andrés Ricardo Barreto López ⓘ, and Paulo Alonso Gaona-García ⓘ

Universidad Distrital Francisco José de Caldas, Bogotá, Colombia
{cmontenegrom,pagaonag}@udistrital.edu.co,
{ldacostac,arbarretol}@correo.udistrital.edu.co

Abstract. Currently, there are many programs that support entrepreneurship as a way to improve economic and social conditions of a country. In this article is designed the model of a fuzzy logic system with the aim of providing a tool that allows generating an initial indicator of the viability of a product or business proposal, based on the model design Canvas and using as a reference the EMIS Benchmarking Score proposed by the Euromoney Institutional Investor Company (EMIS), an organization that provides financial information of companies. The implementation of this prototype taken from experimental data achieved a correlation of 88%, which implies that the model is stable and it fits with the established metrics for the benchmark.

Keywords: Canvas model · Fuzzy logic · EMIS · Feasibility · Correlation

1 Introduction

Entrepreneurship in the world is a driving force behind the economic growth of a country, at least, this is that the GEM report says (Global Entrepreneurship Monitor), which is made annually with the purpose of presenting *"the measurement of entrepreneurship and the identification of factors that, at the institutional, cultural, regulatory and public policy level, determine the level of entrepreneurial activity"*. The report carried out in the period of 2015–2016 covers 61 economies around the world [1].

Within the highlights of the report pointed to the need for agencies offer opportunities, benefits and economic support to these businesses. Thus, it becomes necessary to provide these organizations with tools that can validate the business proposals in an agile and with a high level of certainty.

Take correct decisions becomes the key to success for entrepreneurs, however, it is difficult to propound a model that will guide the business idea proposal to a successful outcome, for this reason this paper proposed a tool that allows management profile users to strengthen decision-making for both investors and entrepreneurs, from the integration between the fuzzy logic and the use of the Canvas model. The main purpose is to generate a first indicator of viability that will indicate whether it is advisable to deepen the business idea.

© Springer International Publishing AG 2017
J.C. Figueroa-García et al. (Eds.): WEA 2017, CCIS 742, pp. 365–377, 2017.
DOI: 10.1007/978-3-319-66963-2_33

This paper is organized as follows. Section 2 is presented a theoretical background related to fuzzy logic and business model Canvas. Section 3 is application case. Section 4 is the implementation of the model. Section 5 is the primary data. Section 6 is the results. Section 7 is results comparison. Finally, we present conclusions.

2   Background

2.1   Fuzzy Logic

The fuzzy logic is a tool that allows to set on the basis of qualitative criteria a series of quantitative values. That is to say, it allows to set values from combinations or truth established values for a series of combined qualities of which is not known. This tool allows to formalize the human mechanics from the transformation of fuzzy concepts to estimations with value and meaning. The fuzzy logic is considered a precise science for the study of the imprecision, where on the basis of elements such as the "Precision" model, the measure of closeness between the reference values vs "coitension" estimates and the translation of the expected results "precisation" we can define a generalization of the behavior of a system that is usually based on linguistic rules [2].

The concept of fuzzy logic was exposed by Lofti Zadeh, who is not in accordance with the classical theory of sets whose truth values allow only two options (membership - not membership) proposed criteria of truth with partial membership (more false - more true), are called fuzzy sets [3].

2.2   Business Model Canvas

The Business Model Canvas is a tool composed of nine blocks of qualitative type in which are defined the possible features that can form a business model, describing "the basics of how an organization creates, develops, and capture value" [4]. Figure 1 presents the interaction of the nine blocks of the model.

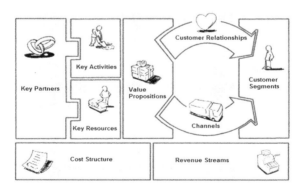

Fig. 1.   The business Canvas model. Taken from Osterwalder, Pigneur (2011, pp. 18–19)

Thanks to the Canvas model is an approach to a global view of the composition of the business, Ferreira [5] establishes the importance of the Canvas as a tool for entrepreneurs, that allows the interaction of concepts such as: entrepreneurship, entrepreneurial, business plan and business in a single work Canvas model, however, it presents a qualitative view, therefore, in spite of knowing the conditions based on the proposal and its composition, it is difficult to establish the viability of the same; since it is not able to establish a quantitative analysis of results that provide a first indicator of the business before performing a feasibility study.

In consideration of the above, it can be shown that the behavior of the tool Canvas allows to propose a fuzzy logic system from a business model and generate a first indicator of project viability.

2.3 Related Work

Within the work toward this type of research was not formally a direct application to the business models with fuzzy logic, however, there are many applications in economic environments and management skills that are associated with our case study. The following are the most relevant sources:

Authors like Rojas et al. [6], present a fuzzy logic system for the assessment of companies oriented to the analysis of some existing corporate valuation methodologies with the aim of identifying impact variables. Jiménez [7], proposes an evaluation model using fuzzy logic that allow to improve the risks analysis related to inflation and macroeconomic growth in the United States. Another proposal made by Angarita and Rios [8], point to the need to improve the security systems with which protects the information generated on the internet. With the use of fuzzy systems can be treated the ambiguity generated in the risks evaluation, as they provide metrics that can have a greater level of certainty with respect to the base of the knowledge.

Other application is presented for Gonzalez et al. [9], identifies the importance of the management of the treasury where it exposes that the payment varies in relation to different factors of the market (Competition - Clients - Regulations), for this uses the zero-based budget (ZBB) as an outline budget and generates a fuzzy system to select the most relevant budget option according to the needs of the organization. And finally, Anagnostopoulos et al. [10], describe a Fuzzy Logic System (FLS) where is modeled the behavior of a buyer in a negotiation process by identifying the dynamics that exist for the assessment of the proposal given by the seller.

The model Canvas has been considered in different areas as noted by Borbinha et al. [11] they identify the risks are exposed to the data in an organization with the purpose of identifying the checks to be carried out and the cost, with the aim of reducing the long-term threats to and increase the gain, from the use of the model Canvas. In the education Guerra et al. [12], makes use of the business model Canvas and the tool Lean launchpad in the educational environment, with the aim of fostering entrepreneurial mindsets in the educational community. Romero et al. [13], sets out the need to implement dynamic systems for the business model Canvas with the purpose of enriching the proposals generated, identifying the variables and constants that may be involved in its preparation.

3   Application Case

Osterwalder and Pigneur [4], identify the four most important areas of the environment, this, to better understand the forces that influence the design of the business model. In each of these areas are identified the forces that are involved, as shown in Fig. 2.

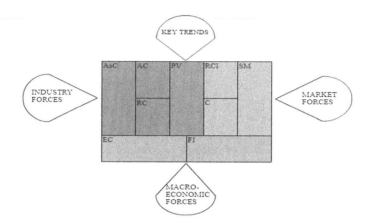

Fig. 2. Environment areas of the business model. Taken from Osterwalder, Pigneur (2011, p. 201)

The four areas identified are:

- Forces of the industry: Identifies and describes what actors there are or who may enter the environment of the business model developed, with the purpose of identifying possible key partnerships and direct and indirect competitors.
- Macroeconomic forces: Identifies the conditions of the global market by presenting the needs of capital, commodities and other resources necessary for business, oriented to the construction of the economic infrastructure of the local market.
- Market forces: identifies issues of the segmented market according to the aspects that impulse it, presenting the needs and demands aimed at defining the behavior of the customers, with the purpose of measuring their capacity, need and desire level to purchase.
- Key Trends: Identifies the technological, regulatory, cultural and socio-economic trends, which may affect the development of the business model.

Based on the identification of the environment areas presented by Osterwalder, it is evident that the characteristics of the key trends are clearly defined within the macroeconomic and market forces. Therefore, it is proposed a restructuring of this area.

To make the fuzzy logic system are identified as inputs, the forces of the industry, market forces and the macroeconomic forces, identified in the model as a product, customers and utility, respectively, for the purpose of controlling the behavior of the system. It is Identified the value proposal within the utility variable as the basis of the analysis performed is a source of value. The grouping was conducted as presented in Fig. 3.

Fig. 3. Grouping of the Canvas model modules.

4 Implementation

For the implementation was used Matlab fuzzy logic simulator where the modeling type Mamdani diffuse of control system is shown in Fig. 4.

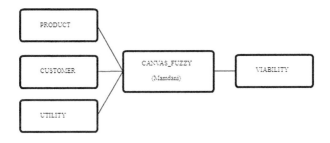

Fig. 4. The proposed system of fuzzy control.

The graphs of behavior are stablished for each factor depending on of the grouping the proposed in the Fig. 3, according to the knowledge base and the analysis of the variables set for the system. As presented hereunder.

For the behavior of the variable "product" presented in Fig. 5 we selected a trend graph similar to the supply and demand curves, depending on the fuzzy value generated for this variable and the parameters that are involved, the objective is to determine if the product is Common, or Innovative.

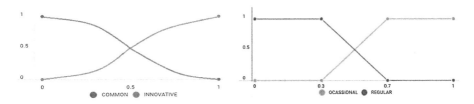

Fig. 5. Product behavior.   **Fig. 6.** Customer behavior.

For the behavior of the variable "customers" shown in Fig. 6, it is selected a trapezoidal graph, the purchasing power, as well as the customer interest are established as occasional or regular according to its behavior in the market and depending on the segmentation, the communication channels and the relation between buyer and seller.

For the behavior of the variable "utility" presented in Fig. 7, we selected a triangular graph, depending on the fuzzy value generated for this variable and the parameters that are involved, the objective is to determine if the interaction of generating value components is set that the utility will be low, variable or high.

Fig. 7. Behavior of the utility.

The output of the system is represented from a triangular graph with four possible states for the viability of the Canvas model to assess, as it is presented in Fig. 8.

Fig. 8. The output of the fuzzy system

5   Primary Data

To validate the functionality of the system is identified the need to compare with existing metrics that display the organizations position currently formalized in the market, with the purpose of comparing it with the generated by the fuzzy logic system. Based on the business models of existing organizations and adjusted to the base of the knowledge generated, it is proposed to stabilize the model in order to provide greater reliability to the fuzzy system to assess business models of future companies to evaluate.

For this is selected the EMIS Benchmarking Score proposed by EMIS; an organization that provides information that covers more than 100 emerging markets with up-to-date information based on different metrics and on the market behavior. This is a private, for-profit organization, gives a score to each company that tracks, indicating the corporate viability of each organization.

To validate the implementation were selected a preliminary basis of 30 companies with the highest market capitalization according to the Colombian Value Stock for March of the year 2017. For the study, it was taken those that have the indicator generated by EMIS, which are presented in Table 1. Validation is performed with existing companies from the hypothesis, that are already qualified and that are models of stable businesses in the market. To adjust the model with the reality of these organizations, we can say that the system is stable and can be implemented for the evaluation of new projects.

Table 1. .

Companies	Abbreviations	EMIS
Ecopetrol S.A.	ECO	41,95
Empresa De Energía De Bogotá S.A. E.S.P.	EEB	81,41
Interconexión Eléctrica S.A.	INTER.ELEC	71,18
Cementos Argos S.A.	CEMEN.ARG	72,61
Isagen S.A.	ISAGEN	69,84
Almacenes Éxito S.A.	ÉXITO	73,73
Cemex Latam Holdings S.A.	CEMEX	68,53
Promigas S.A.E.S.P.	PROMIGAS	76,19
Empresa De Telecomunicaciones De Bogotá S.A.E.S.P.	ETB	46,92
Empresa De Energía Del Pacifico S.A. E.S.P.	EEP	58,93
Productos Familia S.A.	FAMILIA	78,87
Organización Terpel S.A.	TERPEL	69,27
Organización De Ingeniería Internacional S.A.	OII	68,36
Constructora Madera Y Concreto S.A.S.	CONS.MYC	44,59

6 Results

In Table 2 is presented the Canvas model of the fourteen organizations, by weighting each of the nine blocks with values from 0 to 1, in accordance with the information obtained for the authors. Depending on the established metrics in the fuzzy control chart assigned to each group related in Figs. 5, 6 and 7.

After that, it is made the grouping of blocks as shown in Fig. 3, with the purpose of generating the average value of the components of each grouping.

The viability indicator presented in Table 2 is the result that threw the fuzzy logic system for each organization based on the weighted values of each group in the Canvas. Statistical analysis was performed to establish the comparison of the survey results; the results obtained are presented in Table 3:

Table 2. Canvas model results for the selected companies.

Companies	Product	Customer	Utility	Viability (Fuzzy)
ECO	0,501	0,450	0,706	52,900
EEB	0,710	0,750	0,511	80,000
INTER.ELEC	0,870	0,629	0,910	65,900
CEMEN.ARG	0,411	0,957	0,612	78,900
ISAGEN	0,910	0,624	0,890	65,400
ÉXITO	0,511	0,789	0,791	70,000
CEMEX	0,691	0,817	0,712	72,400
PROMIGAS	0,633	0,687	0,550	76,900
ETB	0,655	0,550	0,885	58,600
EEP	0,701	0,550	0,706	57,000
FAMILIA	0,591	0,960	0,911	71,200
TERPEL	0,704	0,650	0,735	63,800
OII	0,690	0,860	0,970	72,600
CONS.MYC	0,560	0,470	0,460	52,500

Table 3. Statistical values

Measurements	EMIS	FUZZY
Medium	69.555	67.95
Median	65.884	67.01
Variance	151.804	77.81
Deviation	12.786	9.15

From the statistical variables, it is generated the dispersion analysis of data, identifying the levels of bias and relational behavior in the indicators generated by the selected sources.

7   Results Comparison

For the results comparison, initially it is established the relationship between the values of the EMIS and those obtained in the fuzzy system, taking the data in Tables 1 and 2, to graphically represent the relationship.

From the results presented in Fig. 9 is evidenced the relational behavior between the theoretical values generated in the fuzzy system and the actual values of the indicator generated by EMIS. It is possible to identify a correlation between the results of the study according to the trend line.

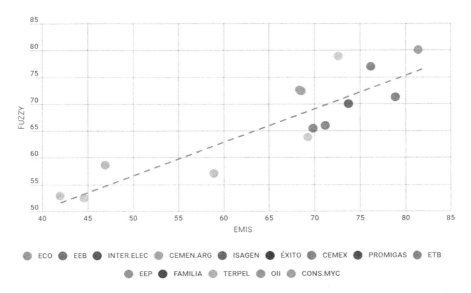

ECO   EEB   INTER.ELEC   CEMEN.ARG   ISAGEN   ÉXITO   CEMEX   PROMIGAS   ETB
EEP   FAMILIA   TERPEL   OII   CONS.MYC

Fig. 9. Relationship of the EMIS indicators and the fuzzy model

In Figs. 10 and 11 it is established the behavior of the values obtained according to the statistical analysis carried out, it is identified the values that are found inside and outside the range of dispersion generated by the fuzzy system and the EMIS, which have a stable behavior according to the ranges of deviation.

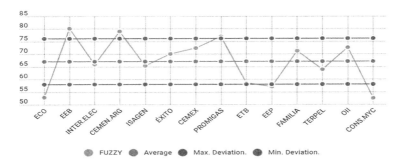

FUZZY   Average   Max. Deviation.   Min. Deviation.

Fig. 10. Fuzzy behavior.

So, it was established for each group of values, which should be considered unfit, for the purpose of identifying those that can reduce the viability of the system. In the case of study, it will be considered all values

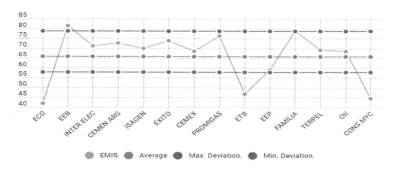

Fig. 11. EMIS behavior.

Using the Pearson correlation coefficient, we established the level of viability of the system from the direct relationship generated between the theoretical data and the actual data represented in Fig. 9; which initially pointed out a linear trend growing in the relationship. To verify the correlation calculations are performed according to the data presented in Table 4. The formula used to calculate correlation [14] is presented in Eq. (1):

$$r = \frac{SS(xy)}{\sqrt{SS(x)SS(y)}} \tag{1}$$

Table 4. Data table for the calculation of the correlation

Companies	EMIS (X)	FUZZY (Y)	X^2	Y^2	XY
ECO	41.95	52.900	1759,80	2798,41	2219,16
BSE	81.41	80.000	6627,59	6400	6512,80
INTER.ELEC	71.18	65.900	5066,59	4342,81	4690,76
CEMEN.ARG	72.61	78.900	5272,21	6225,21	5728,93
ISAGEN	69.84	65.400	4877,63	4277,16	4567,54
SUCCESS	73.73	70.000	5436,11	4900	5161,10
CEMEX	68.53	72.400	4696,36	5241,76	4961,57
PROMIGAS	76.19	76.900	5804,92	5913,61	5859,01
ETB	46.92	58.600	2201,49	3433,96	2749,51
EEP	58.93	57.000	3472,74	3249	3359,01
FAMILIA	78.87	71.200	6220,48	5069,44	5615,54
TERPEL	69.27	63.800	4798,33	4070,44	4419,43
OII	68.36	72.600	4673,09	5270,76	4962,94
CONS.MYC	44.59	52.500	1988,27	2756,25	2340,98
Total	922.38	938.10	62895,61	63948,81	63148,27

From this is performed the calculation for each of the variables to compromise, according to formulas established in (2), (3) and (4)

$$SS(x) = \sum x^2 - \frac{\left(\sum x\right)^2}{n} \tag{2}$$

$$SS(y) = \sum y^2 - \frac{\left(\sum y\right)^2}{n} \tag{3}$$

$$SS(xy) = \sum xy - \frac{\sum x \sum y}{n} \tag{4}$$

It is made the replacement of the values in Eq. (1) to find the value of the correlation coefficient, where it is set r = 0,882108076. This value indicates that there is a linear correlation between the two variables. However, it is clear that the variables X and Y are truly related, that is to say that its correlation was not the result of a coincidence, for this can be from two scenarios:

- $H_0:r = 0 \Rightarrow$ The correlation coefficient comes from a population whose correlation is zero ($\rho = 0$ (correlation coefficient))
- $H_1:r = 0 \Rightarrow$ The correlation coefficient comes from a population whose correlation is zero ($\rho \neq 0$ (correlation coefficient))

With the established hypothesis, it must be checked if the correlation coefficient obtained is within the sampling distribution offered by the null hypothesis. It is calculated as the number of standard deviations that are found in the center of the distribution [18] according to Eq. (5).

$$t = \frac{r_{xy} - 0}{\sqrt{\dfrac{1 - r_{xy}^2}{N - 2}}} \tag{5}$$

It is compared the value obtained with the existing in the tables for a certain level of significance α and N − 2 degrees of freedom $t_{(\alpha, N-2)}$, as well:

- $T > t_{(\alpha, N-2)} \Rightarrow$ rejects the null hypothesis. The correlation does not come from a population whose value $\rho = 0$. Therefore, the variables are related.
- $T \leq t_{(\alpha, N-2)} \Rightarrow$ accept the null hypothesis. The correlation comes from a population whose value $\rho = 0$. Therefore, the variables are not related

It is replaced in Eq. (5) with the known data, t = 6,487062974. Looking for in the Student t table for $\alpha = 0.05$ and 14 − 2 = 12 degrees of freedom, where the value is 2,179. The null hypothesis is rejected, the correlation was obtained between the two indicators where 6,487 > 2,179, it is not appropriate to a population that is characterized by a correlation of zero. That is to say, this correlation is not just a coincidence, this we assure with an estimated error of 0.05.

Finally, the calculation of the typical error S_{yx} [15] of the data according to Eq. (6) and with the data presented in Table 4.

$$\sqrt{\left[\frac{1}{n(n-2)}\right] * \left[n\sum y^2 - \left(\sum y\right)^2 - \frac{\left[n\left(\sum xy\right) - \left(\sum x\right)\left(\sum y\right)\right]^2}{n\sum x^2 - \left(\sum x\right)^2}\right]} \qquad (6)$$

Getting results a typical error of $S_{yx} = 6.3$ units.

8 Conclusions

For the construction of this tool, the Emis Benchmarking Score [16] was taken as reference for established companies in the market and it was proposed to make use of a fuzzy logic system and the principles of the Canvas tool to generate theoretical data to enable the comparison between the theoretical results and the behavior of the selected indicator. The integration of a fuzzy logic system with the Canvas model tool, for the evaluation of projects generated a percentage of correlation of 88%, which implies that the model is stable, presenting the proposed system as a tool to take into account to generate a first indicator of viability in the evaluation of business models.

From the data that are outside of the deviation bounds we were able to identify that it is necessary to adjust the metrics for values assignment to the Canvas model in order to improve the effectiveness because the system presented a typical error of approximately 6.3 units.

References

1. Kelly, D., Singer, S., Herrington, M.: GEM 2015/16 global report. Glob. Entrep. Monit., pp. 1–78 (2015)
2. Zadeh, L.A.: Is there a need for fuzzy logic? Inf. Sci. (NY) **178**, 2751–2779 (2008)
3. Zadeh, L.A.: Fuzzy sets. Inf. Control **8**, 338–353 (1965)
4. Osterwalder, A., Pigneur, Y.: Business Model Generation, p. 285 (2011). (in Spanish). PlanetadeLibros.com
5. Ferreira-Herrera, D.C.: Canvas model in the projects formulation. Coop. y Desarro. **24**, 1–25 (2015). (in Spanish)
6. Rojas López, M.D., Zuluaga Laserna, E., Valencia Corrales, M.E.: Fuzzy logic system for the company valuation. Rev. Ing. Univ. Medellín. **13**, 90–108 (2014). (in Spanish)
7. Jiménez, L.S.: An application of fuzzy logic to the evaluation of the risk balance of inflation and growth macroeconomic. Sci. Soc. **38**, 497–514 (2013). (in Spanish)
8. Angarita, A.A., Tabares, C.A., Rios, J.I.: Definition of a model for measuring risk analysis of security information applying fuzzy logic and systems based on knowledge. Sci. Eng. **9**, 71–80 (2015). (in Spanish)
9. González-santoyo, F., Gil-Lafuente, A.M., Flores Romero, B.: Zero-based budgeting, treasury management in an uncertainty context. (fuzzy logic): technique and application. Rev. Nicolaita Estud. Económicos. **X**, 39–52 (2015). (in Spanish)
10. Kolomvatsos, K., Anagnostopoulos, C., Hadjiefthymiades, S.: A fuzzy logic system for bargaining in information markets. ACM Trans. Intell. Syst. Technol. **3**, 32:1–32:26 (2012)

11. Proença, D., Nadali, A., Borbinha, J.: A pragmatic risk assessment method supported by the business model Canvas. In: Proceedings of Fifth International Symposium Business Modeling and Software Design (BMSD 2015), pp. 156–162 (2015)
12. Guerra, R.C.C., Smith, K.A., McKenna, A.F., Swan, C., Korte, R., Jordan, S., Lande, M., MacNeal, R.: Innovation corps for learning: evidence-based entrepreneurshipTM to improve (STEM) education. In: 2014 IEEE Frontiers in Education Conference Proceedings, 1–5 February 2015 (2014)
13. Romero, M.C., Villalobos, J., Sanchez, M.: simulating the business model Canvas using system dynamics. In: 2015 10th Computing Colombian Conference (10CCC), pp. 527–534 (2015)
14. Johnson, R., Kuby, P.: Elementary Statistics, 11a. edn. Cengage Learning, Mexico City (2012). (in Spanish)
15. Kenney, J.F., Keeping, E.S.: Mathematics of Statistics. Van Nostrand, Princeton (1962)
16. Marqués, F.: Economic models and the company through of excel. Alfaomega. (in Spanish)

A Distance Measure Between Fuzzy Variables

Juan Carlos Figueroa-García[1]([✉]), Eduyn Ramiro López-Santana[1],
and Carlos Franco-Franco[2]

[1] Universidad Distrital Francisco José de Caldas, Bogotá, Colombia
{jcfigueroag,erlopezs}@udistrital.edu.co
[2] Universidad del Rosario, Bogotá, Colombia
carlosa.franco@urosario.edu.co

Abstract. This paper shows some distance measures based on memberships and centroids for comparing fuzzy variables which are commonly
used in fuzzy logic systems and rule-based models. An application example is provided, and some interpretation issues are explained.

1 Introduction and Motivation

Fuzzy logic systems (FLS) relate multiple inputs composed by multiple fuzzy
sets (usually fuzzy numbers) in order to represent a desired output. An FLS is
based on human-like information which contains imprecision/uncertainty, and
there is no a single way to define the shapes and parameters of every fuzzy set,
so there is a need for defining a distance measure between two FLSs to establish
how far/close they are.

An FLS is composed by three components: a set of inputs, a rule base, and a
desired output. A fuzzy variable is defined by a finite number of fuzzy sets whose
shapes and parameters can be defined by different methods such as machine
learning, experts opinions, data driven regressions, etc., with different results.

A *fuzzy variable* is composed by a crisp set of possible values X, a *universe
of discourse* often called Ω, and a set of primary *fuzzy terms* (a.k.a linguistic
labels/partitions) that should be used when describing specific fuzzy concepts
associated to the fuzzy variable. Then, the main problem is how to compare two
fuzzy variables whose linguistic labels are associated to Fuzzy Numbers (FN).

This paper focuses on defining some distances to compare fuzzy variables
(FV) in order to identify differences using a single measure involving all its
individual fuzzy sets (which is useful in decision making, fuzzy logic systems,
fuzzy algebras, etc.). An example is provided and its results are discussed. The
paper is divided into five sections. Section 1 introduces the problem. In Sect. 2,
some basic definitions about FNs are provided; in Sect. 3, some distance measures
for FVs are presented. Section 4 presents an application example; and finally in
Sect. 5, the concluding remarks of the study are presented.

Juan Carlos Figueroa-García is Assistant Professor of the Universidad Distrital
Francisco José de Caldas, Bogotá - Colombia.
Eduyn López-Santana is Assistant Professor of the Universidad Distrital Francisco
José de Caldas, Bogotá - Colombia.
Carlos Franco-Franco is Professor of the Universidad del Rosario, Bogotá - Colombia.

© Springer International Publishing AG 2017
J.C. Figueroa-García et al. (Eds.): WEA 2017, CCIS 742, pp. 378–387, 2017.
DOI: 10.1007/978-3-319-66963-2_34

2   Basics on Fuzzy Sets

A fuzzy set (FS) is denoted by capital letters e.g. A with a membership function $\mu_A(x)$ defined over $x \in X$. A membership function μ_A measures affinity of a value $x \in X$ to a linguistic label/partition A (A is then a word/concept such as *high, medium, low* etc.), so A measures imprecision around X (see Fig. 1).

$$A : X \to [0,1],$$
$$A = \{(x, \mu_A(x)) \mid x \in X\}.$$

where x is the primary variable, and $\mu_A(x)$ is the membership function of A.

2.1   Fuzzy Numbers

A *fuzzy number* (FN) is a fuzzy set whose membership function is normal and convex (a fuzzy subset of $\mathbb{R}$, Zadeh [1]). Thus, $^\alpha A$ is a closed interval for all $\alpha \in [0,1]$, and its support $supp(A)$ is defined over $x \in X$, as shown as follows (the set A in Fig. 1 is also a Fuzzy Number (FN)).

Definition 1 (Fuzzy Number). *Let $\tilde{A} \in \mathcal{F}(X)$. Then, A is a Fuzzy Number (FN) iff there exists a closed interval $[a,b] \neq 0$ such that*

$$\mu_{\tilde{A}}(x) = \begin{cases} 1 & \text{for } x \in [a,b], \\ l(x) & \text{for } x \in [-\infty, a], \\ r(x) & \text{for } x \in [b, \infty] \end{cases} \tag{1}$$

where $l : (-\infty, a) \to [0,1]$ is monotonic non-decreasing, continuous from the right, and $l(x) = \emptyset$ for $x < \omega_1$, and $r : (b, \infty) \to [0,1]$ is monotonic non-increasing, continuous from the left, and $r(x) = \emptyset$ for $x > \omega_2$.

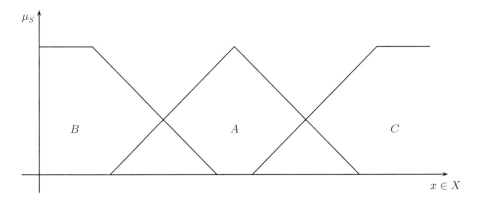

Fig. 1. Fuzzy sets A, B, C

Figure 1 shows three FSs associated to three linguistic labels A, B, C whose universe of discourse is the set X. Since S is characterized by different linguistic labels and their associated membership functions, then we can call it *fuzzy variable*. Note that every fuzzy number is associated to a linguistic label.

A widely used method to represent a fuzzy set A is through α-cuts. The α-cut of a A, namely $^{\alpha}A$, is defined as:

$$^{\alpha}A = \{x \mid \mu_A(x) \geqslant \alpha\}, \tag{2}$$

where $^{\alpha}A$ for a fuzzy number is:

$$^{\alpha}A = \left[\inf_{x \in X}\{\mu_A(x) \geq \alpha\}, \sup_{x \in X}\{\mu_A(x) \geq \alpha\}\right] = [\check{A}_\alpha, \hat{A}_\alpha]. \tag{3}$$

Thus, a fuzzy set A is the union of its α-cuts, $\bigcup_{\alpha \in [0,1]} \alpha \cdot {}^{\alpha}A$, where $\cup$ denotes union (Klir and Yuan [2]).

3 Distance-Based Similarity Between Two FVs

An FV is used to represent perceptions of people about a variable X. While some distance measures between two FNs have been proposed by Chaudhuri and RosenFeld [3], Nguyen and Kreinovich [4], Zheng et al. [5], Xuechang [6], and Hung and Yang [7], Figueroa-García et al. [8], and Figueroa-García and Hernández-Pérez [9], there is no a distance measure between two FVs. The problem of comparing fuzzy partitions has been extensively treated by Anderson et al. [10] and Hüllermeier et al. [11] who were focused to clustering problems where the idea is to measure similarity of elements of a cluster regarding different partitions. This way, our approach goes to compare two FVs using distances to establish if they are either equal or not. To do so, we use the classical axiomatic definitions of distance since every $^{\alpha}A$ can be seen as a crisp set over X.

Let $\mathbb{R}$ be the set of real numbers, and $\mathbb{R}_+$ be its non-negative orthant. X is the universal set; $\mathcal{F}_1(X)$ is the class of all FNs of X; $\mathcal{P}(X)$ is the class of all crisp sets of X, then the distance between A and B namely $d(A, B)$ is called to be a *metric* (or simply distance) if $d(A, B) \in \mathbb{R}_+$ and satisfies the following three axioms:

D1: $d(A, B) = d(B, A)$,
D2: $d(A, A) = 0$,
D3: $d(A, C) \leqslant d(A, B) + d(B, C)$,

Now, in the p-dimensional Euclidean space $\mathbb{R}^p$, the family of L_m Minkowski distances is defined as:

$$d_m(A, B) = \left\{\sum_{i=1}^{p} |x_i - y_i|^m\right\}^{1/m}, \tag{4}$$

where A, B are two points in $\mathbb{R}^p$ with coordinates x_i and y_i.

Now, some useful definitions of distances between intervals, FNs, and the centroids of two FNs are presented. In this paper we adopt the following definition of distance among two interval sets:

Definition 2. *Let $A \in [\underline{a}, \overline{a}]$ and $B \in [\underline{b}, \overline{b}]$ two interval sets defined over $\mathbb{R}_+$, the L_1 distance between A and B is defined as follows:*

$$d(A, B) = |\underline{a} - \underline{b}| + |\overline{a} - \overline{b}| . \tag{5}$$

Kosko [12], and Nguyen and Kreinovich [4] defined the index $A \cap B \subseteq A \cup B$ for crisp/interval sets to evaluate whether $A = B$ or not, so $A = B$ if and only if $A \cap B = A \cup B$. Hence, for crisp (or interval) finite sets. Then, we can establish differences between A and B using the following ratio:

$$R_{A,B} = \frac{|A \cap B|}{|A \cup B|}.$$

If $R_{A,B} = 1$ then $A = B$, so if $R_{A,B} < 1$ then $A \neq B$. As $R_{A,B} \to 0$ as less elements from $A \cup B$ are into $A \cap B$, this is:

$$A = B \Leftrightarrow \mu_A(x) = \mu_B(x)$$

Ramík and Řimánek [13] defined that two fuzzy sets A and B are equal iff $^\alpha A = {}^\alpha B \; \forall \; \alpha \in [0, 1]$, $^\alpha A := [\inf {}^\alpha A, \sup {}^\alpha A]$ and $^\alpha B := [\inf {}^\alpha B, \sup {}^\alpha B]$, this is:

$$A = B \Leftrightarrow \frac{|{}^\alpha A \cap {}^\alpha B|}{|{}^\alpha A \cup {}^\alpha B|} = 1, \; \forall \; \alpha \in [0, 1],$$

Now, the distance between two FNs can be defined as follows:

Definition 3. *Let $A, B \in \mathcal{F}_1(X)$ be two FNs. The distance (metric) d_α between A and B given a set of n α-cuts, $\{\alpha_1, \alpha_2, \cdots, \alpha_n\}$ and $\Lambda = \sum_{i=1}^n \alpha_i$, is:*

$$d_\alpha(A, B) \triangleq \frac{1}{\Lambda} \sum_{i=1}^N \alpha_i \left[\left| \check{A}_{\alpha_i} - \check{B}_{\alpha_i} \right| + \left| \hat{A}_{\alpha_i} - \hat{B}_{\alpha_i} \right| \right], \tag{6}$$

for continuous α we have that $\Lambda = \int_0^1 \alpha \, d\alpha = 1/2$, so d_α is defined as:

$$d_\alpha(A, B) \triangleq 2 \int_0^1 \alpha \left[\left| \check{A}_\alpha - \check{B}_\alpha \right| + \left| \hat{A}_\alpha - \hat{B}_\alpha \right| \right] d\alpha. \tag{7}$$

The centroid of A, $C(A)$ is a crisp number that measures the central trend of A. Now, two FNs A and B are *centroid equal* if their centroids are equal, this is $C(A) = C(B)$, so the L_1 distance between $C(A), C(B)$ is:

$$d_c(C(A), C(B)) = |C(A) - C(B)|. \tag{8}$$

We recall that $A \neq B \not\Rightarrow C(A) \neq C(B)$; and $A = B \Rightarrow C(A) = C(B)$. This means that A and B could be different, this is $d_\alpha > 0$ (see Definition 3) while having equal centroids $C(A) = C(B)$.

3.1   Distances Between FVs

An FLS relates fuzzy variables using different linguistic labels/partitions and a rule base. We address a case where two FVs defined over the same variable X are to be compared; for instance, two FLSs synchronized by machine learning techniques, clustering, genetic optimized methods, etc. To do so, some theoretical definitions about fuzzy variables are provided.

Definition 4. *A linguistic variable S is a triplet (s, X, Ω) where $s = \{A, B, \cdots, K\}$ is a set of linguistic labels defined over a subset X of a universe of discourse Ω, this is $X \in \Omega$. It is said S to be a fuzzy variable if $\{\mu_A, \mu_B, \cdots, \mu_K\} \in \mathcal{F}_1(X)$.*

In this paper, we do not make a distinction between a linguistic label A and its associated fuzzy set μ_A. Figure 1 shows a variable S conformed by three labels $s = \{A, B, C\}$ whose fuzzy sets are FNs $\{A, B, C\} \in \mathcal{F}_1(X)$.

Comparability: Comparability between two FVs S_1, S_2 is an interesting concept. Two sets A, B are comparable if there is a total order relation between both, but when comparing two FVs we have that they can be composed by different linguistic labels and/or over different $X \in \Omega$. Now, we focus on comparing two FVs with the same linguistic labels and defined over the same universe $X \in \Omega$.

Definition 5. *Let S_1, S_2 be two FVs, then they are pairwise comparable $S_1 \perp_p S_2$ only if: (i) they are composed by the same partition $s_1 = s_2 = s = \{A, B, \cdots, K\}$, (ii) its associated fuzzy sets are defined over the same variable $X \in \Omega$, and iiii) the memberships $\mu_{S_{1,j}}, \mu_{S_{2,j}}$ are totally ordered.*

This means that $S_1 \perp_p S_2$ only if S_1, S_2 are equally labeled no matter its membership functions e.g. $s_1 = \{A_1, B_1, \cdots, K_1\}, s_2 = \{A_2, B_2, \cdots, K_2\}$, they are defined over the same universe $X \in \Omega$, and there is a total order for every pair of labels $j \in s$, this is $\mu_{S_{1,j}} \leqslant, \geqslant \mu_{S_{2,j}} \forall j \in s$.

Conversely, two FVs S_1, S_2 are not pairwise comparable $S_1 \|_p S_2$ if they are composed by different linguistic labels/partitions, they are defined over different universes of discourse $X \in \Omega$, or there exists only a partial order between S_1, S_2. If $\mu_{S_{1,j}}, \mu_{S_{2,j}}$ for some $j \in s$ are partially ordered then we propose to compute a distance measure between S_1, S_2 to see how different they are.

Now, the distances d_α, d_c are metrics that helps to see how different $S_1 \perp_p S_2$ or $S_1 \|_p S_2$ are, so the idea is to aggregate all distances between pairs of fuzzy sets using its sum. This way, we propose the following distances between FVs. First, the Minkowski distance between S_1, S_2 is as follows:

Proposition 1. *Let S_1, S_2 be two FVs. The distance d_α between S_1, S_2 given $\{A_1, A_2, B_1, B_2, \cdots, K_1, K_2\} \in \mathcal{F}_1(X)$, a set of n α-cuts $\{\alpha_1, \alpha_2, \cdots, \alpha_n\}$, and $\Lambda = \sum_{i=1}^n \alpha_i$, is:*

$$d_\alpha(S_1, S_2) \triangleq \sum_{j \in \{s\}} d_\alpha(S_{1,j}, S_{2,j}) = d_\alpha(A_1, A_2) + \cdots + d_\alpha(K_1, K_2), \quad (9)$$

where $j \in \{s\}$ is the set of linguistic labels of S_1 and S_2.

Now, the centroid-based L_1 distance between centroids $C(S_1), C(S_2)$ is:

Proposition 2. *Let* S_1, S_2 *be* $S_1 \perp_p S_2$. *The centroid-based* L_1 *distance* d *between* S_1, S_2 *given* $\{C(A_1), C(A_2), \cdots, C(B_1), C(B_2), \cdots, C(K_1), C(K_2)\} \in \mathcal{P}(\mathbb{R})$ *is:*

$$d_c(S_1, S_2) \triangleq \sum_{j \in \{s\}} d_c(C(S_{1,j}), C(S_{2,j}))$$
$$= |C(A_1) - C(A_2)| + |C(B_1) - C(B_2)| + \cdots + |C(K_1) - C(K_2)|\}, \quad (10)$$

where $j \in \{s\}$ *is the set of linguistic labels of* S_1 *and* S_2.

Note that $d_\alpha(S_1, S_2) > 0$ does not imply $C(S_{1,j}) \neq C(S_{2,j})$. It is also clear that if $S_{1,j} = S_{2,j}$ then $C(S_{1,j}) = C(S_{2,j})$, and conversely $C(S_{1,j}) = C(S_{2,j})$ does not mean that $S_{1,j} = S_{2,j}$, in other words:

$$S_{1,j} = S_{2,j} \implies C(S_{1,j}) = C(S_{2,j}),$$
$$C(S_{1,j}) = C(S_{2,j}) \not\implies S_{1,j} = S_{2,j}.$$

Conversely, $d_\alpha = 0$ implies $C(S_{1,j}) = C(S_{2,j})$. It is possible to have $C(A) = C(B)$ while $d_\alpha \neq 0$ since the axiomatic idea that $\mu_{A_1} \neq \mu_{A_2}$ can lead to equal centroids.

4   Application Example

In this example, we compare two FVs S_1 and S_2 composed by three linguistic labels $s = \{A, B, C\}$ defined over the reals $X \in \mathbb{R}$ where B and C are linear sets $L(\check{x}, \bar{x}, \hat{x})$, and A is a triangular set $T(\check{x}, \bar{x}, \hat{x})$ (see Fig. 2 and Table 1). All centroids were computed using the proposal of Figueroa-García [14] (other efficient methods for type reduction were proposed by Melgarejo [15,16], and Wu and Mendel [17,18]).

Table 1. Parameters and centroids for S_1, S_2

Set	B_1	B_2	A_1	A_2	C_1	C_2
$\check{x}$	0	0	4	5	12	12
$\bar{x}$	6	5	10	11	15	17
$\hat{x}$	9	10	16	17	20	20
$C(S_{i,.})$	6.59	7.08	10	11	13.4	13.9

Note that the pairs A_1, A_2 and C_1, C_2 are totally ordered pairs while the pair B_1, B_2 is only partially ordered, this means $S_1 \|_p S_2$. To establish the difference

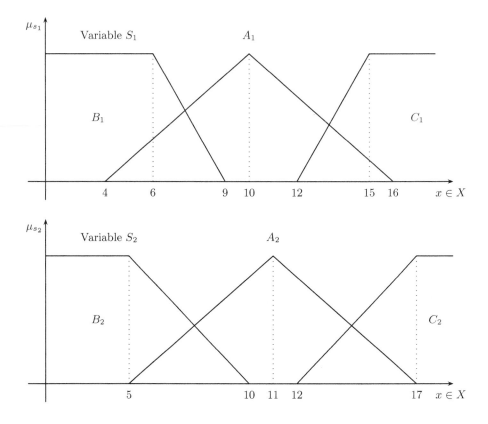

Fig. 2. Fuzzy variables S_1, S_2

between S_1, S_2 we apply the proposed distances d_α and d_c (see Propositions 1 and 2). We recall that as smaller d_α and d, as closer S_1 to S_2. The obtained results are shown as follows:

$$d_\alpha(B_1, B_2) = 0.666, \; d_\alpha(A_1, A_2) = 1, \; d_\alpha(C_1, C_2) = 0.505, d_\alpha(S_1, S_2) = 2.171,$$
$$d_c(B_1, B_2) = 1, \; d_c(A_1, A_2) = 0.5, \; d_c(C_1, C_2) = 0.5, d_c(S_1, S_2) = 2.$$

4.1 Discussion of the Results

The distance $d_\alpha(S_1, S_2) = 2.171$ shows us that $S_1 \neq S_2$, even when they are graphically similar (see Fig. 2). The only case in which $S_1 = S_2$ is when all fuzzy sets are equal.

Regarding $C(S_{i,j})$, we computed $d_c(S_1, S_2) = 3.035$ which means there are some differences between S_1, S_2, so we can conclude that its centroids are different. Figure 3 shows the exact location of $C(S_{1,j}), C(S_{2,j})$ and also shows that even if the shapes of every set seem to be similar, its centroids can be different.

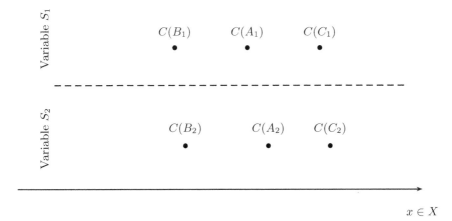

Fig. 3. Ordering of centroids

Conversely, two partially ordered sets could have similar centroids, note that B_2 seems to be on the left of B_1, but clearly $C(B_1) < C(B_1)$. Also note that S_1, S_2 are centroid totally-ordered since $C(S_{1,j}) \leqslant C(S_{2,j}) \, \forall \, j \in s$.

After computing all distances, there is a clear idea about the distance between S_1, S_2: they are not similar, and its centroids are different. This leads us to think that if both sets S_1, S_2 are used in an FLS or a rule-based model, they should produce different results since they are different. If all distances were close to zero then we can assert that S_1, S_2 are similar/equal, so no difference would be detected when using any of them.

5 Concluding Remarks

The proposed distance measures for FVs provide a base for comparing fuzzy logic systems (or rule-based models) which are popular in practice. We also have provided some conditions to establish if two FVs are equal or not by using an L_1 Minkowski crisp distance.

We proposed an L_1 Minkowski distance to compare the centroids of two FVs as well. This helps to measure differences among its centroids (which are widely used defuzzification measures). Also we point out that our proposal does not need big computational efforts and it can be easily implemented.

The membership functions used in the example are trapezoidal and triangular FNs since they are popular in practice. The obtained results are satisfactory since we identified some differences between S_1, S_2, and how distant they are. The same concept was applied to its centroids for which the distance between them was computed.

5.1   Further Topics

The definition of distance measures for *Type-2 fuzzy variables* is a natural step in the analysis. On the other hand, the application of our proposal to decision making problems, including fuzzy differential equations, fuzzy linear programming, among others, appears as an interesting field to be covered in the future (see Chalco-Cano and Román-Flores [19,20]), Figueroa-García and Pachon-Neira [21,22], and Wu and Mendel [23], etc.).

Acknowledgments. The authors would like to thank to Prof. Vladik Kreinovich from the Computer Science Dept. of The University of Texas at El Paso - USA, and Prof. Miguel Alberto Melgarejo-Rey from the Eng. Faculty of the Universidad Distrital Francisco José de Caldas - Bogotá, Colombia for their valuable comments and discussions about the topics addressed in this paper.

References

1. Zadeh, L.: The concept of a linguistic variable and its application to approximate reasoning-I. Inf. Sci. **8**, 199–249 (1975)
2. Klir, G.J., Folger, T.A.: Fuzzy Sets, Uncertainty and Information. Prentice Hall, Upper Saddle River (1992)
3. Chaudhuri, B., RosenFeld, A.: A modified hausdorff distance between fuzzy sets. Inf. Sci. **118**, 159–171 (1999)
4. Nguyen, H.T., Kreinovich, V.: Computing degrees of subsethood and similarity for interval-valued fuzzy sets: fast algorithms. In: 9th International Conference on Intelligent Technologies, InTec 2008, pp. 47–55. IEEE (2008)
5. Zheng, G., Wang, J., Zhou, W., Zhang, Y.: A similarity measure between interval type-2 fuzzy sets. In: IEEE International Conference on Mechatronics and Automation, pp. 191–195. IEEE (2010)
6. Xuechang, L.: Entropy, distance measure and similarity measure of fuzzy sets and their relations. Fuzzy Sets Syst. **52**, 305–318 (1992)
7. Hung, W.L., Yang, M.S.: Similarity measures between type-2 fuzzy sets. Int. J. Uncertainty Fuzziness Knowl. Based Syst. **12**(6), 827–841 (2004)
8. Figueroa-García, J.C., Chalco-Cano, Y., Román-Flores, H.: Distance measures for interval type-2 fuzzy numbers. Discrete Appl. Math. **197**(1), 93–102 (2015)
9. Figueroa-García, J.C., Hernández-Pérez, G.J.: On the computation of the distance between interval type-2 fuzzy numbers using a-cuts. In: IEEE (ed.) Annual Meeting of the North American Fuzzy Information Processing Society (NAFIPS), vol. 1, pp. 1–6. IEEE (2014)
10. Anderson, D.T., Bezdek, J.C., Popescu, M., Keller, J.M.: Comparing fuzzy, probabilistic, and possibilistic partitions. IEEE Trans. Fuzzy Syst. **18**(5), 906–918 (2010)
11. Hüllermeier, E., Rifqi, M., Henzgen, S., Senge, R.: Comparing fuzzy partitions: a generalization of the Rand index and related measures. IEEE Trans. Fuzzy Syst. **20**(3), 546–556 (2012)
12. Kosko, B.: Fuzziness vs. probability. Int. J. Gen. Syst. **17**(1), 211–240 (1990)
13. Ramík, J., Rimánek, J.: Inequality relation between fuzzy numbers and its use in fuzzy optimization. Fuzzy Sets Syst. **16**, 123–138 (1985)
14. Figueroa-García, J.C.: An approximation method for type reduction of an interval type-2 fuzzy set based on α-cuts. In: IEEE (ed.) Proceedings of FEDCSIS 2012, pp. 1–6. IEEE (2012)

15. Melgarejo, M., Bernal, H., Duran, K.: Improved iterative algorithm for computing the generalized centroid of an interval type-2 fuzzy set. In: Annual Meeting of the North American Fuzzy Information Processing Society (NAFIPS), vol. 27, pp. 1–6. IEEE (2008)
16. Melgarejo, M.A.: A fast recursive method to compute the generalized centroid of an interval type-2 fuzzy set. In: Annual Meeting of the North American Fuzzy Information Processing Society (NAFIPS), pp. 190–194. IEEE (2007)
17. Wu, D., Mendel, J.M.: Enhanced Karnik-Mendel algorithms for interval type-2 fuzzy sets and systems. In: Annual Meeting of the North American Fuzzy Information Processing Society (NAFIPS), vol. 26, pp. 184–189. IEEE (2007)
18. Wu, D., Mendel, J.M.: Enhanced Karnik-Mendel algorithms. IEEE Trans. Fuzzy Syst. 17(4), 923–934 (2009)
19. Chalco-Cano, Y., Román-Flores, H.: On new solutions of fuzzy differential equations. Chaos Solitons Fractals 38, 112–119 (2008)
20. Chalco-Cano, Y., Román-Flores, H.: Comparison between some approaches to solve fuzzy differential equations. Fuzzy Sets Syst. 160(11), 1517–1527 (2009)
21. Figueroa-García, J.C., Neira, D.P.: On ordering words using the centroid and Yager index of an interval type-2 fuzzy number. In: Proceedings of the Workshop on Engineering Applications, WEA 2015, vol. 1, pp. 1–6. IEEE (2015)
22. Figueroa-García, J.C., Neira, D.P.: A comparison between the centroid and the yager index rank for type reduction of an interval type-2 fuzzy number. Revista Ingeniería Universidad Distrital 21(2), 225–234 (2016)
23. Wu, D., Mendel, J.M.: Uncertainty measures for interval type-2 fuzzy sets. Inf. Sci. 177(1), 5378–5393 (2007)

Classification by Nearest Neighbor and Multilayer Perceptron a New Approach Based on Fuzzy Similarity Quality Measure: A Case Study

Dianne Arias[1], Yaima Filiberto[1(✉)], Rafael Bello[2], Ileana Cadena[3], and Wilfredo Martinez[3]

[1] Department of Computer Science, Universidad de Camagüey,
Camagüey, Cuba
{dianne.arias,yaima.filiberto}@reduc.edu.cu
[2] Department of Computer Science, Universidad Central de Las Villas,
Santa Clara, Cuba
rbellop@uclv.edu.cu
[3] Department of Civil Engineering, Universidad de Camagüey, Camagüey, Cuba
{ileana.cadenas,wilfredo.martinez}@reduc.edu.cu

Abstract. In this paper the performance of k Nearest Neighbors and Multilayer Perceptron algorithm the is used in a classical task in the branch of the Civil Engineering: predict the level of service in the road. The use of fuzzy similarity quality measure method for calculating the weights of the features allows to performance of KNN and MLP in the case of mixed data (features with discrete or real domains). Experimental results show that this approach is better than other methods used to calculate the weight of the features. The results of the predictions of the level of service show the effectiveness of the method in the solution of problems of traffic engineering.

Keywords: Fuzzy similarity quality measure · Similarity relation · Classification · Level of service of the road

1 Introduction

For the last decade or so, the size of machine-readable data sets has increased dramatically and the problem of data explosion has become apparent. These developments have created a new range of problems and challenges for the analysts, as well as new opportunities for intelligent systems in data analysis and have led to the emergence of the field of Intelligent Data Analysis (IDA), a combination of diverse disciplines including Artificial Intelligence and Statistics in particular. Inside the field of the Artificial Intelligence, the Rough Set Theory (RST) proposed by Pawlak in 1982 offers measures for the analysis of data. The measure called classification quality allows calculating the consistency of a decision system. Its main limitation is being used only for decision systems where the features domain is discrete.

© Springer International Publishing AG 2017
J.C. Figueroa-García et al. (Eds.): WEA 2017, CCIS 742, pp. 388–397, 2017.
DOI: 10.1007/978-3-319-66963-2_35

A new measure (named Similarity Quality Measure) for the case of decisions systems in which the features domain, including the decision feature, does not have to be necessarily discrete, is proposed in [1]. This measure has the limitation of using thresholds when constructing relations of similarity among the objects of the decision system. These thresholds are parameters of the method to be adjusted and parameters are aggravating factors recognized when analyzing any algorithm. The accuracy of the method is very sensitive to small variations in the threshold. Threshold values are also dependent on the application, so an exquisite adjustment process of the thresholds is needed to maximize the performance of the knowledge discovery process. Therefore, it is necessary to incorporate a technique that allows us handling inaccuracy. The Fuzzy Sets Theory, as one of the main elements of soft computing, uses fuzzy relations to make computational methods more tolerant and flexible to inaccuracy, especially in the case of mixed data.

Since Similarity Quality Measure is quite sensitive to similarity values of thresholds, this limitation was tackled by using fuzzy sets to categorize its domains through fuzzy binary relations. This new measure named Fuzzy Similarity Quality Measure based on Fuzzy Sets facilitate the definition of similarity relations (since there are fewer parameters to consider) without degrading, from a statistical perspective, the efficiency of the mining tasks of subsequent data. The Fuzzy Similarity Quality Measure computes the relation between the similarity according to the conditional features and the similarity according to the decision featured.

The method proposed here as a weighing method of features is based on a heuristic search in which the quality of the fuzzy similarity measure of a decision system is used as heuristic value. We use PSO to find the best set W; this method has showed good performance to solve optimization problems [1]. In this problem each particle represents a set of weights W and the quality of particles is calculated by the fuzzy similarity measure. The impact of a new method called PSO+RST+FUZZY, in the k-Nearest Neighbors (k-NN) and Multilayer Perceptron (MLP) algorithm is studied in this paper.

2   The Classification Problem with MLP and k-NN Methods

2.1   Multilayer Perceptron

The most popular neural network model is the Multilayer Perceptron (MLP) and the most popular learning algorithm is the Back-propagation (BP), which is based on correcting the error. The essential character of the BP algorithm is gradient descent, because the gradient descent algorithm is strictly dependent on the shape of the error surface. The error surface may have some local minimum and multimodal. This results in falling into some local minimum and appearing premature convergence [2].

BP training is very sensitive to initial conditions. In general terms, the choice of the initial weight vector W_0 may speed convergence of the learning process towards a global or a local minimum if it happens to be located within the attraction based on that minimum. Conversely, if W_0 starts the search in a relatively flat region of the error surface it will slow down the adaptation of the connection weights [3].

An MLP is composed of an input layer, an output layer and one or more hidden layers, but it has shown that for most problems it is sufficient with a single hidden layer. The number of hidden units is directly related to the capabilities of the network, in our case the number determine what follows $(i + j)/2$, where i is input neurons and j is the output.

Each entry has an associated weight W, which is modified in the so-called learning process. The input layer is responsible for assigning weights Wij to inputs using the proposed PSO+RST+FUZZY method. From there, the information is passed to the hidden layer, and then transmitted to the output layer, that is responsible for producing the network response [4].

2.2 k-Nearest Neighbors

The key idea in the k-NN method is that similar input data vectors have similar output values [1, 5]. This algorithm assumes all instances correspond to points in the n-dimensional space Rn. The target function value for a new query is estimated from the known values of the k nearest training examples.

An obvious refinement to the k-NN algorithm is to weight the contribution of each of the k neighbors according to their distance to the query point X_q giving greater weight to closer neighbors. The k-NN algorithm for approximating a discrete-value target function is given in (2) by [6].

$$f(X_q) \leftarrow argmax_{v \in V} \sum_{i=1}^{k} w_i * \delta(v, f(x_i)) \tag{1}$$

The k-NN method is a simple, intuitive and efficient way to estimate the value of an unknown function. Finding these K nearest neighbors requires the use of distance functions (nominal, numerical or mixed). Similarity functions are often employed in mixed problems, i.e. those with both nominal and numerical attributes [7]. The results presented in [8] show that an important aspect in the methods based on similarity grades, as the k-NN method, is the set of weights assigned to the features, because this improves significantly the performance of the method [9]. In this paper we propose a new alternative for calculating the weights of the features to be associated with the predictive features that appear in the weighted similarity function based on Fuzzy Similarity Quality Measure.

3 The Similarity Quality Measure with Fuzzy Sets

In [10] a fuzzy (binary) relation R was defined as a fuzzy collection of ordered pairs, then a fuzzy relation from X to Y or, equivalently, a fuzzy relation in X ∪ Y, is a fuzzy subset of X × Y characterized by a membership (characteristic) function μR which associates with each pair (x, y) its "grade of membership" μR (x, y), in R. We shall assume for simplicity that the range of μR is the interval [0, 1] and will refer to the number μR (x, y) as the strength of the relation between x and y.

In Fuzzy Similarity Quality Measure, a membership (characteristic) function is defined by a similarity function (4) and (5). This function includes the weights for each feature and local functions to calculate how the values of a given feature are similar.

Given a decision system DS, these two granulations are built using the crisp binary relations R1 and R2 defined in Eqs. (2) and (3):

$$xR1y = F_1(x, y) \tag{2}$$

$$xR2y = F_2(x, y) \tag{3}$$

where *R1* and *R2* are fuzzy relations defined to describe the similarity between objects x and y regarding condition traits and trait decision respectively. Crisp binary relations R1 and R2 are defined by the following functions F1 (4) and (5).

$$F1(x, y) = \sum_{i=1}^{n} w_i *_i (X_i, Y_i) \tag{4}$$

$$F2(x, y) = (d(X), d(Y)) \tag{5}$$

$$\partial_i(X(i), Y(i)) = \begin{cases} 1 - \frac{|X(i) - Y(i)|}{Max(\alpha_i) - Min(\alpha_i)} & \text{if } i \text{ is continuous} \\ 1 & \text{if } i \text{ is discrete and } X(i) = Y(i) \\ 0 & \text{if } i \text{ is discrete and } X(i) \neq Y(i) \end{cases} \tag{6}$$

This establishes a relationship of similarity between two objects *(x, y)* considering the similarity of the same with respect to traits in *A* (calculated as the *F1* function in relation *R1*) and the target trait (calculated according to the function *F2* universe in relation *R2*), the purpose is to find the relations *R1* and *R2* such that *R1(x)* and *R2 (x)* are as similar as possible to any element of the universe. From fuzzy relations *R1* and *R2* can be constructed fuzzy sets *N1(x)* and *N2(x)*. Based on this approach, the sets are built:

$$N1(x) = \{(y, \mu R1(x, y)) \text{ for } \forall y \in U\} \tag{7}$$

$$N2(x) = \{(y, \mu R2(x, y)) \text{ for } \forall y \in U\} \tag{8}$$

The problem is to find functions *F1* and *F2* such that *N1(x) = N2(x)*, where the symbol "=" the greatest possible similarity between *N1(x)* and *N2(x)* sets for every object in the universe. The degree of similarity between the two sets for an object *x* is calculated as the similarity between fuzzy sets *N1(x)* and *N2(x)* can be calculated by expression (9). The expression (9) was presented in [11].

$$\varphi(x) = \sum_{i=1}^{n} \frac{[1 - |\mu R1(x_i) - \mu R2(x_i)|]}{n} \tag{9}$$

Using the expression (9) as the quality of a similarity decision system (DS) with a universe of objects N is defined by (10):

$$\theta(DS) = \sum_{i=1}^{n} \frac{\varphi(x)}{n} \tag{10}$$

This measure represents the degree of similarity of a decision system.

3.1   Algorithm PSO+RST+Fuzzy

The following describes the operation of the PSO+RST+FUZZY algorithm:

Step 1: Initialize a population of particles with random positions and velocities in a D-dimensional space.

Step 2: For each particle, evaluate the quality of the similarity measure (11), D variables.

$$\max \rightarrow \left\{ \frac{\sum\limits_{\forall x \in U} \varphi(x)}{|U|} \right\} \tag{11}$$

Step 3: To compare the quality measure of the current similarity measure each particle with the quality of its best similarity *pbest* previous position. If the current value is better than *pbest*, then assign the current value *pbest* and $Pi = Xi$, i.e. the current location results to be the best so far.

Step 4: Identify the particle in the neighborhood with the highest value for the quality of the similarity measure and assign its index to the variable g and assign the best value quality measure of similarity to m.

Step 5: Adjust the speed and position of the particle according to the Eqs. (12) and (13) (for each dimension).

$$v_i(t+1) = \alpha * v_i(t) + U(0, \varphi 1)(pbest(t) - x_i(t)) + U(0, \varphi 2)(gbest(t) - x_i(t)) \tag{12}$$

$$x_i(t+1) = x_i(t) + v_i(t+1) \tag{13}$$

Step 6: Stop criterion: either maximum iterations or five iterations without improving the overall quality measure similarity *(m)*. Stop if satisfied, otherwise go to Step 2.

4   Experimental Results

We apply both of these methods on a real dataset from the UCI Machine Learning repository (tae, diabetes, iris, hepatitis, postoperative-patient-data, zoo, bridges-version1, biomed, schizo, soybean-small, cars, heart-statlog, liver-disorders, glass).

The variants for calculating the weights for k-NN with $k = 1$ are: the proposed method in [5] (called PSO+RST), the weight obtained by Conjugated Gradient method (k-NN$_{VSM}$), assigning the same weight to each feature (called Standard) and Relief. The results of the accuracy of the general classification of the MLP and the results of the MLP when the different weight calculation methods (Random (MLP-AL), Standard (1/Quantity-Features), KNN$_{VSM}$, PSO+RST weight calculation method proposed in [5] and the proposal of this article PSO+RST+FUZZY) are used, were compared to prove the effectiveness of the PSO+RST+FUZZY method.

The results achieved by the k-NN and MLP for the cases of classification, where the weights are initialized using the mentioned variants, are shown in Tables 1 and 2.

Table 1. Results of the general classification accuracy for k-NN

Datasets	PSO+RST+FUZZY	PSO+RST	KNN$_{VSM}$	Standard	Relief
tae	67.3	63.2	58.94	58.94	58.94
bridges_version1	62.4	52.3	42.4	32.2	45.2
biomed	94.2	99.4	99.4	95.8	97.8
iris	94.5	95.8	94.4	94.4	94.4
zoo	95	71.4	69.4	69.4	71.4
schizo	60.3	75.7	67	48.5	53.5
soybean-small	100	100	100	100	100
cars	86.15	82.3	86.1	75.2	76
heart-statlog	74.4	77.4	77.2	77.5	75.7
liver-disorders	66.4	65.8	65.1	65.1	65.7
glass	83.51	82.3	78.4	72.1	73.9

Table 2. Results of the general classification accuracy for MLP

Datasets	PSO+RST +FUZZY	PSO +RST	1NN$_{VSM}$	Standard	MLP-AL	Relief
tae	59.12	58.94	55.63	49.01	54.3	54.97
diabetes	76.43	74.8	74.22	76.69	75.39	74.74
iris	97.33	97.9	96.67	95.33	97.33	98
hepatitis	84.45	82.01	81.29	78.06	80	79.35
postoperative-patient-data	57.77	57.78	53.33	54.44	55.56	55.56
zoo	97.66	96.04	40.59	73.27	94.29	75.25
bridges-version1	68.03	71.43	41.9	41.9	69.52	60
biomed	92.98	90.7	82.99	83.51	86.08	83.51
schizo	69.54	68.27	62.5	63.46	65.38	63.46
soybean-small	100	100	76.6	78.72	100	74.47
Cars	80.58	80.3	71.17	71.17	78.06	71.17
heart-statlog	83.33	81.85	80.37	80.37	78.15	80.37

In order to compare the results, a multiple comparison test is used to find the best algorithm. In Tables 3 and 4 the results of the Friedman statistical test are shown. There can be observed that the best ranking is obtained by our proposal. Thus, this indicates that the accuracy of PSO+RST+FUZZY is significantly better. Also the Iman-Davenport test was used [12]. The resulting p-value = $0.00015336498 < \alpha$ (with 4 and 40 degrees of freedom) and p-value = $0.000000002666 < \alpha$ (with 5 and 55 degrees of freedom) -for k-NN and MLP respectively- indicates that there are indeed significant performance differences in the group for both methods.

Table 3. Average ranks obtained by each method in the Friedman test for k-NN

Algorithm	Ranking
PSO+RST+FUZZY	2.0455
PSO+RST	2.0909
KNNVSM	2.7727
Relief	3.6818
Standard	4.4091

Table 4. Average ranks obtained by each method in the Friedman test for MLP

Algorithm	Ranking
PSO+RST+FUZZY	1.625
PSO+RST	2
MLP-AL	3.4167
RELIEF	4.2083
Standard	4.7083
KNNVSM	5.0417

There is a set of methods to increase the power of multiple test; they are called sequential methods, or post-hoc tests. In this case it was decided to use Holm [13] test to find algorithms significantly higher. PSO+RST+FUZZY - as the control method-conduct to pair wise comparisons between the control method and all others, and determine the degree of rejection of the null hypothesis.

The results reported in Table 5 reject all null hypotheses whose p-value is lower than 0.025, hence confirming a better performance of the control method [7]. Since the PSO+RST vs. PSO+RST+FUZZY null hypothesis was not rejected, then there is no significant statistical evidence to determine performance differences between the two algorithms and therefore they can be deemed equally effective for a 95% confidence level.

The results shown in Table 6 reject all null hypotheses (its p-values are lower than 0.05), so the test rejects all cases in favor of the best ranking algorithm. It can be noticed that PSO+RST+FUZZY is statistically superior to all compared methods.

Table 5. Holm's table with $\alpha = 0.025$ for 1-NN, PSO+RST+FUZZY is the control method

i	Algorithm	z = (R0 − Ri)/SE	p	Holm	Hypothesis
4	Standard	3.505839	0.000455	0.0125	Reject
3	Relief	2.42712	0.015219	0.016667	Reject
2	KNNVSM	1.07872	0.280713	0.025	It's not rejected
1	PSO+RST	0.06742	0.946247	0.05	It's not rejected

Table 6. Holm's table with $\alpha = 0.05$ for MLP, PSO+RST+FUZZY is the control method

i	Algorithm	z = (R0 − Ri)/SE	p	Holm	Hypothesis
5	KNNVSM	4.473467	0.000008	0.01	Reject
4	Standard	4.037031	0.000054	0.0125	Reject
3	RELIEF	3.382377	0.000719	0.016667	Reject
2	MLP-AL	2.345842	0.018984	0.025	Reject
1	PSO+RST	0.49099	0.623433	0.05	It's not rejected

5 Applications of the Method in the Solution of a Real Problem

In this section a real problem related with the branch of the Civil Engineering is solved, using the following procedure:

Step 1: Build the decision system for the application domain
Step 2: Determine the global similarity function (it was used the expressions 4 and 5) and the local comparison functions for the features (it was used the expression 6)
Step 3: Calculate the weight using the quality of similarity measure (using PSO +RST and PSO+RST+FUZZY)
Step 4: Apply the weight in the classification with MLP and KNN.

The concept of "Level of Service" it was presented as a means to quantify or to classify the operational quality of the service offered by a road to drivers and users. It defined "Level of Service" like a qualitative measure that describes the operational conditions inside the current of the traffic and their perception for the driver and the passenger. A definition of level of service generally describes these conditions in such terms as speed and time of journey, maneuver freedom, interruptions of the traffic, comfort, comfort and security [14].

In the level of service it influences the intensity of the vehicular interaction, the conditions of the road and their environment, and the quality of the regulation and signaling of the road. They have been defined six levels of service for each type of road; assigning them of the letter "A" to the "F", being the level of service "A" the one that represents the best operation conditions and the level of service "F", the worst conditions [14]. The problem is to predict the Level of Service. The description of the dataset is shown in Table 7.

Table 7. Description of the data-set used in the experiment.

Attributes	Description
wide_road	Wide of the road in study
q_bicy	Quantity of bicycles that traffic for the road
ihmd	Intensity time of maxim demands
vel_med_rec	Half speed of journey
level_serv	Level of service of the road (A-F)

The data used for the study were been of counts carried out in different schedules in urban roads in Cuba, in the main arteries of the city of Camagüey. A sample of these data is shown in Table 8.

Table 8. Example of data-set used in the experiment.

wide_road	q_bicy	ihmd	vel_med_rec	level_serv
1.7	0	128	19.46	D
1.7	0	128	25.26	C
2.4	0	252	15.92	E
2.5	232	465	12	F
2.5	232	465	15.31	E
3.9	95	612	29.41	C
3.9	0	376	33	B

To predict service levels of a road allows the engineers to base the decisions that propose in this respect of necessities of new roads, their physical and geometric characteristics assisting at the wanted levels of service. They also allow to fix corrections in existent roads, impacting on the organization of the traffic or envelope the characteristics of the road with the objective of elevating the quality of the operational level. An experimental study for the data-set traffic is performed (Table 9).

Table 9. Results of the general classification accuracy for level of service with MLP and 1NN.

Data set	MLP		1-NN	
	PSO+RST+FUZZY	PSO+RST	PSO+RST+FUZZY	PSO+RST
Traffic	93	93	96	95

6   Conclusions

In this paper has been study a Fuzzy Similarity Measure Quality which using the approach of fuzzy relation based on Fuzzy Set Theory when it combined with MLP and KNN methods. The main contribution is the use of similarity function of Rough Set theory as a membership function. This measure computes the grade of similarity on a decision system in which the features can have discrete or continuous values.

The paper includes the calculus of the features weights by means of the optimization of this measure. The experimental study for problems of classification shows a superior performance of the k-NN and MLP algorithm when the weights are initialized using the method proposed in this work, compared to other previously reported methods to calculate the weight of features. Its application to solve a classification problem of branch of the Civil Engineering has shown satisfactory results.

References

1. Filiberto, Y., Bello, R., Caballero, Y., Larrua, R.: A method to build similarity relations into extended rough set theory. In: 10th International Conference on Intelligent Systems Design and Applications (2010)
2. Fu, X., Zhang, S., Pang, Z.: A resource limited immune approach for evolving architecture and weights of multilayer neural network. In: Tan, Y., Shi, Y., Tan, K.C. (eds.) ICSI 2010, Part I. LNCS, vol. 6145, pp. 328–337. Springer, Heidelberg (2010)
3. Adam, S., Alexios, D., Vrahatis, M.: Revisiting the problem of weight initialization for multi-layer perceptrons trained with back propagation. In: Köppen, M., et al. (eds.) ICONIP 2008, Part II. LNCS, vol. 5507, pp. 308–315. Springer, Heidelberg (2009)
4. Coello, L., Fernandez, Y., Filiberto, Y., Bello, R.: Improving the MLP learning by using a method to calculate the initial weights with the quality of similarity measure based on fuzzy sets and particle swarms. J. CyS. **19**, 309–320 (2015)
5. Filiberto, Y., Bello, R., Caballero, Y., Larrua, R.: Using PSO and RST to predict the resistant capacity of connections in composite structures. In: González, J.R., Pelta, D.A., Cruz, C., Terrazas, G., Krasnogor, N. (eds.) NICSO 2010. SCI, vol. 284, pp. 359–370. Springer, Heidelberg (2010)
6. Mitchell, T.: Machine learning. In: Science/Engineering/Math. McGraw Hill, Portland (1997)
7. Fernandez, Y., Coello, L., Filiberto, Y., Bello, R., Falco, R.: Learning similarity measures from data with fuzzy sets and particle swarms. In: 11th International Conference on Electrical Engineering, Computing Science and Automatic Control, pp. 1–6. IEEE Press, Mexico City (2014)
8. Duch, W., Grudzinski, K.: Weighting and selection features. In: Intelligent Information Systems, pp. 32–36 (1999)
9. Filiberto, Y., Bello, R., Caballero, Y., Frias, M.: An analysis about the measure quality of similarity and its applications in machine learning. In: 4th International Workshop on Knowledge Discovery, Knowledge Management and Decision Support, Mexico, pp. 130–139 (2013)
10. Zadeh, L.A.: Similarity relations and fuzzy orderings. Inf. Sci. **3**, 177–200 (1971)
11. Wang, W.: New similarity measures on fuzzy sets and on elements. Fuzzy Sets Syst. **85**, 305–309 (1997)
12. Iman, R., Davenport, J.: Approximations of the critical region of the friedman statistic. Commun. Stat. Part A Theor. Meth. **9**, 571–595 (1980)
13. Holm, S.: A simple sequentially rejective multiple test procedure. J. Stat. **6**, 65–70 (1979)
14. Cal, R., Reyes, M., Cardenas, J.: Ingenieria deTransito. Fundamentos y Aplicaciones. Felix Varela, La Habana (2013)

Fuzzy Uncertainty in Random Variable Generation: A Cumulative Membership Function Approach

Diana Giseth Pulido-López, Mabel García,
and Juan Carlos Figueroa-García$^{(\boxtimes)}$

Universidad Distrital Francisco José de Caldas, Bogotá, Colombia
diana_141991@hotmail.com, magarcar93@hotmail.com ,
jcfigueroag@udistrital.edu.co

Abstract. This paper presents a method for random variable generation based on the cumulative membership function. The proposed method uses fuzzy numbers and uniformly distributed random numbers to obtain a random variable, mainly used in simulation models.

1 Introduction and Motivation

Fuzzy sets are representations of human-like perceptions around words/concepts. It has been widely applied to fuzzy functions, optimization, differential equations etc., so its use in simulation systems/models is an open field to be covered. Many simulation problems lack of statistical data to use classical methods, and sometimes information comes from experts. This way, fuzzy sets can help to use their opinions/perceptions as primary information sources in simulation models.

Thus, we propose a method to generate fuzzy random variables with non singleton core using the cumulative membership function which is a different method than the proposed by Varón-Gaviria et al. [1] since they addressed fuzzy sets with singleton core using α-cuts. We represent randomness using uniformly random numbers and fuzzyness is defined by an expert. Its potential use in problems based on human-like information, is wide.

The paper is organized as follows: Sect. 1 is an Introductory section. Section 2 presents some basics about fuzzy sets; in Sect. 3, some concepts about random variable generation are provided. Section 4 presents an application example, and Sect. 5 presents the concluding remarks of the study.

D.G. Pulido-López—Undergraduate student at the Universidad Distrital Francisco José de Caldas, Bogotá - Colombia.

M. García—Undergraduate student at the Universidad Distrital Francisco José de Caldas, Bogotá - Colombia.

J.C. Figueroa-García—Assistant Professor at the Universidad Distrital Francisco José de Caldas, Bogotá - Colombia.

© Springer International Publishing AG 2017
J.C. Figueroa-García et al. (Eds.): WEA 2017, CCIS 742, pp. 398–407, 2017.
DOI: 10.1007/978-3-319-66963-2_36

2   Basics on Fuzzy Sets

Firstly, we establish basic notations. $\mathcal{P}(X)$ is the class of all crisp sets, and $\mathcal{F}(X)$ is the class of all fuzzy sets. A fuzzy set A is defined on an universe of discourse X and is characterized by a membership function $\mu_A(x)$ that takes values in the interval $[0,1]$, $A : X \to [0,1]$. A fuzzy set A can be represented as a set of ordered pairs of an element x and its membership degree, $\mu_A(x)$, this is $A = \{(x, \mu_A(x)) \mid x \in X\}$ where $x \in \mathcal{F}(X)$. A fuzzy number is then a convex fuzzy set defined as follows:

Definition 1 (Fuzzy Number). *Let $A \in \mathcal{G}(\mathbb{R})$ where $\mathcal{G}(\mathbb{R}) \in \mathcal{F}(\mathbb{R})$ is the class of all normal, upper semicontinuous, and fuzzy convex sets. Then, A is a Fuzzy Number (FN) iff there exists a closed interval $[a,b] \neq 0$ such that*

$$\mu_A(x) = \begin{cases} 1 & \text{for } x \in [a,b], \\ l(x) & \text{for } x \in [-\infty, a], \\ r(x) & \text{for } x \in [b, \infty] \end{cases} \tag{1}$$

where $l : (-\infty, a) \to [0,1]$ is monotonic non-decreasing, continuous from the right, and $l(x) = \emptyset$ for $x < \omega_1$, and $r : (b, \infty) \to [0,1]$ is monotonic non-increasing, continuous from the left, and $r(x) = \emptyset$ for $x > \omega_2$.

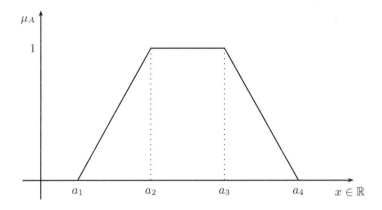

Fig. 1. Fuzzy set A

Figure 1 shows a trapezoidal fuzzy set/number with parameters a_1, a_2, a_3 and a_4. It is defined over the set $x \in \mathbb{R}$, its $supp(A)$ is the interval $x \in [\check{A}, \hat{A}]$, and $core(A) = [a_2, a_3]$.

2.1   The Cumulative Membership Function

The cumulative function $F(x)$ of a probability function $f(x)$ is:

$$F(x) = \int_{-\infty}^{x} f(t)\, dt, \tag{2}$$

where $x \in X$, $t \in X$. Its associated fuzzy definition is the following.

Definition 2 (Figueroa-García and López-Bello [2,3]). *Let $A \in \mathcal{G}(\mathbb{R})$ be a fuzzy number with shapes $l(x)$ and $r(x)$ and $c \in [a,b]$ where $\mu_A(c) = 1$. The cumulative membership function (CMF) of A namely $\psi_A(x)$ is defined as follows:*

$$\psi_A(x) = Ps_A(X \leqslant x), \tag{3}$$

$$\psi_A(x) = \int_{-\infty}^{x} \mu_A(t)\, dt. \tag{4}$$

or in a $l(x), c(x), r(x)$ decomposition:

$$\psi_A(x) = \int_{-\infty}^{x} l(t)\, dt \ , \ -\infty \leqslant t \leqslant x \ ; \ x \in [-\infty, a], \tag{5}$$

$$\psi_A(x) = \int_{-\infty}^{a} l(t)\, dt + \int_{a}^{x} c(t)\, dt, a \leqslant t \leqslant x \ ; \ x \in [a, b], \tag{6}$$

$$\psi_A(x) = \int_{-\infty}^{a} l(t)\, dt + \int_{a}^{b} c(t)\, dt + \int_{b}^{x} r(t)\, dt \ , \ b \leqslant t \leqslant x \ ; \ x \in [b, \infty]. \tag{7}$$

This definition represents the possibility that all elements of X equal or less than a x value has into a set A, $Ps_A(X \leqslant x)$[1]. Figure 2 shows the cumulative membership function $\psi_A(x)$ of a triangular fuzzy set A.

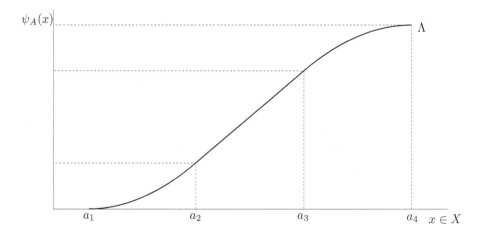

Fig. 2. Cumulative membership function $\psi_A(x)$ of A

When $\mu_A(x)$ is an integrable membership function, then $\psi_A(x)$ is a closed form, while if $\mu_A(x)$ is non-integrable, then $\psi_A(x)$ is only computable by

---

[1] This expression denotes a fuzzy measurement of an event occurs treated as the *Possibility (Ps)*.

numeric methods. Also note that $\mu_A(\infty) > 1$ is not a normalized fuzzy set, so $\sup_{x \in A} \mu_A(x) > 1$. To normalize $\psi_S(x)$ we can divide it by Λ, obtaining a normalized set called $\bar{\psi}_A(x)$:

$$\bar{\psi}_A(x) = \frac{1}{\Lambda} \int_{-\infty}^{x} \mu_A(t) \, dt. \tag{8}$$

where $\bar{\psi}_A(-\infty) = 0$ and $\sup_{x \in A} \bar{\psi}_A(\infty) = 1$.

3 Fuzzy Uncertainty in Random Variable Generation

Simulation models involving fuzzy uncertainty has been widely applied in control and dynamical systems. Fishwick [4] used fuzzy numbers in representation and simulation of qualitative models, and Hüllermeier [5] applied fuzzy sets in simulation of dynamical systems. Other fuzzy-based simulation models (Monte Carlo methods, process simulation and fuzzy variable generation) were proposed by Suresh et al. [6], Zonouz and Miremadi [7], and Huang et al. [8].

We propose to use the cumulative membership function $\psi_A(x)$ of $\mu_A(x)$ to generate fuzzy random variables whose core is an interval, such as presented in Figs. 1 and 2. Although the cumulative membership function exists for any kind of proper membership function (this is, a continuous and Borel-measurable μ_A), we propose its use in cases where $\mu_A(x)$ has non singleton core in order to obtain a proper representation, while for singleton core fuzzy numbers we recommend to use α-cuts or simpler methods.

3.1 Fuzzy Random Variable Generation Using $\psi_A(x)$

Fuzzy sets come from human like information and helps to represent words and concepts via a membership function. Basically, a fuzzy set can be also defined over similar spaces than probabilities, so we can also define a fuzzy space in order to design a method for generating fuzzy random variables.

A fuzzy space is a triplet $(\Omega, \mathcal{D}, \mu_A)$ where Ω is the universe of discourse, $\mathcal{D}$ is a set of possible events (a.k.a σ-algebra), μ_A is a membership function, and A is label/concept/word. A fuzzy random variable $X : \Omega \to \mathcal{D}$ is a measurable function $X(\omega)$ from the sample space to a σ-algebra, so if $\mathcal{D}$ is a topological space then it is called a Borel σ-algebra.

The class $\mathcal{G}(\mathbb{R})$ of fuzzy numbers includes trapezoidal, uncertain-mean gaussian, uncertain-mean exponential, etc. and it is widely used in control problems and dynamical systems, so we first extend some concepts about the area of a fuzzy number before presenting our proposal. In the probabilistic case $F(\infty) = 1$ while in the possibilistic case $1 < \psi(\infty) < \Lambda$, where Λ is a finite value defined itself as the *Total Area* of $\mu_A(x)$.

Definition 3. *Let* $\mu_A \in \mathcal{G}(\mathbb{R})$ *be a fuzzy number, then its area* Λ *is defined as follows:*

$$\Lambda = \int_{-\infty}^{\infty} \mu_A(t)\, dt, \tag{9}$$

$$\Lambda = \Lambda_1 + \Lambda_2 + \Lambda_3 = \int_{x \in \mathbb{R}} l(x)dx + \int_{x \in \mathbb{R}} c(x)dx + \int_{x \in \mathbb{R}} r(x)dx. \tag{10}$$

Definition 4. *Let* $\Lambda_1, \Lambda_2, \Lambda_3$ *be the partial areas of* $\mu_A \in \mathcal{G}(\mathbb{R})$. *Then the normalized areas* $\lambda_1, \lambda_2, \lambda_3$ *of* $\mu_A \in \mathcal{G}(\mathbb{R})$ *are defined as follows:*

$$\lambda_1 = \frac{\Lambda_1}{\Lambda}, \tag{11}$$

$$\lambda_2 = \frac{\Lambda_2}{\Lambda} = \frac{a_3 - a_2}{\Lambda}, \tag{12}$$

$$\lambda_3 = \frac{\Lambda_3}{\Lambda}, \tag{13}$$

$$\lambda_1 + \lambda_2 + \lambda_3 = 1. \tag{14}$$

Random variable generation methods mainly use $f^{-1}(x)$ or $F^{-1}(x)$ to return $X(\omega)$ using a random number $U[0,1]$ (see Devroye [9], and Law and Kelton [10]). As always, as simpler the method as easier to implement, so we propose to use $\psi_A^{-1}(x)$ and U to obtain $X(\omega)$. Our proposal uses the shape of μ_A, their partial areas Λ_1, Λ_2 and Λ_3, its cumulative membership function $\psi_A(x)$, and a uniform random number U_1 to compute $\psi_A^{-1}(x)$ whose image is a random variable $X(\omega)$.

Thus, $Y = U \cdot \Lambda$ where $0 \leqslant y \leqslant \Lambda$ where $F(Y) = \psi_A^{-1}(X)$ is invertible in closed form (or at least continuous over a Borel measurable interval), we can see that $F(Y) = \psi_A^{-1}(X) \to \{X \in F(Y)\} =$, so $\{F^{-1}(y) = U\} = F(F^{-1}(Y)) = y$. This implies that $Y \sim U[0,1] * \Lambda$ since it is the image of X over $\psi_A(x)$ which leads to $F^{-1} : Y \to X$, this is:

$$F^{-1}(y) = \inf\{\, x : F(x) = y, 0 < y < \Lambda \,\}.$$

The proposal is shown in Algorithm 1.

Algorithm 1. Cumulative membership inversion method

Require: $\mu_A \in \mathcal{G}(\mathbb{R})$ (see Eq. (1))
    Compute $\psi_A(x)$ using Definitions 2
    Compute Λ using Definition 3
    Compute $U_1[0,1]$ and $V_1 = U_1 * \Lambda$
    Compute $\psi_A^{-1}(V_1) \to X(\omega)$
    return x as the realization of $X(\omega)$

---

4   Application Examples

4.1   Trapezoidal/Gaussian Fuzzy Set

Gaussian shapes are popular due to its non linearity and similarity to normal probability distributions. However, the trapezoidal/Gaussian membership function is non-integrable, so we propose a special method to generate $X(\omega)$. A trapezoidal/Gaussian shaped membership function is shown in Fig. 3.

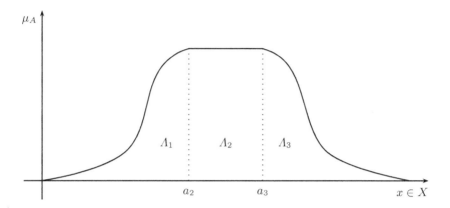

Fig. 3. Trapezoidal/Gaussian fuzzy set A.

Now, the random variable generator for a trapezoidal/Gaussian membership function (see Fig. 3) is as follows: first, we compute the partial and normalized areas Λ, λ as follows:

$$\Lambda_1 = \Lambda_3 = \sqrt{2\pi\delta^2}/2 = 2\sqrt{\pi}\delta,$$
$$\Lambda_2 = a_3 - a_2,$$
$$\Lambda = (a_3 - a_2) + \sqrt{2\pi\delta^2},$$
$$\lambda_1 = \lambda_3 = \frac{2\sqrt{\pi\delta^2}}{(a_3 - a_2) + \sqrt{2\pi\delta^2}},$$
$$\lambda_2 = \frac{(a_3 - a_2)}{(a_3 - a_2) + \sqrt{2\pi\delta^2}}.$$

Now compute $U_1[0,1]$; if $U \leqslant \lambda_1$ then compute U_{11} as follows:

$$U_{11} = U_1 \left(1 + \frac{a_3 - a_2}{\sqrt{2\pi\delta^2}} \right),$$
$$U_{11} \rightarrow N(0,1),$$
$$P(Z \leqslant z_{11}) = U_{11},$$

where z_{11} is normally distributed, and finally $x \in X(\omega)$ is:

$$x = z_{11} \cdot \delta + a_2.$$

If $\lambda_1 \leqslant U_1 \leqslant \lambda_1 + \lambda_2$, then:

$$m_1 = \frac{\lambda_2 - \lambda_1}{a_3 - a_2},$$
$$m_2 = \lambda_2 - ma_3,$$
$$U_{12} = m_1 x + m_2,$$
$$x = \frac{U_{12} - m_2}{m_1}.$$

Finally, if $\lambda_1 + \lambda_2 \leqslant U_1 \leqslant 1$ then $x \in X(\omega)$ is:

$$U_{13} = U_{11} - \lambda_2 \left(1 + \frac{a_3 - a_2}{\sqrt{2\pi\delta^2}} \right) - 0.5,$$
$$U_{13} \to N(0, 1),$$
$$P(Z \leqslant z_{13}) = U_{13},$$

where z_{13} is normally distributed, and finally $x \in X(\omega)$ is:

$$x = z_{13} \cdot \delta + a_3.$$

Example: Table 1 shows 10 simulated variables for $a_2 = 5, a_3 = 10$ and $\delta = 1$, so $\Lambda_1 = \Lambda_3 = 1.253, \Lambda_2 = 5$, and $\lambda_1 = 0.166, \lambda_2 = 0.666$ (Fig. 1).

Table 1. Simulated Gaussian variables x

U_1	V_1	x	$\mu_A(x)$
0.178	$U_{12} = 0.535$	5.088	1
0.135	$U_{11} = 0.407$	4.765	0.946
0.905	$U_{13} = 2.709$	10.566	0.725
0.159	$U_{11} = 0.478$	4.945	0.997
0.765	$U_{12} = 2.291$	9.491	1
0.173	$U_{12} = 0.521$	5.052	1
0.759	$U_{12} = 2.273$	9.446	1
0.606	$U_{12} = 1.815$	8.296	1
0.647	$U_{12} = 1.940$	8.611	1
0.105	$U_{11} = 0.315$	4.518	0.793

In Table 1, the second column shows the area for which x is computed using U_1, and $\mu_A(x)$ is the membership degree of x over the fuzzy set A.

4.2   Trapezoidal Fuzzy Set

Another popular shape is the trapezoidal fuzzy set, defined as follows (Fig. 4):

$$\mu_A = \begin{cases} \dfrac{x - a_1}{a_2 - a_1}, & \text{if } a_1 \leqslant x \leqslant a_2, \\ 1, & \text{if } a_3 \leqslant x \leqslant a_2, \\ \dfrac{a_4 - x}{a_4 - a_3}, & \text{if } a_4 \leqslant x \leqslant a_3, \\ 0, & \text{if } x \notin [a_1, a_4]. \end{cases}$$

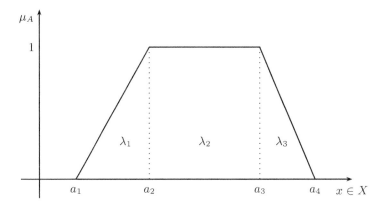

Fig. 4. Non symmetrical triangular fuzzy set A.

First, we compute the partial and normalized areas Λ, λ as follows:

$$\Lambda_1 = \frac{a_2 - a_1}{2},$$
$$\Lambda_2 = a_3 - a_2,$$
$$\Lambda_1 = \frac{a_4 - a_3}{2},$$
$$\Lambda = \frac{a_3 + a_4 - a_1 - a_2}{2},$$
$$\lambda_1 = \Lambda_1/\Lambda, \quad \lambda_2 = \Lambda_2/\Lambda, \quad \lambda_3 = \Lambda_3/\Lambda.$$

Now compute $U_1[0,1]$; if $U \leqslant \lambda_1$ then compute U_{11} and $x \in X(\omega)$ as follows:

$$U_{11} = \frac{(x - a_1)^2}{2(a_2 - a_1)\Lambda},$$
$$x = \sqrt{2(a_2 - a_1)\Lambda U_{11}} + a_1.$$

If $\lambda_1 \leqslant U_1 \leqslant \lambda_1 + \lambda_2$, then:

$$U_{12} = \frac{x - a_2}{\Lambda} + \lambda_1,$$
$$x = U_{12}\Lambda + a_2 - \lambda_1.$$

Finally, if $\lambda_1 + \lambda_2 \leqslant U_1 \leqslant 1$ then $x \in X(\omega)$ is:

$$U_{13} = \frac{2a_4x - x^2 - 2a_4a_3 + a_4^2}{2(a_4 - a_3)\Lambda} + \lambda_1 + \lambda_2,$$

$$x = a_4 - \sqrt{(a_4 - a_3)^2 - 2(a_4 - a_3)(U_{13}\Lambda - \Lambda_1 - \Lambda_2)}.$$

Example: Table 2 shows 10 simulated variables for $a_1 = 23, a_2 = 45, a_3 = 62, a_4 = 98$, so $\Lambda_1 = 11, \Lambda_2 = 17, \Lambda_3 = 18$, and $\Lambda = 46$. Note that the second column is the area for which x is computed using U_1, and $\mu_A(x)$ is the membership degree of x over the original fuzzy set A.

Table 2. Simulated Trapezoidal variables x

U_1	V_1	x	$\mu_A(x)$
0.242	$U_{12} = 11.156$	45.156	1
0.896	$U_{13} = 41.219$	79.447	0.515
0.516	$U_{12} = 23.780$	57.780	1
0.390	$U_{12} = 17.956$	51.956	1
0.510	$U_{12} = 23.473$	57.473	1
0.401	$U_{12} = 18.453$	52.453	1
0.308	$U_{12} = 14.174$	48.174	1
0.589	$U_{12} = 27.100$	61.100	1
0.496	$U_{12} = 22.829$	56.829	1
0.183	$U_{11} = 8.437$	42.268	0.875

5   Concluding Remarks

We have proposed a simple method for generating fuzzy random variables using the membership function ψ_A. Using a uniform random number, we can compute ψ_A^{-1} of a fuzzy number with interval valued core to obtain $X(\omega)$. Our proposal can be used to generate random variables coming from some of the most used fuzzy numbers such as Gaussian, trapezoidal, exponential, etc.

The presented method is intended to be computationally efficient, so it provides closed form equations for generating fuzzy random variables. Its applicability in simulation models and decision making problems where there is no any available statistical information is wide.

Finally, the presented method works for some of the most important interval valued core fuzzy numbers, and it opens the door to use experts opinions and perceptions into simulation models via fuzzy sets/numbers. Its potential use goes to cases where human-like information provides a base for decision making.

Further Topics

Random variable generation based on multi-label fuzzy sets is a challenge to be covered in simulation. Fields such as Markov processes (see Figueroa-García [11], and Figueroa-García et al. [12,13]) or Type-2 fuzzy sets (see Figueroa-García et al. [14–16]) are potential applications of fuzzy simulation.

References

1. Varón-Gaviria, C.A., Barbosa-Fontecha, J.L., Figueroa-García, J.C.: Fuzzy uncertainty in random variable generation: an α-cut approach. In: Huang, D.-S., et al. (eds.) Intelligent Computing Methodologies. LNAI, vol. 10363, pp. 264–273. Springer, Heidelberg (2017). doi:10.1007/978-3-319-63315-2_23
2. Figueroa-García, J.C., López-Bello, C.A.: Linear programming with fuzzy joint parameters: a cumulative membership function approach. In: Annual Meeting of the North American Fuzzy Information Processing Society (NAFIPS), pp. 1–6 (2008)
3. Figueroa-García, J.C., López-Bello, C.A.: Pseudo-optimal solutions of FLP problems by using the cumulative membership function. In: Annual Meeting of the North American Fuzzy Information Processing Society (NAFIPS), vol. 28, pp. 1–6 (2009)
4. Fishwick, P.A.: Fuzzy simulation: specifying and identifying qualitative models. Int. J. Gen. Syst. **19**(3), 295–316 (1991)
5. Hüllermeier, E.: A fuzzy simulation method. In: International Symposium on Soft Computing (1996)
6. Suresh, P., Babar, A., Venkat-Raj, V.: Uncertainty in fault tree analysis: a fuzzy approach. Fuzzy Sets Syst. **83**, 135–141 (1996)
7. Zonouz, S.A., Miremadi, S.G.: A fuzzy-monte carlo simulation approach for fault tree analysis. In: Annual Reliability and Maintainability Symposium, RAMS 2006, pp. 428–433, January 2006
8. Huang, Y., Chen, X., Li, Y.P., Liu, T.: A fuzzy based simulation method for modelling hydrological processes under uncertainty. Hydrol. Proces. **24**(25), 3718–3732 (2010)
9. Devroye, L.: Non-uniform Random Variate Generation. Springer, New York (1986)
10. Law, A., Kelton, D.: Simulation Modeling and Analysis. Mc Graw Hill, Boston (2000)
11. Figueroa-García, J.C.: Interval type-2 fuzzy Markov chains. In: Sadeghian, A., Mendel, J.M., Tahayori, H. (eds.) Advances in Type-2 Fuzzy Sets and Systems, vol. 301, pp. 49–64. Springer, New York (2013)
12. Figueroa-García, J.C., Kalenatic, D., Lopéz, C.A.: A simulation study on fuzzy Markov chains. Commun. Comput. Inf. Sci. **15**(1), 109–117 (2008)
13. Kalenatic, D., Figueroa-García, J.C., Lopez, C.A.: Scalarization of type-1 fuzzy Markov chains. In: Huang, D.-S., Zhao, Z., Bevilacqua, V., Figueroa, J.C. (eds.) ICIC 2010. LNCS, vol. 6215, pp. 110–117. Springer, Heidelberg (2010). doi:10.1007/978-3-642-14922-1_15
14. Figueroa-García, J.C., Chalco-Cano, Y., Román-Flores, H.: Distance measures for interval Type-2 fuzzy numbers. Discrete Appl. Math. **197**(1), 93–102 (2015)
15. Figueroa-García, J.C., Hernández-Pérez, G.J.: On the computation of the distance between interval type-2 fuzzy numbers using α-cuts. In: Annual Meeting of the North American Fuzzy Information Processing Society (NAFIPS), pp. 1–6 (2014)
16. Figueroa-García, J.C., Hernández-Pérez, G.J., Chalco-Cano, Y.: On computing the footprint of uncertainty of an interval type-2 fuzzy set as uncertainty measure. In: Figueroa-García, J.C., López-Santana, E.R., Ferro-Escobar, R. (eds.) WEA 2016. CCIS, vol. 657, pp. 247–257. Springer, Cham (2016). doi:10.1007/978-3-319-50880-1_22

Fuzzy Logic Systems for Assistance in the Anesthesiology Processes

Maria Leandra Guateque[1], Alvaro David Orjuela-Cañón[1(✉)], Wilber Acuña-Bravo[2], and Juan Jose Jaramillo[3]

[1] Universidad Antonio Nariño, Bogota, D.C., Colombia
{mguateque,alvorjuela}@uan.edu.co
[2] Universidad del Cauca, Popayan, Colombia
[3] Universidad del Rosario, Bogota, D.C., Colombia

Abstract. In the anesthesiology area, supporting for surgical interventions are relevant to make these procedures pain-free and comfortable for the patients. Nowadays, complexity in those methods can be simple, where medical doctors perform entire work, or assistance systems for making decisions in this task. The purpose of this paper is to present the comparison between the decision making in anesthesiology process given by medical personnel and a fuzzy logic system output based on the same information. Results based on Kappa index show that fuzzy system can provide information with almost perfect agreement about quantities of gas that have to be supplied to patients in anesthesiology action.

Keywords: Fuzzy logic systems · Anesthesiology process · Support decision making

1 Introduction

In Colombia, inhaled anesthesia is the most common techniques used in surgery rooms. This technique is based on the use of anesthetic substances that are provided by a mixture of gases. Nevertheless, the depth of the anesthetic state is a clinical measure, demanding neurologic monitoring for management of the medications and the waited clinical effect [1].

In this way, anesthesiology processes are important to support surgical interventions, and to make these procedures pain-free and comfortable for patients. This task can be performed using different procedures [2]. A simplest methodology consist in a manual operation, where the anesthesiologist reads physiological measures and makes a decision about the quantity of medication that have to supply for bringing the patient to a level of sleep.

For support the anesthesiologist task, a tool for monitoring the anesthetic depth was approved by the medical community. The Bispectral Index (BIS) was defined as a statistical interpretation, based on mathematical algorithm, taking information from the electroencephalography signals (EEG), giving a measure with the conscience of the patient under anesthesia [3].

© Springer International Publishing AG 2017
J.C. Figueroa-García et al. (Eds.): WEA 2017, CCIS 742, pp. 408–417, 2017.
DOI: 10.1007/978-3-319-66963-2_37

More advanced methods have developed automatic alternatives to support the work of medical personnel, as assessment of dynamic baroreflex sensitivity to monitor cardiovascular regulation under propofol anesthesia [4]. Also, identification tasks for needle insertion site in epidural anesthesia have been developed [5]. Other method, for quantifying the depth of anesthesia based on electroencephalography (EEG) signals and wavelet transform analysis was studied in [6]. Using the same kind of signals, but developing a Bayesian analysis, the assessment in the depth of anesthesia was worked in [7].

Computational intelligence (CI) approaches have shown to be useful as tools in the design of systems to classify or establish the profoundness level of anesthesia in patients. Examples of this are monitoring and alarm systems based on fuzzy logic [8], expert systems for improving clinicians performance and accurately execute repetitive tasks [9], and other proposals employing fuzzy logic and neural networks [10, 11].

In spite of the numerous technological advances, in Colombia, the area of the health systems applications based on computer and technological resources is not advanced. In this case, contributions in this field are necessary to the country development. The objective of this proposal is to present a fuzzy logic system that allows obtaining the amount of anesthesia to be supplied by the anesthesiologist in surgical procedures in the Colombian context. This decision making is developed based on information from heart pulse rate and blood pressure. Output of the system is assessed by the quantity of the exhaled gas used in the anesthesiology process.

2   Methods and Materials

Database and three systems are presented in this section. Development for each one of the fuzzy inference systems is detailed. Used validation measures to assess the performance are described, and information about Kappa index for agreement between medical and fuzzy system is also shown.

2.1   Database

The used database contains information taken from ten subjects with ages between 18 to 60 years and mean of 32 years, generated by the Colombian Cardiovascular Foundation (CCF) in Bogota, Colombia. All subjects were under the effect of sevoflurane in programmed and low complexity surgical procedures. These individuals were classified as I and II patients according with the American Society of Anesthesiologists (ASA) [12]. For this database construction, information acquisition from mean arterial pressure (MAP), heart pulse rate (HPR), and sevoflurane percentage exhaled by the patient was obtained. Each measure was captured in three-minute intervals using the display of the vital signs monitor in the surgery room.

For generalization, database was divided into two sets: one for model development and one more for validation of each system. For the development set, composed by information from five patients, modifications in the models were implemented, searching for improving the results. The validation set was used to measure the performance of the models, employing information from five different patients to the development set. Table 1 shows an example of the MAP, HPR and sevoflurane percentage exhaled values for the patient with the shortest surgical procedure.

Table 1. Values for the patient with the shortest surgical procedure.

Time (minutes)	3	6	9	12	15	18	21
MAP	54	56	54	60	58	58	62
HPR	65	66	79	83	81	85	80
Sevoflurane exhaled (%)	2.0	2.2	2.2	2.2	2.2	2.2	2.2

2.2 Fuzzy Systems Design and Implementation

For the fuzzy system development, the MAP and HPR information were taken as inputs. Also, the anesthesia output (AO), which contains information about sevoflurane exhaled by the patient, was used as output for the design and implementation of the systems. Inputs and output membership functions were adjusted according to the knowledge of the specialist from the CCF and criteria provided in previous works in this topic [8, 14].

At this stage, three fuzzy logic systems were proposed, searching to improve the results. For this, modifications in the membership functions and rules of the models were implemented with supervision of the anesthesiologist. These models are described as follows:

Fuzzy System 1
As mentioned before, information provided by the expert in anesthesia and the literature allowed to define the membership functions as trapezoidal ones. These functions were preferred because of its simpler computations and understanding of the anesthesiologist [14, 15]. Linguistic variables defined for MAP and HPR inputs, and for the AO output are presented in Table 2. Each one with five membership functions according to each physical variable.

Table 2. Membership functions for Fuzzy Systems 1 and 2.

Fuzzy System 1				Fuzzy System 2			
Linguistic variable	MAP	HPR	AO	Linguistic variable	MAP	HPR	AO
Very low	≤60	≤50	≤0	Very low	≤50	≤40	≤0
Low	60–65	50–60	0.5–1.5	Low	55–60	45–55	0.5–1
Normal	65–90	60–80	1.5–2.5	Normal	65–80	60–75	1.5–2.5
High	90–95	80–90	2.5–4	High	85–90	80–90	3–3.8
Very high	≥95	≥90	≥4	Very high	≥95	≥100	≥4
Interval	50–100	40–95	0–4.5	Interval	40–100	30–105	0–4

For inference engine, the Mamdani method was employed to implement the entire system. According with this, rules were created according with the adjustments made by the specialist, and IF - AND connectors were introduced to the system. For the consolidation of the rules were taken into account some cases not valid, which are not possible combinations, because they do not occur in reality. Finally, defuzzification was developed using centroid technique [16].

Fuzzy System 2
In this model, the MAP and HPR ranges were adjusted, as well as the number of membership functions (see Table 2). Five membership functions were settled for both MAP, HPR, and for the output. The implemented modifications were slightly different from the fuzzy system 1. Also, trapezoidal membership functions were used and Mamdani inference method was chosen and the rules were kept the same as in the fuzzy system 1. The specific case given by the rule "IF MAP is very low AND HPR is very low" was considered as invalid.

Fuzzy System 3
As mentioned, improving the results was searched. For this, modifications of the membership functions were developed. In this case, inference engine was maintained the same. The only one difference with previous systems was given when the rule related

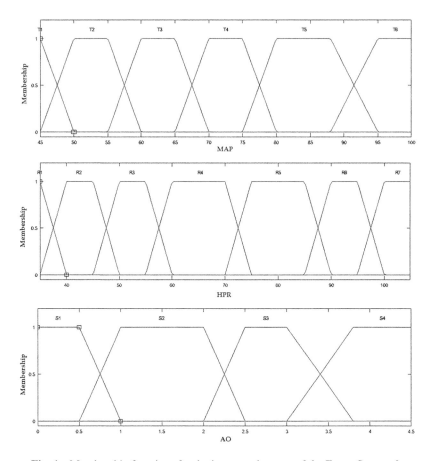

Fig. 1. Membership functions for the inputs and output of the Fuzzy System 3.

with very low for the MAP and the HPR inputs, which was defined as invalid. Figure 1 shows the membership functions for this system, and Table 3 shows the used rules for the three fuzzy systems.

Table 3. Inference engine

If - MAP	and - HPR	then - AO
Very low	Very low	Very low
Very low	Low	Low
Very low	Normal	Low
Low	Very low	Low
Low	Low	Low
Low	Normal	Normal
Normal	Very low	Low
Normal	Low	Normal
Normal	Normal	Normal
Normal	High	High
Normal	Very high	High
High	Normal	High
High	High	Very high
High	Very high	Very high
Very high	Normal	Very high
Very high	High	Very high
Very high	Very high	Very high

2.3   Validation Process

In order to measure the efficiency of each system, different proposals to compute the errors were employed: Mean Absolute Error (MAE), Mean Absolute Percent Error (MAPE) and Mean Square Error (MSE). Expressions for these measures can be seen in formulas (1) to (3):

$$MAE = \frac{1}{n} \sum_{i=1}^{n} \left| \hat{Y}_i - Y_i \right| \tag{1}$$

$$MAPE = \frac{1}{n} \sum_{i=1}^{n} \frac{\left| \hat{Y}_i - Y_i \right|}{\left| Y_i \right|} \tag{2}$$

$$MSE = \frac{1}{n} \sum_{i=1}^{n} \left(\hat{Y}_i - Y_i \right)^2 \tag{3}$$

where n is the number of samples, Y_i is the real value and $\hat{Y}_i$ is the value estimated by the fuzzy systems.

Kappa coefficient is used to measure the inter-observer variability. This is employed when there are differences between studies or approaches to specific problem. The coefficient can be interpreted according with the proportion of agreement when a multi-class classification is implemented [13]. The degree of agreement for the Kappa index is shown in Table 4.

Table 4. Degree of agreement for the Kappa index [13].

Range	Degree of agreement
<0	Less than chance agreement
0.01–0.20	Slight agree
0.21–0.40	Fair agreement
0.41–0.60	Moderate agreement
0.61–0.80	Substantial agreement
0.81–0.99	Almost perfect agreement

3   Results

Figure 2 shows the output surface map for each system. It is possible to see the dependency of AO and MAP HPR inputs. Figure 3 shows the mean and standard deviation of the MAE, MAPE and MSE errors for the development set and Fig. 4 shows the same

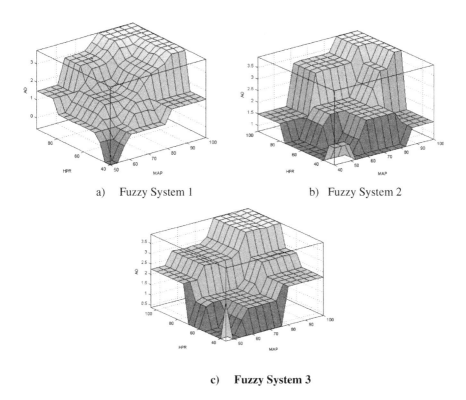

a)   Fuzzy System 1   b)   Fuzzy System 2

c)   **Fuzzy System 3**

Fig. 2. Surface map for the three fuzzy systems.

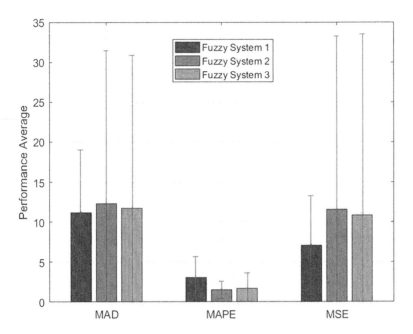

Fig. 3. Results for the implemented fuzzy systems with the development set.

information but computed for the five patients included in the validation set. Table 5 shows the results for each of the five patients used in the validation of the three fuzzy systems, according with the different error measures.

Table 5. Results for each fuzzy system

N° patient	System	MAD	MAPE	MSE
1	Fuzzy 1	5.95	0.29	1.22
	Fuzzy 2	8.85	0.84	2.70
	Fuzzy 3	**2.87**	**0.27**	**0.28**
2	**Fuzzy 1**	**1.75**	**0.14**	**0.128**
	Fuzzy 2	10.14	0.81	4.28
	Fuzzy 3	9.24	0.64	3.56
3	Fuzzy 1	9.08	1.29	4.12
	Fuzzy 2	4.25	0.81	0.90
	Fuzzy 3	**2.01**	**0.33**	**0.20**
4	Fuzzy 1	19.75	4.48	26.00
	Fuzzy 2	18.4	4.17	22.57
	Fuzzy 3	**16.43**	**3.73**	**17.99**
5	Fuzzy 1	7.21	0.186	1.27
	Fuzzy 2	**6.9**	**0.177**	**1.16**
	Fuzzy 3	12.45	0.32	3.8

According to the obtained results, the Fuzzy System 3 performed better than the other two systems (see Figs. 3 and 4). In spite of the results for the development set, where the models were in an adjusting process, it is possible to see that for validation set the fuzzy system 3 obtained the lowest errors. In this way, modifications in the membership functions allow to improve the results. Analyzing the errors for each one of the patients in the validation set, better results and a significant decreasing of the values were obtained in patients one and two when evaluating MAP and HPR entry data.

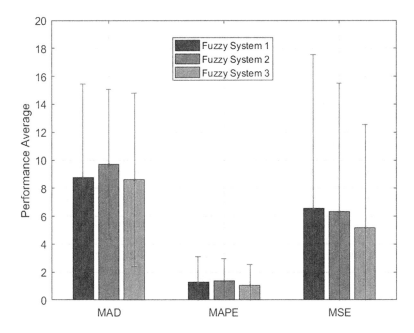

Fig. 4. Results for the implemented fuzzy systems with the validation set.

Information of the Kappa coefficient is detailed in Table 6, which it can be observed that the degree of agreement and response is almost perfect, according to Table 3 for this index [13].

Table 6. Kappa index results for the validation set

System	Index Kappa	Degree of agreement
Fuzzy System 1	1	Almost perfect
Fuzzy System 2	1	Almost perfect
Fuzzy System 3	1	Almost perfect

The total value of exhaled anesthesia against the estimated total value of exhaled anesthesia according to any of the three systems will be used as comparison parameters. In this case under the evaluation of the Kappa index the three systems show concordance with the actual total values of exhaled anesthesia, showing a degree of concordance almost perfect.

It is possible to note that high values in the standard deviation of the results were obtained. A specific example of this can be observed for patient No. 4 (see Table 4), where the highest error measures were found. About it, the specialist manifested that the patient under surgical procedure, also was treated simultaneously with medicaments to maintain the state of hypnosis. In the case, three fuzzy systems had MAD and MSE errors upper than 15, allowing to observe atypical results compared with other patients. This phenomenon was more notorious for the development set (see Fig. 3), where dispersion was major. This can explained due to adjusting process to obtain the final model for each of the fuzzy systems. Other error measures were closer values compared with the results of the other four patients used in the validation tests.

4   Conclusions

The proposed systems in this study present a better approach for the evaluation of the amount of anesthesia to be supplied, since they take into account the maximum and min - (MAP) and the amount of exhaled anesthesia, which allows the control of the doses for the maintenance of the same during the surgical operation. These measures are very useful at the time of a surgical procedure.

Thanks to the criterion of the specialist it is possible to see that the results obtained for the fuzzy systems were affected by the simultaneous use of additional medications with the sevoflurane. This can be explained due to a different physiological response of the patient. In spite of this, three proposed systems had an agreement of almost perfect performance, based on Kappa Index. This measure was useful for performance evaluation of the proposed systems and medical decision. This allowed determining a degree of agreement between the systems and current decision based only in the medical criterion.

According with used error measures, the fuzzy system 3 obtained the best results. In this case, the fuzzy system was composed by five membership function for each input and the anesthesia output and an inference engine of seventeen rules.

Acknowledgments. Authors want to thank the Universidad Antonio Nariño, under project number 2016207 with identification PI/UAN-2017-606GIBIO, Universidad del Cauca and Universidad del Rosario for the support and financial assistance in this work.

References

1. Gómez Oquendo, F.J., Casas Arroyave, F.D., Fernández, J.M., Grisales, Á.G.: Total intravenous anesthesia in a closed loop system: report of the first case in Colombia. Rev. Colomb. Anestesiol. **41**, 306–310 (2013)
2. Jaffe, R.A.: Anesthesiologist's Manual of Surgical Procedures. Lippincott Williams & Wilkins, Philadelphia (2014)
3. Li, T.-N., Li, Y.: Depth of anaesthesia monitors and the latest algorithms. Asian Pac. J. Trop. Med. **7**, 429–437 (2014)

4. Chen, Z., Purdon, P.L., Harrell, G., Pierce, E.T., Walsh, J., Brown, E.N., Barbieri, R.: Dynamic assessment of baroreflex control of heart rate during induction of propofol anesthesia using a point process method. Ann. Biomed. Eng. **39**, 260–276 (2011)
5. Yu, S., Tan, K.K., Sng, B.L., Li, S., Sia, A.T.H.: Automatic identification of needle insertion site in epidural anesthesia with a cascading classifier. Ultrasound Med. Biol. **40**, 1980–1990 (2014)
6. Zoughi, T., Boostani, R., Deypir, M.: A wavelet-based estimating depth of anesthesia. Eng. Appl. Artif. Intell. **25**, 1710–1722 (2012)
7. Nguyen-Ky, T., Wen, P.P., Li, Y.: Consciousness and depth of anesthesia assessment based on bayesian analysis of EEG signals. IEEE Trans. Biomed. Eng. **60**, 1488–1498 (2013)
8. Mirza, M., GholamHosseini, H., Harrison, M.J.: A fuzzy logic-based system for anaesthesia monitoring. In: 2010 Annual International Conference of the IEEE on Engineering in Medicine and Biology Society (EMBC), pp. 3974–3977 (2010)
9. Baig, M.M., GholamHosseini, H., Kouzani, A., Harrison, M.J.: Anaesthesia monitoring using fuzzy logic. J. Clin. Monit. Comput. **25**, 339 (2011)
10. Benzy, V.K., Jasmin, E.A.: A combined wavelet and neural network based model for classifying depth of anaesthesia. Procedia Comput. Sci. **46**, 1610–1617 (2015)
11. Shalbaf, R., Behnam, H., Sleigh, J.W., Steyn-Ross, A., Voss, L.J.: Monitoring the depth of anesthesia using entropy features and an artificial neural network. J. Neurosci. Meth. **218**, 17–24 (2013)
12. Daabiss, M.: American Society of Anaesthesiologists physical status classification. Indian J. Anaesth. **55**, 111 (2011)
13. Viera, A.J., Garrett, J.M.: Understanding interobserver agreement: the Kappa statistic. Fam. Med. **37**, 360–363 (2005)
14. Saraouglu, H.M., Şanlı, S.: A fuzzy logic-based decision support system on anesthetic depth control for helping anesthetists in surgeries. J. Med. Syst. **31**, 511–519 (2007)
15. Duch, W.: Uncertainty of data, fuzzy membership functions, and multilayer perceptrons. IEEE Trans. Neural Netw. **16**, 10–23 (2005)
16. Mamdani, E.H.: Application of fuzzy logic to approximate reasoning using linguistic synthesis. In: Proceedings of the Sixth International Symposium on Multiple-Valued Logic, pp. 196–202 (1976)

Power Systems

Control Optimization of Range Extender's Start-Stop Moment for Extended-Range Electric Vehicle

Zhao Jing-bo[✉], Liu Hai-mei, and Bei Shao-yi

School of Automotive and Traffic Engineering,
Jiangsu University of Technology, Changzhou, China
66822871@qq.com

Abstract. Range extender is the core component of E-REV, its start-stop control determines the operation modes of vehicle. This paper based on a certain type of E-REV, optimized the control strategy for range extender start-stop with different driving cycle conditions and target mileage, and conducted the modeling and co-simulation of E-REV with Advisor and Simulink software. The simulation results with chosen driving cycle conditions indicated that certain target mileage, by correcting the battery SOC of range extender start-stop moment can reduce the running time of the range extender, reached the purpose of meeting the vehicle mileage and reducing consumption and emission at the same time.

Keywords: Extended-range electric vehicle · Range extender · Start-stop time · Control strategy

1 Introduction

Recent years, in response to the global environmental pollution and energy crisis, the electric vehicle as a kind of energy saving, environmental protection car, it does not dependent on oil resources and run smoothly and quietly which has advantages of clean energy vehicles, has become the hot issue of transportation development and the key point of auto industry development. However, because the current battery technology bottlenecks, it is insufficient to provide a high specific energy and power [1], fast charging and relatively inexpensive energy storage device for pure electric vehicles (EV), thus make pure electric cars driving range not yet compete with conventional internal combustion engine vehicles, limiting its large-scale commercial promotion [2]. In this case, as a smooth transition to hybrid electric, the extended range electric vehicle (Extended-Range Electric Vehicle, E-REV) has become an important branch of the current electric cars and drawn more and more attention.

Compared with the BEV, E-REV equipped with a generator and engine with other components, it can provide auxiliary power for the vehicle which called auxiliary power unit (Auxiliary Power Unit, APU) - Range Extender [3], the car generated power, and power transfer to the gearbox entirely provided by the drive motor. As a core component of E-REV, the start-stop control for range extender determines the work mode [4]. Since the E-REV power systems use structure in series, the engine only used for power generation, and not directly output power to drive the vehicle, thus the engine can be adjusted

© Springer International Publishing AG 2017
J.C. Figueroa-García et al. (Eds.): WEA 2017, CCIS 742, pp. 421–432, 2017.
DOI: 10.1007/978-3-319-66963-2_38

in the vicinity of the optimum operating point stable operation [5], for extended-range control system optimization.

In this paper, for a certain E-REV, based on software Advisor and Simulink to get vehicle modeling and co-simulation., in the basic study on the optimal working area of constant temperature and power-following control strategy, combined with the different driving cycles condition and mileage, correcting the range extender SOC (State of Charge) value within the start and stop time of the battery, optimizing control strategy for the range extender to reduce start and stop times and running time, to meet the vehicle driving mileage and reduce fuel consumption and emissions.

2   E-REV Overview and Parameters

2.1   E-REV Structure and Working Mode

A range extender vehicle is a battery electric vehicle that includes an auxiliary power unit (APU) known as a'range extender'. The range extender drives an electric generator which charges a battery which supplies the vehicle's electric motor with electricity. This arrangement is known as a series hybrid drivetrain. The most commonly used range extenders are internal combustion engines, but fuel-cells or other engine types can be used. The key function of the range extender is to increase the vehicle's range. Range autonomy is one of the main barriers for the commercial success of electric vehicles, and extending the vehicle's range when the battery is depleted helps alleviate range anxiety.

The basic structure of a typical E-REV is shown in Fig. 1 [6]. Wherein, engines and generators connected coaxially to form extended-range system is essentially a generator set.

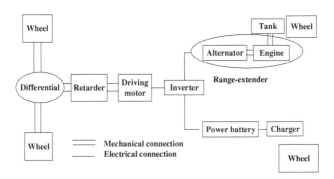

Fig. 1. Basic structure of E-REV

There is no mechanical connection between the engine and the driving wheel of the vehicle, which is only driven by the driving motor. There are two main modes of working mode, which is pure electric mode and extended-range mode shown in Figs. 2 and 3.

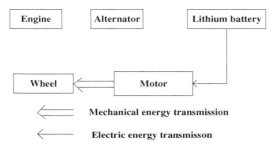

Fig. 2. Pure electric mode

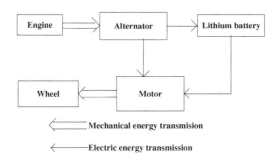

Fig. 3. Extended-range mode

For the pure electric mode, when the battery is fully charged, it provides energy to the drive motor, the motor will transfer electric power into mechanical energy to drive cars, this is equivalent to a pure electric car [7, 8]. The energy transfer method and direction as shown in Fig. 2.

For the extended-range mode, when the battery power is consumed to a certain extent (or the driver has request to start the extended-range), start the process of the range extender system, generate energy to drive the vehicle. In this case, the engine is running to drive generator, part to drive motor to provide energy, making the car continued to running; another part of the power to charge the battery for maintaining its capacity in a range of values, thus it is equivalent to a hybrid vehicle [7, 8]. Its energy transfer and direction is shown in Fig. 3.

A range extending vehicle design can also reduce the consumption of the range extending fuel (such as gasoline) by using the primary fuel (such as battery power), while still maintaining the driving range of a single fuel vehicle powered by a range extending fuel such as gasoline. The range extending fuel is generally considered to be less environmentally and economically friendly to use than the primary fuel source, so the vehicle control system gives preference to using the primary fuel if it's available. However, due to range limitations with the primary fuel source, the range extending fuel allows the vehicle to get many of the cost and environmental benefits of the primary fuel, while maintaining the full driving range of the range extending fuel source.

2.2 E-REV Parameters

As an E-REV is only propelled by the electric motor it can do away with the weight and cost associated with the gearbox transmission system typically used in internal combustion engine cars. Further, as the range extender does not need to increase or decrease output in line with the power needs of the vehicle (this task is handled by the electric motor) the range extender can be sized to satisfy the vehicle's average power requirement rather than its peak power requirement (such as when accelerating).

In this paper, an example of a certain type of electric vehicle in the laboratory is selected, and the basic parameters of the selected vehicle are as shown in Table 1.

Table 1. Model parameters (Basic parameters)

Parameter name	Value
Vehicle length, width, height/mm	$4498 \times 1798 \times 1430$
Axis number	2
Driving form	4×2 FW
Curb weight m1/Kg	1715
Full load mass m/Kg	2015
Wheel radius r/m	0.314
Windward area A/m^2	2.0
Drag coefficient C_D	0.29

The range extender can also operate much closer to its most efficient rotational speed. These design features allow an REEV to convert fossil fuel energy to electric power and vehicle motion very efficiently. When the basic parameters of the vehicle are determined, the design of performance index is shown in Table 2.

Table 2. Performance indicators (Performance parameter)

Parameter name	Value
Maximum speed Vmax/km/h	161
0–100 km/h Acceleration time t_a/s	9
30 km/h climbing gradient α_{max}/%	≥ 30
Pure electric driving range d_1/km	≥ 60
Total mileage d/km	≥ 500

According to 2012 Amendments to the Zero Emission Vehicle Regulations adopted in March 2012 by the California Air Resources Board (CARB), a range-extended electric vehicle should comply, among others, with the following criteria:

The vehicle must have a rated all-electric range, this is higher than the 80 km (50 miles) required of a zero-emission vehicle; The auxiliary power unit (APU) must provide range less than or equal to battery range; The APU must not be capable of switching on until the battery charge has been depleted; The vehicle must meet super ultra low emission vehicle (SULEV) requirements; and the APU and all associated fuel systems must comply with zero evaporative emissions requirements. The parameters of the different power system of E-REV are shown in Table 3.

Table 3. Parameters of power system component

Parameter type	Value
Parameter's type (the following)	Permanent magnet synchronous
Rated power (kw)/Rated speed (r/min)	45/4000
Peak power (kw)/Maximum speed (r/min)	75/9000
Rated torque (N.m)	150
Peak torque (N.m)	240
Rated voltage (V)	300
Power battery type	Lithium iron phosphate
Capacity (A.h)	60
Rated voltage (V)	288
SOC range (%)	30–90
Range-Extender's engine type (the following)	Inline four cylinder
Displacement (L)	1.3
Rated power (kw)/Rated speed (r/min)	38/3500
Peak power (kw)/Maximum speed (r/min)	55/6000
Maximum torque (N.m)/speed (r/min)	130/4250
Range-Extender's generator type (the following)	Permanent magnet synchronous
Rated power (kw)/Rated speed (r/min)	35/4000
Peak power (kw)/Maximum speed (r/min)	60/9000

3   E-REV Control Strategy

3.1   E-REV Energy Management Strategy

The energy management strategy of E-REV can be divided into Depleting Charge period and Charge Sustaining period. During the charge depleting period, the vehicle vehicles rely only on the power of battery, equivalent to pure electric driving, during charge sustaining period, the extender system began to start and power generation vehicle mainly rely on electricity to drive the car [9]. According to the upper and lower threshold SOC of power battery, based on rules of logic threshold switching control strategy to achieve a smooth transition of two period.

In order to ensure the drive motor within normal working voltage, while ensuring the performance of the power battery and prolong the life. In this paper, the SOC is set to 90%–30%.

3.2   Constant Temperature and Power-Following Control Strategy

Constant temperature and power following control strategy is based on the principle of battery SOC threshold and vehicle power requirements which determine the range extender on and off [3, 10]. When the battery SOC reaches the upper threshold, the range extender closed, the generator stops, automotive is under pure electric driving mode and the SOC decreased; when the battery SOC falls below the down threshold, the range extender is on, the generator starts generating to provide power, and the engine always working at high efficiency economic zone, the output power is constant. In this case, the output power priority required for the actual working conditions, if it is higher than the vehicle demand power, the excess will be used to charge the battery; if it is lower than the vehicle demand power, the insufficient part will be provided by battery power.

3.3   Selection of Engine Operating Points

The internal combustion engine in an E-REV cannot drive the wheels; it's sole purpose is to recharge the car's batteries when required. Figure 4 is the curve of engine equivalent fuel consumption rate. E-REV uses tandem type power system, there is no mechanical connection between the engine and the transmission system, the engine output is disconnected with the ground load, and always working in low fuel consumption and low load, in the high fuel economy area. using direct start-stop technology to cancel the engine idle controlling, so that the engine starting work in the speed and torque respectively 3500 r/min and 50 N.m with constant speed and constant torque condition [11] (Fig. 4 point), improving the efficiency of the engine, also reducing exhaust emissions.

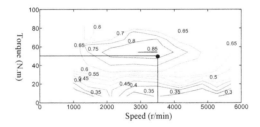

Fig. 4.   Engines equivalent fuel consumption curves

Engine power can be calculated at this time the engine output is constant power 18.3 kW, It can meet the power demand of two driving conditions of the city streets and urban and highway combination.

4   E-REV Control Strategy Optimization

4.1   Prior to Optimize Control Strategies Pure Electric Mileage Sare

Cars with electric driving mode can maximize the use of battery energy from the grid, greatly improving the economic and emissions. For the study of the car in the process of daily driving of pure electric vehicle mileage Sare (developed) range, based on the E-REV vehicle model (Fig. 5) provided in advisor, respectively in NEDC, UDDS and CUDC three typical driving cycle are simulated and calculated.

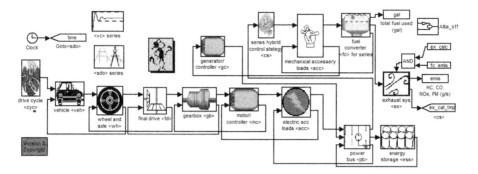

Fig. 5. Model of E-REV

The cycle must be performed on a cold vehicle at 20–30 °C. The cycles may be performed on a flat road, in the absence of wind. However, to improve repeatability, they are generally performed on a roller test bench. This type of bench is equipped with an electrical machine to emulate resistance due to aerodynamic drag and vehicle mass (inertia).

For each vehicle configuration, a look-up table is applied: each speed corresponds to a certain value of resistance (reverse torque applied to the drive wheels). This arrangement enables the use of a single physical vehicle to test all vehicle body styles (Sedan, hatchback, MPV etc.) by simply changing the look-up table. A fan is coupled to the roller bench to provide the vehicle air intakes with an airflow matching the current speed. Many more tests can be performed during vehicle development with this arrangement than with conventional road tests.

The test is conducted with all ancillary loads turned off (Air conditioning compressor and fan, lights, heated rear window, etc.). The relationship between the SOC value of the battery and the mileage of the vehicle under different driving cycles is shown in Fig. 6.

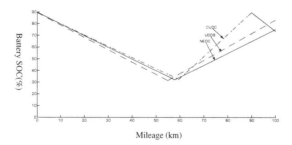

Mileage (km)

Fig. 6. Relationship between SOC and mileage with different cycle conditions

As is shown in Fig. 6, in three different driving cycles, battery SOC value with the vehicle mileage increases continuously decline, before dropping to the 30% threshold, the range-extender is off, it indicated that the car meet various driving cycles of power demand in the period. Due to the different conditions of driving cycle, the power for vehicle's demand Preq are different, the battery SOC change rate is not the same, so the pure electric driving mileage Sare is different.

According to statistics from China's Ministry of Transportation, it shows that the average daily mileage is less than 60 km. Therefore, E-REV basically rely on its own battery power energy to meet the daily needs of people to work and travel without starting the range extender system.

4.2 Optimization of the Control Strategy of the Range- Extender Starting and Stopping Time

By making the petrol engine subservient to the electric motor's needs, as opposed to the other way around, an E-REV is closer conceptually to a pure electric vehicle than other hybrids. When the E-REV target distance D (the mileage adjacent to the two external charging) is greater than that of the pure electric vehicle mileage Sare, target distance will affect the range-extender start-stop times and running time, thus has impact on the vehicle's fuel economy [9], in order to reduce the start-stop times and running time, it should make full use of battery energy. Therefore, when the E-REV is having long-distance travel, it should be reasonable for start-stop time for the range-extender.

According to the original control strategy, the relationship between the SOC value of the battery and the working state of the range-extender with the mileage is shown in Fig. 7.

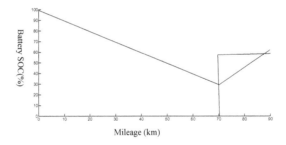

Fig. 7. Change of the SOC (original control strategy)

In initial stage, the vehicle is maintaining pure electric mode, when battery state of charge (SOC) down to the lower threshold value, start the range-extender and enter the road charging mode until the battery state of charge (SOC) reaching the upper threshold, then the range-extender closed.

To shorten the range extender running time, two methods can be used to optimize the original control strategy [11]. In pure electric driving mode, when the SOC value falls to O point, start the system in advance, the simulation results shown in Fig. 8. In the charging mode, when the SOC value is increased to point C, range-extender is stopped in advance and the simulation results as shown in Fig. 9.

In conjunction with Figs. 8 and 9, when the target distance is constant, these two optimization methods for start and stop time can be shortened range extender running time and the range extender power can just to run out before the next external charge.

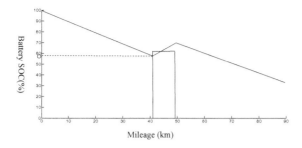

Fig. 8. Change of the SOC (start range extender in advance)

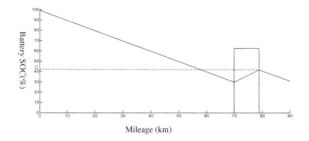

Fig. 9. Change of the SOC (stop range extender in advance)

The optimization strategy can make full use of battery energy, shortening range extender running time, reduce fuel consumption and cost savings.

When the engine is working in a particular point with a constant power output, the difference between the initial value of the battery SOC, the length of the target mileage, driving cycle conditions and other factors will affect the battery SOC decreasing speed, resulting in different start and stop times for range extender and different running time. Therefore, a combination of different driving cycle conditions is needed, to determine the range extender start and stop time.

The initial battery SOC value is set to 90%, with parameters k1, k2, k3 respectively SOC s is dropped to 30%; starting rage extenders SOC charged from 30% to 70%; Close range extenders after SOC decreased from 70% to 30% during the third mileage capacity ratio [4]. According to results of simulation on three previous typical driving cycle conditions, the parameters k1, k2, k3 values are shown in Table 4.

Table 4. Mileage capacity ratio with different cycle condition

Cycle condition	Mileage capacity ratio		
	k1	k2	k3
NEDC	0.88	0.76	0.79
UDDS	1.05	0.68	0.94
CUDC	1.08	0.44	1.06

In pure electric driving with starting the range-extender in advance, the target distance D is obtained when the range extender to start in advance. During the charging process, stop the range-extender in advance. Based on the numerical value of Table 4, the SOC of the starting and stopping time of the range-extender with different cycle conditions can be modified.

4.3 Comparison of Simulation Results Before and After Control Strategy Optimization

To verify the effectiveness of the optimized control strategy, importing the vehicle model established in Advisor/Simulink, selecting the NEDC and UDDS two cycle conditions are simulated, battery SOCs value is set 90% and target D values of mileage is 100 km.

NEDC conditions SOC RE_on and SOC RE_off were 39.4% and 60.5%, and the simulation results shown in Fig. 10. By Fig. 10, under the NEDC cycle condition target mileage is 100 km, according to the original control strategy (Fig. 10a), the range-extender is running 2879 s, after optimize control strategy, during pure electric vehicle driving (Fig. 10b), open the range-extender in advance, the total running time is 1802 s,

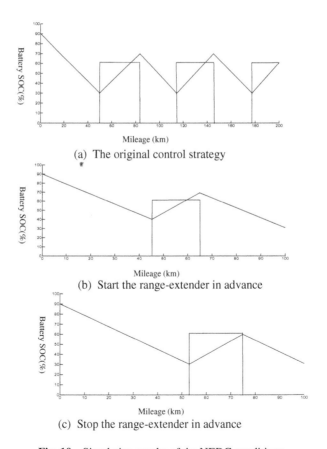

(a) The original control strategy

(b) Start the range-extender in advance

(c) Stop the range-extender in advance

Fig. 10. Simulation results of the NEDC conditions.

during driving charge period (Fig. 10c), shut down the range-extender in advance, accumulating the run time is 2070 s, that's reduced by 37.4% and 28.1% respectively.

UDDS conditions SOC RE_on and SOC RE_off were 46.1% and 51.3%, and the simulation results shown in Fig. 11. By Fig. 11, under the UDDC cycle condition target mileage is 100 km, according to the original control strategy (Fig. 11a), the range-extender is running 2557 s, after optimize control strategy, during pure electric vehicle driving (Fig. 11b), open the range-extender in advance, the total running time is 1515 s, during driving charge period (Fig. 11c), shut down the range-extender in advance, accumulating the run time is 1705 s, that's reduced by 40.7% and 33.4% respectively.

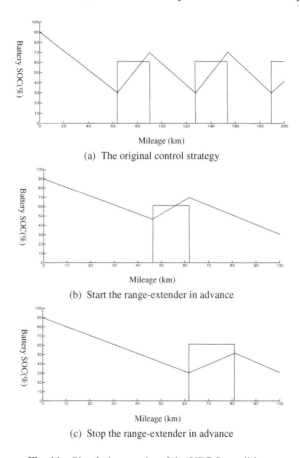

(a) The original control strategy

(b) Start the range-extender in advance

(c) Stop the range-extender in advance

Fig. 11. Simulation results of the UDDS conditions.

According to Figs. 10 and 11, after optimize the control strategy, the running time of two cycles conditions are significantly reduced while reaching the target mileage, besides the power that charged into the battery can basically run out, making full use of the energy of the battery at the same time also ensuring that the car charging power through the outer supply to prepare for the next driving.

5   Conclusions

The range-extender electric vehicle technology has been generally recognized by the industry, the E-REV's start-stop control determines the mode of the car. Using the two methods that during pure electric driving start and stop the range extender in advance to reduce the running time when the target mileage is constant, and correcting the value of the battery SOC to precisely control the start and stop time.

Selecting and simulating two kinds of driving cycle conditions, simulation results show the effectiveness of the control strategy after optimization, while meeting the mileage it can shorten the range-extender running time, improving fuel economy and reducing emissions.

Acknowledgment. Funding from the National Natural Science Foundation of China (Grant No: 61503163), the "333 project" of Jiangsu Province (Grant No: BRA2016440) and the six talent peaks project in Jiangsu Province (Grant No: ZBZZ-024) are gratefully acknowledged.

References

1. Krenek, T., Lauer, T., Geringer, B.: On-board powerplant numerical optimization of internal combustion engines in series hybrid- powertrains. In: Proceedings of the FISITA 2012 World Automotive Congress, pp. 573–584 (2013)
2. Chin, P.F., Miller, J.M., Lehmen, A.J.: Method and apparatus for executing a clutch-driven engine autostart operation. US8956265 (2015)
3. Sah, J.J.F., Heap, A.H., Kaminsky, L.A.: Method and apparatus for controlling an engine disconnect clutch in a powertrain system. US 8989930B2 (2015)
4. Hu, J., Yang, Z., Zhao, J.: Torque control method of the motor drive system in electric vehicle. Adv. Inf. Sci. Serv. Sci. **5**, 1142–1148 (2013)
5. Tate, E.D., Harpster, M.O., Savagian, P.J.: The electrification of the automobile: from conventional hybrid, to plug-in hybrids, to extended-range electric vehicles. SAE Paper, 2008-01-0458 (2008)
6. Zhu, X., Zhang, H., Cao, D.: Robust control of integrated motor-transmission powertrain system over controller area network for automotive applications. Mech. Syst. Sig. Process. **s58–s59**, 15–28 (2015)
7. Zhu, X., Zhang, H., Fang, Z.: Speed synchronization control for integrated automotive motor–transmission powertrain system with random delays. Mech. Syst. Sig. Process. **s64–s65**, 46–57 (2015)
8. Budde-Meiwes, H., Drillkens, J., Lunz, B.: A review of current automotive battery technology and future prospects. Proc. Inst. Mech. Eng. Part D J. Automobile Eng. **5**, 61–776 (2013)
9. Rahman, K., Jurkovic, S., Stancu, C.: Design and performance of electrical propulsion system of extended range electric vehicle (EREV) Chevrolet Voltec. In: Energy Conversion Congress and Exposition, pp. 4152–4159 (2012)
10. Rahman, K.M., Jurkovic, S., Stancu, C.: Design and performance of electrical propulsion system of extended range electric vehicle (EREV) Chevrolet Volt. IEEE Trans. Ind. Appl. **3**, 2479–2488 (2015)
11. Sciarretta, A., Serrao, L., Dewangan, P.C.: A control benchmark on the energy management of a plug-in hybrid electric vehicle. Control Eng. Pract. **6**, 287–298 (2014)

Design and Analytical Studies of a DLC Thin-Film Piezoresistive Pressure Microsensor

Luiz Antonio Rasia[1] ⓘ, Gabriela Leal[2] ⓘ,
Leandro Léo Koberstein[3] ⓘ, Humber Furlan[4] ⓘ, Marcos Massi[5] ⓘ,
and Mariana Amorim Fraga[6(✉)] ⓘ

[1] Universidade Regional do Noroeste do Estado do Rio Grande do Sul,
Ijuí, Brazil
rasia@unijui.edu.br
[2] Universidade Federal de São Paulo, São José dos Campos, Brazil
gabriela.leal@unifesp.br
[3] Faculdade de Tecnologia de São José dos Campos,
São José dos Campos, Brazil
lleok@uol.com.br
[4] Faculdade de Tecnologia de São Paulo, São Paulo, Brazil
humber@fatecsp.br
[5] Universidade Presbiteriana Mackenzie, São Paulo, Brazil
massi.marcos@gmail.com
[6] Universidade Brasil, São Paulo, Brazil
mafraga@ieee.org

Abstract. Diamond-like carbon (DLC) thin films have been investigated for a wide range of applications due to their excellent electrical and mechanical properties. In the last decade, several researches and development activities have been conducted on the use of these thin films as piezoresistors in MEMS pressure sensors. This paper provides an overview on the design of a piezoresistive pressure sensor constituted of a silicon circular diaphragm with four DLC thin-film piezoresistors arranged in the Wheatstone bridge configuration. The sensor was designed from analytical formulas found in the literature.

Keywords: Piezoresistive pressure sensor · Diamond-like carbon (DLC) · Design · Analytical solution

1 Introduction

Piezoresistive semiconductor sensors based on micro-electro-mechanical systems (MEMS) technology have superior performance compared to many conventional sensors in terms of sensitivity, stability, resolution and size. However, harsh-environment sensing measurements have some significant technical challenges to overcome; among them is the development of stable and functional materials to withstand extreme temperatures and corrosive media [1]. In these hard conditions, traditional semiconductor sensors typically exhibit low performance, which is mainly associated to their material properties and packaging technology [2].

© Springer International Publishing AG 2017
J.C. Figueroa-García et al. (Eds.): WEA 2017, CCIS 742, pp. 433–443, 2017.
DOI: 10.1007/978-3-319-66963-2_39

Silicon is the most common semiconductor material used in MEMS piezoresistive sensors. These devices due to physical and electronic properties of the silicon, such as small bandgap energy (1.12 eV), have application limited in harsh environments, particularly at high temperatures. The literature shows that at higher temperatures silicon undergoes creep under minimal load which makes it unsuitable for sensor applications. In addition, it has relatively low values for its Young's modulus, hardness and its fracture toughness [1, 3].

The factors mentioned above have motivated studies on synthesis and processing of different material types (semiconductors, polymers and metals) to replace the silicon in MEMS, especially as sensing material. Carbon-based materials, such as diamond, diamond-like carbon (DLC) and silicon carbide (SiC), are recognized as the promising materials because they possess excellent physical properties that silicon and other materials lack. The excellent electrical, mechanical and thermal properties of carbon-based materials made them an obvious choice for microelectronics device and MEMS sensor applications. These materials exhibit very high Young's modulus, high tensile and fracture strength associated to good piezoresistive properties [4].

The focus of this paper is on the use of DLC thin films as piezoresistive sensing materials. Piezoresistive effect has been shown fundamental in MEMS sensing. The sensitivity of the sensors based in this effect is known as gauge factor (GF) and is defined by:

$$GF = \frac{\Delta R/R}{\varepsilon} \tag{1}$$

Where $\Delta R/R$ is the normalized resistance variation; ε is the mechanical strain.
The electrical resistance R can be written as:

$$R = \frac{\rho.L}{A} \tag{2}$$

where ρ is the electrical resistivity t of the material; L and A are geometric parameters of the resistor (length and the cross-sectional, respectively). This equation can also be written as:

$$R = \frac{\rho.L}{wt} \tag{3}$$

where w is the width and t is the thickness of the resistor.
Based on the orientation of the resistor, the gauge factors can be divided into longitudinal (GF_L) and transverse gauge (GF_T) factors as follows:

$$GF = \frac{\Delta R_L/R}{\varepsilon_L} \tag{4}$$

$$GF = \frac{\Delta R_T/R}{\varepsilon_T} \tag{5}$$

where ΔR_L and ΔR_T are the changes in resistance when the resistors are placed longitudinally and transversely to the applied strain, respectively. The component of strain in the longitudinal direction (ε_L) can be expressed as ratio of change in length to the initial length:

$$\varepsilon_L = \frac{\Delta L}{L} \tag{6}$$

Hooke's law relates the strain longitudinal to the stress (σ) as follows:

$$\sigma = E\varepsilon_L \tag{7}$$

where E is the Young's modulus or the modulus of elasticity of the material.

The transverse strain (ε_T) is proportional to the longitudinal strain (ε_L) within the range of Hooke's law. Hence, the negative ratio of these components is called Poisson's ratio (ν) and can be written as:

$$\nu = -\frac{\varepsilon_T}{\varepsilon_L} \tag{8}$$

Differentiating Eq. (3):

$$\frac{\partial R}{R} = \frac{\partial \rho}{\rho} + \frac{\partial L}{L} - \frac{\partial w}{w} - \frac{\partial t}{t} \tag{9}$$

Therefore, the resistance changes can also be expressed, in two directions when longitudinal and transverse strain is applied respectively as:

$$\frac{\partial R_L}{R} = \frac{\partial \rho}{\rho} + \varepsilon_L + \nu\varepsilon_L + \nu\varepsilon_L = \frac{\partial \rho}{\rho} + (1 + 2\nu).\varepsilon_L \tag{10}$$

$$\frac{\partial R_T}{R} = \frac{\partial \rho}{\rho} - \nu\varepsilon_T - \varepsilon_T + \nu\varepsilon_T = \frac{\partial \rho}{\rho} - \varepsilon_T \tag{11}$$

The choice of a piezoresistive material to develop the piezoresistive sensor is based on the desirable characteristics of the device, such as sensitivity (gauge factor value), nominal electrical resistance, thermal coefficient of resistance (TCR), temperature coefficient of gauge factor (TCGF) and stability.

1.1   Properties of DLC Thin Films

The three possible carbon hybridizations (sp^1, sp^2 and sp^3), which are shown in Fig. 1, make carbon unique due to its various allotropes. Diamond is one of its allotropes and has only sp^3 bond hybridizations. Because of its atomic arrangement, diamond presents high hardness, high electrical resistivity and low wear rate among other properties. Meanwhile the graphite that has only sp^2 bond hybridization presents low hardness, low electrical resistivity and high wear rate [5]. Diamond-like carbon (DLC) is another carbon allotrope that presents both hybridizations: sp^3 and sp^2. This configuration gives the DLC unique properties, merged between diamond and graphite properties, such as high mechanical hardness, chemical inertness, optical transparency and wide band gap [6]. Table 1 compares the properties of DLC and diamond.

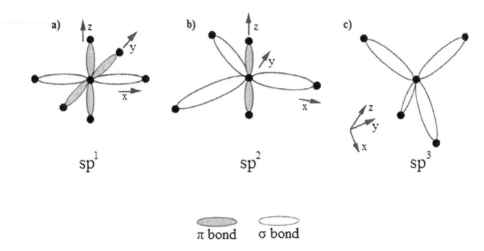

Fig. 1. Schematic representation of carbon hybridizations: (a) sp^1, (b) sp^2 and (c) sp^3 (adapted from [7])

According to Robertson the sp^1 configuration consists in two of the four electrons forming σ bond along x axis and the other two electrons lies in a $p\pi$ orbital in y and z directions [6]. While in sp^2 three of four electron form σ bonds in a plane and the fourth electron lies in a $p\pi$-orbital and in sp^3 each of four electrons form a strong σ bond to adjacent in a tetrahedral configuration. The extreme physical properties of diamond come from its strong directional σ bonds. Thus, the physical properties of DLC depend on the quantity of sp^2 and sp^3 bonds presents in this material.

In Table 1 it can be observed the major properties of amorphous carbon and other carbon materials compared with the quantity of sp^3 bond and hydrogen. The term DLC was used for the first time in 1971 by Aisenberg and Chabot [9], but a variety of names has been used to differentiate the types of DLC. The term a-C is used to all of amorphous carbon materials with a medium portion (40–60%) of sp3 bonds while ta-C term (tetrahedral carbon) is used to carbon materials with high sp3 concentration (more than 70%). The prefix :H is used to indicate that the material is hydrogenated while hydrogen free DLC don't receive this prefix. Some authors choose the use of a-C and ta-C rather than DLC or even the use of other variations as TAC (tetrahedral amorphous carbon) and others [7].

Therefore, as mentioned previously, the properties of DLC depend largely on the amount of sp^2 and sp^3 bonds and of the hydrogen content in the material, being that the mechanical properties depend on these three factors, except the elastic modulus and

Table 1. Summary of the properties of DLC and diamond (adapted from [8]).

Properties	DLC	Diamond
Structural	Amorphous (mixture of sp^2 (graphite) and sp^3 (diamond)	Cubic structure
Physical	• Low thermal expansion coefficient • Thermal conductivity at room temperature (100–700 W m^{-1} K^{-1}) • Dielectric constant (3.0–6.0)	• High melting point (~ 4000 °C) • Low thermal expansion coefficient at room temperature (1×10^{-6} K^{-1}) • High thermal conductivity at room temperature (2000 W m^{-1} K^{-1}) • Low dielectric constant (5.7)
Electronic	• Bandgap (0.8–4.0 eV) • Wide range of electrical resistivities (10^2–10^{12} Ω.cm) • High electric breakdown field (>2.5 MV/cm)	• Wide bandgap (5.45 eV, indirect gap) • High electrical resistivity (10^{13}–10^{16} Ω.cm) • High saturated electron velocity (2.7×10^7 cm/s) • High electric breakdown field (10 MV/cm)
Mechanical	• Hardness (40–60 GPa) • High Young's modulus (200–750 GPa) • Excellent tribological properties • Potential solid lubricant coating	• High hardness (~ 90 GPa) and wear resistance • High Young's modulus (~ 1050 GPa) • High strength/ tensile • (>1.2 GPa) • Low compressibility • (8.3×10^{-3} m^2 N^{-1})
Optical	• High refractive index (1.8–3.0) • Low reflectance • Anti-reflective and scratch resistant coatings for IR optics	• High refractive index (2.41) • Optical transparency • (UV to far IR) • Highly resistant to damage from irradiation
Chemical	• Chemical inertness • Excellent coating material for medical implants	• High resistance to corrosion • Chemically and biologically inert

hardness that depend only on the sp^3 bonds. Meanwhile the electronic properties depend on the fraction and configuration of sp^2 bonds.

According to Takeno et al., although DLC has attractive mechanical properties in order to use this material in sensors, it is necessary to improve its electrical functionality control by light element or metal doping [10]. Characteristics such as electrical resistivity and TCR can be improved by the addition of metal in DLC matrix, forming Me-DLC films [11, 12].

It is known that a wide range of properties can be achieved by varying the synthesis process of DLC. However, DLC is always a thin film, not a bulk [13]. In your paper, Robertson explains that DLC occurs by deposition from energetic ion beams of carbon ions, created by the graphite sputtering or by the formation of an arc from a graphite target, or of hydrocarbon ions created by a discharge or plasma formed in a hydro-carbon gas or by sputtering graphite in hydrogen-containing atmosphere [13].

Currently, PVD (Physical Vapor Deposition) and CVD (Chemical Vapor Deposition) processes are the most used to deposit DLC films. Magnetron sputtering and cathodic vacuum arc are most used PVD techniques. In these techniques, physical processes (ionic impingement on a target and evaporation, respectively) are responsible for the atoms transfer from the source to the substrate [14]. While that, PECVD is the main CVD technique. In this process, the reaction between the precursor gases is stimulated or activated by the plasma [15].

1.2   Piezoresistive Sensors Based on DLC Thin Films

According to Takeno et al. the strain dependence of normalized resistance can be defined by [10]:

$$\frac{\Delta R}{R} = K.\varepsilon \tag{12}$$

Where ΔR is the difference between the resistance with an applied strain and the resistance without strain, ε is strain and k is the gauge factor which can be expressed as:

$$K = 1 + 2\sigma + \pi E \tag{13}$$

Where σ is Poisson ratio, E is Young's module and π is piezoresistive coefficient. Since in metals the effect for the variation of resistance against the strain is small, its piezoresistive coefficient is close to zero, because that they exhibit low GF values (generally between 2 and 4) [16]. However, semiconductor materials present a strong variation in resistivity following a deflection, which result in a gauge factor generally higher than metals [17].

In 1999, Luethje and Brand observed the piezoresistive properties of DLC and Me-DLC thin films [18]. In 2006, Peiner et al. reported for the first time a study of piezoresistive properties of amorphous carbon strain gauges integrated in a silicon cantilever. The gauge factor of a-C films was determined by deflecting the cantilever and measuring the resistance change at compressive and tensile strains as well as under longitudinal and transversal conditions. They concluded that a-C films, besides having favorable mechanical properties, also showed a large piezoresistive effect with the gauge factor varying from 37 to 46 [19]. In the same year, a study comparing the piezoresistive properties among the aforementioned a-C film with an a-C:H thin film deposited by PECVD was reported by Tibrewala et al. [20]. The GF measurements of the a-C:H films were conducted using a test structure based on a silicon boss mem-brane. It was obtained GF values from 100 to 1200. Fraga et al. have found a GF around 70 for sputtered DLC films [21].

2 Design and Analytical Studies of the Pressure Sensor

The purpose is developing a piezoresistive pressure sensor constituted of a circular monocrystaline silicon diaphragm with four DLC thin-film piezoresistors arranged in the Wheatstone bridge configuration as shows Fig. 2. This layout allows using the benefits of DLC as sensing elements associated to well-known silicon microfabrication technologies to form the diaphragm by deep plasma etching. The sensor structure will be fully to design by analytical solution.

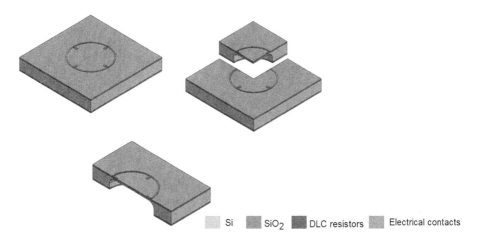

Si   SiO$_2$ DLC resistors   Electrical contacts

Fig. 2. Schematic representation of the pressure sensor

Kanda and Yasukawa demonstrated that the maximum stress of the square diaphragm is 1.64 times as large as that of the circular diaphragm when their diaphragm thickness is the same, i.e. the square diaphragm exhibits better characteristics that a circular [22]. However, from the fabrication viewpoint, the progress in plasma etching technology of silicon has become the circular diaphragm attractive to replace KOH etching.

2.1 Silicon Circular Diaphragm

Thin plate or small deflection theory is often used, and is appropriate for deflections less than 1/5 of the diaphragm thickness [3]. The maximum deflection, w_{max}, of a clamped circular plate under a uniform applied pressure is given by:

$$w_{max} = \frac{3}{16} \frac{(1-v)^2 p r^4}{E t^3} \tag{14}$$

Where E is Young's modulus, U is Poison's ratio, p is the applied pressure, r and t are, respectively, the ratio and the thickness of the circular plate. The small deflection theory determines that:

$$w_{max} \leq \frac{1}{5}t \qquad (15)$$

Substituting the Eq. (14) in (15):

$$\left(\frac{r}{t}\right)^4 \leq \frac{16E}{15p(1 - v^2)} \qquad (16)$$

The material of the diaphragm was considered to be silicon with E = 180 GPa and $v = 0.18$. A uniform pressure of 100 kPa was applied to the entire surface of the circular diaphragm. Therefore,

$$\frac{r}{t} \leq 37.5 \qquad (17)$$

2.2 DLC Thin-Film Resistors

The piezoresistive effect relates the change in electrical resistance of the resistor as a function of the material piezoresistive coefficient and of the longitudinal stress as follows:

$$\frac{\Delta R}{R} = \sigma_l \pi_l \qquad (18)$$

Where π_l is the longitudinal piezoresistive coefficient and the maximum longitudinal stress which is given by

$$\sigma_l = \frac{3}{4}\frac{pr^2}{t^2} \qquad (19)$$

Substituting the Eq. (19) in (18):

$$\frac{\Delta R}{R} = \frac{3}{4}\pi_l p \left(\frac{r}{t}\right)^2 \qquad (20)$$

It is known that the piezoresistive coefficients are sensitive to several quantities such as conductivity type, orientation, temperature and doping level [4]. In this work, we consider the longitudinal piezoresistive coefficient of undoped DLC film ($\pi_l = 2.3 \times 10^{-10}$) [23]. Therefore,

$$\frac{\Delta R}{R} = 1.725.10^{-5} \left(\frac{r}{t}\right)^2 \qquad (21)$$

Substituting the Eq. (21) in (17):

$$\frac{\Delta R}{R} \leq 0.024 \qquad (22)$$

The expressions (17) and (22) determine the maximum values for (r/t) and (ΔR/R) respectively. Figure 3 shows (ΔR/R) as function of (r/t). As the objective is the development of a small sensor with good sensitivity. For this reason, we have selected (r/t) = 25. Therefore, the sensor presents circular diaphragm with r = 500 μm and t = 20 μm.

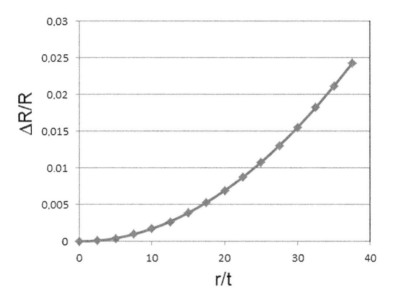

Fig. 3. The fractional change of resistance as a function of (r/t).

3   Conclusions

The benefits of use DLC thin-film resistors in piezoresistive pressure sensors were presented. In addition, we describe a simple and efficient methodology for design a pressure sensor with silicon circular diaphragm using only analytical formulas found in the literature. Using this methodology, it is possible to design the sensor for different pressure ranges.

Acknowledgments. São Paulo Research Foundation – FAPESP (processes number 14/18139-8 and 13/17045-7) and by CNPq (processes number 442133/2014-6 and 305153/2015-3).

References

1. Fraga, M.A., Pessoa, R.S., Massi, M., Maciel, H.S.: Silicon carbide as base material for MEMS sensors of aerospace use: an overview. Matéria 19(3), 274–290 (2014)
2. Casady, J.B., Johnson, R.W.: Status of silicon carbide (SiC) as a wide-bandgap semiconductor for high-temperature applications: a review. Solid-State Electron. 39(10), 1409–1422 (1996)
3. Auciello, O., Pacheco, S., Sumant, A.V., Gudeman, C., Sampath, S., Datta, A., Carpick, R. W., Adiga, V.P., Zurcher, P., Ma, Z., Yuan, H.-C., Carlisle, J.A., Kabius, B., Hiller, J., Srinivasan, S.: Are diamonds a MEMS' best friend? IEEE Microw. Mag. 8(6), 61–75 (2007)
4. Fraga, M.A., Furlan, H., Pessoa, R.S., Massi, M.: Wide bandgap semiconductor thin films for piezoelectric and piezoresistive MEMS sensors applied at high temperatures: an overview. Microsyst. Technol. 20, 9–21 (2014)
5. Vetter, J.: 60 years of DLC coatings: historical highlights and technical review of cathodic arc processes to synthesize various DLC types, and their evolution for industrial applications. Surf. Coat. Technol. 257, 213–240 (2014)
6. Robertson, J.: Diamond-like amorphous carbon. J. Mater. Sci. Eng. R. 37, 129–281 (2002)
7. Silva, S.R.E., Carey, J.D.: Amorphous carbon thin films. In: Nalwa, H.S. (ed.) Handbook of Thin Films, vol. 4, pp 403–506. Elsevier Inc., Burlington (2002)
8. Fraga, M.A., Bosi, M., Negri, M.: Silicon Carbide in microsystem technology – thin film versus bulk material. In: Saddow, S.E., La Via, F. (eds.) Advanced Silicon Carbide Devices and Processing, pp. 1–30. Intech (2015)
9. Aisenberg, S., Chabot, R.: Ion-beam deposition of thin films of diamond like carbon. J. Appl. Phys. 42(7), 2953–2958 (1971)
10. Takeno, T., Miki, H., Sugawara, T., Hoshi, Y., Takagi, T.: A DLC/W-DLC multilayered structure for strain sensing applications. Diam. Relat. Mater. 17(4–5), 713–716 (2008)
11. Petersen, M., Heckmann, U., Bandorf, R., Gwozdz, V., Schnabel, S., Bräuer, G., Klages, C. P.: Me-DLC films as material for highly sensitive temperature compensated strain gauges. Diam. Relat. Mater. 20(5–6), 814–818 (2011)
12. Leal, G., Fraga, M.A., Rasia, L.A., Massi, M.: Impact of high N2 flow ratio on the chemical and morphological characteristics of sputtered N-DLC films. Surf. Interface Anal. 49(2), 99–106 (2017)
13. Robertson, J.: Diamond-like carbon films, properties and applications. In: Sarin, V.K. (ed.) Comprehensive Hard Materials, vol. 3, pp. 101–139. Elsevier Inc., Burlington (2014)
14. Freund, L.B., Suresh, S.: Thin Film Materials: Stress, Defect Formation and Surface Evolution, pp. 1–820. Cambridge University Press, Cambridge (2003)
15. Martin, P.M.: Handbook of Deposition Technologies for Films and Coatings Third Edition. Science Applications and Technology. Elsevier Inc., Burlington (2010)
16. Kenny, T.: Strain gages. In: Wilson, J.S. (eds.) Sensor Technology Handbook, Elsevier Inc., Burlington, pp. 501–529 (2005)
17. Russo, G.P.: Aerodynamic Measurement: From Physical Principles to Turnkey Instrumentation, pp. 1–24. Woodhead Publishing, Elsevier Inc., Burlington (2011)
18. Luethje, H., Brand, J.: German Patent DE 199 54 164 A1. Sensor zur Zustandsbestimmung von Kenngroessen an mechanischen Komponenten (1999)
19. Peiner, E., Tibrewala, A., Bandorf, R., Biehl, S., Lüthje, H., Doering, L.: Micro force sensor with piezoresistive amorphous carbon strain gauge. Sens. Actuators A: Phys. 130–131, 75–82 (2006)

20. Tibrewala, A., Peiner, E., Bandorf, R., Biehl, S., Lüthje, H.: Transport and optical properties of amorphous carbon and hydrogenated amorphous carbon films. Appl. Surf. Sci. **252**(15), 5387–5390 (2006)
21. Fraga, M.A., Furlan, H., Pessoa, R.S., Rasia, L.A., Mateus, C.F.R.: Studies on SiC, DLC and TiO$_2$ thin films as piezoresistive sensor materials for high temperature application. Microsyst. Technol. **18**, 1027–1033 (2012)
22. Kanda, Y., Yasukawa, A.: Optimum design considerations for silicon piezoresistive pressure sensors. Sens. Actuators A **62**, 539–542 (1997)
23. Geremias, M., Moreira, R.C., Rasia, L.A., Moi, A.: Mathematical modeling of piezoresistive elements. J. Phys: Conf. Ser. **648**, 012012 (2015)

Analysis of Power Quality for Connections in the Same Circuit of Metal-Halide, LED and Compact Fluorescent Lamps

Enrique Jácome and Helbert Espitia(✉)

Universidad Distrital Francisco José de Caldas, Bogotá, Colombia
{eejlobo,heespitiac}@udistrital.edu.co

Abstract. This paper shows an estimate of some power quality indices for three different lighting technologies connected in the same electrical circuit. The devices considered are compact fluorescent lamp with electronic ballast, high intensity discharge metal halide lamp, and LED lamp; including nonlinear models of lamps for power quality analysis. These models are obtained by parameter identification, using optimization from the actual measurement of the line current of each lamp. Power analysis are based on IEEE 1459-2010 standard.

Keywords: Compact-fluorescent · Lamps · LED · Metal-halide · Power-quality

1 Introduction

Charges with nonlinear features connected to electrical power systems modify the sine wave nature in AC (Alternate Current) supply producing signal distortion [1]. Some lighting technologies present distortion in these signals, additionally in an electrical installation, the lamps operate independently or simultaneously in the circuit with different or similar nonlinear devices [2–4].

Voltage and current measurements made on lamps connections allow to observe distortion in these signals. Likewise, for Compact Fluorescent Lamps (CFLs) [5], and the same implies for High Intensity Discharge lamps (HIDs), particularly those of metal-halide [6] and for LEDs (Light Emitting Diodes) technologies [7].

About previous analysis for lighting technologies, [8,9] show the effect on secondary distribution circuits, considering the intensive use of Compact Fluorescent Bulbs and LEDs. In [6,10] analysis is carried out for different lighting loads including Incandescent, Halogen, Fluorescent, Compact Fluorescent, and High intensity Discharge lamps. Harmonic studies on a LED lamp in distribution systems are presented in [11]. Additionally, in [12,13] analysis is made considering LED and fluorescent lamps operating together.

This article presents analysis of some power quality indices when CFLs, HIDs and LEDs lighting technologies are connected in the same circuit. The analysis requires the development of a nonlinear model of this lighting technology to

© Springer International Publishing AG 2017
J.C. Figueroa-García et al. (Eds.): WEA 2017, CCIS 742, pp. 444–455, 2017.
DOI: 10.1007/978-3-319-66963-2_40

simulate and evaluate the actual impact of these charges in electrical systems. Nonlinear models are implemented to represent the distortion in electrical signals. Models are based on parameter identification via optimization techniques, using actual current line measurement, obtaining an adequate identification of model parameters [14].

Distribution structure is modeled taking a medium electric power network, an electrical transformer of $11.4V - 0.28Kv$, together with connection set $Dy5$; a conventional electric supply, and a branch circuit $208 - 120V$, where the analyzed lamps are connected [9].

Quality power analysis is based on indices from the standard IEEE 1459-2010, such as rms values for voltage and current, active power, power factor, and current total harmonic distortion. Quality power calculation features are determined together with simulation data [15]. These measurements are made, compared and analyzed at the point of connection of each lamp and at the common coupling point, connecting each lamp independently and in simultaneous operation in the same three-phase circuit.

Finally, in order to exhibit connections setup with deterioration in power quality is presented the different lamps connections with respective power quality indices. All models are implemented in MATLAB® and Simulink®.

2 Model of Distribution System

Figure 1 presents the model of low voltage distribution system utilized to different connection setups for considered lamps; besides, Table 1 summarizes the electrical parameters [16].

Table 1. Distribution system parameter.

Element	Parameters
Transformer	11.4/0.208 KV, 60 Hz, 0.4 MV A, $uk = 4\%$, Losses 5.5 KW, connection group $Dyn5$
Medium voltage network	Penguin, $R = 0.327\,\Omega/\text{Km}$, $X = 0.391\,\Omega/\text{Km}$
Supply	Conductor 1/0 AWG
Feeder	Conductor 1/0 AWG
Branch circuit	Conductor 12 AWG Cu

This model consists of a medium voltage line of 11.4 Kv, a 11.4/208 V transformer, including a connection group $Dy5$, a supply line, a feed line, and the three-phase branch circuit where the lamps are connected [4,16].

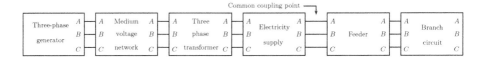

Fig. 1. Distribution model used for simulation.

3   Nonlinear Model of Metal-Halide Lamp

A metal-halide lamp, containing a reactor type electromagnetic ballast, presenting distorted signals of current and voltage. Figure 2 shows the electrical circuit model used for this lamp.

This type of lighting technology works with an electric arc, which is a nonlinear element modeled by Cassie and Mayr differential equations [17]; arc model is presented in Fig. 8. Even though the inductance can behave as a nonlinear element, this model avoids further considerations regarding magnetic saturation; therefore, it is considered a linear element as the condenser.

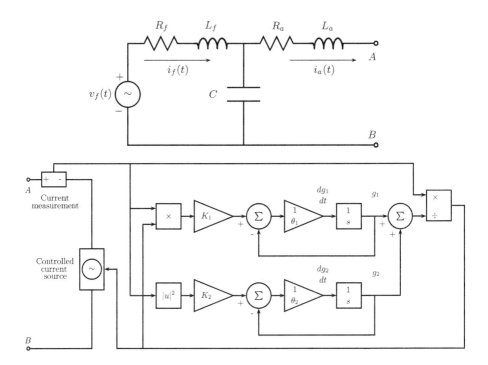

Fig. 2. HID model lamp implemented.

Cassie and Mayr model, is based on differential equations:

$$g = \frac{ui}{U_0^2} - \theta_1 \frac{dg}{dt} \tag{1}$$

$$g = \frac{i^2}{P_0} - \theta_2 \frac{dg}{dt} \tag{2}$$

where:

- g: Dynamic conductance.
- u: Instant tension in tube of discharge.
- i: Instant current in tube of discharge.
- U_0: Constant with tension units.
- θ_1: Constant for time (energy/volume connection).
- P_0: Constant for power due to heat conduction.
- θ_2: Time constant.

In [14] is presented the parameters model identification for an actual metal-halide lamp. Figure 3 show the current simulation for HID lamp.

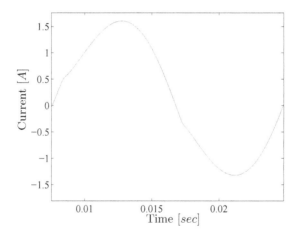

Fig. 3. Current simulation for HID lamp.

4   Nonlinear Model of Compact Fluorescent Lamp

Compact fluorescent lamps have a nonlinear behavior producing distortions and displacements of the voltage and current signals, also causing low power factor and high total harmonic distortion, mainly of the current signal [18–20]. The CLF has an electronic ballast, however for low frequency a compact model can be used for power analysis. Figure 4 displays the CLF model lamp used for simulation [21]. Additionally the current simulation for CLF is presented in Fig. 5.

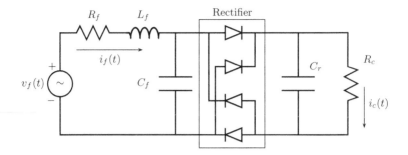

Fig. 4. CLF model lamp implemented.

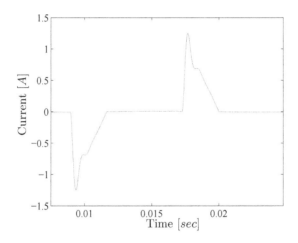

Fig. 5. Current simulation for CLF lamp.

5   Nonlinear Model of LED Lamp

According to [11] the nonlinear model of LED lamp considers a rectifier bridge, resistance line, condenser and a LED driver modeling as a constant current

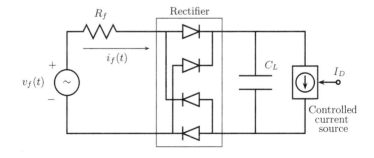

Fig. 6. LED model lamp implemented.

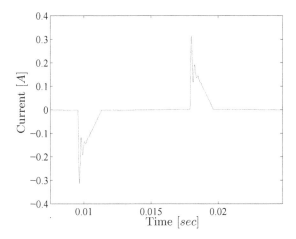

Fig. 7. Current simulation for LED lamp.

source. The nonlinear model LED used is shown in Fig. 6, and current simulation is show in Fig. 7.

6   Process for Parameters Lamp Identification

Figure 8 describes the method employed for model parameter identification. In metal-halide lamp, the parameters identified are K_1, K_2, θ_1, θ_2, R, L, C. For Compact Fluorescent Lamp are R_f, C_f, C_r and R_c. Finally, for LED lamp are R_f, C_L and I_D.

This process is made starting from the measurement of current signal. An optimization process was carried out to validate and guarantee parameter optimal adjustments, where an objective function is implemented for calculating the system dynamic response. Correspondingly, calculations are made to determine the adjustment value, which is optimized [14].

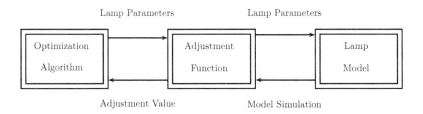

Fig. 8. Process to identify model parameters.

Performance index used is the root of the average quadratic error defined as:

$$J(X) = \sqrt{\frac{1}{N} \sum_{n=1}^{N} [y_r(n) - y_s(n, X)]^2} \tag{3}$$

In Eq. 3, J corresponds to objective function were X is the parameters lamp model; n is the discrete time; y_r represents actual lamp data measured, y_s is the data obtained from the simulation, and N is the number of all data. The optimization techniques implemented to determine the electrical parameters ensure an optimal adjustment for such parameters in this model [16,21].

The Quasi-Newton optimization algorithm is used for parameter lamps identification. In this case an approximation of the Hessian matrix is performed via Broyden-Fletcher-Goldfarb-Shanno (BFGS) method [22,23].

7   Setup for Lamps Connection

In order to observe the lamps effect in power quality, different configurations are simulated. Phases a, b, c and neutral line in the branch circuit are considered for setup connections; those are show in Fig. 9.

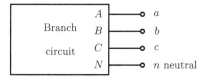

Fig. 9. Branch circuit used for lamps connection setup.

To carry out the analysis, the following lamp connections are considered:

- Case 1: LED connected to $a - n$.
- Case 2: CLF connected to $a - n$.
- Case 3: HID connected to $a - b$.
- Case 4: LED and CLF connected to $a - n$.
- Case 5: LED connected to $a - n$ and HID connected to $a - b$.
- Case 6: CLF connected to $a - n$ and HID connected to $a - b$.
- Case 7: LED, CLF connected to $a - n$ and HID connected to $a - b$.

Power quality is analyzed taking some features based on standard IEEE 1459-2010, such as rms values in voltage and current, active power, power factor and total current harmonic distortion. All measurements are made at the point of common coupling and directly on the respective lamp connection. The Tables 2, 3, 4, 5, 6, 7 and 8 show the results for each case.

Table 2. Power quality values for case 1.

Case 1	LED lamp	Point of common coupling			
Electricity features	$a - n$	a	b	c	n
Current rms [A]	0.0569	0.0569	0	0	0.0569
Voltage rms [V]	119.03	119.03	118.04	118.82	-
Active power [W]	3.45	3.45	-	-	-
Power factor	0.51	0.51	-	-	-
THDi [%]	150	150	-	-	150.26

Table 3. Power quality values for case 2.

Case 2	CLF lamp	Point of common coupling			
Electricity features	$a - n$	a	b	c	n
Current rms [A]	0.3664	0.3664	0	0	0.3664
Voltage rms [V]	119.03	119.03	118.04	118.83	-
Active power [W]	26.16	26.16	-	-	-
Power factor	0.6	0.6	-	-	-
THDi [%]	108.2	108.2	-	-	108.2

Table 4. Power quality values for case 3.

Case 3	HID lamp	Point of common coupling			
Electricity features	$a - b$	a	b	c	n
Current rms [A]	0.98	0.98	0.98	0	0
Voltage rms [V]	206.2	118.89	117.88	118.82	-
Active power [W]	101.03	100.20	99.34	-	-
Power factor	0.5	0.86	0.86	-	-
THDi [%]	6.75	6.75	6.75	-	-

Table 5. Power quality values for case 4.

Case 4	Point of common coupling			
Electricity features	a	b	c	n
Current rms [A]	0.4067	0	0	0.4067
Voltage rms [V]	119.03	118.04	118.83	-
Active power [W]	29.53	-	-	-
Power factor	0.61	-	-	-
THDi [%]	107.1	-	-	107.1

Table 6. Power quality values for case 5.

Case 5	Point of common coupling			
Electricity features	a	b	c	n
Current rms [A]	1.0011	0.98	0	0.0558
Voltage rms [V]	118.88	117.88	118.82	-
Active power [W]	103.54	0.23	-	-
Power factor	0.87	0.002	-	-
THDi [%]	6.6	6.7	-	147.8

Table 7. Power quality values for case 6.

Case 6	Point of common coupling			
Electricity features	a	b	c	n
Current rms [A]	1.16	0.98	0	0.364
Voltage rms [V]	118.88	117.88	118.83	-
Active power [W]	128.24	0.23	-	-
Power factor	0.93	0.002	-	-
THDi [%]	23.55	6.8	-	109.5

Table 8. Power quality values for case 7.

Case 7	Point of common coupling			
Electricity features	a	b	c	n
Current rms [A]	1.164	0.971	0	0.368
Voltage rms [V]	118.89	117.87	118.83	-
Active power [W]	128.7	2.29	-	-
Power factor	0.93	0.02	-	-
THDi [%]	23.6	8.3	-	126

These tables allow to observe the power quality indices when different elements (lamps) with nonlinear characteristics are added. Additionally, when considering the case were the three lamps are connected simultaneously, Figs. 10, 11, and 12 show the simulations carried out.

Figure 10 shows the phase-neutral voltage; in Fig. 11 the respective line currents are shown, finally, Fig. 12 presents the current in neutral line. Furthermore, it is remarkable deformation in currents, which decreases power quality indices.

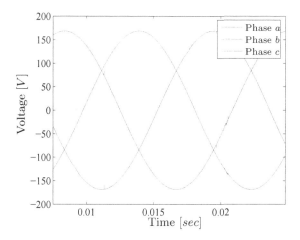

Fig. 10. Phase-neutral voltage.

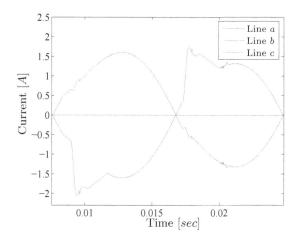

Fig. 11. Line currents.

Due the load imbalance and the nonlinear characteristic of each lamp, it can be seen a distortion in the neutral and line currents. This situation can produce over voltage and/or currents that can cause damage as loss in the insulation or data loss in electronic and electrical devices connected to the system.

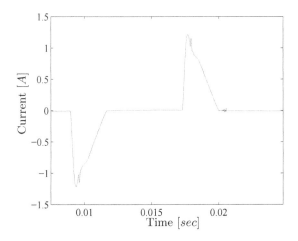

Fig. 12. Current in neutral line.

8   Conclusions

Via power quality calculations under standard IEEE 1459-2010, such as current and tension rms values, active power, power factor, and current total harmonic distortion, the quality power could be analyzed for proposed cases.

The load imbalance and nonlinear characteristic of lamps produce distortion in the line and neutral currents which affects the power quality.

Simultaneous connections of the lamps considered produce distorted current signals at the point of common coupling. This issue raises a risk related to electromagnetic compatibility among these lighting technologies and other nonlinear charges.

References

1. IEEE Standard 519–1992: IEEE Recommended Practices and Requirements for Harmonic Control in Electrical Power Systems April 1993
2. IESNA Illuminating Engineering Society of North America: Lighting Handbook. Reference and Application, 9th edn. (1997)
3. Ministerio de Minas y Energía: Reglamento Técnico de Instalaciones Eléctricas - RETIE, Colombia (2007)
4. Codensa, S.A.: Normas de construcción y especificaciones técnicas, Bogotá (2011)
5. Watson, N., Scott, T., Hirsch, S.: Implications for distribution networks of high penetration of compact fluorescent lamps. IEEE Trans. Power Deliv. **24**(3), 1521–1528 (2009)
6. Abdel, A.F.: Studying the impact of different lighting loads on both harmonics and power factor. In: 42nd International Universities Power Engineering Conference UPEC (2007)
7. Uddin, S., Shareef, H., Krause, O., Mohamed, A., Hannan, M., Islam, N.: Impact of large-scale installation of LED lamps in a distribution system. Turk. J. Electr. Eng. Comput. Sci. **23**, 1769–1780 (2015)

8. Blanco, A.M.: Efecto sobre los circuitos de distribución secundarios debido al uso intensivo de Bombillas Fluorescentes Compactas y LEDs(LightEmittingDiodes). M.Sc. Thesis, Department of Electrical Engineering, National University of Colombia, Bogotá (2010)
9. Pavas, A., Blanco, A., Parra, E.: Applying FBD-power theory to analysing effective lighting devices impact on power quality and electric grid efficiency. Ing. Investig. J. **31**(2), 110–117 (2011)
10. Lin, S., Huang, N., Zhu, M.: The study of the power quality emission characteristics of different types of lamps and their impacts on distribution systems. In: IEEE 11th Conference on Industrial Electronics and Applications ICIEA (2016)
11. Molina, J., Mesas, J.J., Mesbahi, N., Sainz, L.: LED lamp modelling for harmonic studies in distribution systems. IET Gener. Transm. Distrib. **11**(4), 1063–1071 (2017)
12. Tang, Y., Chen, Q., Ju, P., Jin, Y., Shen, F., Qi, B., Xu, Z.: Research on load characteristics of energy-saving lamp and LED lamp. In: IEEE International Conference on Power System Technology POWERCON (2016)
13. Braga, D., Jota, P.: Prediction of total harmonic distortion based on harmonic modeling of nonlinear loads using measured data for parameter estimation. In: 17th International Conference on Harmonics and Quality of Power ICHQP (2016)
14. Jácome, E., Pavas, A., Espitia, H.: Power quality analysis of discharge with metal-halide reactor ballast. In: XX Congreso Internacional de Ingeniería Eléctrica, Electrónica, de Computación y Ramas Afines INTERCON, pp. 75–78 (2013)
15. IEEE Industry Applications Society/Power Engineering Society IEEE Recommended: Definitions for the measurement of electric power quantities under sinusoidal, nonsinusoidal, balanced or unbalanced conditions Standard 1459 (2010)
16. Jácome, E., Pavas, A., Espitia, H.: Power quality analysis for different connections of metal-halide lamps on the same circuit. In: XXI Congreso Internacional de Ingeniería Electrónica, Eléctrica y Computación INTERCON (2014)
17. Lu, S., Cheng, Z., Wu, B., Sotudeh, R.: Modeling of neon tube powered by high frequency converters. In: IEEE 28th Annual Conference of the Industrial Electronics Society IECON (2002)
18. Illuminating Engineering Society of North America IESNA: Approved method for the electrical and photometric measurements of single-ended Compact Fluorescent Lamps. Standard IESNA LM-66-00 (2000)
19. Larsson, E.O.A., Lundmark, C.M., Bollen, M.H.J.: Measurement of current taken by fluorescent lights in the frequency range 2–150 kHz. In: IEEE Power Engineering Society General Meeting (2006)
20. Schinkelshoek, M., Watson, N., Heffernan, B.: The characteristics of CFLs; beyond the harmonics. In: 20th Australasian Universities Power Engineering Conference AUPEC (2010)
21. Lobo, E., Pavas, A., Espitia, H., Parameter identification and power quality analysis for compact fluorescent lamp. In: International Symposium on Power Quality, SICEL, vol. 7, p. 5 (2013)
22. Venkataraman, P.: Applied Optimization with MATLAB Programming, 2nd edn. Wiley, Hoboken (2009)
23. Quarteroni, A., Saleri, F., Gervasio, P.: Scientific Computing with MATLAB and Octave. Texts in Computational Science and Engineering. Springer, Heidelberg (2014)

Multiobjective Genetic Algorithm to Minimize the THD in Cascaded Multilevel Converters with V/F Control

Jorge Luis Diaz Rodriguez$^{(\boxtimes)}$, Luis David Pabon Fernandez, and Edison Andres Caicedo Peñaranda

Universidad de Pamplona, Pamplona, Colombia
jdiazcu@gmail.com, davidpabon@hotmail.es,
eacaicedo@gmail.com

Abstract. This paper deals with the development of a multiobjective optimization algorithm programmed in Matlab, which allows to obtain a voltage vs frequency ratio (V/F) that decreases the voltage value as the frequency is reduced by maintaining the total harmonic distortion (THD) at levels very close to 0% over the entire frequency range of operation. The multiobjective algorithm is applied to a common-source cascaded H-bridge multilevel converter with maximum 15 steps per line voltage. The inverter is simulated by supplying a three-phase induction motor.

Keywords: Multiobjective optimization · Genetic algorithm · Multilevel converter · THD · Induction motor

1 Introduction

The Adjustable Speed Drives (ASD) used in the control of the induction motors (IM) has the ability to modify the synchronous speed of the machine by varying the frequency of the mains power supply. They also change the magnitude of the operating voltage to avoid the circulation of excessive currents due to the saturation of the machine at low speeds [1]. This process is usually performed using a Pulsewidth Modulation (PWM) technique which increase or decrease the frequency and voltage adjusting the pulse duration (width) of the inverter output voltage [2].

The main disadvantage of this type of converters deals with problems affecting its power quality [3], because they have square voltages waveform with high harmonic content, which cause excessive heating of the windings and the generation of opposing parasitic torques in the induction motors [4]. To solve this problem related with power quality, it has been proposed the use of multilevel power converters, because its THD is very low compared to conventional converters [5, 6]. However, it has not been possible to find optimum operating points across the frequency range in the multilevel inverters [7]. This work presents the implementation of a multiobjective genetic algorithm, in a multilevel frequency inverter of 9 steps per phase and 15 steps per lines voltages, which allows obtaining a desired voltage and frequency level with a very low THD.

© Springer International Publishing AG 2017
J.C. Figueroa-García et al. (Eds.): WEA 2017, CCIS 742, pp. 456–468, 2017.
DOI: 10.1007/978-3-319-66963-2_41

2   Cascaded Multilevel Power Converters

The selected multilevel topology is a three-phase H-bridge cascaded converter in an asymmetrical single DC-source configuration, with 2 H-bridges stages and a transformers ratio of 1:3, producing 9 levels of output voltage per phase. The 9 levels generates 15 levels at the line voltage, this topology is shown in Fig. 1 [8].

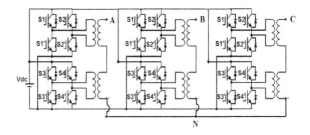

Fig. 1. Cascaded multilevel converter.

3   Mathematical Modeling

In order to obtain a genetic algorithm that allows to simultaneously varying the frequency and the amplitude of the voltage, maintaining a very low value of harmonic distortion (THD). It becomes necessary, to obtain equations that quantify the RMS and THD values of the line voltage waveform in terms of the switching angles per phase. For which the Fourier series of the phase voltages are determined, and the line voltage series is calculated as the difference of the phase voltage Fourier series according Eq. (1):

$$v_{AB}(t) = v_A(t) - v_B(t) \qquad (1)$$

Thus, with the Fourier series of the line voltage, the RMS and THD values are quantified in terms of the harmonics, which are calculated from the *on* and *off* angles of the levels in the first quarter of the phase voltage. Figure 2 shows the first quarter of A phase of a three-phase system with 9 levels per phase.

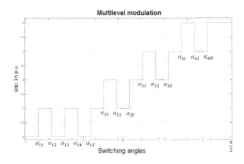

Fig. 2. A modulation first quarter-waveform in terms of the *on* and *off* angles.

Since the shape of the modulation shown has 1/4 waveform symmetry, it is only necessary to define the switching angles in the first quarter of the waveform. The rest of the modulation is constructed by simple trigonometric relationships. In this way, a vector $L = [a\ b\ c\ d]$ is defined which represents the total number of on and off angles at each level. The Fourier series for a periodic waveform:

$$v(t) = \frac{a_0}{2} + \sum_{n=1}^{a} h_n \sin(\omega t + \varphi_n) \tag{2}$$

Where c_n is the peak magnitude of the nth harmonic and φ_n its respective phase shift, which are defined as:

$$h_n = \sqrt{a_n^2 + b_n^2} \tag{3}$$

$$\varphi_n = \tan^{-1}(b_n/a_n) \tag{4}$$

The Fourier series for the phase A waveform is defined by:

$$h_n = \begin{cases} 0 & \text{for } n \text{ even} \\ \dfrac{4V_{dc}}{\pi n} \sum_{i=1}^{4} \sum_{j=1}^{L_i} (-1)^{j-1} \cos n\alpha_{ij} & \text{for } n \text{ odd} \end{cases} \tag{5}$$

$$\varphi_n = 0 \tag{6}$$

Where V_{dc} is the voltage value of each level, and α_{ij} is the angle j of the level i.

For phase B, which has a phase shift of $120°$ electrical degrees to phase A, the Fourier series is defined by:

$$h_n = \begin{cases} 0 & \text{for } n \text{ even} \\ \frac{4V_{dc}}{\pi n} \sum_{i=1}^{4} \sum_{j=1}^{L_i} (-1)^{j-1} \cos n\alpha_{ij} & \text{for } n \text{ old triplen} \\ \frac{4V_{dc}}{\pi n} \sum_{i=1}^{4} \sum_{j=1}^{L_i} (-1)^{j-1} \cos n\alpha_{ij} & \text{for } n \text{ odd no triplen} \end{cases} \tag{7}$$

$$\varphi_n = \begin{cases} - & \text{for } n \text{ even} \\ 0 & \text{for } n \text{ odd triplen} \\ \frac{2\pi}{3}(-1)^{k+1} & \text{for } n \text{ odd no triplen} \end{cases} \tag{8}$$

Where, k is the occurrence of the odd harmonic non-triplen (harmonic multiple of three), i.e. $k = 1$ for harmonic 5, $k = 2$ for harmonic 7, $k = 3$ for harmonic 11, so on.

By developing the respective differences in terms of the Fourier series of phases A and B, we obtain the Fourier series for the line voltage V_{AB}, of which in this work only the amplitude of the harmonics is presented, since the aims is to minimize the THD and to calculate the RMS value, for this the harmonic phase lags are not required, therefore the harmonics amplitudes of the line voltages will be expressed by (9):

$$h_n = \begin{cases} 0 & \text{for } n \text{ even} \\ 0 & \text{for } n \text{ odd triplen} \\ \frac{4\sqrt{3}V_{dc}}{\pi n} \sum_{i=1}^{4} \sum_{j=1}^{L_i} (-1)^{j-1} \cos n\alpha_{ij} & \text{for } n \text{ odd no triplen} \end{cases} \tag{9}$$

3.1 Line Voltage THD

Since the IEEE-519 standard defines total harmonic distortion (THD) as (10) [9]:

$$THD = \sqrt{\sum_{n=2}^{50} h_n^2 / h_1} \cdot 100 \tag{10}$$

Where the harmonic h_1 is the fundamental component and h_n the peak of the harmonic n. Replacing Eq. (9) in (10):

$$THD = \frac{\sqrt{\sum_{n=1}^{50} \left(\frac{1}{n} \sum_{i=1}^{4} \sum_{j=1}^{L_i} (-1)^{j-1} \cos n\alpha_{ij} \right)^2}}{\sum_{i=1}^{4} \sum_{j=1}^{L_i} (-1)^{j-1} \cos 1\alpha_{ij}} \cdot 100 \tag{11}$$

Where n can take odd non-triplen values, i.e. 5, 7, 11, 13, 17, so on, and L_i are the components of the vector $L = [a\ b\ c\ d]$.

Similarly, the RMS value can be defined in terms of harmonics, such as:

$$V_{Line_{RMS}} = \sqrt{\sum_{n=1}^{1} V_{RMS}^2} \tag{12}$$

Replacing the upper bound $h_{max} = 50$ the V_{RMS} is determined by (13), for n non-triple:

$$V_{Line_{RMS}} = \sqrt{\sum_{n=1}^{50} \frac{\left(\frac{4\sqrt{3}V_{cd}}{\pi n} \sum_{i=1}^{4} \sum_{j=1}^{L_i} (-1)^{j-1} \cos n\alpha_{ij} \right)^2}{2}} \cdot 100 \tag{13}$$

By this way, Eq. (10) defines THD as the objective or fitness function to be minimized by the optimization algorithm and constraint Eq. (12). Thus, the algorithm will search for a modulation with a certain RMS value and a minimum of THD. The frequency will depend on the implementation times, so the inverter can reproduce modulations with a certain frequency, voltage level and minimum THD [8].

3.2   Control V/F

In order to avoid saturation of the motor supplied by the frequency inverter, the voltage must be reduced as the frequency drops below its rated value. This decrease is proportional to the decrease in frequency, this variation of V/F is known as scalar control, in this work this control takes the form of the function described by (14):

$$V(f) = \begin{cases} \left(\frac{V_n}{f_n - f_i}\right)(f - f_i) + V_{boost} & \text{para } f < f_n \\ V_n & \text{para } f \geq f_n \end{cases} \tag{14}$$

Where V_n is the rated voltage of the induction motor, f_i, the initial frequency of the operating frequency range, V_{boost} the RMS level of the voltage at the initial frequency and f_n the rated frequency of the machine.

4   Optimization Algorithm

Based on the review of the state of the art and the mathematical problem involved in the deduced equations, it is considered convenient to use the optimization technique known as multiobjective genetic algorithms.

As evidenced in the literary review, this technique has a wide application in the field of optimization of harmonic content in power converters. In addition, this technique has the advantage of considering each angle as a gene independent of the others, within an individual, which improve the optimization, and additionally being multiobjective allows to solve two fitness equations, which is the aims of this work.

Figure 3 shows the consolidated of revised works that have used different optimization techniques in power converters. The revised papers starting in the year 2000 and include conventional and multilevel inverters in single-phase and three-phase configurations. Some references reviewed [10–18].

THD optimization techniques

GA: Genetic Algoritm.
PSO: Particle Swarm Optimization.
DE: Differential Evolution.
BA: Bee Algorithm.
NR: Newton Raphson.
NN: Others and hybrids.
BFA: Bacterial foraging algorithm.

Fig. 3. Summary of techniques used in the optimization of harmonic content.

To perform optimization over the entire frequency range, genetic algorithms are used as the optimization technique, in order to make Eq. 10 as close as possible to zero and the Eq. 12 approach a voltage value given by the V/F control. In this way, the algorithm shown in Fig. 4 is proposed to solve the optimization problem.

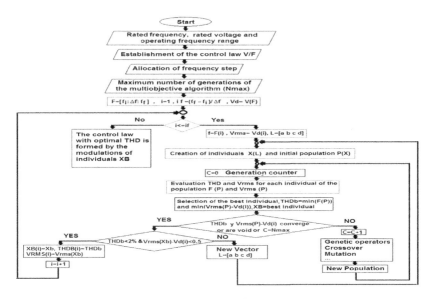

Fig. 4. Multiobjective genetic optimization algorithm applied to V/F control.

In the algorithm the rated values of the machine are assigned, such as line voltage (V_n) and rated frequency (f_n). Enter the frequency range over which the control law [f_i, f_f] is to be performed. The frequency step with which the voltage-frequency ratio (Δf) is to be calculated is also assigned. Finally, the maximum number of generations with which the multiobjective genetic algorithm (N_{max}) is to be operated is assigned.

With the data the algorithm calculates a frequency vector and an RMS voltage vector according to a relation that is designated by a mathematical equation V/F. For this work the selected relationship is given by Eq. 14.

With this relationship, the algorithm calculates the RMS value of the line voltage for each of the frequencies and assigns a vector of switching angles $L = [a \; b \; c \; d]$. The vector L contains information on how many switching angles are required to be generated at each of the four levels of the first quarter waveform of the converter phase voltage. If the desired voltage is low, the upper levels can be annulled, this would be to cancel d, c or even b, and then with this information an initial population P (X) of 20 individuals X is created, that are vectors of the form:

$$X = [\alpha_{11}\alpha_{12} \cdots \alpha_{1a}\alpha_{21}\alpha_{22} \cdots \alpha_{2b}\alpha_{32} \cdots \alpha_{2c}\alpha_{42} \cdots \alpha_{4d}] \tag{15}$$

The algorithm with these data creates an initial population that evolves in terms of the performance of the two fitness functions given by Eqs. 10 and 12. In each generation of evolution, the algorithm selects individuals with lower THD and whose RMS voltage value is closer to the value given by the control law. In this way the evolutionary part of the algorithm ends if one of the following conditions is met: if the THD and the RMS value converge, if the THD is null and the RMS value is the desired or the maximum number of generations is met. However if these conditions are not given the algorithm applies the evolutionary operators to the population and starts with another generation.

If this stage ends, the algorithm verifies that the THD is less than 2% and that the value of the line voltage RMS approaches the desired value with a margin ±0.5 V, otherwise the algorithm assigns a new vector $L = [a \ b \ c \ d]$ and re-iterates the evolutionary part, until the conditions are achieved.

When the conditions are achieved the algorithm stores the vector of switching angles in a matrix, also the RMS voltage and the THD for the given frequency. This increases the index i, and does the same process for the next frequency. This process is repeated until it is terminated with the frequency vector. In this way the V/F control is achieved with optimized modulations.

The algorithms corresponding to the mathematical model of the fitness functions (Eqs. 10 and 12) and their respective optimization using multiobjective genetic algorithms were programmed using the Matlab® and the `gamultiobj` command. The population size for the algorithm is taken from 20 individuals, each individual (X) consisting of the total switching angles in the first quarter of the phase voltage, accompanied by the vector L, which indicates the program in charge of evaluate the objective functions, the angles corresponding to each level.

5   Optimization Results

The rated voltage of the induction motor is set to 220 V, the rated frequency is 50 Hz, the frequency range of operation is [1 Hz–100 Hz] with steps of $\Delta f = 0.5$ Hz, the V_{boost} level is set to 30 Vrms. The data the activation angles of 200 modulations with optimum harmonic content and with RMS values following the V/F control (given by Eq. 14) were obtained as a result. Table 1 shows a fragment of this information.

Table 1.   Angles (degree) of the best individuals.

f	k	a	b	c	d	TC	V_{RMS}	THD	Angles		
1.0	1	121	0	0	0	121	33.80	0.2742	0.07759	0.16753	2.9178
1.5	1	121	0	0	0	121	35.70	0.0754	1.02185	1.03020	2.9183
2.0	1	85	0	0	0	85	37.60	0.0394	2.52739	2.55259	4.3227
2.5	1	89	0	0	0	89	39.50	0.0686	1.64416	1.65871	3.9459
3.0	1	85	0	0	0	85	41.40	0.1286	1.13806	1.16112	4.4966
3.5	1	41	0	0	0	41	43.30	0.0700	3.88632	3.95751	7.8372
4.0	1	41	0	0	0	41	45.20	0.0880	3.93478	4.01100	7.9194
4.5	1	45	0	0	0	45	47.11	0.0280	3.40757	3.46905	7.1465
5.0	1	39	0	0	0	39	49.02	0.0080	3.76383	3.85313	8.6204
5.5	1	39	0	0	0	39	50.90	0.0103	4.25190	4.35025	8.4528

The first column of the table shows the frequency of each modulation. The second column shows k which is the number of steps that the modulation uses in the first quarter of a wave without counting the zero level. The values a, b, c and d define the vector L. The table is only used a due to the low voltage level required for these frequencies. TC is the total number of switching angles. VRMS is the root mean square value of the voltage and THD is the total harmonic distortion of the modulation. As only three angles are shown, there are as many angles as the number indicated in TC.

Figure 5 shows the graph of the V/F control plotted with the RMS values found by the algorithm. Likewise, the behavior of the THD with respect to frequency is shown in Fig. 6. The results show that in most frequencies it is very close to 0%, however in the frequency range of [40.5–42 Hz] the THD exceeds 1% and a maximum peak of 1.8% occurs. These peaks fully comply with the requirement of 5% maximum [9].

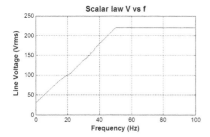 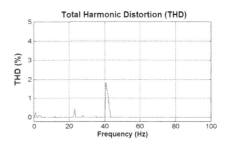

Fig. 5. V/F control.   **Fig. 6.** THD vs. frequency.

In this way, it is verified that the optimization algorithm is capable of generating the V/F control. Determined under a mathematical equation and ensuring minimal harmonic distortion at all frequencies, the THD being always below 5% to meet the requirements [9].

6 Simulation

Next, the results of some modulations at certain frequencies are shown; this data was obtained from the simulation of a multilevel converter of 9 levels per phase. Figure 6 shows the simulation scheme, in which four fundamental stages are observed. As the first phase the power converter, where the six H-bridges are shown together with the transformers at the output of each bridge. In a second box the control signals generation stage

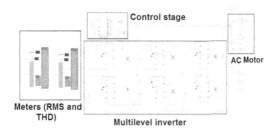

Fig. 7. Simulation scheme.

464   J.L. Diaz Rodriguez et al.

is observed. In another box, the power quality meters and RMS values are demarcated. Finally, the box corresponding to the output of the inverter is displayed (Fig. 7). The first frequency shown is 20 Hz. The waveforms of phase voltage and line voltages are shown in Figs. 8 and 9, respectively. Figure 8 shows that the phase waveform has only 5 levels, because the RMS value of the line voltage must be low, for this case it is measured at 96.44 V. For the line voltages the number of levels increases, presenting a total of 9, due to the appearance of new levels resulting from the differentiation between phases.

As for the harmonic spectra, Fig. 10 shows the spectrum (evaluated by Simulink) of the phase voltage and Fig. 11 shows the spectrum of the line voltage.

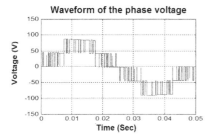

Fig. 8. Phase voltage waveform for 20 Hz.

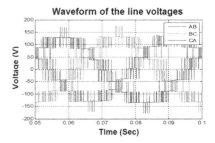

Fig. 9. Line voltage waveform for 20 Hz.

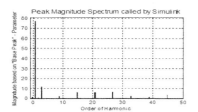

Fig. 10. Phase voltage spectrum for 20 Hz.

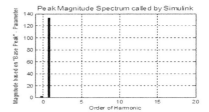

Fig. 11. Line voltage spectrum for 20 Hz.

The third harmonics are only in the phase voltage spectrum. Their presence is not of great importance since the optimization is carried out directly in the line voltage. According to the optimization algorithm and the mathematical model, the third harmonics disappear in the line voltage. This can be verified in Fig. 11, where it is also observed that the harmonic spectrum has no appreciable harmonic components. Thus the THD of line voltage is 0.56%.

As a second sample, the rated frequency at 50 Hz is selected. The waveforms of phase and line voltage are shown in Figs. 12 and 13.

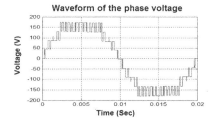

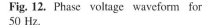

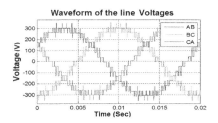

Fig. 12. Phase voltage waveform for 50 Hz.

Fig. 13. Line voltage waveform for 50 Hz.

The waveform of the phase voltage has nine levels because at this frequency the value of the voltage is the rated. The waveform of the line voltage has 15 levels and its RMS value of 215.6 V in the simulation.

As for the harmonic spectra, Fig. 14 shows the spectrum (evaluated in Simulink) of the phase voltage. In this one can observe the third harmonics; this is not of importance, since the optimization is realized to the line voltage.

Figure 15 shows the harmonic spectrum of the line voltage. Where it is verified that the third harmonics disappeared and the harmonic content in the range of the first fifty components is practically zero. The measured THD in the line voltage is 0.273%.

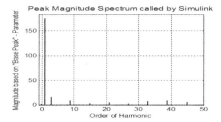

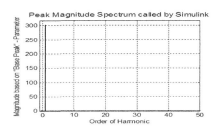

Fig. 14. Phase voltage spectrum for 50 Hz.

Fig. 15. Line voltage spectrum for 50 Hz.

As a last sample, results with a frequency higher than the rated frequency are presented (90 Hz). This frequency is close to the maximum frequency of 100 Hz, so the root mean square (RMS) value of the voltage and the waveform will be equal to those of the modulation of 50 Hz according to V/F control defined by Eq. (14). Establishing that above the rated frequency the voltage must be constant at its rated value, so the machine will not present saturation. The waveforms of the phase and line voltage are shown in Figs. 16 and 17.

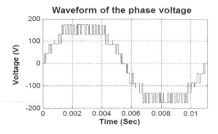

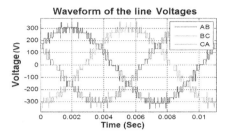

Fig. 16. Phase voltage waveform for 90 Hz.   **Fig. 17.** Line voltage waveform for 90 Hz.

The behavior of the waveforms is identical to the case of the frequency at 50 Hz. The only thing that varies is the duration of the pulses (pulse width). The mean square root (RMS) value measured for this case is 215.6 V. As for the harmonic spectra, Figs. 18 and 19 respectively show the spectrum of phase and line voltages.

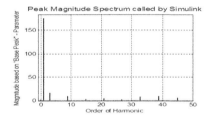

Fig. 18. Phase voltage spectrum for 90 Hz.   **Fig. 19.** Line voltage spectrum for 90 Hz.

The harmonic distortion (THD) measured at the line voltage is 0.273%. The behavior of the spectra is the same as the previous frequencies. In the phase voltage the third harmonics appear, while as expected they disappear in the line voltages.

An example of frequency variation at the output of the converter is shown in Fig. 20. It can be seen how the voltages change shape and frequency in a few cycles.

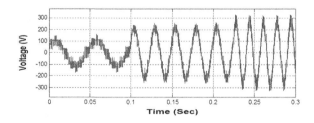

Fig. 20. Line voltage waveform with frequency variation.

7   Conclusions

The contribution of this work is significant, by achieving a wide range of modulations across the frequency range, which have a lower harmonic content in line voltage (THD < 1%). Additionally, within the review of the state of the art it is appreciated that the optimization techniques mostly used in the problem of optimizing the harmonic content of PWM modulations are Particle Swarm Optimization (PSO) and Genetic Algorithms (GA). Thus, being justified the adequate selection of the optimization technique base on multiobjective genetic algorithms for the accomplishment of this work, and verified by its excellent results.

The line voltage THD verifies the validity of the optimization process performed by the multiobjective genetic algorithm. In all tests, the THD is below the limit of the IEEE 519 standard (less than 5%). The lowest value obtained was 0.6% and the highest value was 3%. Both magnitudes are excellent results.

Since the optimization was done directly in to the line voltage; the third harmonics can exist only in the phase voltage and will be totally eliminated at the line voltage. Finally, the developed multiobjective algorithm optimizes the harmonic content of modulations with different frequencies and RMS values. Highlighting the accuracy of the algorithm to find modulations with an RMS value (assigned by user-defined V/F control) and with an optimum total harmonic distortion.

References

1. Mora, J.: Máquinas Eléctricas. McGraw Hill, New York (2005)
2. Fitzgerald, A.E., Kingsley, C., Umans, S.D.: Electric Machinery, 6th edn. McGraw Hill, New York (2003)
3. Sanchez, M.A.: Calidad de la energía eléctrica. Instituto Tecnológico de Puebla, Mexico (2009)
4. Mehmet, Y., Seydi, V., Seci, H.C.: Comparison of output current harmonics of voltage source inverter used different PWM control techniques. WSEAS Trans. Power Syst. 3(11), 695–704 (2008)
5. Malinowski, M., Gopakumar, K., Rodriguez, J., Pérez, M.: A survey on cascaded multilevel inverters. IEEE Trans. Ind. Electron. 57(7), 2197–2206 (2010)
6. Rodriguez, J., Lai, J., ZhengPeng, F.: Multilevel inverters: a survey of topologies, controls, and applications. IEEE Trans. Ind. Electron. 49(4), 724–738 (2002)
7. Barbera, G., Mayer, H.G., Issouribehere, F.: Medición de la emisión armónica en variadores de velocidad y desarrollo de modelos de simulación. In: Encuentro Regional Iberoamericano de CIGRE (2009)
8. Pabón Fernández, L.D., Díaz Rodríguez, J.L., Pardo García, A.: Total harmonic distortion optimization of the line voltage in single source cascaded multilevel converter. WSEAS Trans. Syst. 10, 110–120 (2016)
9. IEEE: IEEE Std. 519-1992 IEEE Recommended Practices and Requirements for Harmonic Control in Electrical Power Systems. IEEE (1992)
10. Ajami, A., Farakhor, A., Ardi, H.: Minimisations of total harmonic distortion in cascaded transformers multilevel inverter by modifying turn ratios of the transformers and input voltage regulation. IET Power Electron. 7(11), 2687–2694 (2014)

11. Diaz Rodriguez, J.L., Pabon Fernandez, L.D., Pardo Garcia, A.: THD Improvement of a PWM cascade multilevel power inverters using genetic algorithms as optimization method. WSEAS Trans. Power Syst. **10**, 46–54 (2015)

12. Kavali, J., Mittal, A.: Analysis of various control schemes for minimal total harmonic distortion in cascaded H-bridge multilevel inverter. J. Electr. Syst. Inf. Technol. **3**(3), 428–441 (2016)

13. Gnana Sundari, M., Rajaram, M., Balaraman, S.: Application of improved firefly algorithm for programmed PWM in multilevel inverter with adjustable DC sources. Appl. Soft Comput. **41**(C), 169–179 (2016)

14. Moeed Amjad, A., Salam, Z., Majed Ahmed, A.: Application of differential evolution for cascaded multilevel VSI with harmonics elimination PWM switching. Int. J. Electr. Power Energy Syst. **64**, 447–456 (2015)

15. Shimi Sudha, L., Tilak, T., Jagdish, K.: Harmonic elimination of a photo-voltaic based cascaded H-bridge multilevel inverter using PSO (particle swarm optimization) for induction motor drive. Energy **107**(C), 335–346 (2016)

16. Vivek Kumar, G., Mahanty, R.: Optimized switching scheme of cascaded H-bridge multilevel inverter using PSO. Int. J. Electr. Power Energy Syst. **64**, 699–707 (2015)

17. Vaniyambadi Sathyanarayanan, B., Mani, G.: Declining multi inverter-based total harmonic distortion with the aid of hybrid optimisation technique. IET Sci. Meas. Technol. **9**(3), 285–293 (2015)

18. Venus, V. and Ramani, K.: Implementation of SVPWM technique based diode clamped five-level inverter direct integration scheme for photovoltaic systems. In: memorias de Emerging Trends in Computing, Communication and Nanotechnology (ICE-CCN) (2013)

Analysis of Current Unbalance and Torque Ripple Generated by Simulations of Voltage Unbalance in Induction Motors

Luis Guasch-Pesquer[1], Adolfo-Andres Jaramillo-Matta[2([⊠])],
Francisco Gonzalez-Molina[1], and Sara Garcia-Rios[1]

[1] Department of Electronic, Electric and Automatic Engineering,
Rovira i Virgili University, Tarragona, Spain
{luis.guasch,francisco.gonzalezm,sara.garcia}@urv.cat
[2] Research Laboratory in Alternative Energy Sources,
Universidad Distrital Francisco José de Caldas, Bogotá, Colombia
ajaramillom@udistrital.edu.co

Abstract. In this paper the effects of voltage unbalance in both the Complex Current Unbalance Factor (*CCUF*) and the Torque Ripple Factor (*TRF*) of a three-phase induction motor have been discussed. The effects of 13060 points of voltage unbalance taken around the limit of standards (*VUF* = 2%) have been analyzed, since the largest number of international standards use this value as the limit. For the analysis, the single cage model of three-phase induction motor was used. The voltage unbalance has been characterized through four parameters: type, module of Complex Voltage Unbalance Factor (*VUF*), angle of Complex Voltage Unbalance Factor (θ_{CVUF}) and positive sequence voltage (V_1). The influence of each parameter in both module and angle of *CCUF* (*CUF* and θ_{CCUF}), and the Torque Ripple Factor (*TRF*) have been analyzed on those 13060 points. Results show that only *VUF* and V_1 parameters have a big influence in *CUF* and *TRF*.

Keywords: Voltage unbalance · Current unbalance · Induction motor · Torque ripple

1 Introduction

Three-phase induction motor is part of the most used electromechanical drives in the world industry, consuming much of the electricity. These motors are designed to work with a balanced three-phase voltages system.

The voltage unbalance disturbances in power systems can be mainly due to single-phase loads being fed from the three-phase supply [1]. When a three-phase motor is supplied by a voltage unbalance system, it can have counterproductive effects on motor, drive and the industrial process. Some effects in the motor are changes in losses, efficiency, power factor, derating factor and temperature [2, 3]. Voltage unbalance can also cause radial vibrations in induction motors because of the increase in magnetic induction [4]. In some industrial applications the torque ripple is the most important effect in the

© Springer International Publishing AG 2017
J.C. Figueroa-García et al. (Eds.): WEA 2017, CCIS 742, pp. 469–481, 2017.
DOI: 10.1007/978-3-319-66963-2_42

drive [5]. The adjustment of the electrical protections of the motor is very important to select the unbalance limits in order to stop the industrial process. In this case, the analysis of the current unbalance and the characteristics of the industrial process can lead to the correct adjustment of the electrical protections.

This work focuses on the effects of voltage unbalance in current unbalance and torque ripple. Recent works have analyzed other effects of the voltage unbalance in the induction motors, such as the temperature [6] or the shaft power. The voltage unbalance has been characterized by four parameters: type, module and angle of voltage unbalance factor (VUF and θ_{CVUF}), and positive sequence voltage (V_1). The influence of each parameter in the module (CUF) and angle (θ_{CCUF}) of the Complex Current Unbalance Factor ($CCUF$) and the torque ripple factor (TRF) have been analyzed. To fulfil this objective, an algorithm has been developed to generate 13060 voltage unbalance points. After that, a second algorithm has simulated the performance of a three-phase induction motor, with 75 kW and 3300 V, providing the waveforms of current and torque for all the voltage unbalance points. Finally, a third algorithm has calculated, from these waveforms, CUF, θ_{CCUF} and TRF.

2   Voltage Unbalance

In Power Quality, two types of perturbations are possible: variations, when the perturbation remains in steady-state, and events, when the perturbation has a beginning and an ending [8]. The voltage unbalance is classified as a variation.

2.1   Types

A classification for voltage unbalance can be seen in [2]: 1: single-phase under-voltage (1Φ-UV); 2: two-phases under-voltage (2Φ-UV); 3: three-phases under-voltage (3Φ-UV); 4: single-phase over-voltage (1Φ-OV); 5: two-phases over-voltage (2Φ-OV); 6: three-phases over-voltage (3Φ-OV); 7: unequal single-phase angle displacement (1Φ-A); 8: unequal two-phases angle displacement (2Φ-A).

The mathematical expressions of the voltages during an unbalance situation can be found in (1).

$$v_a = \sqrt{2}V_a \sin\left(\omega t + 0 + \alpha_a\right)$$
$$v_b = \sqrt{2}V_b \sin\left(\omega t - \frac{2\pi}{3} + \alpha_b\right) \tag{1}$$
$$v_c = \sqrt{2}V_c \sin\left(\omega t + \frac{2\pi}{3} + \alpha_c\right)$$

2.2   Complex Voltage Unbalance Factor

$CVUF$ was presented by Wang [7], and used in other works [5, 12–15]. The expression showed in (2) is defined as the ratio between the phasors V_2 and V_1 (the negative– and positive–sequence voltage components). In other cases, other factors are followed to measure the voltage unbalance, for example, in [15].

$$CVUF(\%) = \frac{V_2}{V_1}100 = \frac{V_2\left(\cos\theta_{V_2} + j\sin\theta_{V_2}\right)}{V_1\left(\cos\theta_{V_1} + j\sin\theta_{V_1}\right)}100 \qquad (2)$$

VUF is the module of **CVUF** and is used in some standards (IEC, GCOI/GCPS, CENELEC, NRS-048 and ANSI) [16], to define the limit of the voltage unbalance in three-phase voltage supply. This index can be found in (3).

$$VUF(\%) = |CVUF(\%)| = \frac{|V_2|}{|V_1|}100 = \frac{V_2}{V_1}100 \qquad (3)$$

In this paper, the **CVUF** is analyzed through its module, VUF, in (4).

$$CVUF = VUF\left(\cos\theta_{CVUF} + j\sin\theta_{CVUF}\right) \qquad (4)$$

2.3 Limits for the Voltage Unbalance Factor (VUF)

Most of standards and references impose $VUF = 2.0\%$ as the voltage unbalance limit. Therefore, in this paper, seven values of VUF were analyzed focusing on that benchmark: 0.5%; 1.0%; 1.5%; 2.0%; 2.5%; 3.0% and 3.5%.

This selection allowed to analyze the effects of balanced ($VUF \leq 2\%$) and unbalanced systems ($VUF > 2\%$) in the current and torque of three-phase induction motors.

2.4 Complex Current Unbalance Factor

In order to analyze the effect of the voltage unbalance in the current, the *Complex Current Unbalance Factor* (*CCUF*) is used (5).

$$CCUF(\%) = \frac{I_2}{I_1}100 = \frac{I_2\left(\cos\theta_{I_2} + j\sin\theta_{I_2}\right)}{I_1\left(\cos\theta_{I_1} + j\sin\theta_{I_1}\right)}100 \qquad (5)$$

I_2 and I_1 are the negative- and positive-sequence current components. In this paper, the CCUF is represented by its module (*CUF*), found in (6).

$$CUF = \frac{I_2}{I_1} \qquad (6)$$

2.5 Torque Ripple Factor

In order to analyze the effect of the voltage unbalance in the torque, the *Torque Ripple Factor*, *TRF*, is used [12]. The expression is showed in (7).

$$TRF(\%) = \frac{T_{pp}}{T_0} 100 \tag{7}$$

Where T_{pp} and T_0 are the peak-to-peak torque and the mean torque, respectively.

2.6 Voltage Unbalance Characterization

To analyze the *CUF*, and *TRF*, the voltage unbalance has been characterized by: type, *VUF* and V_1.

3   Unbalanced Points

In this paper, the unbalanced points have been generated by an algorithm designed for this objective. The total number of points obtained has been 13060, and the conditions to obtain them are summarized in the next points.

3.1   Type of Voltage Unbalance

The final distribution for the 13060 unbalanced points is: 21 points for T1, 1746 for T2, 3288 for T3, 21 for T4, 2151 for T5, 3859 for T6, 21 for T7, and 1953 for T8.

3.2   Module of *CVUF* (*VUF*)

The algorithm generates: 781 points of unbalance with $VUF = 0.5\%$, 1274 points with $VUF = 1.0\%$, 1787 points with $VUF = 1.5\%$, 2197 points with $VUF = 2.0\%$, 2376 points with $VUF = 2.5\%$, 2340 points with $VUF = 3.0\%$ and 2305 points with $VUF = 3.5\%$, for a total of 13060 unbalanced points.

3.3   Angle of *CVUF* (θ_{CVUF})

The algorithm has been designed without any restriction for θ_{CVUF}, in order to analyze the effects of this parameter.

3.4   Positive-Sequence of Voltage (V_1)

In this case, the selected restrictions have been related to the modules and angles of phase voltages. In order to have symmetrical limits, the selected values for the algorithm were $100 \pm 15\%$.

According to the change in the angle of the phase voltage, the values selected by the algorithm were $\pm 15°$.

With these restrictions, the value of positive-sequence voltage could be found between 0.85 and 1.15 pu for the 13060 points generated.

4 Motor 1

Initially one induction motor has been chosen, hereinafter referred as Motor 1, with the following characteristics: 75 kW, 3300 V, 50 Hz, 15.3 A, 484 Nm and 1455 min^{-1}. The motor drives a mechanical load with parabolic torque versus mechanical speed.

The single-cage model, with five constant parameters, has been used to simulate the performance of the motor for each selected unbalanced point.

5 Currents and Torque Waveforms Under Voltage Balance

As an example from the total of 13060 voltage unbalance points analyzed, only one has been chosen to show the evolution of the voltage, current and torque. The characteristics of the selected unbalance voltage point are: Type T5, $VUF = 3.5\%$ and $\theta_{\text{CVUF}} = 107.6°$. This point has been selected because it has the highest values of CUF and TRF on the induction motor.

Figure 1 shows the time evolution of the phase voltages. Values are shown in pu, taking the maximum value of the voltage in rated conditions as base value, obtained from (8).

$$v_{pu} = \frac{v}{\sqrt{2}\,V_N} \tag{8}$$

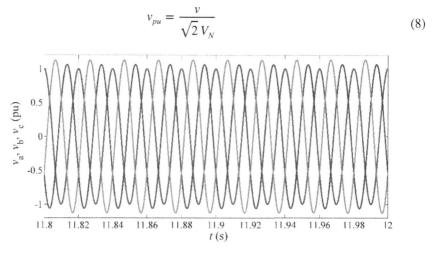

Fig. 1. Time evolution of the phase-to-ground voltages, when the 75 kW and 3300 V induction motor is under a voltage unbalance Type T5 with $VUF = 3.5\%$ and $\theta_{\text{CVUF}} = 107.6°$

Figure 2 shows the temporal evolution of currents. These values are shown in pu, based on the maximum value of the current at rated conditions, obtained from (9).

$$i_{pu} = \frac{i}{\sqrt{2}\,I_N} \tag{9}$$

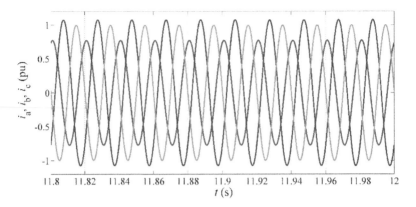

Fig. 2. Time evolution of currents, when the 75 kW and 3300 V induction motor is under a voltage unbalance Type T5 with $VUF = 3.5\%$ and $\theta_{CVUF} = 107.6°$

A visual comparison of Figs. 1 and 2 shows a current unbalance larger than the initial voltage unbalance. It is also noted that the voltage unbalance is produced by two phases with module above the nominal value, leading to a different type of unbalance for the currents.

Figure 3 shows the temporal evolution of torque, in pu values, based on the rated torque value, calculated from (10).

$$T_{pu} = \frac{T}{T_N} \tag{10}$$

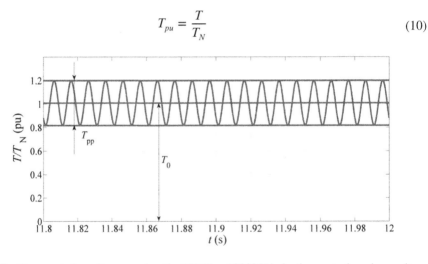

Fig. 3. Time evolution of torque, when the 75 kW and 3300 V induction motor is under a voltage unbalance Type T5 with $VUF = 3.5\%$ and $\theta_{CVUF} = 107.6°$

The torque presents a ripple around its rated value, losing its distinctive constant value when the motor is powered by a system of balanced voltages.

This ripple causes vibrations in the motor [12], and its frequency is equal to twice the frequency of the system voltage.

Unlike the torque, the speed maintains its value very close to the rated value, and oscillations are not observed. This behavior is repeated with every unbalanced point analyzed. For this reason the influence of voltage unbalance on the speed is not discussed in the following sections.

6   Effects on Motor 1

In this section the performance of the motor for each of the 13060 unbalanced points has been analyzed. For this task, the CUF and TRF have been obtained from the current and torque simulated waves. The designed algorithm locates the maximum points of current waves in one period to calculate the module and angle of each current phase. After that, the Fortescue transformation is applied to obtain the positive- and negative-sequence currents. Finally, CUF can be calculated by (6). In the same period of the torque waveform, the maximum, minimum and average values have been located to calculate TRF using (7).

6.1   Influence in the CUF

Figure 4 shows the CUF versus voltage unbalance type for the 2197 unbalanced points with $VUF = 2\%$. All values of CUF are very close to the average value, 9.69%, and the same performance has been observed for all values of VUF.

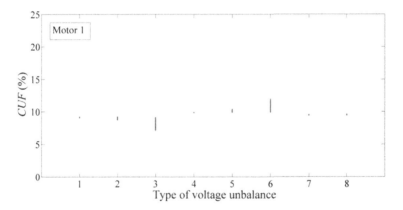

Fig. 4. CUF versus voltage unbalance type for the 2197 unbalanced points with $VUF = 2.0\%$ for Motor 1

Figure 5 illustrates the CUF having a linear trend versus the VUF for each value of V_1. To obtain this figure the unbalanced points selected were: $V_1 = 0.90 \pm 0.005$, $V_1 = 0.95 \pm 0.005$, $V_1 = 1.00 \pm 0.005$, $V_1 = 1.05 \pm 0.005$ and $V_1 = 1.05 \pm 0.005$.

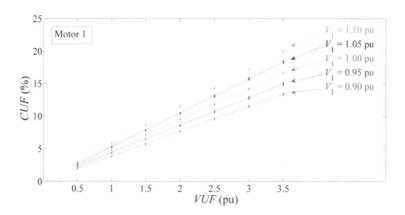

Fig. 5. *CUF* versus *VUF* for the 4289 unbalanced points with the selected values of V_1 for Motor 1

CUF versus V_1 is showed in Fig. 6. Here, a clear lineal relation is observed for each value of *VUF*.

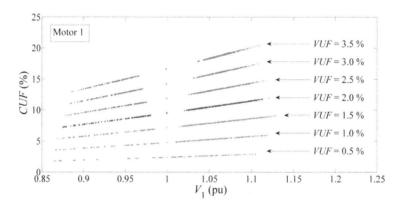

Fig. 6. *CUF* versus V_1 for the 13060 unbalanced points for Motor 1

Finally, only the *VUF* and V_1 have influence on *CUF*. The type of voltage unbalance and $\theta_{\mathbf{CVUF}}$ do not have effects in *CUF*.

6.2 Influence on the θ_{CCUF}

The obtained results show that the θ_{CCUF} does not affect the severity of the voltage unbalance and therefore the graphical results are not presented.

6.3 Influence on the *TRF*

Results presented in Figs. 7, 8, and 9 for the *TRF*, have been very similar to the *CUF*. For this reason, the conclusions are similar too: a linear performance between *TRF* and *VUF* is observed, for each value of V_l (Fig. 8), and a linear performance between *TRF* and V_l, for each value of *VUF* (Fig. 9).

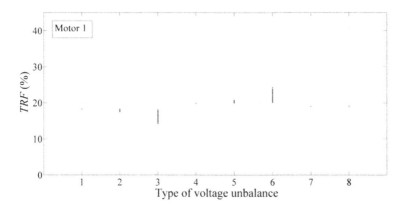

Fig. 7. *TRF* versus type of voltage unbalance for the 2197 unbalanced points with *VUF* = 2.0% for Motor 1

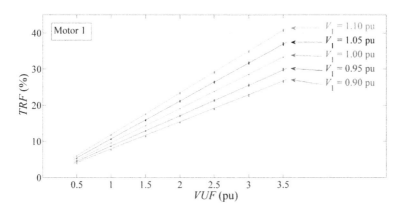

Fig. 8. *TRF* versus *VUF*, for the 4289 unbalanced points with the selected values of V_l for Motor 1

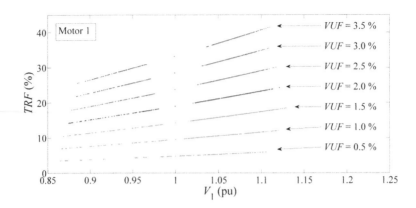

Fig. 9. *TRF* versus V_1 for the 13060 unbalanced points for Motor 1

7   Analysis of the Results

In this section, the effects of *VUF* and V_1 on *CUF* and *TRF* are shown, and compared, for Motor 1 and for an additional motor (Motor 2).

7.1   Motor 2

A second motor has been added to confirm the previous results. The main characteristics of this second motor are: 7.5 kW, 400 V, 50 Hz, 15.3 A, 39.7 Nm, 1460 min^{-1}. Similar to the operating conditions for Motor 1, Motor 2 drives a mechanical load with parabolic torque versus mechanical speed.

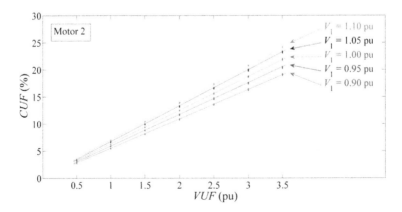

Fig. 10. *CUF* versus *VUF*, for the 4289 unbalanced points with the selected values of V_1 for Motor 2

7.2   Influence of *VUF* and *V₁*

The graphical results obtained for Motor 2 are very similar to the ones obtained in the previous section using Motor 1. Figure 10 shows *CUF* versus *VUF* for Motor 2, showing a linear performance between both for each value of V_1. This conclusion was already observed for Motor 1 in Fig. 5.

Other linear trend is observed in Fig. 11 between *CUF* and V_1 for each value of *VUF* for Motor 2 again, this performance was also obtained for Motor 1 in Fig. 6.

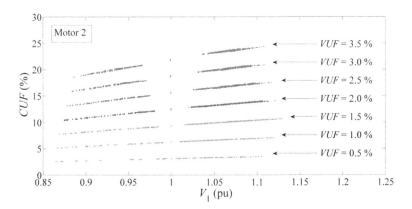

Fig. 11. *CUF* versus V_1 for the 13060 unbalanced points for Motor 2

In Fig. 12, for Motor 2, a linear performance between *TRF* and *VUF* for each value of V_1 is observed. This conclusion was also observed for Motor 1 in Fig. 8.

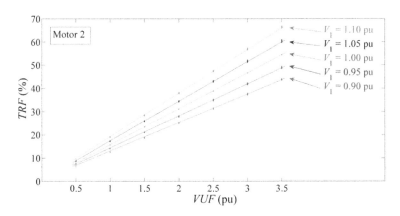

Fig. 12. *TRF* versus *VUF*, for the 4289 unbalanced points with the selected values of V_1 for Motor 2

Finally, in Fig. 13 Motor 2 shows the linear trend between *TRF* and V_1 for each value of *VUF*. The same performance was shown for Motor 1 in Fig. 9.

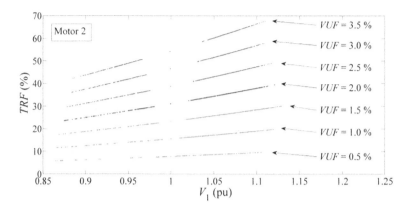

Fig. 13. *TRF* versus V_I for the 13060 unbalanced points for Motor 2

8   Conclusions

Voltage unbalance can be characterized by: type, *VUF*, θ_{CVUF} and V_1.

Voltage unbalance generates current unbalance and torque ripple in three-phase induction motors.

Current unbalance has been characterized by *CUF* and θ_{CCUF}, but only *CUF* seems to be a good factor to analyze the effect of the voltage unbalance on the current.

For voltage unbalance, only *VUF* and V_I have influence in the current unbalance and torque ripple. Type and θ_{CVUF} do not have influence.

A voltage unbalance with *VUF* = 2%, the limit used in some standards, can determine important current unbalance and torque ripple in induction motors. These facts can trip the electrical protections stopping the industrial process and generating intolerable torque ripple in some drives.

The *CUF* is greater than the *VUF* for the analyzed motors in all the values of *VUF* and V_1.

A linear trend is observed between *CUF* and *TRF* versus *VUF* for a constant value of V_1.

Finally, another linear trend is observed between *CUF* and *TRF* versus V_1 for a constant value of *VUF*.

References

1. Gómez-Expósito, A., Conejo, A.J., Cañizares, C.: Electric Energy Systems: Analysis and Operation, 1st edn. CRC Press, Boca Raton (2009)
2. Lee, C.Y., Chen, B.K., Lee, W.J., Hsu, Y.F.: Effects of various unbalanced voltages on the operation performance. In: Proceedings of the Industrial and Commercial Power Systems Technical Conference, Philadelphia, PA, USA, pp. 51–59 (1997)
3. Dekhandji, F.Z., Refoufi, L., Bentarzi, H.: Quantitative assessment of three phase supply voltage unbalance effects on induction motors. Int. J. Syst. Assur. Eng. Manag. **8**(S1), 393–406 (2017)

4. Silaev, M.A.: Tul'Skii, V.N., Kartashev, I.I.: The effect of fast changes in voltage unbalance on vibration characteristics of asynchronous motors. Russ. Electr. Eng. **85**(6), 382–388 (2014)
5. Guasch-Pesquer, L., Youb, L., González-Molina, F., Zeppa-Durigutti, E.R.: Effects of voltage unbalance on torque and current of the induction motors. In: Proceedings of the International Conference on Optimization of Electrical and Electronic Equipment, Brasov, Romania, pp. 647–652 (2012)
6. Sousa, V., Viego, P.R., Gómez, J.R., Quispe, E.C., Balbis, M.: Shaft power estimation in induction motor operating under unbalanced and harmonics voltages. IEEE Lat. Am. Trans. **14**(5), 2309–2315 (2016)
7. Wang, Y.J.: Analysis of effects of three-phase voltage unbalance on induction motors with emphasis on the angle of the complex voltage unbalance factor. IEEE Trans. Energy Convers. **16**(3), 270–275 (2001)
8. Le-Huy, H., Perret, R., Feuillet, R.: Minimization of torque ripple in brushless DC motor drives. IEEE Trans. Industry Appl. **22**(4), 748–755 (1986)
9. Bollen, M.H.J., Gu, I.Y.: Signal Processing of Power Quality Disturbances. Signal Processing of Power Quality Disturbances, 1st edn. Wiley, Hoboken (2006)
10. Ebadi, A., Mirzaie, M., Gholamian, S.A.: Torque analysis of three-phase induction motor under voltage unbalance using 2D FEM. Int. J. Eng. Sci. Technol. **3**(2), 871–876 (2011)
11. Sandhu, K.S., Chaudhary, V.: Steady state modelling of induction motor operating with unbalanced supply system. WSEAS Trans. Circ. Syst. **8**(2), 197–206 (2009)
12. Faiz, J., Ebrahimpour, H., Pillay, P.: Influence of unbalanced voltage on the steady-state performance of a three-phase squirrel-cage induction motor. IEEE Trans. Energy Convers. **19**(4), 657–662 (2004)
13. Quispe, E.C., Lopez-Fernandez, X.M., Mendes, A.M.S., Marques Cardoso, A.J., Palacios, J.A.: Influence of the positive sequence voltage on the derating of three-phase induction motors under voltage unbalance. In: Proceedings of the IEEE International Electric Machines and Drives Conference, Chicago, IL, United States, pp. 100–105 (2013)
14. Ferreira Filho, A.L., Garcia, D.C., Nascimento, F.A.O., Cormane, J.A.A.: Study of voltage unbalance conditions based on the behavior of the Complex Voltage Unbalance Factor (CVUF). In: Proceedings of the IEEE/PES Transmission and Distribution Conference and Exposition: Latin America, Sao Paulo, Brazil, pp. 184–189 (2010)
15. Craciunescu, A., Ciumbulea, G.S., Dumitrica, C.N.: Space phasor geometrical loci in polar coordinates as voltage unbalance monitoring tool. In: 8th International Symposium on Advanced Topics in Electrical Engineering, Bucharest, Romania (2013)
16. Ferreira Filho, A.L., de Oliveira, M., Silva Pinto, M.G.: A computational tool to analyze, quantify and classify voltage imbalance in electrical power systems. In: Transmission and Distribution Conference and Exposition: Latin America, Caracas, Venezuela (2006)

Emulation of a Photovoltaic Module Using a Wiener-Type Nonlinear Impedance Controller for Tracking of the Operation Point

Oswaldo López-Santos[1(✉)], María C. Merchán Riveros[1], María C. Salas Castaño[1], William A. Londoño[1], and Germain Garcia[2]

[1] Universidad de Ibagué, 730001 Ibagué, Colombia
{oswaldo.lopez,maria.merchan,william.londono}@unibague.edu.co,
2420131018@estudiantesunibague.edu.co
[2] LAAS-CNRS, Université de Toulouse, Toulouse, France
garcia@laas.fr

Abstract. This paper proposes a control method to provide the function of Solar Panel Emulation (SPE) to a low-cost programmable DC source. The proposed control operates with base on the error between measurement of the conductance connected at the output of the SPE and the conductance obtained evaluating the I-V characteristic of the panel model. The principle of operation is that the output of the controller modifies the value of the voltage introduced into the W-Lambert function to obtain the corresponding current enforcing the regulation of the measured conductance. In this paper, a controller composed by a nonlinear static gain and a conventional PI controller is proposed. The controller architecture configures a Wiener system structure which ensures the stable convergence of the real SPE variables to the values defined by the model. Simulation results are presented evaluating the dynamic performance of the system for irradiance and load variations. SPE method is implemented using simple measurement and conditioning circuits interacting with an application developed in LabVIEW through a data acquisition card. This implementation provides a complete solution highly applicable in research and industrial development.

Keywords: Solar panel emulator · Photovoltaic modules · Non-linear control · Impedance controller · Wiener-type structure · W-Lambert function · LabVIEW · Graphic user interface

1 Introduction

Photovoltaic (PV) solar energy is one of the topics with more development in research among the more relevant renewable resources in the world. However, research efforts focused in its development and application heavily depends on environmental conditions because of the need of acceptable irradiance levels for test processes. To face this difficulty, sun simulators and photovoltaic array emulators have been developed allowing the test of microinverters, module integrated converters and maximum power point trackers (MPPT) in the laboratory under any environmental conditions. Simulators

© Springer International Publishing AG 2017
J.C. Figueroa-García et al. (Eds.): WEA 2017, CCIS 742, pp. 482–494, 2017.
DOI: 10.1007/978-3-319-66963-2_43

and emulators require less area, avoid the use of interconnection elements, include additional protections and allow emulating any type of solar panel under any temperature and solar irradiance conditions. However, commercial versions of emulators offer a wide variety of functions which increases their cost, then limiting the access to industrial and high-level research facilities. This limitation can be solved with the development of low-cost emulators also providing interactivity, flexibility, reliability and accuracy of the commercial products.

In the last years, different types of photovoltaic panel emulators have been proposed and developed around the world [1–15]. Most of the documented works are focused on the selection and design of optimum DC-DC converter topologies which are controlled locally or remotely [1–5]. For instance, half-bridge converter is selected in [1], full-bridge is selected in [2], buck-boost and buck converters are used in [3] and [13], respectively. Many other proposed emulators use programmable DC supplies working with proprietary software applications or embedded programmable devices as controllers [6–12]. The use of a power converter to provide the voltage and current in SPE has as main advantages the rapidity of the control loops and the possibility to change the operational point only manipulating the duty cycle [10, 11]. On the other hand, the use of programmable power sources (PPS) is also common [8, 13, 16]. These solutions show as advantage, the heritage to the emulator the flexibility and reliability of the PPS. However, its main drawback is the limited acquisition rate which imposes the sample rate of the control loop and then the frequency response of the emulator.

The majority of these last developments are based on different circuit type models of the PV module. Among these models, it can be referenced the single diode model [13], the well-known two diodes model [14], and the models including the effect of the bypass diode [17]. To obtain a useful mathematical expression representing the static behaviour of the PV modules, the use of the Lambert W function plays a key role in order to simplify the solution of the circuit model equations.

In addition to the power component of the SPE, another key part is the software application providing the control functions and the interaction with users. The first versions of SPE including Graphical User Interfaces (GUI) were developed using C programming language [1, 3]. In the most recent, the use of MATLAB/Simulink in this application becomes common, as it is evidenced in [8, 13, 14, 16]. However, as it was illustrated in [6, 7], LabVIEW platform is also preferred because it provides simple programming and better tools to develop GUI and real-time control, making this option the most versatile to accomplish our implementation objectives.

In order to achieve the emulation of a PV module, the control problem can be divided in to main tasks: (1) to ensure the accurate definition of the output voltage corresponding to the expected operation point, and (2) to ensure a rapid convergence to a new operation point when a change appears in the configuration parameters manipulated by the user (irradiance, temperature) or a disturbance is applied at the output. In these last two cases, the impedance changes and in consequence the operation point moves. Several methods to control the convergence of the SPE output to a point in the I-V curve of a PV module are proposed in the literature. The basic approach presented in [4] uses a piece-wise representation of the I-V curve using discrete values allocated in a table in order to determine the needed voltage with the aim to arrive to this value after two or three iterations increasing or decreasing the output voltage. Other works such as [6, 7] use measurements of voltage and current in order to determine the resistance line and its intersection with the I-V curve. In [8], it is proposed a control based on two PI regulators operating over the current and voltage output values simultaneously which improves the dynamic performance of the emulator.

The current and voltage, as the main variables to describe the electrical behavior of PV module have constrained ranges and this fact implies limitations using them as manipulated variables. Then, the use of resistance or, which is the same, the conductance, allows having a wider range of operation ($0 \rightarrow \infty$) which is an advantage in terms of control implementation. However, the conductance as a function of the other variables of the panel has also an accentuated nonlinear nature what prevents that a conventional proportional-integral (PI) controller operate properly for the whole range.

This paper describes the development of a real-time SPE based on the use of a programmable DC source. The single diode model (SDM) of the solar panel represented by the use of the Lambert W function, which allows determining the current of the panel as a function of its voltage and the instantaneous environmental conditions. A nonlinear controller is proposed to achieve conductance tracking in such a way that the emulator provides the voltage corresponding to the connected load. The proposed scheme includes a PI controller preceded by a nonlinear static gain configuring what is named as Wiener structure. This control shows advantages in terms of dynamic performance but its use implies a high computational cost, which is not relevant when the control has a computer based implementation but can be inacceptable for embedded solutions. Control and GUI of the SPE are developed in LabVIEW allowing the user to vary the environmental conditions (temperature and irradiance), to modify the characteristics of the panel in real time, to visualize the point of operation of the system in the representative graphs and exporting and importing panel parameters from PSIM software. The rest of the paper is organized as follows: Sect. 2 explains the mathematical modelling employed. Control approach is developed in Sect. 3 and simulated results are presented in Sect. 4. The main aspects of the implementation of the proposed emulator are presented in Sect. 5. Finally, conclusions and future work are presented in Sect. 6.

2   Photovoltaic Modelling

The equivalent electric circuit or model of a solar panel can be represented as a current source in parallel with a diode representing the behavior of semiconductor materials, a series resistance representing the internal voltage drops and a parallel resistance representing other external effects. By performing circuit analysis, the current of the PV module can be described as a function of the voltage providing an approximate model. To this previous model, it can be added the bypass diode which is conventionally used in order to protect the panels when they are connected in series. The resulting model is well known as the bypass diode model [17]. Figure 1a depicts the circuit model including the bypass diode which can be represented using the Lambert W function [18]. The circuit model is composed by the light induced current generator I_{ph}, diode D, series resistance R_s, shunt resistance R_h and the bypass diode D_b. The equations describing the operation of the circuit were extracted from [15].

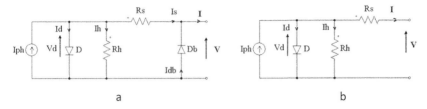

Fig. 1. Circuit model of a PV module: (a) Bypass diode circuit model, (b) single diode model (SDM).

Using Kirchhoff voltage and current laws is obtained PV output current and can be expressed as a non-linear function of voltage as:

$$I = \frac{\left[R_h\left(I_{ph} + I_{sat,d}\right) - V\right]}{\left(R_h + R_s\right)} + I_{sat,db}\left(e^{\frac{V}{nV_{t,db}}} - 1\right) - \frac{nV_{t,d}}{R_s}LambertW(\theta), \qquad (1)$$

where

$$\theta = \frac{(R_h//R_s)I_{sat,db}\, e^{\left[R_h R_s\left(I_{ph}+I_{sat,d}\right)+R_h V/nV_{t,d}\left(R_h+R_s\right)\right]}}{nV_{t,d}} \qquad (2)$$

In the proposed SPE, the bypass diode will not be considered since it does not have a significant effect on an individual panel and the calculations required by the model decrease. The single diode circuit model is shown in Fig. 1b. Considering that the value of shunt resistance is much greater than the series resistance value, PV current can be expressed in simplified form of expressions (1) and (2) as:

$$I = I_{ph} + I_{sat,d} - \frac{V}{\left(R_h + R_s\right)} - \frac{nV_{t,d}}{R_s}LambertW\left(\frac{R_s I_{sat,d}e^{\left(\frac{R_s\left(I_{ph} + I_{sat,d}\right) + V}{nV_{t,d}}\right)}}{nV_{t,d}}\right) \qquad (3)$$

3   Control Approach

The operation point of the PV module is defined by the impedance connected at its output, in such a way that, among all the possibilities, this point is unique. Figure 2 depicts two surfaces representing the voltage of the PV module as either a function of the irradiance and the conductance or a function of the temperature and the conductance. Using this representation, it is easy to understand that the PV module can be easily emulated considering that for an irradiance value and a temperature value, the operation point is determined only by the connected conductance. Then, measuring the connected conductance at the output of the emulator and considering this measurement as the reference, the system can enforce the convergence of the PV module model to this value in the I-V characteristic, which corresponds to the connected inductance. As expected, the proposed control objective involves nonlinear relations.

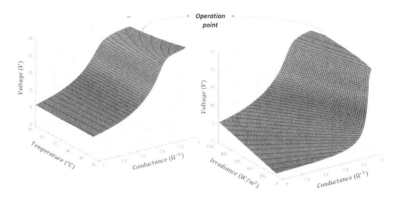

Fig. 2. 3D surfaces representing the voltage as a function of: (a) temperature and conductance, and (b) irradiance and conductance.

In the approach presented in this paper, the model of the PV module is the mathematical expression (3) which gives a current value as output for a voltage value as input. Considering the conductance as the controlled variable, the voltage programmed in the source is then the manipulated variable. The relation between these two variables has a nonlinear nature which affects the control loop. As the first part of the proposed control, nonlinear function (4) is suggested in order to linearize the control loop.

$$v_{ctr} = K_p \left(e^{-k_{lin} \cdot g_{mes}} - e^{-k_{lin} \cdot g_{mod}} \right) + K_i \int_0^t \left(e^{-k_{lin} \cdot g_{mes}} - e^{-k_{lin} \cdot g_{mod}} \right) dt \tag{4}$$

As expected, this control approach solves properly the nonlinear problem for a given value of irradiance. Hence, a compensation of this effect using parameter scheduling of the input nonlinear function is proposed. Parameter K_{lin} is defined as $K_{lin} = m + nE$ where m and n are positive parameters, and E is the instantaneous irradiance. Figure 3 depicts the compensated static relation G-V related with its nonlinear version.

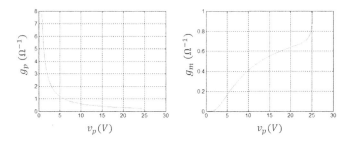

Fig. 3. G-V characteristics of a PV module and its linearized version Gm-V.

Using this linearization method, the control loop can be represented in the form of a Wiener-type structure as it is shown in Fig. 4 in which it is identify the parameter scheduling introduced in the input nonlinear function to compensate the effect of the irradiance in the PV model. It is worth to remember that the irradiance is settled by the user in the software application either directly or by means of a programmed test bench.

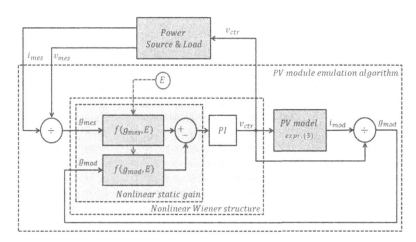

Fig. 4. Block diagram of the proposed control scheme.

Expected operation of the emulator is depicted in Fig. 5 where the responses to two possible transitions of variables are evaluated. In the first case, resistance suddenly decreases enforcing the system to converge to the new operational point in two jumps which will occur during a sample period of the programmable source. As it can be observed in Fig. 5a, after change, voltage keeps constant intersecting the line corresponding to the new applied load. After that, control system reacts increasing the programmed voltage until the panel characteristic is achieved in the model. In the second case in Fig. 5b, a change of irradiance is applied what produces a direct displacement of the system to the new point since controller will attain the new curve in less than a sample period.

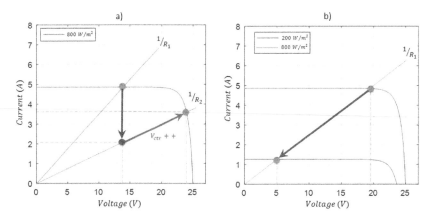

Fig. 5. Trajectories described by the output of the emulator represented in the I-V plane: (a) load variations; (b) irradiance variations.

4   Simulated Results

In order to validate the proposed control several simulations was performed using PSIM software. Simulation uses the solar module model available in the software with the parameters listed in Table 1.

Table 1.   Solar module parameters.

Parameter	Symbol	Value	Units
Number of cells	N_s	36	–
Open-circuit voltage	V_{oc}	21.1	V
Short-circuit current	I_{sc}	3.8	A
Band energy	E_g	1.12	eV
Ideality factor	A	1.2	–
Series resistance	R_s	0.008	Ω
Shunt resistance	R_{sh}	1000	Ω
Saturation current	I_{so}	2.16×10^8	A
Temperature coefficient	C_t	0.0024	A/K

Parameters of the proposed controller were settled as $K_p = 2$, $K_i = 1 \times 10^6$, $m = 0.6$ and $n = 0.001$. The first test consist on applying resistance disturbances at the output of the simulated power source which is accomplished by commuting a load between 0.005 and 0.1 Ω^{-1} with a frequency of 20 Hz and a duty cycle of 50%. The same test was applied for loads commutating between 0.01 and 0.2 Ω^{-1}, between 1 and 5 Ω^{-1}. A triangular ripple was added to the steady state of the load in order to assess the frequency response of the close loop system. The amplitude of the ripple was selected as 0.005 Ω^{-1}, 0.1 Ω^{-1} and 0.5 Ω^{-1}, respectively. All results demonstrate the effectiveness of the control proposal. As it can be observed in all depicted cases in Fig. 6, the performance of the system is satisfactory for both increasing and decreasing transitions.

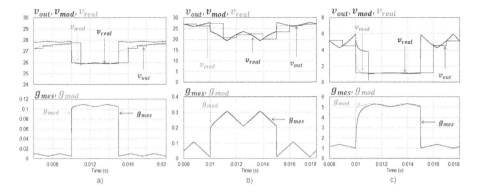

Fig. 6. Simulated results for conductance sudden disturbances: (a) from 0.005 to 0.1 Ω^{-1} with a triangular ripple of 0.005 Ω^{-1}, (b) from 0.01 to 0.2 Ω^{-1} with a triangular ripple of 0.1 Ω^{-1}, and (c) from 1 to 5 Ω^{-1} with a triangular ripple of 0.25 Ω^{-1}.

Complementary, a set of simulations were applied considering sudden disturbances on the irradiance values from 250 to 500 W/m^2 at 0.01 s, returning to 250 W/m^2 after 50 ms (see Fig. 7a), and from 500 to 1000 W/m^2 returning to 500 W/m^2 with the same time intervals (see Fig. 7b). For these test the conductance was kept constant using a value of 0.5 Ω^{-1}. The results demonstrate the appropriate operation of the parameter scheduling in the nonlinear static gain of the controller.

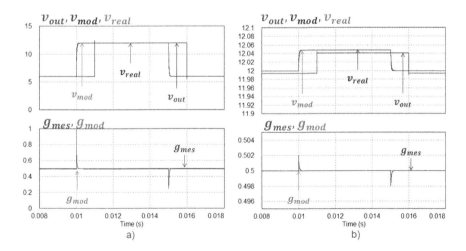

Fig. 7. Simulated results for irradiance sudden changes: (a) from 250 to 500 W/m^2 and (b) from 500 to 1000 W/m^2.

As it was demonstrated using simulation results, the convergence of the proposed control to the operating point is achieved with a good dynamic response obtaining settling times below ten of microseconds without overshoots or important deviations.

Also, the applied test used ripple content in the applied impedance showing the ability of the method to track not only constant reference but also time varying references.

5   System Implementation

5.1   General Description of the System

The operating principle of the proposed SPE is based on the control of a programmable power supply (PPS) in order to enforce its operation as a solar panel. The PPS is the power stage of the system and its output voltage is defined by means of signals produced by the control which is embedded in a computer application. Controller takes measurements of both voltage and current in order to define the control voltage. This voltage corresponds to a point within the characteristic curve of the desired solar panel based on the connected external load and the model of the solar panel.

The proposed SPE is composed by a software component developed in LabVIEW and a hardware component interconnected through an acquisition card. Then, from the implementation perspective, the system can be decomposed into three blocks: (a) programmable power source; (b) measurement and conditioning circuits; and (c) acquisition card and computational application. The blocks (a) and (b) will be described hereinafter as the hardware component whereas the block (c) will be treated as the software component. Description of hardware and software components is based on the same methodology as in [19]. The diagram in Fig. 8 depicts the signal flow between the three blocks. As it is observed, the programmable power source voltage receives voltage and current configuration signals (v_{ctr} and i_{lim}) which are given by the software component. The output voltage and output current of the power source are measured (v_{out} and i_{out}), after that, they are conditioned and acquired by the software component (v_{mes} and i_{mes}).

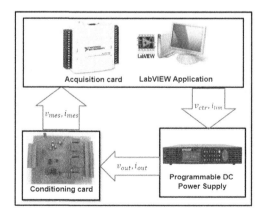

Fig. 8. Descriptive block diagram of the proposed solar emulator system.

5.2   Hardware Component

The hardware component is integrated by a current sensor and a voltage divider obtaining measurements of signals i_{mes} and v_{mes} respectively, and analogue conditioning circuits. Current is measured by using an isolated closed-loop hall-effect transducer CAS-15-NP. All these circuits are integrated on a single circuit board giving the conditioned signals to an acquisition card DAQ NI USB-6008.

5.3   Software Component

The software component of the system is represented by the computer application SunnySIM performed in LabVIEW, which contains graphical user's interface (GUI), signal acquisition and generation, and computing of the control routine. The GUI of the emulator allows visualization and real-time interactivity with users, configuration of parameters and execution of different registration and data storage functions.

Figure 9 shows GUI of the proposed emulator highlighting: visualization of current-voltage curve (I-V), visualization of the power-voltage curve (P-V), visualization of the power-conductance curve (P-G) and signalling of the operational point. Also, it is possible to identify a frame dedicated to the manual configuration of PV parameters and numerical visualization of the irradiance, access to registration functions and a pop-up window to import and export PV module parameters from and to PSIM respectively.

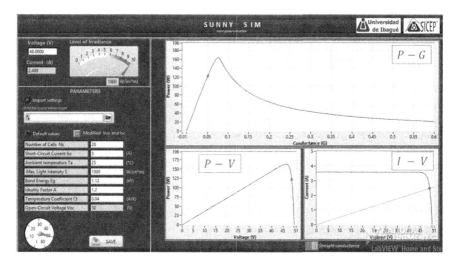

Fig. 9. Graphical user interface highlighting visualization of characteristic curves of a solar panel.

Moreover, the software component has the following computational functions: modify the irradiance to generate the curves of the emulated panel in real time, calculate the operating point of the system in different curves based on the mathematical model and the acquired signals and calculate the values of current and voltage for the convergence of the emulator to the curve of the solar panel. Figure 10 shows experimental results of the signals of the SPE during on-line operation coping with sudden changes of the conductance and the irradiance. As it can be observed, the proposed control reacts recuperating the stable behaviour in the new desired or expected condition.

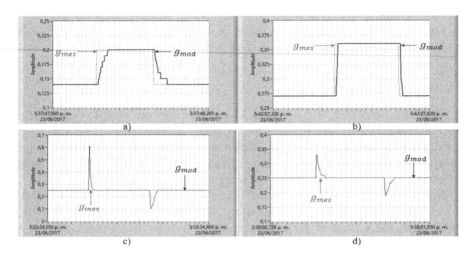

Fig. 10. LabVIEW captures of experimental results for conductance sudden load disturbances: (a) from 0.143 to 0.2 Ω^{-1} (b) from 0.27 to 0.37 Ω^{-1}; and irradiance disturbances (c) from 200 to 500 W/m^2 (d) from 600 to 800 W/m^2.

6   Conclusions and Future Work

An innovative control scheme providing the SPE function to a Programmable Power Source was presented. The control is based on a conductance regulator represented in the form of a Wiener structure in which a nonlinear function and a PI controller are integrated. The performance of the proposed controller was demonstrated by means of simulated results in which an appropriate transient response allows to converge to the photovoltaic module model before a new sample of the signal programming the source is taken. Transient response to external load changes and user irradiance programmed changes were evaluated obtaining a reliable and accurate behavior of the SPE. The algorithm was implemented in a LabVIEW application to obtain experimental validation which was partially presented in the paper.

Acknowledgements. This research is being developed with the partial support of the Gobernación del Tolima under Convenio de cooperación 1026-2013. The results presented in this paper have been obtained with the assistance of students from the Research Hotbed on Power Electronic Conversion (SICEP), Research Group D+TEC, Universidad de Ibagué, Ibagué-Colombia.

References

1. Kulkarni, S.S., Thean, C.Y., Kong, A.W.: A novel PC based solar electric panel simulator. In: Proceedings of the Fifth International Conference on Power Electronics and Drive Systems (PEDS), pp. 848–852 (2003)
2. Thean, C.Y., Junbo, J., Kong, A.W.: An embedded microchip system design for programmable solar panel simulator. In: Proceedings of the International Conference on Power Electronics and Drives Systems (PEDS), pp. 1606–1610 (2005)
3. Lu, D.D., Nguyen, Q.N.: A photovoltaic panel emulator using a buck-boost DC/DC converter and a low cost micro-controller. Sol. Energy **86**(5), 1477–1484 (2012)
4. Singh, A., Hota, A.R., Patra, A.: Design and implementation of a programmable solar photovoltaic simulator. In: Proceedings of the International Conference on Power, Control and Embedded Systems (ICPCES), pp. 1–5 (2010)
5. Espinar, C.M.: Diseño e implementación de un emulador fotovoltaico para el testeo de inversores en un entorno de programación Simulink y desarrollo de una interfaz HMI. Doctoral Dissertation, Universidad Politécnica de Catalunya (2011)
6. Dolan, D.S., Durago, J., Taufik, T.: Development of a photovoltaic panel emulator using Labview. In: Proceedings of the 37th IEEE Photovoltaic Specialists Conference (PVSC), pp. 1795–1800 (2011)
7. Bhise, K., Pragallapati, N., Thale, S., Agarwal, V.: Labview based emulation of photovoltaic array to study maximum power point tracking algorithms. In: Proceedings of the 38th IEEE Photovoltaic Specialists Conference (PVSC), pp. 2961–2966 (2012)
8. Kadri, R., Andrei, H., Gaubert, J.-P., Ivanovici, T., Champenois, G., Andrei, P.: Modeling of the photovoltaic cell circuit parameters for optimum connection model and real-time emulator with partial shadow conditions. Energy **42**(1), 57–67 (2012)
9. Jiang, T., Putrus, G., McDonald, S., Conti, M., Li, B., Johnston, D.: Generic photovoltaic system emulator based on lambert omega function. In: Proceedings of the 46th International Universities' Power Engineering Conference (UPEC), pp. 1–5 (2011)
10. Azharuddin, M., Babu, T.S., Bilakanti, N., Rajasekar, N.: A nearly accurate solar photovoltaic emulator using a dSPACE controller for real-time control. Electr. Power Compon. Syst. **44**(7), 774–782 (2016)
11. Tapfumanei, T.B., Mouton, H.D.T., Rix, A.J.: Solar array emulator. In: Proceedings of the 4th Southern African Solar Energy Conference (SASEC), pp. 1–8 (2016)
12. Barrera, L.M., Osorio, R.A., Trujillo, C.L.: Design and implementation of electronic equipment that emulates photovoltaic panels. In: Proceedings of the IEEE 42nd Photovoltaic Specialist Conference (PVSC), pp. 1–5 (2015)
13. Gonzalez-Llorente, J., Rambal-Vecino, A., Garcia-Rodriguez, L.A., Balda, J.C., Ortiz-Rivera, E.I.: Simple and efficient low power photovoltaic emulator for evaluation of power conditioning systems. In: Proceedings of the IEEE Applied Power Electronics Conference and Exposition (APEC), Long Beach, CA, pp. 3712–3716 (2016)
14. Orozco-Gutierrez, M.L., Ramirez-Scarpetta, J.M., Spagnuolo, G., Ramos-Paja, C.A.: A method for simulating large PV arrays that include reverse biased cells. Appl. Energy **123**, 157–167 (2014)
15. Tornez-Xavier, G.M., Gomez-Castañeda, F., Moreno-Cadenas, J.A., Flores-Nava, L.M.: FGPA development and implementation of a solar panel emulator. In: Proceedings of the 10th International Conference on Electrical Engineering, Computing Science and Automatic Control (CCE), pp. 467–472 (2013)

16. Ardila-Franco, C.E., Soto-Gómez, J.A., Arango-Zuluaga, E.I., Ramos-Paja, C.A., Serna-Garcés, S.I.: Desarrollo de un Sistema Emulador de Arreglos Fotovoltaicos en Tiempo Real Considerando Variaciones en las Condiciones Climáticas. TecnoLógicas, 151–163 (2013)
17. Petrone, G., Spagnuolo, G., Vitelli, M.: Analytical model of mismatched photovoltaic fields by means of Lambert W-function. Sol. Energy Mater. Sol. Cells **91**(18), 1652–1657 (2007)
18. Weisstein, E.W.: Lambert W-Function. [En línea]. Disponible en. http:// mathworld.wolfram.com/LambertW-Function.html. Accessed 17 Feb 2017
19. Lopez-Santos, O., Arango-Buitrago, J.S., Gonzalez-Morales, D.F.: On-line visualization and long-term monitoring of a single-phase photovoltaic generator using SCADA. Commun. Comput. Inf. Sci. (CCIS) **657**, 295–307 (2016)

Control of a Bidirectional Cûk Converter Providing Charge/Discharge of a Battery Array Integrated in DC Buses of Microgrids

Oswaldo Lopez-Santos[1(✉)], David A. Zambrano Prada[1],
Yeison A. Aldana-Rodriguez[1], Harold A. Esquivel-Cabeza[1],
Germain Garcia[2], and Luis Martinez-Salamero[3]

[1] Program of Electronics Engineering, Universidad de Ibagué, Ibagué, Colombia
{oswaldo.lopez,david.zambrano}@unibague.edu.co,
aleoj30l@gmail.com, haec88@hotmail.com
[2] LAAS-CNRS, Univ de Toulouse, INSA, Toulouse, France
germain.garcia@laas.fr
[3] Universitat Rovira i Virgili, Tarragona, Spain
luis.martinez@urv.cat

Abstract. This paper presents a proposal to charge and discharge valve-regulated lead-acid (VRLA) battery arrays integrated into microgrids by using the bidirectional Cûk converter with a multi-mode multi-loop control scheme based on sliding-mode control. The proposed control integrates the constant current - constant voltage - constant voltage charge method (CC-CV-CV) which is implemented using an inner current loop based on the sliding mode control of the input current of the converter and two nested outer loops based on the voltage and current of the battery. Conversely, the discharge is studied using two operational modes, one using a current reference given by a high level on a hierarchical structure and other using a current reference given by an outer Proportional-Integral (PI) controller regulating the voltage of the DC bus. The modelling of the bidirectional Cûk converter in these applications and its operational modes besides the analysis of the inner loop and the design criteria used in the synthesis of the outer loops are addressed. Simulation results are presented validating the control proposal.

Keywords: Microgrids · Battery charge · Battery energy storage system · Sliding-mode control · Bidirectional Cûk converter

1 Introduction

The batteries are an essential part of modern energy structures such as microgrids integrating generation, storage and consumption in localized power systems [1, 2]. The elements composing microgrids interacts through power buses, which can have AC or DC nature [3], being this last the more used to integrate renewable energy resources (RES) and energy storage systems (ESS) [4]. As a solution to the intermittence in the power availability of renewable resources, the batteries allow the storage of energy in order to obtain autonomy in the absence of the grid. To attain this target, an electronic

© Springer International Publishing AG 2017
J.C. Figueroa-García et al. (Eds.): WEA 2017, CCIS 742, pp. 495–507, 2017.
DOI: 10.1007/978-3-319-66963-2_44

device must be inserted between a DC power bus and batteries covering the charging method requirements as a function of the type of battery. For many years, the CC-CV-CV method has been used to charge VRLA batteries as an improvement of the traditional constant current-constant voltage method since it yields a better use of the battery without increasing the complexity of the electronic control [5, 6]. However, its application is conditioned to the availability of an energy source at least a period long enough to accomplish the charge, which may become up to eight hours [7].

The power converter interfacing the batteries with the DC bus must have bidirectional power flow capability in order to provide charge and discharge regime. The discharge of the battery can be made at a constant current rate which value is defined by a high level in hierarchical control architecture or by power demand in order to ensure the stability of the bus providing voltage regulation. Figure 1 depicts a device based scheme of an Extra Low Voltage DC (ELVDC) bus integrating two RES, a battery array, local loads and interaction with a Low Voltage DC (LVDC) bus through the bidirectional converter denoted as Interlink converter (ILC).

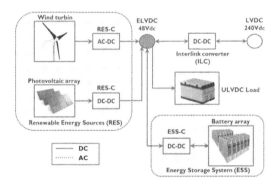

Fig. 1. Energy storage system integration in a ELVDC bus of a microgrid

ESS is composed by bidirectional converter ESS-C and a lead-acid battery array. Operation mode of ESS depends on the ones that the converter exhibits. Indistinctly of the used power converter, it must operate in three modes: The first mode corresponds to the charge of the battery, the second corresponds to discharge of the battery at limited current and the last mode corresponds to the discharge of the battery regulating the bus voltage. Changing between modes depends on the power balance of the DC bus.

Selection of the DC-DC power converter (ESS-C) and its control is a key task of the system design, since afore mentioned settings only modify the reference values of the internally regulated variables. This DC-DC converter must provide compatibility between the DC bus and the battery, which means avoiding the high frequency components in both input and output connection ports. In this sense, the Cûk converter is a converter topology with buck and boost capability, which has inductors in both input and output ports covering the aforementioned requirements guarantying that the current at the DC bus side and the current at the battery side have continuous nature [8, 9].

Like most DC-DC converters, the Cûk converter has also a non-linear nature; hence, it is classified as a variable structure system. Because of this fact, the sliding-mode approach is an interesting choice to guarantee robustness and stability with a relatively simplicity in the circuit implementation [10, 11]. With this in mind, an indirect stabilization of the output voltage is obtained enforcing a sliding motion on the input current by means of an inner control loop based on hysteresis comparison [12]. The use of a cascade control topology as in [13–15], allows applying sliding mode control in bidirectional converters by modifying the current reference as a function of the voltage error. Consequently, if required as in this case, an additional outer loop can modify the reference of the outer voltage loop to attain all control aims. In this work, in order to charge batteries, the first outer loop (voltage loop) is composed by a PI compensator which modifies the current reference of the inner loop in order to attain a desired output voltage in every operational condition regardless of power losses, voltage drops, input voltage disturbances or output current changes. The outermost loop allows regulate the charge current during the constant current mode by reducing the output voltage set-point until the required value. Discharge of batteries is accomplished by using a similar control configuration, in which the converter can have two functionalities, discharge the battery at constant current rate or regulate the DC bus voltage. In both modes, the current is controlled by means of a current control loop based on sliding-mode whereas only in the second mode the current value is instantaneously determined by an outer loop in the same manner as in the charge mode. Although a unified control can be proposed covering both charge and discharge operation, this paper focuses in these two modes independently.

The rest of the paper is organized as follows: Battery charging requirements and the ESS control scheme are presented in Sect. 2. Section 3 presents the modelling of the converter and the control synthesis for charging and discharging modes. After that, the design and analytical predictions are validated using simulation results in Sect. 4. Finally, conclusions are given in Sect. 5.

2 Energy Storage System Description

2.1 CC-CV-CV Charging Method Description

As shown in Fig. 2, three different behaviors are identified in the CC-CV-CV charging method. At the start, during the interval $t_0 < t \leq t_1$, the output current is limited to a value between 0.1C and 0.4C (C is the rated capacity of the battery) until the output voltage reaches the references value V_{bref1}. This is called either constant current or bulk charge interval. After that, during the interval $t_1 < t \leq t_2$ the output voltage is regulated to the reference value V_{bref1} until the output current falls below a defined minimum value, which is about of 0.002C. This is called either constant voltage or absorption interval. After that, the output voltage is regulated permanently to the value V_{bref2} which is lower than that used in the above interval. This is called either standby or floating voltage interval. The voltage values V_{bref1} and V_{bref2} are defined in the range of float voltages given by the battery manufacturers [12].

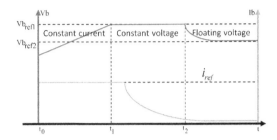

Fig. 2. Battery waveforms in the CCCV-CV charging method

2.2   Proposed Control Scheme

The block diagram of the proposed control scheme is depicted in Fig. 3. A multi-feedback control system with output voltage regulation and/or output current limitation capabilities can be easily identified. The reference values of the control loops are tuned in such a way that different operational points can be attained for all variables. Operation of the system charging or discharging the batteries is defined by means of the signals EN_{ch} and EN_{dch} which are given by a high level decision control.

For the charging mode, the output voltage v_{C_2} (battery side), is regulated by using a dual-loop controller which has a sliding-mode controller in the inner loop operating over the input current i_{L_1} (ELVDC bus side) determining the instantaneous value of the discrete manipulated variable $u_1 \in \{0, 1\}$. The reference of this control loop (I_{ref1}) is given by a first outer loop, which has a PI compensator acting over the output voltage error. The reference of this loop can be either the equalization voltage $V_{b_{ref1}}$ or the floating voltage $V_{b_{re2}}$ (see Fig. 2). Like the current given to the battery i_{bat} is a function of the output voltage and the instantaneous battery impedance, charge current limitation is obtained by modifying the reference of the voltage loop. Hence, an outermost loop allows controlling the output current (average value of i_{L_2}) through other PI compensator acting over the battery current error. This implementation considers that PI controller has a filtering action, which makes negligible the effect of the high frequency ripple of the current. Also, it is worth to note that this loop only operates during the constant current interval of the battery charge regime where it is necessary reducing the output voltage to limit the current at the desired value (I_{ref}). This fact implies the existence of a limiter for positive values at the output of the controller which is named as V_{comp} in the block diagram of Fig. 3.

For the discharging mode, the control of the converter is accomplished using a sliding mode controller stabilizing the input current i_{L_2} at the reference value I_{ref2} using the discrete manipulated variable $u_2 \in \{0, 1\}$. The current reference I_{ref2} is provided by a dual channel selector allowing using either an externally defined constant value I_{lim2} or the output of a PI controller in an outer voltage regulation loop (ELVDC bus side). The variable $Disc_{mode}$ select the reference since it is the reset of the PI controller and the enable of the constant reference as shown Fig. 3. The constant reference is used when the ELVDC bus is regulated by other power conversion stage in the microgrid. The control signals u_1 and u_2 are applied as the gate signals of the power switches of the converter when signals EN_{ch} and EN_{dch} are activated. These signals cannot be active simultaneously. The implementation of the sliding-mode based controllers is performed through hysteresis comparators with a band $\pm\ \delta$ over the reference current. This choice implies a simple implementation.

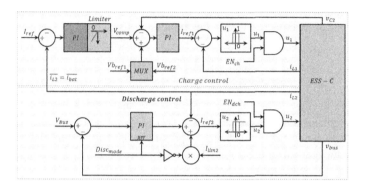

Fig. 3. ESS-C charge-discharge control system.

3 Modelling and Control of Bidirectional Cûk Converter

3.1 Cûk Converter Modeling and Control Onsidering Bus to Battery Power Flow

The circuit diagram of the Cûk converter integrated to an ELVDC bus is shown in Fig. 4. The ELVDC bus is represented by the constant voltage source (v_{bus}), the resistive load (R_{bus}) and the bus capacitance (C_3). The bilinear Eq. (1) represents the model of modified Cûk converter during charging mode.

$$
\begin{aligned}
\frac{di_{L_1}}{dt} &= \frac{v_{bus}}{L_1} - \frac{v_{C_1}}{L_1}(1 - u_1) \\
\frac{di_{L_2}}{dt} &= \frac{v_{C_1}}{L_2}u_1 - \frac{v_{C_2}}{L_2} \\
\frac{dv_{C_1}}{dt} &= \frac{i_{L_1}}{C_1}(1 - u_1) - \frac{i_{L_2}}{C_1}u_1 \\
\frac{dv_{C_2}}{dt} &= \frac{i_{L_2}}{C_2} - \frac{(v_{C_2} - v_b)}{R_bC_2}
\end{aligned}
\tag{1}
$$

To stabilize the output voltage of the converter in an indirect form, a sliding surface is proposed using the current on the inductor L1, $S(x) = i_E - i_{L_1}$. i_E is the instantaneous value of the reference for a desired input current in charging mode, which allows

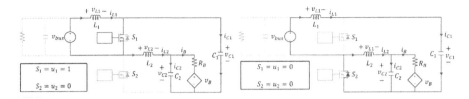

Fig. 4. Circuit diagram of the modified Cûk converter in charging mode.

to indirectly obtain a steady-state value in the output voltage v_{C_2}. By applying the equivalent control method, we obtain the expression (2).

$$u_{1_{eq}} = 1 - \frac{v_{bus}}{v_{C_1}} + \frac{L_1}{v_{C_1}} \frac{di_E}{dt} \qquad (2)$$

$u_{1_{eq}}$ is the average value of the control signal that allows reaching the sliding surface and remain on it. However, it is worth to recall that its value is physically constrained between 0 and 1, which are the possible real values of the control signal u_1. By replacing the equivalent control in (1), a third-order sliding dynamic represented by the system Eq. (3) is obtained.

$$\frac{di_{L_2}}{dt} = \frac{v_{C_1}}{L_2} \left(1 - \frac{v_{bus}}{v_{C_1}} + \frac{L_1}{v_{C_1}} \frac{di_E}{dt} \right) - \frac{v_{C_2}}{L_2}$$

$$\frac{dv_{C_1}}{dt} = \frac{i_{L_1}}{C_1} \left(\frac{v_{bus}}{v_{C_1}} - \frac{L_1}{v_{C_1}} \frac{di_E}{dt} \right) - \frac{i_{L_2}}{C_1} \left(1 - \frac{v_{bus}}{v_{C_1}} + \frac{L_1}{v_{C_1}} \frac{di_E}{dt} \right) \qquad (3)$$

$$\frac{dv_{C_2}}{dt} = \frac{i_{L_2}}{C_2} - \frac{(v_{C_2} - v_b)}{R_b C_2}$$

The battery internal impedance has been represented with the constant resistance R_b considering the fact that the time constant related with its dynamic is many times longer that the time constants of the converter dynamics. So, in steady-state the sliding mode on the input current leads to (4).

$$\bar{i}_{L_1} = I_{ref}$$

$$\bar{i}_{L_2} = I_{ref} \frac{v_{bus}}{\left(\dfrac{v_b + \left(v_b^2 + 4v_{bus} i_E R_b \right)^{\frac{1}{2}}}{2} \right)}$$

$$\bar{v}_{C_1} = v_{bus} + \left(\frac{v_b + \left(v_b^2 + 4v_{bus} i_E R_b \right)^{\frac{1}{2}}}{2} \right) \qquad (4)$$

$$\bar{v}_{C_2} = \frac{v_b + \left(v_b^2 + 4v_{bus} i_E R_b \right)^{\frac{1}{2}}}{2}$$

By linearizing (3) around (4) and applying the Laplace transform, we obtain the transfer function from input current to output voltage $G_1(s) = V_{C_2}(s)/I_E(s)$ which is required to the synthesis of the outer control loops.

$$G_1(s) = \frac{\frac{L_1}{L_2C_2}s^2 - \frac{L_1A(B-1)}{L_2C_1C_2}s + \frac{B}{L_2C_1C_2}}{s^3 + \frac{1}{L_2C_1C_2}\left(\frac{L_2C_1}{R_b} + L_2C_2AB\right)s^2 + \frac{1}{L_2C_1C_2}\left(C_1 + MBC_2 + \frac{L2AB}{R_b}\right)s + \frac{1}{L_2C_1C_2}\left(\frac{MB}{R_b} + AB\right)},$$

$$(5)$$

where

$$A = \frac{I_{ref}}{\left(\frac{v_b + \left(v_b^2 + 4v_{bus}i_E R_b\right)^{\frac{1}{2}}}{2}\right)}$$

$$B = \frac{v_{bus}}{v_{bus} + \left(\frac{v_b + \left(v_b^2 + 4v_{bus}i_E R_b\right)^{\frac{1}{2}}}{2}\right)}$$

$$(6)$$

$$M = \frac{\left(\frac{v_b + \left(v_b^2 + 4v_{bus}i_E R_b\right)^{\frac{1}{2}}}{2}\right)}{v_{bus}}$$

3.2 Cûk Converter Modeling Considering Battery to Bus Power Flow

The two different states that the Cûk converter has operating in the two proposed discharging modes is showed in Fig. 5. In order to distinguish the states the variable $Disc_{mode}$ is defined. When the converter is operating in limited current discharging mode, $Disc_{mode}$ is equal to cero and conversely, when converter operated in bus control discharge mode, $Disc_{mode}$ is equal to one. Expression (7) is the bilinear equation system modeling the Cûk converter in discharging mode including the $Disc_{mode}$ variable.

$$\frac{di_{L_1}}{dt} = \frac{v_{C_1}}{L_1}u_2 - \frac{v_{bus}}{L_1}$$

$$\frac{di_{L_2}}{dt} = \frac{v_{C_2}}{L_2} - \frac{v_{C_1}}{L_2}(1 - u_2)$$

$$\frac{dv_{C_1}}{dt} = \frac{i_{L_2}}{C_1}(1 - u_2) - \frac{i_{L_1}}{C_1}u_2 \qquad (7)$$

$$\frac{dv_{C_2}}{dt} = \frac{(v_b - v_{C_2})}{R_bC_2} - \frac{i_{L_2}}{C_2}$$

$$\frac{dv_{C_3}}{dt} = Disc_{mode}\left[\frac{i_{L_1}}{C_3} - \frac{v_{C_3}}{R_{bus}C_3}\right]$$

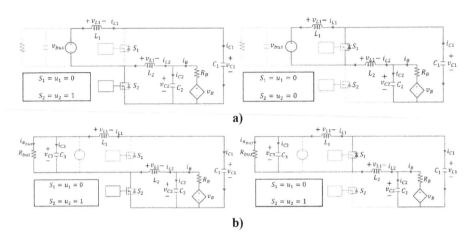

Fig. 5. Circuit diagram of the modified Cûk converter in discharging mode. (a) Limited current discharging mode (Disc$_{mode}$ = 0), (b) Bus control discharging mode (Disc$_{mode}$ = 1).

To stabilize the output voltage of the converter in an indirect form, a sliding surface is proposed using the current on the inductor L_2, $S(x) = i_E - i_{L_2}$. i_E is the instantaneous value of the reference for a desired input current in discharging mode, which allows to indirectly enforce a steady-state value in the output voltage v_{C_3}. The same way for (2), by applying the equivalent control method, we obtain the expression (8).

$$u_{2_{eq}} = 1 - \frac{v_{C_2}}{v_{C_1}} + \frac{L_2}{v_{C_1}} \frac{di_E}{dt} \qquad (8)$$

By replacing the equivalent control in (7), a fourth-order sliding dynamic represented by the system Eq. (9) is obtained.

$$
\begin{aligned}
\frac{di_{L_2}}{dt} &= \frac{v_{C_1}}{L_2}\left(1 - \frac{v_{C_2}}{v_{C_1}} + \frac{L_2}{v_{C_1}}\frac{di_E}{dt}\right) - \frac{v_{C_2}}{L_2} \\
\frac{dv_{C_1}}{dt} &= \frac{i_{L_1}}{C_1}\left(\frac{v_{C_2}}{v_{C_1}} - \frac{L_2}{v_{C_1}}\frac{di_E}{dt}\right) - \frac{i_{L_2}}{C_1}\left(1 - \frac{v_{C_2}}{v_{C_1}} + \frac{L_2}{v_{C_1}}\frac{di_E}{dt}\right) \\
\frac{dv_{C_2}}{dt} &= \frac{i_{L_2}}{C_2} - \frac{(v_{C_2} - v_b)}{R_b C_2} \\
\frac{dv_{C_3}}{dt} &= Disc_{mode}\left[\frac{i_{L_1}}{C_3} - \frac{v_{C_3}}{R_{bus}C_3}\right]
\end{aligned}
\qquad (9)
$$

So, in steady-state the sliding mode on the input current leads to the equilibrium point in (10).

$$\bar{i}_{L_1} = I_{ref} \frac{(v_b - I_{ref}R_b)}{\bar{v}_{C_3}}$$

$$\bar{i}_{L_2} = I_{ref}$$

$$\bar{v}_{C_1} = v_b - I_{ref}R_b + \bar{v}_{C_3} \qquad (10)$$

$$\bar{v}_{C_2} = v_b - I_{ref}R_b$$

$$\bar{v}_{C_3} = (1 - Disc_{mode})[v_{bus}] + Disc_{mode}\left[\sqrt{\frac{I_{ref}(v_b - I_{ref}R_b)}{R_{bus}}}\right]$$

By linearizing (9) around (10) and applying the Laplace transform, we obtain two transfer function. To limited current, from input current to output current $G_2(s) = I_{L_1}(s) / I_E(s)$ (Expression (11)), and to bus control, from input current to output voltage $G_3(s) = V_{C_3}(s) / I_E(s)$ (Expression (12)). Both transfer function is required to the synthesis of the outer current and voltage loops.

$$G_2(s) = \frac{\frac{L_2C_2}{L_1}s^3 + \frac{1}{L_1C_1}\left(\frac{L_2C_1}{R_b} + L_2A(B-1)\right)s^2 + \frac{1}{L_1C_1}\left(C_1 + \frac{L_2A(B-1)}{R_b}\right)s + \frac{A(B-1)}{L_1C_1}}{\left(s^2 + \frac{L_1AB}{L_1C_1}s + \frac{MB}{L_1C_1}\right)\left(sC_2 + \frac{1}{R_b}\right)} \qquad (11)$$

$$G_3(s) = \frac{\frac{L_2C_2}{L_1C_3}s^3 + \frac{1}{L_1C_1C_3}\left(\frac{L_2C_1}{R_b} + L_2ABC_2\right)s^2 + \frac{1}{L_1C_1C_3}\left(C_1 + BC_2 + \frac{L_2AB}{R_b}\right)s + \frac{1}{L_1C_1C_3}\left(\frac{B}{R_b} + A(B-1)\right)}{\left(s^3 + \frac{1}{L_1C_1C_3}\left(\frac{L_2C_1}{R_{bus}} + L_1C_3AB\right)s^2 + \frac{1}{L_1C_1C_3}\left(C_1 + MBC_3 + \frac{L_2AB}{R_b}\right)s + \frac{1}{L_1C_1C_3}\left(\frac{MB}{R_{bus}} + AB\right)\right)\left(sC_2 + \frac{1}{R_b}\right)}, \qquad (12)$$

where

$$A = \frac{I_{ref}}{\bar{v}_{C_3}}$$

$$B = \frac{v_b - I_{ref}R_b}{v_b - I_{ref}R_b + \bar{v}_{C_3}} \qquad (13)$$

$$M = \frac{\bar{v}_{C_3}}{v_b - I_{ref}R_b}$$

3.3 Design Criteria for the Outer Voltage Loops and the Outermost Current Loop of Charging Mode

Having determining the transfer function of the remaining sliding dynamic, the current controlled converter can be considered as a stable high order system in both charging and discharging modes. Like the PI controller has a free position real zero and one integrator, the zero can be placed left than the real pole of the inner loops with the aim to attract it and reduce its influence in the close loop response. Voltage controller parameters can be synthesized using a conventional design method for linear controllers such as root loci, frequency response or PI tuning. From our concept the Robust Loop Shaping approach documented in [15] can be useful to accomplish the control aims considering similitude in the application and the resulting order of the loop transfer function. No details are given about this controller in the paper because it can be obtained applying any classic design method for linear controllers.

Regardless of the fact that the output voltage remains unregulated during the constant current interval of the charge mode, it is not expected that it suffers considerable changes because the time constants of the battery variables are considerably slow. Thus, it is possible to define that the transient response of the outermost loop is at least ten times lower than that the voltage regulation loop. In this case, because the impedance of the battery changes extremely slower respect to the voltage regulated converter dynamic, we can define a more accentuated relation (twenty time, for example). However, it is worth to recall that an excessively slow response prevents a reliable reaction at the start-up event. As in the case of the voltage regulator, no details are given about this controller in the paper.

4 Simulated Results

In order to verify the functionality of the proposed charge/discharge control scheme and the dynamic performance of the controllers, PSIM simulations were implemented. Nominal characteristics and parameters of the power converter used in all simulations are: Input voltage, 48 VDC; DC bus resistive load, 10Ω; Battery voltage, 24 VDC; Battery resistance, 0.6Ω; Inductor L_1, 270 µH; Inductor L_2, 1.8 mH; Capacitor C_1, 10 µF; Capacitor C_2 and Capacitor C_3, 680 µF, and; Hysteresis band $\pm\delta$, ±0.5 A. All controllers in the system have the form $C(s) = (K_p s + K_i) s^{-1}$. The charge and discharge systems uses $K_p = 0.8$ and $K_i = 200$ in the voltage regulation loops and the charge system uses $K_p = 0.1$ and $K_i = 90$ in the current regulation loop.

In charging mode, a complete test was applied in simulation in order to verify the correct operation of the battery charge controller regarding the constant-current interval and both constant voltage intervals. As it can be observed in Fig. 6, between 0 and 0.6 s, system operates in constant current mode using a set-point of 3 A on the outermost control loop. During this interval the voltage applied to the battery increases until reach the equalization voltage reference value (28.8 V) and from there this voltage reference is keep as constant. Once the battery current reduces below 0.2 A at 1 s, transition for float charging is applied obtaining a first order type response with a settling time of 2 ms arriving to the new equilibrium point at 27 V verifying the correct operation of the entire charging mode control.

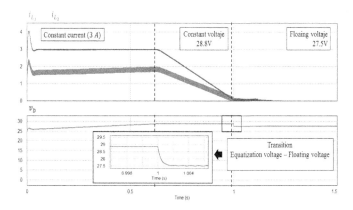

Fig. 6. Simulated results for CC-CV-CV battery charge method

In discharging mode in order to test the two different discharge modes, a simulation was made introducing changes valuating the performance of each mode and the transition between them (see Fig. 7). At 0 s, the start-up of the system is evaluated by defining a constant current reference of 3 A. System reaches the steady state after 400 ms showing an overshoot of 30%. After that, the reference is suddenly changed to 4 A at 1 s. As it is observed, only transient response appears in converter currents recuperating steady-state after 500 ms with a deviation below 20%. After that, at 2 s, the voltage source representing the regulated bus voltage is disconnected in order to enforce the operation of the voltage regulation mode. The steady state is recuperated in less than 50 ms with a maximum deviation of 3% in the bus voltage and a first order transition in the converter currents.

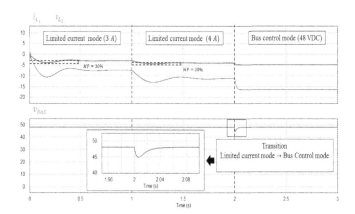

Fig. 7. Simulated results for different discharge modes.

5 Conclusions

A control approach allowing integration of battery arrays to DC buses in microgrids are presented. The bidirectional version of the Cûk converter was selected considering the non-pulsating nature of its input and output currents and the advantage of this characteristic to extend the life-time of batteries and the reliability of the entire system. Proposed voltage regulation loops use multi-loop controllers for both charge and discharge modes, which were differentiated in order to give a more didactic explanation of the control requirements, although they can be integrated in a seam-less control structure. As was demonstrated by means of simulation results, the proposed control is suitable for the studied application and its real implementation is really simple and flexible allowing the use of both analogue and digital electronics.

Acknowledgements. This research is being developed with the partial support of the *Gobernación del Tolima* under *Convenio de cooperación 1026–2013*. The results presented in this paper have been obtained with the assistance of students from the Research Hotbed on Control and Power Electronics (SICEP), Research Group D + TEC, Universidad de Ibagué, Ibagué-Colombia.

References

1. Soshinskaya, M., Crijns-Graus, W.H.J., Guerrero, J.M., Vasquez, J.C.: Microgrids: experiences, barriers and success factors. Renew. Sustain. Energy Rev. **40**, 659–672 (2014)
2. Marietta, M.P., Samaniego, B., Guinjoan, F., Velasco, G., Piqué, R., Valderrama-Blavi, H.: Integration of a Pb-acid battery management algorithm into optimization control strategies for microgrid systems. In: Proceedings of the 26th IEEE International Symposium on Industrial Electronics, pp. 1–7 (2017)
3. Nejabatkhah, F., Li, Y.W.: Overview of power management strategies of hybrid AC/DC microgrid. IEEE Trans. Power Electron. **30**(12), 7072–7089 (2015)
4. Elsayed, A.T., Mohamed, A.A., Mohammed, O.A.: DC microgrids and distribution systems: an overview. Electr. Power Syst. Res. **119**, 407–417 (2015)
5. Chen, B.Y., Lai, Y.S.: New digital-controlled technique for battery charger with constant current and voltage control without current feedback. IEEE Trans. Ind. Electron. **59**(3), 1545–1553 (2012)
6. Wong, Y.S., Hurley, W.G., Wölfle, W.H.: Charge regimes for valve-regulated lead-acid batteries: performance overview inclusive of temperature compensation. J. Power Sources **183**(2), 783–791 (2008)
7. Cheng, P.-H., Chen, C.-L.: A high-efficiency fast charger for lead-acid batteries. In: Proceedings of the IEEE 28th Annual Conference of the Industrial Electronics Society, pp. 1410–1415 (2002)
8. Erickson, R.W.: Fundamentals of Power Electronics. Springer Science & Business Media, New York (2007)
9. De Sá, M.V.D., Andersen, R.L.: Dynamic modeling and design of a Cûk converter applied to energy storage systems. In: Proceedings of the IEEE 13th Brazilian Power Electronics Conference and 1st Southern Power Electronics Conference, pp. 1–6 (2015)
10. Utkin, V.: Sliding Mode Control in Electro-Mechanical Systems, 2nd edn. CRC Press, Boca Raton (2009)

11. Chen, Z.: PI and sliding mode control of a Cûk converter. IEEE Trans. Power Electron. **27**(8), 3695–3703 (2012)
12. Lopez-Santos, O., Martinez-Salamero, L., Garcia, G., Valderrama-Blavi, H.: Sliding-mode indirect control of the quadratic boost converter operating in continuous conduction mode or discontinuous conduction mode. In: Proceedings of the IEEE 4th Colombian Workshop on Circuits and Systems, pp. 1–6 (2012)
13. Barrado, J.A., Aroudi, A.E., Valderrama-Blavi, H., Calvente, J., Martinez-Salamero, L.: Analysis of a self-oscillating bidirectional DC-DC converter in battery energy storage applications. IEEE Trans. Power Deliv. **27**(3), 1292–1300 (2012)
14. Albiol-Tendillo, L., Vidal-Idiarte, E., Maixe-Altes, J., Mendez-Prince, S., Martinez-Salamero, L.: Seamless sliding-mode control for bidirectional boost converter with output filter for electric vehicles applications. IET Power Electron. **8**(9), 1808–1816 (2015)
15. Lopez-Santos, O., Martinez-Salamero, L., Garcia, G., Valderrama-Blavi, H., Sierra-Polanco, T.: Robust sliding-mode control design for a voltage regulated quadratic boost converter. IEEE Trans. Power Electron. **30**(4), 2313–2327 (2015)

Logistics and Operations Management

A Two-Phase Heuristic for the Collection of Waste Animal Tissue in a Colombian Rendering Company

Eduwin J. Aguirre-Gonzalez$^{(\boxtimes)}$ and Juan G. Villegas$^{(\boxtimes)}$

Departamento de Ingeniería Industrial, Facultad de Ingeniería,
Universidad de Antioquia, Medellín, Colombia
{eduwin.aguirre,juan.villegas}@udea.edu.co

Abstract. This work addresses the planning of the collection of waste animal tissue in a Colombian rendering company. Over a week, the rendering company visits more than 800 slaughterhouses, butchers, and supermarkets in the Aburra's Valley, the metropolitan area of Medellín (Colombia) to supply their plant (located in the outskirts of the city) with raw material that are transformed into value-added products. The underlying vehicle routing problem have several distinguishing features: periodicity, consistency, clustered customers and heterogeneous fleet. To solve this rich VRP we present a two-phase heuristic. The first phase of the heuristic groups the collection points using a capacitated concentrator location problem (CCLP). Then, in the second phase a mixed integer program schedules the visits of the collection points in each cluster to balance the number of visits performed daily based on the capacities of the available vehicles. These two phases aim at getting consistent and evenly spread visits during the week. Preliminary results with the data of the current operation reveal a savings potential of 5 out of 15 vehicles, and a better spread of the visits over the planning horizon.

Keywords: Clustering · Scheduling · Rendering · Waste collection

1 Introduction

Human beings do not consume between a third and a half of each animal raised to produce meat, milk, eggs or fiber [1]. Besides, in 2014 the Colombian consumption of meat per capita was about 50 kg [2]. These two reasons highlight the importance of the rendering industry dedicated to recycling waste animal tissue (WAT). Rendering companies spent a big part of their logistic resources in the collection and transportation of WAT from the (many) geographically-spread collection points (slaughterhouses, butchers, and supermarkets) to their production plants. Furthermore, transportation is the single most expensive process in companies that include collection or distribution operations within their supply chain [5]. Therefore, companies in the rendering industry has to search for cost reduction in order to keep their competitiveness in a growing environment.

© Springer International Publishing AG 2017
J.C. Figueroa-García et al. (Eds.): WEA 2017, CCIS 742, pp. 511–521, 2017.
DOI: 10.1007/978-3-319-66963-2_45

One alternative to achieve this goal is by planing better the use of the available resources (the fleet in this case).

The collection of WAT can be framed into the well know vehicle routing problem (VRP) [25]. As a logistic optimization tool, the VRP is defined as a combinatorial optimization problem that selects the optimal routes performed by a fleet of vehicles that departs from a depot to visit a given set of suppliers (or customers) to collect its supply (serve its demand). The attributes of the customers, and the vehicles, as well as the operative constraints on the routes give rise to different VRP extensions [16].

Therefore, this paper describes a two-phase heuristic for the planning of the collection of WAT for a Colombian rendering company located in Medellín (Colombia). The proposed heuristic follows the cluster-first route-second approach based on Bramel and Simchi-Levy location heuristic [8]. Therefore, we focus our attention to the first two phases, namely the clustering of the collection points; and the scheduling of the visits over the week. With the output of these two phases a well-known traveling salesman problem (TSP) [15] has to be solved to find the sequence followed by each vehicle each day of the week.

In this case, the 800+ WAT collection points visited by the rendering company are geographically spread over the Aburra's Valley (Medellín's metropolitan area). They are visited periodically with visiting frequencies depending on their WAT generation rate; and they have relatively stable collection requirements over the planning horizon (a week). Moreover, there is a consistency requirement, i.e., the collection points have to be visited by the same vehicle and approximately at the same hour each time they are served. Additionally, collection points located at nearby sites (e.g., several butchers at a traditional market place or at the same street) are clustered so that all of them are visited by the same route. Finally, the fleet operated by the company comprises several types of vehicles with varying collection capacities, operation cost, and storage/refrigeration characteristics. To the best of our knowledge the only work that tackles a similar problem is [10]. In this work the authors describe and solve a WAT collection problem appearing in Belgium and northern France. Contrary to them, we face a large problem with more than 800 collection points, whereas their larger instance comprises only 262 collection points.

The remaining of this paper is structured as follows. Section 2 presents a brief literature review of the VRP extensions related to the collection problem under study. Then, Sect. 3 describes the heuristic method proposed to assign the vehicles and to schedule the visits to each collection point. Section 4 presents the results of the case study comparing the current practice of the company with the scenario obtained with the heuristic. Finally, Sect. 5 summarizes the main finding and concludes the paper outlining possible extensions of this work.

2   Literature Review

The VRP is a classical combinatorial optimization problem. In its most widely studied variant (the capacitated VRP, CVRP) the main constraint is the hauling capacity of the vehicles [11]. In the CVRP the set of customers is served by an homogenous fleet of vehicles that perform routes departing from and finishing at a single depot. Each customer is visited exactly once by these routes; and the total demands of the customers assigned to a route does not exceed the hauling capacity of the vehicles. In this section we briefly review the relevant VRP literature, considering mainly the VRP extensions related with the characteristics of the WAT collection problem faced by the rendering company, more precisely: the periodic VRP, the consistent VRP, the clustered VRP, and the heterogeneous fleet VRP (Fig. 1). Additionally, we outline the different approaches used to solve these and other related VRPs.

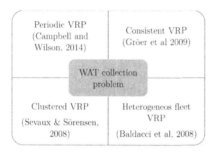

Fig. 1. VRP extensions related to the WAT collection problem.

2.1 Periodic Vehicle Routing Problem

In the periodic vehicle routing problem (PVRP), the customers (or suppliers) have to be visited one or more times during a planning horizon and there is a set of feasible visiting options denoted as *(visiting) scenarios*. Then, in addition to the routing decisions, the assignment of customers to (feasible) scenarios that visit them the required number of times is also considered. Once this assignment is performed a single VRP for each day is solved. The most common objective functions for the PRVP are the minimization of the size of the fleet or the total distance traveled by the vehicles in the entire planning horizon. Other objectives include the total cost (including the traveled distance cost and the fleet cost), the balancing of the number of customers or workload among the days, and the improvement of the service quality perceived by the customers. For a complete review of the variants, applications and solution methods for the PVRP, we refer the interested reader to [9].

The PVRP is widely used to model the collection operations of raw materials [18], solid waste [7], and recyclable materials [13]. Particularly, in [10] the authors describe a PVRP application to a closely related WAT collection operation. In this, case periodic collection routes visit roughly two hundreds of butchers, slaughterhouses and supermarkets in Belgium and northern France to collect their animal waste. Animal waste is classified into three different risks levels, and depending on these risk levels the visiting frequency can be predefined or can be determined as a decision of the model.

2.2   Clustered Vehicle Routing Problem

As its name suggest, in the Clustered VRP (CluVRP) customers are grouped into clusters. As in the CVRP all customers has to be visited once, but in the CluVRP the vehicle that visits a customer in a given cluster has to visit all the customers in its cluster. Moreover all the customers in a given cluster must be visited sequentially before serving customers in a different cluster. The CluVRP was introduced in the context of parcel delivery where the orders of customers in predefined zones are stored into containers that must be completely emptied before processing the next container in the delivery truck [22]. As pointed in [26], the CluVRP is a seldom studied problem with few works tackling it [6,26].

2.3   Heterogeneous Fleet Vehicle Routing Problem

The heterogeneous fleet VRP (HFVRP) is a natural extension of the VRP since fleets grow and change dynamically over time. This gives rise to routing problems with heterogeneous vehicles having different hauling capacities as well as different operation costs. Real world application of the HFVRP include the distribution of fresh milk in Greece [23], the distribution of furniture in France [20] and the collection of solid waste in the US [21]. In [3] and [17] the authors provide two comprehensive reviews of the literature dedicated to the HFVRP.

2.4   Solution Methods

Solution methods for VRPs can be classified into four categories: exact methods [4], heuristics [19], metaheuristics [14], and matheuristics [12]. As pointed in [9], solution methods for PVRPs include approaches in these four categories, heuristics and metaheuristics being the preferred approach for large scale problems (as the one tackled in this case). According to [7] solution methods for PVRPs follow four main solution strategies: the so-called monolithic approach solves the entire problem without decomposing it. The other three strategies decompose the problem into several phases to solve simpler problems tackling at each time one or two of the main decisions of the PVRP. The first strategy decomposes the problem in two parts, the first correspond to the assignment of the customers to the days of visit (scenarios) and the solution of several VRPs (one for each day). The second one also includes the assignment of the customers to the vehicles in the first stage so that the routing part is tackled as a TSP that is solved for each vehicle in each day of the planning horizon. The last strategy decomposes the problem in three parts. The first one assign the customers to the visiting scenarios, then a second stage assign customers to vehicles for each day of the planning horizon, and finally, a TSP is used to find the routing of the vehicles for each day in the planning horizon. In this work we follow a solution approach that resembles this last approach. However, we follow a cluster-first route-second strategy [8,19] in order to ensure the consistency of the solution (i.e., the same vehicle serves a customer in all the visits over the planning horizon).

3 A Heuristic Approach for the Waste Animal Tissue Collection Problem

3.1 Problem Definition and Notation

In the WAT collection problem faced by the company there is a set of collection points (butchers, slaughterhouses and supermarkets) I with known (weekly) supply s_i, additionally each collection point has a number of required visits f_i assigned by the company according to its WAT generation rate. The planing horizon comprises a set of days D, that can be combined in a set of different visiting scenarios C. Binary parameter a_{ct} is equal to one if day $t \in D$ is selected (to visit collection points) in scenario $c \in C$, and parameter f^c counts the number of days included in scenario c. The collection points are served by a heterogeneous fleet of vehicles K each one with capacity Q_k that are located at a plant (denoted by 0). Moreover, there is a distance c_{ij} between collection points $i, j \in I \cup \{0\}$, and nearby collection points are grouped together to be served by the same vehicle and with the same frequency. The aim of the WAT collection problem is to design collection routes for each day in the planning horizon ensuring that collections points are visited by the same vehicle the number of required times over the planning horizon without surpassing the hauling capacity of the vehicles in the fleet and aiming at minimizing the cost of the operation, and also balancing the number of collection points visited by each vehicle each day.

3.2 Heuristic Method

To solve the WAT collection problem we propose a two-phase heuristic that groups and schedules the collection points in consistent clusters. Each phase of the heuristic solves a mathematical programming model. The first one groups the collection points into clusters that will be served by the same vehicle during the planning horizon (to ensure consistency). The second one assigns visiting scenarios to the collection points in each cluster to balance the number of visits performed by the vehicle over the days. For the sake of brevity, the detailed routing of the collection points visited in each cluster for each day is not discussed since it corresponds to the well-known TSP [15].

Clustering phase. For the first phase we use the location based heuristic proposed in [8] to cluster the collection points. This phase solves a capacitated concentrator location problem (CCLP) that can be described as follows. There is a given set of terminals (collection points) I with known supplies s_i for each terminal $i \in I$, and a set of possible locations for concentrators (vehicles) J with capacities Q_k. Additional parameters include (CF_k) the cost of opening a concentrator of size Q_k (i.e., cost of operating a vehicle of this size), and the distance (c_{ij}) between concentrator $j \in J$ and terminal $i \in I$. The aim is to locate and select capacity of the concentrators and assign each terminal to exactly one concentrator so that the total cost of installing concentrators and the cost of assigning terminals to concentrators is minimized and the capacities of the concentrators is enough to handle the weekly supply of terminals assigned to them. Two binary variables are used in this first model: variable y_{jk} is equal to one if a concentrator of size Q_k is located at candidate point j and zero otherwise; whereas, variable x_{ij} is equal to one if supplier i is assigned to concentrator j, and zero otherwise. Using this notation the CCLP is formulated as follows:

$$\min \sum_{i \in I} \sum_{j \in J} c_{ij} x_{ij} + \sum_{j \in J} \sum_{k \in T} CF_k y_{jk} \tag{1}$$

subject to:

$$\sum_{j \in J} x_{ij} = 1 \qquad\qquad \forall i \in I \tag{2}$$

$$l \sum_{k \in T} y_{jk} \le \sum_{i \in I} x_{ij} \le h \sum_{k \in T} y_{jk} \qquad\qquad \forall j \in J \tag{3}$$

$$\sum_{i \in I} s_i x_{ij} \le |D| \sum_{k \in T} Q_k y_{jk} \qquad\qquad \forall j \in J \tag{4}$$

$$\sum_{j \in J} y_{jk} \le m_k \qquad\qquad \forall k \in T \tag{5}$$

$$x_{ij} \le \sum_{k \in T} y_{jk} \qquad\qquad \forall i \in I, \ \forall j \in J \tag{6}$$

$$\sum_{k \in T} y_{jk} \le 1 \qquad\qquad \forall j \in J \tag{7}$$

$$x_{ij} \in \{0, 1\} \qquad\qquad \forall i \in I \ \forall j \in J \tag{8}$$

$$y_{jk} \in \{0, 1\} \qquad\qquad \forall j \in J \ \forall k \in T \tag{9}$$

The objective function (1) seeks to minimize the total cost of traveling distance among all the terminals and the total cost of opening the concentrators. Constraints (2) ensures that each terminal is connected to exactly one concentrator. Constraints (3) ensures that (if open) each concentrator (cluster) has a minimum (l) and a maximum (h) of assigned terminals. Constraints (4) represent the capacity constraint of the concentrators (measured over a period of length $|D|$). Constraints (5) represent a maximum number (m_k) of available concentrators (vehicles) of each capacity Q_k. Constraints (6) ensures that terminals are assigned to open concentrators. Constraints (7) ensures that only one capacity is selected for each open concentrator. Finally, constraints (8) and (9) define the domain of the variables.

Scheduling phase. The second phase consists in performing the scheduling process for each cluster. This phase assigns a specific scenario $c \in C$ to each terminal $i \in I$, which corresponds to its collection frequency. This second phase guarantees compliance with the periodicity restrictions while keeping the capacity constraints of the vehicles. This phase aims at obtaining a more balanced working schedule to the drivers and also ensures a more smooth flow of WAT in the plant over the week. This is obtained using as objective function the balancing the number of collection points visited by each vehicle each day of the planning horizon.

Therefore, for the set of collection points in a given cluster (served by a vehicle of capacity Q_k) the heuristic solves a frequency assignment problem with binary variables r_{ic} equal to one if supplier i is assigned to scenario c and zero otherwise. Three auxiliary integer variables are used in the mathematical formulation of this problem z_d representing the number of suppliers visited in day d of the planning horizon, wl is the minimum number of collection points visited per day, and wh is the maximum number of collection points visited per day. The frequency assignment problem follows:

$$\min \ wh - wl \tag{10}$$

subject to:

$$\sum_{c \in C: f^c = f_i} r_{ic} = 1 \qquad\qquad \forall i \in I \tag{11}$$

$$\sum_{i \in I} \sum_{c \in C: f^c = f_i} a_{ct} r_{ic} = z_t \qquad\qquad \forall d \in D \tag{12}$$

$$wl \le z_d \le wh \qquad\qquad \forall d \in D \tag{13}$$

$$\sum_{i \in I} \sum_{c \in C} \frac{s_i}{f_i} a_{cd} r_{ic} \le Q_k \qquad\qquad \forall d \in D \tag{14}$$

$$r_{ic} \in \{0, 1\} \qquad\qquad \forall i \in I, \ \forall c \in C \tag{15}$$

$$wl, wh \in \mathbb{Z}^+ \tag{16}$$

$$z_d \in \mathbb{Z}^+ \qquad\qquad \forall d \in D \tag{17}$$

The objective function (10) seeks to minimize the difference between the maximum and the minimum number of visits per day. Constraints (11) ensure that each collection point is assigned to exactly one visiting scenario (among those with the same number of required visits). Constraints (12) count the number of visits made to the collection points on each day, whereas constraints (13) define the balance between days in terms of visits to collection points. Constraints (14) represent the capacity constraint of the vehicle selected to serve the collection points assigned to the corresponding cluster in the previous phase. Finally, constraints (15), (16) and (17) define the domain of the variables.

4   Results and Analysis

The two phases of the proposed heuristic were implemented in Xpress-MP using their modeling language (MOSEL). Using the data of the collection operation performed between January and March 2017 we estimate the weekly collection need (s_i) for each one of the 853 points visited by the company during this period and also assign a collection frequency (f_i) based on their WAT generation rate. Distances between collection points and the plant were calculated using QGIS [24]. This section presents the preliminary results calculated from the solution obtained with the proposed heuristic and its comparison with the current operation.

4.1 Clustering

The first phase of the heuristic grouped the collection points into ten clusters. Remarkably, this represents a reduction of five vehicles with respect to the current operation that uses fifteen vehicles (i.e., a 33% reduction of the fleet size). Given that the company operates an heterogeneous fleet, it is important to see the detail of this fleet reduction. Table 1 presents a detailed comparison of the usage of the vehicles in the fleet. In this table, vehicles are presented in ascending order of their capacity. This table shows that the heuristic suggest to increase the use of vehicles whit medium capacity (B and D) rather that the smallest and largest vehicles (A and E). This fleet reduction represents roughly an annual savings of 185.000 US$ in the fixed cost of the operation. Figure 2 presents the geographical distribution of the collection points over the Aburra's Valley metropolitan area and the corresponding assignment of them to the ten clusters (with different colors in the figure). The compactness of the resulting clusters and the differences in their size (due to the heterogeneous capacity of the fleet) can be seen in the figure. Nonetheless, the capacity constraint of the concentrators (vehicles) produces a few isolated points that can't be assigned to the vehicle that serves nearby collection points. Additional, (compactness oriented) constraints must be added to the model to improve this feature of the solution.

Table 1. Comparison of the usage of the different types of vehicles

Vehicle type	A	B	C	D	E
Hauling capacity (Kg)	4,000	5,000	5,200	7,000	10,000
Vehicles used by the company	4	4	5	1	1
Vehicles used in the heuristic solution	1	2	0	7	0

4.2 Scheduling

Once collection points are assigned to a given cluster/vehicle the second phase aims at balancing the number of visits performed over the days of the week. The complete results of this balancing phase are highlighted in Fig. 3 that shows how the solution of the proposed heuristic has a much balanced number of visits over the week (the high unbalance of Monday in the current solution is clear). The balance in the total number of visits each day allows for more collection points to be served each day. Increasing the number of collection points per day and decreasing the number of

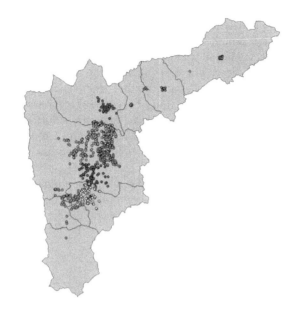

Fig. 2. Results of the clustering phase

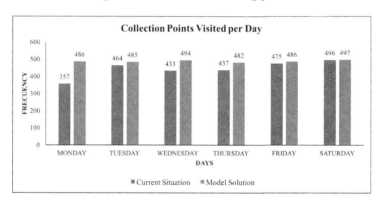

Fig. 3. Distribution of the number of visits per day

vehicles used by the solution, represents an increase in the utilization of the fleet (97%+) that produces an important saving in the cost of each kilogram of collected material. Moreover, the reduction of the variability on the number of collection points visited each day smooths the material flow in the downstream process (the production plant), and allows for a better planning of the rendering process.

5   Conclusions

In this work we present a two-phase heuristic to solve the waste animal tissue collection problem faced by a Colombian rendering company. The proposed heuristic relies in two mathematical programming models that cluster and schedule the 800+ collection points visited by the company each week. The design of the heuristic provides a solution with some desired features: consistency, balance and heterogeneity of the fleet. The first phase of the heuristic aims at obtaining a consistent clustering of the collection points, whereas the second phase aims at balancing the visits over the planning horizon taking into account the heterogeneity of the fleet. The comparison of the heuristic solution and the current operation of the company reveals that the fleet size can be reduced by 33%, and that an even distribution of the collection points visited during a week can be obtained. The analysis of this preliminary experiments also suggest some possible research directions, the first one is the need for additional constraints to obtain more compact clusters (without isolated points). Likewise, the implementation of a third phase to find the sequence of the collection points visited in each cluster each day is under development.

References

1. Aldrich, G., Andreson, D., Basu, L., Bisplinghoff, F.: Lo impresindible del reciclaje todo sobre la industría de los subproductos de origen animal (2009)
2. ANIF: Mercados industriales (2014)
3. Baldacci, R., Battarra, M., Vigo, D.: Routing a heterogeneous fleet of vehicles. In: The Vehicle Routing Problem: Latest Advances and New Challenges, pp. 3–27. Springer, New York (2008)
4. Baldacci, R., Mingozzi, A., Roberti, R.: Recent exact algorithms for solving the vehicle routing problem under capacity and time window constraints. Eur. J. Oper. Res. **218**(1), 1–6 (2012)
5. Ballou, R.H.: Business logistics/supply chain management: planning, organizing, and controlling the supply chain. Pearson Education India (2007)
6. Battara, M., Erdogan, G., Vigo, D.: Exact algorithms for the clustered vehicle routing problem. Oper. Res. **62**(1), 58–71 (2014)
7. Bianchi-Aguiar, T., Carravilla, M.A., Oliveira, J.F.: Municipal waste collection in Ponte de Lima, Portugal - a vehicle routing application. OR Insight **25**(4), 185–198 (2012). http://link.springer.com/10.1057/ori.2011.23
8. Bramel, J., Simchi-Levi, D.: A location based heuristic for general routing problems. Oper. Res. **43**(4), 649–660 (1995)
9. Campbell, A.M., Wilson, J.H.: Forty years of periodic vehicle routing. Networks **63**(1), 2–15 (2014). http://doi.wiley.com/10.1002/net.21527
10. Coene, S., Arnout, A., Spieksma, F.C.R.: On a periodic vehicle routing problem. J. Oper. Res. Soc. **61**(12), 1719–1728 (2010). http://dx.doi.org/10.1057/jors.2009.154
11. Cordeau, J.F., Laporte, G., Savelsbergh, M.W., Vigo, D.: Vehicle routing. Handb. Oper. Res. Manage. Sci. **14**, 367–428 (2007)
12. Doerner, K.F., Schmid, V.: Survey: matheuristics for rich vehicle routing problems. In: International Workshop on Hybrid Metaheuristics, pp. 206–221. Springer, New York (2010)
13. Ferreira, J.A., Costa, M., Tereso, A., Oliveira, J.A.: A multi-criteria decision support system for a routing problem in waste collection. In: International Conference on Evolutionary Multi-Criterion Optimization, pp. 388–402. Springer, New York (2015)

14. Gendreau, M., Potvin, J.Y., Bräysy, O., Hasle, G., Løkketangen, A.: Metaheuristics for the vehicle routing problem and its extensions: a categorized bibliography. In: The Vehicle Routing Problem: Latest Advances and New Challenges, pp. 143–169. Springer, New York (2008)

15. Gutin, G., Punnen, A.P.: The traveling salesman problem and its variations, vol. 12. Springer Science & Business Media, New York (2006)

16. Irnich, S., Toth, P., Vigo, D.: The family of vehicle routing problems. In: Vehicle Routing: Problems, Methods, and Applications, pp. 1–36. SIAM, Philadelphia (2014)

17. Koç, Ç., Bektaş, T., Jabali, O., Laporte, G.: Thirty years of heterogeneous vehicle routing. Eur. J. Oper. Res. **249**(1), 1–21 (2016)

18. Lahyani, R., Coelho, L.C., Khemakhem, M., Laporte, G., Semet, F.: A multi-compartment vehicle routing problem arising in the collection of olive oil in Tunisia. Omega **51**, 1–10 (2015). http://dx.doi.org/10.1016/j.omega.2014.08.007

19. Laporte, G., Semet, F.: Classical Heuristics for the Vehicle Routing Problem. Les cahiers du GERAD (1999)

20. Prins, C.: Efficient heuristics for the heterogeneous fleet multitrip VRP with application to a large-scale real case. J. Math. Model. Algorithms **1**(2), 135–150 (2002)

21. Sahoo, S., Kim, S., Kim, B.I., Kraas, B., Popov, A.: Routing optimization for waste management. Interfaces **35**(1), 24–36 (2005)

22. Sevaux, M., Sörensen, K.: Hamiltonian paths in large clustered routing problems. In: Proceedings of the EU/MEeting 2008 workshop on Metaheuristics for Logistics and Vehicle Routing, EU/ME 2008, pp. 4:1–4:7. Troyes, France (2008)

23. Tarantilis, C.D., Kiranoudis, C.T.: A meta-heuristic algorithm for the efficient distribution of perishable foods. J. Food Eng. **50**(1), 1–9 (2001)

24. Team, Q.G.D.: Quantum GIS Geographic Information System (2017). http://qgis.osgeo.org

25. Toth, P., Vigo, D.: Vehicle Routing: Problems, Methods, and Applications. SIAM, Philadelphia (2014)

26. Vidal, T., Battarra, M., Subramanian, A., Erdogan, G.: Hybrid metaheuristics for the clustered vehicle routing problem. Comput. Oper. Res. **58**, 87–99 (2015)

Success Probability Applied to Inventory Routing Problem with Time Windows

Francisco Morales[1](✉), Carlos Franco[2],
and Germán Andres Mendez-Giraldo[1]

[1] Universidad Distrital Francisco José de Caldas, Bogotá, D.C, Colombia
fjmoralesg@correo.udistrital.edu.co,
gmendez@udistrital.edu.co
[2] Universidad del Rosario, Bogotá, Colombia
carlosa.franco@urosario.edu.co

Abstract. The objective with the present paper is to find a solution method for the inventory routing problem, in which have been added several characteristics that resemble their behavior to the current companies' reality. Between them the hard time windows, a dynamic component and a success probability applied to the routes between the nodes. In that case we use the dynamic programming with finite stages in order to optimize the routing of vehicles in each period, taking into account the dynamical changes implicit in the nodes and the other IRP characteristics.

Keywords: Inventory routing problem · Disruption networks · Dynamic programming

1 Introduction

The *Inventory Routing Problems*, or IRP are based on a set of suppliers and customers defined which interact within a planning horizon; both, the supplier and the consumer incur in an inventory maintenance costs and each customer has a defined capacity to store inventory [1]; The first studies referring to this kind of problems date from 1957 by Clarens and Hurdle, and later one of the most relevant in 1984 by Federgruen and Zipkin [2] who defined it as an extension of the *Vehicle Routing Problem* or VRP [3].

Factors such as traffic, transportation policies, the possibility of traffic accidents, the vehicle's reliability, are factors which can influence the delivery of products; It indicates a variant scenario in which we must modify the approach of the delivery routes including the possible variation in factors in order to satisfy the demand in the established times with the lowest possible cost.

It is important to clarify that the objective of this paper is not to establish a success probability for the IRP; the objective is the application of a success threshold previously established for each possible routes in a determined system in order to optimize the routing to do under the specified conditions.

© Springer International Publishing AG 2017
J.C. Figueroa-García et al. (Eds.): WEA 2017, CCIS 742, pp. 522–531, 2017.
DOI: 10.1007/978-3-319-66963-2_46

1.1   Dynamic Component

The dynamic component adds realism to IRP performance; In the classic models as in Archetti et al. [4] the number of nodes as well as the demand for each of them in each time period is known and constant as shown in Fig. 1.

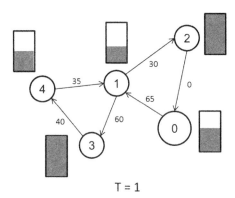

T = 1

Fig. 1. Classic IRP

On the other hand, in the present paper a dynamic component is introduced in the quantity of nodes which have demand in each time period; Is to say that the number of clients is not constant, but can vary over time so we have to define for each period a different routing according to the nodes that have been activated and the demand of each one of them.

Figure 2 shows an example of IRP with the dynamic component, in this figure appears a new node with its respective demand and known inventory level, as well as with a transport cost determined which allows to analyze the best route in order to satisfy the demand of all the active nodes in that period of time.

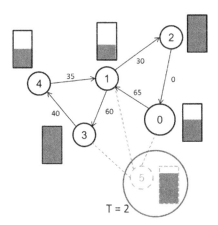

T = 2

Fig. 2. IRP with dynamic component

It is important to clarify that we do not create nodes randomly, as well as their demand or level of inventory; We randomly activate or deactivate some nodes of a previously total known whose characteristics are established. This in order to simulate the dynamic behavior of total demand.

1.2 Success Probability

In this paper we pretend to assign to each possible route between two nodes a success threshold, conditioning the decisions to a new probability restriction that will tell us what is the minimum probability that we can assume to take a certain path.

This success threshold depends directly of the different characteristics mentioned before, like the traffic or the possibility of traffic accidents; in a real case this success threshold must be defined with a study of the real comportment of the vehicles when make the routes and how it's change with the time. In this paper we defined the success threshold for each possible route randomly because we are adapting existed instances to prove our algorithm (Fig. 3).

Fig. 3. Success threshold

It opens the door for two scenarios, the first is a scenario with disruptions which takes into account the success probabilities among the nodes to define the best possible route; the second one is a scenario without disruptions which ignores the success probabilities among the nodes for which the probability constraint is not applied.

2 Theoric Framework

The IRP is an optimization problem in which one or more suppliers control the level of inventory of their customers in order to find the most efficient way of satisfy the demand of each one of them minimizing the costs in which should be incurred, such as transportation costs and inventory maintenance costs [5]. This problem is known as a variation of the VRP first introduced by Dantzig and Ramser [6], as the VRP, the IRP has had several variations and solution methods proposed such as IRPTW "Inventory *Routing problem with Time Windows*" [2]; multi suppliers problems and with *n* numbers of customers [7], cyclic planning problems or reactive planning [8], as bi objectives problems solved by heuristics [9].

In 1998 Flavio Baita et al. performed a paper called DRAI (*Dynamic Routing and Inventory Problems*) making a review of the papers concerning the IRP which have a dynamic component framing in the field of distribution logistics [2]. In 2005 Alfredo Núñez presented a dynamic IRP solution based on genetic algorithms, in this article the authors were based on a problem of door-to-door passenger delivery formulating as a predictive hybrid control problem [10]. In 2006 Jamison M. Day et al. made a study case in Indiana about a company that manages inventory of carbon dioxide (CO_2) at about 900 customers [11].

In 2007 Pablo Eidelman and Alejandro Valdez propose an optimization system for the vehicles dynamic routing with time windows [12]; Clara Novoa and Robert Storer in 2008 present a paper which study the dynamic programming algorithms for problems of a single vehicle with stochastic demand, considering the calculus of the relation *Cost to go* applied to the Monte Carlo simulation along with a Method of forward search deployment in two stages [13]. In 2012 Yugang Yu et al. made a paper about SIRPSD *(stochastic Inventory Routing Problem with Split delivery)* which allows the demand is satisfied by using two or more vehicles for each node in a given period [14].

In 2013 Coelho and Laporte proposed a Branch and Cut algorithm to give exact solution to different kind of IRP, especially to the IRP multivehicle with homogeneous and heterogeneous fleet of which performed an extensive computational analysis [1]. In 2014 Nekooghadirli presents an bi objective model that considers a multi - period and multi vehicle system; it has two objectives, minimize transport costs and travel time for which are used MOICA algorithms *(Multi Objective Imperialist Competitive Algorithm)* Demonstrating its efficacy for the proposed problem [9].

3   Model

The IRP model is based on the model proposed by Archetti et al. [4], adding the time windows randomly generated based on a uniform distribution according to the Pérez Kaligari paper [15] in which a supplier *"1"* manufacture product for a set of nodes $Vp = \{2, ..., n\}$, in a time horizon P. The supplier produces and releases a certain amount of product rt_t each period $T = \{1, ..., P\}$.

For each period $t \in T$, the customers have a demand dt_i which must be less than their warehouse capacity C_i, just as each client defines an initial inventory $I0_i$ and a safety stock L_i which must be less than the final inventory of each period I_{it} which in turn is a decision variable calculated by the model; to the supplier the final inventory depend besides of the quantity of product manufactured by period rt. The distance between nodes c_{ij} is given by the sum of the absolute value of the differences between their coordinates on the x axis px_i and the y axis py_i, looking more like the distance between the points in this way that Calculate it according to Euclidean distance; this distance is at the same time

Each client is visited in period t for the vehicle $k = \{1, ..., K\}$ receiving a quantity $q_{i,}^{k,t}$; $Y_{i,k,t} = \{0,1\}$ is the binary variable that controls whether or not the respective node visited by the route $X_{i,j,k,t} = \{0,1\}$ express whether or not covered the distance between the two related nodes. This quantity received should be less than the vehicle capacity Qk because it is a homogeneous fleet.

It is defined as $e_{i,k,t}$ the start service time for each node i by the vehicle k in period t which must be greater than the lower limit of the time window of each node a_i and in turn less than the upper limit of the time window each node b_i; It should be aware that the service time of each node s_i directly affect the travel time and therefore the time of arrival and the start of service on each client.

Pe_{ij} represents the success probability that would have a route between the respective nodes i, j and Pb the minimum probability accepted to take certain route. Pe_{ij} must be greater or equal to Pb; However, this restriction does not apply in all cases since there is a possibility to obtain a greater gain by ignoring it, for this we use a dynamic programming model with finite stages [16].

In this way, the model can be expressed as follows.

$$MIN\ Z = \sum_{i \in V} \sum_{t \in T} h_i I_i^t + \sum_{i \in V} \sum_{j \in V} \sum_{k \in K} \sum_{t \in T} c_{ij} X_{ij}^{kt} \tag{1}$$

$$I_1^t = I_1^{t-1} + rt - \sum_{i \in Vp} \sum_{k \in K} q_i^{kt} \quad t \in T \tag{2}$$

$$I0^t \geq t \in T \tag{3}$$

$$I_i^t = I_i^{t-1} + \sum_{k \in K} q_i^{kt} - dt_i^t \quad i \in Vp, t \in T \tag{4}$$

$$I_i^t \geq 0 \quad i \in Vp, t \in T \tag{5}$$

$$I_i^t \geq L_i \quad i \in Vp, t \in T \tag{6}$$

$$I_i^t \leq C_i \quad i \in Vp, t \in T \tag{7}$$

$$\sum_{k \in K} q_i^{kt} \leq C_i - I_i^{t-1} \quad i \in Vp, t \in T \tag{8}$$

$$\sum_{k \in K} q_i^{kt} \leq C_i \sum_{j \in V} \sum_{k \in K} X_{ij}^{kt} \quad i \in Vp, t \in T \tag{9}$$

$$\sum_{k \in K} q_i^{kt} \leq Qk \quad t \in T, k \in K \tag{10}$$

$$q_i^{kt} \leq Y_i^{kt} C_i \quad i \in Vp, t \in T, k \in K \tag{11}$$

$$\sum_{j \in V} X_{ij}^{kt} = \sum_{j \in V} X_{ji}^{kt} \quad i \in Vp, t \in T, k \in K \tag{12}$$

$$\sum_{j \in V} X_{ij}^{kt} = Y_i^{kt} \quad i \in Vp, t \in T, k \in K \tag{13}$$

$$\sum_{j \in Vp} X_{1j}^{kt} \leq 1 \quad k \in K, t \in T \tag{14}$$

$$\sum_{k \in K} Y_i^{kt} \leq 1 \quad i \in Vp, t \in T \tag{15}$$

$$X_{ij}^{kt}, Y_i^{kt} \in \{0,1\} \qquad i,j \in Vp, i \neq j, t \in T, k \in K \tag{16}$$

$$e_i^{kt} + s_i + c_{ij} - e_j^{kt} \leq \left(1 - X_{ij}^{kt}\right) M_{ij} \qquad i \in V, j \in Vp, k \in K, t \in T, i \neq j \tag{17}$$

$$e_i^{kt} \geq a_i \qquad i \in Vp, k \in K, t \in T \tag{18}$$

$$e_i^{kt} \leq b_i \qquad i \in Vp, k \in K, t \in T \tag{19}$$

$$e_1^{kt} = 0 \tag{20}$$

$$If \begin{cases} GEM_i^t = GEC_i^t \rightarrow Pe_{ij}X_{ij}^{kt} \geq PbX_{ij}^{kt} & i \in V, j \text{ in } V, k \in K, t \in T \\ GEM_i^t = GES_i^t \rightarrow The\ restriction\ does\ not\ apply \end{cases} \tag{21}$$

The model proposed by Archetti et al. [4] includes constraints from 2 to 16, constraints 17 to 20 are taken based on the Pérez Kaligari paper [15], and restriction 21 is proposed for the work of the IRPTW through the dynamic programming model. The objective of this model is to minimize the sum of inventory costs h_i and transportation costs c_{ij} incurred for each of the nodes in the established routes.

3.1 Dynamic Programming with Finite Stages for Decision Making

Given the dynamical changes of the nodes that has been raised in the problem, implement a probability constraint in which case all possible routes should meet a minimum probability required by the supplier, could skew the results and not allow to make the best decision. This is dynamic programming with finite stages is used [16], this process will decide to which arcs the constraint expressed in Eq. 21 applies and which, on the other hand, are not subject to it; based on the Expected Gain without Disruption GES_i^t and the Expected Gain with Disruption for each node i in each period t which determined the GEC_i^t Maximum Expected Gain GEM_i^t.

Each arc (i, j) has an associated success probability; For this case two politics are managed, one of them is taking into account the scenarios with disruption, and the other one is ignoring these scenarios, their respective matrices of transition and gains are determined according to the distance between the nodes and how the travel time can increase proportionally to the success probability.

The dynamic programming model with finite stages starts from the most distant period, to decrease in each iteration until reaching the first period, taking the decisions in descending stages.

3.2 Modifications for Dynamic Component

Another of the main elements is the dynamic component that is added to the IRPTW base [4]; This together with the success probability make up the main variants of the model. For this purpose, a matrix Dt_i^t is created according to which if the node i is active in a certain period t then $Dt_i^t = dt_i$ otherwise $Dt_i^t = 0$; The activation or not of the nodes is considered as a random variable.

From the base equations of model (1) to (21), a new restriction must be added which will ensure that no quantity of the product is sent to a node that is not active, it means their demand is 0, for this we introduce the Eq. (22)

$$q_i^{kt} = 0 \quad i \in Vp, k \in K, t \in T, Dt_i^t = 0 \tag{22}$$

Besides, Eq. (17) must be modified and replaced by Eq. (23), which, given the dynamic and probabilistic character of the problem, allows travel through nodes that, although they are not active, can exceed the accepted minimum probability Pb.

$$\textit{If} \begin{cases} Dt_i^t > 0 \rightarrow e_i^{kt} + s_i + c_{ij} - e_j^{kt} \leq \left(1 - X_{ij}^{kt}\right) M_{ij} \\ Dt_i^t = 0 \rightarrow e_i^{kt} + c_{ij} - e_j^{kt} \leq \left(1 - X_{ij}^{kt}\right) M_{ij} \end{cases} \quad i \in V, j \in Vp, k \in K, t \in T, i \neq j \tag{23}$$

Finally, the most important change will be given in the operation of the dynamic programming model with finite stages, since the dimensions of the transition and gains matrices will vary for each period t according to the active nodes; for this reason this process besides to being repeated in each time period will have a slight variation since they must iterate from the period equal to the planning horizon P to the period t in which they are, to make the decisions of that period based on the gains matrix that would have been achieved if these active nodes had been maintained.

4   Model Application and Results

The model was programmed in the software *FICO XPRESS 7.9* version, using the Coelho and Laporte instances [1], modified by generating time windows based on the Pérez Kaligari paper [15]; To perform an adequate analysis of the operation of the algorithm, we will compare the results obtained in the proposed algorithm with the results when making 3 modifications.

- Modification 1 – Without Probability
- Modification 2 – Without Nodes Dynamic
- Modification 3 – Without Probability and nodes Dynamic

The Table 1 shows the results for one of the instance used, the Table 2 shows the summary of results for all the instance used to probe the algorithm. The original algorithm; Although it obtains the lowest Z value of all in most cases, satisfies a percentage of the demand equal or similar to the other modifications. In this way, we can verify that the algorithm allows to obtain a solution close to the scenarios with modifications even taking into account a greater number of variables that present uncertainty as the success probability and the dynamic of the nodes.

Table 1. Summary of results for instances COST HIGH H3

	HIGH COST H3			
	Org. Algorithm	Mod. 1	Mod. 2	Mod. 3
$AbsIn5\ Z$	2579.38	2579.38	3328.9	3328.9
% dt_i^t Satisfied	44.54%	44.54%	50.37%	50.37%
$AbsIn10\ Z$	4781.35	4385.01	0	5220.94
% dt_i^t Satisfied	31.52%	31.52%	0.00%	37.27%
$AbsIn15\ Z$	5810.16	5757.2		6495.73
% dt_i^t Satisfied	25.78%	25.23%		33.33%
$AbsIn25\ Z$	7561.01	7549.01	9472.47	9121.17
% dt_i^t Satisfied	24.61%	24.61%	33.33%	33.33%
$AbsIn30\ Z$	11968.4	11968.4	12892.3	12801.8
% dt_i^t Satisfied	17.71%	20.84%	34.89%	33.33%
$AbsIn35\ Z$	11968.4	11225.3		11757.7
% dt_i^t Satisfied	13.30%	14.36%		32.59%

Table 2. Summary of average percentage of unmet demand

	Percentages average of Satisfied Demand			
	Org. Algorithm	Mod. 1	Mod. 2	Mod. 3
High Cost H3% dt_i^t Satisfied	26.24%	26.85%	29.65%	36.70%
High Cost H6% dt_i^t Satisfied	32.47%	32.25%	16.94%	41.63%
Low Cost H3% dt_i^t Satisfied	22.85%	18.92%	33.46%	33.33%
Low Cost H6% dt_i^t Satisfied	33.73%	33.73%	42.00%	40.86%

Another one of the main observations that we can identify based on the results is the relation between the dynamic of the nodes and the time of iteration or operation of the algorithm, when is not considered those characteristics (modification 2), in many cases There was no optimal solution to the problem or iteration time increased considerably.

Therefore, taking into account the real demands of the instant of time that is analyzed improves the effectiveness of the system.

5   Conclusions

The present paper shows the advantages of taking into account the success thresholds of the routes that lead from one customer to another, thus achieving a routing with the highest success probability. In the same way, it allows to show the utility of the algorithm to propose a route scheme that satisfies the greatest quantity of demand possible considering great uncertainty variables such as the probability of success and the dynamism of the nodes; factors that have not been talked into account at the same time in the literature.

However, in the application to real life we observe that exist several problems to take into account since these thresholds depends on factors which can change in the time, especially the traffic that changes suddenly and under special conditions as the climate can fluctuate considerably being complex to define a specific threshold for certain route that allows the algorithm to work properly in real time.

The success probability of a determinated route in real time has a dynamic comportament because depends of different causes like the mencionated before. It makes to the algorithm an approximation for the reality based on historic data; even if we want to work with the real characteristics, we have to define a form to recopilet the data at real time and define the best route taking into account the characteristics of a classic IRP and the real traffic.

On the other hand, as future work the possibility of using soft time windows should be evaluated; In the same way, other characteristics should be taken into account in the future such as deferred demand over time, or the possibility of demand being satisfied by more than one vehicle; giving a more realistic character to the problem. However, given the computational complexity of the problem, an approximation algorithm must be considered to obtain a near optimal response sooner.

References

1. Coelho, L.C., Laporte, G.: The exact solution of several classes of inventory-routing problems. Comput. Oper. Res. **40**(2), 558–565 (2013)
2. Baita, F., Ukovich, W., Pesenti, R., Favaretto, D.: Dynamic routing-and-inventory problems: a review. Transp. Res. Part A Policy Pract. **32**(8), 585–598 (1998)
3. Federgruen, A., Zipkin, P.: A combined vehicle routing and inventory allocation problem. Oper. Res. **32**, 1019–1037 (1984)
4. Archetti, C., Bianchessi, N., Irnich, S., Speranza, M.G.: Working papers department of economics and management formulations for an inventory routing problem (2013)
5. Eliseo Pérez Kaligari, W.J.G.R.: Optimization methods for the inventory routing problem, pp. 31–49 (2015)
6. Pillac, V., Gendreau, M., Guéret, C., Medaglia, A.L.: A review of dynamic vehicle routing problems. Eur. J. Oper. Res. **225**(1), 1–11 (2013)
7. Lou, S.Z., Wu, Y.H., Xiao, J.W.: Study on integrated inventory-routing problems. In: Proceedings of the 2009 IEEE International Conference on Intelligent Computing and Intelligent Systems, vol. 1, no. 1, pp. 42–46 (2009)
8. Raa, B.: Cyclic versus reactive planning for inventory routing. Procedia - Soc. Behav. Sci. **111**, 909–917 (2014)
9. Nekooghadirli, N., Tavakkoli Moghaddam, R., Ghezavati, V.R., Javanmard, S.: Solving a new bi-objective location-routing-inventory problem in a distribution network by meta-heuristics. Comput. Ind. Eng. **76**, 204–221 (2014)
10. Núñez, A., Sáez, D., Cortés, C.E.: Problema de ruteo dinamico de una flota de vehiculos con un enfoque de control predictivo hibrido basado en algoritmos geneticos, p. 13 (2005)
11. Day, J.M., Wright, P.D., Schoenherr, T., Munirpallam, V., Gaudette, K.: Improving routing and scheduling decisions at a distributor of industrial gasses.PDF. Science Direct, p. 11 (2006)
12. A.P.L.U., Lerena, V., Alejandro, L.U., Dra, D., Loiseau, I.: Sistema de optimización para el ruteo dinámico de vehículos con ventanas de tiempo' Resumen (2007)

13. Novoa, C., Storer, R.: An approximate dynamic programming approach for the vehicle routing problem with stochastic demands. Eur. J. Oper. Res. **196**(2), 509–515 (2009)
14. Yu, Y., Chu, C., Chen, H., Chu, F.: Large scale stochastic inventory routing problems with split delivery and service level constraints. Ann. Oper. Res. **197**, 135–158 (2012)
15. Perez, E.: Ruteo de inventarios con ventanas de tiempo fuertes, pp. 1–53 (2015)
16. Kulkarni, V.G.: Introduction to modeling and analysis of stochastic systems (2010)

Routing Analysis and Improvement for the Pick-up Service of Raw Material for a Company Specialized in Plastic Injection

Sánchez-Partida Diana[(⊠)] ⓘ, Zamudio Karen ⓘ,
Caballero-Morales Santiago-Omar ⓘ,
and Martínez-Flores José Luis ⓘ

Universidad Popular Autónoma del Estado de Puebla, Puebla, Mexico
{diana.sanchez, santiagoomar.caballero,
joseluis.martinez01}@upaep.mx,
arelyzamudio.ort@gmail.com

Abstract. For all organizations in the manufacturing and service sectors, transportation has become an important topic for the economic decision-making process. This is due to the high quality and versatility standards that today the industries have established to follow a strict guideline focused on Just-In-Time (JIT). In this context, the present paper extends on the analysis and improvement of a real-world routing problem of a Mexican company dedicated to the manufacturing of plastic products. The value chain of the company has its origin at the gathering (picking-up) of raw materials and components from different suppliers located in the United States. Currently, a third-party company (carrier) has been hired to perform the pickup process, however there is uncertainty regarding the optimality of its routes and their associated costs. The present research analyses the current routing scheme that is performed by the carrier to verify compliance of the requirements of the company which are minimization of costs and travel times. Then, the Capacitated Vehicle Routing Problem (CVRP) is performed for improvement of the current routing scheme. In addition, a new location for a depot (or collection center) is proposed to allow the company to manage its own raw material, avoiding the need to consider a third-party company for the picking-up services by means of the p-Median Problem (PMP). Optimization for the CVRP and PMP was performed with a specialized software and the results obtained by this research present an improved cost-efficient routing scheme for the picking-up process of the plastic company.

Keywords: Capacitated vehicle routing problem · Capacitated p-Median problem · Optimization · Operations research

1 Introduction

In the present globalized world, logistics strategies for efficient movement and constant flow of the value chain in the business, products and services industries, has become a crucial element of the supply chain. Some examples of the practical application and

© Springer International Publishing AG 2017
J.C. Figueroa-Garca et al. (Eds.): WEA 2017, CCIS 742, pp. 532–543, 2017.
DOI: 10.1007/978-3-319-66963-2_47

effective implementation of network design and logistic planning are: distribution (goods and services), manufacturing, strategic planning of projects, location of facilities, material handling, and resource management.

Recently, the problem of transportation has become a very important issue during the economic decision-making process for all companies. This is due to the high standards of quality and versatility that are sought by the industries, in particular the automotive industry. With the arrival of international automobile manufacturers in Mexico such as General Motors, Mazda, Honda, Ford, and particularly Volkswagen and Audi to the city of Puebla in Mexico, the suppliers of these automobile manufacturers are required to comply with their demands by creating a strict guideline focused on JIT (Just-In-Time). According to Thot [14], JIT is focused on producing the elements that are needed, in the quantities and time required, thus avoiding losses in surplus stores of raw material or overproduction. Hence, logistic strategies are important to establish well-planned supply chains in order to meet the time restrictions of a company and supply their demands as required on time to keep scheduled production and delivery to the customers on the dates agreed upon, avoiding delays and minimizing the transportation costs of goods [14].

For this reason, one of the main developments in the field of Operations Research (OR) has been the rapid progress, both in the methodology and in the implementation, of optimization models for distribution networks [8]. Within this context, the Capacitated Vehicle Routing Problem (CVRP) is one of the fundamental routing models for logistic network design and supply chain management. It was first proposed by Dantzig and Ramser [3] and an extensive specialized literature has been published through the years regarding different variants of this problem. Also, due to its computational complexity, many approaches have been proposed to solve it, from exact methods to approximate methods [1, 4, 6, 10].

The CVRP consists of a set of nodes to be visited (i.e., suppliers) by a set of vehicles which depart from (and return to) a particular node (i.e., depot or collection center). The goal is to determine the routes (ordered sequence of nodes) for the vehicles that minimize the total transportation cost or distance. It is important to mention that this goal implies the following constraints: (1) a node cannot be visited by more than one vehicle, and it must be visited only once; and (2) the requirements of the nodes assigned to a route cannot exceed the capacity of the vehicle assigned to it [1, 2].

In addition to the CVRP, the p-Median Problem (PMP) has become one of the most important models for facility location. The PMP can be described as follows: given a set of n nodes (i.e., suppliers or customers), each of them with a known requirement (i.e., demand), it is required to find p medians (centers, depots) and assign each node to exactly one median such that the total distance of assigned nodes to their corresponding medians is minimized [12].

In real problems, the number of serviced customers takes the value of several thousands and the number of candidate locations for a facility (or facilities) can take this value as well. Thus, finding the most suitable locations for p centers in order to serve n nodes becomes a task of high computational complexity [12].

Within the context or a real-world case study, this research performs the analysis and improvement of the current pick-up routes of a company specialized in plastic injection by means of the CVRP. Additionally, the PMP is used to estimate a location for a new depot that will be managed by the company. This proposal is presented because there are uncertainties associated to the cost efficiency of the pick-up routes which are currently served by a third-party company (carrier). Solutions for the CVRP and PMP were obtained with a specialized optimization software. This led to an improved cost-efficient routing scheme for the picking-up process and an efficient alternative for a new service depot.

2 Capacitated Vehicle Routing Problem

The Capacitated Vehicle Routing Problem (CVRP) is one of the most studied combinatorial optimization problems in logistics and supply chain management [9]. This is due to its practical relevance for distribution and collection of goods. As an example of its real-world relevance, a case of success regarding the use of the CVRP for minimization of transportation costs for a Colombian company focused on collection of hazardous solid waste is described in [15].

For our real-world case study, we consider the static and deterministic version of the CVRP with the following characteristics: deliveries are performed for all customer nodes by a set of vehicles which are identical (homogeneous fleet with equal capacities); the demands of the customers are deterministic, known in advance and may not be split; all vehicles depart from a specific node (depot node), travel to serve a set of customer nodes, and after all vehicles have visited their assigned customers, they return to the departing node; the travel cost between each pair of customer nodes is the same in both directions (symmetric CVRP); the objective is to determine the traveling sequences of customer nodes that ensure the minimal cost for each route without compromising the restrictions of capacity of the vehicles assigned to them [9].

The mathematical formulation of the CVRP is presented as follows: A is the capacity of each vehicle, V is the maximum number of vehicles, F_{ij} is the flow of cores from node i to node j, Z is the total transportation cost, d_i is the demand of the customer node i, c_{ij} is the distance or cost between node i and node j, N is the number of nodes, and x_{ij} is a binary decision variable where xij equal one if the vehicle moves from node i to j and zero otherwise. Then, the objective function of the CVRP mathematical formulation can be written as follows:

$$Min\ Z = \sum_{i=1}^{N} \sum_{j=1, j \neq i}^{N} c_{ij} x_{ij} \tag{1}$$

subject to

$$\sum_{l=2, k \neq l}^{N} x_{lk} + x_{lk} = 1\ \forall k \tag{2}$$

$$\sum_{l=2, k \neq l}^{N} x_{kl} + x_{kl} = 1\ \forall k \tag{3}$$

$$\sum_{k=2}^{N} x_{lk} \leq V \tag{4}$$

$$\sum_{j=1, j\neq i}^{N} x_{ij} = \sum_{j=1, j\neq i}^{N} x_{ji} \quad \forall i \tag{5}$$

$$x_{kk} = 0 \quad \forall k \tag{6}$$

$$x_{lk} + x_{kl} = 1 \quad \forall k, l, k \neq l \tag{7}$$

$$\sum_{j=1, j\neq i}^{N} F_{ij} = \sum_{j=1, j\neq i}^{N} F_{ji} + d_{ji} \quad \forall i, i > 1 \tag{8}$$

$$d_i x_{ij} \leq F_{ji} \quad \forall i, j, i \neq j \tag{9}$$

$$F_{ij} \leq \left(A - d_{ij}\right) x_{ij} \quad \forall i, j, i \neq j \tag{10}$$

As presented, the objective function (1) of the CVRP model is aimed to minimize the total traveled distance. Constraints (2) and (3) state that there is exactly one departure from node i. Constraint (4) states that the total number of vehicles cannot be exceeded. Constraint (5) provides balance between incoming and outgoing arcs at a given node. Constraint (6) eliminates flow from node i to node i. Constraint (7) is a trivial sub-tour elimination constraint. Constraints (8), (9) and (10) provide balance between total inflow and outflow for all nodes.

3 p-Median Problem

Location planning involves the decision task of determining the physical location of facilities to provide efficient delivery of services. Examples of facilities include hospitals, restaurants, ambulances, retail and grocery stores, schools, etc. There are a variety of different models to address facility location planning, and for this case study we consider the PMP.

As discussed in [13], from the point of view of public decision making, the objective of the PMP consists on maximizing the accessibility in terms of average proximity of customers to a facility. Thus, it is required to place p facilities to minimize an average distance between a demand node (i.e., customer) and its servicing facility.

The mathematical formulation of the PMP is presented as follows: p is the total number of facilities to be located, and Yij and Xj are binary decision variables such that Yij equal one if the demand node $i \in I$ is assigned to facility located at $j \in J$, and zero otherwise. And Xj equal one if facility is located at $j \in J$ and zero otherwise. Then, the objective function of the PMP mathematical formulation can be written as follows:

$$Min\ Z = \sum_{j \in J} \sum_{i \in I} h_i d_{ij} Y_{ij} \qquad (1)$$

subject to:

$$\sum_{j \in J} Y_{ij} = 1, \forall i \in I \qquad (2)$$

$$Y_{ij} - X_j \leq 0, \forall i \in I, j \in J \qquad (3)$$

$$\sum_{j \in J} X_j = p \qquad (4)$$

$$X_j \in \{0, 1\}, \forall j \in J \qquad (5)$$

$$Y_{ij} \in \{0, 1\}, \forall i \in I, j \in J \qquad (6)$$

The objective (1) is aimed to minimize the total distance over all facilities and demand nodes. Note that this distance, defined by $d_{ij}Y_{ij}$, is weighted by h_i. Constraint (2) implies that a demand node i can only be serviced (i.e., assigned to) by one facility. Constraint (3) states that a demand node i can be serviced by a facility at j only if there is a facility at j. Note that if $X_j = 0$ then $Y_{ij} = 0$. Constraint (4) states that exactly p facilities must be placed. Finally, constraints (5) and (6) define that the decision variables are binary [11].

4   Description of the Real-World Instance

The outsourcing of transport is a practice that, according to the literature, has been growing in recent years. This has been successfully generalized in activities which were initially considered as peripheral. Outsourcing is the process in which a firm identifies a portion of its business process that could be performed more efficiently and /or more effectively by another corporation [7].

Currently, the pick-up service of raw material for the company, which is specialized in plastic injection, is performed by an external (third-party) company (carrier) under an outsourcing model. This carrier decides the pick-up routes to be served according to the requirements that are provided by the company like strategic flexibility and cost-benefit comparison. However in many cases the carrier does not provide an efficient service. While the carrier performs the picking route, it temporally stores the raw material in a depot (collection center) before delivering it to the company.

For the purposes of this research, the Null hypothesis is based on the assumption that "the pick-up routes of the carrier are optimal and were efficiently planned to establish the best price". Then, the Alternative hypothesis is defined as "the pick-up routes of the carrier are not optimal and the carrier does not perform the best routing, generating uncertainty in delivery times and generating additional costs that are paid by the contracting company". Given this situation, an analysis and optimization of the network is proposed to improve the pick-up routes and minimize the associated costs and travel times. Then, a comparison of the improved routes with the current pick-up routes will be performed to analyze the performance of the carrier and assess the compliance of the Null hypothesis.

The company has 15 suppliers of raw material (see Table 1). Each supplier meets a certain demand required by the company, and this demand is picked-up by the carrier.

Table 1. Monthly demand supplied in kilograms (kg).

Number	Supplier	Monthly demand (kg)
1	A	8,835
2	B	500
3	C	1,372
4	D	463
5	E	19,051
6	F	11,250
7	G	55
8	H	847
9	I	9,225
10	J	14
11	K	4,122
12	L	3,173
13	M	2,110
14	N	182
15	O	108

In Fig. 1 the geographic locations of the suppliers are presented where the yellow star represent the depot and the red balloons represent the suppliers.

Fig. 1. Locations of the current depot and suppliers.

Then, an array of distances expressed in kilometers (km) was obtained considering all these locations by using the *Google Maps©* application. This allowed us to come closer to the reality of the travel distances, according to the direction of the streets and their availability. This information is shown in Table 2.

Table 2. Distance matrix through all locations (km): depot at node 1.

	1	2	3	4	5	6	7	8	9	10	11	12	13	14	15	16
1	0	68	37.02	1111	472	1873	63.3	23	56.4	125	1086	79	1099	83	255	12.2
2	68	0	138	1096	425	1724	105	77	82	98	981	118	1050	121	184	53
3	37	138	0	1057	479	1794	42.3	16	26.1	114	996	55.3	1040	60.3	276	47.6
4	1111	1096	1057	0	1460	1867	1063	1090	1079	1251	1696	1058	1961	1048	1048	1118
5	472	425	479	1460	0	1906	530	488	515	415	1156	546	846	550	330	447
6	1873	1724	1794	1867	1906	0	1907	1883	1892	1811	780	1923	1349	1927	1956	1883
7	63	105	42	1063	530	1907	0	44	20	184	1121	18.2	1134	22	293	59
8	23.6	77	16.4	1090	488	1883	44.1	0	21	143	1094	58	1107	63	267	33
9	56	82	26	1079	515	1892	20	21	0	168	1110	34.02	1123	38	278	44
10	125	98.3	114	1251	415	1811	184	143	168	0	1023	198	1052	202	231	128
11	1086	981	996	1696	1156	780	1121	1094	1110	1023	0	1172	598	1176	1205	1132
12	79.1	118	55	1058	546	1923	18.6	58	34.3	198	1172	0	1147	16	295	71
13	1099	1050	1040	1961	846	1349	1134	1107	1123	1052	598	1147	0	1152	1015	1107
14	83.2	121	60.01	1048	550	1927	22	63	38	202	1176	16.41	1152	0	312	78.3
15	255	184	276	1048	330	1956	293	267	278	231	1205	295	1015	312	0	241
16	12.5	53.2	47	1118	447	1883	59	33.1	44	128	1132	71.8	1107	78	241	0

5   Optimization of the CVRP and PMP Models

The CVRP model was solved using LINGO which provided an effective solution. In this case, due to the size of the instance (16 nodes), the method of Branch-and-Bound (B&B) provided a fast and exact (optimal) solution. As presented in Table 3, the optimal solution represents a monthly traveled total distance of 12,613.8 km.

Table 3. Optimal pick-up routes generated by Lingo: carrier-owned depot.

Vehicle	Route	Traveled distance (km)
1	1 10 3 14 1	382.5
2	1 7 9 1	139.3
3	1 6 1	3746
4	1 12 2 16 15 5 13 4 8 1	4,741.6
	Total	9,009.4 km

The carrier currently has a depot that serves as storage center for the collected material. However, and additional goal of the present research is to propose a new and optimal location for a company-owned depot because it is estimated that the depot of the carrier is generating extra costs for the company. Thus, after solving the CVRP with the current depot (which is carrier-owned) an optimal location for the new depot is determined (which will be managed and owned by the company).

For this task, the first step consisted on obtaining candidate locations for the new depot. With respect to the candidate depots, they were strategically selected for permits, laws and all land available for purchase in the United States, trying to get these candidates close to the concentration of suppliers and the industrial zone with the greatest influence on the country. In addition, the total distances from each candidate location to each supplier were computed. The second step consisted on using the PMP model to minimize distances and therefore costs. It is important to emphasize that management, transportation and operative costs of this new depot will be the company's own. Table 4 presents the coordinates of three candidate locations for the depot and the total distance traveled once was applied the model in Lingo.

Table 4. Candidate locations for the new depot and results obtained.

	Latitude	Longitude	Distance
Node 1	42.364	−83.398	8,510 km
Node 2	39.445	−84.185	10,706 km
Node 3	42.850	−85.526	12,614 km

Programming of the PMP model with LINGO provided the optimal location for the new depot which is the Node 1 with 8,510 km. Subsequently, it was necessary to define the routes to be served by each vehicle from the new depot. Thus, the CVRP model was solved with the location of the new depot which is owned by the company. As presented in Table 5, the updated routes with the new depot represent a monthly traveled total distance of 8,510 km which is a reduction of 8.8%. Although this proposal implies an important investment for the company, a further discussion presented in the following section supports this decision.

Table 5. Optimal pick-up routes generated by Lingo: new company-owned depot.

Vehicle	Route	Traveled distance (km)
1	1 6 11 3 1	3,686
2	1 7 12 9 8 1	159
3	1 14 4 15 5 13 10 1	4,532
4	1 16 2 1	133
	Total	8,510 km

Figure 2 shows the routes shown in Table 5 which were obtained according to the capacity of each vehicle and the amount of raw material collected from each supplier.

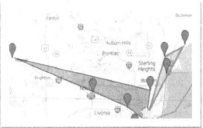

Fig. 2. Route mapping with the new company-owned depot.

6 Economic Analysis of the New Depot Proposal

In order to assess the suitability of the proposed solution (minimum transportation costs), an economic analysis of costs and comparison with the current routing scheme were performed. It must be mentioned that for future economic projections, a detailed study of costs and depreciation is important to obtain a more accurate framework of the investment required by the proposal which involves depots and a fleet of trucks.

1. Current Routing Scheme (no optimization with carrier's depot). The company of plastic injection hires a carrier that performs individual and consolidated pick-up services. According to the load volume of its customers it sets different rates. Individual services have an average transportation cost of $52,470 MXN with a load capacity of 114,522 cubic meters or 20,411 kg. In Fig. 3 and Table 6 the details of the current routes and their transportation costs are presented.

2. Proposed Routing Scheme (optimization with company's depot). As previously discussed, the proposal consists on an optimized network via CVRP modelling with a new location for the depot. The optimized pick-up routes, which are presented in Table 6, assume that the company will purchase the vehicles for their exclusive use.

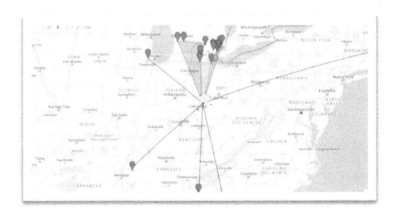

Fig. 3. Current pick-up routes performed by the carrier.

Table 6. Costs of the current routing scheme.

Current routes	Traveled distance (km)	Transportation cost (MXN)
1 (1-14-12-1)	178	$ 52,470.00
2 (1-10-15-1)	581	$ 52,470.00
3 (1-7-1)	127	$ 52,470.00
4 (1-2-1)	136	$ 52,470.00
5 (1-9-8-16-3-1)	194	$ 13,203.54
6 (1-4-1)	2,222	$ 22,604.58
7 (1-5-1)	944	$ 5,688.00
8 (1-6-1)	3,746	$ 52,470.00
9 (1-11-1)	2,173	$ 1,120.00
10 (1-13-1)	2,198	$ 32,472.00
Total (km) monthly	**12,499**	
Total (km) annual	**149,988**	
Total ($) monthly		**$ 337,438.12**
Total ($) annual		**$ 4,049,257.44**

Table 7. Costs involved in the proposed routing scheme.

Investment	Year 0	Year 1	Year 2
Truck investment	$ 5,120,000.00		
Fixed asset investment	$ 50,000.00		
Permissions and licenses	$ 80,000.00		
Maintenance	$ 45,000.00	$ 45,000.00	$ 45,000.00
Depot rental	$ 120,000.00	$ 1,440,000.00	$ 1,440,000.00
Operational wages	$ 238,968.00	$ 238,968.00	$ 238,968.00
Administrative salaries	$ 180,000.00	$ 180,000.00	$ 180,000.00
Diesel consumption cost (MXN)		$ 503,249.76	$ 503,249.76
Total	$ 5,833,968.00	$ 1,903,968.00	$ 1,903,968.00

Hence, Table 7 provides an estimated breakdown of the investment and operation costs associated with this proposal. It is considered that four vehicles will be bought to serve the four routes, thus, the purchase cost of the trucks, as well as the salaries and wages of drivers and people in charge of loading and unloading materials to and from the trucks, are presented in Table 8. The transportation costs were obtained by the supplier's quotations of trucks KENWORTH®. The costs of licenses, salaries and consumption of gasoline were estimated considering US data.

The loss of value suffered by a physical asset as a consequence of its use through the time is known as depreciation. Most assets, except land, have a useful life over a finite period of time. Useful life is understood as the time during which the property, plant and equipment will contribute to the generation of income. In order to determine depreciation it is necessary to consider the legal useful life which is regulated by the Tax Statute. In the course of such period, these assets diminish their value, and this loss

Table 8. Annual depreciation of fixed assets

Depreciative assets	Useful life	% Annual depreciation
Constructions and buildings	20 years	5%
Machinery and equipment	10 years	10%
Office equipment	10 years	10%
Communication and computer equipment	5 years	20%
Fleet and transport equipment	5 years	20%

is reflected by the depreciation [5]. Table 8 presents the annual depreciation percentage of fixed assets that must be considered.

Depreciation of the transport equipment was based on the purchase price which includes taxes on sales of customs and others. For example: Acquisition value $ 1,280,000.00, Acquisition date 2017, Depreciation percentage 20%, thus the Depreciated value (1,280,000.00–256,000.00) = 1,024,000.00. By considering this information, Table 9 presents the cost values of the annual depreciation for the transport equipment.

Table 9. Annual depreciation of the transport equipment.

Year	Annual depreciation	Accumulated depreciation	Total value
0			1,280,000
1	256,000	256,000	1,024,000
2	256,000	512,000	768,000
3	256,000	768,000	512,000
4	256,000	1,024,000	256,000
5	256,000	1,280,000	0

This proposal represents an important opportunity for the company because, while the first year (Year 0) the investment is approximately $5.8 million (see Table 8), for the following years the costs associated to transportation would be less than $2.0 million. Table 10 presents the comparison of costs associated to the annual distance traveled by the carrier and the costs of the annual distance traveled under the proposal with the opening of a new depot. In the long-term, the proposal represents a saving of nearly 50.0% in operational costs. These findings reject the Null hypothesis and provide the support for an improved pickup service that can be managed by the company.

Table 10. Comparison of annual costs of current situation versus proposal.

Current annual costs	Annual costs of the proposal	Annual savings
$4,049,257.44	$1,903,968.00	$2,145,289.44

7 Conclusions

As a conclusion it is possible to see that operations research models have been and still are of great support in making strategic decisions. With this analysis and results obtained the plastic company can take a decision that helps to optimize their resources. Whatever the decision, it has been proven that the carrier company´s current routing has an opportunity to reduce by 27% in mileage and therefore in costs. If the company takes the second option to implement it will have more benefits in terms of costs and a reduction of mileage by 31% may have more activities that would not be core business, but will have more opportunity to take action and be able to increase or maintain the level of service without relying on the service operator.

References

1. Baldacci, R., Mingozzi, A., Roberti, R.: Recent exact algorithms for solving the vehicle routing problem under capacity and time window constraints. Eur. J. Oper. Res. **218**, 1–6 (2012)
2. Clarke, G., Wright, J.W.: Scheduling of vehicles from a central depot to a number of delivery points. Oper. Res. **12**, 568–581 (1964)
3. Dantzig, G.B., Ramser, J.H.: The truck dispatching problem. Manage. Sci. **6**, 80–91 (1995)
4. Desrosiers, J., Soumis, F., Desrochers, M.: Routing with time windows by column generation. Networks **14**(4), 545–565 (1984)
5. Díaz, A., Aguilera, V.: Matemáticas financieras, 4th edn. McGraw Hill, Mexico (2008)
6. Fisher, M.L., Jaikumar, R.: A decomposition algorithm for large-scale vehicle routing. Working Paper No. 78-11-05, Department of Decision Sciences, University of Pennsylvania, pp. 1–27 (1978)
7. Gillett, B.E., Miller, L.: A heuristic algorithm for the vehicle dispatch problem. Oper. Res. **2**, 340–349 (1974)
8. Hiller, S., Lieberman, G.: Introducción a la Investigación de Operaciones, 9th edn. McGraw-Hill, Mexico (2006)
9. Kir, S., Yazgan, H.R., Tüncel, E.: A novel heuristic algorithm for capacitated vehicle routing. J. Industrial Eng. Int. **57**, 1–8 (2017)
10. Kumar, S., Panneerselvam, R.: A survey on the vehicle routing problem and its variants. Intell. Inf. Manage. **4**, 66–74 (2012)
11. Daskin, M., Maass, K.: The p-Median problem. In: Laporte, et al. (eds.) Location Science, pp. 21–45. Springer International Publishing, New York (2015)
12. Montoya, M., Bernabé, M., González, R., Martínez, J., Bautista, H., Sánchez, A., Macias, F.: A solution proposal for the capacitated P-median problem with Tabu search. Res. Comput. Sci. **121**, 59–67 (2016)
13. Piccolo, C.: Mathematical models to support territorial reorganization decisions in the public sector. Ph.D. Dissertation, University of Naples Federico II (2014)
14. Toth, P., Vigo, D.: Models, relaxations and exact approaches for the capacitated vehicle routing problem. Discrete Appl. Math. **123**(1–3), 487–512 (2002)
15. Zuñiga, J., López, A., Lozano, Y.: Vehicle routing problem [VRP] and its applications in Colombian medium-sized companies. Ingenium **10**(27), 29–36 (2016)

Model of Optimization of Mining Complex for the Planning of Flow of Quarry Production of Limestone in Multiple Products and with Elements for the Analysis of the Capacity

Holman Ospina-Mateus[1](✉) 📵, Jaime Acevedo-Chedid[1],
Katherinne Salas-Navarro[2], Natalie Morales-Londoño[1,3],
and Jairo Montero-Perez[4]

[1] Department of Industrial Engineering, Universidad Tecnológica de Bolívar,
Cartagena, Colombia
{hospina, jacevedo}@unitecnologica.edu.co
[2] Department of Industrial Management, Agroindustry and Operations,
Universidad de la Costa, Barranquilla, Colombia
Ksalas2@cuc.edu.co
[3] Ciptec Research Group, Industrial Engineering Program,
Fundación Universitaria Tecnológico Comfenalco, Cartagena, Colombia
namoraleslo@hotmail.com
[4] Industrial Engineering Program,
Corporación Universitaria del Caribe (CECAR), Sucre, Colombia
jairo.monteroperez@gmail.com

Abstract. Activities in mining complexes contain multiple decisions that affect the operations of the system for the extraction, transformation, transport and storage of various subsoil components. The purpose of this research is the planning of continuous flow production systems for mixed products, in non-metallic mining extraction processes, considering bottlenecks and capacity planning. This paper presents a model for production, based on mathematical optimization, that facilitates the planning and management of operations in the area of extraction, crushing and transformation of a quarry of aggregates for construction, considering the resources and the constraints that allow to define effective strategies in the increase of the productivity of the lines of low production environment by scenarios. This research develops an analysis of bottlenecks and contrasts the nature of the production system by means of a mathematical model of optimization, which considers the capacities and balances in the flows of the Limestone production line. The mathematical model that maximizes profits can be adapted to systems of continuous flow production in mining complexes where their products are part of a reverse logistics process, analysis of alternatives of extraction, transformation and transport.

Keywords: Production scheduling · Flow shop · Mining complex · Sensitivity analysis · Bottleneck

© Springer International Publishing AG 2017
J.C. Figueroa-García et al. (Eds.): WEA 2017, CCIS 742, pp. 544–555, 2017.
DOI: 10.1007/978-3-319-66963-2_48

1 Introduction

Mining is the set of techniques and activities related to the discovery and exploitation of mineral deposits. In the strict sense, the term is associated with underground operations aimed at starting and treating an ore or associated rock, even though in practice it includes open pit operations, quarries, dredging and combined tasks involving the treatment and transformation underground or surface. The mining chain in the nonmetallic minerals sector is made up of glass, clay, non-refractory ceramics, cement, lime, gypsum and concrete products, enabling the construction industry to supply materials Housing and civil works.

In the functional dimension, problems in mining operations often include open pit and underground mine scheduling, which consists of determining the optimum production schedule over the life of the reservoir, from the feasibility study to the termination phase. The assignment and shipment of the trawl and load equipment in the mine, which consists of the efficient deployment of trucks and excavators, according to some performance criteria, maintaining a constant and reliable supply of the mineral to the processing plants. Processing, in which physical and chemical processes are carried out to improve the quality of the mineral, through the application of classification, concentration and agglomeration operations. The mixture, which consists of mixing the ore through an adequate storage and recovery, both in the yard of collection in the mine and in the port, in order to deliver the ore with the required quality specifications. Programming and dispatch, which effectively involves the routing and control of the movement towards the customer [1].

The mathematical formulation of the model for the planning of a mining production system is composed of the lot size, the capacity expansion, the location of facilities on the network and the design decisions, such as the management of production levels in the mine and its corresponding transformation process in the feeding of material in the processing plants, as well as the transformation of the material into granules.

Among the various studies that plan mining complexes, we find: [2] carried out an analysis of the transport and distribution of construction materials using discrete simulation. For their part, [3] propose a mathematical model for the strategic planning of the capacity of a mining system that includes the zones of exploitation, multimodal transport, zones of shipment in ports and final distribution. [4] described a method for modeling a complex export supply chain using a combination of discrete event optimization and simulation techniques to allow capacity analysis and evaluation of expansion options of Coal in an area of Indonesia. [5] proposed a non-conventional approach for the estimation of reserves or understanding of mineral deposits throughout the mining chain, optimization of mining planning, and forecasting of production, integrating two elements: simulation and Mathematical optimization. [6] posed a supply chain model for coal mine planning through linear programming for production scheduling. The purpose of the optimization model is to maximize sales volumes with constraints on the customer's supply chain, lead times, capacity and inventory. [7] designed a model for optimizing capacity planning in mineral supply chains, which tends to minimize the cost of infrastructure expansion for any scenario based on future demand. [8] developed a global optimization model for scheduling the production of open pit mining complexes with uncertainty. [9] developed a model to obtain the value of stored mineral reserves for future processing, once the mine is exhausted and how it affects the optimal extraction rate.

The different investigations conclude that the storage option can significantly increase the profits in the mines and propose, among other things, the inclusion of elements that cover the effects of economies of scale in mathematical models.

The use of mathematical models becomes an essential tool for the design and implementation of production chains. [10] suggests two basic aspects in supply chain modeling: "chains must be modeled for their own management, and the integration and coordination of processes need to be modeled". Hence, the model must be able to capture the complexity of the supply chain and integrate its resources [11]. Several efficient methodologies have been developed in environments for the problem of scheduling mining production: [12–15].

One of the difficult managerial problems in supply chains of mineral resources is capacity planning, which aims at finding a cost-effective expansion of the infrastructure in order to satisfy a forecasted increase in demand. Capacity planning is crucial for supply chains of mineral resources due to the multi-million-dollar cost associated with capacity expansion, the long lead-time for building the additional infrastructure and the difficulty of withdrawing from building projects and purchasing commitments [16].

The capacity planning as a long-term planning problem needs data aggregation. However, this aggregation should not diminish the significance of the multi-stage nature of supply chains of mineral resources [17, 18]. It is well known that neglecting the scheduling can distort capacity estimates so far as to make the results of capacity planning invalid. This leads to a difficult trade-off – aggregation versus the necessity to take care of queues and congestions [19].

According to [20], the collaborative capacity allows to determine the plan of capacity contracted or available with your customers, to negotiate a level of minimum and maximum capacity, so that it does not affect the production, nor the costs of both. For [21] typical of collaborative capacity aims to provide additional flexibility for the manufacturer (the consumer), being conceived as an example of collaboration related to the service: the exchange of information of suppliers and consumers on demand and the availability of production services. In this sense, a manufacturer (consumer) collaborates with a subcontractor (provider) around the use of production facilities of the subcontractor, based on the master plan of the manufacturer, therefore the manufacturer seeks to make sure that he gets a booking for a specific amount of capacity, without knowing the level used for the production capacity and the product being manufactured, so the collaborative capacity is usually triggered by the consumer.

This research aims to offer a new model to optimize the production flow of a mining complex that considers the method of extraction, processing and transformation of nonmetallic minerals, as well as the quality of material extracted by reservoir uncertainty, so as to Critical points of the productive process, their capacities and their limiting resources. This model provides a source of competitive advantage and allows the planning and control of production under different scenarios, in accordance with the growing needs of the markets.

The content of this research is structured as follows: The introduction in Sect. 1, which indicates a context of the problem and state of the art. The methods in Sect. 2, present the elements of nonmetallic mining for mathematical formulation. In Sect. 3, the results. In Sect. 4, presents an analysis of productive capacity by means of sensitivity to the mathematical model. Finally, the conclusions (Sect. 5) of the model and case study.

2 Method

2.1 Overview

The research is oriented in the field of nonmetallic mining, for the extraction of aggregate materials, which are usually used in construction, more specifically in extractors and crushed in limestone quarries. All phases of the mineral extraction, crushing and transformation process are described below.

The flow of the process for the productive system begins in the phase of the deposit, where the activities of choice, classification and segmentation of the land are developed. In these activities the machine is planned and the selection of ground for the extraction of the earth banks. These blocks of land are segmented by terraces (reservoir), by means of imaginary levels of extraction that cover from 2 to 3 m approximately from top to bottom, which determine the properties of the terrain and affect the conditions of final products, such as aggregate which can be generated. At this stage, there is a high uncertainty component due to geological properties. After the excavation, we move to the main shaking phase, where the material taken from the mine is exposed to strong vibrations, in order to segment it. To develop this activity, the material must be transported from the mine by means of a magazine and pour it on the sash. The extracted material separates the material, from the thinnest to the thickest. Of the total of the shaken material, this one has percentages of yield in a set of byproducts. From this stage, all the unprocessed bulk material is transported to the production line. Then the crushing line has the objective of turning the stones into commercial size and cleaning them by removing the amount of fines. This percentage depends on the level of the reservoir from which it is extracted.

The production line is divided into an unloading ramp where the material extracted from the mine is located, followed by a feeder which acts as a squeegee, which allows the filling material to be removed from a conveyor belt. The thicker material passes to the primary crusher, which crushes the material by breaking it down into smaller material. All the processed material passes to the platform, to a conveyor belt that receives the material in the squeegee, whose objective is to clean the material removing the greater amount of fines to the bigger stone. The material that transports the squeegee leaves a conveyor belt, which ends in the storage of dust. The material that does not pass through the squeegee is taken to a discharging and pre-sorting shuttle, which is dosed the material little by little towards a secondary cone or crusher, which aims to break the stones to bring them to the commercial size.

The crushed material passes to the last platform by means of a discharging and pre-sorting shuttle, followed by a new conveyor belt connecting to the second squeegee. Once the material is entered, it is shaken, releasing more fines, which pass to a conveyor belt that allows to store dust for sale, as well as a new internal mesh classifies the material, leaving each one by different conveyor bands for its storage. The material that does not pass the main mesh of the squeegee, returns to the secondary crusher through a conveyor belt that takes this material to the reprocessing.

2.2   Fundamental Assumptions and Notation

Next, we present a Lineal Programming model developed to plan the production of the quarry, describing the mathematical formulation developed as a productivity management strategy. Likewise, the assumptions that were adopted for the development of the model are stated, as follows: The inventory of the initial phase of the process is unlimited, One working day of operation is 6 h with the time of preparation, A work month consists of 20 days with the time of maintenance, Each workstation is dedicated to a particular operation, The production line platform for transformation allows for inventory at the start, The extraction is related by deposits, levels and periods, Inventories can be unlimited, Multiple products are generated on the production line, with effects of reverse movements on the line for some products.

Declaration of Indices

t Index of the type of reservoir where material is extracted, where $t : 1, 2, 3, \ldots, T$.

n Index that identifies the level of the reservoir (Depth) where material is extracted, where n: 1, 2, 3, ..., N.

p Index that identifies the period where material is extracted, where $p : 1, 2, 3, \ldots, P$.

k Index identifying the type of products transformed, where $k : 1, 2, 3, \ldots, K$.

Statement of Variables

X_{tnp} Amount of stone extracted from the t-field of level n in period p. (Ton/Sem)

I_{tnp} Inventory of reservoir t of level n in phase 0 in period p. (Ton/Week)

W_{tnp} Amount of stone that is processed from the t-field at level n in phase 1 in period p. (Ton/week)

$I1_{tnp}$ Inventory of reservoir t of leven in phase 1 in period p. (Ton/week).

Y_{tnp} Stone transported from t-field to production line in period p. (Ton/week)

$I2_{tnp}$ Inventory at the beginning of the production line (platform 4) of the t-field of level n in period p. (Ton/week)

Z_{tnp} Quantity of stone that is processed at the beginning of the production line (platform 4) of the t-field at level n in period p. (Ton/week)

O_{tnp} Amount of stone that is processed in the middle of production line (platform 5) of the t-field of level n in period p. (Ton/week)

K_{tnp} Amount of stone processed at the end of the production line (platform 6) of the t-field of level n in period p. (Ton/week)

PF_{tnp} Outgoing product k of the production line of the t-field of level n. (Ton/week)

FPF_{pk} Final product k in period p. (Ton/week)

Declaration of Parameters

Cap_t	Capacity to extract productive force at the t-field in (Stage 0). (Ton/week)
$Caproc_t$	Processing capacity in t-fields in phase 1. (Ton/week)
$Captran_t$	Number of tons transported from stage 1 to production line (Ton/week)
$Caplat(4,5,6)_t$	Maximum processing capacity of platform 4, 5 and 6. (Ton/week)
FR_{tn}	Recovery factor of reservoir t of level n in phase 1.
$FR4_{tn}$	Recovery factor of platform t of level n.
$FR5_{tn}$	Recovery factor of platform t of level n.
$FRetorno_{tn}$	Return factor of what leaves platform 6 to platform 5.
$FFinos_{tn}$	Factor of fines of the deposit t in level n.
FRP_{tnk}	Recovery factor for product k of the t-field of level n on platform 6.
V_k	Selling price of the product k. ($/Ton)
CX	Extraction cost - Phase 0. ($/ton)
CTR	Cost of transportation. ($/Ton)
$CPF1$	Shaking cost - Phase 1. ($/ton)
$CP(4,5,6)$	Production Cost in ptform 4, 5 and 6. ($/ton)
$CIF0$	Inventory cost in phase 0 ($/ton)
$CIF1$	Inventory cost in phase 1. ($/ton)
$CIP4$	Inventory cost on platform (4.$/ton)

The productive process was plotted by placing each of the variables, parameters and costs, which are part of the model, for a better analysis of each of the data involved in the model (see Figs. 1).

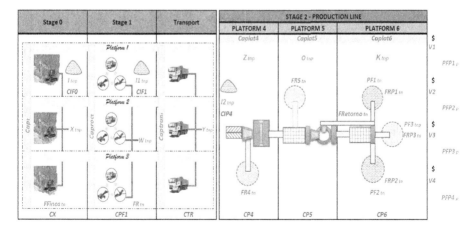

Fig. 1. Location of variables, parameters and costs of the PL model of the productive process.

2.3   Optimization Model

Once the variables have been defined, the formulation is as follows:

$$FO(Max) = \sum_{t:1}^{T} \sum_{n:1}^{N} \sum_{p:1}^{P} \sum_{k:1}^{K} \left(\begin{array}{c} \left(FPF_{pk} * V_k\right) - \left(CX * X_{tnp}\right) - \left(CPF1 * W_{tnp}\right) \\ -\left(CTR * Y_{tnp}\right) - \left(CP4 * Z_{tnp}\right) - \left(CP5 * O_{tnp}\right) \\ -\left(CP6 * K_{tnp}\right) - \left(CIF0 * I_{tnp}\right) - \left(CIF1 * I1_{tnp}\right) \\ -\left(CIP4 * I2_{tnp}\right) \end{array} \right) \quad (1)$$

S/A:

$$\sum_{n:1}^{N} X_{tnp} \leq Cap_t, \forall t \in T, p \in P \quad (2)$$

$$X_{t3} \leq X_{t2} \leq X_{t1}, \forall t \in T \quad (3)$$

$$\sum_{n:1}^{N} W_{tnp} \leq Caproc_t, \forall t \in T, p \in P \quad (4)$$

$$\sum_{n:1}^{N} Y_{tnp} \leq Captran_t, \forall t \in T, p \in P \quad (5)$$

$$\sum_{t:1}^{T} \sum_{n:1}^{N} Z_{tnp} \leq Caplat_4, \forall p \in P \quad (6)$$

$$\sum_{t:1}^{T} \sum_{n:1}^{N} O_{tnp} \leq Caplat_5, \forall p \in P \quad (7)$$

$$\sum_{t:1}^{T} \sum_{n:1}^{N} K_{tnp} \leq Caplat_6, \forall p \in P \quad (8)$$

$$I_{tnp} = I_{tnp-1} + X_{tnp} - W_{tnp}, \forall t \in T, n \in N, p \in P \quad (9)$$

$$I1_{tnp} = I1_{tnp-1} + W_{tnp} - \left(W_{tnp} * (1 - FR_{tn})\right) - Y_{tnp}, \forall t \in T, n \in N, p \in P \quad (10)$$

$$I2_{tnp} = I2_{tnp-1} + Y_{tnp} - Z_{tnp}, \forall t \in T, n \in N, p \in P \quad (11)$$

$$O_{tnp} = Z_{tnp} * FR4_{tn}, \forall t \in T, n \in N, p \in P \quad (12)$$

$$K_{tnp} = O_{tnp} * FR5_{tnp} + \left(Fretorno_{tn} * K_{tn}\right), \forall t \in T, n \in N, p \in P \quad (13)$$

$$PF_{pk} = K_{tnp} * FRP_{tnk}, \forall t \in T, n \in N, p \in P, k \in K \quad (14)$$

$$FPF_{pk} = \sum_{t:1}^{T} \sum_{n:1}^{N} PF_{tnpk}, \forall p \in P, k \in K : (1,2) \quad (15)$$

$$FPF_{pk} = \sum_{t:1}^{T} \sum_{n:1}^{N} PF_{tnpk} + \left(O_{tnp} * (1 - FR5_{tn})\right), \forall k \in K : 3 \quad (16)$$

$$FPF_{pk} = \sum_{t:1}^{T} \sum_{n:1}^{N} \left(Z_{tnp} * (1 - FR4_{tn})\right) + \left(W_{tnp} * (1 - FR_{tn})\right), \forall k \in K : 4 \quad (17)$$

$$\sum_{t:1}^{T} \sum_{n:1}^{N} FPF_{tnpk} * FFinos_{tn} \leq Calidad * \sum_{t:1}^{T} \sum_{n:1}^{N} FPF_{tnpk}, \forall p \in P, k \in K : (1,2) \quad (18)$$

$$X_{tnp}, I_{tnp}, W_{tnp}, I1_{tnp}, Y_{tnp}, I2_{tnp}, Z_{tnp}, O_{tnp}, K_{tnp}, PF_{tnk}, FPF_{pk} \geq 0, \quad (19)$$
$$\forall t \in T, n \in N, p \in P, k \in K$$

Equation (1) maximizes the profit obtained by the sale of products less costs incurred in the production process (Extraction, sanding, shredding, transportation, processing and inventories). The Eq. (2) determines the quantity of tons that can be extracted from the deposits. The Eq. (3) determines the quantities to be extracted from the reservoirs depending on the levels. Equation (4) defines the tons that can be processed in the shaking in Phase 1. Equation (5) determines the tons that can be transported from Phase 1 to Platform 4. The Eqs. (6, 7 and 8) determines the quantity of tons that can be processed in Platform 4, 5 and 6 respectively. Equation (9) indicates the inventory of Phase 0. Equation (10) indicates the inventory of Phase 1. Equation (11) indicates the inventory quantity at the start of Platform 4. Equation (12) ensures The balance of Platform 4 to Platform 5. Equation (13) guarantees the product flow balance of Platform 5 to Platform 6. Equation (14) determines the quantity of Product k leaving platform 6. Equation (15) determines the final total quantity of product 1 and 2. Equation (16) determines the quantity of Product 3 taking into account that leaving Platform 6 and the quantity not retrieved from Platform 5. The Eq. (17) determines the final total quantity of product 4 taking into account the quantity not recovered from Platform 4 and the quantity of tons not recovered in Phase 1. The Eq. (18) determines the minimum quality that should have Product 1 and 2 With respect to the percentage of Maximum permissible fines for this product. The quality varies for the type of product per level. The last Eq. (19) conditions the non-negativity of the variables for a linear programming problem.

3 Results

The model was programmed using GAMS and the problem was solved optimally using the CPLEX resolution libraries. For this, a computer with an Intel® CoreI7 2.66 GHz processor, 24 GB of RAM and a professional Windows 8 operating system was used. The objective function of this model raises the profit maximization, with a solution of COP $3'274,932,743.5 And, to find this value, 84 iterations of the possible 2,000,000,000 were made.

The results showed that the amount of extracted material X(tnp) for the four periods was 11,571 tons, while the inventory I (tnp) is fluctuating and handles low inventories between 771 and 1,542 tons. In the case of the variable W(tnp) it shows that its maximum capacity is used in all the periods.

The tons that are transported to the production line first enter Platform 4, which has a maximum capacity of 6,500 tons per week, of which 4,463.4 are used, which corresponds to 69% of its maximum capacity. Most of the tons that are processed in Platform 4 go to Platform 5. This platform has a capacity of 3,660 tons per week, of which 100% is being used. Platform 6 has a capacity of 7,850 tons per week, of which 4,967.1 are used, equivalent to 63% of its total capacity. it is determined that the variables Z and K, associated to the quantity of product processed in Platforms 4 and 6 respectively, are constant, since these variables are adjusted to the capacity of Platform 5. The variable O, which determines the quantity processed in Platform 5, is also kept constant in all periods, being used the capacity to 100%. With respect to variable K, it is also kept constant, since it depends on the capacity of the previous platform. It is evident that the bottleneck is found in Platform 5, where resources are being used at 100%, while other platforms are used between 63% and 69%. After analyzing the variables involved with the processes, we then present the quantities obtained by the proposed model for scheduling the production of each of the products by periods. It is observed that 1,390.8 tons of Aggregate 1″, 1,896.9 tons of Aggregate 1/2″, 431, 4 tons of powder and 2,961.7 tons of Graded - Aggregate were obtained on average.

It should be noted that the graded-aggregate product is the one that is generated the most, because it emerges in two different parts: in the shaking out phase and in Platform 4. It is important to clarify that this product, like dust, is waste That are generated of the productive process, and these are used to be commercialized by the great advantages that they possess. In the case of Graded - Aggregate, it is used as a filler; And the dust is used as a base for cement and brick making. Given this situation, it can be determined that these products are part of a reverse logistics process, because the waste is recovered from the manufacturing process and, as a waste, the company seeks to market them in order to seek an economic benefit.

4   Sensitivity Analysis

It is evident that the capacity of the resource associated to Platform 5 of the production line is much lower than that of other resources, thus having a bottleneck to be exploited, represented by the processing capacity of the secondary cone or crusher. It is known that the product that generates the highest Throughput is the product 2 triturated of ½″. However, the production system does not allow to produce this exclusively, since the production line performs all the corresponding operations for the process of the raw material and this is concatenated. If the production of Crushers increases, the production of dust (powder) and graded-aggregate will also increase according to the recovery factors already established by the system in the different platforms. After the results of the linear programming model, different scenarios were proposed to analyze the behavior of the model according to the bottleneck, adjusting in the mathematical model in condition to vary the capacity of the system.

4.1   Scenario 1: Increased Capacity of the Bottleneck

Currently, the capacity of Platform 5 is equal to 3,660 tons per week, determined by the capacity of the cone crusher. For the sensitivity analysis, in this scenario the capacity of this platform was increased, increasing it to 35%, 70% and 100%. However, increasing the capacity to 100% remains the same as if it were increased to 75% since in this scenario, there is now a new restrictive resource that would be the resources aligned with the variable Z, which reaches its maximum capacity in Platform 6.

The company's profits increase with the variation of capacity, going from COP $3'274, 932,743.5 to COP $4'339.200.222, this being an additional 32.5% to the current data of the model. For the 35% scenario, the objective function increases by 42.3% and in the scenario of 100% it remains the same as in the scenario of 75%.

Taking into account the cost data, it is considered to increase the capacity of the resource restriction by 35%, with an effectiveness (ROI), which for each weight that is invested in this option were obtained 6.8 back.

4.2   Scenario 2. Increase of 1 Shift

In this second scenario, the daily shifts were increased, from 1 single shift to 28 h shifts each, which means that a total of 16 h per day would be worked. For the development of this model, it is taken into account that the costs of production of the second shift increase by 30%. The objective function finds an optimal value of COP $6'510,740,548.0 of which COP $3'274,932,743.6 correspond to the first turn, value thrown in the analysis of the main model, and COP $3'235.807.804,4 to the second turn. If it is increased to 2 shifts, the company would have the ability to meet the demand and handle an Aggregate 1/2″ inventory that normally holds a high demand and the organization currently cannot cover it. With respect to the other products, it would increase the inventory of finished products, which means that it increases the risk of losses due to the obsolescence of material.

4.3   Scenario 3. Changing Production Line Configuration

The configuration change considers an alteration of the meshes of the production line, so that it can classify one product more than another. With respect to the end products, the aggregate 1/2″ material has increased, which is considered satisfactory. However, it is not considered desirable since as Product 2 increases, Product 1 decreases. And this is the second product that generates the highest value to the company. In addition, Products 3 and 4 increase, thus increasing your inventory. Due to the sales prices that are handled in the market and the demand that is given for the products, it is considered that it is not convenient to carry out the configuration of the production line, since this would lead to losses due to obsolescence of material.

4.4   Scenario 4. Changing the Demand Configuration and Restrictions on Inventories

The model considers the missing ones that suppose a lost sale. This value does not generate an impact on the Objective Function, but it does in the market, being a cost difficult to calculate. Of course it is reflected in customer losses and lack of credibility, affecting the good name of the company. Also, the model will handle the costs of inventories of final products, taking into account the loss factor due to material obsolescence. New variables were considered in the problem as they are: $IFPF_{pk}$ = Final product inventory k in period p; FAL_{pk} = Product missing k in period p; $Demp_{pk}$ = Demand of product k in period p.

And it is included in the following Eq. (20):

$$IFPF_{pk} = IFPF_{p-1,k} + FPF_{pk} + FAL_{pk} - Dem_{pk}, \forall p \in P, k \in K \qquad (20)$$

Demand values for 1″ , 1/2″, powder and shredding products were 750, 2,500, 250 and 1,500 ton/Weekly. The linear programming model with demand yields an optimal value of COP $1'524.059.405.9 since it considers not to sell everything that is produced but to cover the demand of its Products handling an inventory of finished products.

The new model of linear programming determines that the demand for its main product, which is the aggregate 1/2″, is not met, and therefore it generates a number of in each period. This, in turn, leads to the lack of finished products of this kind in inventories. When performing the analysis of the scenarios, it is possible to identify as the most convenient the context where the capacity of the restrictive resource is increased by 35%, in which the model finds the values of each of the variables optimum and maximizes its objective function from COP $3,274,932,743.5 to COP $4,339,200,222 as a profit for the company, which is equivalent to approximately 33% in increase of its profits.

5   Conclusions

This research accomplishes the design of optimization strategies for mining complexes, where the production flow in the development of mixed products must be considered, through the results of the management of the restriction and the sensitivity analysis, yielding financial benefits, such as shown by the results of the mathematical model.

The model allows to distinguish the restrictions within a productive system of this nature, with their respective bottlenecks, which, with a post-optimal analysis and sensitivity, derives in the approach of different scenarios that help to define alternatives for planning of capacity.

As an investigative contribution, it was shown that it is possible to model and optimize the conditions of uncertainty in performance and material quality, within production systems that have alternatives of flow and sequencing in the development of various products, where profit maximization is desirable by means of the search of conditions necessary for the restrictive resource to reach its peak in production and, therefore, the generation of money for the companies.

After identifying the bottleneck of the productive system and after making the necessary changes to generate the different scenarios, it is important to emphasize that its exploitation becomes obligatory to find alternatives that allow to cover the demand and generate an added value. Future work will include performance variables with stochastic behavior and variation of processing alternatives in productive capacity.

References

1. Pimentel, B.S., Mateus, G.R., Almeida, F.A.: Mathematical models for optimizing the global mining supply chain. In: Intelligent Systems in Operations: Methods, Models and Applications in the Supply Chain, pp. 133–163 (2010)
2. Gómez, R.A., Correa, A.A.: Análisis del transporte y distribución de materiales de construcción utilizando simulación discreta en 3D. Boletín de Ciencias de La Tierra **30**, 39–52 (2011)
3. Pimentel, B.S., Mateus, G.R., Almeida, F.A.: Stochastic capacity planning in a global mining supply chain. In: 2011 IEEE Workshop on Computational Intelligence in Production And Logistics Systems (CIPLS), pp. 1–8. IEEE (2011)
4. Bodon, P., Fricke, C., Sandeman, T., Stanford, C.: Modeling the mining supply chain from mine to port: a combined optimization and simulation approach. J. Min. Sci. **47**(2), 202–211 (2011)
5. Dimitrakopoulos, R.: Stochastic optimization for strategic mine planning: a decade of developments. J. Min. Sci. **47**(2), 138–150 (2011)
6. Zhao, Y., Zhou, Y., Li, C., Cao, Z.: SCM-based optimization of production planning for coal mine. In: 2012 9th International Conference on Fuzzy Systems and Knowledge Discovery (FSKD), pp. 968–972. IEEE (2012)
7. Fung, J., Singh, G., Zinder, Y.: Capacity planning in supply chains of mineral resources. Inf. Sci. **316**, 397–418 (2015)
8. Goodfellow, R.C., Dimitrakopoulos, R.: Global optimization of open pit mining complexes with uncertainty. Appl. Soft Comput. **40**, 292–304 (2016)
9. Zhang, K., Kleit, A.N.: Mining rate optimization considering the stockpiling: a theoretical economics and real option model. Resour. Policy **47**, 87–94 (2016)
10. Vernadat, F.B.: Enterprise integration: on business process and enterprise activity modelling. Concurrent Eng. **4**(3), 219–228 (1996)
11. Vélez, J.G.D., Otero, L.F.R.: Modelo matemático para la optimización de una cadena de suministro global con consideraciones de cupos de compra y periodos de pago. El Hombre y la Máquina **38**, 6–21 (2012)
12. Benndorf, J., Dimitrakopoulos, R.: Stochastic long-term production scheduling of iron ore deposits: integrating joint multi-element geological uncertainty. J. Min. Sci. **49**(1), 68–81 (2013)
13. Godoy, M., Dimitrakopoulos, R.: Managing risk and waste mining in long-term production scheduling of open-pit mines. SME Trans. **316**(3), 43–50 (2004). https://www.researchgate.net/profile/Roussos_Dimitrakopoulos/publication/43458583_Managing_risk_and_waste_mining_in_long-term_production_scheduling/links/0f31752f9977473219000000/Managing-risk-and-waste-mining-in-long-term-production-scheduling.pdf
14. Lamghari, A., Dimitrakopoulos, R., Ferland, J.A.: A variable neighbourhood descent algorithm for the open-pit mine production scheduling problem with metal uncertainty. J. Oper. Res. Soc. **65**(9), 1305–1314 (2014)
15. Montiel, L., Dimitrakopoulos, R.: Stochastic mine production scheduling with multiple processes: application at Escondida Norte, Chile. J. Min. Sci. **49**(4), 583–597 (2013)
16. Fung, J., Singh, G., Zinder, Y.: Capacity planning in supply chains of mineral resources. Inf. Sci. **316**, 397–428 (2015). http://dx.doi.org/10.1016/j.ins.2014.11.015
17. Shapiro, J.: Modeling the Supply Chain. Brooks/Cole-Thomson Learning, Pacific Grove (2001)
18. Crainic, T.G., Laporte, G.: Planning models for freight transportation. Eur. J. Oper. Res. **97**, 409–438 (1997). doi:10.1016/S0377-2217(96)00298-6
19. Solberg, J.J.: Capacity planning with a stochastic workflow model. AIIE Trans. **13**, 116–122 (1981). doi:10.1080/05695558108974543
20. Mehrjerdi, Z.: The collaborative supply chain. Assembly Autom. **29**(2), 127–136 (2009)
21. Stadtler, H.: Supply chain management and advanced planning –basics, overview and challenges. Eur. J. Oper. Res. **163**, 575–588 (2005)

Solving the Interval Green Inventory Routing Problem Using Optimization and Genetic Algorithms

Carlos Franco[1(✉)], Eduyn Ramiro López-Santana[2],
and Juan Carlos Figueroa-García[2]

[1] Universidad del Rosario, Bogotá, Colombia
carlosa.franco@urosario.edu.co
[2] Universidad Distrital Francisco José de Caldas, Bogotá, Colombia
{erlopezs,jcfigueroag}@udistrital.edu.co

Abstract. In this paper, we present a genetic algorithm embedded with mathematical optimization to solve a green inventory routing problem with interval fuel consumption. Using the idea of column generation in which only attractive routes are generated to the mathematical problem, we develop a genetic algorithm that allow us to determine speedily attractive routes that are connected to a mathematical model. We code our genetic algorithm using the idea of a integer number that represents all the feasible set of routes in which the maximum number allowed is the binary number that represents if a customer is visited or not. We approximate the fuel consumption as an interval number in which we want to minimize the overall fuel consumption of distribution. This is the first approximation made in the literature using this type of methodology so we cannot compare our approach with those used in the literature.

Keywords: Green inventory routing problem · Optimization · Genetic algorithms · Interval optimization

1 Introduction

One of the biggest challenges in logistics is to deal with the inventory management and the distribution networks. To face this situation several theories and models have been developed in order to minimize the total logistic costs. A best known theory for solving this situation is known as the Vendor Manage Inventory strategy (VMI) in which the decisions of distributions and inventory management are made by retailers with the objective of the minimization of costs [1].

A mathematical approximation to the VMI strategy is the Inventory Routing Problem (IRP) which is an extension of the classic Vehicle Routing Problem (VRP). The IRP is an attractive problem due to its mathematical and computational complexity and for its applicability. In fact, this problem is NP-Hard because can be reduce to the traveling salesman problem (TSP) [1].

The IRP and its extensions usually looks for minimizing the overall logistics cost (routing and inventory). This traditional model does not take into account the emissions of greenhouse gases. In this way, green logistics refers to the design of models that consider the emissions and other factor that affect the environment in the process of distribution.

© Springer International Publishing AG 2017
J.C. Figueroa-García et al. (Eds.): WEA 2017, CCIS 742, pp. 556–564, 2017.
DOI: 10.1007/978-3-319-66963-2_49

Policy makers has been interested in contributing to the global environment, for this reason, supply chain management is not excluded of design distribution networks that help to reduce the environmental impact [2].

Transportation is one of the most significant contributor to the global warming in the world because of the uses of fossil fuels for energy [3]. In this paper, we model the problem of determined the set of routes that satisfied a set of requirements by minimizing the fuel consumption using an interval approximation. The objective of the model is to design a network of transportation over a planning horizon, determining the inventory levels at the customers and the routes but considering that in the distribution network the fuel consumption is the impact to the environment.

The paper is organized as follows: Sect. 2 contains a literature overview of the Green approximations to the VRP and IRP. Section 3 presents the mathematical model that is used and Sect. 4 shows the genetic algorithm approach. Some results are presented in Sect. 5. Finally, Sect. 6 states the conclusions and future works.

2   Related Literature

The term of green logistics is a related new field of study in the literature. Nevertheless it has gain high attention by researcher because of the global warming and several factors in the climate change. In this way some authors have developed different models, approximations and algorithms for facing this situation.

Most of the articles deals with the problem of distribution networks (VRP) with green factors. In this review we will mention some of the most relevant articles about Inventory Routing Problems considering green factors.

Cheng et al. [4] developed a model for the IRP with heterogeneous fleet considering green factors in the objective function representing the fuel emission by using the fuel consumption by the load, distance, speed and vehicle characteristics. They proposed a branch and cut algorithm for solving some random instances.

Another approximation is made by Cheng et al. [5] in which the fuel consumption rate is the approximation to the impact of carbon emission. They proposed some nonlinear mix integer problems and linearization techniques are used. Also a heuristic is developed in order to reduce the computational time.

Another branch and cut algorithm is developed by Qiu et al. [6], but in this case is developed for the production routing problem. The green factor is consider as the carbon cap-and-trade.

Mirzapour et al. [7] Developed a green approach for the multi-product inventory routing problem by considering the relation between the transportation cost and the greenhouse gas emission level. They proposed a mixed integer programming and it is solved using a commercial software.

A real application of the petrochemical industry is developed by Treitl et al. [8], in this article authors focuses on the analysis of the process of transportation measuring the environmental effects or routing decisions with vertical collaborations.

Nasir et al. proposed a mathematical formulation taking into account the CO_2 emissions [9]. The main idea is to identify the effect of the total emission on the inventory and routing decisions over the planning horizon.

Malekly develop also a model for the green inventory routing problem [10] but considering uncertainty. They want to determine the economic and environmental consequences of transport routing decisions in a supply chain with vertical collaboration. An optimization model and a solution method is presented in which inventory and transportation costs and emissions as well as demand uncertainty concerns are explicitly incorporated.

Finally an Inventory Routing Model for perishable products is developed by Rahimi et al. [11]. One of the objective function used is the consideration of the Greenhouse Gas (GHG) emissions, produced by different IRP activities, finally they developed a multiobjective optimization algorithm for obtain the Pareto-frontier.

To conclude our research contributes to the literature of the IRP by introducing an interval number to the fuel consumption, using a genetic algorithms for reduce the computational time and performing numerical tests to provide managerial insights.

3   Problem Definition

In this section the mathematical model is presented as follows, this mathematical model has been adapted from other models proposed in [12–14] and we have added the fuel consumption in the objective function:

3.1   Mathematical Model

Sets	
T	Set of period time
V	Set of nodes
Vp	Set of customers $=\{2,\dots,n\}$

Parameters	
rt	Amount of product available at the depot for each period time
$dt_i{}^t$	Demand for each customer i, for each period time t
Li	Lower bound of inventory for each customer i
Ci,	Upper bound of inventory for each customer i
cij	Travel cost between customer i and customer j
Qk	Capacity of each vehicle
si	Service time for each customer i
h_i	Inventory holding cost for each customer i
FC_{ij}	Fuel consumption between two pair of nodes i,j

Variables	
I_i^t	Inventory levels for each node i for each period time t
X_{ij}^{kt}	=1 if the arc i,j is traversed by vehicle k in a period time t
q_i^{kt}	Amount of product delivery to customer i by vehicle k in a period time t
Y_i^{kt}	=1 if a customer i is visited by vehicle k in a period time t
e_i^{kt}	Time of beginning of a service for a customer i in a period time t for a specific vehicle k

Model Formulation.
The mathematical formulation for the problem is presented as follows: the objective function given in Eq. (1) is used to minimize the total fuel consumption between each pair of nodes.

$$min\ Z = \sum_{i \in V} \sum_{j \in V} \sum_{k \in K} \sum_{t \in T} FC_{ij} X_{ij}^{kt} \tag{1}$$

$$I_i^t = I_i^{t-1} + \sum_{k \in K} q_i^{kt} - dt_i^t \quad \forall i \in Vp, t \in T \tag{2}$$

$$I_i^t \geq L_i \quad \forall i \in Vp, t \in T \tag{3}$$

$$I_i^t \leq C_i \quad \forall i \in Vp, t \in T \tag{4}$$

$$\sum_{k \in K} q_i^{kt} \leq C_i - I_i^{t-1} \quad \forall i \in Vp, t \in T \tag{5}$$

$$\sum_{k \in K} q_i^{kt} \leq C_i \sum_{j \in V} \sum_{k \in K} X_{ij}^{kt} \quad \forall i \in Vp, t \in T \tag{6}$$

$$\sum_{k \in K} q_i^{kt} \leq Qk \quad \forall t \in T, k \in K \tag{7}$$

$$q_i^{kt} \leq Y_i^{kt} C_i \quad \forall i \in Vp, t \in T, k \in K \tag{8}$$

$$\sum_{j \in V} X_{ij}^{kt} = \sum_{j \in V} X_{ji}^{kt} \quad \forall i \in Vp, t \in T, k \in K \tag{9}$$

$$\sum_{j \in V} X_{ij}^{kt} = Y_i^{kt} \quad \forall i \in Vp, t \in T, k \in K \tag{10}$$

$$\sum_{j \in Vp} X_{1j}^{kt} \leq 1 \quad \forall k \in K, t \in T \tag{11}$$

$$\sum_{k \in K} Y_i^{kt} \leq 1 \quad \forall i \in Vp, t \in T \tag{12}$$

$$I_i^t \geq 0 \quad \forall i \in Vp, t \in T \tag{13}$$

$$X_{ij}^{kt}, Y_i^{kt} \in \{0, 1\} \quad \forall i, j \in Vp, i \neq j, t \in T, k \in K \tag{14}$$

$$q_i^{kt} \geq 0 \quad \forall i \in Vp, t \in T, k \in K \tag{15}$$

Equation (2) ensures the balance inventory constraints. Constraints (3) and (4) ensures that for each customer the inventory levels can't exceed the minimum and maximum level respectively. With constraints (5) and (6) are modeled the quantities of product that can be delivered to each customer. With Eq. (7) is guaranteed that the amount of product delivered in a vehicle exceed its capacity. With constraints (8) the consistency between amount of product delivered and the activation of a route is given. Equations (9) and (10) represents the flow conservation and activation constraints respectively. With constraints (11) and (12) is ensure that a vehicle only can begin in one route from the depot. Equations (13), (14) and (15) defines the type of variable. In this formulation we have not added the well-known sub tour elimination constraints because in our approximation via genetic algorithm we can guarantee that the solution doesn't contain subtours.

3.2 Fuel Consumption as an Interval Number

It can be determine that the fuel consumption is not a deterministic number and depend of different factors, hence, it can't be known with absolutely certainty. Some studies have tried to determine the fuel consumption as a mathematical function for different factors [15, 16].

In our proposal we used a interval approximation to estimate the fuel consumption between each pair of nodes. For this reason, the fuel consumption has a linguistic uncertainty between each pair of nodes and between an interval function as follows in Eq. (16):

$$FC_{ij} \in \left[FC_{ij}^-; FC_{ij}^+ \right] i,j \in V \tag{16}$$

3.3 Mathematical Reformulation

For solving this type of problems Delgado et al. [17] prove that the solution of the problem can be obtained by reformulating with a multi-objective auxiliary model in which all the possible values of the objective functions are used. The auxiliary model used is as follows (17):

$$\max z = \left[c^1 x, c^2 x, \dots, c^n x \right]$$
$$s.t.$$
$$x \leq 0, \alpha \in [0,1], c_j^k \in \left\{ g_j^{-1}(1-\alpha), h_j^{-1}(1-\alpha) \right\} \tag{17}$$
$$j = 1, \dots, n; \quad k = 1, \dots, 2^n$$

4   Genetic Algorithm Approach

As we can see in the mathematical model presented previously and as extension of the classical vehicle routing problem (VRP) this is a NP-Hard problem in which the mathematical model only can solve instances with a reduce number of customers. In this way and as it can be find in other approximations to this problem [2, 18], we have developed a genetic algorithm that allow us to reduce the complexity of the problem. Instead of using a column generation approach, we have combine a genetic algorithm that allow us to obtain a set of feasible and attractive routes embedded with a mathematical model that determines the quantities of products delivered taking into account the constraints of inventories and capacities.

4.1   Encoding the Genetic Algorithm

For encoding our genetic algorithm we want to create attractive routes for each period time. In this way, our genetic algorithm must be encoded to determine feasible routes that can vary for different period's time.

In our codification of the GA we divide our chromosome into the t periods time, this means that in each chromosome we obtain a set of feasible routes for the planning period. Now, in other to determine how we will create the routes, for each period time we use an integer number which describe all the possible routes. For example, if we have three customers the routes can be: 1-0-0, 0-1-0, 0-0-1, and all the combinations between them. To get fast and easy calculations we transform the binary routes into integer numbers, for this reason the maximum number in a field is $2^{number\ of\ customers} - 1$ and that number allow us that all the possible routes can be generated and that can be generated easily. In the Fig. 1 we can see an example of our codification:

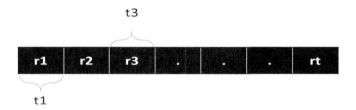

Fig. 1. Example of codification

4.2   Selection of Population

During each iteration, a part of the total population is selected to breed a new generation based on this new population. We have selected two types of population that we will select in each iteration, the first one is those which its objective value are prominent. The second one is those with worst objective function. We have limited the new population by an integer number of P, and the size of each type of population is P/2. In this step we use Roulette Wheel that allow us to generate solutions based on the fitness but also using a distribution probability.

4.3   Crossover and Mutation

To generate new population based on those selected in the previous step, we use a random number between the intervals [0, 1]. After the number is generated, we compare with a predefine number for the crossover process. If the random number is greater than the predefine number the crossover doesn`t occurs. The method use for crossover is the one-point crossover in which we select a point of the interval and determine that the new population generated is a combination between the two parents using both information. Child chromosomes are then constructed from the characters of the first parent occurring before the crossover point and the characters of the second parent occurring after the crossover point.

The mutation operator consist in using a probability of mutation in which if a random number is greater than this probability of mutation then the current solution of the chromosome is perturbed. In our case the mutation is doing by generating a new number between 1 and the maximum number of customers (in the integer number) and adding this number to the current solution.

4.4 Termination Criteria

We have used multiple termination criteria for the genetic algorithm and the mathematical model because we are using them embedded. The first termination criteria is a maximum top of total time. The second criteria used is the maximum number of iterations without an improving in the objective function and finally a maximum number of iterations is used.

5 Results

We have adapted some instances from the literature proposed by Coelho et al. [12–14, 19] in which the number of customers, the demand and distance between each pair of nodes is given. The number of customer vary between 5 and 25, and the number of periods time are 3 or 5. Results of our algorithm are presented in Table 1.

Table 1. Results of the algorithm

Instance	# Customers	# Periods time	Time (s)
abs1n5	5	3	8
abs1n10	10	3	230
abs1n15	15	3	600
abs1n20	20	3	740
abs1n25	25	3	870
abs1n5	5	5	35
abs1n10	10	5	429
abs1n15	15	5	856
abs1n20	20	5	953
abs1n25	25	5	1129

The interval objective function is obtained by adapting the distance between each pair of nodes. We have tested in some of the instances in the literature as we can see in the table presented below. We can see that our algorithm combined with mathematical modeling can solve the instances in a considerable reduce number of time given the multiple objective functions because of the interval fuel consumption number, this doesn't mean that we have developed a multi-objective algorithm and find a Pareto region, for each route generated with the encoding we have determine its fitness for each scenario.

6 Conclusions

In this article we have developed a mathematical model an approximation using genetic algorithms for the Inventory Routing Problem with interval fuel consumption. In this article a new model for take into account the green factors into the Inventory Routing Problem is presented. The genetic algorithm developed allow us to reduce the computational complexity of the problem by separating decisions of routing and decisions of inventory management for customers, nevertheless these two decisions are working simultaneously because the routes generated by the genetic algorithm are the input for the mathematical model that determines the quantities of product send to customers and the inventory levels. Future work will focus on the stochastic version of the fuel consumption and adding some other features for determining another approximations to the greenhouses emissions.

References

1. Federgruen, A., Zipkin, P.: A combined vehicle routing and inventory allocation problem. Oper. Res. **32**, 1019–1037 (1984)
2. Franco, C., López-Santana, E.R., Méndez-Giraldo, G.: A column generation approach for solving a green bi-objective inventory routing problem. In: Montes-y-Gómez, M., Escalante, H.J., Segura, A., de Dios Murillo, J. (eds.) IBERAMIA 2016. LNCS, vol. 10022, pp. 101–112. Springer, Cham (2016). doi:10.1007/978-3-319-47955-2_9
3. Boden, T.A., Andres, R.J., Marland, G.: Global, Regional, and National Fossil-Fuel CO2 Emissions. https://www.epa.gov/ghgemissions/global-greenhouse-gas-emissions-data
4. Cheng, C., Yang, P., Mingyao, Q., Rousseau, L.: Modeling a green inventory routing problem with a heterogeneous fleet. Transp. Res. Part E **97**, 97–112 (2017)
5. Cheng, C., Qi, M., Wang, X., Zhang, Y.: Multi-period inventory routing problem under carbon emission regulations. Int. J. Prod. Econ. **182**, 263–275 (2016)
6. Qiu, Y., Qiao, J., Pardalos, P.: A branch-and–price algorithm for production routing problems with carbon cap-and-trade. Omega **68**, 49–61 (2017)
7. Mirzapour Al-e-hashem, S.M.J., Rekik, Y.: Multi-product multi-period inventory routing problem with a transshipment option: a green approach. Int. J. Prod. Econ. **157**, 80–88 (2014)
8. Treitl, S., Nolz, P.C., Jammernegg, W.: Incorporating environmental aspects in an inventory routing problem. a case study from the petrochemical industry. Flex. Serv. Manuf. J. **26**, 143–169 (2014)
9. Alkawaleet, N., Hsieh, Y.-F., Wang, Y.: Inventory routing problem with CO2 emissions consideration. In: Golinska, P. (ed.) Logistics Operations, Supply Chain Management and Sustainability, pp. 611–619. Springer, Cham (2014)
10. Malekly, H.: The inventory pollution-routing problem under uncertainty. In: Fahimnia, B., Bell, M.G.H., Hensher, D.A., Sarkis, J. (eds.) Green Logistics and Transportation, pp. 83–117. Springer, Cham (2015)
11. Rahimi, M., Baboli, A., Rekik, Y.: Inventory routing problem for perishable products by considering customer satisfaction and green criteria. In: Freitag, M., Kotzab, H., Pannek, J. (eds.) Dynamics in Logistics. Springer, Cham (2017)
12. Coelho, L.C., Laporte, G.: The exact solution of several classes of inventory-routing problems. Comput. Oper. Res. **40**, 558–565 (2013)

13. Archetti, C., Bertazzi, L., Laporte, G., Speranza, M.G.: A branch-and-cut algorithm for a vendor-managed inventory-routing problem. Transp. Sci. **41**, 382–391 (2007)
14. Coelho, L.C., Laporte, G.: Optimal joint replenishment, delivery and inventory management policies for perishable products. Comput. Oper. Res. **47**, 42–52 (2014)
15. Feng, Y., Zhang, R.-Q., Jia, G.: Vehicle routing problems with fuel consumption and stochastic travel speeds. Math. Probl. Eng. **2017**, 1–16 (2017)
16. Chang, R.C.: Examination of excessive fuel consumption for transport jet aircraft based on fuzzy-logic models of flight data. Fuzzy Sets Syst. **269**, 115–134 (2015)
17. Delgado, M., Verdegay, J.L., Vila, M.A.: A general model for fuzzy linear programming. Fuzzy Sets Syst. **29**, 21–29 (1989)
18. Franco-Franco, C., Figueroa-García, J.C.: A column generation-based algorithm for solving combined inventory and routing problems. Ingeniare **24**, 305–313 (2016)
19. Coelho, L.C., Cordeau, J.-F., Laporte, G.: Consistency in multi-vehicle inventory-routing. Transp. Res. Part C Emerg. Technol. **24**, 270–287 (2012)

A Meta-Optimization Approach for Covering Problems in Facility Location

Broderick Crawford[1(✉)], Ricardo Soto[1], Eric Monfroy[2], Gino Astorga[1,3],
José García[1,4], and Enrique Cortes[1,5]

[1] Pontificia Universidad Católica de Valparaíso, 2374631 Valparaíso, Chile
{broderick.crawford,ricardo.soto}@pucv.cl
[2] LINA, Universite de Nantes, Nantes, France
Eric.Monfroy@univ-nantes.fr
[3] Universidad de Valparaíso, 2361864 Valparaíso, Chile
gino.astorga@uv.cl
[4] Centro de Investigación y Desarrollo Telefónica, 7500961 Santiago, Chile
joseantonio.garcia@telefonica.com
[5] Universidad de Playa Ancha, Leopoldo Carvallo 270, 2340000 Valparaíso, Chile
enrique.cortes@upla.cl

Abstract. In this paper, we solve the Set Covering Problem with a
meta-optimization approach. One of the most popular models among
facility location models is the Set Covering Problem. The meta-level
metaheuristic operates on solutions representing the parameters of other
metaheuristic. This approach is applied to an Artificial Bee Colony metaheuristic that solves the non-unicost set covering. The Artificial Bee
Colony algorithm is a recent swarm metaheuristic technique based on
the intelligent foraging behavior of honey bees. This metaheuristic owns
a parameter set with a great influence on the effectiveness of the search.
These parameters are fine-tuned by a Genetic Algorithm, which trains
the Artificial Bee Colony metaheuristic by using a portfolio of set covering problems. The experimental results show the effectiveness of our
approach which produces very near optimal scores when solving set covering instances from the OR-Library.

Keywords: Covering problems · Facility location · Artificial bee colony
algorithm · Swarm intelligence

1 Introduction

Facility Location is an important research area in strategic planning of public
and private firms. One of the most popular models among facility location models is covering problem, this is due to its applicability in real-world problems.
Covering Problems were introduced in [22] to model and locate emergency service facilities as a Set Covering Problem (SCP). The following applications for
covering problems were mentioned in [18]: Bus stop location, Fire equipment
allocation, Fire company relocation, Fire service sitting and Terrain visibility.

© Springer International Publishing AG 2017
J.C. Figueroa-García et al. (Eds.): WEA 2017, CCIS 742, pp. 565–578, 2017.
DOI: 10.1007/978-3-319-66963-2_50

Also, in [11] were presented some general applications of the gradual covering problem: The delivery problem; Competitive location; Dense competition; The radio, TV, or cellular transmitter problem and Medical facility location problem.

Often Facility Locations and Covering Problems are NP-Hard. Thus, exact solutions are not expected to be found easily. Thus, we are interested in to find alternative ways of solving SCP, specifically using metaheuristics.

The Set Covering Problem can be formally defined as follows. Let $A = (a_{ij})$ be an m-row, n-column, zero-one matrix. We say that a column j can cover a row i if $a_{ij} = 1$. Each column j is associated with a nonnegative real cost c_j. Let $I = \{1, ..., m\}$ and $J = \{1, ..., n\}$ be the row set and column set, respectively. The SCP calls for a minimum cost subset $S \subseteq J$, such that each row $i \in I$ is covered by at least one column $j \in S$. A mathematical model for the SCP is stated in the following:

$$Minimize \quad f(x) = \sum_{j=1}^{n} c_j x_j \tag{1}$$

subject to

$$\sum_{j=1}^{n} a_{ij} x_j \geq 1, \quad \forall i \in I \tag{2}$$

$$x_j \in \{0, 1\}, \quad \forall j \in J \tag{3}$$

If the costs c_j are equal for each $j \in J$, the problem is referred to as the unicost SCP, otherwise, the problem is called the weighted or non-unicost SCP, where $J_i = \{j \in J : a_{ij} = 1\}$: the subset of columns covering row i and $I_j = \{i \in I : a_{ij} = 1\}$: the subset of rows covered by column j.

The goal is to minimize the sum of the costs of the selected columns, where $x_j = 1$ if the column j is in the solution, 0 otherwise. The constraints ensure that each row i is covered by at least one column.

Different solving methods have been proposed in the literature for the Set Covering Problem. In recent years, there has been an important development of research lines applying swarm intelligence continuous metaheuristics to solve SCP. Because they are continuous metaheuristics and SCP is a combinatorial problem, these metaheuristics must be accompanied by a binarization mechanism. In the literature, we find the main binarization technique used to solve SCP corresponds to transfer functions, for more details on binarization techniques see [4,12]. Among the main algorithms that use this technique we found a cat swarm [5], a binary Firefly Optimization [3], a Binary Cuckoo Search (BCS) [21] and artificial bee colony [14]. Specific binarization techniques have also been developed to solve SCP, among the most efficient are: a Teaching-learning binarization [17], a Binary Black Hole (BBH) [13], and a specific Jumping Particle Swarm Optimization (JPSO) method [1].

Depending on the algorithm that has been used, the quality of the solution wanted and the complexity of the SCP chosen, it is defined the amount of customization effort required. Conveniently, this work proposes a meta-optimization approach where the task of customization is transferred to another metaheuristic (a "high level" metaheuristic) which can handle the task of parameters adjustment for a low level metaheuristic [9].

Concretely, the main design of the proposed approach considers a Genetic Algorithm (GA) for parameter setting and an ABC algorithm at a lower level using an Automatic Parameter Tuning approach. The Automatic Parameter Tuning is carried by the GA which searches for the best parameters in the parameter space in order to tune the solver automatically.

This approach is considered as meta-optimization since there are two metaheuristics covering tasks of parameter setting, for the former, and problem solving, for the latter [7].

The rest of this paper is organized as follows. In Sect. 2, we briefly survey the ABC algorithm. In Sect. 3 we present the meta-optimization approach. In Sect. 4, we present the experimental results obtained. Finally, in Sect. 5 we conclude the paper and give some perspectives for further research.

2 Artificial Bee Colony Algorithm

ABC is one of the most recent algorithms in the domain of the collective intelligence [16]. Created by Dervis Karaboga in 2005, who was motivated by the intelligent behavior observed in the domestic bees to take the process of foraging [15]. ABC is an algorithm of combinatorial optimization based on populations, in which the solutions of the problem of optimization, the sources of food, are modified by the artificial bees, that fungen as operators of variation. The aim of these bees is to discover the food sources with major nectar.

In the ABC algorithm, the artificial bees move in a multidimensional search space choosing sources of nectar depending on its past experience and its companions of beehive or fitting his position. Some bees (exploratory) fly and choose food sources randomly without using experience. When they find a source of major nectar, they memorize his position and forget the previous one. Thus, ABC combines methods of local search and global search, trying to balance the process of the exploration and exploitation of the space of search. The pseudocode of Artificial Bee Colony is showed in Algorithm 1.

Algorithm 1. $ABC()$

- **Step 1:** Initialize Food Sources;
- **Step 2:** Evaluate the nectar amount of Food Sources;
- **Step 3:** Phase of Workers Bees;
- **Step 4:** Phase of Onlookers Bees;
- **Step 5:** Phase of Scout Bees;
- **Step 6:** Update Optimum();
- **Step 7:** If not TerminationCriterion go to Step 3;
- **Step 8:** Return BestSolution;

The procedure for determining a food source in the neighborhood of a particular food source which depends on the nature of the problem. Karaboga [14] developed the first ABC algorithm for continuous optimization. The method for determining a food source in the neighborhood of a particular food source is based on changing the value of one randomly chosen variable while keeping other variables unchanged. This is done by adding to the current value of the variable the product of a uniform value in [−1, 1] and the difference in values of this variable for this food source and some other randomly chosen food source. This approach can not be used for discrete optimization problems for which it generates at best a random effect.

Singh [19] subsequently proposed a method, which is appropriate for subset selection problems. In his model, to generate a neighboring solution, an object is randomly dropped from the solution and in its place another object, which is not already present in the solution is added. The object to be added is selected from another randomly chosen solution. If there are more than one candidate objects for addition then ties are broken arbitrarily. In this work we use the ABC algorithm described in [2] and extending the work presented in [7].

3   A Meta-Optimization Approach to Solve the SCP

Metaheuristics, in their original definition, are solution methods that orchestrate an interaction between local improvement procedures and higher level strategies. Thus, metaheuristics create a process capable of escaping from local optima and performing a robust search of a solution space.

Over time, these methods have also come to include any procedures that employ strategies for overcoming the trap of local optimality in complex solution spaces. The use of one or more neighborhood structures as a means of defining admissible moves to transition from one solution to another, or to build or destroy solutions in constructive and destructive processes are examples of such procedures.

3.1   Parameter Setting

The selection of an adequate set of values for parameters improves the performance of metaheuristic methods. To perform the parameter setting the first approach is a brute-force search. This implies in determining the best parameter values evaluating the performance of each possible parameter configuration experimentally performing systematic experiments with different settings. This makes tuning process a very high consuming time task. Moreover, the choice of parameter values requires a user with a lot of experience.

Since the parameter setting is an optimization problem itself we can search for optimal settings using a meta-level optimizer.

3.2   Meta-Optimization

A meta-optimization approach can be considered as two or more metaheuristics where a higher level metaheuristic controls the parameters of a lower level one, which is at charge of dealing more directly to the problem. Our ABC algorithm employs four control parameters which are: number of food sources, the value of limit, % of Columns to add, and % of Columns to eliminate. Different combinations of parameters are evaluated by the upper-level GA algorithm relieving the task of manual parameterization. Each GA individual encodes the parameters of an ABC algorithm generating an ABC instance. In the following, we give the details of each component of the proposed approach.

3.3   The GA Component

In the GA component, the chromosome genes are: *"Food sources"*, it is the number of initial solutions for ABC (which is equal to the number of workers or onlookers bees), it will take values between 50 and 500. The second gene, *"Limit"*, it takes values between 0 and 100. Similarly, the third and fourth genes, *"% Columns to Add"* and *"% Columns to Eliminate"*, they take values between 0.01 and 10.

During each generation of the GA algorithm, in order to produce offsprings, a tournament selection method is used to select a set of individuals from the population as follows. Given the size k of the tournament group and a probability p, the k individuals are sorted using their fitness value and a random value r is generated. If $r \leq p$, the best individual is choosen, otherwise the probability p is incremented, a new random value is generated and the tournament group is reduced by one. This process is repeated at most k times. If no individual is chosen after k attempts, the worst individual belonging to the tournament group is selected. To select n individuals this selection procedure is carried out n times.

The operator randomly selects two chromosomes from the population and performs the crossover as follows. It generates randomly a binary crossover mask with the same length as the chromosomes. If the value of a bit is 1, chromosome information is copied from the first parent. If the value is 0, the genes from the second parent are used and vice-versa for the second offspring.

The mutation operator is applied with a certain rate replacing the value of a gene with a value drawn uniformly from its domain.

3.4   The ABC Component

In the ABC component, a first step is performed in order to initialize the parameters of ABC as size of the colony, number of workers and onlookers bees, limit of attempts and maximum number of cycles (iterations). To generate the initial population we cross every row of the counterfoil of constraints and by every row a column is selected at random. This column is part of the solution which is represented by means of an entire vector. This vector considers the columns chosen in one solution. To complete this vector a procedure is performed for all the rows in such a way that the generated solution complies with all the constraints. Then, the evaluation of the population fitness is performed using the objective function, see (1). Afterwards, the modification of the position and selection of sites for worker bees is performed as follows. A hard-working bee modifies its current position selecting a food source randomly. If a hard-working bee duplicates a solution, it is transformed to an explorer bee. Otherwise, it proceeds to add a certain random number of columns between 0 and the maximum number of columns to be added. Then, it proceeds to eliminate a certain random number of columns between 0 and the maximum number of columns to be eliminated. If the new solution does not meet the constraints, it is repaired.

Algorithm 2 shows a repair method where all rows not covered are identified and the columns required are added. So in this way all the constraints will be covered. The search of these columns are based in the relationship showed in the Eq. 4.

$$\frac{cost\ of\ one\ column}{amount\ of\ columns\ not\ covered} \qquad (4)$$

Once the columns are added and the solution is feasible, a method is applied to remove redundant columns of the solution. A redundant column are those that are removed, the solution remains a feasible solution. The algorithm of this repair method is detailed in the Algorithm 2.

Algorithm 2. *Repair Operator*()

- **Step 1:** $w_i \leftarrow |S \cap J_i| \ \forall i \in I$;
- **Step 2:** $U \leftarrow \{i | w_i = 0\}, \forall i \in I$;
- **Step 3:** Find the first column j in J_i that minimize $\frac{c_j}{|U \cap I_j|} S \leftarrow S \cap j$;
- **Step 4:** $w_i \leftarrow w_i + 1, \forall i \in I_j$;
- **Step 5:** $U \leftarrow U - I_j$;
- **Step 6:** If $i \in U$ go to Step 3;
- **Step 7:** If $w_i \geq 2, \forall i \in I_j$ then $S \leftarrow S - j$ and $w_i \leftarrow w_i - 1, \forall i \in I_j$;
- **Step 8:** If $j \in S$ go to Step 7;

After this, the fitness of the solution is evaluated by means of the objective function of the SCP and if the fitness is minor that the solution previously obtained, the solution is replaced. Otherwise, the number of attempts for improving this solution is increased and the algorithm continues evaluating another hard-working bee.

3.5   Putting It All Together

Algorithm 3 shows the meta-optimization approach developed to solve the SCP. Once the GA population is generated, each individual is taken to run the ABC algorithm until a certain cutoff. Then, the genetic operators are applied and a termination criterion is evaluated in order to stop the parameter setting. Once the termination criterion is achieved, the best individual from the GA contains the best parameter set which is selected to run the ABC algorithm.

Algorithm 3. *Tuning ABC()*

- **Step 1:** SetUp Genetic Algorithm Population();
- **Step 2:** For each GA Individual x_i do Run ABC(x_i,cutoff);
- **Step 3:** Apply Genetic Algorithm Operations();
- **Step 4:** If not TerminationCriterion then go to Step 2;
- **Step 5:** Best Individual ← select Best Individual();
- **Step 6:** Run ABC(bestIndividual);

---

4   Experimental Results

The ABC algorithm has been implemented in C in a 2.5 GHz Dual Core with 4 GB RAM computer, running windows 7. ABC has been tested on 65 standard non-unicost SCP instances available from the OR-Library[1].

Table 1 summarizes the characteristics of each of these sets of instances, each set contains 5 or 10 problems and the column labeled. Density shows the percentage of non-zero entries in the matrix of each instance. ABC was executed 30 times on each instance, each trial with a different random seed.

The Genetic Algorithm used to obtain the best values of the ABC parameters was implemented using the Java Genetic Algorithm Package[2] (JGAP) version 3.5. The basic behavior of a GA implemented using JGAP contains three main steps: a setup phase, the creation of the initial population and the evolution of the population. The parameters of the GA component are shown in Table 2. We give to GA a time limit of 720 s.

Table 3 contains the parameters value of the best chromosome obtained per each instance set. It is important to note that best parameter values set depends on the problem at hand. Different instances of the same problem can strongly vary in terms of their search space. In this work GA searched a parameter settings for each instance set.

---

[1] http://people.brunel.ac.uk/~mastjjb/jeb/info.html.
[2] http://jgap.sourceforge.net.

Table 1. Details of the 65 test instances

Instance set	No. of instances	m	n	Cost range	Density (%)	Optimal solution
4	10	200	1000	[1, 100]	2	Known
5	10	200	2000	[1, 100]	2	Known
6	5	200	1000	[1, 100]	5	Known
A	5	300	3000	[1, 100]	2	Known
B	5	300	3000	[1, 100]	5	Known
C	5	400	4000	[1, 100]	2	Known
D	5	400	4000	[1, 100]	5	Known
NRE	5	500	5000	[1, 100]	10	Known
NRF	5	500	5000	[1, 100]	20	Known
NRG	5	1000	10000	[1, 100]	2	Unknown
NRH	5	1000	10000	[1, 100]	5	Unknown

Table 2. GA parameters

Parameter	Value	Parameter	Value
Number of generations	20	Mask probability	0.5
Population size	30	Mutation rate	0.025
Crossover type	Uniform crossover	Selector tournament size	3
Crossover rate	0.4	Tournament selector parameter (p)	0.75

Table 3. Parameters values from best chromosome

Instance set	Food sources	Limit	% Columns to add	% Columns to eliminate
4	83	30	0.4	1
5	77	40	0.7	1.2
6	106	37	0.6	1.3
A	93	53	0.6	1.1
B	85	50	0.2	1.7
C	100	70	0.5	1.4
D	112	66	0.2	1.5
NRE	98	38	0.3	1.5
NRF	200	51	0.3	1.7
NRG	103	70	0.3	1.6
NRH	107	53	0.4	2

Table 4. Results solving SCP benchmarks - problem set 4

Instance		4.1	4.2	4.3	4.4	4.5	4.6	4.7	4.8	4.9	4.10
Z_{opt}		429	512	516	494	512	560	430	492	641	514
New approach											
ABC	Z_{min}	430.0	512.0	516.0	494.0	512.0	561.0	430.0	493.0	643.0	514.0
	Z_{avg}	430.5	512.0	516.0	494.0	512.0	561.7	430.0	494.0	645.5	514.0
	RPD	0.2	0.0	0.0	0.0	0.0	0.2	0.0	0.2	0.3	0.0
Previous approaches											
BCSO	Z_{min}	459	570	590	547	545	637	462	546	711	537
	Z_{avg}	480	594	607	578	554	650	467	567	725	552
	RPD	7	11.3	14.3	10.7	6.4	13.8	7.4	11	10.9	4.5
BFO	Z_{min}	429	517	519	495	514	563	430	497	655	519
	Z_{avg}	430	517	522	497	515	565	430	499	658	523
	RPD	0	0.97	0.58	0.2	0.39	0.53	0	1.01	2.18	0.97
BSFLA	Z_{min}	430	516	520	501	514	563	431	497	656	518
	Z_{avg}	430	518	520	504	514	563	432	499	656	519
	RPD	0.23	0.78	0.78	1.42	0.39	0.54	0.23	1.02	2.34	0.78
BELA	Z_{min}	447	559	537	527	527	607	448	509	682	571
	Z_{avg}	448	559	539	530	529	608	449	512	682	571
	RPD	4.20	9.18	4.07	6.68	2.93	8.39	4.19	3.46	6.40	11.09
BABC	Z_{min}	430	513	519	495	514	561	431	493	649	517
	Z_{avg}	430	513	521	496	517	565	434	494	651	519
	RPD	0.23	0.20	0.58	0.20	0.39	0.18	0.23	0.20	0.93	0.58

We use the relative percentage deviation (RPD) in order to evaluate the quality of a solution. The RPD value quantifies the deviation of the objective value Z from Z_{opt}. We report the optimum, the best value found using our approach and its average. To compute RPD we use $Z = ABC\ Best$ and $Z_{opt} = Optimum$ from Tables 4, 5 and 6. This measure is computed as follows:

$$RPD = \frac{(Z - Z_{opt})}{Z_{opt}} \times 100 \qquad (5)$$

We compared our algorithm solving the complete set of 65 standard non-unicost SCP instances from the OR-Library with recent approaches for solving SCPs based on modern bio-inspired metaheuristics, namely Binary Cat Swarm Optimization (BCSO) [5]; Binary Firefly Optimization (BFO) [6]; Binary Shuffled Frog Leaping Algorithm (BSFLA) [8]; Binary Electromagnetism - Like

Table 5. Results solving SCP benchmarks - problem set 5

Instance		5.1	5.2	5.3	5.4	5.5	5.6	5.7	5.8	5.9	5.10
Z_{opt}		253	302	226	242	211	213	293	288	279	265
New approach											
ABC	Z_{min}	254.0	309.0	228.0	242.0	211.0	213.0	296.0	288.0	280.0	266.0
	Z_{avg}	255.0	310.2	228.5	242.0	211.0	213.0	296.0	288.0	279.2	267.0
	RPD	0.4	2.3	0.9	0.0	0.0	0.0	1.0	0.0	0.4	0.4
Previous approaches											
BCSO	Z_{min}	279	339	247	251	230	232	332	320	295	285
	Z_{avg}	287	340	251	253	230	243	338	330	297	287
	RPD	10.3	12.3	9.3	3.7	9	8.9	13.3	11.1	5.7	7.5
BFO	Z_{min}	257	309	229	242	211	213	298	291	284	268
	Z_{avg}	260	311	233	242	213	213	301	292	284	270
	RPD	1.58	2.31	1.32	0	0	0	1.7	1.04	1.79	1.13
BSFLA	Z_{min}	254	307	228	242	211	213	297	291	281	265
	Z_{avg}	255	307	230	242	213	214	299	293	283	266
	RPD	0.4	1.66	0.88	0	0	0	1.37	1.04	0.72	0
BELA	Z_{min}	280	318	242	251	225	247	316	315	314	280
	Z_{avg}	281	321	240	252	227	248	317	317	315	282
	RPD	10.67	5.30	7.08	3.72	6.64	15.96	7.85	9.38	12.54	5.66
BABC	Z_{min}	254	309	229	242	211	214	298	289	280	267
	Z_{avg}	255	309	233	245	212	214	301	291	281	270
	RPD	0.40	2.32	1.33	0	0	0.47	1.71	0.35	0.36	0.75

Algorithm (BELA) [20]; and Binary Artificial Bee Colony (BABC) [10]. The column Z_{opt}, for instance executed, the column Z_{avg} represent the average objective function value respectively and finally, RPD, the minimal relative percentage deviation calculated.

The following tables show the detailed results obtained by the algorithms: The Table 4 show the results obtained for instances from group 4, where ABC had the best optimal values compared to the results by the previous approaches, only BFO exhibit a good performance for this data with two global optimums.

The Table 5 shows the results obtained for instances from group 5, where ABC obtained four optimal values and in the previous approaches BCS, BBH, BFO, BSFLA and BABC presents global optimums in their results.

The Table 6 shows the results obtained for instances from groups B and C. ABC shows again optimal values for most of the instances. On the other hand, BFO find only one optimal value, BSFLA find two optimal values, being the best performing, and BABC find two optimal values. The Instance namely NRH, we observe that the RPD obtained by the proposed approach had optimal values in all the instances, while the previous approaches had a low performances in the instances.

Table 6. Results solving SCP benchmarks - problems set B, C and H

Instance		B.1	B.2	B.3	B.4	B.5	C.1	C.2	C.3	C.4	C.5	H.1	H.2	H.3	H.4	H.5
Z_{opt}		69	76	80	79	72	227	219	243	219	215	63	63	59	58	55
New approaches																
ABC	Z_{min}	69.0	76.0	80.0	79.0	72.0	230.0	219.0	244.0	220.0	215.0	63.0	63.0	59.0	58.0	55.0
	Z_{avg}	69.0	76.0	80.0	79.0	72.0	231.0	219.0	244.5	224.0	215.0	63.0	63.0	59.0	58.0	55.0
	RPD	0.0	0.0	0.0	0.0	0.0	1.3	0.0	0.4	0.5	0.0	0.0	0.0	0.0	0.0	0.0
Previous approaches																
BCSO	Z_{min}	79	86	85	89	73	242	240	277	250	243	70	67	68	66	61
	Z_{avg}	79	89	85	89	73	242	241	278	250	244	71	67	70	67	62
	RPD	14.5	13.2	6.3	12.7	1.4	6.6	9.6	14	12.3	13	11.1	6.3	15.3	13.8	10.9
BFO	Z_{min}	71	78	80	80	72	230	223	253	225	217	69	66	65	63	59
	Z_{avg}	72	78	80	81	73	232	224	254	227	219	70	66	67	65	60
	RPD	2.89	2.63	0	1.26	0	1.32	1.82	4.11	2.73	0.93	9.52	4.76	10.16	6.77	7.27
BSFLA	Z_{min}	70	76	80	79	72	229	223	253	227	217	68	66	62	63	59
	Z_{avg}	70	77	80	80	73	231	225	253	228	218	69	66	64	64	63
	RPD	1.45	0	0	0	0	0.88	1.83	4.12	3.65	0.93	7.94	4.76	5.08	8.62	7.27
BELA	Z_{min}	86	88	85	84	78	237	237	271	246	224	70	71	68	70	69
	Z_{avg}	87	88	87	88	81	238	239	271	248	225	71	71	70	72	69
	RPD	24.64	15.79	6.25	6.33	8.33	4.41	8.22	11.52	12.33	4.19	11.11	12.70	15.25	20.69	25.45
BABC	Z_{min}	70	78	80	80	72	231	222	254	231	216	70	69	66	64	60
	Z_{avg}	70	79	80	81	74	233	223	255	233	217	71	72	67	64	61
	RPD	1.45	2.63	0	1.27	0	1.76	1.37	4.53	5.48	0.47	11.11	9.52	11.86	10.34	9.09

Table 7 summarizes the time (in seconds) of the experiments. For each instance the table shows the average running times considering the time consumed in the parameter settings process.

When manually solving parameter setting of ABC we consumed 5 h. This time was apportioned between all the instances because we used the same set of values in all of them: 100; 50; 0,5 and 1,2.

With GA we consumed 720 s searching the best parameter setting for each instances set, then we apportioned this effort between the number of instances of each set. Consequently, we showed that the manual setting of ABC parameters can be improved using a meta-optimization approach.

Table 7. Comparison of ABC with manually and automatically tuned parameters

Instance	Manual tuned	Auto tuned	Instance	Manual tuned	Auto tuned	Instance	Manual tuned	Auto tuned
4.1	282.0	77.1	6.3	287.2	154.3	D.5	344.3	211.4
4.2	281.7	76.8	6.4	286.0	153.1	NRE.1	366.0	233.1
4.3	281.8	76.9	6.5	290.0	157.1	NRE.2	375.7	242.8
4.4	282.3	77,4	A.1	288.8	155.9	NRE.3	381.8	248.9
4.5	282.5	77.6	A.2	288.1	155.1	NRE.4	370.1	237.2
4.6	282.0	77.1	A.3	287.7	154.7	NRE.5	374.6	241.7
4.7	281.9	77.0	A.4	288.5	155.6	NRF.1	607.3	474.4
4.8	282.3	77.4	A.5	287.6	154.7	NRF.2	559.5	426.5
4.9	281.2	76.3	B.1	316.3	183.4	NRF.3	585.4	452.5
4.10	282.5	77.6	B.2	314.6	181.6	NRF.4	602.0	469.1
5.1	283.9	79.0	B.3	311.7	178.8	NRF.5	601.2	468.2
5.2	283.0	78.1	B.4	318.6	185.7	NRG.1	374.5	241.5
5.3	284.3	79.4	B.5	312.9	179.9	NRG.2	373.8	240.9
5.4	283.1	78.2	C.1	294.1	161.2	NRG.3	371.3	238.4
5.5	283.5	78.6	C.2	294.2	161.3	NRG.4	369.4	236.5
5.6	283.6	78.7	C.3	295.7	162.8	NRG.5	369.7	236.8
5.7	284.2	79.3	C.4	294.5	161.5	NRH.1	809.3	676.4
5.8	283.0	78.1	C.5	294.6	161.6	NRH.2	810.8	677.9
5.9	283.0	78.1	D.1	355.5	222.6	NRH.3	834.1	701.1
5.10	283.1	78.1	D.2	351.2	218.3	NRH.4	842.7	709.8
6.1	288.5	155.6	D.3	351.5	218.6	NRH.5	816.0	683.1
6.2	287.6	154.7	D.4	343.1	210.1			

5   Conclusion

A meta-optimization approach has been tested on different SCP benchmarks showing to be very effective. The interest to solve the SCP lies in that this is the most popular model representing Facilities Locations Problems. We have presented an Artificial Bee Colony Algorithm for the Set Covering Problem where its parameters were tuned using a Genetic Algorithm. We performed experiments through all ORLIB instances, our approach has demonstrated to be very effective, providing an unattended solving method, for quickly producing solutions of a good quality.

Experiments shown interesting results in terms of robustness, where using different parameters for different set of instances giving good results.

It is clear that to use an automatic tuning method instead of using a set of recommended parameter values was a good choice.

This does not require any user interactions and although the meta-optimization approach consumes time running sequentially different instances of ABC, this time is a relatively low value in comparison with the total time consumed when manual setting of ABC was used. The promising results of the experiments open up opportunities for further research. The fact that the presented framework is easy to implement, clearly implies that it could also be effectively applied using others metaheuristics. Furthermore, our approach could also be effectively applied to other combinatorial optimization problems.

Acknowledgements. Broderick Crawford is supported by grant CONICYT/ FONDECYT/REGULAR 1171243 and Ricardo Soto is supported by Grant CONICYT/FONDECYT/REGULAR/1160455, Gino Astorga is supported by Postgraduate Grant, Pontificia Universidad Catolica de Valparaíso, 2015 and José García is supported by INF-PUCV 2016. This research was partially funded by CORFO Program Ingeniería 2030 PUCV - Consortium of Chilean Engineering Faculties.

References

1. Balaji, S., Revathi, N.: A new approach for solving set covering problem using jumping particle swarm optimization method. Nat. Comput. **15**(3), 503–517 (2016)
2. Crawford, B., Soto, R., Cuesta, R., Paredes, F.: Application of the artificial bee colony algorithm for solving the set covering problem. Sci. World J. **2014**(189164), 1–8 (2014)
3. Crawford, B., Soto, R., Surez, M.O., Paredes, F., Johnson, F.: Binary firefly algorithm for the set covering problem. In: 2014 9th Iberian Conference on Information Systems and Technologies (CISTI), pp. 1–5, June 2014
4. Crawford, B., Soto, R., Astorga, G., García, J., Castro, C., Paredes, F.: Putting continuous metaheuristics to work in binary search spaces. Complexity **2017** (2017). Pages 19
5. Crawford, B., Soto, R., Berríos, N., Johnson, F., Paredes, F., Castro, C., Norero, E.: A binary cat swarm optimization algorithm for the non-unicost set covering problem. Math. Probl. Eng. **2015** (2015)
6. Crawford, B., Soto, R., Olivares-Suárez, M., Paredes, F.: A binary firefly algorithm for the set covering problem. In: Silhavy, R., Senkerik, R., Oplatkova, Z.K., Silhavy, P., Prokopova, Z. (eds.) Modern Trends and Techniques in Computer Science. AISC, vol. 285, pp. 65–73. Springer, Cham (2014). doi:10.1007/ 978-3-319-06740-7_6
7. Crawford, B., Soto, R., Palma, W., Johnson, F., Paredes, F., Olguín, E.: A 2-level approach for the set covering problem: parameter tuning of artificial bee colony algorithm by using genetic algorithm. In: Tan, Y., Shi, Y., Coello, C. (eds.) Advances in Swarm Intelligence, vol. 8794, pp. 189–196. Springer, Cham (2014)
8. Crawford, B., Soto, R., Peña, C., Palma, W., Johnson, F., Paredes, F.: Solving the set covering problem with a shuffled frog leaping algorithm. In: Nguyen, N.T., Trawiński, B., Kosala, R. (eds.) ACIIDS 2015. LNCS (LNAI), vol. 9012, pp. 41–50. Springer, Cham (2015). doi:10.1007/978-3-319-15705-4_5
9. Crawford, B., Valenzuela, C., Soto, R., Monfroy, E., Paredes, F.: Parameter tuning of metaheuristics using metaheuristics. Adv. Sci. Lett. **19**(12), 3556–3559 (2013)

10. Cuesta, R., Crawford, B., Soto, R., Paredes, F.: An artificial bee colony algorithm for the set covering problem. In: Silhavy, R., Senkerik, R., Oplatkova, Z.K., Silhavy, P., Prokopova, Z. (eds.) Modern Trends and Techniques in Computer Science. AISC, vol. 285, pp. 53–63. Springer, Cham (2014). doi:10.1007/978-3-319-06740-7_5

11. Drezner, T., Drezner, Z., Goldstein, Z.: A stochastic gradual cover location problem. Nav. Res. Logist. (NRL) **57**(4), 367–372 (2010). doi:10.1002/nav.20410

12. García, J., Crawford, B., Soto, R., Carlos, C., Paredes, F.: A k-means binarization framework applied to multidimensional knapsack problem. Appl. Intell. 1–24 (2017)

13. García, J., Crawford, B., Soto, R., García, P.: A multi dynamic binary black hole algorithm applied to set covering problem. In: Del Ser, J. (ed.) Harmony Search Algorithm, pp. 42–51. Springer, Singapore (2017)

14. Karaboga, D.: An idea based on honey bee swarm for numerical optimization. Technical report-tr06, Erciyes University, Engineering faculty, Computer Engineering Department (2005)

15. Karaboga, D., Basturk, B.: A powerful and efficient algorithm for numerical function optimization: artificial bee colony (ABC) algorithm. J. Glob. Optim. **39**(3), 459–471 (2007)

16. Karaboga, D., Gorkemli, B., Ozturk, C., Karaboga, N.: A comprehensive survey: artificial bee colony (ABC) algorithm and applications. Artif. Intell. Rev. **42**(3), 21–57 (2014)

17. Lu, Y., Vasko, F.J.: An or practitioner's solution approach for the set covering problem. Int. J. Appl. Metaheuristic Comput. (IJAMC) **6**(4), 1–13 (2015)

18. Schilling, D.A., Jayaraman, V., Barkhi, R.: A review of covering problem in facility location. Locat. Sci. **1**(1), 25–55 (1993)

19. Singh, A.: An artificial bee colony algorithm for the leaf-constrained minimum spanning tree problem. Appl. Soft Comput. **9**(2), 625–631 (2009). doi:10.1016/j.asoc.2008.09.001

20. Soto, R., Crawford, B., Muñoz, A., Johnson, F., Paredes, F.: Pre-processing, repairing and transfer functions can help binary electromagnetism-like algorithms. In: Silhavy, R., Senkerik, R., Oplatkova, Z., Prokopova, Z., Silhavy, P. (eds.) Artificial Intelligence Perspectives and Applications. Advances in Intelligent Systems and Computing, vol. 347, pp. 89–97. Springer, Cham (2015). doi:10.1007/978-3-319-18476-0_10

21. Soto, R., Crawford, B., Olivares, R., Barraza, J., Figueroa, I., Johnson, F., Paredes, F., Olguín, E.: Solving the non-unicost set covering problem by using cuckoo search and black hole optimization. Nat. Comput. **16**, 1–17 (2017)

22. Toregas, C., Swain, R., ReVelle, C., Bergman, L.: The location of emergency service facilities. Oper. Res. **19**(6), 1363–1373 (1971). doi:10.1287/opre.19.6.1363

Manufacturing Cell Formation with a Novel Discrete Bacterial Chemotaxis Optimization Algorithm

Camilo Mejia-Moncayo[1]($^{(\boxtimes)}$) ⓘ, Alix E. Rojas[1] ⓘ, and Ruben Dorado[2] ⓘ

[1] Universidad EAN, Bogotá, Colombia
{cmejiam,aerojash}@universidadean.edu.co
[2] École de Technologie Supérieure, Université du Québec, Montreal, Canada
ruben.dorado-sanchez.1@etsmtl.com

Abstract. In this paper, we present a novel optimization algorithm named Discrete Bacterial Chemotaxis Optimization Algorithm DBCOA to solve the formation of manufacturing cells (MCs) problem, which consists in assigning machines and parts to a specific cell or family, considering the similarities in their manufacturing processes. The algorithm is based on BFOA with a discrete and hierarchical chemotaxis process that explore the search space to get the best solution. To evaluate the performance of the proposal, we use seven benchmark problems. The results were compared with the optimum solution and the performance of a Genetic Algorithm. In all benchmark problems, the proposed algorithm outperformed the baseline, giving the optimum solution in a short time.

1 Introduction

Manufacturing systems have evolved in the context of optimization of resources through the implementation of various design strategies. Group technology is a philosophy for manufacturing system design that is based on grouping parts and machines based on their similarities [1]. Generally, the application of group technology results in the arrangement of manufacturing cells (MCs), which operate like specialized factories of certain part families. MCs are widely used in batch production systems when there is a high variety of products and the production volume is variable [2]. MCs promote significant reductions in processing times, setups, materials handling, furniture, and space required to increase job satisfaction and quality [3]. In this context, this work presents a novel method to solve the manufacturing cell formation problem by means of a novel optimization algorithm named Discrete Bacterial Chemotaxis Optimization Algorithm. This document begins with a brief review of manufacturing cell formation including the mathematical model used in this work, followed by the presentation of the Discrete Bacterial Chemotaxis Optimization Algorithm, then the methodology is addressed, results and discussion and finally the conclusions.

© Springer International Publishing AG 2017
J.C. Figueroa-García et al. (Eds.): WEA 2017, CCIS 742, pp. 579–588, 2017.
DOI: 10.1007/978-3-319-66963-2_51

2   Manufacturing Cell Formation

The implementation of MCs begins with the definition of machine cells and part families. In this process, the parts are grouped based on similarities in their manufacturing processes and/or geometry. Likewise, the machines are grouped into cells based on the similarities of their manufacturing process and/or the types of parts that they can produce. MCs formation is commonly addressed using incidence matrices that relate the parts and machines. An incidence matrix a_{ij} is a binary array where, $a_{ij} = 1$, if the part j is processed by the machine i, in other case $a_{ij} = 0$.

MCs formation problems have been addressed using several approaches including descriptive methods, cluster analysis, graph partitioning, mathematical programming, and artificial intelligence, among other heuristic and meta-heuristic approaches [4–7]. Descriptive methods can be classified into three types: part family identification, machine group identification, and simultaneous identification. Procedures based on cluster analysis can be classified into array-based clustering techniques, hierarchical clustering techniques, and non-hierarchical clustering techniques. The graph partitioning methods are designed to obtain disconnected sub-graphs to identify the manufacturing cells.

Mathematical programming methods can be classified depending on the formulation of the problem into linear programming (LP), linear and quadratic programming (LQP), dynamic programming (DP), and goal programming (GP). Heuristic methods are popular for its multiple applications and because they provide an alternative solution to the problems with sub-optimal response in a reasonable time.

Meta-heuristics techniques have been developed to solve NP-hard combinatorial problems such MCs formation. Prominent methods include: simulated annealing (SA) [8], Tabu search (TS) [9], Ant Colony Optimization (ACO) [10], Particle Swarm Optimization (PSO) [11], bacterial foraging optimization (BFO) [12–14] and genetic algorithms (GAs) [15–19]. Saeedi [20] proposed a mathematical model for the problem of the formation of manufacturing cells and compared the results obtained by solving the model with GA, ACO and SA. Their results showed that the GA were the most effective methods for solving the cell formation problem. Considering that there are a few number of works based in bacterial foraging, this proposal gives another point of view to solve MCs formation.

The problem of formation of manufacturing cells (MCs) has been modeled and evaluated in different ways. In this work, the objective function minimizes the Manhattan distance between the machines and parts for each cell or family under the hypothesis that by minimizing the distances or differences between the elements of a group, it is possible to get a good grouping; similar to the graphical method developed by [1], where the layout of manufacturing cells is defined by linking the machines through kinship circles. The mathematical model implemented is described as follows.

minimize:
$$f(X,Y) = DM + DP \tag{1}$$

$$DM = \sum_{k=1}^{mc} \left[\frac{(\sum_{i=1}^{m} \sum_{i'=1}^{m} X_{ik} X_{i'k} dm_{ii'})(mn - \sum_{j=1}^{n} \sum_{i=1}^{m} X_{ik} Y_{jk} a_{ij})}{1 + \sum_{j=1}^{n} \sum_{i=1}^{m} X_{ik} Y_{jk} a_{ij}} \right] \tag{2}$$

$$DP = \sum_{k=1}^{mc} \left[\frac{(\sum_{i=1}^{m} \sum_{i'=1}^{m} Y_{ik} Y_{i'k} dp_{ii'})(mn - \sum_{j=1}^{n} \sum_{i=1}^{m} X_{ik} Y_{jk} a_{ij})}{1 + \sum_{j=1}^{n} \sum_{i=1}^{m} X_{ik} Y_{jk} a_{ij}} \right] \tag{3}$$

subject to:

$$\sum_{k=1}^{mc} X_{ik} \ k = 1, \ \forall i, \ i = 1, , m \tag{4}$$

$$\sum_{k=1}^{mc} Y_{jk} \ k = 1, \ \forall j, \ j = 1, , n \tag{5}$$

where:

m : number of machines
n : number of parts
mc : maximum number of cells
i : machine index; $i = 1, , m$
j : part index; $j = 1, , n$
k : cell index; $k = 1, , mc$
dm_{ii} : Manhattan distance between machines
dp_{jj} : Manhattan distance between parts
$X_{ik} = 1$, if the machine i belong to cell k, in other case $X_{ik} = 0$
$Y_{jk} = 1$, if the part j belong to cell k, in other case $Y_{jk} = 0$
$a_{ij} = 1$, if the part j is processed by the machine i, in other case $a_{ij} = 0$

The decision variables are X_{ik} and Y_{jk}. They are binary and allow the assignation of machines (i) and the parts (j) to the cells or families (k). The objective function (Eq. 1) is subjected to two restrictions of unicity, the first one (Eq. 4) assures that each machine can only be assigned to one cell, the second (Eq. 5) assures that each part can only be assigned to one family. The characteristics of each system are defined by an incidence matrix (a_{ij}), which establishes if one part is processed by a machine or not.

3 Discrete Bacterial Chemotaxis Optimization Algorithm

Bacterial Foraging Optimization Algorithm (BFOA) was developed by [21], considering the bacterial foraging process of E. Coli as an optimization process applied in many situations [22, 23]. Figure 1 shows BFOA pseudocode, where each artificial bacterium executes the chemotaxis process which consists of movements in the search space following a trace of food. This process is repeated Nc times. Next, it executes a reproduction by duplication. In this step, only the fittest will be duplicated to continue. Next, it repeats the chemotaxis and reproduction processes until the maximum number of cycles of reproduction (Nre) is obtained and executes the elimination and dispersion process. This works by randomly eliminating bacteria to create others in different locations in order to disperse the bacteria and to explore other possible solutions. This process is repeated Ned times where the algorithm stops.

```
Pseudocode BFOA
Begin
   Generation of initial bacteria
   Evaluation of objective function
   for l = 1 to Ned do
      for k = 1 to Nre do
         for j = 1 to Nc do
            Chemotaxis
         end for
         Reproduction
      end for
      Elimination and Dispersion
   end for
 end
```

Fig. 1. Pseudocode BFOA

Discrete Bacterial Chemotaxis Optimization Algorithm uses the original structure of BFOA as defined by [21]. At the same time, previous works [13, 14] are taken for the definition of chemotaxis. Chemotaxis is the core of the algorithm. It allows exploring the search space to find better solutions on each step. Additionally, it has a simple structure that allows getting good results. This process creates a new artificial bacterium by modifying through different operations. The sequence of this process is described in Fig. 2, where the original bacterium is replaced by the new bacterium if the new bacterium has a better value when calculating the objective function. The original bacterium is conserved in any other case (see Fig. 2).

3.1 Variables Coding

Coding based on group or order is constructed considering the description of [24], where each bacterium is defined by five vectors; the first corresponds to the permutations of machines, the second to the permutations of parts, the third the number of cells or part families and the two remaining corresponding to the limits or

```
Pseudocode Chemotaxis
Begin
  Create a new bacterium modifying the machines permutation
  if (new bacterium is better than original) then
    Replace the original bacterium with the new
  else
    Create a new bacterium modifying the parts permutation
    if (new bacterium is better than original) then
      Replace the original bacterium with the new
    else
      Create a new bacterium modifying the limits of machines
      if (new bacterium is better than original) then
        Replace the original bacterium with the new
      else
        CCreate a new bacterium modifying the limits of parts
        if (new bacterium is better than original) then
          Replace the original bacterium with the new
        else
          Create a new bacterium modifying the number of cells or families
          if (new bacterium is better than original) then
            Replace the original bacterium with the new
          endif
        endif
      endif
    endif
  endif
end
```

Fig. 2. Pseudocode chemotaxis DBCOA

boundaries at the positions of permutations of the groups of machines and parts to form cells and families. For the example of Fig. 3 the cells and part families would be formed as follows: Cells[(6, 4) (3, 1, 2) (5)], Families [(3) (4, 1) (2)].

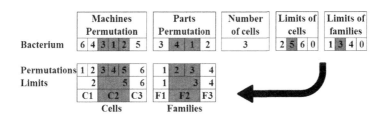

Fig. 3. Example of coding

3.2   Generation of Initial Bacteria

In this case the permutations are generated for the machines and parts, disordering an arrangement that goes from 1 to the number of machines or parts. The number of cells is assigned with a random number between 1 and the maximum number of cells, which defines the quantity of limits in the positions to form the cells and families, assigning randomly to these the machines or parts remaining in the intervals that they define.

3.3 Elimination and Dispersion

Elimination and dispersion are random processes. If a bacterium obtains a random number less than the probability of elimination, a new bacterium is created by using the operators of generation of initial bacteria.

4 Methodology

In general terms, the process begins with the definition of the mathematical model. The algorithm was implemented considering the coding to manage the restrictions and leave them embedded. The setup of the parameters of the algorithm is shown in Table 1. The experimental process is focused on evaluating the performance of the proposed algorithm applied to a set of benchmark problems with a unique solution. The dataset was developed for this work and is presented in Tables 2, 3 and 4, along with its optimal solution. For each problem, we ran the algorithm 100 times to obtain the results in the same computer.

Table 1. Parameters of algorithm

Parameter	Value
(S) Number of bacteria	50
(Nc) Number of chemotaxis cycles	2
(Nre) Number of reproduction cycles	5
(Ned) Number of elimination and dispersion cycles	100
(Ped) Probability of elimination and dispersion	0.5

Table 2. Benchmark problems 7×9, 10×8 and 11×9.

7 machines and 9 parts	10 machines and 8 parts	11 machines and 9 parts
	1 0 0 0 0 0 1 1	0 0 1 0 1 0 1 0 0
0 0 1 1 0 0 0 0 1	0 0 1 1 0 1 0 0	0 1 0 0 0 1 0 0 1
1 1 0 0 0 1 1 0 0	1 0 0 0 0 0 1 1	0 1 0 0 0 1 0 0 1
0 0 0 0 1 0 0 1 0	0 0 1 1 0 1 0 0	0 0 1 0 1 0 1 0 0
0 0 1 1 0 0 0 0 1	1 0 0 0 0 0 1 1	1 0 0 1 0 0 0 1 0
1 1 0 0 0 1 1 0 0	1 0 0 0 0 0 1 1	1 0 0 1 0 0 0 1 0
0 0 0 0 1 0 0 1 0	0 0 1 1 0 1 0 0	0 0 1 0 1 0 1 0 0
0 0 1 1 0 0 0 0 1	0 1 0 0 1 0 0 0	0 1 0 0 0 1 0 0 1
	1 0 0 0 0 0 1 1	0 0 1 0 1 0 1 0 0
Cells: (3, 6) (2, 5) (1, 4, 7) Families: (5, 8) (1, 2, 6, 7) (3, 4, 9)	Cells: (1, 3, 5, 6, 9) (2, 4, 7) (8, 10) Families: (1, 7, 8) (3, 4, 6) (7, 8)	Cells: (1, 4, 7, 9) (2, 3, 8) (5, 6, 10, 11) Families: (3, 5, 7) (2, 6, 9) (1, 4, 8)

Table 3. Benchmark problems 11×12 and 14×12.

11 machines and 12 parts	14 machines and 12 parts
	0 0 0 0 0 0 1 1 0 0 1 0
	0 0 1 0 0 0 0 0 0 0 0 1
0 0 1 1 1 0 0 0 1 0 0 0	0 0 0 0 0 0 1 1 0 0 1 0
1 0 0 0 0 0 1 1 0 0 0 1	0 1 0 1 0 1 0 0 1 1 0 0
1 0 0 0 0 0 1 1 0 0 0 1	0 0 0 0 0 0 1 1 0 0 1 0
0 1 0 0 0 1 0 0 0 1 1 0	0 0 1 0 0 0 0 0 0 0 0 1
0 1 0 0 0 1 0 0 0 1 1 0	0 1 0 1 0 1 0 0 1 1 0 0
1 0 0 0 0 0 1 1 0 0 0 1	1 0 0 0 1 0 0 0 0 0 0 0
0 1 0 0 0 1 0 0 0 1 1 0	0 0 0 0 0 0 1 1 0 0 1 0
0 1 0 0 0 1 0 0 0 1 1 0	0 0 1 0 0 0 0 0 0 0 0 1
0 0 1 1 1 0 0 0 1 0 0 0	0 1 0 1 0 1 0 0 1 1 0 0
	0 0 1 0 0 0 0 0 0 0 0 1
	1 0 0 0 1 0 0 0 0 0 0 0
	0 1 0 1 0 1 0 0 1 1 0 0
Cells: (2, 3, 6, 11) (4, 5, 7, 8, 10) (1, 9) Families: (1, 7, 8, 12) (2, 6, 10, 11) (3, 4, 5, 9)	Cells: (8, 13) (2, 6, 10, 12) (4, 7, 11, 14) (1, 3, 5, 9) Families: (1, 5) (3, 12) (2, 4, 6, 9, 10) (7, 8, 11)

Table 4. Benchmark problems 15×15 and 16×16.

15 machines and 15 parts	16 machines and 16 parts
1 0 1 0 0 0 0 0 0 0 1 1 1 0 0	0 1 0 0 0 0 0 1 0 0 0 0 0 1 1 0
1 0 1 0 0 0 0 0 0 0 1 1 1 0 0	1 0 0 1 1 0 0 0 0 0 0 0 1 0 0 0
0 0 0 0 1 0 1 1 0 1 0 0 0 1 0	1 0 0 1 1 0 0 0 0 0 0 0 1 0 0 0
0 1 0 1 0 1 0 0 1 0 0 0 0 0 1	0 0 0 0 0 1 0 0 1 0 1 0 1 0 0 0
0 0 0 0 1 0 1 1 0 1 0 0 0 1 0	0 0 1 0 0 0 1 0 0 1 0 0 0 0 0 1
0 0 0 0 1 0 1 1 0 1 0 0 0 1 0	0 0 0 0 0 1 0 0 1 0 1 0 1 0 0 0
0 1 0 1 0 1 0 0 1 0 0 0 0 0 1	0 0 1 0 0 0 1 0 0 1 0 0 0 0 0 1
1 0 1 0 0 0 0 0 0 0 1 1 1 0 0	0 0 0 0 0 1 0 0 1 0 1 0 1 0 0 0
1 0 1 0 0 0 0 0 0 0 1 1 1 0 0	0 0 1 0 0 0 1 0 0 1 0 0 0 0 0 1
0 0 0 0 1 0 1 1 0 1 0 0 0 1 0	1 0 0 1 1 0 0 0 0 0 0 0 1 0 0 0
1 0 1 0 0 0 0 0 0 0 1 1 1 0 0	0 1 0 0 0 0 0 1 0 0 0 0 0 1 1 0
0 1 0 1 0 1 0 0 1 0 0 0 0 0 1	0 0 1 0 0 0 1 0 0 1 0 0 0 0 0 1
0 0 0 0 1 0 1 1 0 1 0 0 0 1 0	1 0 0 1 1 0 0 0 0 0 0 0 1 0 0 0
0 1 0 1 0 1 0 0 1 0 0 0 0 0 1	0 1 0 0 0 0 0 1 0 0 0 0 0 1 1 0
0 1 0 1 0 1 0 0 1 0 0 0 0 0 1	0 0 1 0 0 0 1 0 0 1 0 0 0 0 0 1
	0 1 0 0 0 0 0 1 0 0 0 0 0 1 1 0
	0 0 0 0 0 1 0 0 1 0 1 0 1 0 0 0
Cells: (3, 5, 6, 10, 13) (4, 7, 12, 14, 15) (1, 2, 8, 9, 11) Families: (5, 7, 8, 10, 14) (2, 4, 6, 9, 15) (1, 3, 11, 12, 13)	Cells: (4, 6, 8, 16) (1, 10, 13, 15) (5, 7, 11, 14) (2, 3, 9, 12) Families: (6, 9, 11, 13) (2, 8, 14, 15) (3, 7, 10, 16) (1, 4, 5, 12)

5   Results and Discussion

The results obtained by the experimental process are shown in Table 5, Figs. 4 and 5; on them it is possible to observe the comparison between Discrete Bacterial Chemotaxis Optimization Algorithm DBCOA and Genetic Algorithm GA, under the consideration of the average of the percentage of deviation respect to the optimal solution and the average time to get the best solution on each iteration.

Table 5. Comparison of average results of GA and DBCOA by benchmark problem

Problems		% Deviation to optimum		Average time (sec)	
m × p	Optimum	GA	DBCOA	GA	DBCOA
7 × 9	23,31	0,00	0,00	5,13	0,20
10 × 8	26,36	0,07	0,00	7,64	0,19
11 × 9	22,38	1,24	0,00	16,82	0,34
11 × 12	25,93	1,91	0,00	31,32	0,77
14 × 12	69,62	1,13	2,95	44,03	24,45
15 × 15	23,07	3,63	0,00	60,73	2,23
16 × 16	56,47	3,80	1,00	43,60	27,30

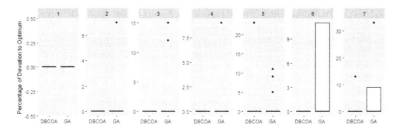

Fig. 4. Comparison of percentage of deviation to optimal between GA and DBCOA by benchmark problem

As seen in Table 5, Discrete Bacterial Chemotaxis Optimization Algorithm gets solutions with an average of percentage of deviation to optimal solution equal to 0.0% in five of the seven problems, which is possible given that DBCOA has less dispersion than GA (see Fig. 4). On the other two problems, DBCOA obtains a deviation lower than 3%, when compared with GA these results are better because GA obtains, in the first problem only, a result equal to 0.0%. In addition, considering the time needed to obtain the best solution for the iteration, DBCOA in all problems has values smaller and less disperse than GA, as shown in Fig. 5. Given this, DBCOA has a better performance than GA because is faster, has a better accuracy and less variability in the solution of the cases analyzed in this work.

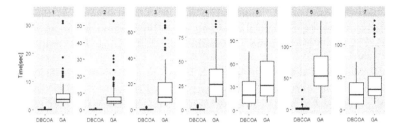

Fig. 5. Comparison of average time to get the best solution between GA and DBCOA by benchmark problem

6 Conclusions

Considering the percentage of deviation of optimal solution and time, it is shown that the simple structure of the Discrete Bacterial Chemotaxis Optimization Algorithm is faster, accurate and efficient than Genetic Algorithm for solving the benchmark problems analyzed in this work. One important element of this process is coding, which allows manage the restrictions without the implementation of other operations and reduce the search space only to feasible solutions. Additionally, the coding and objective function used in this work allow transforming a grouping problem into a permutation problem. The advantage of this approach is the possibility of an easier exploration, through simple operators like interchange, insertion and inversion of the elements of the permutation. An important contribution of this work is the possibility to use Discrete Bacterial Chemotaxis Optimization Algorithm to solve other combinatorial problems like TSP, scheduling, facility layouts and others.

References

1. Mejia-Moncayo, C., Lara-Sepulveda, D.F., Cordoba-Nieto, E.: Technological kinship circles. Ing. e Investig. **30**, 163–167 (2010)
2. Heragu, S.S.: Facilities Design, 3rd edn. CRC Press, Clermont (2008)
3. Romero, G.A., Mejia-Moncayo, C., Torres, J.A.: Mathematical models for the definition of cell manufacturing layout. Literature review. Rev. Tecnura **19**, 135–148 (2015)
4. Selim, H.M., Askin, R.G., Vakharia, A.J.: Cell formation in group technology: review, evaluation and directions for future research. Comput. Ind. Eng. **34**, 3–20 (1998)
5. Papaioannou, G., Wilson, J.M.: The evolution of cell formation problem methodologies based on recent studies (1997–2008): review and directions for future research. Eur. J. Oper. Res. **206**, 509–521 (2010)
6. Yin, Y., Yasuda, K.: Similarity coefficient methods applied to the cell formation problem: a comparative investigation. Comput. Ind. Eng. **48**, 471–489 (2005)
7. Yin, Y., Yasuda, K.: Similarity coefficient methods applied to the cell formation problem: a taxonomy and review. Int. J. Prod. Econ. **101**, 329–352 (2006)

8. Tavakkoli-Moghaddam, R., Rahimi-Vahed, A.R., Ghodratnama, A., Siadat, A.: A simulated annealing method for solving a new mathematical model of a multi-criteria cell formation problem with capital constraints. Adv. Eng. Softw. **40**, 268–273 (2009)

9. Lei, D., Wu, Z.: Tabu search approach based on a similarity coefficient for cell formation in generalized group technology. Int. J. Prod. Res. **43**, 4035–4047 (2005)

10. Li, X., Baki, M.F., Aneja, Y.P.: An ant colony optimization metaheuristic for machine part cell formation problems. Comput. Oper. Res. **37**, 2071–2081 (2010)

11. Duran, O., Rodriguez, N., Consalter, L.A.: A PSO-based clustering algorithm for manufacturing cell design. In: First International Workshop on Knowledge Discovery and Data Mining, (WKDD 2008), pp. 72–75 (2008)

12. Nouri, H., Hong, T.S.: Development of bacteria foraging optimization algorithm for cell formation in cellular manufacturing system considering cell load variations. J. Manuf. Syst. **32**, 20–31 (2013)

13. Mejia-Moncayo, C., Garzon-Alvarado, D.A., Arroyo-Osorio, J.M.: Solution of cell manufacturing layout problem through a discrete hybrid Bfoa-Ga. In: 3rd International Conference Engineering Optimization, vol. 1, pp, 1–5 (2012)

14. Mejia-Moncayo, C., Garzon, D.A., Arroyo, J.M.: Discrete methods based on bacterial chemotaxis and genetic algorithms to solve the cell manufacturing. Cienc. e Ing. Neogranadina **24**, 6–28 (2014)

15. Al-Sultan, K.S., Fedjki, C.A.: A genetic algorithm for the part family formation problem. Prod. Plan. Control **8**, 788–796 (1997)

16. Mak, K.L., Wong, Y.S., Chan, F.T.S.: A genetic algorithm for facility layout problems. Comput. Integr. Manuf. Syst. **11**, 113–127 (1998)

17. Mak, K.L., Wong, Y.S., Wang, X.X.: An adaptive genetic algorithm for manufacturing cell formation. Int. J. Adv. Manuf. Technol. **16**, 491–497 (2000)

18. Mahdavi, I., Paydar, M.M., Solimanpur, M., Heidarzade, A.: Genetic algorithm approach for solving a cell formation problem in cellular manufacturing. Expert Syst. Appl. **36**, 6598–6604 (2009)

19. Deljoo, V., Mirzapour Al-e-hashem, S.M.J., Deljoo, F., Aryanezhad, M.B.: Using genetic algorithm to solve dynamic cell formation problem. Appl. Math. Model. **34**, 1078–1092 (2010)

20. Saeedi, S.: Heuristic approaches for cell formation in cellular manufacturing. J. Softw. Eng. Appl. **3**, 674–682 (2010)

21. Passino, K.M.: Biomimicry of bacterial foraging for distributed optimization and control. IEEE Control Syst. **22**, 52–67 (2002)

22. Niu, B., Fan, Y., Tan, L., Rao, J., Li, L.: A review of bacterial foraging optimization part I: background and development. In: Huang, D.-S., McGinnity, M., Heutte, L., Zhang, X.-P. (eds.) ICIC 2010. CCIS, vol. 93, pp. 535–543. Springer, Heidelberg (2010). doi:10.1007/978-3-642-14831-6_70

23. Niu, B., Fan, Y., Tan, L., Rao, J., Li, L.: A review of bacterial foraging optimization part II: applications and challenges. In: Huang, D.-S., McGinnity, M., Heutte, L., Zhang, X.-P. (eds.) ICIC 2010. CCIS, vol. 93, pp. 544–550. Springer, Heidelberg (2010). doi:10.1007/978-3-642-14831-6_71

24. Gen, M., Lin, L., Zhang, H.: Evolutionary techniques for optimization problems in integrated manufacturing system: state-of-the-art-survey. Comput. Ind. Eng. **56**, 779–808 (2009)

Project Scheduling with Dynamic Resource Allocation in a Multi-project Environment. Case: Bogotá Electricity Distributor

Feizar Javier Rueda-Velasco[✉], Carlos Efraín Cubaque[✉], and
Juan Martin Ibañez Latorre[✉]

Universidad Distrital Francisco José de Caldas, Bogotá, Colombia
fjruedav@udistrital.edu.co, charcubaque@yahoo.es,
jmibanezl@correo.udistrital.edu.co

Abstract. Into the engineering projects is usual to see significant deviations from the planning global duration time to the real achieved. This situation presents some questions about the schedule planning activities effectiveness or control during the execution. The present work develops an algorithm for multi-project scheduling with dynamic resource allocation. The algorithm uses variable total resource availability and priority rules in order to schedule activities and renewable resources, like the manpower or the equipment. System performance has been measured on overall project makespan. The model has been proved using activity networks modeled on dynamic systems software for a case of study in a Bogotá- Colombia electricity distributor. The results have shown a time reduction on the global projects duration time.

Keywords: Project management · Project control · Activity network · Renewable resources · Dynamic system

1 Introduction

The Project planning and execution control are widely used techniques into the industry and engineering development, for instance civil work, infrastructure development, market investigation and development, according to Project Management Institute [1], a Project is any temporal effort aimed to create a unique product or service and is executed by people, is planned, executed, controlled and is resource constrained.

The project scheduling looks for a sequence and activities or projects schedule in order to achieve the goals planned for the case under consideration. This problem is well known as the "project sequencing problem", and the latest application includes the resources restriction problem.

The basic instance for this problem has been focused in the global duration minimization considering the precedence relation between activities and resources, being the resources analysis an important focus to deal with, mainly the renewables as the manpower or machines.

© Springer International Publishing AG 2017
J.C. Figueroa-García et al. (Eds.): WEA 2017, CCIS 742, pp. 589–600, 2017.
DOI: 10.1007/978-3-319-66963-2_52

According to Hartmann [2], the basic instance for this problem, considers that the availability of renewable resources is constant for time unit, this assumption is not always true due to factors like absenteeism, fatigue, motivation, machine breakdown or overheat, producing deviations from the initial solution and final execution.

The literature about the project scheduling problem has been enhanced during last years, however, just a few works have been focused on analyzing the problem considering the variables as stochastic, even more according to Canonico [3], the rules type are not applied to the practical or real context.

In this paper a System Dynamics approach provides the ability to prove, into a simulated instance, the effectiveness of each of the rules proposed for execution planning and controlling. Chavez [4] states an effective technique for the policies, rules or option evaluation, even more its main functionality as a simulation tool is based on the ability to include or use feedback cycles, based on the automatic control theory, thus its application is justified for sociotechnical systems. In the contextual review was found that has been used for project simulation for contrast instances but not using information from real projects.

2   Reach and Assumptions for the Multiple Project Sequencing Under Restricted Renewable Resource Problem

The resource-constrained project scheduling problem (RCPSP) has been a widely researched problem in operations research literature. The RCPSP problem is caused when the total resource demand in a group of scheduled activities is greater than the total resource availability [5]. Therefore the better sequences in the project activities are searched without overpass the total resources availability.

The most usual objective for the RCPSP has been the minimization of project makespan [6], which is one of the most relevant performance measures in engineering practice, however other objectives have been worked for others authors such a the quality maximization [7], cost minimization [8], the time/cost ratio [9–11], the resources leveling [12], among others. The involved resources, due to Bey [7], are categorized into the next categories:

1. Renewable Resources: Are they such the availability by unit time is amount limited, and its consumption can't exceed its availability so the total resource use at every time instant is constrained but renewed at the beginning time instant, e.g. Machines, manpower, process tools or space.
2. Nonrenewable Resources: These kinds of resources are amount constrained for the entire project so is not renewed at any time or period, e.g. money, raw materials or energy.
3. Doubly Constrained Resources: These kinds of resources are amount constrained for the entire project and for period or unit time, e.g. cash flow which could be restricted not just for the entire project both for each period or unit time due to the budget.
4. Partially renewable resources: Initially proposed by Botcher [14], these kind of resources are available just for a specific time period, being would compose by any

combination of the three last resources kind, e.g. manpower from an employee who works for a fixed time in ordinary time and could work a limited extra time per week, so the composition for the extra time along the week may vary depending on the extra time allow.

According to the resource classification, a set of assumptions in the classic RCPSP and its main extensions- the multimode resource-constrained project scheduling problem (MRCPSP) an the resource constrained project scheduling problem under time parameter variation (RCPSP/τ) are detailed in Table 1.

Table 1. Resource types and assumptions.

Assumption	*RCPSP*	*MRCPSP*	*RCPSP/τ*
Entire Project renewable resources constant availability.	■	■	
Time Period renewable resources constant availability, Time Period variable.			■
Resource renewable constant requirement for the entire project	■	■	
Resource renewable constant requirement for time periods (t)			■
Unique mode execution.	■		
Mutiple mode execution.		■	
Knowing Anticipated of resource availability.	■	■	■
Knowing Anticipated of resource requirement.	■	■	■
Constant requirement efficiency	■	■	■

Table 1 shows that the analyzed problems suppose mainly the availability, efficiency and resource requirement for time periods, however, at the practice, these assumptions are not accomplished totally, due to the resources are not available all the time, or its efficiency would vary into the time periods even respect to the planning, and this effect increased depending on the units time planning (days, weeks, months). In this paper, we propose an algorithm for generates a dynamic resource availability and a dynamic resource allocation. This proposal tries to reduce the gaps between RCPSP assumptions and project management practice.

In recent years only a few models have considered dynamic resource allocation. In [15] a mathematical programming model under conditions of dynamic resource allocation in continuous time was proposed. Nevertheless, the authors state an increase of computational time. In our proposal, and due to a combination of systems dynamic simulation and priority project scheduling rules, the computational times are low. The same problem was found in [16] which try to solve computational problem trough a hybrid metaheuristic. Neither consider a combination with queuing theory nor use a multiproject framework.

3   Case: Bogotá Electricity Distributor

The interconnection process for a small unit from the grand central for a feasible project is composed by the necessary steps to connect and electrify small units from the electricity network, those electrification projects are executed by the network operator who will be the electricity provider to the final client.

Nowadays the interconnection process involves more than five operators and the completion time for a project would spend between 21 and 80 working days. The delays produce less client satisfaction; even sometimes a provisional connection is made which is not able to manage the demand capacity, producing electricity falls and poor quality service.

Although the electrification projects are coordinated from a unique administrative unit and are independent between them, they share resources, for this reason for the present work this problem was dealt with multiple project sequencing problem.

3.1   Electrificación Project Characterization

The Project Electrification Characterization was obtained from experts and official operator documents, obtaining the activities, durations, precedence relations, and the resource requirements. Figure 1 show the activity network obtained.

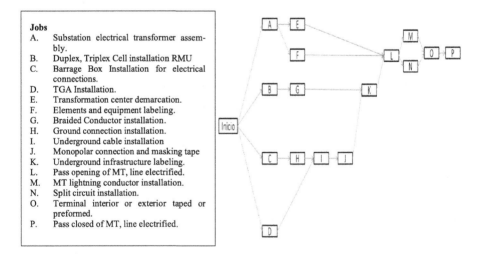

Jobs

A.   Substation electrical transformer assembly.
B.   Duplex, Triplex Cell installation RMU
C.   Barrage Box Installation for electrical connections.
D.   TGA Installation.
E.   Transformation center demarcation.
F.   Elements and equipment labeling.
G.   Braided Conductor installation.
H.   Ground connection installation.
I.   Underground cable installation
J.   Monopolar connection and masking tape
K.   Underground infrastructure labeling.
L.   Pass opening of MT, line electrified.
M.   MT lightning conductor installation.
N.   Split circuit installation.
O.   Terminal interior or exterior taped or preformed.
P.   Pass closed of MT, line electrified.

Fig. 1. Electrification project activity network.

The main restriction is the total resource availability like the workers crew (renewable resource), currently only two crew are available and are allocated according to the electrical power needs, less than 150 kVA and more than 150 kVA.

This situation generates a classic RCPSP since the total resource demand exceeds the resource availability. RCPSP solution is not enough because multiple interconnection services are required at the same time, producing a queue composed by two project lined and two servers (specialized crew). the present work proposes a dynamic resource allocation algorithm to solve the depicted problem.

4 Dynamic Constrained Renewable Resources Allocation Model

Based on the problem described in the previous paragraphs, the proposed model, as the same RCPSP [17], assumes non-splitting activities, this assumption does not allow to stop the activity execution once it has been started until it has been finished. Additionally the mode execution has been considered not allowed to change during the project completion.

Analyzing the system structure is important to note that is similar to a multiple servers queue system, being the projects the clients and the crews the servers, executing one project per time. Figure 2 presents the scheme proposed for the system.

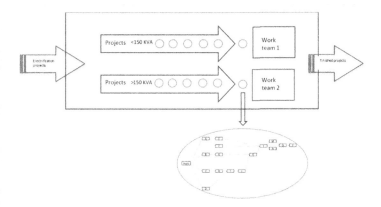

Fig. 2. System structure

Modeling the problem as queue system, each Project has to be finished before another project starts, and is not allowed to change the resources assignation (crews) during project execution, considering the project as a unique unit job or indivisible. A dynamic model proposed allows a dynamic resource assignation between the projects, in order to obtain the resource level which reduces the global cost and time completion.

Like the basic formulation for the Project scheduling, the RCPSP assumes constant resource availability for each period time into the whole planned time, this has been shown in the models proposed by Klein [18], Browning and Yassine [19] and D. Krüger and A. Scholl [20], therefore the resource availability is used like a parameter, for the present work this assumption was changed and is considered as variable, allowing a dynamic resource assignation.

In order to solve the problem described above, we proposed two steps:

1. The first step develops two dynamic resource allocation strategies. These strategies are based on an algorithm which increases the number of resources available for a

project if the total resource capacity allows it. If this is not possible, a rule-based method to solve the RCPSP is used. The difference between the two proposed strategies is the way to fit the total resource demand in the project: In the first strategy once a project increases its resource capacity, do not return to the total resource capacity. In the second strategy, if a resource capacity for a project exceeds the demand, the surplus is returned to the capacity and could be used in another project. The expected result with the first step is to generate a resource usage profile more similar to the resource demand profile.

2. The second step applies the strategies for the real case; this application first calculates the maximum number of project would be executed at the same time, for this purpose, the maximum queue length is obtained using discrete event simulation. After that, the dynamic allocation strategies depicted in the previous step are used.

4.1   Resource Assignation Strategy Design

Looking for the use resources optimization is possible to control each activity however this would mean an over cost; the present work is based on the hypothesis that the use of the priority rules for the activities and resources scheduling would reduce the total completion time for a project set, the rules or assignation strategies to consider are present bellow:

Assignation Strategy 1.   The allocation strategy proposed for the present work looking to make dynamic the resource restriction through the algorithm shown in Fig. 3.

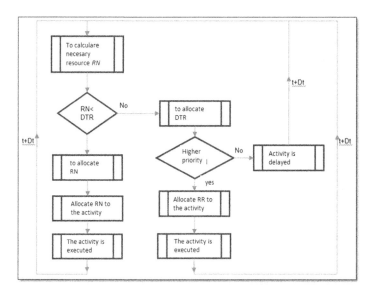

Fig. 3.   Resource allocation algorithm.

The variable RN represents the total resource demand in a time, that means the sum of individual resource demand RR for a group of activities scheduled in the time t. The parameter DTR represents the total resource availability for all projects; finally Dt means the next time step in the algorithm.

The resource assignation has two main functions; the first is to forward check the activity network obtaining the resources requirements in the next time, if the requirement is less than the availability then the resource is assigned.

The second function is showed when the amount required is higher than the amount available, prioritizing the assignation for the activities using static rules, therefore the model allocates the resource to the higher priority activities.

The rule used, and best performed, to evaluate the priority was based on the Most Total Successors (MTS). For the strategy design was consider the resource requirement profile, which is shown at Fig. 4.

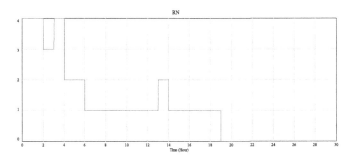

Fig. 4. Resource requirement profile

The resource requirement profile presented above, shows the requirement for the electrification projects from the Activity I, the amount required resource is around one work team until the end, except for the activity M and N, and those activities would be executed in parallel.

For this strategy when the total resource requirement reduces to a one work team, the resources are available for be used in other projects. Figure 5 shows the resource requirement profile to the first project using the assignation resource strategy proposed.

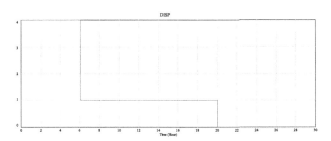

Fig. 5. Resource requirement profile assigned to the project 1.

Assignation Strategy 2. The main objective of the resource restriction is to make dynamic the resource assignation, this strategy assigns the resource to the *RN* variable and liberate the resources which are not using by the next project, in this way the resource assignation will be more adjusted to the resource requirement profile for the set of the electrification projects RN, like is shown in Fig. 6.

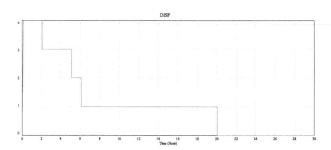

Fig. 6. Resource assigned profile to the project 1 by strategy 2

5 Impact Over Project Makespan of the Resources Allocation Strategies

In order to measure the impact over project makespan and project cost of the two strategies presented before, we did two linked simulations.

First, a maximum number of projects in the queue is calculated using discrete event simulation. For this, goodness to fit test, over the project input rate, was run. The results show a maximum and mode number of projects in queue equals to four (Fig. 7).

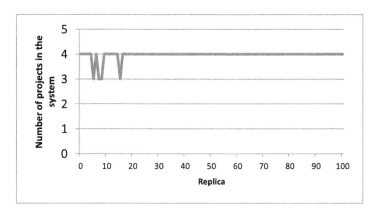

Fig. 7. Number of projects in queue

Second, a system dynamics model was used for testing the designed strategies. In this simulation, was modeled four projects to be executed simultaneously according to the previous step. The part of the Forrester model which allows allocating the resource is shown below (Fig. 8).

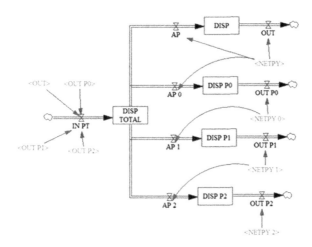

Fig. 8. Resource availability, forrester diagram.

The figure presents a level called *DISP TOTAL* which represents the total resource capacity in the system, the others four levels represent resource availability for a single project. Information flows controls new resources orders and resource releases. Variables as *NETPY* have the function to calculate the total resource requirement one step ahead and allocate – if it is possible- the resource requirement to each project through the variables called *AP, AP0, AP1* and *AP2*. Finally the variables with the name *OUT* return to the resources to the level *DIP TOTAL* when these resources are not needed. The full experiment to test the strategies has the next conditions:

- Maximum number of parallel projects: 4
- Number of jobs for project: 16
- Network complexity level: 1.06
- Resource cost [$/hour]:
- Scenarios: renewable resources availability: {2, 3}

Jobs and precedence relationships were presented in Fig. 1. Two scenarios were defined with total resource availability equals to 2 and 3. In the case of study this means 2 or 3 work teams assigned to the system. In the current system strategy, the total resource availability is static and no changes in the resource allocation are allowed. The objective of the scenarios analysis is to determine a good solution for the total resource availability in the electrification projects. A results summary of the full experiment is presented in the next table (Table 2):

Table 2. Experiment summary

	Strategy	Total resources cost	Resource usage cost	Idle resource cost	Makespan [Hours]	New projects to be processed/ year
Scenario 1: Total resource availability = 2	Current strategy	$40.996.700	$33.653.900	$7.342.800	104	
	Strategy 1	$33.865.700	$33.653.900	$211.800	95	8
	Strategy 2	$33.865.700	$33.653.900	$211.800	95	8
	Difference between current and strategy 1	−17%	0%	−97%	−9%	
	Difference between current and strategy 2	−17%	0%	−97%	−9%	
Scenario 2: Total resource avaiability = 3	Current strategy	$58.321.100	$33.653.900	$24.667.200	100	
	Strategy 1	$37.853.700	$33.653.900	$4.199.800	78	26
	Strategy 2	$34.690.900	$33.653.900	$1.037.000	76	29
	Difference between current and strategy 1	−35%	0%	−83%	−22%	
	Difference between current and strategy 2	−41%	0%	−96%	−24%	

The total resource cost includes the resource usage cost and idle resource cost. The experiment shows worst performance in current strategy in both scenarios, and the best performance in scenario 2 with strategy 2. The current strategy in both scenarios presents the same resource usage cost but higher idle resource cost. This fact is explained by the static resource allocation rule which generates a longer projects overall makespan.

Also, we found better performance when resource flexibility increases, in strategy 2, each project can order new resources, and also return it if are no longer needed.

Finally, flexibility in resource allocation makes possible to execute more projects in a planning horizon (a year).

6   Conclusions and Future Work

Through the case of study we identified a particular kind of systems which combines classic queue systems and multi-project networks.

This kind of system has characteristics as multiple projects waiting to be attended by a finite number of resources and, once the jobs have started, projects presents constraints about the total resources available and precedence relationships.

For this reason this paper combines tools from both approaches. Queuing theory allows to calculate the queue length and project network analysis allows doing the jobs scheduling and the resource allocation.

Additionally we proposed an algorithm for resource allocation. The main idea in this algorithm is to make a flexible and dynamic resource allocation.

With this purpose the algorithm evaluates the resource requirement one step in advance, and order new resources if these are needed. If the resources required are available, these resources are assigned to the job, otherwise the project schedule is modified according to a set of priority rules used to resolve the resource constraints.

Through the application of this algorithm we simulate the main effects in the case of study. We found high differences in the reduction of project makespan and resource utilization cost.

Future work could include the design of control policies in order to minimize deviations in the total budget or time baseline.

Furthermore, new policies for resource allocation could be generated, for example completely dynamic resource allocation. In this type of policies projects not only could request new resources when needed, but also release resources to other projects when they are not.

References

1. Project Management Institute: Guía de los fundamentos para la dirección de proyectos, vol. 87, no. 11 (2013)
2. Hartmann, S., Briskorn, D.: A survey of variants and extensions of the resource- constrained project scheduling problem. Eur. J. Oper. Res. **207**, 1–14 (2010)
3. Canonico, P., Söderlund, J.: Getting control of multi-project organizations: combining contingent control mechanisms. Int. J. Proj. Manag. **28**(8), 796–806 (2010)
4. Chavez Guillén, R.M.: Dinamica de sistemas. Diagramas causales, pp. 1–49 (2010)
5. Ballestín González, F., Verdejo, V.: Nuevos métodos de resolución del problema de secuenciación de proyectos con recursos limitados. Tesis doctorals. Universitat de València, Servei de Publicacions, València, p. 1 disc òptic (CD-ROM) (2002)
6. Kolisch, R., Padman, R.: An integrated survey of deterministic project scheduling. Omega **29**(3), 249–272 (2001)
7. Bey, R.B., Doersh, R.H., Patterson, J.H.: The net present value criterion: its impact on project scheduling. Proj. Manag. Q. **12**(2), 35–45 (1981)
8. Icmeli, T., Rom, W.: Ensuring quality in resource constrained project scheduling. Eur. J. Oper. Res. **103**, 483–496 (1997)
9. Elmaghraby, S.: Activity networks: project planning and control by network models, pp. 417–433. Wiley-Interscience Publication, New York (1977)
10. Deckro, R., Herbert, F.: Resource constrained project crashing. Int. J. Manag. Sci. **17**, 69–79 (1989)
11. Deckro, R.F., Hebert, J.E., Verdini, W.A.: A decomposition approach to multi-project scheduling. Eur. J. Oper. Res. **51**, 110–118 (1990)
12. Bandelloni, M., Tucci, M., Rinaldi, R.: Optimal resource leveling using non-serial dyanamic programming. Eur. J. Oper. Res. **78**(2), 162–177 (1994)

13. Vanhoucke, M., Debels, D.: The impact of various activity assumptions on the lead time and resource utilization of resource-constrained projects. Comput. Ind. Eng. **54**(1), 140–154 (2008)
14. Schilling, M.A., Vidal, P., Ployhart, R.E., Marangoni, A.: Learning by doing something else: variation, relatedness, and the learning curve. Manage. Sci. **49**(1), 39–56 (2003)
15. Naber, A.: Resource-constrained project scheduling with flexible resource profiles in continuous time. Comput. Oper. Res. **84**, 33–45 (2017)
16. Tritschler, M., Naber, A., Kolisch, R.: A hybrid metaheuristic for resource-constrained project scheduling with flexible resource profiles. Eur. J. Oper. Res. **262**(1), 262–273 (2017)
17. Rueda, F., Gonzalez, L.: Modelo para la Medición del impacto de la Variabilidad en Recursos Renovables para la Gestión de Proyectos, Memorias del 7° Congreso Latinoamericano de Dinámica de Sistemas (2009)
18. Klein, R.: Scheduling of Resource-Constrained Projects. Springer, New York (2000)
19. Browning, T.R., Yassine, A.A.: Resource-constrained multi-project scheduling: priority rule performance revisited. Int. J. Prod. Econ. **126**(2), 212–228 (2010)
20. Krüger, D., Scholl, A.: A heuristic solution framework for the resource constrained (multi-)project scheduling problem with sequence-dependent transfer times. Eur. J. Oper. Res. **197**(2), 492–508 (2009)

A Hybrid Genetic Algorithm and Particle Swarm Optimization for Flow Shop Scheduling Problems

Lindsay Alvarez Pomar$^{(\boxtimes)}$ (D), Elizabeth Cruz Pulido (D), and Julián Darío Tovar Roa (D)

Universidad Distrital Francisco José de Caldas, Bogotá, Colombia
lalvarez@udistrital.edu.co,
{ecruzp,jdtovarr}@correo.udistrital.edu.co

Abstract. The hybrid algorithm proposed by Liou, Hsieh [1] is a combination between genetic algorithm and particle swarm optimization that can be applied to the flow shop scheduling with constraints of families, setup times, transportation times, batch processing in some machines, and postponement of activities at the end of the work day, $F_m|fmls, s_{i,k}, t_{i,j,k}, prmu, batch, day|C_{max}$. In this hybrid algorithm, each sequence is a chromosome and at the same time an individual of a swarm, individuals produce new generations and die (like in genetic algorithms), and the decision of which chromosomes will undergo the application of the mutation and crossover operators is made on the basis of the individuals gbest and lbest (like in particle swarm optimization). Finally, the algorithm was benchmarked using Taillard's instances and was applied in a real case, eleven real sequences of production were measured and the C_{max} decreased 16.45% on average, this is measured as the percent change of C_{max} given by the algorithm with respect to the C_{max} observed in the real case.

Keywords: Flow shop · Job families · Setup times · Transportation times · Batch processing · Postponement of activities · Particle swarm optimization · Genetic algorithms

1 Introduction

The company Café Semilla S.A.S. belongs to the industry of milling and roasting of coffee in Bogotá, Colombia. This company has three families of products: traditional coffee, gourmet coffee, and organic coffee. For the elaboration of finished product, the products must pass through all of the work stations: selection, hulling, roasting, milling, packing, weighing, sealing, labeling, lettering, and boxing. Product sizes are ¼ pound, ½ pound, 1 pound, and 5 pounds. The production system is a flow shop [2]. The real sequences mentioned in the abstract were taken in this company.

Using the notation of Pinedo [2] the scheduling model is $F_m|fmls, s_{i,k}, t_{i,j,k}, prmu, batch, day|C_{max}$ because is a flow shop (F_m), three families of products are produced (*fmls*), there are setup times when a change of family must happen in the machines ($s_{i,k}$), there are transportation times of each job between every pair of machines ($t_{i,j,k}$),

© Springer International Publishing AG 2017
J.C. Figueroa-García et al. (Eds.): WEA 2017, CCIS 742, pp. 601–612, 2017.
DOI: 10.1007/978-3-319-66963-2_53

the permutation of jobs is held constant during the production (*prmu*), some machines do batch processing (*batch*), and the activities that can't be finished on a work day are postponed to the next day (*day*). The activities are: the processing of a job, the setup of a machine, and the transportation of a job. The objective function is C_{max}.

The flow shop scheduling problem is an NP-hard problem [3], therefore the resolution of the model $F_m|fmls$, $s_{i,k}$, $t_{i,j,k}$, *prmu, batch, day*$|C_{max}$ is also NP-hard. This specific model hasn't been described in the literature, but was based on the hybrid algorithm of Liou, Hsieh [1].

Flow shop systems problems with groups and setup times are known as FSDGS problems, for "Flow Shop Sequence Dependent Group Scheduling". Franca et al. [4] developed genetic algorithms and a memetic algorithm for the FSDGS problem. Salmasi et al. [5] proposed a programming model for the FSFGS, which they solved with a hybrid algorithm of tabu search and ant colony optimization. Naderi, Salmasi [6] proposed a hybrid metaheuristic of genetic algorithms and simulated annealing for the FSDGS problem. Other metaheuristics have been applied to solve problems in flow shop systems [7]. The former examples show that metaheuristics can be used to solve problems in flow shop systems. Other problems, like parallel machines, have also been treated with heuristics [8].

Genetic algorithms require the definition of chromosomes, an objective function (makespan), and two operators defined for the sequences of mutation and crossover [9, 10]. Swarm particle optimization was developed initially by Kennedy, Eberhart [11] and sequences are individuals of a swarm, each one with a value of the objective function. Two types of individuals are defined: gbest and lbest, gbest is the sequence of all the swarm with the best value of the objective function. The swarm is divided in subgroups; lbest is the sequence with the best value of the objective function in each subgroup [10]. The particle swarm optimization has already been used in the solution of the flow shop problem [12] and the hybrid algorithm of Liou, Hsieh [1] can be applied independent of the specific form that the equations of completion times may have.

The remainder of the paper is organized as follows. The model formulation is presented in Sect. 2. In Sect. 3, the proposed flowchart to represent the hybrid algorithm of Liou, Hsieh [1] is presented. In Sect. 4 is shown the benchmarking of the algorithm created compared with the example of Liou, Hsieh [1] and the instances of Taillard [13]. Section 5 are presented the results of the model, including the model's error and the improvement found. Conclusions are found in Sect. 6.

2   Model Formulation

For the production of roasted coffee, in the processes of hulling, roasting, and milling the machines do batch processing and the processing time per batch is fixed in those machines, the amount of coffee to process is near to the machine capacity. Below follows the model formulation of the model $F_m|fmls$, $s_{i,k}$, $t_{i,j,k}$, *prmu, batch, day*$|C_{max}$.

2.1 Subscripts, Parameters, and Variables of the Model

Subscripts

b auxiliary subscript for batches
i position of the families in the sequence, $i = 1, 2, ..., g$
j position of the jobs in the sequence, $j = 1, 2, ..., N$
k machine, $k = 1, 2, ..., m$

Parameters

g number of families
N total number of jobs
m number of machines
n_i number of jobs in the family i
$p_{i,j,k}$ processing time of the job j from the family i in the machine k (minutes)
$s_{i,k}$ setup time between families $i - 1$ and i in the machine k (minutes)
$t_{i,j,k}$ transportation time of the job j from the family i between machines k and $k + 1$ (minutes)
$pBatch_{i,k}$ processing time per batch of jobs from the family i in the machine k (minutes)
cap_k capacity of the machine k if it does batch processing (pounds)
$mJb_{i,j}$ mass of the job j from the family i (pounds)
L_k binary parameter, 1 if the machine k does batch processing and 0 otherwise
mt duration of the work time per day (minutes)
mD duration of the day (minutes)

Variables

$C_{i,j,k}$ completion time of job j from the family i in the machine k (minutes)
$jbIn_i$ position (inside the sequence) of the initial job from the family i
$jbFn_i$ position (inside the sequence) of the final job from the family i
$bat_{i,j,k}$ number of the batch of the machine k in which the job j from the family i will complete its production. The count restarts in each family
$batT_{i,k}$ total number of batches of the family i in the machine k
$jbInB_{i,j,k}$ position (inside the family) of the initial job from the jobs that are completed in the same batch as the job j from the family i in the machine k
$jbFnB_{i,j,k}$ position (inside the family) of the final job from the jobs that are completed in the same batch as the job j from the family i in the machine k
$jbBat_{b,i,k}$ amount of jobs from the family i to complete in the batch b in the machine k
$CtT_{i,j,k}$ total transportation time of the job j from the family i between machines k and $k + 1$ (minutes)
$CsT_{i,k}$ total setup time in the machine k between families $i - 1$ and i (minutes)
$CdT_{i,j,k}$ total processing time of the job j from the family i in the machine k, without considering the day restriction (minutes)
$day_{i,j,k}$ day of completion of the job j from the family i in the machine k

$dayt_{i,j,k}$ day when finishes the transportation of the job j from the family i between the machines k and $k + 1$

$days_{i,k}$ day when finishes the setup of the machine k between families $i - 1$ and i

2.2 Mathematical Definition of the Variables

The listed variables can be mathematically expressed as follows,

$$jbIn_i = 1 + \sum_{i=1}^{i-1} n_i \tag{1}$$

The position of the initial job of each family in the sequence is equal to 1 plus the summation of the sizes of the previous families.

$$jbFn_i = \sum_{i=1}^{i} n_i \tag{2}$$

The position of the final job of each family in the sequence is equal to the summation of the sizes of previous families including the current family in the sequence.

$$bat_{i,j,k} = \left\lceil \frac{\sum_{j=jbIn_i}^{j} mJb_{i,j}}{cap_k} \right\rceil \tag{3}$$

The $bat_{i,j,k}$ equation shows that the batch in which a job j from the family i is completed on the machine k is a whole number. The number of the batch in which a job is completed augments along with the sum of the mass of the jobs from the initial job of the family i until the current job j, and the bigger the capacity of the machine k, the less the amount of batches required. The count of batches in a machine is independent for each family.

$$batT_{i,k} = \left\lceil \frac{\sum_{j=jbIn_i}^{jbFn_i} mJb_{i,j}}{cap_k} \right\rceil \tag{4}$$

The $batT_{i,k}$ equation is very similar to the $bat_{i,j,k}$ equation, the difference is that the summation doesn't go to j but to $jbFn_i$ which eliminates the subscript j in $batT_{i,k}$. This number represent the total quantity of batches that machine k will make of family i.

$$jbBat_{b,i,k} = \overset{count}{\underset{b \le batT_{i,k}}{j \ge jbIn_i}} \{bat_{i,j,k}, b\} \quad j \le jbFn_i \tag{5}$$

The $jbBat_{b,i,k}$ equation uses the "count" function which returns the number of times that the second argument is repeated among the values inside a set or array located in the first argument. Thus $jbBat_{b,i,k}$ is the number of times that b is repeated inside the set of the values that $bat_{i,j,k}$ takes by varying j from $jbIn_i$ to $jbFn_i$. The variable $jbBat_{b,i,k}$ measures the amount of jobs from the family i that are completed in the batch b of the machine k.

$$jbInB_{i,j,k} = \sum_{\hat{b}=1}^{bat_{i,j,k}-1} \left(jbBat_{\hat{b},i,k} \right) + 1 \tag{6}$$

To determine the jobs that belong to a batch to be processed by machine k, notice that the cumulative sum over the subscript b of the variable $jbBat_{b,i,k}$ always coincides with the position of the final job of the batches to make in machine k, this implies that if 1 is added to the cumulative sum of $jbBat_{b,i,k}$ the position of the first job of the next batch is obtained. To know the first job not from the next batch but from the current one, the cumulative sum should be done until the previous batch, i.e. $bat_{i,j,k} - 1$.

$$jbFnB_{i,j,k} = \sum_{\hat{b}=1}^{bat_{i,j,k}} jbBat_{\hat{b},i,k} \tag{7}$$

The equation to determine the final job of a given batch will be the cumulative sum over the subscript b of the variable $jbBat_{b,i,k}$ to the value $bat_{i,j,k}$.
For the completion times,

$$CdT_{i,1,k} = L_k * \left(pBatch_{i,k} * bat_{i,1,k} \right) \\ + (1 - L_k)\left(p_{i,1,k} \right) + \max\left(CtT_{i,1,k-1}, CsT_{i,k} \right) \tag{8}$$

$$CdT_{i,j,k} = L_k * \left(pBatch_{i,k} * \left[bat_{i,j,k} - bat_{i,j-1,k} \right] \right) \\ + (1 - L_k)\left(p_{i,j,k} \right) + \max\left(CtT_{i,j,k-1}, C_{i,j-1,k} \right) \tag{9}$$

In the two previous equations, there is a factor multiplied by L_k and other by $1 - L_k$, the value of the parameter L_k determines which of the two factors will affect the equation. Both factors are comparable in that $pBatch_{i,k} * bat_{i,1,k}$ and $pBatch_{i,k} * [bat_{i,j,k} - bat_{i,j-1,k}]$ are similar in meaning to $p_{i,j,k}$ because they measure the processing time of the batches or of the individual jobs respectively.
The time interval that lasts the workday of a given day is: $[(day_{i,j,k} - 1) * mD, mt + (day_{i,j,k} - 1) * mD]$, it is required to subtract 1 to the day in order to obtain the moment of start of the day. If there is no time left in a day to complete an activity then it is postponed to the next day. Now for the completion times of the first job of each family,

$$C_{i,1,k} = \begin{cases} CdT_{i,1,k} & , \text{if } CdT_{i,1,k} \leq mt + \left(day_{i,1,k} - 1 \right) * mD \\ L_k\left(pBatch_{i,k} * bat_{i,1,k} \right) + (1 - L_k)\left(p_{i,1,k} \right) + day_{i,1,k} * mD, \text{ otherwise} \end{cases} \tag{10}$$

For the next day only the processing is postponed, regardless of that the machine does batch processing or not.

The completion times of the remaining jobs of each family, $j > 1$ are,

$$
C_{i,j,k} = \begin{cases} CdT_{i,j,k} & , if\ CdT_{i,j,k} \leq mt + \left(day_{i,j,k} - 1\right) * mD \\ L_k\left(pBatch_{i,k} * \left[bat_{i,j,k} - bat_{i,j-1,k}\right]\right) + (1 - L_k)\left(p_{i,j,k}\right) + day_{i,j,k} * mD\,, otherwise \end{cases} \tag{11}
$$

The activities of transportation and setup can also be postponed to the next day; in the following the respective equations are presented.

For transportation activities in machines that do batch processing ($L_{k+1} = 1$),

$$
CtT_{i,j,k} = \begin{cases} \max_{\hat{j}} \left\{ C_{i,\hat{j},k} + t_{i,\hat{j},k} \right\}, & if\ \max_{\hat{j}} \left\{ C_{i,\hat{j},k} + t_{i,\hat{j},k} \right\} \leq mt + \left(dayt_{i,j,k} - 1\right) * mD \\ \max_{\hat{j}} \left\{ t_{i,\hat{j},k} \right\} + dayt_{i,j,k} * mD, otherwise \end{cases} \tag{12}
$$

Where $\hat{j} \in \left[jbInB_{i,j,k+1} + \sum_{i=1}^{i-1} n_i, jbFnB_{i,j,k+1} + \sum_{i=1}^{i-1} n_i \right]$

For the transportation activities in the rest of machines ($L_{k+1} = 0$),

$$
CtT_{i,j,k} = \begin{cases} C_{i,j,k} + t_{i,j,k}, & if\ C_{i,j,k} + t_{i,j,k} \leq mt + \left(dayt_{i,j,k} - 1\right) * mD \\ t_{i,j,k} + dayt_{i,j,k} * mD, & otherwise \end{cases} \tag{13}
$$

If the machine $k + 1$ doesn't do batch processing, then the moment when the jobs arrive to the machine $k + 1$ is calculated as $C_{i,j,k} + t_{i,j,k}$. If the machine $k + 1$ does batch processing, then it must wait for the arrival of all the jobs in the batch, hence it will start processing when the last job arrives i.e. $\max\{C_{i,j,k} + t_{i,j,k}\}$ varying j.

The setup of the first family is always made in day 1 of production,

$$
CsT_{1,k} = s_{1,k} \tag{14}
$$

For the remaining families $i > 1$

$$
CsT_{i,k} = \begin{cases} s_{i,k} + C_{i-1,n_{i-1},k}, & if\ s_{i,k} + C_{i-1,n_{i-1},k} \leq mt + \left(days_{i,k} - 1\right) * mD \\ s_{i,k} + days_{i,k} * mD, & otherwise \end{cases} \tag{15}
$$

3 Hybrid Algorithm

The description of the hybrid algorithm is show in Fig. 1. The population is shaped by all the sequences, *Iter* is the current iteration, N is the number of jobs to be sequenced, *ms* is the size of the subgroups, s1 is a counter, G_order is an array that saves the order of the families in a given sequence, *rCro* is the crossover rate, *rMut* is the mutation rate,

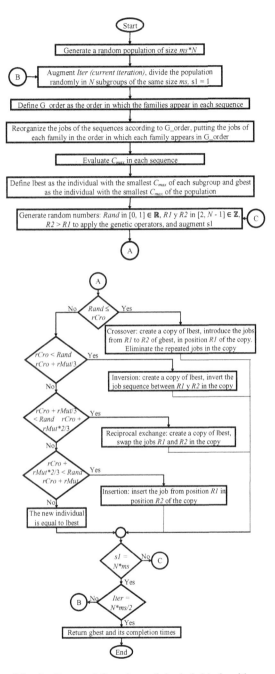

Fig. 1. Proposed flowchart of the hybrid algorithm

it must be complied that *rCro* + *rMut* ≤ 1. Liou, Hsieh [1] recommend a value of *ms* = 6, and a quantity of iterations equal to *ms* * *N/2*.

In the hybrid algorithm of Liou, Hsieh [1] each sequence is a chromosome and at the same time an individual of a swarm. In this hybrid algorithm individuals produce new generations and die (like in genetic algorithms), and the decision of which chromosomes will undergo the application of the mutation and crossover operators is made on the basis of the individuals gbest and lbest (like in particle swarm optimization).

4 Benchmarking of the Algorithm

To test the proper functioning of the algorithm, the example that appears in the paper of Liou, Hsieh [1] was done. If the algorithm created in this paper works appropriately, then the outcome must be at least as good. Five of Taillard's instances where also taken to compare the performance of the algorithm.

4.1 Example of Liou, Hsieh [1]

The smallest makespan found by Liou, Hsieh [1] in their example has a value of 185 time units. The algorithm created in this work gave the same outcome of 185 time units.

It could be thought that the algorithm created in this work, found the solution of 185 time units by chance. To see the probability of this occurrence, the size of the search space must be considered. The example has 10 jobs and 4 machines, the search space is made of 10! possible sequences. Let A be the event of finding by chance the solution in which the makespan is 185 time units, then P(A) = 1/10! = 0.000000276. As it can be seen, that event is highly unlikely. The sequence that was found in the paper of Liou, Hsieh [1] is: [5, 4, 3, 7, 6, 8, 9, 10, 1, 2] this sequence was also found by the algorithm created in this work.

Due to the stochastic nature of genetic algorithms, it was necessary to repeat the execution of the algorithm to check that the outcome was always the same makespan of 185 time units. The execution of the algorithm was repeated more than 30 times and in this replication, it was found that more than one sequence exists with a makespan of 185 time units. In the paper of Liou, Hsieh [1] only one such sequence is given, and the existence of other solutions is not specified. Using our algorithm coded in VBA, the following sequences with the stated makespan were found: [5, 3, 4, 7, 6, 8, 9, 10, 1, 2], also [5, 4, 3, 6, 7, 8, 9, 10, 1, 2], [5, 3, 4, 6, 7, 8, 9, 10, 1, 2], and also the first one [5, 4, 3, 7, 6, 8, 9, 10, 1, 2].

As an example, the completion times for the sequence [5, 3, 4, 6, 7, 8, 9, 10, 1, 2] is show in Table 1.

Table 1. Completion times for the sequence [5, 3, 4, 6, 7, 8, 9, 10, 1, 2] from the example of Liou, Hsieh [1]. The machines are in the rows, the jobs are in the columns.

	5	3	4	6	7	8	9	10	1	2
1	9	21	31	43	63	79	83	102	124	137
2	23	41	61	79	90	112	118	133	151	169
3	40	59	75	95	111	122	142	149	161	176
4	57	61	96	111	124	141	147	159	179	185

4.2 Taillard's Instances

Liou, Hsieh [1] didn't make benchmarking of their algorithm using instances available internationally. Five of Taillard's instances where randomly taken and the algorithm created in this work was applied to those instances, the aforementioned instances are,

- Instance 3 of Taillard 20 jobs 5 machines: Taillard20x5(3)
- Instance 9 of Taillard 20 jobs 10 machines: Taillard20x10(9)
- Instance 8 of Taillard 20 jobs 20 machines: Taillard20x20(8)
- Instance 4 of Taillard 50 jobs 5 machines: Taillard50x5(4)
- Instance 1 of Taillard 50 jobs 10 machines: Taillard50x10(1)

The next table shows the main results of the benchmarking (Table 2),

Table 2. Results related to Taillard's instances

	Upper bound (t.u)*	Outcome (t.u)*	Absolute error (t.u)*	Percentage error	Average computational time (s)
Taillard20x5(3)	1081	1098	17	1.57%	8.10
Taillard20x10(9)	1593	1636	43	2.70%	16.21
Taillard20x20(8)	2200	2261	61	2.77%	31.51
Taillard50x5(4)	2751	2765	14	0.51%	131.42
Taillard50x10(1)	3025	3153	128	4.23%	267.41

*t.u: time units

Although the algorithm was always near to the upper bound, but it was never reached; because of the additional constrains (families, setup times, and transportation times). The average percentage error of the algorithm created in this work with respect to the upper bound is 2.36%, and the average absolute error is 53 time units. The computational time grows with the size of the problem. The algorithm was executed on an Intel Core i5-4210U processor, with a speed of 1.70 GHz, 8 GB of RAM, in Excel 32 bits, with all programs closed except Excel, and PC plugged to the electrical current.

5   Results of the Model

Improvements were found in the scheduling of Café Semilla S.A.S., mainly the reduction of the makespan by 16.45% or 1376.37 min on average. A total of 1070 completion times were measured to revise how valid is the model. Some noteworthy results are: the average of the average absolute error is 13.88 min; the maximum of the average absolute error is 23.59 min, and the average of the average percentage error is 0.52%. Table 3 shows the results related to the model's error.

Table 3. Results of the model's error

Average of the average absolute error	Minimum of the average absolute error
13.88 min	11.14 min
Maximum of the average absolute error	Average of the maximum absolute error
23.59 min	48.58 min
Minimum of the maximum absolute error	Maximum of the maximum absolute error
28.10 min	141 min
Average of the average percentage error	Minimum of the average percentage error
0.52%	0.30%
Maximum of the average percentage error	Average of the maximum percentage error
0.81%	4.07%
Minimum of the maximum percentage error	Maximum of the maximum percentage error
2.20%	4.77%

All errors are greater than zero, but with low values. A source of error is the technique used to measure the real completion times, because workers reported the time of completion. On the other hand, one of the most important results of this work is the makespan reduction; Table 4 shows the main results of the improvement. The smallest improvement is a reduction of 276.68 min in the makespan. Moreover, the maximum improvement is a reduction of 2712.49 min. Absolute improvement is 1376.37 min on average, which corresponds to 16.46% of improvement.

Table 4. Results of improvement

Average absolute improvement	Minimum absolute improvement
1376.37 min	276.68 min
Maximum absolute improvement	Average percentage improvement
2712.49 min	16.46%
Minimum percentage improvement	Maximum percentage improvement
3.63%	26.55%
Average of days of production decreased by the solution of the algorithm	
1 day	

6 Conclusions

In this paper the model $F_m|fmls, s_{i,k}, t_{i,j,k}, prmu, batch, day|C_{max}$ was presented, which was fitted to a real case that belongs to the industry of roasting and milling of coffee. The productive system is a flow shop with product families, setup times between families in a machine, transportation times of jobs between machines, batch processing in some machines, and postponement of activities at the end of the day.

We compared the makespan of the sequences that the company plans to produce with the sequences provided by the proposed algorithm. The flexibility of the created code program goes beyond, if, for example, the transportation times are eliminated, one must simply replace them with zeroes; if, in the future, the company decides to change its standards of production, the algorithm can be rerun with the new changes; likewise, if a new family is created (in fact the company is starting to produce a new line of low price coffee with low quality compared to the other established families) the new family can be included and rerun the algorithm.

References

1. Pinedo, M.: Scheduling, Theory, Algorithms, and Systems, 4th edn. Springer, New York (2012). doi:10.1007/978-1-4614-2361-4
2. Garey, M., Johnson, D., Sethi, R.: The complexity of flowshop and jobshop scheduling. Math. Oper. Res. **1**(2), 117–129 (1976). doi:10.1287/moor.1.2.117
3. Liou, C., Hsieh, Y.: A hybrid algorithm for the multi-stage flow shop group scheduling with sequence-dependent setup and transportation times. Int. J. Prod. Econ. **170**(1), 258–267 (2015). doi:10.1016/j.ijpe.2015.10.002
4. Franca, P., Gupta, J., Mendes, A., Moscato, P., Veltink, K.: Evolutionary algorithms for scheduling a flowshop manufacturing cell with sequence dependent family setups. Comput. Ind. Eng. **48**(3), 491–506 (2005). doi:10.1016/j.cie.2003.11.004
5. Salmasi, N., Logendran, R., Skandari, M.: Total flow time minimization in a flowshop sequence-dependent group scheduling problem. Comput. Oper. Res. **37**(1), 199–212 (2010). doi:10.1016/j.cor.2009.04.013
6. Naderi, B., Salmasi, N.: Permutation flowshops in group scheduling with sequence-dependent setup times. Eur. J. Ind. Eng. **6**(2), 177–198 (2012). doi:10.1504/ejie.2012.045604
7. Shao, W., Pi, D.: A self-guided differential evolution with neighborhood search for permutation flow shop scheduling. Expert Syst. Appl. **51**(1), 161–176 (2016). doi:10.1016/j.eswa.2015.12.001
8. Wang, X., Cheng, T.: Heuristics for parallel-machine scheduling with job class setups and delivery to multiple customers. Int. J. Prod. Econ. **119**(1), 199–206 (2009). doi:10.1016/j.ijpe.2009.02.005
9. Holland, J.: Adaptation in Natural and Artificial Systems. The University of Michigan Press, Ann Arbor (1975)
10. Sivanandam, S., Deepa, S.: Introduction to Genetic Algorithms. Springer, Heidelberg (2008). doi:10.1007/978-3-540-73190-0
11. Kennedy, J., Eberhart, R.: Particle swarm optimization. In: International Conference on Neural Networks, Perth, Australia (1995)

12. Zhang, C., Ning, J., Ouyang, D.: A hybrid alternate two phases particle swarm optimization algorithm for flow shop scheduling problem. Comput. Ind. Eng. **58**(1), 1–11 (2010). doi:10.1016/j.cie.2009.01.016
13. Taillard, E.: Benchmarks for basic scheduling problems. Eur. J. Oper. Res. **64**(2), 278–285 (1993). doi:10.1016/0377-2217(93)90182-m

Miscellaneous

Early Warning Systems, Recurrent Risks and Location of Sensors in Bogotá

Roberto Ferro[1(✉)], Gabriel Alzate[1], and Helmer Muñoz[2]

[1] Universidad de Universidad Distrital Francisco José de Caldas,
Bogotá, Colombia
roberto.ferro@gmail.com
[2] Corporación Unificada Nacional CUN, Bogotá, Colombia

Abstract. In Bogota Colombia early warning systems are a source of useful information on the care and prevention of disasters. This document will be the SIDISAT (district early warning system) network which has different types of sensors that record measurements of different variables such as rainfall, temperature, humidity, shock that could generate disasters or affect the safety, health, or tranquility of citizens, the network of air of Bogota as well as information about the recurrent risks affecting the working area monitoring.

Keywords: Early alerts · Risk management · SAT · SIDISAT

1 Introduction

.

Defining the processes to identify, analyze and quantify the possible threats that may occur in the city of Bogotá defined by the IDIGER and the Ministry of environment through the records historical calamities that occurred throughout the territory gets a great tool for the prevention and correction of various factors that surround these potential threats, the same as its side effects or loss representing.

The relationship between society and nature has taken much in environmental policies in recent years having relevance in the Plan of Territorial Planning (POT) [1] in chapter risk management and climate change in the city of Bogotá; Bearing in mind that disasters are global incidence, it is necessary to take as priority the social, environmental and economic impact that this represents, as the destination of resources to emergency care is greater than to its prevention, resources that can well be invested in other types of programs in the State.

As pioneers in Latin America in search of systems of prevention and attention of disasters since the disaster produced by Avalanche caused by activation of the volcano del Ruiz in 1985 which produced 25,000 victims and lost economic around 211.8 million dollars the creation of a system to the prevention and care of disasters, reason by which the national system for the prevention and attention of disasters (SNPAD) as institutional network is created to fulfil this function [2] is taken as a priority. Thus Colombia has been one of the countries with more vision front possible methodologies to follow in the prevention and treatment of risks and disasters [3]. As a

© Springer International Publishing AG 2017
J.C. Figueroa-García et al. (Eds.): WEA 2017, CCIS 742, pp. 615–624, 2017.
DOI: 10.1007/978-3-319-66963-2_54

result the district system of early alerts (SIDISAT) is established under the framework of the Plan district of risk management and climate change for Bogota D.C., 2015–2050.

2 District Early Warning System (SIDISAT)

A SAT is an articulated mechanism of procedures that enables you to collect information for timely decision-making in the prevention and treatment of recurrent disasters, that aims to the minimization of physical and social harm improving the response time of the organs of response and coordination in alert situations, attention or evacuation. SIDISAT is the union of two data acquisition networks related to natural phenomena that can cause disasters, data collection is in real time and runs along the city of Bogotá

2.1 Bogotá Hydro-meteorological Network (RHB)

In order to anticipate and mitigate the impact of disasters caused by natural phenomena associated with the field of Hydrometeorology is set the RHB which consists of 1 base and 40 weather stations, of which 7 stations measure River along the route of the Bogotá River and the river Tunjuelo, 39 precipitation, 24 temperature and relative humidity. These 40 stations are divided into the following technologies: 8 Seba, 12 Campbell and 20 Motorola.

The measurements are recorded throughout the city of Bogotá, especially in the mountainous area of the city. River level measurements are carried out along the route of the Bogotá River and the Tunjuelo River, at the same time in the low watersheds of the streams Limas and Chiguaza [5].

The information recorded by the sensors can be consulted through the portal of the SIDISAT but does not offer the possibility of obtaining historical information, therefore only is to question the portal.

Fig. 1. SIDISAT measurements places recorded in the system.

The network has thresholds, alerts, and warnings set forth in the following way:

- Red, Orange and yellow alerts by the Tunjuelo and Bogotá rivers rising levels.
- Alert by overview of threshold of precipitation for the Chiguaza Creek basin.
- Alert for the shower dam: alert 1: from 1 m before arriving to the overflow up to start to overflow. Alert 2. From 0.5 m³ of overflow to infinite m³ of overflow.
- Notice greater or equal to 5 mm rainfall in 10 min for all seasons.

All alerts and warnings are issued automatically via email and text messages. In addition, the Bogotá aqueduct company - EAB provides information to the RHB, with report via radio of the record of discharge rate reported by manual operations in dams Chisaca and the shower. Continuous monitoring of information generated from other entities with open access to the public is performed at the same time. Specific information is as follows:

- Bogotá water company - EAB: levels of Rio Bogota, Cundinamarca canal, and river Teusaca data. Level data and discharge rate of reservoir bottom San Rafael, wetland Jaboque, Tunjuelo river and La Regadera. The thresholds for Bogotá river have not been updated regarding the latest adjustments made.
- IDEAM: Make a day rainfall forecasts with a stopover on Bogotá (5 km) also performs measurements of wind speed and temperature.
- EMGESA: State Alicachín gates, level and flow of the river Bogota.
  Civil Aeronautical hydrometeorological radar report reflectivity (intensity of the returning wave after contact with a particular white) on the savannah of Bogotá that allows a real-time view of the conditions of cloudiness and precipitation in the city and short-term forecasting with high reliability.
- Colombian Geological Service: Real-time reports of seismic activity in the country.

It is part of a hydrometeorological radar hydrometeorological network band whose use to locate precipitation, calculate their trajectories and types of precipitation that may occur, which is in configuration phase and calibration.

3 Monitoring Network of Quality Air in Bogotá - RMCAB

The RMCAB consists of 13 fixed monitoring stations and a mobile station located in different places in the city, equipped with the latest technology that allow continuous monitoring of concentrations of particulate matter (PM10, PST PM2.5); pollutants (SO2, NO2, CO, O3) and meteorological variables precipitation, speed and wind direction, temperature, solar radiation, relative humidity and barometric pressure, not all stations all measurements recorded.

3.1 Recurrent Risks

Recurrent risks are those associated with weather conditions that affect the lives and property of people, generate damages and losses in networks to provide services, mobility and housing affecting both comfort and health of the population. Mainly present as floods, puddles, landslides and forest fires. Similarly, these recurring risks in Bogota are associated with the effects of "El Niño" and "La Niña".

During the period there "El Niño" rainfall deficit in Colombia, resulting in droughts, shortages of drinking water and the marked increase in forest fires. During the occurrence of cold episodes, "La Niña", there is an increase in rainfall and consequently more floods, slope instability by mass movements and effects on human lives, homes, land routes, agriculture, among others.

Floods overflow. Floods account for one of the highest percentages of loss of housing in the country. This phenomenon of meteorological origin is characterized by generating localized impacts and high frequency, i.e., they affect specific areas are presented in more recurrently, and historically have generated higher monetary losses geological risks in the country as seen in Fig. 2.

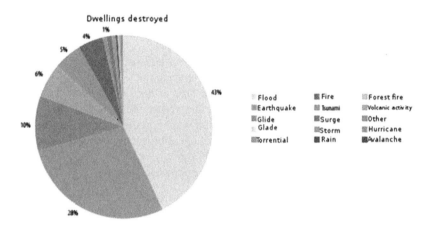

Fig. 2. Losses of housing by the type of event 1970-2011 [2] in which the houses caused by the eruption of the volcano Nevado del Ruiz in 1985 are excluded.

In Bogotá, the identification of areas prone to overflow flooding and zoning studies have been carried out. The main areas of study are the Bogotá River Basin and the Tunjuelo River basin as (see Fig. 1), Flood Zoning in Bogotá, Taken of web page IDIGER. Each classification has the following features:

High threat

- Zone in which the probability of flood (65%) is given at least once every 10 years.
- It is delimited by the line produced by the flood generated by the overflow of the channel, regardless of the cause of the flood.
- Depth equal to or greater than 0.50 m from the water sheet of the overflow, with potential effects in generating serious damages due to flow, speed and duration of the flood (Fig. 3).

Fig. 3. Flood zonification in Bogotá.

Average threat

- Zone in which the probability of flood (10%–65%) is given at least once every 10 and 100 years.
- It is delimited by the line produced by the flood generated by the overflow of the channel, regardless of the cause of the flood.
- Potential effects on generating moderate damage due to flow, speed and duration of flooding.

Low threat

- Zone in which the probability of flood (<10%) is given at least once every 100 years.
- It is delimited by the line produced by the flood generated by the overflow of the channel, regardless of the cause of the flood.
- Potential effects in generating slight damages by flow rate, speed and duration of the flood.

In this way the prevention of this type of recurrent risk should be focused on the anticipation of floods mainly in these areas in order to respond quickly in case of flood. This shows that the total area of the urban perimeter of the city is 38,427 hectares, of which 5,104 are in danger of flooding due to an overflow equivalent to 13% of the total urban area. Of the total area under threat, 931 hectares are in high threat, 3,193 in medium threat and 980 in low threat. The localities with the highest percentage of threat from this recurrent risk are Suba and Engativá.

The area most prone to flooding are visible. Suba with 55.2% and Engativá with 12% in Table 5. Likewise in Table 5 the distribution of high flood threat associated with each locality is more clearly seen in comparison with the others (Fig. 4).

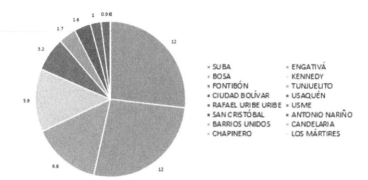

Fig. 4. Total area in high threat by locality. Taken from IDIGER

Forest Fires. A forest fire or fire of vegetation cover is defined as "fire that spreads uncontrollably over the plant material (stubble, scrub, savannah, grassland, moors, crops and forest plantations). It occurs when they occur in the same place and at the same time heat, oxygen (air) and fuel (plant material). In the city of Bogotá, this recurring risk makes more presence during the months of December, January and February, where we find low cloudiness, higher hours of sunshine and a low relative humidity which, accompanied by a high temperature, increases the probability of its being generated. A fire of this type over some cover along the eastern hills. Within the framework of the District Plan for Risk Management and Climate Change for Bogota 2015–2018, the district made a data collection of the SIRE system (an information system designed to support the administration in the processes of attention and mitigation of recurring risks).

The reference shows the number of hectares affected in the 16 years of data collected, where only seven years ago the intervention process began, showing a depressing panorama due to the little intervention that is done in comparison to the recorded damage; Of about 3000 hectares affected by the fires in the established period only 245 hectares have been intervened, of which only 5.4 have been recovered. The recovery of hectares under intervention is equivalent to 0.18% of the total hectares lost due to this recurrent risk.

Figure 5 shows a portion of very small recovered area therefore it cannot be shown in the figure.

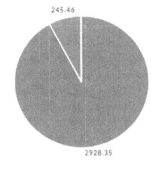

Fig. 5. Area affected by forest fires.

4 Sensor Location

The location of sensors is an important factor in the task of preventing disasters that may be caused and of efficiently mitigating those that cannot be anticipated. For this its location must take into account diverse factors and it is recommended to use different technologies for its implementation.

Flood prevention sensors. The use of satellite images as support in obtaining information facilitates the location of the sensor because the satellite orbits around the earth, there are several possibilities between existing satellites. Wei Zheng poses the use of images generated from RADARSAT for the most difficult to reach areas, due to the ability of radar images to penetrate cloud cover [2]. On the other hand, researchers from Malasya propose the use of satellite images obtained by the Quick Bird satellite and through an algorithm to identify the flood zones in real time [3]. Complementing the possible use of satellite images of radar researchers in India point out the advantages of using these images which, unlike satellite images that do not use radar technology, do not need lighting or good weather conditions to perform the Data Capture [4]. The location of sensors at points of interest depends on the definition of high risk areas, it does not make sense to place sensors in places where it is not probable that disasters occur, in this order of ideas it is necessary through historical records to generate maps with the vulnerable areas where floods have occurred in recent years. In this way, according to US studies, observing the threat zones and the range of the sensors that are decided to use should be placed in the points near the flood zone barometric pressure measurement sensors, wind direction and wind speed [5], as well as rain gauges that together with the satellite images can predict the directions of the storms before they reach the sites of high vulnerability. It is useful to keep in mind that most floods occur near drainage; therefore, a detailed map of the drainage of the area is necessary in conjunction with the map of threat zones [6]. The use of wireless sensors based on ZigBee due to their low power consumption are being used to monitor and predict floods [7] and forest fires [8].

Forest fire prevention sensors. There are different methods to define the location of the sensors depending on their purpose, it is important to find the location where the efficiency of the sensor is maximized, i.e. where its range is not limited by external factors and their measurements are not altered by its location [9]. As the purpose of the sensors is the prevention of forest fires, it is necessary to take into account for their location different points of view. A geostatistical analysis is useful, processing the information of the historical records of the fires that have occurred over the years, it is an efficient way to know the places with more risk of a forest fire [10]. To make a more efficient location it is necessary to make a classification of the vegetation cover of the forest areas [11], that is, to classify through satellite image analysis processes each of the different plants that exist in the area and identify the most prone to fires, this because different plant species retain different amounts of water, some absorb more.

5   Proposal

Due to the geographical location of the headquarters of the Francisco José de Caldas District University and based on the information presented in this article is to take into account that the inclusion of these points within the already established sensor network will allow more truthful information and of greater utility.

Table 1. Location headquarters District University

Headquarters	Location	Latitude	Length
Ingeniería	Carrera 7 No. 40B-53	4°37'40.56"N	74° 3'55.56"O
Macarena	Carrera 3 No. 26 A-40	4°36'48.86"N	74° 3'50.00"O
Vivero	Carrera 5 Este No. 15-82	4°35'49.51"N	74° 3'48.47"O
Tecnológica	Calle 68D Bis A Sur No. 49F-70	4°34'45.12"N	74° 9'28.84"O

Table 1 shows the different locations of the headquarters where it is proposed the inclusion of variable measurement sensors that contribute to improve the decision-making and the response time of the agencies responsible for emergency care. The spatial location of each of these four sites makes them key points due to their proximity to the hills, generating more precise information because of the properties of the hill where more clouds are generated.

Fig. 6. Location of the headquarters of the District University with respect to the hill.

As shown in Fig. 6 it is clear the proximity of the sites raised for inclusion as points of data collection, although the university has more locations, these particular points are connected to each other and because of their location important sites In the dynamics of the city.

In order to corroborate if the proposed sensor installation points are valid, we proceeded to implement precipitation sensors in the engineering and environmental faculties to generate a comparison frame with the Paraiso station 1 of the capital district which is between the two Faculties. The sensor implemented in an Internet network of the things that work inside the university was the rain sensor RG11, optical detector used in the stations of monitoring district, this allows to check if the proximity to the eastern hills of the sensors affects in Measure the measurements. For this, measures were taken every 10 min as recorded by SIDISAT at the times indicated in the district reports. A total of 432 measurements of each sensor were taken.

Data Analysis. In the initial univariate statistical analysis the parameters were determined by averaging the results of the two control points of the university and taking those of the Paraiso 1 station. The data are stored as a CVS file and analyzed with the RCommander program.

- Average University 1.5 mm, middle district 1.2 mm
- Highest value University 2.3, highest value district 1.6
- Minimum university value 0, minimum district value 0
- University deviation 0.2, deviation district 0.4

We verified data consistency using the Shapiro test for normality of the data set.

- University data 0.93, p-value = 0.0004321, district data 0.838, p-value4.532e-09
- Test performed with an alpha of 0.9, so there is no normality.

The value of the correlation between the two variables is analyzed to verify that the data are not significantly different from each other, presenting a correlation of 0.988, which corroborates that the two sources of information coincide in their forms and values.

6 Conclusion

The main problems with areas of flood are related to an expansion of the urban helmet without measure, the neighborhoods of invasion or subnormal neighborhoods are those that have more affection due to its systems of self-construction and its illegal constructions made in the river round, evidenced by The areas of high threat of flood which correspond mainly to locations near the Bogotá. The systems implemented to date are the basis for building a better system for risk management, the implementation of new systems must take into account new factors associated with new knowledge generated, that is to establish new temperature measurement points, Relative humidity, atmospheric pressure for the prevention of fires, it is advisable to first make an analysis of coverings in the vegetation zones in order to know the groups of plants with a greater probability of catching fire in times of phenomenon "El Niño".

The addition of new points of data collection is necessary due to the great extension of the territory and its constant growth dynamics. In the same way, when considering the eastern hills as the lung of Bogotá becomes imperative the conservation of the species of fauna and flora that are there, this is also part of the prevention due to the contribution that these plants make in the permeability of the soil, the firmness of the same and the purification of the air making.

References

1. Ana, C.G., Niels, H.-N., Carolina, D.G., Diana, R.V., C.P, Carlos, R., Fernando, R.C., Dickson, E.: Análisis de la gestión del riesgo de desastres en Colombia: Un aporte para la construcción de políticas públicas. Banco Mundial, Bogotá, Colombia (2012)
2. Zheng, W.: The flood monitoring information system framework based on multi-source satellite remote sensing data. In: 2012 International Conference on System Science and Engineering (ICSSE), Dalian, Liaoning, pp. 306–309 (2012)
3. Ahmad, R.F., Malik, A.S., Qayyum, A., Kamel, N.: Disaster monitoring in urban and remote areas using satellite stereo images: a depth estimation approach. In: 2015 IEEE 11th International Colloquium on Signal Processing and its Applications (CSPA), Kuala Lumpur, pp. 150–155 (2015)
4. Senthilnath, J., Omkar, S., Mani, V., Prasad, R., Rajendra, R., Shreyas, P.: Multi-sensor satellite remote sensing images for flood assessment using swarm intelligence. In: 2015 International Conference on Cognitive Computing and Information Processing (CCIP), Noida, pp. 1–5 (2015)
5. Dykes, N., Easley, L., Powell, J., Mitchell, J.E., Hayden, K.L.: Charles creek flood zone modeling: a correlation study of environmental conditions versus water level in the Pasquotank watershed. In: 2012 IEEE International Geoscience and Remote Sensing Symposium, Munich, pp. 966–969 (2012)
6. Anees, M.T., Abdullah, K., Nawawi, M.N.M., Kadir, M.O.A.: Morphometric analysis for delineation flood hazard zone of Batang Padang catchment, Perak, Peninsular Malaysia. In: 2015 International Conference on Space Science and Communication (IconSpace), Langkawi, pp. 231–236 (2015)
7. Chan, K.-H., Cheang, C.-S., Choi, W.-W.: ZigBee wireless sensor network for surface drainage monitoring and flood prediction. In: 2014 International Symposium on Antennas and Propagation (ISAP), Kaohsiung, pp. 391–392 (2014)
8. Zhang, J.: Forest fire detection system based on a ZigBee wireless sensor network. Front. For. China 3, 369–374 (2008)
9. Ball, M.G., Wesolkowski, S.: Sensor network placement for maximizing detection of vehicle tracks and minimizing disjoint coverage areas. In: 2015 IEEE International Symposium on Systems Engineering (ISSE), Rome, pp. 7–11 (2015)
10. Castello, C.C., Fan, J., Davari, A., Chen, R.-X.: Optimal sensor placement strategy for environmental monitoring using wireless sensor networks. In: 42nd South Eastern Symposium on System Theory (2010)
11. Yoon, G.-W., Park, J.-H., Choi, K.-H.: Land-cover supervised classification using user-oriented feature database. In: Geoscience and Remote Sensing Symposium IGARSS (2004)

Postural Control Assessment in Multiple Sclerosis by Diffusion Analysis on Kinect Skeleton Data

Germán D. Sosa[1], Albert Montenegro[1], Juanita Sánchez[3],
Xiomary Bermúdez[2], Angélica Ramírez[1], and Hugo Franco[1(✉)]

[1] Universidad Central, 110311 Bogotá, Colombia
hfrancot@ucentral.edu.co
[2] Fundación para la Esclerosis Mútltiple (FUNDEM), Bogotá, Colombia
[3] Facultad de Ciencias de la Salud, Universidad Manuela Beltrán,
111221 Bogotá, Colombia

Abstract. Multiple Sclerosis (MS) is a central nervous system disease widely known for being a non-reversible degeneration process that affects young adults as well as elder people. Such disease affects the equilibrium function of the postural control system required to perform vital tasks such as walking or hold upright position. To palliate the long-term effects associated to MS, physicians perform therapeutic interventions on patients in order to preserve their motor capabilities as best as possible. In order to evaluate the effectiveness of therapeutic interventions, representative measurements or scores are used to assess the actual state of each patient. This work presents an exploratory approach to provide quantitative mediolateral and anteroposterior balance descriptors in MS through Diffusion Analysis on balance data acquired with a low-cost computational system using a Kinect device. The obtained results were compared against a subset of exercises of the Berg Balance Scale.

Keywords: Multiple Sclerosis · Postural control · Kinect · Balance · Diffusion analysis

1 Introduction

Multiple Sclerosis (MS) is an autoimmune inflammatory disease of the Central Nervous System (CNS) caused by the presence of focal areas of inflammatory demyelination of the white matter in the brain and spinal chord [1], described as an autonomous neurodegenerative process, similar to that observed in Alzheimer that causes irreversible neural damage [2]. Some of the most common symptoms of MS are cognitive impairment as well as hypoesthesia and spasticity of muscles [3], producing a disorder of the postural control system (PCS) equilibrium functions, required to perform walking or even hold upright position [4]. Due to its irreversible nature, most of patients with MS have no full recovery of their symptoms, while they tend to increase over lifetime.

© Springer International Publishing AG 2017
J.C. Figueroa-García et al. (Eds.): WEA 2017, CCIS 742, pp. 625–637, 2017.
DOI: 10.1007/978-3-319-66963-2_55

World Health Organization [5] shows that MS has a global prevalence around 30 per 100.000 people, with Europe and North America having the highest values (80/100.000 and +100/100.000 respectively). The same study reveals that most of MS patients start onset symptoms between 25 and 30 years and become chronic after 20 years after onset. In Colombia, the prevalence of MS is between 1.4 and 4.98 per 100.000 habitants with a high presence of women (around 73%) which start onset symptomatology around 43 years [6]. In Colombia, MS is considered as an "orphan disease" with high treatment costs [7]. Despite MS symptoms are irreversible, early physical therapy is useful to mitigate the long-term effects of MS and provide a better quality of life [8]. To ensure a positive impact, physicians agree that therapy programs have to be performed regularly (1–4 times a week) [9] and should involve objective assessment stages able to describe patient current status and predict the disease outcome [10].

One of the most prevalent aspects to be improved with therapy interventions is the stability of patients in static and dynamic balance, i.e. during walking, sitting or upright position. In order to report changes and performance over time, physicians have performed PCS assessment by observing and qualifying the performance of patients during the execution of different physical tasks like those in the Berg Balance Scale (BBS) [11] and Tinetti balance test [10]. Recently, the use of force platform (FP) to evaluate balance in terms of the displacement of the center-of-pressure (COP) have allowed medical community to produce a new set of objective measures and plots, known as stabilograms, accurately describing the balance function of a patient over time [12]. However, the implementation of measurement systems based on force platform (FP) is expensive and demands considerable space requirements. For such reason, engineers have addressed the design and validation of low-cost motion capture devices (s.a Kinect) to measure postural and body-movement variables [13].

This work presents a computational system intended to perform diffusion analysis over balance measures obtained with a Kinect as a motion capture device during the execution of a subset of 5 physical trials adopted from those reported in the Berg Balance Scale. Such approach was implemented over a set of 5 subjects with MS from FUNDEM and presents balance measures for each trial in terms of mediolateral balance (MLB) and anteroposterior balance (APB). The obtained motion data was post-processed using diffusion analysis to produce plots and coefficients in the fashion of those obtained in stabilometry from force-platform data. To evaluate the validity of such plots and coefficients to assess the state of postural control system in MS, a comparison against the traditional Berg Balance Scale was performed. The evaluation will tell whether the results generated by this system can provide additional information associated to the current state of a MS patients in terms of balance.

1.1   Stabilometry for Postural Control Assessment

The use of stabilograms as an assessment tool for postural control is considered a truly objective measure for stance in absence of external perturbations [14]. Traditional stabilometry displays the trajectories of the center-of-pressure (COP) over a two-dimensional space corresponding to the surface plane defined by the area delimited by a force platform device used to calculate COP location in real-time.

1.2 Stabilogram-Difussion Plots

Stabilograms are good enough to represent present the behavior of the balance in a visual way. Beyond that, there are two recognized approaches to summarize stabilometry data: the first one, proposed by Kaptein et al. [14] and consists of the direct application of RMS value of an electric signal to represent the dissipated energy, based on the variability of the signal; the second is the Diffusion Analysis, proposed by Collins et al. [15], which provide representative coefficients related to behavior of PCS. Diffusion analysis models the COP trajectory over the FP as a fractional Brownian motion involving an stochastic process, to calculate diffusion coefficients as well as stabilogram-diffusion plots which have demonstrated to be effective to distinguish the PCS behavior between healthy people and patient with with physical disability (PD).

Traditional stabilometry [16] allows physicians to obtain sway information in terms of displacement of COP along x and y coordinates in function of time determined by a FP device. Such information may be used to generate displacement vs. time graphs known as stabilograms. A well-constructed stabilogram is enough to present the behavior of body sway in a visual way, however it requires the interpretation of an expert to provide a description of PCS condition involving certain level of subjectivity associated to the expert perception of stabilogram. For such reason, different mathematical procedures have been proposed to summarize stabilometry information into functional scores or biomarkers such as RMS values or stabilometry diffusion analysis (SDA).

2   Materials and Methods

The proposed approach consists of a computational system based on Kinect skeletal tracking for acquisition and processing of balance data from patients with MS. The experimental setup used to evaluate the data consist of three basic stages: First, the description of the population and the performed physical test, then, some details about the computational system in terms of the physical setup, software application and reported measures, and finally, a brief summary of the coefficients and plots obtained through a post-acquisition diffusion analysis.

2.1 Subjects

The evaluated subjects consist of five patients from *Fundación para la Esclerosis Múltiple* (FUNDEM) located in Bogotá, Colombia. All subjects were adults with variety of age (min: 35, max: 63, mean: 50.4) and gender (3 men and 2 women). None of the patients exceed the 20 years after the MS onset (min: 5, max: 17, mean: 11.75). 20 years or less is recommendable because MS have not become chronic in most cases. All patients for testing were required to hold upright position for at least one minute with no assistance of third-party people or orthesis. Additionally, all patients fulfilled an informed consent before any evaluation involving the proposed experiment.

2.2 Physical Test Description

BBS is widely used to assess posture in physical disabled and elderly people. This test was chosen as the baseline for this proposed physical test due to: (a) it is approved by clinical standards for assessment of posture in physical disabled people; (b) it is possible to perform the conventional evaluation through direct observation of a physician simultaneously with the computational system; and (c) several exercises provided by the test can be executed in frontal-view with respect to the Kinect with no rotations nor object interactions. to avoid artifacts during motion capture. Exercises which involve side-view position, rotations around longitudinal axis or interaction with external objects were neglected. Thus, from all 14 trials included in the BBS, 5 were selected which are described as follows:

1. **Standing unsupported (BP-WB):** Standing for 2 min.
2. **Standing with closed eyes (BP-CE):** Standing for 10 s.
3. **Standing with feet together (BP-FT):** Standing for 1 min.
4. **Standing with one foot in front (TANDEM):** Hold Tandem position for 30 s, patient can try step ahead one foot.
5. **Standing on one foot (MP):** Standing on one leg as long as possible.

2.3 Movement Capture System

The operation of the developed computational system acquisition and registration of balance measures can be described as a sequence of three processes as shown in Fig. 1. The physical setup associated to spatial requirements and the equipment used for balance data acquisition; the software specially developed for registration of balance angles using Kinect skeletal tracking [17]; and the post-processing stage that takes balance data from software to produce balance and diffusion plots representative of the performance of patients in terms of balance.

Physical Setup: A Kinect sensor (v1.0) produces color and depth streams, which are sent to a computer via USB. The z-axis in the Kinect coordinate system is aligned with the point of view (Fig. 1(a)). Kinect effective field-of-view is $54°$ and $39°$ for horizontal and vertical directions and its effective depth-of-field is between 1.0 and 3.0 m [18]. For these work, it was found out that an adequate working distance for human standing motion registration is about 2.5 m from Kinect.

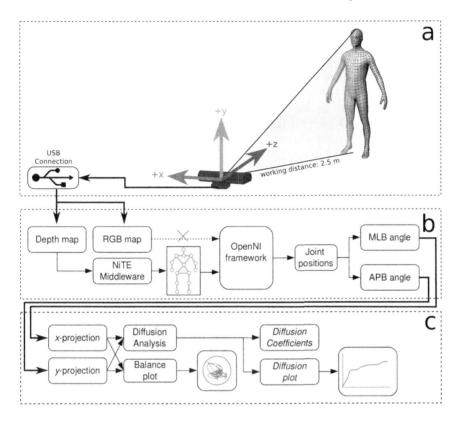

Fig. 1. Diagram of the proposed computational system based on Kinect skeletal tracking to acquire balance and diffusion measures: (a) physical setup, spatial conditions and equipment required to provide depth and color streams during test execution; (b) acquisition software to produce balance angles APB and MLB vs. time from Kinect depth data stream; (c) offline implementation of Diffusion Analysis by using the projection of APB and MLB onto a two-dimensional surface.

Software Application: The position of the joints included in the skeleton model provided by OpenNI libraries and NiTE middleware [19] are used to estimate APB and MLB (Fig. 1(b)). Joint positions were recorded at 30 frame-per-second, and, at each frame, APB and MLB angles are estimated by calculating the angle between the vector defined by *neck* (n) and *torso* (t) joints and an unitary vector $\hat{j}$ in the y-axis as shown in the set of Eq. (1). Since joints positions are 3D, they have to be decomposed in two-dimensional vectors projected onto the xy-plane and yz-plane for APB (α) and MLB (β) angle estimation respectively.

$$\alpha = \cos^{-1}\left(\frac{(n_{xy} - t_{xy}) \cdot \hat{j}}{\|n_{xy} - t_{xy}\|}\right) \quad \beta = \cos^{-1}\left(\frac{(n_{yz} - t_{yz}) \cdot \hat{j}}{\|n_{yz} - t_{yz}\|}\right) \quad (1)$$

Offline Diffusion Analysis: Although APB and MLB angles can be used as objective measures to support postural control assessment, they are not widely accepted both in medicine and biomechanics. On the other hand, there is an interesting approach presented by Collins et al. [15], widely recognized in biomedical engineering, that assumes COP trajectories can be modeled as an stochastic process related to Brownian motion. Thus, this work presents a similar approach using APB and MLB angles from Kinect instead of COP measures produced by a force platform.

Since COP trajectories are 2D dynamical data, and APB/MLB angles are 3D and kinematic, a post-processing stage is required in order to make both types of measures comparable. To do that, it is assumed that the center-of-mass (COM) is highly determined by the position and orientation of the trunk segment [20], and COM is biomechanically related to COP during stance [21]. The estimation of the orientation of the trunk onto a 2D surface is achieved by projection of APB and MLB angles using biometric information of the trunk length T for each subject as shown in Fig. 2.

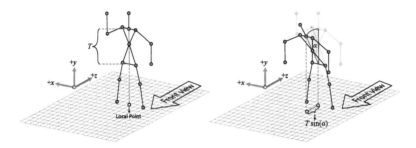

Fig. 2. Example of the projection of the APB angle onto the floor (xz-plane) using trigonometric functions to produce balance plots and posterior diffusion coefficients

2.4 Diffusion Analysis from Balance Data

The framework presented by Collins et al., states that COP trajectories are representative of the activity of the PCS in order to preserve equilibrium. Despite those trajectories are highly unpredictable overtime, it is possible to use statistical mechanics in order to find relations between time and displacement. In that way, the simplest assumption is the Brownian motion, studied by Einstein [22], which shows that mean square displacement in one-dimension $\overline{\Delta x^2}$ and the time interval Δt are related by a diffusion coefficient D resulting in the expression $\overline{\Delta r^2} = 2D\Delta t$. The last equation can be extended to two, three and higher dimensions; for those cases, the term $\overline{\Delta r^2}$ represents the mean square distance in an euclidean space of $\mathbb{R}^n$ where n is the number of dimensions.

As COP trajectories can be modeled using Brownian motion, this work assumes that two-dimensional projections of the trunk sway can also be described in the same way. Thus, the mean square of projected APB and MLB angles,

$\overline{\Delta x^2}$ and $\overline{\Delta y^2}$ respectively, and radial projection $\overline{\Delta r^2}$, can be related to the time interval Δt using Brownian motion equation. For those calculations, x, y and r time-series were calculated using $x = L_{trunk}sin(\alpha)$, $y = L_{trunk}sin(\beta)$ and $r = \sqrt{x^2 + y^2}$ respectively.

To produce diffusion plots, i.e. mean square displacement vs. time elapsed, it is necessary to calculate $(\overline{\Delta x^2}, \overline{\Delta y^2}, \overline{\Delta r^2})$ from $(x, y$ and $r)$ time-series, as well as Δt from the time-marks provided by the software application. To do that, Eq. (2) describes the mean square displacement $(\overline{\Delta r^2})$ calculation, in function of a time interval Δt, (a similar calculation is performed for $\overline{\Delta x^2}$ and $\overline{\Delta y^2}$). N is the number of frames of the balance time-series and m is the width of the time interval limited to 5 s at 30 frames-per-second $(m = 1, 2, 3, ...150)$.

$$\overline{\Delta r^2}(\Delta t) = \frac{\sum_{i=1}^{N-m} (r_{(i+\Delta t)} - r_i)^2}{N - m} \quad \text{for a given } \Delta t = t_m - t_0 \quad (2)$$

As is it will be explained in Sect. 3, diffusion plots are hard to approximate to a linear function as the Brownian motion model suggest. The results of Collins et al. also pointed out such behavior in COP trajectories and determined that mean square displacement grows almost linearly with a high slope for low time intervals, called the *short-term* region, and suddenly changes to a lower slope growing, called the *long-term* region, after a critical-point for a small value of Δt. In this study, the critical points $(\Delta t_{xc}, \Delta t_{yc}, \Delta t_{rc})$ were found by evaluating the change of slope in function of the time interval Δt. After that, the slope of the *short-term* regions (D_{xs}, D_{ys}, D_{rs}) and *long-term* regions (D_{xl}, D_{yl}, D_{rl}) were estimated by applying a regular linear regression process.

3   Results

The experimental evaluation comprises two assessment methods carried out simultaneously during the execution of each test for each subject, separately. One method consists of the traditional BBS using an ordinal scale from 0 to 4 (being 4 the best score); BBS was performed by a physical therapist through direct observation of patient trial execution. The second method is the proposed system which provides one balance plot, one diffusion plot, and a set of 9 diffusion coefficients for each one of the five physical trials. Both plots and coefficients will be analyzed in conjunction with BBS to see how these objective variables can support the assessment of postural control in patients with physical disability, particularly Multiple Sclerosis.

3.1   Berg Balance Scale Results

Third column of Table 1 shows the performance of subjects according to the BBS. This postural assessment scale scores with a 4 when patients is able to maintain equilibrium during the full-time established for a specific trial, and 0 when is unable to hold equilibrium in one position by itself. Intermediate values

Table 1. Diffusion coefficients and critical points discriminated by patients and trials

Patient	Exercise	BBS score	Δt_{xc}	Δt_{yc}	Δt_{rc}	D_{xs}	D_{ys}	D_{rs}	D_{xl}	D_{yl}	D_{rl}
P1	BP-WB	4	0.7	0.93	0.73	442.33	125.59	572.06	12.79	13.71	27.02
	BP-CE	4	–	–	–	–	–	–	–	–	–
	BP-FT	3	0.4	1.43	1.1	147.86	47.56	112.56	0.19	9.39	8.65
	TANDEM	4	1.47	2.13	1.67	274.72	124.86	410.12	−45.87	−62.36	−104.24
	MP	4	0.47	0.73	0.23	1778.35	355.67	3890.63	89.94	91.39	222.55
P2	BP-WB	4	0.53	0.87	0.7	220.71	160.56	360.02	5.91	16.28	22.57
	BP-CE	4	–	–	–	–	–	–	–	–	–
	BP-FT	4	0.4	0.3	0.4	2042.15	529.11	2444.9	59.48	10.07	68.79
	TANDEM	4	–	–	–	–	–	–	–	–	–
	MP	3	0.67	1.83	0.47	398.46	266.3	1283.73	143.54	78.14	234.68
P3	BP-WB	4	1.8	0.73	0.97	490.29	661.74	1276.57	13.42	−5.04	56.39
	BP-CE	0	–	–	–	–	–	–	–	–	–
	BP-FT	3	0.23	0.27	0.27	7062.65	2487.49	9550.14	114.2	256.62	370.82
	TANDEM	0	–	–	–	–	–	–	–	–	–
	MP	0	–	–	–	–	–	–	–	–	–
P4	BP-WB	4	0.67	0.9	0.73	339.8	64.46	401.7	12.93	2.75	15.91
	BP-CE	4	–	–	–	–	–	–	–	–	–
	BP-FT	4	0.27	1.63	0.3	2105.88	115.36	2387.85	128.62	−18.45	137.19
	TANDEM	4	0.7	0.6	0.7	579.85	61.38	672.15	21.59	19.34	34.46
	MP	4	0.4	0.9	0.5	762.57	127.45	790.65	23.29	16.64	41.05
P5	BP-WB	4	0.8	0.7	0.77	347.41	208.67	558.34	22.02	3.82	25.85
	BP-CE	4	–	–	–	–	–	–	–	–	–
	BP-FT	4	0.73	0.4	0.57	439.76	646.42	1033.49	14.65	93.19	109.26
	TANDEM	4	2	0.8	0.4	491.92	132.57	1434.37	6.58	17.82	176.37
	MP	3	0.43	1.57	2.13	1687.6	413.89	1372.48	629.95	−153.21	118.09
Average			0.74	0.98	0.74	11153.66	384.06	1679.51	73.71	22.94	92.08
Standard deviation			±0.51	±0.50	±0.48	±1662.09	±577.84	±2243.64	±147.66	±80.22	±107.82

are assigned when patient is able to hold equilibrium only during a fraction of the time established, or when external assistance is required.

Despite the small sample size, The BBS Scores show an observable variability in balance performance between subjects. For 4 of the 5 subjects included in Table 1 the performance was particularly good (between 3 and 4), such results were expected since none of the patients exceed the 20 years after onset. In contrast, patient $P3$ exhibits a noticeable affection of its balance and postural control. This is an interesting finding because it means that a high variability is also expected in the results obtained by the computational system, allowing a test-to-test comparison to check how diffusion analysis can represent the behavior of postural control during stance.

3.2   Diffusion Coefficients and Plots

For each trial registered by the system, the diffusion analysis provides one diffusion plot involving one critical point Δt_c that divides the plot into two regions, the *short-term* region with slope D_s and the *long-term* region with slope D_l. Each trial was also evaluated in 2D (x and y) in addition to the distance from the 2D projection coordinate origin, i.e. $r = \sqrt{x^2 + y^2}$. Thus, for every trial, three critical points ($\Delta t_{xc}, \Delta t_{yc}, \Delta t_{rc}$) and 6 diffusion coefficients ($D_{xs}, D_{ys}, D_{rs}, D_{xl}, D_{yl}, D_{ls}$) were calculated in conjunction with the BBS scores (Table 1).

To understand the physiological meaning of those values, Collins et al. describe both regions in the following way: during *short-term* stance, the PCS produces a high muscular activity, looking for a comfortable equilibrium position. This process can be observed in the acquired data as a high stochastic activity, i.e. a higher value for the diffusion coefficient D_s. This phase belongs to lower time intervals before the critical point (Δtc, around one second). For larger time intervals, i.e. the *long-term* region, PCS reaches a more stable posture, so the stochastic activity decreases; this process is described by the value of the diffusion coefficient D_l where $D_l < D_s$.

4   Discussion

The values presented in Table 1 show critical points Δt_c varying from 0.23 to 2 s, and diffusion coefficients with noticeable magnitude variability in their units (10^2 to 10^3 for *short-term* region D_s, and 10^1 to 10^2 for *long-term* region D_l). However, both types of variation seems to be related since large magnitudes of

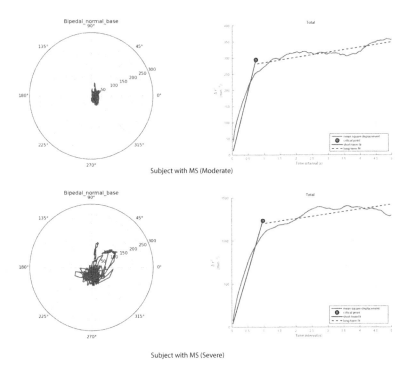

Fig. 3. Balance and diffusion plots for P4 (top) and P3 (down) during the execution of the standing unsupported trial

D_s correspond to small values of Δt_c and vice versa. Another interesting finding is that for those cases where Δt_{xc}, Δt_{yc} and Δt_{rc} are very similar, the diffusion coefficient D_r can be approximated to the sum of D_x and D_y, analogous to the Brownian motion equation, since $r^2 = x^2 + y^2$. As drawbacks, it can be seen several empty spaces corresponding to those trials that could not be performed by the subject (BBS Score: 0), or where trial duration was too short to calculate mean-square-displacement for all Δt in a significant way. There are also some unexpected negative values for diffusion coefficients, maybe due to artifacts during acquisition such as fatigue and loss of concentration caused by the physical exigence of the test (approximately 5 min of standing trials) which may be quite demanding for a patient with MS.

Balance and diffusion plots generated by the computational system display relevant information supporting balance assessment by visual inspection. To illustrate that, the balance and diffusion plots for the two patients with the best and worst BBS score (P4 and P3) are shown for the normal bipedestation trial (Fig. 3) and bipedestation with feet together (Fig. 4).

For the case of normal bipedestation (Fig. 3), P4 (moderate affection, BBS score: 4) shows a balance plot with low variations in balance for APB and MLB, with MLB oscillations being moderately lower than APB. The diffusion plot

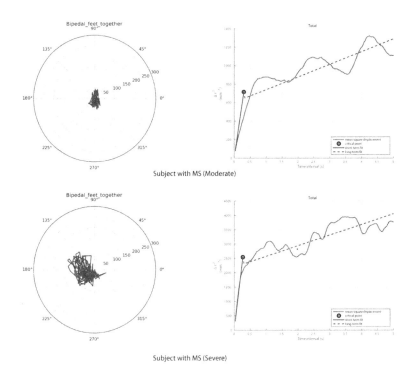

Fig. 4. Balance and diffusion plots for P4 (top) and P3 (down) during the execution of the standing with feet together trial

for the combined value r shows a critical point with coordinates $\Delta t_{rc} = 0.73$ s and $\overline{\Delta r^2} = 293\,\text{mm}^2$. Diffusion coefficients values were $D_{rs} = 401.7$ and $D_{rl} = 15.91$. On the other hand, P3 (severe affection, BBS score: 4) exhibits a worse performance since the oscillations on the balance plot are wider in both APB and MLB with respect to P4. Can also be seen that P3 achieves critical point for a larger time interval $\Delta t_{rc} = 0.97$ in comparison with P4. Moreover, the value of $\overline{\Delta r^2} = 1238\,\text{mm}^2$ at critical points considerably higher in magnitude than the value obtained for P4. P3 has also higher diffusion coefficient values: $D_{rs} = 1276.57$ and $D_{rl} = 56.39$.

For bipedestation with feet together (Fig. 4), P4 (moderate affection, BBS score: 4) shows a balance plot with low variations in balance for APB and MLB, with MLB oscillations lower than APB. The diffusion plot for r presents a critical point in $\Delta t_{rc} = 0.3$ s and $\overline{\Delta r^2} = 716\,\text{mm}^2$. Diffusion coefficients values were $D_{rs} = 2387.5$ and $D_{rl} = 137.19$ which are higher than the same values for normal bipedestation as expected since this trial is more demanding cause the shorten support basis. In contrast, P3 (severe affection, BBS score: 3) has wider oscillations for APB and MLB where MLB has a tendency to the left side. The critical point of P3 is located at $\Delta t_{rc} = 0.27$ and $\overline{\Delta r^2} = 2578$ what is noticeably higher than P4. P3 has also higher diffusion coefficient values: $D_{rs} = 9550.14$ and $D_{rl} = 370.82$.

5   Conclusions and Future Work

This work presents an exploratory implementation of a computational system intended to provide balance measures for postural control assessment, similar to those obtained through COP trajectories of stabilogram diffusion analysis, but using only postural information based on the skeletal tracking model provided by the NiTE middleware for Kinect. This preliminary results point out that the estimated coefficients by themselves are not fully representative of the balance performance. However, balance and diffusion plots are more consistent with the Berg Balance Scale scores assigned by a physical therapist during the proposed test.

Incoming stages of this work should consider physical test with tasks not exceeding 30 s of execution. Finally, since the nature of projected trunk sway and COP are not the same (trunk sway is kinematic measure that does not consider limbs movement, whereas COP is a kinetic measure representative of the whole muscular activity of th body), an additional processing stage may be required on balance measures to achieve a behavior similar to that exhibited by COP trajectories.

References

1. Trapp, B.D., Nave, K.A.: Multiple sclerosis: an immune or neurodegenerative disorder? Annu. Rev. Neurosci. **31**, 247–269 (2008)
2. Stadelmann, C.: Multiple sclerosis as a neurodegenerative disease: pathology, mechanisms and therapeutic implications. Curr. Opin. Neurol. **24**(3), 224–229 (2011)
3. Kalron, A., Dvir, Z., Achiron, A.: Effect of a cognitive task on postural control in patients with a clinically isolated syndrome suggestive of multiple sclerosis. Eur. J. Phys. Rehabil. Med. **47**(4), 579–586 (2011)
4. Massion, J.: Postural control system. Curr. Opin. Neurobiol. **4**(6), 877–887 (1994)
5. World Health Organization, et al.: Atlas: multiple sclerosis resources in the world 2008 (2008)
6. Sánchez, J., Aguirre, C., Arcos-Burgos, O., Jiménez, I., Jiménez, M., León, F., Pareja, J., Pradilla, G., Uribe, B., Uribe, C.S., et al.: Prevalencia de la esclerosis múltiple en Colombia. Rev. Neurol. **31**, 1101–1103 (2000)
7. Romero, M., Arango, C., Alvis, N., Suarez, J.C., Duque, A.: Costos de la esclerosis múltiple en Colombia. Value Health **14**(5), S48–S50 (2011)
8. Di Fabio, R.P., Soderberg, J., Choi, T., Hansen, C.R., Schapiro, R.T.: Extended outpatient rehabilitation: its influence on symptom frequency, fatigue, and functional status for persons with progressive multiple sclerosis. Arch. Phys. Med. Rehabil. **79**(2), 141–146 (1998)
9. Solari, A., Filippini, G., Gasco, P., Colla, L., Salmaggi, A., La Mantia, L., Farinotti, M., Eoli, M., Mendozzi, L.: Physical rehabilitation has a positive effect on disability in multiple sclerosis patients. Neurology **52**(1), 57–57 (1999)
10. Bohannon, R.W.: Objective measures. Phys. Ther. **69**, 590–593 (1989)
11. Berg, K.O., Wood-Dauphinee, S.L., Williams, J.I., Maki, B.: Measuring balance in the elderly: validation of an instrument. Can. J. Public Health (Revue canadienne de sante publique) **83**, S7–S11 (1991)
12. Bonde-Petersen, F.: A simple force platform. Eur. J. Appl. Physiol. **34**(1), 51–54 (1975)
13. Bonnechere, B., Jansen, B., Salvia, P., Bouzahouene, H., Omelina, L., Moiseev, F., Sholukha, V., Cornelis, J., Rooze, M., Jan, S.V.S.: Validity and reliability of the Kinect within functional assessment activities: comparison with standard stereophotogrammetry. Gait Posture **39**(1), 593–598 (2014)
14. Kapteyn, T.S., Bles, W., Njiokiktjien, C.J., Kodde, L., Massen, C.H., Mol, J.M.: Standardization in platform stabilometry being a part of posturography. Agressologie **24**(7), 321–326 (1983). DIRECTIONS, I.O.
15. Collins, J.J., Luca, C.: Open-loop and closed-loop control of posture: a random-walk analysis of center-of-pressure trajectories. Exp. Brain Res. **95**(2), 308–318 (1993)
16. Terekhov, Y.: Stabilometry as a diagnostic tool in clinical medicine. Can. Med. Assoc. J. **115**(7), 631 (1976)
17. Sosa, G.D., Sánchez, J., Bermúdez, X., Ramírez, A., Franco, H.: Evaluation of computer vision based objective measures for complementary balance function description and assessment in multiple sclerosis. In: Torres, I., Bustamante, J., Sierra, D. (eds.) VII Latin American Congress on Biomedical Engineering CLAIB 2016, Bucaramanga, Santander, Colombia, 26–28 October 2016. IFMBE Proceedings, vol. 60, pp. 377–380. Springer, Singapore (2017)
18. Dutta, T.: Evaluation of the Kinect sensor for 3-D kinematic measurement in the workplace. Appl. Ergon. **43**(4), 645–649 (2012)

19. OpenNI Community: OpenNI User Guide (2010)
20. Plagenhoef, S., Evans, F.G., Abdelnour, T.: Anatomical data for analyzing human motion. Res. Q. Exerc. Sport **54**(2), 169–178 (1983)
21. Benda, B.J., Riley, P., Krebs, D.: Biomechanical relationship between center of gravity and center of pressure during standing. IEEE Trans. Rehabil. Eng. **2**(1), 3–10 (1994)
22. Einstein, A.: Investigations on the Theory of the Brownian Movement. Courier Corporation (1956)

Achievement and Motivation Analysis in Mathematics for Elementary Students with the Interactive Tool Kinect Park

Erika Lorena Villamizar Franco(✉) ⓘ,
Michael Alexander Salazar Ortega ⓘ,
and Fernando Martínez Rodriguez ⓘ

Universidad Distrital Francisco José de Caldas, Bogotá, Colombia
{elvillamizarf,masalazaro}@correo.udistrital.edu.co,
fmartinezr@udistrital.edu.co

Abstract. This article presents the importance of complementary technological tools in the student education and analyzes the impact on mathematics learning of students in fourth grade based on motivation and performance variables involved in each process of instruction conducted in the classroom with the implementation of the interactive tool Kinect Park developed by the authors.

The analysis of the students behaviour in their interaction with the educational tool will make it possible to assess the importance of the inclusion of IT in the classroom which for a long time have been guided by traditional methodologies.

Keywords: Interactive learning · Kinect · Mathematics · Motivation · Technology and innovation

1 Introduction

The implementation of educational testing at the national and international level in Colombia extends from several years ago, among which are annual tests, such as PISA, SERCE, TIMSS, ICFES; the results of the Colombian students associated with academic areas and skills, according to international agencies confirm that reach average levels of performance when compared with countries of Latin America and low levels compared to students from international countries.

The majority of young population in Colombia is at a low level of performance or insufficient in the national tests "Pruebas Saber" because of low-prepared teachers, traditional methodologies inadequate, poor infrastructure, lack of educational materials and ineffective guidelines in search of knowledge. To ensure that a significant percentage of students improve their performance, it is clear that those conditions must be improved, since they are fundamental to ensuring education and quality learning.

This article proposes the analysis of the factors which affect the learning based on the collection of quantitative and qualitative data on the interaction of the students with Kinect Park, an interactive learning tool in mathematics for students in fourth grade developed by the authors, which implements the natural interface Kinect device whose

© Springer International Publishing AG 2017
J.C. Figueroa-García et al. (Eds.): WEA 2017, CCIS 742, pp. 638–646, 2017.
DOI: 10.1007/978-3-319-66963-2_56

purpose is to facilitate the learning process and improve the performance of students in the area of mathematics.

2 Benchmark

A technological education tool adjusted to the academic conditions and the needs of the end user, requires the identification of significant factors in the current training of students for the definition of a proper and effective proposal focused on complementing the traditional learning methodology.

One of these key factors in the pedagogical process is the achievement, because it is a clear evidence used in various international projects to take a measurement of the education quality and in which the country is not among one of the most prominent. Specifically, in the mathematics area this situation is evidenced in the national and international applied tests.

One of the tests in Colombia is the "Prueba Saber". Once the results of the last two years were analysed, it is evidence that in third and fifth grade there is a better achievement of the year 2015 to 2016, but in terms of the overall level of the third grade in front of the fifth-grade results are unfavourable.

At the national level, the percentage of students who are in the category of advanced maths achievement in third grade is higher compared to fifth grade and the opposite happens with the indicator of the percentage of students in level too low. See Table 1.

Table 1. Comparison results "Pruebas Saber" year 2015 and 2016.

Maths performance (%)		Third grade		Fifth grade	
		2015	2016	2015	2016
Advanced	National	27	30	13	14
	Bogotá D.C.	38	36	22	19
Insufficient	National	19	18	36	36
	Bogotá D.C.	8	10	20	23

According to the above analysis it was decided to direct the tool to students in fourth grade, because at this level it is necessary to strengthen the different math skills in order to improve the results in the fifth grade so that the percentage of advanced level is predominant on the insufficient.

It is important to deepen in the process of searching techniques, tools and methodologies, best practices for the training of elementary school children with the purpose of generating a greater benefit in the learning of mathematics students and thus produce a significant impact on education.

Vrellis, Mikropoulo and Moutsioulis [3] carried out a study about the attitude of students toward gesture-based interfaces. A simple construction activity was designed and tested both with Kinect and the traditional mouse. The main finding was that Kinect is preferred over the mouse; although it was less easy to use, it is identified that was intuitive for students. Therefore, it strengthens the idea of implementing the Kinect device as a means of interaction with the system.

Blair and Davis [4] established that through the use of the Kinect can be taught in a simple, fast and effective way a series of relatively complex concepts, being a familiar and attractive platform to students because it provides tangible, meaningful and enjoyable interactivity with the device. One of the successful solutions was the working with school groups interested in the fields of science, technology, engineering and mathematics (STEM).

It is important to bear in mind that the Kinect device is similar to a web camera and enables person to interact with an Xbox 360 or a computer in three-dimensional space using a depth infrared research camera and a standard RGB camera [5]. J. Sánchez highlights the relevance of the appropriation of the interactive learning for the success of the focused-environments education that allow the user to navigate through it and display the relevant information through the use of various input devices [6].

On the other hand, in the context of the Guide to the Basic Rights of learning that the Ministry of National Education puts at the disposal of the entire educational community, it is specified the knowledge and skills that every student must learn at the end of fourth grade and on which emphasis should be made in the search for effective teaching techniques.

3 Educational Tool

The tool was born as an idea of project at the Universidad Distrital F.J.C., developed by the authors of this article to contribute to the district in the mitigation of the current problems in educational institutions.

Kinect Park is the end product of the development of a tool for interactive learning in mathematics that uses the natural interface device Kinect, created to facilitate the learning process and improves the performance of students in fourth grade [8].

The virtual world to which the user can access consists of different islands, each with an environment characterized by particular elements to a season of the year. Students have the opportunity to interact in each island with a game developed for the learning of a main theme of the fourth-grade mathematics.

These topics were selected and grouped based on the guide of basic learning resulting in five major categories sets, basic operations, fractions, geometric shapes and angles. See Fig. 1. In each of the activities are test the knowledge and skills to overcome challenges that increase their difficulty allowing the student to strengthen their education.

Fig. 1. Kinect park modules.

In Fig. 2 there is one of the games included in the tool which aims to strengthen the knowledge with the basic operations such as addition, subtraction, multiplication and division. Given an operation with an incognito, the student has to complete the equation using the voice recognition and gestures included in the Kinect device.

Fig. 2. Island dry leaves.

In the Dark Island, the student must use their knowledge of mathematics to face the ultimate challenge forming with their arms the angle shown to lead a power to the evil magician who in turn will launch attacks in order to put an end to the intentions of the player; the student will be more assertive than the enemy in the launch of the attacks and in avoiding them by agile movements as displayed in Fig. 3.

The set of all games, educational thematic and multimedia elements give life to the interactive tool Kinect Park that will complement the educational process and will significantly increase the motivation and performance of students in the area of mathematics.

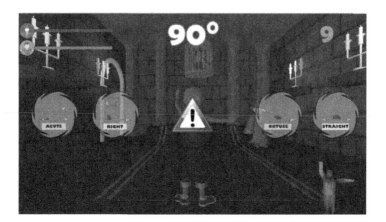

Fig. 3. Dark Island.

The results of the activities (hits, mistakes, time) are stored by the application for further analysis and generation of reports that will be useful for teachers, parents and educational institutions because allow to visualize the progress that students have in mathematics area.

4   Implementation

In this process is too important to the observation of the student's interaction with Kinect Park and the analysis of their reactions.

The presentation of the prototype is made in the San Jorge de Inglaterra School, in order that their students interact with the system to know the perception of the tool, the score and reaction times, the variation of the motivation, determining the degree of effectiveness of the implementation in a classroom.

According to the field work, it is identified that students can interrupt the reading of the Kinect in front of the user who is active in the game, due to external factors such as relocation of the student, need to get out of the classroom, among others.

For this reason, it is proposed a scheme of installation as shown in Fig. 4 where are listed seven main elements listed in the table, which are needed to optimize the interaction with the system and improving the student's learning experience.

It is important to highlight in this section the cooperative learning, as evidenced in the event, because despite the fact that only two students interact in real-time directly with the system, the other students contributed by encouraging and expressing the answer if their schoolmates had difficulties.

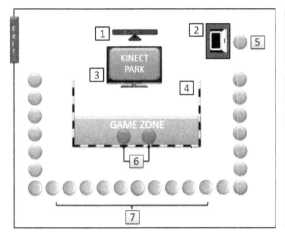

Convention	Equivalent
1	The Kinect device
2	Computer
3	Tv or projector
4	Play area delimitation
5	Teacher
6	Active Students
7	Students participating

Fig. 4. Installation diagram.

In the event were participating four courses, organized according to Fig. 4 and its graphic conventions. The study tool applied was an interview, which was divided into four sections in the following order:

1. Personal data: general information to identify the interviewee.
2. Before the practice: Questions about mathematics and educational video games.
3. Results: Record of the score and times obtained with the prototype.
4. After the practice: a series of questions about the experience with Kinect Park.

5   Results

It is of importance to the analysis of the information collected on the implementation of the tool in the educational institution since it allows to visualize the impact generated by the project in math students and generate a meaningful feedback for the improvement of Kinect Park.

One of the most important variables that are intended to analyse is the performance of students, being necessary to establish an indicator based on the difference of the scores obtained by the user in the activities development in the interactive tool. See Table 2.

Table 2. Results in the students' performance.

Interpretation	Indicator	No. of students
A very high improve	>7	6
High improve	5–7	13
Presents median improvement	3–4	19
Low improve	2	8
No improvement	<2	4
Total students	N/A	50

Based on the collected information is presented in Fig. 5 an overview of the performance obtained by students, considering that only 8% of children presented no improvement in carrying out the activity with the learning tool, but the 76% of the students presented an improvement classified at medium, high or very high.

Performance with Kinect park use

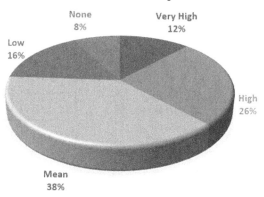

Fig. 5. Students performance.

After the practical activity with the educational tool is made an analytic exercise based on the perception that took students, aimed at determining the impact it had on the stimulation for the learning of mathematics; obtaining as a result that the 70% of the children prefer learning with Kinect Park in front of the use of traditional methodologies (Fig. 6).

Do you feel more enthusiasm to learn math by using Kinect park

Fig. 6. Motivation with Kinect Park.

It is possible to identify in the applied interview the enthusiasm of students by the activity carried out and the construction of different modules focused on other subjects, for example, Natural Sciences and Social Sciences; highlighting the interest in learning languages with this tool (Fig. 7).

Which other subjects do you like to learn with Kinect park

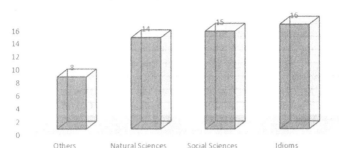

Fig. 7. Subjects of interest with Kinect Park.

6   Conclusions

With the implementation of the educational tool Kinect Park it is concluded that students demonstrate greater interest in learning mathematics with a technological device to involve body movements and other senses different to those used in traditional learning.

To ensure that students will gain a better performance in mathematics it is important that the tool is adapted to the progress of each one of the students, although they are all in the same grade: fourth grade, the knowledge and skills differ on an individual basis.

This adaptation is key to children do not feel frustration if the exercises are too complex or lose the motivation to not be generated new challenges for minds in constant development.

The inclusion of IT tools generates added value for educational institutions to provide the opportunity to improve the educational processes in the area, allowing their students benefit and strengthen their skills and knowledge.

References

1. Clavijo, S.: Desempeño educativo de Colombia: pruebas Pisa de 2013. La República, Bogotá D.C. (2014)
2. Osorio Villada, A.: Problemáticas educativas, docentes investigadores y política pública educativa de Bogotá. Instituto para la investigación educativa y el desarrollo pedagógico
3. Vrellis, I., Moutsioulis, A., Mikropoulos, T.: Primary school students' attitude towards gesture based interaction: a comparison between Microsoft kinect and mouse. In: IEEE 14th International Conference on Advanced Learning Technologies (2014)
4. Blair, T., Davis, C.: Innovate engineering outreach: a special application of the Xbox 360 Kinect sensor. In: IEEE Frontiers in Education Conference (FIE) (2013)

5. Sharma, S., Chen, W.: Multi-user VR classroom with 3D interaction and real-time motion detection. In: International Conference on Computational Science and Computational Intelligence (2014)

6. Sánchez, J.: Agentes animados en Macromedia Flash con síntesis de voz para ambientes de aprendizaje. Universidad de las Américas, Puebla (2005)

7. Sánchez Mena, F.: Estrategia de motivación en educación primaria. Universidad de Valladolid (2014)

8. Salazar Ortega, M., Villamizar Franco, E.: Prototipo de una Herramienta de Aprendizaje Interactivo que Implementa el Kinect para Estudiantes de Cuarto Grado de Primaria. Universidad Distrital F.J.C., Bogotá D.C. (2016)

Varicella Incidence Rate Forecasting in Bogotá D.C. (Colombia) by Stochastic Time Series Analysis

Wilson Sierra[1,2], Camilo Argoty[1], and Hugo Franco[1(✉)]

[1] Universidad Central, Bogotá, D.C. 110321, Colombia
{wsierra,cargotyp,hfrancot}@ucentral.edu.co
[2] Universidad Jorge Tadeo Lozano, Bogotá, D.C. 110321, Colombia

Abstract. This work presents a specific implementation of the Allard approach to the epidemiological time series analysis by ARIMA and SARIMA modeling, intended to describe and predict the epidemic behavior of Varicella in the city of Bogotá D.C. (Colombia). Model selection and preliminary forecast evaluation supported on the official accounts of Varicella incidence rate are performed and reported for the interval 2010–2015. This approach yields a SARMA(3,0,1)(1,0,1) model, whose forecasting results were evaluated against real data of the year 2016. Performance comparison with alternative models and their potential use in the support of epidemic surveillance are also discussed.

Keywords: Epidemiology · Time series analysis · Data analysis · Varicella · ARIMA · SARIMA

1 Introduction

Current research in epidemiology is increasingly focused on the development of models and tools for quantitative analysis of epidemic data, particularly time series consisting of incidence and prevalence accounts alongside environmental data related to each disease aetiology.

This is the case of Varicella (known as Chickenpox in native English speaking countries), a highly contagious disease whose aetiologic agent is the Varicella–Zoster Virus (VZV). Humans that have not suffered from varicella are especially prone to be infected. People get immune to VZV either after getting infected for the first time or by means vaccination [1]. Communication of the virus is the result of direct contact or air transmission, with a mean incubation time between 14 to 17 days. Two days before the end of this period, the infectious stage begins, lasting an average of 5 days [2].

Bogotá, the most populous Colombian city, has also the highest Varicella incidence in the country (about 201.002 cases between 2011 and 2015). According to the Instituto Nacional de Salud[1] (INS), this is almost one third of all

---

[1] Colombian National Institute of Health http://ins.minsalud.gov.co.

© Springer International Publishing AG 2017
J.C. Figueroa-García et al. (Eds.): WEA 2017, CCIS 742, pp. 647–658, 2017.
DOI: 10.1007/978-3-319-66963-2_57

varicella cases in Colombia (around 610.930 [3]). Beyond its intrinsic periodicity (probably related to regular school and vacation times in the educational calendar [4]), Varicella incidence data has a noticeable variability (see Fig. 1), characteristic of random processes. Thus, the studies of the Varicella epidemic dynamics is moving from deterministic approaches [5] to stochastic models, s.a. Markov chains involving Montercarlo methods [6], among others. Indeed, the combination of such models and approaches could yield interesting results for both epidemic dynamics description and incidence forecasting [7].

Allard [8] proposed a formal approach to apply time series analysis in epidemiological research and practice. This work adopted ARIMA and seasonal ARIMA (SARIMA) models to understand, from an stochastic point of view, the epidemic dynamics, and to provide methodological tools for epidemic forecasting. Since then, ARIMA and SARIMA models have been usually applied in recent literature to describe the epidemic dynamics of different diseases (mainly of contagious nature). In this line, Trottier et al. [9] studied the stochastic dynamics of several childhood contagious diseases by using a simple ARIMA model. In 2008, Kristotakis et al. [10] proposed a measure of the temporal effect of antibiotics using Vancomycin-resistant Enterococcus, using ARIMA models. In 2012, Critselis et al. [11] studied the seasonality of hospitalized varicella cases in Greece for the period 1982–2003, by means of ARIMA.

This paper presents a detailed implementation of the Epidemiology–oriented scheme of Allard [8] (Sect. 2), intended to define an ARIMA/SARIMA model which fits the best for the official accounts [3] of Varicella incidence in Bogotá D.C.(Colombia), and to evaluate its forecasting capabilities (Sect. 3). This method was applied to the interval 2010–2015, obtaining a SARMA(3,0,1)(1,0,1) model, whose forecast performance was tested against the real data accounted by the INS for the year 2016. Finally, a brief discussion of the obtained results and potential future activities is presented in Sect. 4.

2   Materials and Methods

2.1   Varicella Incidence Rate Data Acquisition and Preparation

This work is supported by official data from the Colombian public health surveillance system SIVIGILA[2], which is aimed to collect and organize the epidemiological information submitted by first level health institutions along the country, and its main repository is accessible via web browser and direct URL access, in MS Excel (XLSX) format. Specifically, incidence data are then represented by individual files per year. For this work, data for "Individual Varicella" (code 831 according to the CIE-10 standard [12]) were automatically downloaded and extracted from the corresponding link, then converted to plain UTF-8 comma separated values (CSV) files using the open source application ssconvert.

---

[2] Sistema Nacional de Vigilancia Epidemiológica (SIVIGILA) http://www.ins.gov.co/lineas-de-accion/Subdireccion-Vigilancia/sivigila/Paginas/sivigila.aspx.

These CSV files were merged into a single data file for Varicella, from the first record in the collection (January, 2007) to the current (updated) data (March, 2017), Universidad Central (Colombia). As usual for epidemiological systems, data records have a weekly basis (epidemiological week or *"epi–week"*). Since the Colombian official accounts became reliable around 2010, the Varicella incidence rate[3] data for the interval between 2010 to 2015 will be used as case study, while data for the year 2016 will support the selected model.

2.2   ARIMA Model Formulation for Varicella Incidence in Bogotá

Under this approach, it is essential to identify the inter-variable correlation for each of the random processes. This can be carried out by using the autocorrelation function, which measures the dependence level for every pairs of variables Y_t and Y_{t-k} in the time series by means of the corresponding correlation coefficients ρ_k, whose graphical representation is the "correlogram" given by the GNU R function acf() [13]. In addition, the Partial Autocorrelation function is included to estimate the relationship between Y_t and Y_{t-k}, but now excluding the dependence each of these variables has on the intermediate variables $Y_{t-1}, Y_{t-2}, ..., Y_{t-k+1}$. The forecast package function pacf() performs the necessary regressions to determine and represent the coefficients P_k.

Model Identification. An early exploration of incidence rate data can check seasonality features by performing a classical Fourier analysis, which is implemented in GNU R by using the function spec.pgram(). The first step in the Allard scheme [8] is the analysis of stationarity in a broad sense: verify if the time series has constant mean and variance along the set of observations and if the covariance between any pair of variables Y_{t_1}, Y_{t_2} depends only on the constant separation k between them.

Variance analysis: If the time series does not met the constant variance condition (or *homoscedasticity*), it is necessary to perform a Box-Cox transformation with parameter λ:

$$Y_t^\lambda = \begin{cases} \frac{Y_t^\lambda - 1}{\lambda} \to \lambda \neq 0 \\ ln(Y_t) \to \lambda = 0) \end{cases} \tag{1}$$

The best value for this parameter is estimated by invoking the function BoxCox.lambda(), which optimizes the likelihood function [14].

Mean analysis: To determine if the time series met the stationarity condition and deterministic trends, it is possible to use a graphical method as it is usual in the ARIMA/SARIMA literature. The inspection of both the autocorrelation plot (or

---

[3] The quotient of the new confirmed cases of disease in a particular location during an epidemiological week, divided by its total population.

"correlogram") from the Autocorrelation Function (ACF), and the Partial Auto-correlation Function ($PACF$) plot, allow the identification of significant correlations between the stochastic process variables by detecting correlation values outside the Bartlett bands[4]. Furthermore, correlation coefficients (ρ_k) could exhibit an oscillating behavior if there are relations among variables due to seasonal periodicities (i.e. the series corresponds to a *ciclostationarity* process [15]). This could prevent the rapid decay of the values for ρ_k associated to an uncorrelated time series, as it is further required by the ARIMA approach.

Thereafter, it can be necessary to apply a differentiation operator between Y_t and Y_{t-1} and/or Y_{t-s}, where s corresponds to each seasonal period, thus obtaining the values for parameters d y D of the non-seasonal and seasonal components of a SARIMA model, respectively. This step, implemented by the function diff(), must be applied once or more times on each component until the stationarity condition is reached.

Another approach is to identify the existence of unit roots within the autoregressive polynomial by the Augmented Dickey-Fuller (ADF) test [16] –applied to the ordinary component of a seasonal series–, or the Osborn, Chui, Smith and Birchenhall (OCSB) test –applied to the seasonal component of time series [17]. These hypotheses tests are implemented by their corresponding GNU R functions ndiffs() and nsdiffs(), which return the proper number of differentiations. The function ur.df from the urca package, determines the existence of roots within the unit circle and determines if including constants related to deterministic and stochastic tendencies is required.

Once the necessary differentiations are performed, new ACF and PACF graphs are obtained to identify the order of the parameters p, q, P and Q of the autoregressive and moving average polynomials. Finally, the Augmented Dickey–Fuller Extended test is applied to determine the average parameters in the deterministic and stochastic trend to be included in the final model. The function ur.df() is used to test the null hypothesis in accordance to the t-values.

Parameter Estimation. The model identification process yield a set of models suitable to represent the time series under study, in accordance to the corresponding statistical criteria. After that, it is performed the actual estimation of the best values for the parameters $(p, q)(P, Q)$ (equivalent to estimate the parameters of a SARMA model). Among several methods in the literature, the most common implementation relies on the Maximum Likelihood Estimation [13], assuming initial values for Y_t and for the white noise variables ϵ_t. For this calculation, the implicit optimization process is performed by the function Arima(), which tests for the different orders of the non-seasonal and seasonal components, together with the transformation parameters and the trend terms included in the model.

---

[4] This is the interval $[-2/T, 2/T]$ where T is the time series length.

Model Diagnostic and Selection. In this stage, the resulting candidate models are analyzed by a residual analysis, verifying if residuals have the same distribution of a white noise process and comply the condition of homoscedasticity. If these conditions are not achieved, the corresponding model is rejected; otherwise, it is marked as valid to perform forecast tasks in the context of the specific time series. To apply such tests (using the function `Box.test()` from the package `stats`), an inspection of the residual ACF graph is performed, and a Ljung-Box test [13] is applied to check that there are no significant correlations, i.e. that every correlation coefficient equals zero, assumed as null hypothesis:

$$H_0 : \rho_1, \rho 2, ...\rho k = 0 \tag{2}$$

To establish which candidate model best approaches the stochastic process that generates the data (noted as $\widehat{M}$) there are several statistical criteria in the literature. The Akaike information criterion (AIC) employs the likelihood function to find the model whose parameters provide the best fit to $\widehat{M}$, i.e., the model with lower value for the expression

$$\text{AIC} = -2ln\widehat{L} + 2(p + q + P + Q + k + 1) \tag{3}$$

where $\widehat{L}$ is the maximum likelihood function value, and the second term penalizes model overfitting. The Bayesian Information Criterion (BIC) looks for the best model approximating the real data source by constraining the probability of obtaining the actual time series Y_n to the very existence of the estimated ideal model, given the statistical structure of the candidate model under evaluation M (noted as the parameter set θ), thus leading to the conditional probability $P(Y_n \mid \theta, M)$. Under such approach, the BIC is stated [18] as

$$\text{BIC} = -2ln\widehat{L} + ln(T)(p + q + P + Q + k + 1) \tag{4}$$

where T is the time series length, then penalizing model overfitting. BIC calculation is implemented within the function `Arima()`.

These tests allow the selection of the best candidate model in the diagnostic stage, but do not provide further detail on the goodness-of-fit obtained by each model for the training data, nor the forecast performance of the model under evaluation. Therefore, both the Root Mean-Squared Error (RMSE) and the Mean Absolute Percent Error (MAPE) are used in this work to report the model deviation from the expected behavior for both fitting and forecasting processes

$$\text{RMSE} = \sqrt{\frac{1}{T} \sum_{i=1}^{T} \left| \widehat{Y}_t - Y_t \right|} \qquad \text{MAPE} = \frac{1}{T} \sum_{i=1}^{T} \frac{\left| \widehat{Y}_t - Y_t \right|}{Y_t} \times 100 \tag{5}$$

where T the length of the time series. Finally, since the ARIMA family consists of linear models, the quality of each model can be assessed in terms of the determination coefficient, which describes the variability ratio of Y_t.

2.3   Model Forecast Performance Evaluation

Predictive capabilities are among the most interesting features of ARIMA models. The GNU R function `forecast()` (from the `forecast` package) performs single point and interval predictions at confidence levels of 90% and 95%. In the first case, the forecast is obtained by using the Y_t estimation given by the selected model. The second case considers the standard deviation and the invertibility property of the series [19]. Thus, to evaluate the forecasting performance of the selected model, a forecast evaluation stage is carried out along the model diagnostic and selection phase, and the corresponding MAPE is calculated to assess the deviation of the forecast data from the observed data for a predefined testing interval (in this work, varicella incidence rate for the year 2016).

3   Results

3.1   Dataset Construction

To obtain a correct estimation of Varicella incidence rate for Bogotá D.C. (new cases in each epidemiological week over the size of the entire population) the raw incidence values from SIVIGILA were normalized using the official population estimate (*Secretaría de Planeación de Bogotá D.C.*). This rate, the main input for model identification and selection processes, constrained to the period between 2010 and 2016 (as mentioned above), is shown in Fig. 1. It is remarkable that the time series exhibits a slight decline since 2015, where the second semester peak appears less prominent with respect to the first semester peak than it was observed for previous years.

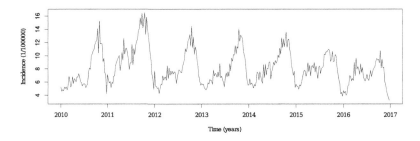

Fig. 1. Incidence rate of the varicella in the Bogotá D.C. (Colombia). Source: own elaboration.

3.2   Model Identification

Seasonality. The spectral analysis of Varicella incidence rate for the interval 2010–2016 confirms the presence of two main periods: 53.50 weeks and 26.78 weeks. The first of these periods is outside the annual cycle and the second is placed next to the middle of the year (though with little lags between cycles). This is consistent with the main contagious mechanism due to direct contact in scholar institutions [4], according to the Colombian educational calendar.

Stationarity

Variance analysis: In order to reduce variance, we applied a Box-Cox transform with $\lambda = -0.1$ for the interval 2010–2015. Using this potential transformation on the time series, a corrected version is obtained.

Mean analysis: Annual cycles oscillate around an almost constant mean value, except for 2011 (marked by specialized personnel as an epidemic year). There is no noticeable deterministic trend in the first order component. However, Fig. 2 shows an evident cyclostationarity, in consistency with the basic spectral analysis of the time series. On the other hand, Fig. 3 presents positive correlations up to the 10th week, where this relationship become inverse until week 43. The ACF also has an oscillatory nature with peaks at 52 and 104 lags, in consistency with such annual periodicity, induced by the original process. The slow correlogram decay points out that there is no seasonal trend, supporting the assumption of cyclostationarity (or "periodically correlated process [15]).

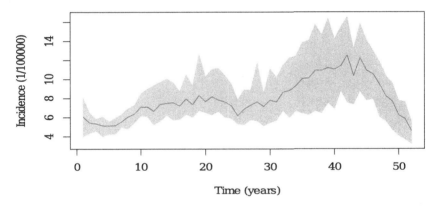

Fig. 2. Seasonal mean of the varicella incidence rate for the city of Bogotá D.C. 2010–2015 (blue line) and its corresponding variation (gray band) (Color figure online)

The unit root contrast test for the period 2010–2015 (performed by invoking the function ur.df), indicates that the Box-Cox transformed version of the series is stationary, even without differentiations, since the t-value equals -3.72, lying under the test critical value (tau3 $= -3.42$) at significance level of 5%. This leads to the rejection of the null hypothesis (unit root existence in the series autoregressive polynomial). Given a regression including a linear trend parameter, the statistic (phi2 equals 4.97, lying outside the acceptance region 4.71; thus, the hypothesis of unit root existence is rejected while confirming the inclusion of drift and time-dependent trend, at a significance level of 5%.

This result is confirmed by the return value of the ndiffs() function, indicating that no differentiation is required. However, the PACF plot in Fig. 3(b) presents a fast decay from the third lag and also a significant decay from around the annual period. This suggests that the model must have autorregressive ordinary and seasonal components of order 3 and 1, respectively, with parameters $d = D = 0$, including deterministic-trend parameters. The identification of a possible moving average process is not conclusive.

Parameter Estimation. Table 1 presents the parameter values obtained for the best models suggested by the unit root contrast test, i.e. SARIMA(3,0,0)(1,0,0) and SARIMA(3,0,1)(1,0,1) –as they are returned by invoking the function `Arima()` for the interval 2010–2015.

Table 1. SARIMA model coefficients representing the varicella incidence rate in Bogotá D.C. between 2010–2015

Parameter	SARIMA(3,0,1)(1,0,1)		SARIMA(2,0,0)(1,0,0)	
	Estimated value	Std. error	Estimated value	Std. error
ar1	−0.5815	0.0494	0.4247	0.0509
ar2	0.8971	0.0305	0.5008	0.0509
ar3	0.5060	0.0498		
ma1	0.9984	0.0073		
sar1	0.9985	0.0070	0.5469	0.0518
sma1	−0.9406	0.1331		
mean	−1.8486	0.1335	1.7877	0.1272

Model Diagnostic and Selection. Table 2 and the Fig. 4 show the residual tests and the model adjustment in the learning stage. According to those results, the SARIMA$(2, 0, 0)(1, 0, 0)$ do have a high residual correlation (Fig. 4(a)), so it does not pass the Ljung-Box test. On the other hand, the residuals of the SARIMA$(3, 0, 1)(1, 0, 1)$ model passed the Ljung-Box test and in the first lags

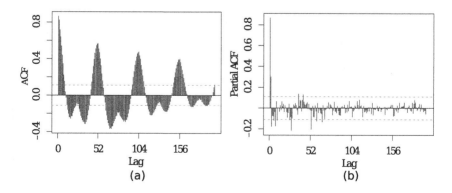

Fig. 3. Autocorrelation functions (ACF) and partial autocorrelation functions (PACF) of model residuals without differentiation

Table 2. Statistical tests for the varicella incidence rate series for Bogotá D.C. in the interval 2010–2015 (learn)

Model	R^2	Ljung-Box	AIC	BIC	RMSE	MAPE
SARIMA (2,0,0)(1,0,0)[52]	88.1%	3.077e−06	−573.2	−554.5	0.920	8.7%
SARIMA (3,0,1)(1,0,1)[52]	91.8%	0.081	−617.5	−587.6	0.764	7.1%

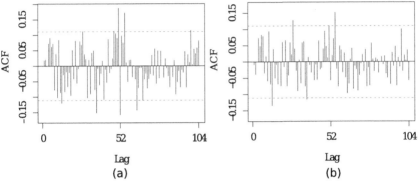

Fig. 4. Autocorrelation functions (ACF) for the model (2,0,0)(1,0,0)[52] (a) and Autocorrelation functions (ACF) for the model (3,0,1)(1,0,1)[52] (b)

of the ACF (Fig. 4(b)) does not exhibit a level of significance outside the lattice bands. In addition, the numerical tests of normality KS and LF with a significance level of 95% were within the acceptance zone of the null hypothesis, with p-value = 0.7477 and p-value = 0.3194 respectively. Then, the selected model for the varicella incidence rate time series for Bogotá D.C. between the years 2010 and 2015 is explicitly represented by the expression

$$(1 + 0.58L - 0.89L^2 - 0.50L^3)(1 - 0.99L^{52})Y_t$$
$$= -1.84 + (1 - 0.99L)(1 + 0.94L^{52})\epsilon_t \tag{6}$$

3.3   Forecast Evaluation

According to model selection, the SARIMA(3,0,1)(1,0,1) is capable of producing forecast values of varicella incidence rates in an epidemiological week basis. Figure 5(b) presents the corresponding point for the year 2016, while Fig. 5(a), in the sake of checking the model selection process robustness, shows the result of adjusting the model for the interval 2010–2014 to forecast the incidence rate of varicella in Bogotá D.C. for the year 2015.

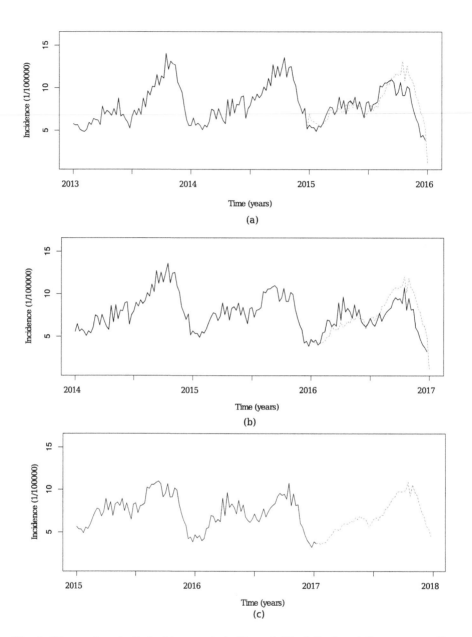

Fig. 5. Observed varicella incidence rate in Bogotá (black line) and the corresponding forecast (red line) for the training intervals 2010 to 2014 (a) –2015 forecast– and 2010 to 2015–2016 forecast. Independent selection model processes for each training interval yield a SARIMA$(3, 0, 1).(1, 0, 1)_{52}$ model. Preliminary forecast for the year 2017 yield by the selected model (c) is also shown. Source: own elaboration (Color figure online)

The RMSE and MAPE were calculated for the testing data, corresponding to the year 2016, after using the interval 2010–2015 as training data, yielding values of 1.6106 and 19.4% respectively. These values show that the model SARIMA(3,0,1)(1,0,1) provides reliable predictions, especially for the first half of the testing year, which exhibits lower variability.

4 Discussion and Future Work

The working data do have a seasonal nature with two main periods: a main 53 week period, whose length is close to the duration of an epidemiological year (52 weeks). The second one, between 26 and 27 weeks, lies near the half of the epidemiological year and could be related to the vacation time in the Colombian educational calendar. Another important aspect is that the function *auto.arima()* from the R package *forecast* suggested a seasonality process (given that one of the main periods is within the annual cycle and the other correspond to the annual cycle itself), in consistency with the model selection, which neglected non-seasonal and seasonal differentiations. This choice is supported by the unit root test and the visual inspection of ACF and PACF.

According the BIC criterion, the best choice within the autoregressive, mean average model family for the interval 2010–2015 is the SARIMA(3,0,1)(1,0,1) (Sect. 3.2); however, this structure is not preserved for the interval 2010–2016 (intended to forecast the incidence rate for the year 2017), since it didn't pass the residual test, and the entire model identification process applied to those data pointed out to a SARIMA(3,0,3)(1,0,1) as the suggested model (Fig. 5(c)).

The forecast capabilities of SARIMA(3,0,1)(1,0,1) were examined by using the evaluation method proposed in Sect. 2.3. In accordance to the forecast error (defined as the MAPE in this work), this SARIMA model yields a consistent forecast for the previously defined evaluation scenario. Thus, the model for Varicella incidence rate in Bogotá depends on both the three previous weeks and the previous year incidence values, but also on the variability of the previous week and the previous year, proving the seasonality of the Varicella incidence. Furthermore, the model dependence on the mentioned variability could be related to disease features s.a. the incubation period of this contagious disease.

Future work: Another stochastic or combined approaches, s.a. EGARCH or DSARIMA, could be evaluated under a similar scheme, looking for models with robust forecast potential effectively tested by rigorous statistical methods.

Future incidence reports should also take into account varicella incidence for younger children who will attend the scholar activities in next years, so it will be possible to evaluate the impact of vaccination (introduced around early 2015) on the overall epidemic dynamics.

References

1. Bardach, A., Cafferata, M., Klein, K., Cormick, G., Gibbons, L., Ruvinsky, S.: Incidence and use of resources for chickenpox and herpes zoster in Latin America and the Caribbean - a systematic review and meta-analysis. Pediatr. Infect. Dis. J. **31**(12), 1263–1268 (2012)
2. Masresha, B., Fall, A., Eshetu, M., Sosler, S., Alleman, M., Goodson, J., et al.: Progress towards measles pre-elimination, African region, 2011–2012. Wkly Epidemiol. Rec. **4**(14), 141–150 (2014)
3. Instituto Nacional de Salud: Reporte anual 2016, December 2016
4. Silhol, R., Boëlle, P.Y.: Modelling the effects of population structure on childhood disease: the case of varicella. PLoS Comput. Biol. **7**(7), e1002105 (2011)
5. Zibolenová, J., Ševĉoviĉ, D., Baška, T., Rošková, D., Malobická, E., Szabóová, V., Švihrová, V., Hudeĉková, H.: Mathematical modeling of infectious childhood diseases [matematické modelovanie infekĉných ochorení detského veku]. Cesko-Slovenska Pediatrie **70**(4), 210–214 (2015)
6. Ferrante, M., Ferraris, E., Rovira, C.: On a stochastic epidemic SEIHR model and its diffusion approximation. Test **25**(3), 482–502 (2015)
7. Hans, H., Roy, M., Viggo, A.: Modeling infectious disease dynamics in the complex landscape of global health. Science **347** I, aaa4339 (2015)
8. Allard, R.: Use of time-series analysis in infectious disease surveillance. Bull. World Health Organ. **76**(4), 327–333 (1998)
9. Trottier, H., Philippe, P., Roy, R.: Stochastic modeling of empirical time series of childhood infectious diseases data before and after mass vaccination. Emerg. Themes Epidemiol. **3**, 9 (2006)
10. Kritsotakis, E., Christidou, A., Roumbelaki, M., Tselentis, Y., Gikas, A.: The dynamic relationship between antibiotic use and the incidence of vancomycin-resistant enterococcus: time-series modelling of 7-year surveillance data in a tertiary-care hospital. Clin. Microbiol. Infect. **14**(8), 747–754 (2008)
11. Critselis, E., Nastos, P., Theodoridou, K., Theodoridou, M., Tsolia, M., Hadjichristodoulou, C., Papaevangelou, V.: Time trends in pediatric hospitalizations for varicella infection are associated with climatic changes: a 22-year retrospective study in a tertiary Greek referral center. PLoS ONE **7**(12), e52016 (2012)
12. Rivadeneira, A.G.: Clasificación internacional de enfermedades (cie): Descifrando la cie-10 y esperando la cie-11. Monitor Estratégico (7), Enero-junio 2015
13. Wei, W.W.: Time Series Analysis - Univariate and Multivariate Methods, 2nd edn. Pearson Addison-Wesley, Boston (2006)
14. Hyde, S.: Likelihood based inference on the Box-Cox family of transformations: SAS and MATLAB programs. Ph.D. thesis, Montana State University (1999)
15. Gardner, W.A., Napolitano, A., Paura, L.: Cyclostationarity: half a century of research. Sig. Process. **86**(4), 639–697 (2006)
16. Said, S.E., Dickey, D.A.: Testing for unit roots in autoregressive-moving average models of unknown order. Biometrika **71**(3), 599–607 (1984)
17. Osborn, D.R., Chui, A.P., Smith, J.P., Birchenhall, C.R.: Seasonality and the order of integration for consumption. Oxford Bull. Econ. Stat. **50**(4), 361–377 (1988)
18. Montesinos López, A.: Estudio del aic y bic en la selección de modelos de vida con datos censurados (2011)
19. Hyndman, R.J.: Forecast: forecasting functions for time series and linear models. R package version 8.0 (2017)

Adaptation of a Teaching Laboratory of Mechatronics Area for an Undergraduate Mechanical Engineering Program

Alberto Enrique Loaiza García(✉)🆔, Ruth Edmy Cano Buitrón🆔,
Phil Anderson Pontoja Caicedo🆔, and José Isidro García Melo🆔

Universidad del Valle, Cali 760001, Colombia
{alberto.loaiza, ruth.cano, phil.pontoja,
jose.i.garcia}@correounivalle.edu.co

Abstract. Considering the impact of technological advances in mechanical engineering applications, the program offered in this profession at the University of Valle, Cali, Colombia added more than a decade the area of mechatronics. In consequence, it was necessary to adequate current infrastructure to complement the theoretical knowledge acquired in this new area. This paper presents the strategy used to adapt an infrastructure that facilitates learning through experimentation with the "mechatronics principles" course. Many aspects of user-centered design techniques were considered, such as usability, ergonomics, functionality, costs, among others. Thus, a functional prototype of mechatronics workstation was designed and manufactured.

Keywords: Lab design · Mechanical engineering · Mechatronics · User centered design

1 Introduction

The School of Mechanical Engineering at the Universidad del Valle has the mission of training personnel, through the generation, diffusion and transfer of knowledge in the fields of Mechanical Engineering, having as its thematic axes research, teaching and extension (industry research), contributing to the generation, adaptation and transfer of strategic knowledge for the region and country development. To accomplish this, the university development plan 2015–2025 identifies five strategic issues to formulate lines of action that favor the university community, including the permanent updating of didactic resources and laboratories for each academic programs. To reach an effective infrastructure in laboratories is necessary a correct planning of the use of the personnel, technical and economic resources.

According to the quality management system of laboratories at the Universidad del Valle, training laboratories can be classified into three groups: development, research and education. Where, developmental laboratories focus on the taking of experimental data under controlled conditions solving specific questions of a phenomenon, oriented to the design and development of products or prototypes and their validation. For their part, research laboratories are used to expand knowledge of a specific area and

© Springer International Publishing AG 2017
J.C. Figueroa-García et al. (Eds.): WEA 2017, CCIS 742, pp. 659–666, 2017.
DOI: 10.1007/978-3-319-66963-2_58

education labs are designed to complement theoretical knowledge in different educational programs [1]. The last group being a growing need within the academic program of mechanical engineering at the Universidad del Valle.

The accelerated development of technology has created a gap between the teachings of traditional mechanical engineering education and the skills that graduates are expected to acquire before participating in the industrial sector, the future professionals are increasingly faced with automated systems and must have a basic knowledge of their operation and use [2]. To respond to this growing need, the academic program of mechanical engineering through resolution 075 of 2002 updated the academic pensum adding the mechatronics line to the traditional three lines of work: solids, thermal and fluids. This scenario generated a growing need for a teaching laboratory infrastructure that would allow students to be familiar with the non-mechanical technologies needed to make a modern electromechanical product. In this way, the teaching methodology try to use experimentation with emphasis on electronics and software to educate students with interdisciplinary knowledge [3]. In this context, this article shows a procedure carried out for the design and construction a test laboratory for the experimental practices of the "mechatronics principles" course of the academic program of Mechanical Engineering at the Universidad del Valle located in the city of Cali, Valle del Cauca, Colombia.

The article is divided into five sections. The following section presents some background related with didactic workstations developed in different universities. Then, a description of the methodological procedure for the procedure design is presented. Next, the design and manufacture of a functional prototype is presented. Finally, relevant comments are presented in the conclusions.

2 Background

According to [2], mechatronics is an integrative discipline in the mechanical, electronic, electrical, control, measurement and computer science areas, which aims to provide innovative solutions in the products, processes and systems developed. The role of a mechanical engineer in mechatronics can be understood by two aspects, design and mechanical operations, therefore, a successful mechatronics system must take into account the parameters of the mechanical system embedded in it, any change in these parameter will change the conditions of control and operation of the mechatronic system. In this context, the mechatronic solutions given in industry can vary regionally, nationally and even internationally. In the educational sector, a search was made of the different alternatives used for teaching mechatronics in the mechanical engineering program in different universities of the world. Below are presented some of the workstations developed in different institutions taken into account in this work as background.

In the University of Southern California [4] is used a module called EVB development for the course "Microcontrollers in mechanical engineering". At the University of Santa Barbara [5] the course "laboratory sensors, actuators and computer interfacing" has a design control system laboratory dedicated to teaching. The laboratory contains ten stations, which can be occupied by two students, for a total of twenty students. The Mechanical Engineering program at the University of Kattering [6] has fifteen microcontroller trainers TLCS 900H and evaluation boards (EVBs), which were integrated with a general interface and a display (GIDB), a conditioning signal board (SCB) and a high current controller board (HCDB). The Universidad Nacional de Cuyo [7] implemented a laboratory to teach mechatronics in the mechanical engineering program.

Based on this information a decision matrix was performed (see Table 1). to compare some features in each laboratory, aspects as modularity, ergonomics, functionality, maintenance, cost and auxiliary components were considered, in order to identify which of these alternatives could be adapted to the needs of the mechatronics laboratory required by the academic program of Mechanical Engineering at the Universidad del Valle. The results allowed to identify that none of the workstations developed in other institutions completely fit in full to the programmatic content of the course "principles of mechatronics", for this reason, it was decided to design a learning workstation to the particular needs of the course.

Table 1. Decision matrix features learning modules. (a) Modularity, (b) Ergonomics, (c) Functionality, (d) Maintenance, (e) Cost and (f) Auxiliary components.

Backgrounds	Comparison features					
	(a)	(b)	(c)	(d)	(e)	(f)
EVB development module	x		x			x
Microprocessor trainer and evaluation board			x		x	x
Learning module ALECOP	x		x			x
FESTO workstations	x	x	x	x		x
Ball and pendulum positioning system			x		x	x
Modular mechatronics learning kit	x		x	x		x

3   Procedure for the Mechatronics Laboratory Adaptation

A sequential methodological procedure was structured for the development of the experimental laboratory (workstation), which starts with a bibliographical query to establish the requirements, followed by a design phase of the test workstation. Once the basic design was finished, a detailed design was carried out. Finally, the manufacturing specifications were made that allowed a later construction.

4   Workstation Design

The requirements and detailed design of each components of the workstation are described below.

4.1   Structure of the Workstation

Ergonomic requirement. The design of the workstation not only had to meet the teaching needs, but also had to comply with the requirements of the regulations related to the design of workstations. Some aspects considered in those regulations are: the configuration of the workstation, the furniture and the posture. In this way, the workstation should consider ergonomic aspects that favor safety, health and working condition. Some of the ergonomic factors considered were: position and posture, work plans, reach area of the upper limbs, optimization of the disposition working area, planning works methods, workspace security conditions and visual fields. The set of these requirements allowed to define the structure of the workstation, and the distribution of the laboratory space, which are explained in the following sections.

Specifications of the structure. The desk dimensions were defined (see Fig. 1). It has a working radius of 650 mm, a work surface of 0°, this to avoid slippage elements, also, it has a panel in 50° to facilitate assembly of the elements, to provide a larger work area on the surface of the desk. The inclined panel is 249 mm length, allowing the student to extend his arms as norms recommended.

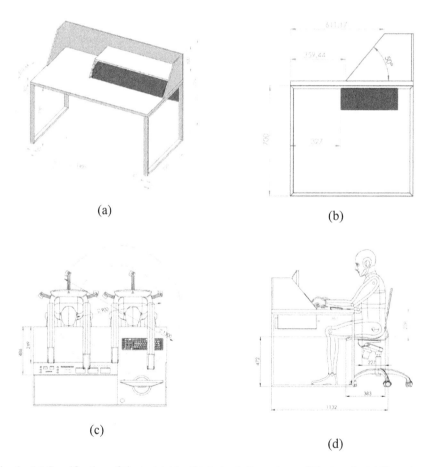

(a)

(b)

(c)

(d)

Fig. 1. (a) Specification of the test table, (b) Lateral dimensions of the bench, (c) Top view of the workstation and the user, (d) Side view of the bank and the user (units in mm).

4.2   Design of Electronic, Electrical and Mechanical Systems for Experimental Practices

Next, the processes for the design of the electronic, electrical and mechanical systems will be described.

Hardware requirements. Requirements electronic and electrical of each laboratory practices to be performed in the laboratory are presented (see Fig. 2). Considering common characteristics of mechatronic equipment, it is observed that for the course "mechatronics principles" six practices must be addressed: control sensor (position and speed), timing system (interruptions), communication (serial), motor control (pwm), digital inputs and outputs (switches, buttons and leds) and concept integration.

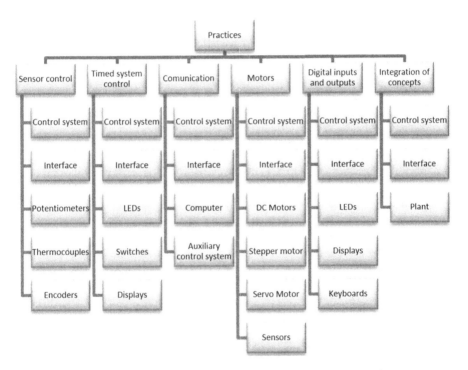

Fig. 2. Requirements for electrical and electronic laboratory practices.

Control System Requirements. The control system (microcontrollers) must have the minimum specifications to carry out the tasks of the objectives set out in the course. In this way, the microcontroller must have: digital inputs and outputs, analog-digital converters, PWM outputs, USB communication, TWI communication and SPI communication, this should also be programmable in a C and/or C++ language, and an open source platform. According to these requirements, an Arduino DUE was selected for the control system. This device has features as memory into two blocks of 256 KB, each of the pins can be used as inputs or outputs, has eight PWM outputs, and so on.

Specifications of the practice interfaces. The system must have different interfaces for the input and output of digital signals, global inputs and outputs, DC motor control, AC power devices and the control panel. Below are the specifications of some of the interfaces required for the practices to be performed on the workstation.

- Interface Digital input: The digital inputs, can couple the all inputs, switches and buttons with Arduino DUE.
- Interface Digital Output: The digital output allows to visualize the output state of the development board.
- Control panel: The control panel has all electronic and mechanics components connection (see Fig. 3).

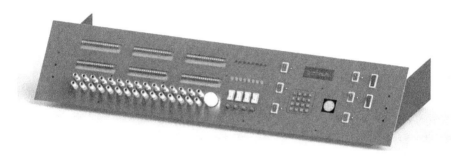

Fig. 3. Mechatronics workstation panel.

4.3   Manufacturing and Implementation of a Functional Prototype

The construction and use of mechatronics workstations (see Fig. 4) have favored the strengthening of the theoretical concepts, through the different practices carried out in it, as well as the development of an integrative project, as part of the evaluation method of the course "mechatronics principles".

Additionally, the laboratory was distributed in three areas. An exhibition area, that allows the teacher to present the theoretical concepts (area A). An area where twelve modules are placed or experimentation area (area C) and an assembling area (area B), (see Fig. 5).

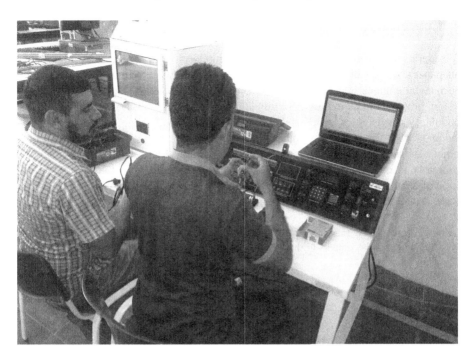

Fig. 4. Use of the functional mechatronics workstation prototype.

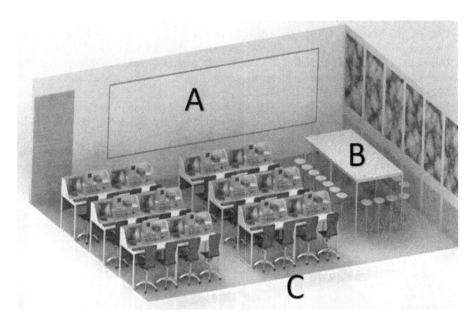

Fig. 5. Workbench for course of mechatronics, (a) Exhibition area, (b) Assembling area, (c) Experimentation area.

5 Conclusions

Considering the need to educate mechanical engineers in electronics and informatics, this paper discusses the adequacy of an experimental infrastructure in the context of the mechanical engineering program of the Universidad del Valle. Thus, a user-centered design process oriented in the fulfillment requirements of various types, such as: modularity, ergonomics, functionality, costs, maintenance, among others. In this way, not only were the minimum conditions ensured for learning by experience in this subject, but also a sustainability over time. This work encourages the development of a laboratory infrastructure by the academic programs and not only consider the acquisition of commercial solutions that are traditionally expensive and do not fully conform to the academic contents of the program.

Acknowledgment. To the School of Mechanical Engineering, Universidad of the Valley, Cali-Colombia, for the support in the construction and development of the mechatronics workstations of this work.

References

1. Feisel, L.D., Rosa, A.J.: The role of the laboratory in undergraduate engineering education. Eng. Educ. **94**(1), 121–130 (2005)
2. Ceccarelli, M., Erika, O., Giuseppe, C.: A role of mechanical engineering in mechatronics. In: Improving Stability in Developing Nations through Automation 2006, pp. 31–36. Elsevier Science and Technology, Vienna (2006)
3. Carryer, J.E.: Mecatrónica: El Impacto de la Ubicuidad de la Información en la Educación de los Ingenieros mecánicos. An. mecánica y Electr. Asoc. Ing. del ICAI, pp. 3–5 (2002)
4. Giurgiutiu, V., Lyons, J., Rocheleau, D., Liu, W.: Mechatronics/microcontroller education for mechanical engineering students at the University of South Carolina. Mechatronics **15**(9), 1025–1036 (2005)
5. Ranaweera, A., Bamieh, B., Par, V.: Sensors, actuators, and computer interfacing laboratory course at the University of California at Santa Barbara. Mechatronics **15**(6), 639–650 (2012). Sci. Intell. Mach.
6. Hargrove, J.: Curriculum, equipment and student project outcomes for mechatronics education in the core mechanical engineering program at Kettering University. Mechatronics **12**(2), 343–356 (2012). Sci. Intell. Mach.
7. Puglesi, A.E., Bernasconi, M.S.: Equipo educativo para La Enseñanza de la Mecatrónica. Sistema De Bola y Barra, vol. 16, pp. 57–70 (2012)

A New Method to Detect Apneas in Neonates

Carlos Marcelo Pais$^{(\boxtimes)}$ and Santiago Arévalo González$^{(\boxtimes)}$

Cybernetics Laborary, Faculty of Engineering, Universidad Nacional de Entre Ríos,
Ruta Provincial 11, Km 10, 3100 Oro Verde, Entre Ríos, Argentina
cpais@ingenieria.uner.edu.ar, sarevalog@correo.udistrital.edu.co

Abstract. In this work it was developed a new method to detect apneas in neonates infants through ECG and oximetry records.

The work has been carried out and evaluated using The Apnea-ECG Database. The developed method analyzes automatically the register of the electrocardiogram and oximeter records and identifies periods of the normal breath and apneic incidents. The base of the proposed method is a system of pattern recognition that identifies the apnea through the analysis based on the domain of the frequency and the time of the ECG signal and the time domain of the oximeter signal. The method was evaluated using a crossed validation with 10 iterations and presents an error of 4.77 %. There is a specificity of 95.78% and a sensibility of 94.61% obtained.

Keywords: Neonates pathology · Sleep apnea · Fisher discriminant · Pattern recognition · ECG · Oximetry · Machine learning · Supervised learning

1 Introduction

Infant mortality is defined as the number of deaths that affect the pediatric population during their first year of life. It is a sensitive and commonly used indicator for measuring the health status of the population, as it relates to different social, cultural and economic aspects. Infant mortality is linked, among other reasons, with hypoxia, which represents, one of the leading causes of neonatal deaths (34.7% of all neonatal deaths [13]). To achieve their reduction, considerable investment and resources are required. This work will focus on the reduction of this mortality facing one of its possible causes: apnea of the newborn. In general, in the newborn population, apnea can produce hypoxia (directly related to the duration of the apnea episode), which can lead to alterations in central respiratory control, motor tone, and cardiac function. These ventilatory pauses have immediate blood and cardiovascular effects. In addition, it is necessary to take into account the long-term repercussions that repeated episodes of pathological apnea may have on subsequent neurodevelopmental development or the progression of others processes, such as retinopathy of prematurity, etc. [9].

The cardio-respiratory system of adults and neonates were analyzed. The purpose is the comprehension of the anatomy and physiology of these systems

© Springer International Publishing AG 2017
J.C. Figueroa-García et al. (Eds.): WEA 2017, CCIS 742, pp. 667–678, 2017.
DOI: 10.1007/978-3-319-66963-2_59

and in this way, to understand the causes and effects of the studied pathology. The special features of the neonates are identified. These are related to the adult population and it is concluded that, from the point of view of the apneic episodes etiology, the major part of the anatomic differences of the intra-uterine life are closed physiologically in the first hours of life after the birth [5]. This permits that the development and the analysis of the method of records of adults could be extrapoled to the neonatal infants. This comparison is briefly exposed in this work as it focuses on the discriminant model performed.

To end up with the theoretical analysis, there are shown different techniques, which were used on the basis of the ECG and the oximeter records for the identification of the apneas. These particular signals are analyzed because the state of the art exposes relevant features in the discrimination of apneic events.

2   Physiology of the Newborn

The cardio-respiratory system has physiological changes at birth which require the initiation of complex mechanisms of homeostasis, maturation of organs and systems necessary to survive outside the maternal uterus. All these complex modifications that occur during the neonatal period are called adaptations. It is the stage of greatest vulnerability in the life of the human being and where there are more chances of getting sick and dying or presenting severe sequelae, particularly neurological ones. Many of the problems that afflict the newborn are closely related to some flaw in this adaptive mechanism [9].

The delivery of oxygen in a fetus in the uterus varies considerably with that of a newborn. The fetus has particular mechanisms that maximize the efficiency of circulation, but once the baby is born, the circulatory system begins to resemble that of an adult.

It is understood that it is feasible to make analogies between the cardio-respiratory system of the term neonate and the adult, in view of the proportions of oxygen saturation between the adult and the neonates correspond to the same proportions (between 92% and 98%) and are not altered by the anatomical features of the neonate without pathology (anatomical shunts). In addition, the heart rate and respiratory frequency ranges are perfectly established for both adults and neonates [18]. Considering that the model used is based on supervised learning, the result is adapted to the population delivered for training. However, preterm neonates are excluded in this project due to the immaturity (ductus arteriosus persistence, intraventricular and immaturity communications of the nervous system) that can modify the ECG morphology along with the time-related variables.

3   Introduction to the Apnea

An apnea is an episode of absence of respiratory flow lasting more than 20 s, irrespective of the clinical repercussion, or episodes of absence of flow in the lower airway accompanied by cardiocirculatory repercussion (bradycardia and/or hypoxemia).

For accurate apnea diagnosis, various records are required: toric impedance, cardiac frequency, oxygen saturation, and nasal flow measurement. The importance of home supervision is summarized in the timely detection of alterations in respiratory registers that are indicative of metabolic alterations, caused by the presence of more prolonged apneas than the system allows. These alterations can break the homeostasis of the organism and can lead to a hypoxia that can be fatal.

4   Measurement of Respiratory Signs and Assessment of Apnea

The control of physiological indexes provides data that allow to respond to therapy and trends to avoid any catastrophe. Physiological records can be obtained by direct or indirect methods. The direct ones are those that record the movement or other property of the airflow that enters and leaves the lungs, coupling a sensor in the airway. In contrast, indirect monitoring does not sense air movement, but variables related to air are measured.

Indirect methods are preferred for supervision in children, due to it does not require contact with the airway or with the flow of air entering and leaving the lungs, and they are noninvasive which makes them easier to connect.

It will be detailed in electrocardiography and oximetry in view that they have been found to have properties that allow the identification of apneic events. They also have the advantage of being non-invasive methods suitable for home supervision of neonates.

4.1   Heart Rate Variability

The intervals between the beats of a heart (cardiac period) show differences in duration that result in changes in heart rate. The new computational methods have facilitated the measurement and storage of these intervals, promoting the study of their variability over time, which is known as the Heart Rate Variability (HRV). The HRV can be analyzed in the frequency domain (spectral analysis). The spectrum is divided into frequency bands and on this basis the spectral density of each band expressed in ms^2 is estimated. The definition of the bands are defined in Table 1.

Previous work has shown that the energy in the VLF band is an element that allows the identification of apneic events [22, 24].

There are statistical methods that use measurements in the time domain of the HRV signal. These methods are simple to perform and have been evaluated as apnea discriminant. For example, different investigations concluded that the typical deviation of the RR intervals (SDNN (ms)), the mean RR intervals [3, 20] and the square root of the mean sum of the squared differences between RR intervals (RMSSD (ms)) [3] are relevant features in the automatic detection of apneas.

Table 1. Spectral elements of HRV signal [24]

Power	Frequency range
VLF	0.003–0.04 Hz
LF	0.04–0.15 Hz
HF	0.15–0.4 Hz

4.2 Oximetry

The measurement of the relative concentration of O_2 in the blood in the body can be carried out by the infrared absorption spectroscopy technique.

The term SpO_2 refers to peripheral SaO_2 (Oxygen saturation in the arteries) Rajadurai et al. [19] compared SpO_2 and SaO_2 in neonates and demonstrate the linear relationship ($SpO2 = 0.75SaO_2 + 24.43$). Similar to the ECG signal, previous studies have used temporal and frequency elements of this signal for the diagnosis of apneas. The temporal characteristics of this signal include the percentage of time below a certain level of saturation, the mean of the signal and the number of drops in oxygen saturation per hour [4,10,14]. Among the frequency-based features are the location and the energy of the frequency peaks in the SpO_2 spectrum [12,15,25]. There are some other methods, such as EMD (empirical mode decomposition) [21], that explore in a different way the manifestations of apnea.

During the apnea, the time response of the oximetry is sufficiently rapid to detect changes in SpO_2 (5 to 7 s), no calibration requires and can remain continuously installed. Although many authors [1,2,25] has demonstrated that oximetry offers high specificity (100%), it has a very low sensitivity (31–36%). Because of this, the oximeter produces many false negative readings when used as a single input in an apnea detector [11].

5 Features Based on Oximeter Signals and HRV

5.1 Model

This study has adopted components that come from the field of pattern recognition using supervised learning. In general terms, a data set must be delivered with the "correct answer" and the aim of the algorithm is to generate more correct answers. In other words, the system processes the data and places them as "normal breathing" or "apnea event". This can be represented as two-block process sequence: Generation of candidates and Classification of those candidates. A *candidate* is a section of the record with a unspecified size; Window defined by a fixed time fraction [6]. Chazal demonstrates that 60 s is probably the natural time scale associated with an apnea [3]. The classifier takes incoming candidates, and recognizes or identifies similarities between classes of interest. That is, if it is similar to some of the inter-class, then it emits a "positive assumption", otherwise throw a "negative assumption". To design the classifier, initially relevant elements are obtained in the discrimination of apneas in the training samples. These training samples are based on the criteria of medical experts, in other words, derived from the opinion of the medical doctor whether or not there is apnea in that fraction of the record. Within the classifier an element called *the descriptor* is defined. It distributes the windows in a "feature space" in such a way that the inter-elements are grouped in a given region and separated from the rest. The descriptor is defined as a column vector of n elements $x = \begin{bmatrix} x_1 \\ \vdots \\ x_n \end{bmatrix}$.

Each element of the descriptor is a feature that allows the identification of the class of information. It is to be expected that the greater the number of features the better the descriptor, but this has a high computational cost which is not desired. Therefore, one of the important tasks is to identify which features are most relevant and which can be omitted (this is called regularization).

On the other hand, in order to delineate the different regions of the feature space, it is necessary to create a *boundary* separating the apneic events from the others. Boundaries can be simple or complex, they can be seen as hyperplanes or hypersurfaces. In the present work the most simple border is used (see next section): a straight plane perpendicular to the feature space that divides it into two parts. The equation of the hyperplane is defined as:

$$w_0 + \sum_{i=1}^{n} w_i x_i = 0 \tag{1}$$

In the above equation we have the components of the vector that defines the hyperplane and of course, the coordinates within the feature space where that hyperplane is defined.

The physiological knowledge of the manifestation of apnea in the HRV and the oximeter signal is used to identify the best descriptors.

5.2 Data Base

It was shown that for the recognition of apneas in neonates, adult SpO_2 and cardiac frequency records can be used, on account that their interpretation is not affected by the physiological peculiarities of the neonates (anatomical shuts and fetal hemoglobin). The high metabolic rate of neonates makes the ranges of the instantaneous cardiac and respiratory frequency signals different from that of adults, however, the sudden percentile changes, due to the apneas observed in adults are similar to those in neonates.

For this reason, it was used the database 'The Apnea ECG Database' developed by Dr. Thomas Penzel of the University of Phillips, Marburg, Germany and entered into the PhysioNet PhysioBank file [8]. The database has a digital characterization file of electrophysiological signals (ECG, Abdominal respiratory effort signals obtained by thoracic inductance plethysmography, oronasal flow measurements using nasal thermistors, SpO_2 and apnea annotations) and related data for the use of the biomedical research community. The records come from 25 men and 7 women with an average age of 41 years (27–63 years).

The extraction and computation of the data were done on Matlab® mathematical software of Mathworks, version R2015a.

5.3   Descriptors

Some of the descriptors that have shown the best results in the state of the art [3,10,20] have been chosen. The elements considered in the study are:

– Features in the frequency domain of heart rate variability.
– Features in the time domain of heart rate variability.
– Features in the time domain of the oximetry signal.

It is worth noting that none of the measures mentioned above takes into account the ECG morphology. It is implicitly assumed that the processes that produce apnea occur in a place outside the heart and therefore do not directly affect the potential cardiac outputs generated (reason why preterm neonates are excluded in this model).

Descriptors based on the HRV signal. The HRV can be computed from any signal that identifies a given phase of the cardiac cycle; such as sounds, echocardiographic images, doppler effects, and any other form of cardiac activity recording. However, as already mentioned, ECG is the most used tool because it allows very simple recordings and with very accurate references, such as the waves of the ventricular complex QRS (in particular the R wave). We performed the detection of RR intervals of the registers by the Pan-Tompkins algorithm. This algorithm is one of the most recognized methods for detecting the QRS complex, detecting 99.3% of the QRS complexes [17]. The implementation of the Pan-Tompkins algorithm by Hooman Sedghamiz from Linkoping University for Matlab was used [23].

Descriptors based on the oximetry signal. Three features in the time domain of the SpO_2 register have been extracted: The mean SpO_2 value, the minimum SpO_2 value and the number of values lower than 92% of the saturation in each of the windows of 60 s.

Spectral analysis. The energy derived from the power density spectrum of the HRV in the very low frequency band (FMB (ms^2)) of each of the candidates has been evaluated. For this, it is necessary to find the distribution of the power of the signal as a function of the frequency. This is known as the power spectral density (PSD). It is given by the expression:

$$PSD(f) = \frac{1}{f_s N}|X(f)|^2 \tag{2}$$

The spectral compute ($X(f)$) was performed with the non-parametric Welch analysis technique. This was done with the aim of reducing the discontinuities in the window edges of the time-domain truncation generated by the Fourier transform-based techniques and the spectral leakage problems.

Figure 1(a) and (b) shows the PSD expressed in dB/Hz. It is evident that there is a fall in the average value of the power spectral density in the VLF band of candidates with an apnea event with respect to the qualified candidates with normal breathing.

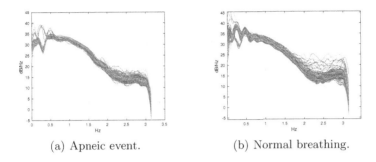

(a) Apneic event.   (b) Normal breathing.

Fig. 1. PSD candidates

The energy (E) of the signal in the frequency domain is given by:

$$E = \sum_{k=0}^{N-1} |PSD(k)|^2 \tag{3}$$

where k is a given discrete frequency and N represents the total of frequencies. In the particular case of obtaining the energy of the VLF band, k takes values between 0.003 and 0.04.

Temporal analysis. The following features which were extracted from the HRV signal were generated for use as apnea classifiers:

- Typical onset of each RR interval (ms)
- Mean RR intervals (ms)
- RMSSD (ms) (Root mean square successive difference)

The RMSSD is defined as the root square of the average of the differences between the adjacent NN intervals. It is defined in Eq. 4.

$$RMSSD = \sqrt{\frac{1}{N-1} \sum (RR_{i+1} - RR_i)^2} \tag{4}$$

where RR_i is a given interval, RR_{i+1} is the next interval and N is the total number of intervals (in the 1 min window).

Seven descriptors that several studies recommend for the apnea discrimination are obtained. Each window with a sample f_s of 100 times per second and 60 s of duration has 6000 elements, the window becomes a candidate described as a vector column of 7 elements. With the selected descriptors, the pattern recognition method proposed in Fig. 2 is used.

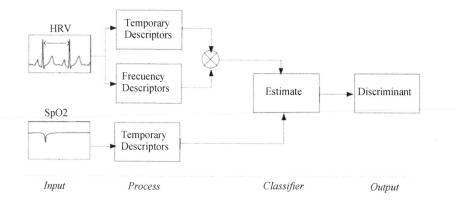

Fig. 2. Apnea identification system. Modified from [4].

6   Classification and Evaluation

There are many ways to combine descriptors, the problem is to decide which combination is the best and the easiest method to detect apneas.

The combinations of the features extracted from the oximetry isolated were performed. Likewise, the features that were obtained from the HRV isolated were combined. It is observed that a linear discriminant in the features spaces obtained from the HVR might not be the most appropriate. So, the features of the HVR have been combined with the features of the oximetry. Some of the results are shown in the Fig. 3. This has generated feature spaces that are not only suitable for linear discriminants but also for other classifiers.

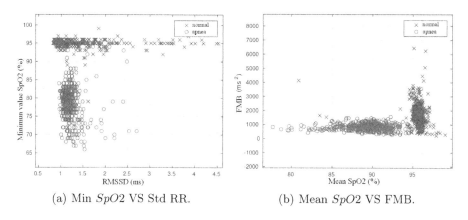

(a) Min $SpO2$ VS Std RR.   (b) Mean $SpO2$ VS FMB.

Fig. 3. Feature spaces based on temporal and frequency characteristics of the HRV signal and oximetry

The boundary was performed with one of the most popular techniques used to classify: Linear discriminant analysis (LDA). The purpose of this is finding discriminant functions or decision rules $C = C(x_1, ..., x_n)$, which allow to assign each of the descriptors or vectors of interest to a specific population, minimizing the error rate. Where C is a linear function [7]. The LDA is similar to the analysis of variance (ANOVA) that works by comparing the means of the variables, based on these assumptions:

- The predictors are independent
- Values are normally distributed
- Variations between groups are similar

The creation of the discriminants was done either using the MATLAB® Statistics and Machine Learning Toolbox.

To verify the normality assumption, the Jarque-Bera test was performed on the extracted features of the signals. In the features: Values less than 92% of SpO_2 (less92), Mean SpO_2, Minimum value SpO_2 (min SpO_2), Typical Deviation RR (RR std), Mean RR and RMSSD, the P (significance) value is less than 0.01 which rejects the hypothesis of normality. For this, the Box-Cox transformation is performed in these features to correct the biases in the distribution and heteroscedasticity, for this the statistical software environment R was used.

We chose the two features of each of the signals that presented the best answers with LDA individually and in pairs according to the criteria of classification error. These features are combined with each other to obtain new descriptor spaces. In these descriptors it was decided to fix the two best features of the oximetry, in view of they showed outstanding answers regarding the features of the HRV.

$$x_1 = \begin{bmatrix} minSpO_2 \\ less92 \\ meanRR \end{bmatrix}, x_2 = \begin{bmatrix} minSpO_2 \\ less92 \\ FMB \end{bmatrix}, x_3 = \begin{bmatrix} minSpO_2 \\ less92 \\ FMB \\ meanRR \end{bmatrix} \quad (5)$$

In these descriptors vectors the following evaluation criteria were obtained (Table 2).

Table 2. Classification performance of the different feature vectors. a: accurate b: sensibility c: specificity d: precision

Feature space	Parameter				
	a	b	c	d	True cases
x_1	0.9523	0.9461	0.9578	0.9513	95.23%
x_2	0.9493	0.9395	0.9578	0.9510	94.92%
x_3	0.9518	0.9450	0.9578	0.9513	95.18%

The best descriptor is x_1 and requires less computational effort than x_2 and x_3. The discriminant function with P-value less than 0.05 is statistically significant at a confidence level of 95.0%. The discriminant function is:

$$D = 52.4127 + 0.3004 * min_s pO2 - 0.0022 * less92 - 7.5860 * meanRR \quad (6)$$

The obtained descriptor space is shown in Fig. 4.

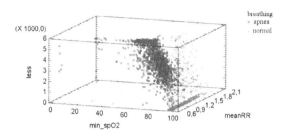

Fig. 4. Feature space of x_1

The evaluation of this function on is done by means of the cross-validation technique of K-rations. Cross-validation of x_1 with $K = 10$ was performed. The cross-validation error for x_1 is $Ecv = 4,77\%$. This shows that for new samples the predictions will have a margin of error of less than 5%. The results are compared with similar works. Schrader [22] obtains a sensitivity and specificity of 90.8% and 92.7% respectively. Mendez [16] obtained a sensitivity and specificity of 89.34% and 83.37% respectively, using 4 characteristics extracted from the HRV signal in its descriptor. The ROC curve of cross-validation can be seen in Fig. 5. It is seen in the ROC curve that the selected discriminant has a good performance and is very close to the ideal classifier. Nevertheless, the impact on clinical practice has yet to be established, it remains to be elucidated until that our prediction will be validated in independent sleep laboratories in newborn suspected of suffering from apnea events.

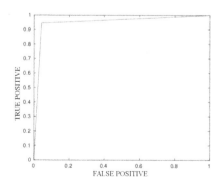

Fig. 5. Feature space and ROC of the obtained descriptor

7   Conclusion

The oximetry signal is the most prominent for the detection of apneas, however, when combined with the HRV signal, benefits are obtained with respect to using the signals separately. The combination is more robust and improves the parameters used in the assessment as compared to the use of the signals in isolation due to the apnea events are linked to oxygen desaturation and changes in heart rhythm.

It was decided to obtain the HRV from the ECG signal, although it is a measured that can be extracted from the photoplethysmography. Because in this way the low sensitivity of the oxymetry can be increased. In addition to that, in this way to add features that can be extracted from the EDR in a later work. It has been shown that information can be used from different sensors to pose a feature space a particular pathology, it is possible to use this model to perform the detection of different pathologies.

It is expected that this model will be the basis for the detection of apneas in home monitoring, it has the advantage of using descriptors that use very few resources. In addition, the LDA is mathematically more simple than nonlinear models. On the other hand, the possibility of studying other classifiers (Bayesians, neural networks, quadratic, adaboost) with these same descriptors is open since their dispersion diagram exposes a distribution that would be appropriate to nonlinear boundaries.

References

1. Anderson, J.: Symposium on pulse oximetry and neonatal medicine. In: The Accuracy of Pulse Oximetry in Neonates: Effects of Fetal Hemoglobin and Bilirubin. Colorado Springs, Colorado (1988)
2. Brouillette, R.T., Morielli, A., Leimanis, A., Waters, K.A., Luciano, R., Ducharme, F.M.: Nocturnal pulse oximetry as an abbreviated testing modality for pediatric obstructive sleep apnea. Pediatrics $105(2)$, 405–412 (2000)
3. de Chazal, P., Penzel, T., Heneghan, C.: Automated detection of obstructive sleep apnoea at different time scales using the electrocardiogram. Physiol. Meas. $25(4)$, 967–983 (2004)
4. Cohen, G., de Chazal, P.: Detection of sleep apnoea in infants using ECG and oximetry signals (2013)
5. Cunningham, D.J.C., Lloyd, B.B.: The Regulation of Human Respiration (1963)
6. Duda, R.O., Hart, P.E., Stork, D.G.: Pattern Classification, 2nd edn. Wiley, Hoboken (2000)
7. Fisher, R.A.: The use of multiple measurements in taxonomic problems. Ann. Eugenics $7(7)$, 179–188 (1936)
8. Goldberger, A.L., Amaral, L.A.N., Glass, L., Hausdorff, J.M., Ivanov, P.C., Mark, R.G., Mietus, J.E., Moody, G.B., Peng, C.K., Stanley, H.E.: PhysioBank, PhysioToolkit, and PhysioNet: components of a new research resource for complex physiologic signals. Circulation $101(23)$, e215–e220 (2000)
9. Avery, G.B., Fletcher, M.A., MacDonald, M.G. (eds.): Avery's Neonatology: Patophysiology and Management of the Newborn. Lippincott Williams & Wilkins, Philadelphia (2005)

10. Guilleminault, C., Hagen, C., Huynh, N.: Comparison of hypopnea definitions in lean patients with known obstructive sleep apnea hypopnea syndrome (OSAHS). Sleep Breathing 13(4), 341–347 (2009)
11. Hilton, M., Bates, R., Godfrey, K., Chappell, M., Cayton, R.: Evaluation of frequency and time-frequency spectral analysis of heart rate variability as a diagnostic marker of the sleep apnoea syndrome. Med. Biol. Eng. Comput. 37(6), 760–769 (1999)
12. Lazareck, L., Tarassenko, L.: Detection of apnoeic and breathing activity through pole-zero analysis of the SpO2 signal. In: 28th Annual International Conference of the IEEE Engineering in Medicine and Biology Society, EMBS 2006, vol. Supplement, pp. 6573–6576, August 2006
13. Leon Lopez, R., Gallegos Machado, B., Estevez Rodriguez, E., Rodriguez Garcia, S.: Mortalidad infantil: analisis de un decenio. Revista Cubana de Medicina General Integral 14, 606–610 (1998)
14. Magalang, U.J., Dmochowski, J., Veeramachaneni, S., Draw, A., Mador, M.J., El-Solh, A., Grant, B.J.: Prediction of the apnea-hypopnea index from overnight pulse oximetry. Chest 124(5), 1694–1701 (2003)
15. Marcos, J.V., Hornero, R., Alvarez, D., del Campo, F., Zamarron, C.: Assessment of four statistical pattern recognition techniques to assist in obstructive sleep apnoea diagnosis from nocturnal oximetry. Med. Eng. Phys. 31(8), 971–978 (2009)
16. Mendez, M.O., Ruini, D.D., Villantieri, O.P., Matteucci, M., Penzel, T., Cerutti, S., Bianchi, A.M.: Detection of sleep apnea from surface ECG based on features extracted by an autoregressive model. Conf. Proc. IEEE Eng. Med. Biol. Soc. 2007, 6106–6109 (2007)
17. Pan, J., Tompkins, W.J.: A real-time QRS detection algorithm. IEEE Trans. Biomed. Eng. BME–32(3), 230–236 (1985)
18. Park, M.: Manual de Cardiologia Pediatrica. Manual práctico de Mosby. Elsevier, Amsterdam (2003)
19. Rajadurai, V.S., Walker, A.M., Yu, V.Y., Oates, A.: Effect of fetal haemoglobin on the accuracy of pulse oximetry in preterm infants. J. Paediatr. Child Health 28(1), 1034–4810 (1992). (Linking)
20. Rangayyan, R.M.: Biomedical Signal Analysis. IEEE Press Series in Biomedical Engineering, 2nd edn. Wiley, Hoboken (2015)
21. Schlotthauer, G., Di Persia, L.E., Larrateguy, L.D., Milone, D.H.: Screening of obstructive sleep apnea with empirical mode decomposition of pulse oximetry. Med. Eng. Phys. 36(8), 1074–1080 (2014)
22. Schrader, M., Zywietz, C., von Einem, V., Widiger, B., Joseph, G.: Detection of sleep apnea in single channel ecgs from the physionet data base. Comput. Cardiol. 2000, 263–266 (2000)
23. Sedghamiz, H.: Matlab implementation of Pan Tompkins ECG QRS detector (2014). https://de.mathworks.com
24. Wang, X., Eklund, J., McGregor, C.: Parametric power spectrum analysis of ECG signals for obstructive sleep apnoea classification. In: 2014 IEEE 27th International Symposium on Computer-Based Medical Systems (CBMS), pp. 8–13, May 2014
25. Zamarron, C., Gude, F., Barcala, J., Rodriguez, J.R., Romero, P.V.: Utility of oxygen saturation and heart rate spectral analysis obtained from pulse oximetric recordings in the diagnosis of sleep apnea syndrome. Chest 123(5), 1567–1576 (2003)

Author Index

Printed in the United States
By Bookmasters